THE ALLEGORY OF THE CHURCH

Romanesque Portals and Their Verse Inscriptions

THE ALLEGORY OF THE CHURCH

Romanesque Portals and Their Verse Inscriptions

Calvin B. Kendall

with photographs by Ralph Lieberman

UNIVERSITY OF TORONTO PRESS
Toronto Buffalo London

Toronto Buffalo London
Printed in Canada

ISBN 0-8020-4262-7

Printed on acid-free paper

Canadian Cataloguing in Publication Data

Kendall, Calvin B.
The allegory of the church : romanesque portals and their verse inscriptions

Includes bibliographical references and index.
ISBN 0-8020-4262-7

1. Doorways, Romanesque – Europe. 2. Church doorways – Europe.
3. Architectural inscriptions – Europe. 4. Inscriptions, Latin – Europe.
5. Christian art and symbolism – Europe. I. Title.

NA4950.K45 1998 726.5′1822′09409021 C97-932536-6

University of Toronto Press acknowledges the financial assistance to its publishing program of the Canada Council for the Arts and the Ontario Arts Council.

To Eleanor

Contents

List of Illustrations, Text Figures, and Maps

Illustrations

Text Figures

Maps

Preface

This book examines Romanesque portals through the lens of the verses inscribed on their sculptural programs. The burden of its argument is that the Romanesque church was a material allegory and that the portal with its verse inscriptions spoke the allegory in the voice of Christ and the Church. The portal was designed to assist medieval Christians in experiencing the church as a mystical space that was both the dwelling place of God and the place where one entered into his or her own better nature. This dynamic interaction between the portal and its intended audience was a function of the art and architecture of the Romanesque church that is particularly difficult for modern viewers to grasp; the verses that accompanied the images of the portals are therefore an important source of information and understanding.

Verse inscriptions in stone appeared in abundance on the façades of churches in the eleventh and twelfth centuries. They are found all over Europe, but their heaviest concentration, if the surviving evidence bears any relation to original patterns of distribution, was in a broad geographical area that included northern Italy, southern France, and northern Spain. They were usually associated with the sculptural programs of the portals. Gothic artists abandoned the practice; hence, verse inscriptions are diagnostically characteristic of the Romanesque period.

This body of material constitutes a largely unexplored 'archive' of texts. The inscriptions tell more than one tale; although I concentrate on the allegory of the church, other topics that they suggest, such as interest in the techniques of visual narrative, wordplay and visual punning as stimulants for meditation, the self-promotion of abbots and artists, fashion, and the economic consequences of pilgrimage, receive passing attention. The inscriptions are collected for purposes of reference in the Catalogue at the end of the book. The Catalogue cannot claim to be exhaustive, but I hope that no inscriptions of major, and relatively few of minor, importance have been overlooked.

In the first chapter, I argue that the method of allegorical exegesis that was developed for the purpose of interpreting the Bible was applied to the material structure of the medieval church. The church was allegorized as the temple of Solomon, the body of Christ, the community of the faithful, and the heavenly Jerusalem. Chapters 2 and 3 trace the history of the application of verse inscriptions to church buildings from the time of Constantine to the Romanesque period, and show how they came to be used to express the allegory of the church.

Chapter 4 sets forth the premise that Christ's metaphor 'I am the door' was the fundamental organizing principle of many, if not most, Romanesque portals. Chapter 5 looks at the language and form of the inscriptions that gave voice to the portals, while chapters 6 and 7 take up both the extent to which the voice of Christ or the Church might have been felt to be effectively present in the portals themselves and the perceived danger that sculptural images above the portals might be mistaken for the Deity that they represented. One of the best attested aspects of the dynamism of Romanesque portals is their penitential function. The moral and anagogical implications of the allegory of the church contribute to this function and are the themes of chapters 8 through 10. Chapter 11 presents what is to me a fascinating sidelight on the allegory of the church – that is, the projection, in the form of images, of the multiple levels of medieval allegorical interpretation onto the archivolts of some notable Aquitainian churches.

The last three chapters of the book serve two purposes. First, they stand as a reminder that the allegory of the church was not the only thing on the minds of builders and artists in the Romanesque period. The 'allegory of the church' makes no claims to being a General Theory of Romanesque. Romanesque portals were complex and endlessly varied, and these chapters give me an opportunity to glance at a few of the other ideas that informed them. Second, they chronicle the decline of the allegory as a formative influence. Even before the abandonment of the use of verse inscriptions, there is evidence that the allegory of the church had come to be thought of as symbolic of a transcendent reality rather than as a reality inherent in the material church, and the allegory itself was finally subsumed and exhausted in the Gothic period in elaborate sculptural programs that represented all aspects of the relationship between the visible and invisible worlds.

For books of the Bible I have followed the abbreviations suggested in the *Chicago Manual of Style* with the following exceptions: my 1, 2 Kings = 1, 2 Samuel; 3, 4 Kings = 1, 2 Kings; 1, 2 Para. [Paralipomenon] = 1, 2 Chronicles; Apoc. [Apocalypse] = Revelation. I generally use the spelling of proper names in the Vulgate, but Isaiah, Jeremiah, and Ezekiel are so spelled. The system I use for transcribing verses and other inscriptions, both in the Catalogue and in the text and notes, is described in the 'Key to transcriptions' in the introduction to the Catalogue, pp. 199–200.

My fascination with verse inscriptions goes back some twenty years to a sabbatical spent in the south of France, which gave my wife Eleanor and myself an opportunity to view at first hand many of the major monuments of Romanesque architecture and sculpture. In the spring of 1978, our good friends Ted and Jerry Wright guided us north from Provence into Burgundy along a meandering path that took us past such extraordinary churches as Conques and Autun. I wondered about the verses on their tympana, and how they might be related to the curious verses I had previously seen on the interior nave wall of Saint-Trophime of Arles and the equally curious verses on the exterior wall of Vaison-la-Romaine. On returning home to Minnesota, I discovered to my surprise that no study of Romanesque verse inscriptions had ever been made. This was the inspiration for the present book.

With financial support from the Bush Foundation, the Graduate School of the University of Minnesota, and the MacKnight Foundation, Eleanor and I explored Romanesque Europe with notebook, binoculars, and cameras in hand. At first we searched more or less at random, wandering from one remarkable church to the next, and recording inscriptions when we stumbled upon them. Though I did not learn about it until several years after the fact, Robert Favreau and his colleagues had already published the initial volumes in the *Corpus des inscriptions de la France médiévale*, which soon became our guide to more systematic collecting in France. Paging through Kingsley Porter's collection of photographs in *Romanesque Sculpture of the Pilgrimage Roads* and the photographs in the ongoing series of volumes on Romanesque art and architecture published by Zodiaque, among others, brought many additional inscriptions to our attention.

A resident fellowship at the Camargo Foundation in Cassis, France, enabled me to gather these scattered materials into preliminary catalogue form. It was there, too, that I had leisure to sort through the various themes suggested by the inscriptions and first glimpse the direction that this book would take. I am grateful to the Foundation's director, Michael Pretina, for his cooperation and support. A chance meeting in Verona gave me the opportunity to draw upon Fred Gettings's knowledge of medieval astrological lore. Another chance meeting, this one in the parvis in front of the west façade of Conques, introduced us to Ralph Lieberman and his wife, Valerie. Ralph's photograph of the tympanum of Conques (fig. 1) is a memento of that day. Our paths separated, but fortuitously intersected again ten years later, at which time Ralph agreed to undertake the two photographic campaigns that produced the splendid illustrations for this book. Katharine Kendall is responsible for the graphic design of the text figures and maps.

László Scholz obtained photographs of the sculptural remains from the abbey of Moreaux that are now in the Allen Memorial Art Museum of Oberlin College, which enabled me better to understand that portal. He and his wife, Katalin Halacsy, were our hosts and guides in Hungary. David and Sonia Simon shared their expertise in Spanish Romanesque sculpture with us under the shelter of the west porch of Jaca cathedral.

Jill Keen did invaluable bibliographical work as my research assistant early in the project, particularly in Italian sources. I am grateful to Joseph Alchermes, Susan Caldwell, Rita Copeland, Allen Frantzen, Michael Hancher, and Marguerite Ragnow for their critiques of drafts of different chapters of the book. Special thanks are owing to Margery Durham and David Simon for reading and commenting on the manuscript in its entirety. Steven Davis, Oliver Nicholson, and David Wallace gave me expert help and advice on various specialized matters. The anonymous readers for the University of Toronto Press and John St James, copy-editor, made a number of constructive suggestions that I have thankfully adopted. I have been saved from numerous errors of fact and judgment by the expert knowledge and collective wisdom of them all. The faults that remain are my own.

Portions of chapters 6, 7, and 9 appeared in substantially different form under the title, 'The Gate of Heaven and the Fountain of Life: Speech-Act Theory and Portal Inscriptions,' in *Essays in Medieval Studies* 10 (1993), 111–28. Chapter 10 is a revised and altered version of 'The Verse Inscriptions of the Tympanum of Jaca and the Pax Anagram,' originally published in *Mediaevalia* 19 (1996), 405–34. I am grateful to the Illinois Medieval Association and to the Center for Medieval and Early Renaissance Studies of the State University of New York at Binghamton, respectively, for permission to reprint these essays.

Finally, I want to acknowledge that this book is the joint effort of

Eleanor and myself. We have worked on it together on the road and in the study. Over the many months and years and in the course of tens of thousands of miles of travel in pursuit of the evidence on which it is built, there has been much pleasure and some pain. No matter how trying the circumstances, her enthusiasm and her determination to carry the project through to the end have never wavered. The book is dedicated to her with my deepest gratitude and love.

Part One

The Making of Meaning

1

The Allegory of the Church

For more than a thousand years after the emergence of Christianity as an organized religion in the first century AD, the most powerful minds in Christendom focused on a single problem: how to read and interpret the word of God in the book of the Bible and the book of nature. The building in which Christians worshipped did not escape this scrutiny; it was interpreted by the same exegetical methods that were developed to interpret the Bible. The church was a multilevel allegory and every part of it was infused with meaning. It was read as the heavenly Jerusalem and the universal Church. It was the home of God, and Mary, and all of the saints. If the church had a dome, it was the vault of heaven.[1] Its entrance doors symbolized the apostles and their columns the bishops and doctors of the Church. On a more profound level, the portal was identified with, or as, Christ.

The allegory of the church was so much a part of the mental landscape of the earlier Middle Ages that everyone from illiterate peasants to the most educated members of the aristocracy and clergy would have believed that they were entering the dwelling place of God when they passed through the portal of their church. An early-ninth-century Anglo-Latin poet by the name of Æthelwulf described the spiritual inhabitants of his own monastic church: 'This is the house which the mother of the exalted divinity inhabits and occupies beneath the vast dome of the sky ... All the saints haunt the midmost floor of the church, and occupy it at all times, mustering in countless troops.'[2] Crossing the threshold of the church must have been an awesome experience. Faith, energized by the allegorical imagination and the effects of liminal spiritual transformation,[3] stimulated a devotion that produced tens of thousands of extraordinary buildings in stone in the Romanesque period – a period, by our

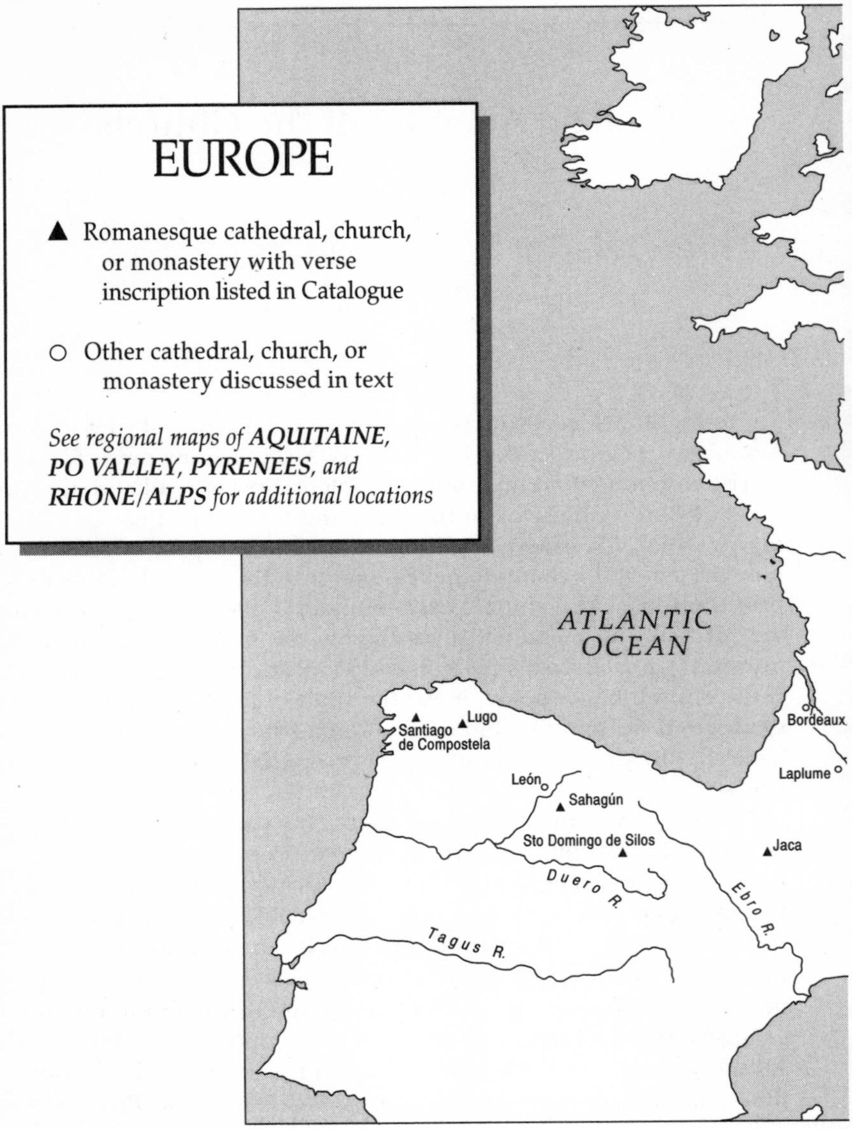

EUROPE
▲ Romanesque cathedral, church, or monastery with verse inscription listed in Catalogue
○ Other cathedral, church, or monastery discussed in text
See regional maps of AQUITAINE, PO VALLEY, PYRENEES, and RHONE/ALPS for additional locations
ATLANTIC OCEAN
Santiago de Compostela
Lugo
León
Sahagún
Sto Domingo de Silos
Jaca
Bordeaux
Laplume
Duero R.
Ebro R.
Tagus R.

Ruthwell
Wearmouth
NORTH SEA
Gellerup
Ribe
Schleswig
Kilpeck
Dinton
Egmond Binnen
Zwolle
Weser R.
Königslutter
Corvey
Goslar
Rhine R.
Maastricht
Elnone
Huy
Aachen
Centula
Seine R.
St-Denis
Reims
Rothenkirchenhof
Würzburg
Loire R.
Bellegarde
Strasbourg
Regensburg
Danube R.
Fleury
Alpirsbach
Tours
Poitiers
Déols
Bourges
Dijon
Autun
Augsburg
Moosburg
Isen
Salzburg
Esztergom
AQUITAINE
St Gall
Payerne
Lyon
Bordeaux
Beaulieu
Mauriac
Agen
Le Puy
Milan
Laplume
Moissac
Conques
Rhone R.
RHONE/ ALPS
Venice
Po R.
Toulouse
PYRENEES
Jaca
Arles
PO VALLEY
Ebro R.
LIGURIAN SEA
Trogir
Barcelona
Torre de Passeri
MEDITERRANEAN SEA
Rome
Nola

standards, of desperate poverty, massive ignorance, and limited technological resources.

Throughout Europe Latin verses that helped express the allegory of the church were carved on church façades in conjunction with the sculptural programs of their portals. Portals, with their images and verses, guided and directed Christians in their passage into the interior of the church. The portal was not only the boundary between secular and sacred space, it was also, like the cross, a sign of Christ. The allegory of the church was multilayered – a complex of meanings and messages inherent in the building and the portal. What the allegory was, how it affected the design of the Romanesque portal, and the way the verses mediated between the allegory and its intended audience are the themes of this book.

Little documentary evidence exists to help us understand how the allegory would have been perceived. The scattered remains of the verses that once covered the portals in profusion and that still survive in surprising abundance therefore assume a particular importance.[4] When these verses are read in conjunction with the sculptural programs they accompany, they permit inferences to be drawn about contemporary medieval understandings of, and responses to, the allegory. The images sculpted above the portal gave visible expression to Christ's invisible presence and the verses gave spatial form to the words he addressed to the worshippers who came to enter the church. In the hearts of the faithful the portal was Christ. When the allegory of the church was a reality in local space and time and its effects were immediate, crossing the threshold of the church transported the worshipper directly into the heavenly city. This response to the allegory appears to have been widespread in the eleventh and early part of the twelfth century.

As the twelfth century wore on, however, the development of a different perception of the allegory of the church can be inferred from the evidence of the verses and portal sculptures. In a world of thought in which objects were assumed to have multiple layers of meaning, a shift took place from predication to representation. Sign became symbol. It is the difference between the statements 'the portal is Christ' and 'the portal symbolizes Christ,' or, to take an example from a more charged sphere, the difference between the claim that the bread of the Eucharist is the body of Christ and that it merely represents his body. Symbolic representation drew the mind to a reality that was not in the church but beyond it.[5]

In concert with the shift toward representational symbolism, the decoration of many later twelfth-century portals overtly reflected the ambition of their patrons and the genius of their artists, drawing attention to human agency at the expense of divine signification. The synthesis of verse and image that was the hallmark of so many Romanesque portals began to break down. Gothic artists took the decoration of the portal to new heights of elaborate grandeur and thematic complexity, but they had no need for the verses that had articulated the voice of the Romanesque portal. Eventually, the allegory of the church itself was forgotten.

The allegory of the church that is reflected in the construction and decoration of Romanesque churches and monastic complexes was an outgrowth of the methods developed by Christian scholars for use in interpreting the Bible. Medieval commentators working in the 'Alexandrian' tradition of exegesis[6] looked for multiple layers of meaning in biblical texts. They began with the premise that the actors and actions of history (especially the history recorded in the Bible) constituted a sacred language, part of God's message to mankind, the meaning of which was obscure and difficult to comprehend without investigation. One of their chief concerns was to find significant relationships between the Old and New Testaments. A person or event in the Old Testament was interpreted as a 'figure' or 'type' of another person or event in the New Testament, which was its 'fulfilment' or 'antitype.' When commentators found a moral in an Old Testament story that applied to Christians in the present, or 'sixth age' of the world, as the Venerable Bede liked to call it,[7] they were, in effect, adding a second level of interpretation – a moral, or 'tropological' level.

There were two principal strands to this tradition of allegorical interpretation – the 'threefold' method, which goes back to Origen, Jerome, and Gregory, and the 'fourfold' method, which can be traced to Augustine and Cassian.[8] The threefold method involved the assumption that a text could reveal any one of three senses – a literal or historical sense, a moral sense, and a sense variously referred to as 'intellectual,' 'mystical,' or 'allegorical.' In his Epistle to Bishop Leander, Pope Gregory the Great (590–604) described the threefold method he employed in interpreting the Book of Job: 'You should know that I read and interpret certain things in a historical sense, other things allegorically by figural analysis, and still other things by means of moral allegory alone. And some things I ascertain by all these means, investigating with greater care in three ways simultaneously. For first I lay the foundations of history; then I erect the fabric of the mind into a citadel of faith by figural interpretation;

and finally I also clothe the edifice with added colour by the grace of morality.'[9]

A double interpretation of every Old Testament figure was potentially available – its immediate fulfilment occurring in the person or event of the New Testament, and its ultimate fulfilment in the anticipated event of Last Judgment.[10] This gave rise to the fourfold method, in which a text was assumed to have, potentially, a literal, a 'typological,'[11] a moral, and an anagogical sense. John Cassian (ca. 360–ca. 435) wrote of the fourfold method: 'Theoretical knowledge is divided into two parts, that is, into historical interpretation and spiritual understanding ... But there are three kinds of spiritual knowledge: tropological, allegorical, and anagogical.'[12] Cassian went on to define tropology as 'the moral explanation pertaining to the improvement of life and practical instruction'; typology (*allegoria*) as being the sense when 'those things that truly happened are said to have prefigured the form of some other mystery'; and anagogy as the sense that rises 'to certain even more sublime and sacred secrets of heaven.'[13]

In practice, exegetes tended not to distinguish carefully between the two methods, nor were they ever as strictly employed as this formulation might seem to suggest.[14] The fundamental distinction was between the literal sense of the text and its spiritual meaning or meanings, however these might be defined or labelled.[15]

Logically speaking, there was no reason to suppose that history had ceased to be meaningful in the sixth age, and the concept of 'figure' or 'type' was therefore extended to 'imitation.' Just as the saints of the sixth age recapitulated or imitated the *acta* and *passio* of Christ,[16] so medieval European churches, as Richard Krautheimer has shown, imitated influential prototypes in the Holy Lands. Imitation did not produce faithful replicas of the originals. Revered churches like the Holy Sepulchre at Jerusalem were not copied exactly; instead, the unity of the original design was disintegrated into its constituent elements, these elements were then selectively transferred to the copy, and reshuffled to form the new construction, which nevertheless reproduced the original *typice* and *figuraliter* with all of its allegorical signification.[17] Although the Rotunda of the Holy Sepulchre was round, copies of it could just as well be polygonal, since the polygon was regarded as being interchangeable with the circle. And although the Rotunda was carried by twenty supports – eight piers and twelve columns, either eight supports or twelve would suffice for an imitation. Both numbers carried a heavy load of allegorical meanings. The number twelve could be associated with the number of Christ's disciples, and eight was a perfect number signifying resurrection. Therefore, on one level, a church like the Baptistery of Pisa was a type of the Holy Sepulchre, while on another, it figured the promise of eternal life.[18]

Allegorical interpretation, then, was crucially implicated in the construction and meaning of medieval churches. The Venerable Bede (ca. 673–735) was one of the earliest commentators to provide a clear formulation of the fourfold method.[19] In his textbook on rhetoric, *De Schematibus et Tropis,* he attempted a synthesis of the Alexandrian tradition with Augustine's theory of signs.[20] For Bede, allegory was at one and the same time a rhetorical figure, a method of interpretation, and a reality inherent in the natural world. Because he used the allegory of the church to illustrate what allegory was and because his writings were widely diffused and influential in the Middle Ages, his textbook is a convenient point of departure. Anglo-Saxon missionaries carried *De Schematibus et Tropis* to the Continent in the ninth century, where it was quickly diffused from centres like Saint Gall, Lorsch, Murbach, and Reichenau into northern and central France, Germany, Austria, Spain, and Italy. Thirty-six Continental manuscripts from the twelfth century or earlier survive and many more are known to have existed. The work continued to be copied right through the sixteenth century.[21]

Bede added two refinements to the conventional treatment of allegory, which are helpful for understanding the allegory of the church in the Romanesque period. First, he drew a distinction between 'historical allegory' and 'verbal allegory.'[22] This enabled him to steer a middle course between Origen's distrust of the literal sense of the Old Testament and Augustine's insistence upon its historical veracity. Historical allegory was the procedure to be used when the language of the biblical narrative was 'straight' and 'factual.' The particular historical reality described in such language could be read as if it were a figure of speech or trope. It would therefore have a double meaning, referring both to itself and to some meaning outside of itself.

Historical allegory as Bede understood it rested on the assumption that 'things' as well as 'words' could be signs – that the physical world, like the Bible that recorded a portion of its history, was the word of God. In his treatise *On Christian Doctrine,* Augustine had argued that some things in the physical world were also signs:

> I have here called a 'thing' that which is not used to signify something else, like wood, stone, cattle, and so on; but not that wood concerning which we

> read that Moses cast it into bitter waters that their bitterness might be dispelled, nor that stone which Jacob placed at his head, nor that beast which Abraham sacrificed in place of his son. For these are things in such a way that they are also signs of other things.[23] There are other signs whose whole use is in signifying, like words. For no one uses words except for the purpose of signifying something. From this may be understood what we call 'signs'; they are things used to signify something. Thus every sign is also a thing, for that which is not a thing is nothing at all; but not every thing is also a sign.[24]

There was no method that could be used to determine whether a particular thing was, or was not, a sign. Augustine took his examples of things that were also signs from the Bible, but he did not exclude things that happen not to be found there. Every thing was *potentially* a sign. (Not until the thirteenth century did Thomas Aquinas specifically restrict the operation of allegory to sacred history leading up to the Redemption.[25]) Thus, allegorical interpretation or something akin to it easily passed from Scripture into natural history, where it ceased to have any specific historical application. Bestiaries and the like, in which animals, plants, and minerals were assumed to have moral meanings for man, flourished in this climate of thought.[26] More important, historical allegory opened up the possibility of finding meaning – a divine significance – in the things and events of the contemporary world.

Verbal allegory, by contrast, was Bede's solution to the problem of dealing with metaphorical and prophetic language in the Bible – language that was not 'straight' and 'factual,' language either that 'literally' made no sense or that lacked any immediate historical referent. Such language could only be read as a trope; its meaning was the interpretation which was placed on it. Bede gives as an example of verbal allegory the statement of the prophet Isaiah: 'There shall come forth a rod out of the root of Jesse, and a flower shall rise up out of his root' (Isa. 11:1). In Bede's view, these words have no literal meaning or historical reference, because no 'rod' ever has or ever will come from the 'root' of Jesse. The sole meaning of the statement is its allegorical one, that 'our Savior was to be born of the Virgin Mary from the race of David.'[27] Strictly speaking, Bede's historical allegory is not a device of language, although it might be said to be a figure of speech in God's rhetoric, which is the speech that constitutes the world; whereas verbal allegory is purely linguistic in the sense that we ordinarily understand.

Bede's second refinement of the allegorical method was to propose that the meaning of an allegory could be either literal ('historical') or spiritual. An allegory with a literal meaning is one that refers to some historical reality other than Christ or the Church. The relationship between the allegory and the thing or event it refers to is real (that is, intended by God), but its spiritual meaning, if any, is prospective. Both figure and fulfilment belong to the unredeemed world, which may be defined either as the world before the arrival of the Redeemer, Christ, or as the world of the sixth age, the contemporary world insofar as it has not fully accepted redemption. The literal level of interpretation in Bede's methodology is not to be confused with the thing or event being interpreted (which as a verbal description or narrative may be referred to as the 'letter' of the text).

Thus, for Bede, there were four possible levels of interpretation of a biblical text once the meaning of the letter of the text (or lack of it) had been determined, a literal level and three spiritual levels – typological, tropological, and anagogical.[28] The literal level referred to some reality in the unredeemed world. The three spiritual levels offered a spiritual meaning of the text with respect to the past, the present, and the future of the reader. A typological allegory referred to Christ or the Church; a tropological, or moral, allegory referred to the moral experience of the individual Christian in the present; and an anagogical allegory referred to the joys of heaven that the Christian might look forward to. Two or more things or texts could have the same allegorical meaning, one thing could have several meanings on the same level, and a single thing could have one or more levels of interpretation. Nothing would preclude an allegory from having, for example, two tropological interpretations and no anagogical one.

Bede gives two examples of an allegory which may be interpreted in all four senses. One is the verbal phrase or material object *templum Domini*, 'the temple of the Lord':

> Sometimes a single historical or verbal allegory will figuratively reveal a literal sense, a mystical [= typological] sense concerning Christ or the Church, a tropological sense, and an anagogical sense all at the same time. For example, the temple of the Lord in the literal sense is the house which Solomon built; allegorically [= typologically], it is the Lord's body, of which Christ said: 'Destroy this temple, and in three days I will raise it up' [John 2:19], or his Church, to whom the apostle Paul said: 'For the temple of the Lord is holy, which you are' [1 Cor. 3:17]; tropologically, it is each of the faithful, to whom the Apostle said: 'Know you not, that your bodies are the temple of the holy Spirit, who is in you?' [1 Cor. 3:16; 6:15, 19]; anagogically, it is the

> joys of the heavenly mansion, for which the Psalmist sighed, when he said: 'Blessed are they that dwell in your house, O Lord; they shall praise you for ever and ever' [Ps. 83:5].[29]

The phrase *templum Domini*, as Bede uses it, is not a specific quotation from the narrative of the building of the temple of Solomon in 3 Kings 6–7 and 2 Chronicles 3, but a general term that could be applied to any church.[30] On the literal level, *templum Domini*, 'church' (either the word or the thing as sign), refers historically to the house that Solomon built, according to the Old Testament narrative. The temple of Solomon belonged to the unredeemed world; although it was the place where the true God was worshipped before the coming of Christ, its chief significance for the medieval Christian was as a type or figure of the Church (that is, the temple of Solomon in the Old Testament had the same three spiritual meanings as the phrase *templum Domini*).[31] Typologically, a church refers to the body of Christ, or to Christ's Church. Tropologically, it refers to each of the faithful. Anagogically, it signifies the joys of the heavenly mansion.[32]

Bede's second example of an allegory that may be interpreted in all four senses is the word or thing 'Jerusalem' in the verse of the Psalmist '"Praise the Lord, O Jerusalem; praise your God, O Sion. Because he has strengthened the bolts of your gates, he has blessed your children within you" [Ps. 147:12–13]. This trope can rightly be taken as referring literally to the citizens of the earthly Jerusalem, allegorically [= typologically] to the Church of Christ, tropologically to each saved soul, and anagogically to the celestial homeland.'[33] The three spiritual levels of interpretation of Jerusalem are virtually identical to the spiritual interpretations of the temple of the Lord. Thus the *church* and the *city* are interchangeable images, as is Sion, the *mountain*, which is parallel to Jerusalem in the verse Bede quotes.[34] On the literal level of interpretation, 'the citizens of the earthy Jerusalem' are not identical with either the word or the physical entity, Jerusalem, which is the sign. The citizens of the earthly Jerusalem in Psalm 147 would have been in Bede's eyes the unredeemed Jews of the Old Testament, but by extension any unsaved inhabitants, pagan or Christian, of any city could be meant by the literal allegory. The implied reference is not only to the era before the advent of Christ but also to the spiritually untransformed world of everyday reality in the sixth age. On the spiritual level Jerusalem was the city of God. Bede's parallel interpretations of the church and Jerusalem are indicative of the close relationship between the allegory of the church and Christian pilgrimage. Any pilgrimage to a distant or nearby shrine was both a mirror of the great pilgrimage to Jerusalem and a ritual means of entering sacred space. The allegory of the church turned the act of entering the church, even one's local church, into a form of pilgrimage.

The allegory of the church can be distinguished from the tradition of typological allegory in Christian art that stems from Prudentius and Paulinus of Nola.[35] Typological allegory played a part in the allegory of the church, but the allegory of the church was not a system of typological correspondences between the Old and New Testaments. It can also be distinguished from the piecemeal symbolic interpretation of the parts of the church that was derived from it. The monk Bernard of Angers, who travelled to the abbey of Sainte-Foy of Conques in 1013 to investigate the miracles of Saint Foy and became such an ardent admirer that he wrote a *Book of Miracles* celebrating her, described the church that preceded the present one in language that Paulinus of Nola might have used six centuries earlier: 'From the outside, the basilica is made up of three forms by the division of the roofs, but on the inside these three forms are united across their width to shape the church into one body. And thus this trinity that fuses into unity seems to be a type of the highest and holy Trinity, at least in my opinion.'[36] When Bruno of Asti (d. 1123) discussed the church as a sign, he moved seamlessly between the allegory of the church and the symbolism of its parts:

> For indeed the church itself certainly signifies the Church, that is, the assembly of people, which is contained in it. Hence it is also called a church, because it contains the Church. The grammarians call this figure of rhetoric, when that which contains is substituted for that which is contained, metonymy. Such is the figure that the Lord used when he said in the gospel: 'Jerusalem, Jerusalem, you who kill the prophets' [Matt. 23:37], since it was certainly not Jerusalem itself, but its inhabitants who killed the prophets. And thus we are accustomed to say: that house is good, because it has good inhabitants, and that one is bad, because bad inhabitants live in it. According to this sense of the word, therefore, this church, constructed of wood and stones, signifies the Church, which is built from living stones; its stones are joined and unified not with lime but with charity; its foundation is Christ; its portals are the apostles; its columns are the bishops and doctors. In it each stone gleams by so much the more as it is the more faithful and better.[37]

As an interpretative framework the allegory of the church influenced and shaped the architecture of medieval churches and the decoration of their portals. The church building was a thing that was also a sign, the meanings of which were realities intended by God. Furthermore, the realities predicated by the allegory of the church tended to be identified closely with the sign itself. That is, the consecrated Christian church was at one and the same time a material structure in the unredeemed world, the body of Christ, the community of each of the faithful, and the heavenly Jerusalem. It was filled in the here and now with the presence of God. Evidence for this from earlier periods is fragmentary, but by the eleventh and twelfth centuries it comes in abundance both directly from verse inscriptions and inferentially from the design of portals and their sculptural programs.[38] It is convenient to take up the evidence in accordance with the Bedan model, which is the clearest medieval exposition of the allegory of the church that we have, but this is not to imply that abbots and builders necessarily thought in terms of the fourfold method or that they were all acquainted with Bede's writing. The allegory of the church was part of their mental and spiritual outlook, and there would have been no need for them to consult a particular written source.

The Church as a Literal Allegory

As a literal allegory, the Romanesque church was from the perspective of the worshipper the material embodiment in the sixth age of the temple of Solomon or, more generally, of the unredeemed world – the world of the Old Man subject to the Old Law. It was the arena where the struggle for salvation reached its climax, the issue of which remained in doubt. Solomon, said Isidore of Seville, was the type of the man 'whose beginnings were good, but his endings bad.'[39]

The allegorical relationship between the church on the literal level as the temple of Solomon and on the anagogical level as the kingdom of heaven was well understood. Otto von Simson calls attention to a miniature in the *Liber Floridus* from Saint-Bertin (ca. 1120) that placed an image of the Heavenly Jerusalem above the biblical description (2 Para. 2) of how Solomon built the temple. As Simson remarks, 'The twofold relationship makes it quite clear that the church was conceived as an image of the Celestial Jerusalem, but that the Celestial Jerusalem in turn was thought to have been prefigured in the Solomonic Temple.'[40] However, specific allusions to the literal allegory of the church as the temple of Solomon are comparatively rare in Romanesque architecture and sculpture. There are a pair of knotted columns, which were formerly part of the porch of the west portal of the cathedral of Würzburg, that are inscribed *Iachim* and *Booz*, the names of the pillars that Solomon set up in front of his temple (3 Kings 7:21). These were probably added to the cathedral in the thirteenth century, but Walter Cahn has shown that the motif of knotted and twisted columns, which is common in the Romanesque period, invested the space it enclosed with 'special significance,' and may have carried Solomonic associations.[41] The oxen that support the second storey of the central porch at the cathedral of Piacenza have been cited as a reference to Solomon's temple (cf. 3 Kings 7:29).[42]

Images of the natural world belong to this level of the allegory. The cycles of time, the year, the seasons, the months, and the days, and the labours connected with them were the conditions under which mankind was condemned to live after the Fall and which still obtained. Emile Mâle protested against overzealous nineteenth-century attempts to find symbolic meaning in every piece of decorative flora and fauna in Romanesque churches.[43] Nevertheless these images, which are as common inside the churches as out, reminded their viewers that the house of God was a material structure built by human hands, and subject like themselves to the ravages of time and evil in the natural world. Even the monstrous hybrids, two-headed beasts, and other grotesque creatures, which were so beloved of Romanesque sculptors and to which Bernard of Clairvaux took such strenuous exception, may be seen as projections of the fears and terrors of the unredeemed world. And yet the natural world also had encoded in it signs of the possibility of redemption. Not every image of nature was hostile or threatening.

The Church as a Typological Allegory

The cruciform basilican church signified Christ. Medieval architectural terminology anthropomorphized the building accordingly: in a *Vita* of Raymond Gayrard (d. 1118) the apse and transepts of the basilica of Saint-Sernin of Toulouse are referred to as *capitis membrum* ('the portion of the head'); the nave as the *corpus* ('body').[44] The portal was the boundary between the external, spiritually untransformed world of experience, and the internal sacred space. To cross the threshold was the decisive act, since spiritual transformation could be expected at the moment of entering. Portal and interior sculptures assisted in the transformation. The allegory of the church as the body of Christ carried an overlay of masculine symbolism, whereas the allegory of the church as *ecclesia* – the Bride of Christ – entailed feminine symbolism.[45] To enter was in a physical sense a kind of incorporation into Christ and the Church. This may explain the presence in churches of grossly obscene sexual imagery both male and female, as on the capital in the west aisle of the south transept, just inside the portal, at Santiago of Compostela.[46] Sex in the unredeemed world was a kind of natural parody or perversion of spiritual transformation.

The typological allegory of the church as Christ is visually predicated in every sculptural program in which Christ appears symmetrically positioned on the central, vertical axis above the portal (in subsequent discussions of apse mosaics or tympana above doorways, I refer to this position on the vertical axis as 'the axial position'). This was the single most important element of design in the typical Romanesque monumental portal.[47] Inscriptions sometimes made this predication verbally explicit.

The other primary typological allegory, the church as an allegory of *ecclesia*, the universal Church, did not have as profound an effect. When the Church spoke through the medium of verse inscriptions, it spoke as *ecclesia*, but this gave rise to very few visual representations. One is a keystone medallion in the nave of Sainte-Marie-Madeleine of Vézelay that shows a seated woman, who is crowned and holds a standard in her right hand and a church in her left. A verse inscription around the rim of the medallion declares in her voice: 'Now I am smoke-stained, but later I will be beautiful.'[48] The verse articulates the typological analogies between the material church, which had been damaged by a fire in 1120 and was in the course of reconstruction, and the universal Church, which is imperfect in the present world of the sixth age but which will shed its imperfections in the glory of the time to come.

Toward the end of the Romanesque period, that is, for the most part, after the middle of the twelfth century, the typological equation of the Virgin Mary with *ecclesia*, the Church, a commonplace of biblical commentators since the time of Gregory the Great,[49] began to generate portal designs with the Virgin and Child in the axial position.

The Church as a Tropological Allegory

The Apostle Paul wrote in his first letter to the Corinthians (3:16–17): 'Know you not, that you are the temple of God, and that the Spirit of God dwells in you? But if any man violate the temple of God, him shall God destroy. For the temple of God is holy, which you are.' Bede quoted from this passage in his discussion of tropology, and it was the basis for the Spanish poet Prudentius's allegory of the soul, the *Psychomachia*. Prudentius (348–ca. 405) describes the marriage of the feminine soul (*anima*) with the masculine Holy Spirit.[50] After the soul has been purged of her sins, she is entered by Christ, who builds in her a temple of gold that is adorned with the jewels of the virtues for the pleasure of wisdom.[51] The task of building the temple of the soul is what Solomon accomplished when he built his temple; and Prudentius borrows the details of construction from the description of the New Jerusalem (Apoc. 21:10–21).[52]

Tropological allegory is slippery; except when it takes the form of a moral exhortation (delivered typically in the voice of Christ or the Church), it is difficult to disentangle it from the literal and anagogical levels. The Christian in the sixth age was not assured of his or her place in the heavenly city; the struggle for the crown of virtue was yet to be won. If the church was by tropological allegory the community of the faithful, as in Bede's formulation, then each of the faithful was a smoke-stained block in hopes of being washed clean, and tropology was grounded in the unredeemed world of everyday experience. But if the church was the community of each saved soul, as is implied by Bede's strictly parallel allegory of Jerusalem, then tropology rose to the level of anagogy. Bede gives a beautiful illustration of the dual aspect of the tropological allegory of the church when he remarks in *The Ecclesiastical History* (4.3): 'A plague sent from heaven came upon [the Christians of Lichfield] which, through the death of the body, translated the living stones of the church [*vivos ecclesiae lapides*] from their earthly sites to the heavenly building.'[53] But it must be noted that Bede has allegorized his fellow Christians rather than the stones of their church. Despite his central role in popularizing the allegory of the church, it is an arresting fact, as Arthur Holder points out, that Bede never himself offered an allegorical interpretation of a Christian church building.[54]

The Church as an Anagogical Allegory

Just as in Romanesque art the heavenly Jerusalem was represented architecturally as a structure with round-arched portals or arcades, so the Romanesque church with its rounded arches was an allegory of the heavenly city and its portal was the gate of heaven.

Anagogical allegory tended to generate self-referential imagery. On the tympanum of Conques, the heavenly city is shown on the lower left, balanced by Satan's infernal empire on the lower right (fig. 1). The tympanum master represented the heavenly city as an arcade with seven arches (fig. 2). Abraham is enthroned under the middle arch; he holds two of the saved in his embrace. The middle arch stands beneath a gable-shaped roof and two crenelated towers. Six of the arches rest on columns; the seventh, on the far right, is part of a portal. An angel stands in the open door, welcoming the souls of the saved into heaven. The three central arches are the same size, while the two arches on either side of them decrease in height. The seven arches of the heavenly city correspond to the seven radiating chapels of the basilica of Conques – the three central ones to the three chapels of the apse; the two smaller ones on either side to the two chapels of each transept (the outermost chapels of the transepts are also much reduced in size). Square crosses between the centre and the outer arches mark the separation of the apse chapels and the transept chapels. The peaked roof and the two towers above the middle arch represent the west façade.[55] It is as though we were looking through transparent walls at a flattened-out elevation of the apse and façade of the earthly church, within which are Abraham and the other inhabitants of the heavenly city.

The façade of Saint John Lateran in Rome displays a notable example of twelfth-century anagogical allegory. This basilica, the cathedral of the city of Rome and the 'Mother and Head of all the churches of the City and the World,' has been several times reconstructed and much altered over the course of time. The present main façade (the east front) is the work of Alessandro Galilei (1733–5), but the architrave of the portico preserves an inscription from the portico of the Romanesque façade, which was constructed by Niccolò di Angelo in about 1170.[56] The inscription, which reaffirms the ancient dedication of the basilica to Christ the Saviour,[57] proclaims, in six leonine hexameters: 'By papal decree and also by imperial decree it is granted that I be the mother (and) head of all churches. From henceforward, after everything has been finished [= the 12th-century reconstruction], they [= the pope and the Holy Roman emperor] have consecrated this heavenly kingdom [= the basilica by anagogy] with the name of the Saviour and Creator. Thus we (have been) persuaded wholly by humble prayer that this our celebrated temple be your home, Christ.'[58] The church, or the Church, speaks by anagogy as the kingdom of heaven. This is, in a sense, *the* authoritative Romanesque expression of the allegory of the church.

Part Two

The Early History of Christian Verse Inscriptions

2

Constantine and the Mosaics of Rome

The story of how verse inscriptions came to play an important role in the design and meaning of Romanesque portals and in the articulation of the allegory of the church can be said to begin with the Gospel accounts of Christ's Passion.[1] According to Luke, the soldiers mocked Jesus and offered him vinegar and said: '"If thou be the king of the Jews, save thyself." And there was also a superscription written over him in letters of Greek, and Latin, and Hebrew: "This is the King of the Jews."'[2] The inscription was doubly ironic. Its putative authors would have meant the irony to be self-evident; the ignominy of the crucifixion – a slave's punishment – proclaimed its falsity. But in the narratives of the Evangelists, the irony worked on a second level. This was not the 'King of the Jews,' but the Son of God. With the triumph of Christianity in the late Roman Empire, a third level of irony was added. Under Christ the King, the successors of Peter and Caesar gained dominion over this world and the next. The cross was metamorphosed into the church, and the church was inscribed with the message of its supremacy.[3]

Verse inscriptions began to appear as part of the decoration of Christian churches as soon as Christianity became the authorized religion of the Empire. Rome was a city of inscriptions. The stately carved capital letters of the dedicatory inscriptions on the porticoes of public buildings and triumphal arches reflected Roman power and assurance. Until the Christian revolution, most building inscriptions were in prose. Verse and verse inscriptions, however, were employed for two religious or quasi-religious purposes in the Roman world that could not fail to have been noticed or remembered by Christians in the fourth century and beyond. First, pagan epitaphs were often composed in hexameters or elegiacs, both in Greek and in Latin, and Christians followed suit.[4] Second, verses were used in a variety of ways in connection with famous oracles. Verses were inscribed upon their altars, and recorded the names of pilgrims. Oracular pronouncements were often delivered in hexameters or other classical metres.[5]

In AD 315 the Roman Senate erected the Arch of Constantine to commemorate the emperor's epoch-making victory over Maxentius at the Battle of Mulvian Bridge three years earlier. On the eve of battle Constantine had adopted the cross; his victory tipped the scales in favour of Christianity. The Arch still displays on its north and south faces, above the central arch, the prose dedicatory inscription, originally in letters of bronze (only the undercuttings in the stone remain) (fig. 3): 'The Senate and the People of Rome have dedicated (this) arch, conspicuous with (scenes of his) triumphs to the emperor Constantine the Great, *Pius, Felix*, Augustus, because by divine inspiration (and) greatness of mind, with his army he avenged the State against both the tyrant and his whole army, at one (and the same) time, with righteous arms.'[6] The monuments of imperial Rome, like the pyramids of Egypt, seem grandiose relics of a vanished civilization. It is difficult for a modern visitor, standing in front of the Arch, to connect it in any meaningful way with the Christian culture that was taking shape around it. Nevertheless, the inscription on the Arch played a significant role in the development of the convention of verse inscriptions on Christian churches.

About fifteen years after the construction of the Arch, Constantine, having declared Christianity the state religion, undertook to build a church, dedicated to Saint Peter, on the site of a temple of Apollo in what is now Vatican City.[7] Old Saint Peter's was constructed on the basilican cruciform plan. A chancel or 'triumphal' arch marked the passage from the nave into the transept. The triumphal arch was decorated with a mosaic of Constantine presenting a model of the church to Christ and Saint Peter, with an inscription in letters of gold.[8] The analogy between the arch in the interior of the church and the triumphal arches of Rome was probably as evident to Constantine and the builders of the fourth century as it is to us, because the inscription, in Latin hexameters, read:

> Quod, duce te, mundus surrexit in astra triumphans,
> Hanc Constantinus victor tibi condidit aulam.[9]
> *(Because the world rose triumphant to the stars under your leadership, Constantine the victorious built this church for you.)*

These verses employ the same syntactic and thematic formula that the dedicators used for the inscription on the Arch. 'The Senate/Constantine // dedicated/built // the arch/church // for the emperor/Christ, // because (*quod*) under his/your leadership // the state/world // was avenged/triumphed.' The theme of sacralized political triumph has been transferred from earthly to spiritual empire. It seems reasonably certain that Constantine, or his writer, deliberately imitated the inscription on the Arch, and that the idea of triumph was part of the meaning of the chancel arch in basilican churches from the beginning.[10]

There are other points of similarity and contrast between these two inscriptions and the structures on which they were set that are worth exploring, given the enduring vitality of the tradition of verse inscriptions that was inaugurated here. Both inscriptions were accompanied by images to which the inscriptions refer. On the Arch of Constantine the sculpture is formally isolated from the inscription. Much of the sculpture was taken from earlier monuments, but the frieze that extends around the four outer faces of the Arch above the level of the two smaller side arches is contemporary. It shows the scenes of Constantine's triumphs over his enemies mentioned in the inscription as well as his triumphal procession. Human figures tend to line up side by side, either facing forward or moving in procession toward a goal. They belong to an authorized version of the past, not distant (at the time the Arch was built), but safely contained. The inscription calls our attention to this visually narrated history. Its words mediate between the present time of the dedicators, the Senate, and the present time of us, the viewers. They invite our uncritical acceptance of the *res gestae* of the sculpture.

The mosaic of the triumphal arch of Old Saint Peter's disappeared in 1525 when the arch was destroyed.[11] We do not know the precise disposition of the figures in the mosaic or how the verse inscription was placed in relation to them. But there is no great mystery. The sixth-century mosaic of the triumphal arch of San Lorenzo fuori le Mura seems to have been modelled on it. Christ in Majesty[12] is in the centre, above the arch, flanked by three standing figures on each side. These include Saint Lawrence, Saint Peter, Saint Paul, and Pope Pelagius II (579–90) on the far left, who offers a model of the church in veiled hands. A verse inscription, which follows the curve of the arch beneath their feet, declares: 'Deacon, you once endured martyrdom in flames. Your venerable light has justly returned to your church.'[13] Although this is a slightly more complicated scheme than the mosaic of Old Saint Peter's, it very likely makes use of the same arrangement of visual image and inscription. The mosaic figures occupy the space on the chancel arch that corresponds to the inscription panel in the attic above the central arch on the Arch of Constantine. The image rather than the inscription carries the burden of the message. The image exists in the timeless present of eternity; the inscription, which is reduced to a subordinate, decorative location, provides a bridge from the temporal world of the viewer to this eternal scene.

The inscription in the mosaic of Old Saint Peter's addressed Christ in the second person ('Because the world rose triumphant to the stars under your leadership, Constantine the victorious built this church for you'). Second-person address implies a first-person speaker. This tentative shift of voice to the first person, with its intimacy and involvement of the viewer, is a harbinger of a more radical use of the first-person voice in the Romanesque period. It points to the influence of the epitaph on the development of monumental verse inscriptions. In pre-Christian Latin verse epitaphs, the deceased person sometimes speaks in his own voice and is sometimes addressed in the second person by the mourner.[14] Christian epitaphs employed the same conventions, which were then applied to inscriptions honouring the saints and martyrs. A poem composed by Pope Damasus (366–84) for the reliquary tomb of Saint Agnes can still be seen inscribed on a stone panel in the staircase to the narthex of Sant'Agnese fuori le Mura. It concludes: 'O dear noble woman, holy glory of chastity, whom I venerate, I pray that you, celebrated martyr, favour the prayers of Damasus.'[15]

The couplet from Old Saint Peter's Basilica is, so far as I am aware, the earliest monumental verse inscription on a Christian church of which we have any record. Several other verses were inscribed on its interior surfaces later in the fourth or fifth century.[16] An apse mosaic behind the altar showed Christ in Majesty flanked by Saint Paul and Saint Peter; beneath them were two processions of sheep coming from Jerusalem and Bethlehem toward the Lamb of God in the centre.[17] The mosaic was created in the mid-fourth century, but it was remodelled by Pope Innocent III (1198–1216). The verses on the horizontal inscription band below the Lamb of God frieze must have been added during the remodelling, because they displayed full leonine rhyme – something unheard of in inscriptions before the Romanesque period – but they may have replaced unrhymed verses in the same position.[18]

The mosaics of Old Saint Peter's fixed for centuries to come two schemes for combining images with verse. One is the scheme of the triumphal arch, in which the mosaic is laid out in the flat, rectangular surface above the arch and the verse inscription is placed in a narrow, semicircular band around the arch. (A variant of this scheme occurs when the surface in front of the apsidal semidome is treated like a triumphal arch. It is an unfortunate fact that this surface is often referred to, also, as a 'triumphal arch.' The two architectural elements are different, and ought to be distinguished. I refer to the surface in front of the apsidal semidome as an 'apsidal arch.') The other is the scheme of the apse, in which the mosaic is laid out in the concave interior surface of the apsidal semidome and the verse inscription is placed in a broad, rectangular band around the semidome's curved base. If it were projected on a flat plane, an apse mosaic would have precisely the form of a Romanesque tympanum. A tympanum with an inscription running around the rim of the arch owes something to the first scheme, while a tympanum with a horizontal inscription on the lintel corresponds to the second.

In Rome we can distinguish three periods of renewed interest in church mosaics after the imperial age of Constantine and his successors. There are the mosaics of the sixth and seventh centuries; those of the ninth century, associated particularly with Pope Paschal I; and those of the twelfth and thirteenth centuries. Artists and patrons alike tended to be conservative; the themes and formulas of the fourth century were repeated over and over again.

In the sixth and seventh centuries, the presentation of a model of the church was frequently shown in the apse mosaic above a Lamb of God frieze. The donor was no longer the emperor but the pope. Pope Felix IV (526–30) constructed the basilica of Santi Cosma e Damiano from a pre-Christian, probably public, building in the Roman Forum, in honour of the martyrs Cosmas and Damian. According to legend, these twin brothers were physicians who practised medicine as a charity among the poor and were martyred in Syria for their faith. In the apse mosaic, Christ stands in clouds above the river Jordan (fig. 4). Pope Felix, Saint Cosmas, and Saint Paul are on the left; Saint Peter, Saint Damian, and Saint Theodore are on the right. Pope Felix offers the church. A Lamb of God frieze is beneath their feet and, below that, a verse inscription that lays stress upon the glittering mosaic tiles of the church: 'Beautified with bright mosaic tiles, the house of God shines, in which the precious light of faith shines more. Certain hope of eternal health came to the people after the doctors became martyrs, and from that sacred honour this place has grown. Felix has presented this gift, worthy of a bishop, to the Lord, so that he may live in the supernal citadel of heaven.'[19]

The apse mosaic of Sant'Agnese fuori le Mura shows Pope Honorius I

(625–38) offering the church to Saint Agnes.[20] An inscription band beneath their feet is filled with six elegiac couplets. Inspired, it would seem, by the verses in Santi Cosma e Damiano, the poet introduces every variation on the theme of light playing on the mosaic tiles that he can think of, not always to the advantage of syntax and sense:

> The golden picture arises from the cut tesserae, and having been embraced as well, the day itself is confined within. You might believe that the dawn is climbing up from snowy fountains, watering the fields with dew after the clouds have been chased away, or rather that it will bring forth light like a rainbow among the stars, and shining with colour like the purple peacock itself. He, who was able to restore day and light, has banished chaos henceforth from the tombs of the martyrs. With a single command, Bishop Honorius gave that which is discerned by all above, these prayers of his having been devoted [to the project?]. His features are represented by his clothing and deeds, and he gleams in appearance, displaying a shining heart.[21]

A variation on these images and ideas occurs in the apse mosaic of the chapel of San Venanzio in the Baptistery of Saint John Lateran. The mosaic was probably commissioned by Pope John IV (640–2) and finished by Pope Theodore (642–9). Christ in Majesty appears in the clouds flanked by two angels on either side (all half-figures). Beneath, instead of a Lamb of God frieze, we see the Virgin in the *orans* position flanked by four figures on either side. Among them, on the left, is Pope John with a model of the chapel in his veiled hands, and, on the right, Pope Theodore, holding a reliquary casket.[22] There are three elegiac couplets in the inscription band, which read: 'Bishop John offered pious prayers to the martyrs of Christ the Lord, with God giving his blessing. But being prudent he urgently united this work with the glittering mosaic to the similar one of the sacred fountain [= the Baptistery]. From which place anyone approaching and falling prone in adoration of Christ sends his prayers, which he has poured out, to heaven.'[23]

The modern visitor views these apse mosaics in the even, steady illumination of electrical lighting (frequently interrupted by the expiration of time purchased on a meter!). Awe-inspiring as they now are, one can only imagine how much more awesome they must have been in the flickering light of hundreds of lamps and candles. Roman worshippers might or might not have been impressed by the monumentality of the church or by the representation of human and divine figures on a large scale. Despite administrative disorder and the devastation of barbarian invasions, Rome still offered endless prospects of grandeur. But the play of light on the mosaics was unique, as the verse inscriptions make clear. This light was a metaphor for the eternal light; it gave the faithful a glimpse of the order that lay beyond chaos. To enter the church was to move into a divine palace (*aula*). In the apse mosaic of God's palace on earth one could see through this world into the next. Radiant beauty became a way of transcending temporal cares. The verses in their inscription band, like a great open scroll, are the last visual expression of the human world before the eye is lifted up and beyond.

Almost two centuries separate the mosaics of the late-antique basilicas of Rome from the mosaics of Pope Paschal I (817–24). Although in the interim the classical world had faded away to be replaced by the Europe of the Carolingian Empire, one's first impression, judging from the mosaics, is that Rome was sleeping in a dream of the past. The same images appear in the vaults of the apse; the same words in the inscriptions. Rome was always resistant to change. Nevertheless, on closer examination, some novel elements show up against the background of continuity.

The apse mosaic of Santa Maria in Domnica displays for the first time in an apse the Virgin in Majesty with the Child in her lap (fig. 5). Paschal had it built during his papacy. As the inscription in the apse mosaic suggests, it replaced an earlier church. The Virgin is flanked by angels (the celestial choir) in a field of flowers and by the kneeling figure of Paschal who is depicted with a square blue halo (indicating that he was still alive). He grasps the Virgin's right foot in his hands. Paschal's monogram appears above her head. On the upper face of the apsidal arch, Christ in Majesty in a mandorla is at the top between two standing angels. Six apostles approach him on either side. Saint Paul carries a model of the church in his veiled hands. On the inscription band around the base of the mosaic are the verses: 'This church had long since fallen in ruins. Now it shines continually, decorated with various precious stones, and, behold, his (?) glory shines like Phoebus [Apollo] in orbit, he, virtuous Bishop Paschal, who afterwards, driving away the black veils of horrid night, joyously built this church, which should remain through the ages, for you, Virgin Mary.'[24]

The church of Santa Prassede is nearly swallowed up now in the urban sprawl that surrounds Santa Maria Maggiore, although before its nave was truncated it was very nearly as long as the great basilica. It was built by Pope Paschal on the site of an earlier fifth-century church. He had a crypt readied beneath the altar as the resting place for a huge number of relics of popes and martyrs that he ordered to be gathered from the catacombs and carried in procession to Santa Prassede.

So the Palace of God (*aula Dei*), while never ceasing to be that, became as well the domicile for all the saints whose relics it possessed. Santa Prassede housed the relics of Saint Praxedes, who was believed to be one of two virgin daughters of the Pudens mentioned in passing by Saint Paul in 2 Timothy 4:21. Her sister's church, Santa Pudenziana, is just three hundred metres away. And, as the verse inscription of Santa Prassede informs us, Saint Praxedes' bones were not alone. The *translatio* of relics had become an industry. Another powerful motive behind Paschal's interest in them may have been the demand for relics in the churches of northern and western Europe beyond the Alps. Since the Fifth Council of Carthage (401), the Roman Catholic Church had required that every altar contain relics (although this was not binding throughout the West and was not enforced in Rome for centuries). Before Willibrord undertook his mission to Frisia, he hurried to Rome to obtain relics from Pope Sergius I (687–701) for the churches that he hoped to establish.[25] Carolingian ecclesiastics, re-emphasizing the requirement, began importing relics in large quantities.[26] Rome was the most plentiful and prestigious source of supply. Paschal's churches were, in a sense, way stations for the translation of saints' relics along the routes to the north as well as focal points for pilgrimages to the relics they retained.

In the apse mosaic of Santa Prassede we see Christ standing against the background of the river Jordan with Saint Peter, Saint Pudentiana, and Saint Zeno on his left, and Saint Paul, Saint Praxedes, and Pope Paschal on his right.[27] Paschal, with a square halo, presents a model of the church. Paschal's monogram is above Christ's head. A Lamb of God frieze separates Christ and the saints from the mosaic inscription band around the base that displays these verses: 'The church, decorated with various precious stones, gleams in honour of holy Praxedes, who is pleasing to the Lord in heaven above, through the care of the supreme pontiff, father Paschal of the apostolic see, who, burying bodies everywhere, places a great many bodies of the saints beneath these walls, trusting that he may deserve to approach the threshold of heaven.'[28] Crowds of standing figures packed tightly together in the mosaics of the triumphal arch and the spandrels of the apsidal arch hint at the multitude of relics in the crypt.

Paschal's passion for collecting relics is reflected in another church that he had rebuilt, the church of Santa Cecilia in Trastevere. The apse mosaic is similar to the one in Santa Prassede. Christ stands against a background of thin clouds in a field of flowers. Paschal, Saint Agatha, and Saint Paul are on his right. Saint Peter, Saint Cecilia, and Saint Valerian are on his left. Paschal, with his square halo, holds a model of the church. Beneath their feet is a Lamb of God frieze. The Lamb of God with a Chi-Rho monogram inscribed in his halo stands on a tiny hill in the centre. Six lambs on each side move in procession from the cities of Bethlehem and Jerusalem. The Hand of God is above Christ's head, and Paschal's monogram is above that, on the underside of the arch. The nine hexameters in the inscription band read: 'This spacious house, constructed with various precious stones, which once in an earlier age had been ruined, sparkles. Wealthy Bishop Paschal has built this house of the Lord for the better, forming it with a bright foundation. This golden sanctuary of the temple echoes with gems. Here, joyous with the love of God, he has united the holy bodies with Cecilia and her companions. Here the youth in their prime shine brightly, those blessed limbs which long ago rested in death in the catacombs [*in cruptis*]. Rome, forever embellished, always exulting, resounds.'[29] The crypts of medieval churches were a development and extension of the *confessiones*, the burial places of martyrs, of early Christian churches. In Rome Christians commemorated martyrs at their tombs in Rome's suburban catacombs and cemeteries. Regular worship took place in urban churches, many of which seem to have originated in *tituli* (private houses where Christian services were held). These urban churches acquired relics and exhibited them in a *confessio*, which might be a small recessed chamber beneath or behind the altar. As traffic in relics increased in the Carolingian period, the *confessio* became in some instances a full-size lower-level church or crypt into which pilgrims could descend via stairs from the main church above.[30] The Plan of Saint Gall, which is almost exactly contemporary with Pope Paschal's churches in Rome, shows just such an arrangement, and the new space beneath the main altar is labelled a 'crypt,'[31] the word that for Paschal still signified the catacombs.

Paschal's vigorous campaign of relic-hunting, his support of art, and the development of the crypt in place of the *confessio* may all have been responses to the suppression of the cult of the saints in the East during the iconoclastic persecutions that were particularly strong in Constantinople in the eighth and ninth centuries.[32] Hostility to the representation of the human figure in art must have driven some Byzantine mosaicists to the West.[33] Their influence has been detected in the apse mosaic of Santa Cecilia, where Christ gives his benediction in the Eastern manner (fourth finger touching the thumb). Both the art and the collections of relics in Paschal's churches were powerful statements of the papal position in the controversy.

After the ninth century there was another hiatus in the art of mosaic decoration in Rome. The next, and final, flowering occurs in the Romanesque period. Despite their resemblance to earlier Roman mosaics, three features help identify the apse mosaics of San Clemente and Santa Maria in Trastevere as twelfth-century work or remodelling. First, in a general way they exhibit a certain anecdotal quality. There is a greater variety of scenes, including ones alluding to typological relationships between the Old and New Testaments. Second, the inscription band moves up to become a border between the central scene of the apse semidome and the Lamb of God frieze. Third, the verses display leonine rhyme.

Although they may preserve some elements of the design of a much older mosaic, the mosaics of the basilica of San Clemente belong to the world of the twelfth century.[34] The present church was rebuilt on top of the rubble-filled ruins of the fourth-century church by Cardinal Anastasius, the Titular of San Clemente from ca. 1099 to 1125.[35] The older church had been severely damaged by a fire set by Robert Guiscard in 1084.[36] The decision to rebuild was taken ca. 1100, during the pontificate of Paschal II (1099–1118), who was Anastasius's predecessor as Titular of San Clemente. Walter Oakeshott dates the mosaics to about 1125.[37]

The apse mosaic depicts the Crucifixion of Christ, with Mary and John on either side of the Cross. Twelve doves are on the Cross; a chrismon – a Chi-Rho monogram – with the Alpha and Omega is above it, and the hand of God above that. There is a foliage design growing from the base of the Cross and filling the background with spiral circles. Thirsting harts are placed at the base of the Cross, with scenes from everyday life beside them. A mosaic inscription band encircles the base. Below this is the traditional Lamb of God frieze.

The verses of the inscription band present problems of continuity and reference. They read:

Ecclesiam Cristi viti similabimus isti
De ligno crucis. Iacobi dens Ignatiique
In suprascripti requiescunt corpore Cristi
Quam lex arentem set crus facit esse virentem.[38]

(We will liken the Church of Christ to this vine from the wood of the Cross – the tooth of James and [the tooth] of Ignatius rest in the body of the already-mentioned / depicted-above ? Christ –, which the [Old] Law desiccates but the Cross makes green.)

Oakeshott suggests that the first and fourth verses, which belong together, might have been reproduced from the apse mosaic of the fourth-century church.[39] This cannot be so, because they display full leonine rhyme, which was never used in early mosaics. The second and third verses seem to be a crude interpolation (there are false quantities in *crucis* and *Iacobi*). A fifteenth-century pilgrim's guide mentions that the relics of Saint Ignatius were among those displayed in San Clemente.[40] Oakeshott, who interprets these verses slightly differently from the way I have, implies that the relics of Saint James and Saint Ignatius, that is, the teeth, are depicted in the mosaic in the body of Christ on the cross. If so, they are difficult to see.

The spandrel mosaics of the apsidal arch depict the martyrs Lawrence and Clement with Saints Paul and Peter above Isaiah and Jeremiah. Two more leonine hexameters accompany these scenes. Isaiah instructs Lawrence to carry out Paul's teaching about the cross, and Jeremiah directs Clement to behold Christ (presumably in the apse mosaic of the Crucifixion) whom he had foretold.[41] Thus, the mosaics proclaim, in typical medieval fashion, the importance of the prophets of the Old Testament as harbingers of Christ.

Pope Innocent II (1130–43) reconstructed the basilica of Santa Maria in Trastevere about 1140, after Bernard of Clairvaux managed to bring an end to the schism between Innocent and the antipope Victor IV.[42] The apse mosaic reflects the new emphasis on Mary, so typical of sculptural programs later in the century. Christ and Mary are seated in majesty, side by side (the two thrones are displaced to the left, so that Christ is in the axial position). In the ancient manner of nearly all Roman mosaics, standing figures of saints and popes line up on the right and left. Among them, on the far left, is Pope Innocent, who holds a model of the church. The verses of the inscription band, which combine disyllabic end rhyme (1/2, 5/6) with full leonine rhyme (3/4), read: 'This very brilliant basilica shines with the divine glory of beauty in your honour, Mother of honour. The seat remains forever in which you sit, Christ. She, whom the golden clothing covers, is worthy of (sitting on) your right. Since the old building was about to fall down, Pope Innocent the Second, who came from here, restored it.'[43]

At the very end of the thirteenth century Pietro Cavallini added a series of six panels of the Life of the Virgin underneath the mosaics of the apsidal arch and the apse. Unrhymed hexameters accompany each panel. One of the panels shows Joseph, seated at the lower left, facing a small church and round tower. A little stream flows from the door of the church to a river. This is a visual reference to a medieval legend which maintained that on the very site of Santa Maria in Trastevere a spring of oil miraculously flowed from the ground on the night of the Nativity.[44] Although they complement and humanize the majestic scene above them, these panels seem unrelated to the hierarchical iconography of the Roman mosaic tradition. We are abruptly in the presence of a pictorial world derived from the frescoes of the late thirteenth century.

By their placement in the interiors of the buildings Roman mosaic inscriptions in verse were hidden from the sight of casual passers-by. In this respect, they represented a radical departure from the public inscriptions, civic and religious, of pagan Rome. But in verbal content they remained constant to the old Roman tradition of proclaiming the magnificence of the patron – first the emperor and then the popes. And, like the mosaics they accompanied, as the centuries passed, they remained remote, stiff, and hierarchical – mirroring the authoritarian pretensions of an increasingly imperial papacy.

3

Portal Inscriptions, Liminal Transformation, and the Creation of Sacred Space

The practice of adding inscriptions to churches spread widely throughout western Europe. Verses accompanied apse mosaics, just as they did in Rome, but other parts of the church also received inscriptions. Most of these have long since disappeared, as have the buildings that displayed them. Nevertheless, enough evidence remains to show that verses were often displayed on exterior walls and with increasing frequency above the portals of churches and other buildings in monastic complexes, where they exhibited a new tone and focus. They concerned themselves with the spiritual well-being of worshippers, and they served to create and delineate sacred space.

A basilica erected in Reims before AD 367 by the Roman general Jovinus carried a verse inscription on its façade in letters of gold.[1] A century later, when Bishop Patiens of Lyon (450–94) constructed his cathedral on the bank of the river Saône, he commissioned three poets, Constantius, Secundinus, and Sidonius Apollinaris, to write verses for it. Hexameters by Constantius and Secundinus were placed on the walls adjoining the apse. Sidonius (ca. 430–ca. 487) composed a thirty-line poem in hendecasyllables for the 'far ends' (*extimis*) of the building. It was apparently inscribed at the end of the church opposite the apse. Addressing the viewer in the second person, it celebrated among other glories the play of light on the gold leaf of the ceiling: 'Light gleams within, and thus the sun is enticed to the gilded ceiling, so that it plays over the gold leaf in the same colour.'[2]

The mosaics of Ravenna, which rival those of Rome in splendour, preserve verses from the sixth century in the church of Sant'Apollinare in Classe[3] and in the narthex of the chapel of Sant'Andrea in the Archbishop's Palace. The palace chapel was commissioned by Bishop Peter II

(494–519). At one end of the narthex – a low, barrel-vaulted chamber – there is a mosaic of Christ, with a book in his hand, standing on a lion and an asp. The barrel vault is covered with a mosaic of a field of birds and flowers. Inscription panels face each other on the long walls that support the vault. Audience, patronage, tradition, and purpose all played a part in determining what themes a poet would consider appropriate for a church. Bishop Peter could not resist the obvious puns on his name; his pride in his own patronage and his delight in the reflection of light on the mosaic tiles is evident.[4] But one poem strikes a different note: 'Coming hither, let him pour forth laments, which will produce joys, making firm the contrite mind in the stricken breast. In order that he may not die, let him lie down on the ground, and reveal hidden diseases plainly to the physician with hastening care. Often the fear of death becomes the cause of a blessed life.'[5] The visible expression of these emotional, penitential themes with their emphasis on the recuperative, transforming experience of entering the church owes much to the contemporary development of sacred space in monastic churches that were the goals of pilgrimage.

European monasticism was a product of two contradictory human impulses – the urge to wander and the desire to find a stable dwelling place. The men and women who set out on distant journeys to visit the *loca sancta* and other holy places[6] were often the same men and women who sought refuge for the spirit within fixed walls. Movement and stasis were characteristically linked in the lives of two monks of the fourth century who are of immediate concern to this narrative – Saint Martin of Tours (ca. 316–97) and Paulinus of Nola (ca. 355–431).

Saint Martin journeyed far before coming to rest on the banks of the Loire. He was born in Pannonia in what is now Hungary. His most famous gesture – dividing his cloak in half to share it with a poor beggar – took place in Amiens. He was baptized in Poitiers by Saint Hilary. Later, he retraced his steps to Pannonia, went on to Illyricum (roughly Slovenia, Croatia, and Bosnia), and to Milan. Returning to France, he settled as a hermit in a ruined Roman villa at Ligugé near Poitiers, where disciples gathered about him and formed the first monastery in Gaul.[7] Still later, he was acclaimed bishop of Tours, but he continued to live as a monk in the monastery of Marmoutier near the town. The fame of his cult spread both because of his reputation as a worker of miracles and because of a popular biography of him, written by his friend Sulpicius Severus.

Pilgrims flocking to the shrine of Saint Martin after his death required ever larger facilities. Saint Perpetuus, bishop of Tours (458–88), enclosed the chapel that housed the relics with a far grander structure, which he consecrated in 470.[8] He invited Sidonius Apollinaris to write a poem for the walls of the new church. Sidonius obliged him with twenty lines of elegiac verse in which he compared Perpetuus's building to the temple of Solomon.[9] Gregory of Tours (ca. 539–94) rebuilt the Merovingian basilica after a fire damaged it in 558. According to his description: 'It is one hundred and sixty feet long by sixty feet broad; and its height up to the beginning of the vaulting is forty-five feet ... In the whole building there are fifty-two windows, one hundred and twenty columns and eight doorways, three in the sanctuary and five in the nave.'[10] A poem composed by Saint Martin of Braga (ca. 515–80) was inscribed above the south portal.[11]

Five poems, together with some other prose legends, which are said to be from the basilica, appear in several ninth- and tenth-century manuscripts of Sulpicius Severus's *Life of Saint Martin.*[12] Rubrics in the manuscripts indicate, approximately, the location of these poems and legends in the church. The evidence reveals that the *portals* were decorated with scenes from the Bible and the life of Saint Martin and that some of the verse inscriptions addressed the faithful as they were about to enter the church.[13] This suggests a conception of the spiritual mission of the Church that has more in common with the ideas of Paulinus of Nola (discussed below) than it does with papal attitudes in Rome. Whereas the popes, following the imperial example of Constantine, looked upon the churches they financed as personal gifts to the supreme ruler in heaven, the abbots and monks of Saint-Martin of Tours regarded their church as an instrument for the salvation of others. Rather than being a human message to God, the church had become a divine messenger to mankind.

One of the five poems is a twenty-five-line poem on the subject of Saint Martin, which was composed by Paulinus of Périgueux (fl. ca. 459–72). A poem of this length would have been too long to be effectively integrated into mural decorations. It was probably presented on a separate inscription plaque, rather like the page of a book set into the wall. The poem addressed the viewer. It begins: 'Each of you, bent to the ground, has plunged your face in the dust, and has pressed your moist eyes to the beaten earth. Lifting up your eyes, conceive the miracles with anxious sight and assign the cause to your distinguished patron saint. No inscription plaque can comprehend such great power, although the rough rocks and stones themselves may be inscribed with these *tituli* [= labels in prose or verse].' This is the voice of the Church instructing worshippers in the penitential attitude they should adopt before entering through the portal. The last lines return to the theme: 'Whoever attends weeping, joyfully returns. All the clouds yield. What disturbs merit, the art of medicine makes serene. Seek help. You do not knock on these doors in vain. Piety so prodigal goes forth into the entire world.'[14] There can be little doubt that the inscription plaque was set on the *exterior* of the basilica in conjunction with scenes from the life of the saint.

Edmond Le Blant tentatively identified the poem that begins *Quisquis templa Dei* as the poem of Martin of Braga above the south portal. The south portal was probably damaged or destroyed in the fire of 558. Martin is known to have visited Tours in or about the year 560, so the poem (if the identification is correct) may belong to that year.[15] Like the previous one, this poem is a liminal inscription that addresses the worshipper as a penitent: 'Whoever you are who are about to enter the church of God with a pure mind, you enter to ask for pardon for your recent sins. You must not hesitate in mind, you must not hesitate in faith. What you seek you get if you ask with a pure heart. As He himself says, you believe, so salvation will be yours.'[16]

Other portals were similarly inscribed. Another of the poems was for a portal in the entrance tower. According to the rubric the tower was in the east (*in turre a parte orientis*); how it stood in relation to the apse is uncertain.[17] The poem, which is in elegiacs, plays on the conceit that the lowly shall be exalted and the proud humbled:

> Entering the church, lift your face to the heights [*Ingrediens templum refer ad sublimia vultum*], deep faith looks up at lofty entrances. Be humble in understanding but pursue with hope the person who is calling. Venerate the doors which Martin opens. This tower thrown up against agitated, proud persons is safe, excluding puffed-up hearts, protecting gentle ones. But that [tower is] higher which, spiralling up with star-bearing paths, carried Martin to the citadel of heaven, from which place he, who, having led the way and entered [heaven], sanctified the starry journey, calls the peoples to the goods of Christ.[18]

Emile Mâle saw in the metaphor of the second tower evidence that the Merovingian basilica had a crossing tower that was taller than the entrance tower and that appeared like a pedestal from which Saint Martin could have been imagined as mounting toward heaven.[19]

Another poem was located 'in the other direction' (*a parte alia*) from the portal in the entrance tower. The first line makes it clear that this too was a portal inscription: 'You who are about to enter the church, venerating the threshold of Christ [*Intraturi aulam venerantes limina Christi*], drive out worldly cares from your mind, and free your mind from profane desires. May he who prays for righteous things come back out with his wishes fulfilled.'[20]

Finally, a poem in elegiac couplets, which was inscribed above the western portal (*in introitu a parte occidentis, super ostium historia picta viduae*), accompanied a mural painting or mosaic of the Widow's Mite, drawing the moral lesson implicit in the parable of the poor woman who gave all she had to the Church (Mark 12:41–4; Luke 21:1–4).[21]

Two prose legends were inscribed above a portal that faced the Loire. Since the Loire is to the north of the church this must have been a north portal, perhaps a north nave portal. One of the legends apparently accompanied a mural decoration in three scenes of Jesus and the Disciples Walking upon the Water.[22] The other inscription implies that there was a mural decoration representing a church in Palestine. According to the inscription, the church possessed the throne of the apostle James and the column on which Christ was scourged: 'The most holy church of Christ which is the mother of all churches. The apostles had founded this church in which the Holy Spirit descended upon them in the likeness of tongues of fire. In it is placed the throne of the apostle James and the column on which Christ was flagellated.'[23] (Cf. Acts 2:3.) The church depicted in the mural was evidently the church of Saint Mary on Mount Sion in Jerusalem. According to Bede, the apostles founded the church of Saint Mary on the spot where the Holy Spirit descended upon them, and the marble column on which Christ was scourged stood in the middle of the church.[24] These subjects suggest an interest in associating the experience of local pilgrims with the *loca sancta* of Palestine.

William Loerke argues that the systematic liturgical organization, beginning in the fourth century, of the sites in Palestine connected with the remote events of the Bible transformed the experience of pilgrims by lifting those events into the present through a reading of texts and prayers at the very place where each event occurred. This created a new realism in a 'progressive past tense' in Christian art.[25] The affective emotionalism of this art could be utilized in the holy places of western Europe. Tours was a pilgrimage church, and these murals indicate that the monks were aware of the impact on pilgrims of the *loca sancta* and the relics of Palestine. Perhaps they hoped that by associating the portals of their own basilica with the life of Saint Martin and the Holy Lands they would enable the pilgrims to Tours to experience a similar transformation of the spirit at the moment of entrance.

Paulinus of Nola does not loom so large in the standard introductions to monasticism in the West. It could even be debated whether he has any title to be called a monk at all.[26] Nevertheless, the ideals of monasticism and the spirit of religious revival stimulated by Saint Martin inspired Paulinus and his work at Nola. To read about Paulinus is to be reminded of the immense scale and enduring vitality of the late Roman Empire. He was born Meropius Pontius Paulinus in the Roman province of Aquitania in Gaul about 355 to a wealthy Gallo-Roman noble family, which possessed vast estates in Aquitaine, in Campania in Italy, and in Spain. His teacher at Bordeaux was the poet Ausonius, with whom he studied rhetoric and the law. He entered state service at an early age, and held a number of important offices, advancing to senatorial rank and, probably, the consulship. On a trip to Spain he met and married Therasia, who came from another wealthy noble family and was a pious Christian. The couple lived for a time near Bordeaux, where Paulinus was baptized, and then moved to Spain, where they had a son who died shortly after birth.[27] At some point Paulinus came under the influence of Saint Martin; Sulpicius Severus claimed that Martin cured him of an affliction of the eyes.[28]

After the death of their son, Paulinus and Therasia agreed to live chastely as brother and sister in Christ, and Paulinus clothed himself as a monk. Progressively selling off his estates, he gave the proceeds to the poor. At the insistence of the people of Barcelona he was made a priest in December of 394. Shortly thereafter he and Therasia travelled through Rome to his rich family estate at Nola in southern Italy, about sixteen miles east of Naples. In Nola he developed a special veneration for the confessor and priest Saint Felix of Nola (d. 260). He spent his time in the work of providing municipal services for the town and restoring and building a cluster of churches in honour of Felix. He turned the ground floor of his house into a guest-house for pilgrims and the poor. On the second floor, he and some friends followed a monastic routine, which included a daily recital of the divine office. It will surprise no one to learn that it fell to Therasia to act as housekeeper for the community. Paulinus became bishop of Nola between 404 and 415, and exercised that office until his death on 22 June 431.[29]

There were already several churches at Nola when Therasia and Paulinus took up permanent residence there in 396. The most important was the cathedral church of Saint Felix. Paulinus undertook to restore and decorate the old cathedral. In accordance with normal practice in the fourth-century churches of Rome and the West, the façade of the cathedral faced east and the apse was in the west ('reverse orientation').[30]

Even before the restoration, the church of Felix had become a popular pilgrimage shrine. Paulinus speaks several times of the throngs of people crowding into the basilica. Perhaps overcrowding was one reason why he decided to build yet another church, but a more important motive may have been his desire to create a self-contained sacred space for meditation – a kind of monastic complex *avant la lettre.* The new church, the church of the Apostles, was not to be an independent structure. Instead, Paulinus decided that the old church of Felix and the new church should comprise a single unit. Thus, when he constructed the new church between 401 and 404, he abandoned reverse orientation and laid the building out on a north-south axis, with the façade facing the north side of the old basilica.[31] The arrangement of the two buildings can be envisaged as an upside-down T. The old church of Felix is the crossbar at the bottom, its apse to the left (west). The new church of the Apostles is the ascender, its apse to the top (north). However, the new building was not directly attached to the old. An atrium, or forecourt, extended south from the façade of the church of the Apostles. The atrium in turn opened onto a smaller courtyard on the north side of the church of Felix. Paulinus was immensely proud of the *transenna* that joined the atrium to the smaller courtyard. The *transenna* was a kind of screen with three arched portals through which either church could be seen from the other.[32] One imagines something like the entrance to the atrium of Sant'Ambrogio of Milan, where three inner arched portals opened into the courtyard (now bricked up on the outside except for the central door), or the entrance to the atrium of Old Saint Peter's, as reconstructed by Kenneth J. Conant.[33] The three portals of the *transenna* corresponded to the three portals of the south façade.

Verse inscriptions were to be seen everywhere in the new complex. Paulinus was fascinated with the signs and symbols of Christianity. He took pains to point out the hidden meaning of images as well as structures. The apse mosaic of the church of the Apostles was devoted to the Trinity. It was accompanied by a fourteen-line poem, which both described and explained it:

> The Trinity gleams in its full mystery: Christ appears as a lamb, the voice of the Father thunders from heaven, and the Holy Spirit issues forth through a dove. A wreath encircles the cross in a bright circle, and the apostles make a wreath for that wreath. They are figured in the chorus of doves. The holy unity of the Trinity is combined in Christ, who also has the very signs of three-ness: the voice of the Father reveals God, and the Spirit; the cross and

the lamb make known the holy sacrifice; the purple and the palm indicate the kingdom and the triumph. He himself, the rock of the Church, stands upon a rock, from which four sounding streams flow, the Evangelists, the living rivers of Christ.[34]

Another poem was set beneath the apse mosaic, probably just behind and above the main altar. The altar contained the relics of martyrs and a fragment of the true cross, which was a gift to Paulinus from Saint Melania. Paulinus found a special meaning in the association of these relics: 'How fitting that the bones of the pious martyrs are joined with the wood of the cross, so that there may be rest in the cross for those who were killed for the cross.'[35] Hexameter couplets identified the functions of the two sacristies on either side of the apse, and others were placed on the lintels of four side chapels in the nave.

The practice of placing verse inscriptions on or above the portals of the church of the Apostles and the *transenna* connecting it with the church of Felix marks an important stage on the road leading to the allegorized Romanesque portal, which came to rival the apse in the mystery and power of its numinous liminal space. Paulinus copied thirteen portal inscriptions in a letter to his friend Sulpicius Severus.[36] They cannot all be precisely located, but it is clear that there were verses above the triple portals on the exterior side of the south façade and on both sides of the three openings of the *transenna* that separated the atrium from the small courtyard. Repeatedly, Paulinus stressed how the layout of his complex projected the symbolism of unity in Trinity. The poem above the central arch on the inner side of the *transenna* began: 'Just as Jesus, our peace, broke down the middle wall [between the unredeemed world of the flesh and the spiritual world] and, destroying the division with the Cross, made the two into one, so we see that the new roofs, with the dividing line of the old roof having been pulled down, are joined by the bond of the portals.'[37] One of the side arches displayed this poem: 'The two churches have been laid open through the three arches, and each marvels at the elegance of the other through their common entrances.'[38] And a poem on the other side of the *transenna* declared: 'One faith which worships one God under three names receives those who are one in heart through a triple entrance.'[39]

Writing for these portals created a sense of audience in Paulinus. He began to address the person or persons whom he imagined to be entering. The doors of one portal were inscribed: 'Peace be with you, whoever you are who, being pure, with a peaceful heart, enter the sanctuary of

Christ the God.'[40] A cross was painted above this portal with the inscription: 'Behold the wreathed cross of Christ the Lord standing above the porch, which promises lofty rewards for hard labour; take up the cross, you who wish to carry off the wreath of victory.'[41] Is this Paulinus speaking, or is it the portal? Two uninspired poems addressed the crowds thronging through the *transenna* on their way from the church of Felix to the church of the Apostles. But an entrance to the church from the cloister garden brought out Paulinus's better qualities as a poet: 'Enter the celestial paths through pleasant lawns, Christians; it is also fitting that the entrance to this place is from fertile gardens. From here an exit into the sacred paradise is given to those who merit it.'[42] Not only did Paulinus turn the church complex into a symbolic reminder of the possibility of salvation, but by his emphasis on portals he made their liminal spaces a locus for reflection and spiritual transformation.

Mural paintings of scenes from the New Testament decorated the nave of the old church of Felix; scenes from the Old Testament decorated the nave of the new church of the Apostles. Each scene was labelled with a verse inscription, so that the people might know what they were looking at. Representations of human beings were not yet common in churches; Paulinus justified their presence with the argument that they could help cut down on gluttony and drunkenness among the illiterate peasants! As he explained it, the country folk, clinging to the customs of their pagan ancestors, celebrated the feasts of the saints by feasting and drinking throughout the night, carrying their cups into the churches. His hope was that the pictures would fill the people with admiration and wonder, and distract them, at least temporarily, from their evil habits.[43] But he was surely pleased with the visual splendour of the scenes and the artful way he had intertwined the Old Law and the new church with the New Law and the old church.[44]

By what may be only a curious coincidence, a collection of poems by Prudentius seems designed to accompany just such mural scenes as Paulinus had painted for his churches at Nola.[45] The *Dittochaeon*[46] or *Tituli Historiarum* is a sequence of forty-nine hexameter quatrains. The first twenty-four describe scenes from the Old Testament, like the Offering of Abel and Cain (no. 2) or Samson and the Foxes (no. 18); the next twenty-four describe scenes from the New Testament, like the Annunciation (no. 25) or the Raising of Lazarus (no. 38). The final quatrain (no. 49) concerns the Twenty-four Elders of the Apocalypse.[47] In the judgment of F.J.E. Raby, 'It is probable that they were inscriptions for mosaics or pictures in a Spanish basilica. One side of the great arcade would contain the twenty-four scenes of the Old Testament, and the other side the twenty-four scenes of the New, while the apse might be crowned with the elders of the Apocalypse praising the Lamb ...'[48] It is unclear whether or not Prudentius's poem anticipated the juxtaposition of scenes from the Old and New Testaments on opposite walls of the nave in churches in Rome, notably in Old Saint Peter's.[49] Be that as it may, the assumptions of typological exegesis had permeated the imagination of Christian-Latin poets and artists by the end of the fourth century. Prudentius was one of the most widely read authors in western Europe until at least the thirteenth century.[50] The *Dittochaeon* was imitated in the sixth century by a certain Rusticius (or Rusticus) Helpidius, who composed twenty-four verse inscriptions for related scenes from the Old and New Testaments for an unknown church in Italy.[51] Bede tells how Benedict Biscop, the abbot of the monastery of Wearmouth in which he had grown up as an oblate, brought back from Rome in 684 a wealth of treasure, which included 'a set of pictures for the monastery and church of the blessed apostle Paul, consisting of scenes, very skilfully arranged, to show how the Old Testament foreshadowed the New [*imagines ... de concordia ueteris et noui Testamenti ... conpositas*]. In one set, for instance, the picture of Isaac carrying the wood on which he was to be burnt as a sacrifice was placed immediately below that of Christ carrying the cross on which He was about to suffer. Similarly the Son of Man lifted up on the cross was paired with the serpent raised up by Moses in the desert.'[52] In the *Psychomachia* Prudentius enlarged the potential of typological allegory to embrace the moral conflict between the virtues and vices. The *Psychomachia* inspired numerous visual as well as verbal imitations.[53] Prudentius's poetry may have been as influential as the labours of the biblical commentators in perpetuating the allegorical habit of mind in the art of the Middle Ages.

During his tenure as Abbot of Tours (796–804), Alcuin had in the basilica of Saint-Martin a model for the practice of inscribing verses above portals. He borrowed the phrase *ingrediens templum* from the poem for the entrance tower for a poem he composed for the abbey church of Saint-Hilaire-le-Grand of Poitiers.[54] The basilica of Saint-Martin as Alcuin knew it was destroyed by the Vikings in 853 and 903.[55] It was reconstructed in 903–18 and again in 997–1014 (and rebuilt between 1050 and 1175), only to be destroyed finally in the French Revolution.[56] It is not certain whether verses were inscribed on these later structures, but one bit of evidence may be offered in the affirmative. When the abbey church of Saint-Pierre of Mozac, near Clermont, was built shortly after the abbey was affiliated with Cluny in 1095, the first line of the poem for the entrance tower at Tours and the first line of the poem for the portal 'in the other direction' from the entrance tower were inscribed on an archivolt which is now above the portal of the north porch at Mozac:

> Ingrediens templum referat ad sublimia vultum;
> Intraturi aulam veneransque limina Cristi.[57]

Both verses are slightly garbled, as though they had been imperfectly remembered, although this could be simply the result of later attempts to make sense of what was assumed to be a unified couplet. Perhaps the designer of the Mozac portal wished to invoke the prestige of the great pilgrimage centre of France by an allusion to two poems that were familiar to generations of pilgrims.[58]

Alcuin busied himself while he was at Tours composing verses for use in churches throughout the Carolingian empire.[59] In so doing he was imitating the practice of Christian poets of the fourth through the sixth centuries, like Paulinus of Nola, Prudentius, and Venantius Fortunatus (ca. 540–600), the bishop of Poitiers.[60] Alcuin's poems were topical. The poem in eight elegiac couplets that can still be seen inscribed on the lintels above the central piers of the interior octagon of the cathedral of Aachen is typical of his work, whether or not he was the author. It celebrates Charlemagne as the founder of the church: 'When the living stones are joined by a compact of peace, and everything is assembled into equal proportions, the work of the Lord shines – he who constructs the entire church and gives effect to the pious studies of men, whose structure of perpetual beauty will remain perfect, so long as its Author may protect and guide it. Thus may God will that this church, which Emperor Charles built, be secure on a stable foundation.'[61]

Alcuin died more than a decade before the councils of 816 and 817 at Aachen, where controversies were aired and decisions taken concerning the organization of monasteries within the Carolingian empire. In the library of the abbey of Saint Gall in Switzerland, there is preserved a comprehensive diagram of a Carolingian monastery with a significant number of inscriptions that may reflect contemporary practice. The diagram, known as the Plan of Saint Gall, is a unique document; nothing quite like it has come down to us from antiquity or the Middle Ages. It may be a copy of a paradigmatic scheme for a normative Benedictine monastery agreed to at the councils of Aachen. Abbot Haito of Reichenau (806–23) had the Plan prepared at Reichenau, perhaps between 826 and 830, and sent it to Abbot Gozbert (816–836/7) of Saint Gall, who was contemplating rebuilding his abbey.[62]

The Plan indicates in red ink the layout of all the monastic buildings. Numerous inscriptions provide information on everything from the dimensions of the main church to the location of the monks' privies. Many of them are no more than a word or a phrase indicating the function of an interior room or the nature of the item represented by some particular diagram. But among the inscriptions are thirty-six hexameters and five elegiac couplets.[63]

The thirty-six hexameters are used primarily to identify separate buildings. These verses are usually written on the Plan on the outside of the entrance walls to the buildings.[64] In the north range of the monastery hexameters label the house for distinguished guests, the outer school, and the abbot's house. In the west range the six service buildings south of the entrance road are each labelled with a hexameter. It is probable that the large building north of the entrance road, which was rubbed out on the Plan to gain space for copying the last chapter of a life of Saint Martin, was also given a hexameter. In the south range the buildings that are labelled with hexameters are the hospice for pilgrims and paupers, the house for horses and oxen and their keepers, the house of coopers and wheelwrights, the monks' bake and brew house, the collective workshop, and the granary. Even the goose house and the hen house – two round buildings in the east range – are labelled with hexameters. The verses are inscribed within two concentric circles that enclose the central structures. Horn and Born interpret the outer circles as representing a fence enclosing a fowl run and the inner circles as the wall of the coops.[65] The gate, or door, through the 'fence' is clearly marked on both structures. In both the verse begins to the right of the gate, as you would face it *from inside*, and runs clockwise entirely around the building.

The five elegiac couplets are exclusively associated with sacred space. One of them is laid out in the western approach road to the church:

> Omnibus ad sanctum turbis patet haec via templum.
> Quo sua vota ferant unde hilares redeant.
> *(This road to the church is open to all peoples in order that they may bring their prayers to the church and come back out gladdened in spirit.)*

There is no building for which this would be a suitable inscription. However, the Plan does not include the outer walls of the monastic complex with the main entrance gate to the monastery, and, arguably, the inscription could be imagined as being placed on the entrance gate. Another couplet is laid out in the church between the piers on either side of the nave, and a third couplet is in the access porch leading from the church to the guest house and the outer school. The remaining two elegiacs on the Plan are in the monks' cemetery, which is shown planted with fruit trees.

What, if anything, can we deduce about the use of verse inscriptions in Carolingian monasteries from the Saint Gall Plan? The fact that both the church and many of the other monastic buildings are labelled with verses may reflect the reality that churches in the early ninth century were provided with inscriptions of the kind that Alcuin loved to write. It would be going too far to imagine that the entrance to every monastic chicken coop was adorned with a hexameter, but it is not unreasonable to conclude that the distribution of verse inscriptions on the Plan corresponds in some measure to medieval practice.

Corroborating evidence is fragmentary, and comes from different times and scattered regions, but it all points in the same direction. At the beginning of the ninth century, Abbot Iosue of the monastery of San Vincenzo al Volturno in west-central Italy commemorated his patronage of his new church by means of two hexameters inscribed across the whole width of the upper façade in metal letters of gold fastened into shallow settings in stone.[66] A brief prayer in prose is set into the ninth-century *Westwerk* of the abbey church of Corvey high above the central portal: 'Lord, surround this city [= the abbey] and may your angels watch over its walls.'[67] Numerous *tituli* from the eighth and ninth centuries survive in manuscript collections. These are short poems, almost always in hexameters, composed for a church, a chapel, or other building, or for an altar or a cross. In most cases, we have no way of knowing whether they were ever inscribed on the building or object for which they were designed. Possibly some of them began as school exercises in the composition of Latin verse. But after all reservations are taken into account, it remains clear that there was a demand for inscriptions for churches and other monastic buildings. Boniface, Alcuin, Theodulfus, Hrabanus Maurus, Walahfrid Strabo, Florus of Lyon, Sedulius Scottus, Mico, Fredegarius, and Hincmar are some of the Carolingians who worked in this genre. Alcuin composed verses for at least seven different monasteries, including the abbeys of Saint-Amand of Elnone (near Tournai), Saint-Vedast, Fleury (Saint-Benoît-sur-Loire), Saint-Hilaire-le-Grand of Poitiers, and Saint Peter of Salzburg. Among them are verses suitable for a monastic library,[68] for a refectory,[69] for a dormitory,[70] and even for a latrine: 'As you sense the putrid dung with your nose, reader, learn to know the luxury of your greedy belly. Then you will flee the gluttony of your belly in your mouth: fast for a fixed period of time.'[71] Alcuin's friend, the Spanish Visigothic poet Theodulfus (ca. 760–ca. 821), who became bishop of Orléans, wrote verses that would have been suitable for a monastic guest house[72] and for a library.[73] Walahfrid Strabo (808/9–849), the abbot of Reichenau, wrote a poem for the window by his bed and another to put over his bed, in which he prayed that a phalanx of guardian angels might watch over him and that the path used by the demonic choirs might be blocked.[74] Among the *tituli* that survive from the great Carolingian abbey of Centula or Saint-Riquier, in the north of France, near Abbeville, are ones for the scriptorium,[75] the hospice for the poor,[76] and the lavatory: 'Here I wash the surface of my body, but that the supreme grace of God may cleanse the sins of my mind is my humble prayer.'[77] There was even a *titulus* for the apple orchard: 'Here hanging apples customarily fill the air with their fragrance in autumn, but they drop in the stiff chill of winter.'[78]

Fewer *tituli* were written in the tenth century than in the two preceding.[78] Perhaps the troubled years before the turn of the millennium did not offer adequate leisure for such a comparatively minor art. Nevertheless, the practice of inscribing lintels and other parts of ancillary conventual buildings with verses continued into the Romanesque period, when we begin to find material evidence for the practice in extant inscriptions.

Sometime around the year 1100 (as I guess), a monk in the abbey of Saint-Honorat of Lérins scratched a prayer in the form of a clever little poem onto the side of a lavabo, which was placed in the south walk of the cloister facing the refectory:

> Criste, tua dextra que mundat et intus et extra,
> Interius munda mundare quod hec nequit unda.[80]
> *(Christ, with your right hand which purifies both within and without, purify inwardly that which this water cannot purify.)*

The monk was a competent scribe, but not an experienced craftsman in stone. The letters are so shallow that the inscription can easily go unnoticed in the dim light of the cloister walk. We have no idea who the author of the poem was – a monk of Lérins, no doubt, and perhaps the same man who did the carving. Yet the poem reveals something about him. He was, I should say, a traveller. He may have seen sculptured portals and inscribed lintels in more than one abbey. Their message to the wayfarer was often simple: purify yourself before crossing the threshold. With the means at his disposal, he transformed the wash basin of his cloister into a reminder of the need for spiritual purification.

Another touching prayer is inscribed on a fragment of a gable-shaped lintel from the entrance to the night-stairs of the collegiate church of Sainte-Radegonde, now on display in the Musée Sainte-Croix in Poitiers. The poet embellished it with a remarkable anticipation or imitation of the triple rhymes of Bernard of Cluny:

Tu qui es
praeclara dies
nos, Criste guberna.
Noctibus omnibus
intro iacentibus
esto lucerna.[81]

(Guide us, O Christ, you who are the shining day. Be the lamp for all those who are lying within.)

The monastic refectory rivalled the church and the cloister in symbolic significance in the life of the monks. Chapter 38 of the Rule of Saint Benedict prescribed that a reader should be appointed to read to the brethren during the meals, so that their souls might be nourished while they fed their bodies. Verses on the tympanum of the refectory portal of Rothenkirchenhof in the Rhineland expressed this sentiment succinctly: 'In this place you will give bread to the flesh [and] the word to the ear. You are fed better by the delights of the word than by the bread.'[82]

In its heyday in the twelfth century, the abbey of Sainte-Foy of Conques, perched on the steep hillside above the confluence of two streams, would have presented to the eyes of the local populace, visiting pilgrims, and its own Benedictine monks an unending prospect of verse inscriptions. The enormous tympanum of the west façade displayed within its sculptural program three hexameter couplets, two elegiac couplets, and two simple hexameters (fig. 1). Judging from the fragmentary evidence that survives, nearly every door of the monastery may have had a couplet carefully incised on its lintel. There were verses inscribed on the tomb of Abbot Bego. Even the jewelled reliquary caskets that were made in its workshop were provided with verses. Only an abbey of considerable means would have been able to adorn itself so lavishly. Conques had a monastic school where monks could be trained in the art of composing Latin verse, and teams of sculptors and masons who could carve the verses in stone.

When Prosper Mérimée visited the abbey in June 1837 in his capacity as Inspector General of Historic Monuments, he saw a ruined portal opening off from the cloister, which had been almost entirely dismantled earlier in the century.[83] A lintel over the portal bore the verse inscription: 'Bless these doors, good King, you who save the world, and at the same time snatch us all from the gates of death.'[84] Mérimée was unable to guess to what part of the abbey the portal, which no longer exists, led.[85] He also found a lintel from the entrance door to a storage room that may have been connected with the monastic school. His remarks do not make clear whether this door was still standing at the time of his visit, or whether he inferred its existence from the verse inscription on the lintel: 'This is the place both of the masters and the boys. When they wish, they send to this place the things which they do not want to lose.'[86] Neither lintel can be precisely dated, but they may be associated with the completion of the cloister under Abbot Bego III (ca. 1087–ca. 1107). If such a minor room as the storage closet of the school were graced with a verse inscription, it seems likely that other doorways in the abbey complex were similarly adorned. Four stone fragments, with inscriptions, are preserved in the treasure of Conques.[87] Unfortunately, not enough remains of any of the inscriptions to permit the fragments to be identified or located, but they may include the remains of other inscribed lintels.

These monastic *tituli* confirm the impression given by the Saint Gall Plan that in the period from the ninth to the twelfth century not only churches but also many other conventual buildings in the major monasteries of western Europe displayed verse inscriptions. The preferred location for these inscriptions was the lintels of the principal doors. In a rigidly ordered space, where every activity of monastic life had its prescribed location, doorways marked significant thresholds of transition. Inscriptions articulated the hopes and fears of monks and worshippers, spoke for them and to them, and in some cases may have functioned as talismans against lurking demons. Above all, they made the portal of the monastic church a place of spiritual transformation.

Part Three

Visions and Voices: Allegorizing the Romanesque Church

4

'I am the door': Typological Allegory and the Design of the Romanesque Portal

The allegory of the church concentrated the full power of Christological typology on the main portal through which the laity entered to worship and to venerate the relics of the saints. The portal was interpreted in light of the figure of speech that Jesus applied to himself: 'I am the door. By me, if any man enter in, he shall be saved' (John 10:9). These words are inscribed around the rim of the early twelfth-century tympanum of Christ in Majesty above the west portal of Alpirsbach in Baden-Württemberg,[1] and on the open book in Christ's hand in the mosaic Deesis (Christ enthroned between Mary and Mark) on the interior wall above the west portal of San Marco in Venice.[2] But there was scarcely any need for this explicit assertion. When the figure of Christ was aligned on the vertical axis of the portal, it visually projected the metaphor of Christ the door as a typological reality.

As the cult of relics flourished and churches became the focal point of local and even international pilgrimages, portals began to receive decoration as elaborate as that which had always been lavished on the interior of apses. Romanesque façades with their monumental portals bear little resemblance to the plain façades of ancient Christian basilicas in Rome.[3] Mosaics and mural paintings were placed on exterior-wall surfaces around the portals of Merovingian and Carolingian basilicas, but monumental sculpture in stone does not seem to have been employed in the decoration of portals until the eleventh century. The typological association of Christ with the door generated the most widespread and influential conception of the monumental Romanesque portal. Its formative power can be detected in the earliest examples of portal sculpture that are known to us.

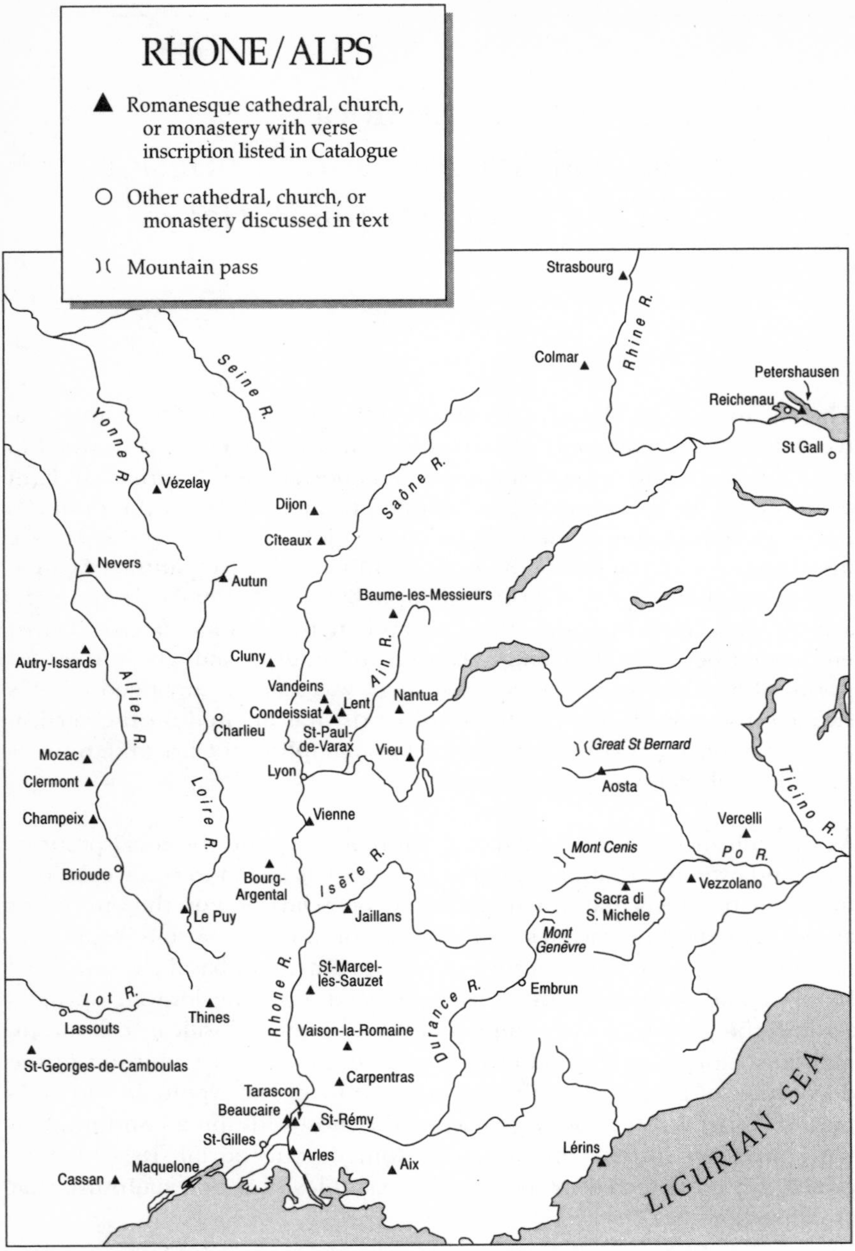
RHONE/ALPS
Romanesque cathedral, church, or monastery with verse inscription listed in Catalogue
Other cathedral, church, or monastery discussed in text
Mountain pass
Strasbourg
Rhine R.
Colmar
Petershausen
Reichenau
St Gall
Seine R.
Yonne R.
Vézelay
Dijon
Cîteaux
Saône R.
Nevers
Autun
Baume-les-Messieurs
Autry-Issards
Allier R.
Cluny
Ain R.
Vandeins
Lent
Nantua
Condeissiat
Charlieu
St-Paul-de-Varax
Vieu
Great St Bernard
Mozac
Clermont
Lyon
Aosta
Loire R.
Ticino R.
Champeix
Vienne
Vercelli
Mont Cenis
Brioude
Bourg-Argental
Isère R.
Po R.
Vezzolano
Sacra di S. Michele
Le Puy
Jaillans
Mont Genèvre
Rhone R.
St-Marcel-lès-Sauzet
Embrun
Lot R.
Durance R.
Thines
Lassouts
Vaison-la-Romaine
St-Georges-de-Camboulas
Carpentras
Tarascon
Beaucaire
St-Rémy
St-Gilles
Arles
Lérins
Maquelone
Aix
Cassan
LIGURIAN SEA

Stone sculpture began to appear on the façade above the portal in the first half of the eleventh century. Two important examples come from Roussillon in French Catalonia: the lintel of Saint-Genis-des-Fontaines (1019/20) (fig. 6) and the lintel and façade sculptures of Saint-André-de-Sorède (ca. 1030).[4] These sculptures show how the allegory of the church affected the organization of Romanesque portals.[5] They have in common three elements of design. First, Christ, who is the central figure in a horizontal rectangular composition, is placed in the axial position above the portal. At Saint-André, a chrismon on a Greek cross set into the tympanum area above Christ's head extends the axial line. Second, Christ is enlarged and isolated from the other figures in the composition by a frame. In both of these lintels, he is framed by a mandorla within which he is seated in majesty. Third, Christ is flanked by symmetrically arranged supporting figures – angels and apostles – on the horizontal plane of the lintel. The combination of these three elements of design fixes the typological allegory of Christ tightly to the vertical axis that bisects the portal.

These elements have antecedents in earlier Christian art. The most important are found in the apse mosaics of Italy and the Eastern Empire of the fourth through the sixth centuries, where an enlarged figure of Christ is aligned on the central axis, often seated in majesty, and almost always flanked by symmetrically arranged supporting figures. He is not, however, within a frame or above a portal. Thomas Mathews describes the organizational principle of these earlier mosaics as 'processional composition' and traces it backwards into the pre-Christian art of the Greco-Roman world and forward into Romanesque, Gothic, and even Renaissance art.[6] There are significant traces of processional composition in Romanesque portal design, and yet the location of the design above the portal radically alters the meaning of the composition. In the interior of the church, processions, whether liturgical or in art, move *toward* a fixed point – the altar or Christ in Majesty. But portal design involves or implies movement *through* the portal, from exterior to interior. Hence, the element of procession is de-emphasized and reordered, though rarely entirely lost. It may be manifested in a line of apostles beneath Christ's feet, or in a procession approaching Christ from his right side only, or in a group of the saved moving from left to right toward Christ and a group of the damned moving in the same direction away from him. Personal transformation and incorporation into sacred space rather than adoration are the end terms of the worshipper's experience of the design of the portal.

These three elements of design centred on Christ – Christ placed in the axial position above the portal, Christ enlarged and isolated within a frame, and Christ flanked by symmetrically arranged supporting figures on the horizontal plane – govern the sculptural programs of most major Romanesque portals in France and northern Europe. With some important modifications they also govern the programs of many portals in Spain. Italian artists were familiar with these elements of design, but they rarely used them to project the typological allegory of Christ the door, and took the development of the portal in a somewhat different direction.

In the larger pilgrimage churches that were constructed in the eleventh century a double portal was sometimes employed to facilitate heavy traffic. In these the vertical axis of the façade bisected the mural surface between the two doors. This, rather than the axis of either doorway, proved to be the more important site for the typological allegory of Christ the door. The western transept of Saint Emmeram of Regensburg is entered from the north by two doors recessed under semidomed arches. The doors are flanked by splayed buttresses that end in engaged pilasters. Three large limestone reliefs are set into the pilasters above the height of the doors (ca. 1050). The relief of Christ in Majesty is on the central one; that is to say, it is on the vertical axis of the double portal, although it is not above either door. The relief on the left pilaster represents Saint Emmeram; Saint Dionysius is on the right. The plaques appear to have been designed for the relative positions that they now occupy since Saint Emmeram's head is turned to the right, and Saint Dionysius's to the left, looking at Christ in the centre.

Some thirty years later the same configuration was used for the double portal of the south transept of Saint-Sernin of Toulouse (the Porte des Comtes). Here, however, a plaque with the martyr Saint Sernin, the church's patron, was set in the axial position in place of Christ – a substitution that is remarkable outside of Italy.[7] The figure of Sernin, which has been destroyed, was framed by columns under an arch; two lions flank this central plaque.

The twelfth-century *Pilgrim's Guide*[8] informs us that a figure of Christ was placed in the axial position between the double portals of both the north and south transepts of Santiago of Compostela. Christ in Majesty surrounded by the symbols of the four Evangelists stood on the top of a column between the double north portal (the Puerta de la Azabachería).[9] (The Romanesque sculptural program of the north portal was destroyed in the eighteenth century to make way for a neo-classical façade.) Likewise, the *Guide* describes a standing figure of Christ with Saint Peter on his left and Saint James on his right on the upper façade of the double south portal (the Puerta de las Platerías) above the four doors ('super quatuor valvas'), that is, in the axial position. Apparently this figure of Christ was replaced by the early thirteenth-century statue of Christ that now occupies this position.[10]

The tympanum, that most characteristic innovation of the Romanesque portal, may have been invented independently more than once in the last two decades of the eleventh century.[11] It can be looked upon as a projection onto a flat plane of the semidome of the apse: a kind of transfer of sacred space from the sanctuary to the exterior of the portal,[12] or as a logical extension of the Romanesque love of the rounded arch. Wherever they appeared, tympana tended to attract verse inscriptions. Their employment and characteristic arrangement on the tympanum constitute the critical final element of design that enabled the allegory of the church to be fully articulated.

One of the earliest Romanesque tympana still extant is a west-portal tympanum at the priory of Charlieu near Cluny that is generally believed to date from a little before 1094. The church, which was completed in 1094, has been replaced, but the portal with its tympanum was incorporated into the later church. The three elements of design operate just as they did in Roussillon. In the tympanum the outsize figure of Christ, who is seated in majesty with his right hand raised in blessing and his left hand on a book, is in the axial position. He is framed within a mandorla, and the mandorla is flanked on the same horizontal plane by two supporting angels. The apostles, who at Saint-Genis (fig. 6) and Saint-André provided an additional number of symmetrically arranged flanking figures, are instead lined up on the lintel beneath Christ's feet, still framed between columns under semicircular arches.[13] Since they are twelve in number, no one of them is in the axial position. Charlieu was a dependency of Cluny, and the design of the tympanum (exclusive of the lintel) is similar to what is known of the no-longer-extant west-portal tympanum of the abbey church of Cluny (Cluny III): at Cluny the outsize, axial figure of Christ in Majesty in a mandorla was flanked by two supporting angels and the Four Animals – the symbolic winged man, lion, bull, and eagle representing the Evangelists Matthew, Mark, Luke, and John.[14] One theory is that the tympanum of Charlieu was carved by an artist who was familiar with the designs for the tympanum of Cluny. The Cluny tympanum was not erected until ca. 1106/12, but its design might go back to the time when work began on the church in 1088, and the idea could have been copied before the tympanum itself was carved.[15]

There are no inscriptions with the tympanum of Charlieu, and there may have been none with the tympanum of Cluny (although verse inscriptions were extensively employed elsewhere at Cluny). Three Burgundian churches clustered east of the Saône near Bourg-en-Bresse, whose portals were influenced by Cluny and Charlieu, illustrate how verses were incorporated into the design of the tympanum early in the twelfth century. The church of Condeissiat is undistinguished except for its early-twelfth-century west portal. The tympanum displays a Christ in Majesty within a mandorla. A prose inscription invoking Christ, Mary, and Saint Julian the Martyr follows the curve of the arch of the tympanum and the lower edge of the lintel, framing the scene. The rim of the mandorla provides an inscription band for an unrhymed hexameter. It is the voice of the church speaking on the tropological level as the community of the faithful: 'Sitting thus in heaven, you bless us, Christ.'[16]

The tympanum of the west portal of the nearby church of Saint-Paul-de-Varax is similar in conception to Condeissiat. Christ is seated in majesty within a mandorla, which is supported by two angels. The twelve apostles gaze up at him from the lintel; Mary is between them in the axial position directly under Christ's feet. Inscriptions around the arch of the tympanum and on both the upper and lower edges of the lintel frame the two scenes of the tympanum and the lintel. The inscription around the arch invokes Christ, Mary, Saint Paul, and all the saints of God.[17] A rhyming hexameter couplet is laid out on the lower edge of the lintel. The inscription is damaged and garbled, but the verses clearly conveyed a penitential message: 'If they (?) would pour forth tears with their prayers on entering [*ingredientes*], ... on exiting [*egredientes*].'[18]

The west-portal tympanum of Saint-Pierre of Vandeins combines elements of Condeissiat and Saint-Paul-de-Varax in a more elaborate design (fig. 7). Vandeins, like Charlieu, was a dependency of Cluny. In the tympanum Christ in Majesty is seated within a mandorla supported by two angels above a gable-shaped lintel of the Last Supper and (on the far right) the Washing of the Feet. An inscription is carried around the arch of the tympanum. Another inscription follows the lower edge of the lintel and continues above the Last Supper on the lower edge of the tympanum. These inscriptions, like those at Saint-Paul-de-Varax, frame the scenes of the tympanum and lintel. However, the inscription around the arch is itself framed by a repetitive decorative moulding on the outside and a broader, foliate moulding on the inside, so that the tympanum appears to be enclosed by concentric archivolts. As at Condeissiat, there is an inscription around the rim of the mandorla, which addresses Christ in the second person (but in prose): 'May you also bless this house, Majesty of the Lord.'[19] The inscription around the arch of the tympanum is a rhymed couplet, which uses the same rhyme-pair that appears at Saint-Paul: 'May the omnipotent Goodness hear the prayers of those who enter [*ingredientes*], and his angel watch over those who go out [*egredientes*].'[20] Another rhymed couplet with a penitential application frames the lintel of the Last Supper: 'When the sinner approaches the table of the Lord, it is proper for him to repudiate his sins with all his heart.'[21]

The two greatest extant tympana of Burgundy – the Last Judgment tympanum of Saint-Lazare of Autun (fig. 8) and the tympanum of the Apostolic Mission of Sainte-Marie-Madeleine of Vézelay (fig. 9) – are considerably more complex, but the basic elements of the Charlieu/Cluny design remain the same. Christ in Majesty, seated within a mandorla, occupies the axial position above the portal. He is flanked by symmetrically positioned groups of figures (saints and angels on Christ's right, sinners and devils on his left at Autun; the apostles at Vézelay). A well-defined lintel under his feet is filled with a horizontal line of figures (the dead waiting for judgment at Autun; the races of mankind at Vézelay). The borders, which were emphasized by the inscription bands at Condeissiat and Saint-Paul-de-Varax, that is, the arch of the tympanum, the upper and lower edges of the lintel, and the rim of the mandorla, also define the tympana of Autun and Vézelay. But at Autun and Vézelay the arches of the tympana are encircled by elegantly carved concentric archivolts. These tympana were the work of sculptors from Cluny. The Cluny Master directed the workshop at Vézelay that created the historiated capitals of the nave and aisles as well as the three tympana of the west portals. He brought with him from Cluny his chief assistant, the sculptor Gislebertus. Gislebertus worked briefly at Vézelay before going on to head the workshop at Autun.[22]

At Autun Gislebertus inscribed verses around the rim of the mandorla and along the upper edge of the lintel (fig. 8).[23] He omitted them from the lower edge of the lintel and, so far as one can now judge, from the archivolts (the inner archivolt has been deprived of its decoration). The cathedral was built on the western slope of a hill above the river Arroux.[24] The steps leading up to the west portal are steep, the tympanum towers above the viewer, and Gislebertus kept the inscription bands narrow. Nevertheless, the inscriptions stand out clearly amid the immensity of the tympanum and the crowded profusion of its sculpture. Furthermore, he did not make the mistake of the sculptors at Condeissiat and Vandeins, who inscribed their verses on the concave surfaces of the mandorla, which partially blocked the inscriptions from the view of worshippers looking up at them from below. Instead, he flattened the mandorla's outer edge, creating a visible inscription band.

The Cluny Master did not put inscriptions in any of the usual places on the tympanum at Vézelay (fig. 9). The upper and lower borders of the lintel and the rim of the mandorla are bare. But there is an inscription on the base of the statue column of John the Baptist, which stands on an engaged pilaster of the central pier that supports the lintel. The statue is in the axial position beneath Christ's feet. John's head crosses in front of the line of the lintel and his halo lies against a pedestal which supports a block on which Christ's mandorla appears to rest. Thus the trumeau merges with the tympanum, and the vertical axis (Christ + John the Baptist + trumeau) intersected by the horizontal axis of the lintel forms a gigantic cross.[25] The statue column of John the Baptist is badly damaged. John holds the Lamb of God in a circular dish or mandorla; his face is gone, and only the outline of the Lamb can be seen. Two leonine hexameters on the base of the statue column identify the Lamb as God: 'Let all realize [*agnoscant*] that this is meant to be John when he holds the attention of the people, pointing out Christ with his finger.'[26] *Agnoscant* puns on *agnus*, incorporating the knowledge of the Lamb in the people. Although Christ's mandorla does not have an inscription, the mandorla of the Lamb, which is, of course, on the same axis, once did. Traces of letters can still be seen on the lower rim.

As at Autun, one archivolt at Vézelay depicts the Labours of the Months and the Signs of the Zodiac in a series of medallions. These belong to the literal level of the allegory of the church. The rims of the medallions are now blank, except for the last one on the far right, which shows a man holding a cup of wine – the month of December. It is inscribed with an oddly uninformative leonine hexameter: 'In all its parts the image of December represents ...'[27] The thought appears to be incomplete, and there is room for another verse, which might have clarified the meaning of the medallion or suggested its relevance to the program of the tympanum as a whole.

Tympana first appeared above portals in Languedoc at about the same time as they did in Burgundy, and the same three elements of design deriving from the typological allegory of Christ the door are found in them. Even the earliest of them exhibit extraordinary thematic complexities, often as part of sculptural programs that spilled over into other areas around the portal. The present-day visitor to the basilica of Saint-Sernin of Toulouse can have no inkling of the fact that the west façade and its double portal, which are disappointingly bare, were once magnificently ornamented with sculptures and inscribed with numerous verses.[28] But the Porte Miègeville, set into the south nave wall, partially redeems the loss of the decoration of the west façade. Although it is not uncommon for a portal to be located in the south wall of the nave, it is unusual to find one as elaborately decorated as this competing with major portals in the west façade and the north and south transepts. To appreciate the significance of the Porte Miègeville it is necessary to take into account the site of the church and the cult of Saint Sernin (or Saturninus). The Porte Miègeville is so named because it faces the main street leading from the centre of the old city of Toulouse (*mieja vila*, 'milieu de la ville') where Saint Sernin was martyred in the third century. Therefore, it is likely that the cult of the saint involved processions from the spot where the martyrdom occurred to the basilica where his relics were displayed. This would explain the emphasis on the portal.

The focal point of the portal is the tympanum of the Ascension of Christ above a lintel of the Twelve Apostles (ca. 1110–15) (fig. 10). Christ is in the axial position and he is flanked on the horizontal plane by symmetrically arranged supporting figures, but he is not framed within a mandorla. The artist has chosen to emphasize the moment in time when the human Christ ascended into heaven with the apostles looking on (Acts 1:9). Neither the arch of the tympanum nor the edges of the lintel are framed with inscription bands in the Burgundian manner.

Despite these differences, this is a variation of the three-element design, although I do not mean to imply that the Saint-Sernin master was dependent on Burgundian models. Cross-fertilization was the rule at the beginning of the twelfth century, and the same ideas appear simultaneously in widely scattered regions. Here, where the focus is on the humanity of the resurrected Christ, isolation and framing are accomplished by the two small angels who squeeze against the sides of the outsize, dominating figure of Christ and hold him under the arms, by his prominent halo (which almost takes the place of the mandorla), and by the vertically aligned rectangular block of stone that barely contains the three figures. The idea of divine majesty which is a corollary of isolation and framing is made explicit by inscriptions on Christ's cruciform halo. The arms of the cross are inscribed with the letters R/E/X, 'King,' the words DEVS and PATER appear in the upper two quadrants formed by the arms of the cross, and the Alpha and Omega are in the lower two quadrants.[29]

The tympanum master at Moissac borrowed elements of the Porte-Miègeville design for the elaborate south portal of the church's west tower-porch. The subject of the tympanum is Christ in Majesty surrounded by the Four Animals and the Twenty-four Elders. The axial figure of Christ is tightly framed by the Animals, which are in turn framed by two elongated angels and in a broad upright horseshoe pattern by the Elders. The effect is nearly claustrophobic; only Christ's overwhelming size and presence renders him independent of the teeming life that almost engulfs him. A horizontal row of eight circular rosettes of acanthus leaves decorates the lintel, which is supported by a trumeau of crossed lions. Therefore, as at Vézelay (fig. 9), the vertical axis of Christ and the trumeau plus the horizontal axis of the lintel form a gigantic cross.[30]

Variations on the theme of Last Judgment appeared on tympana in the second quarter of the twelfth century at such widely scattered places as Autun in Burgundy (fig. 8), Beaulieu on the river Dordogne, and Saint-Denis outside of Paris (fig. 11). In the context of Last Judgment, as also of Christ in Majesty, the typological allegory of Christ the door emphasizes the anagogical level of the allegory of the church. All these tympana exhibit the three elements of design that shape so many Romanesque portals – Christ is placed in the axial position above the portal; his outsize figure is framed and isolated within a mandorla; and he is flanked by symmetrically arranged supporting figures on the horizontal plane. As a tympanum subject the theme of Last Judgment may have originated with the tympanum of Conques in the region of Rouergue in south-central France (fig. 1). Like the others I have named, the tympanum of Conques is often assumed to be a work of the second quarter of the twelfth century.[31] In my opinion, it is almost certainly earlier (ca. 1105–15).[32]

According to Marcel Durliat, the capital of Last Judgment from the cloister of La Daurade, which is now in the Musée des Augustins in Toulouse, and which he dates to ca. 1100 or a little later, is the earliest representation of the theme of Last Judgment in monumental sculpture. Given the complexity of the design of the tympanum of Conques, its utilization of features found in Burgundy and Languedoc, and the vexed question of its dating, the possibility that it was influenced by the capital from La Daurade is a matter of great interest. The capital and the tympanum share so many features that some connection between them seems certain. Among the features of the capital that are relevant to Conques are the following: Christ seated in majesty within a mandorla flanked by angels;

angels sounding the trumpets of Last Judgment; angels supporting the arms of a cross with their hands; the resurrection of the dead from their coffins; the archangel Michael holding the balance; an angel holding the Book of Life; and a banderole inscribed with a phrase (at La Daurade the phrase is IN IGNEM ETERNVM; at Conques it is DISCEDITE A ME) taken from the same verse in Matthew – Christ's words in judgment: 'Depart from me [*discedite a me*], you cursed, into everlastinc fire [*in ignem aeternum*]' (Matt. 25:41).[33]

Pilgrims approaching the west façade of Conques saw an immense scene carved in stone above the portal. The tympanum, which is twenty-two feet in width, is one of the largest ever carved. It is divided into three principal registers by an upper and a lower inscription band. Christ in Majesty in a mandorla flanked by four angels occupies a rectangular block of stone in the centre of the middle register. This block interrupts the upper inscription band, dividing it into two parts. In the upper register two angels hold a great cross, the lower arm of which extends down behind the Christ in Majesty. The Heavenly City and Hell are carved on two gable-shaped lintels in the lower register. The gables provide another inscription band, and in effect divide the lower register into upper and lower portions. The lower edge of the left-hand lintel (the Heavenly City) also carries an inscription.

Both verse and prose inscriptions are used on the tympanum. All the non-metrical inscriptions are within the pictorial scenes, for instance, on the cross, on banners held by angels, on an open book, and so forth, as opposed to the verse inscriptions, which are found on the frames that enclose the scenes.[34]

Christ in Majesty dominates the tympanum by his size and axial position, and is surrounded by a multitude of standing figures, symmetrically arranged on either side of the central axis. He is seated in Judgment, in accordance with the account in Matthew:

> And when the Son of man shall come in his majesty, and all the angels with him, then shall he sit upon the seat of his majesty: and all nations shall be gathered together before him, and he shall separate them one from another, as the shepherd separates the sheep from the goats: and he shall set the sheep on his right hand, but the goats on his left. Then shall the king say to them that shall be on his right hand: Come, ye blessed of my Father, possess you the kingdom prepared for you from the foundation of the world ... Then he shall say to them also that shall be on his left hand: Depart from me, you cursed, into everlasting fire which was prepared for the devil and his

angels ... And these will go into everlasting punishment: but the just, into life everlasting. (Matt. 25:31–34, 41, 46)

Christ is enthroned in an elliptical mandorla studded with stars. His halo is inscribed with a cross in the manner of Christ's halo in the Ascension tympanum of Saint-Sernin (figs. 2, 10). The word R/E/X is carved on the arms of the cross (the letter R has been chipped away[35]) and the word IV/D/E/X in the spaces between the arms.

The artist has fixed in stone the dramatic moment in the future when Christ will pronounce the words reported by the Gospel text: 'Come, ye blessed of my Father, possess you the kingdom prepared for you' and 'Depart from me, you cursed.' These words are inscribed on little streamers that two angels unroll on either side of his head. Four angels are in the clouds at Christ's left. The inner pair are liturgical angels: the lower angel swings a censer; the upper one holds the Book of Life inscribed, 'The book of life is sealed.'

On Christ's right, the chosen ones approach the Judgment seat. The elect form a procession in which the scale of the figures gradually diminishes from the observer's right to left. Several of the persons in the procession carry staffs. As a group, they typify the pilgrims making their way to the shrine of Saint Foy. The procession is led by the Virgin Mary, who thus assumes her traditional position on the immediate right-hand side of Christ.[36] Next to her is Saint Peter, holding the keys to the kingdom of heaven. Secular authority, in the person of a crowned king, is back in the middle of the procession. The king is taken firmly in hand by an abbot, who is both one step closer to Christ and slightly larger in size than the king. Conques, like Saint-Sernin,[37] seems to have wanted to proclaim its allegiance to the papacy and its view of the subordinate role of lay rulers.

The decisive moment in the drama of Last Judgment takes place in the block directly beneath Christ's feet. The archangel Michael faces a devil, and holds a scale between them (the balance arm and chains holding the platters were made of iron and have rusted away). Michael looks grim and the devil grimaces back. Despite the devil's attempt to cheat (he has his finger on the scale), the good deeds, which are figured by tiny crosses inside the platter, outweigh the bad, symbolized by a hideous mask in the other platter. Christ the door has opened the way to the heavenly kingdom.

A distinct type of tympanum made its appearance in Aragon at the cathedral of San Pedro of Jaca (fig. 12). The cathedral stood on the southern pilgrimage route, which, according to the *Pilgrim's Guide*, after passing through Toulouse crossed the Pyrenees via the Somport Pass and dropped down to Jaca.[38] Its west-portal tympanum is probably older than any of the French tympana with the possible exception of Charlieu, although the exaggerated claim that it belongs to the mid-eleventh century has been abandoned.[39] At present most scholars agree that it was carved late in the eleventh century, probably in the 1090s.[40] It may have been the first Romanesque tympanum to be accompanied by verse inscriptions. At first glance it would seem to have nothing in common with the French tympana that we have discussed. The centre of the tympanum is entirely filled by a chrismon that resembles an eight-spoked wheel. Between each spoke of the wheel there is a ten-petalled daisy. Two lions stand guard over the chrismon. The only human figure on the tympanum is a hooded man who is prostrated beneath one of the lions. Such abstraction is worlds apart from the design of French tympana, where God usually has a human face and there are often dozens, if not hundreds, of other human figures.

However, the similarities are as important as the differences. The chrismon is a sign that stands for Christ. With the understanding that the sign substitutes for the image of Christ in Majesty, the tympanum of Jaca conforms to the three elements of design that we have been following. Christ (the Chi-Rho monogram) is in the axial position above the portal; Christ is framed by the rim of the wheel; Christ is flanked by the symmetrically arranged supporting figures of the lions. In the tympana of Burgundy, the rim of the mandorla was used for an inscription band; at Jaca the rim of the wheel of the chrismon serves the same function. Verse inscriptions frame the tympanum in a single line along its lower edge and in two lines in the background above the lions' heads.

The Jaca design was imitated immediately in the smaller tympana of the nearby churches of Santa Cruz de la Serós (fig. 13), San Martín of Uncastillo, and Navasa.[41] Its influence may be detected in the numerous chrismons that are placed in the axial position above the portal in churches on both sides of the Pyrenees. But portals with tympana in the French manner were also prevalent in Spain. Even at Jaca the cathedral's south portal may have had a tympanum of Christ in Majesty with the Four Animals. The centre of this tympanum has been replaced by a sixteenth-century papal coat of arms. Two tiny tympana turned on their sides flank the coat of arms. These display the animal symbols of Mark and Luke. Serafín Moralejo Alvarez argues that they were originally placed horizontally within the larger tympanum in a design similar to that of the tympana of the cathedral of Oloron-Sainte-Marie (fig. 14) and the priory church of Sainte-Foy of Morlaàs in the French Pyrenean region of Béarn.[42] And Marcel Durliat adds the observation that the larger tympanum was probably flanked by the statues of two saints in a composition subsequently taken up for the Porte Miègeville and for the two southern portals of San Isidoro of León.[43]

How it is that these separate, but related, conceptions of the tympanum could have sprung forth independently, fully developed, in widely scattered areas of south-western Europe in the closing years of the eleventh century is a question that may never be satisfactorily answered.[44]

In Aquitaine, a characteristic type of monumental portal without a tympanum developed. The portal was typically recessed within splayed jambs; and the arch above the portal was surmounted by a nested sequence of concentric archivolts. This design did not lend itself to the kind of unified theme, like the Ascension of Christ or Last Judgment, that is usually found in tympana. Very few verse inscriptions are associated with these portals, and the allegory of the church is reflected in them in a different way. However, representations of Christ (the Lamb of God; the Hand of God; Christ in or beside a miniature portal) were sometimes placed in the axial position (the keystone voussoir) in the archivolts above the portal where they were flanked by symmetrically arranged figures in the archivolts.[45]

The monumental Gothic portals of northern France might be said to combine the elaborately carved archivolts of Aquitaine with the figured tympana of Burgundy and Languedoc.[46] To the extent that the recarved façade of the central portal of Saint-Denis represents the original intention of Abbot Suger and his tympanum master, it conforms to this pattern (fig. 11). The Dove, Christ holding the Lamb of God,[47] and Christ in a frame are represented in three of the axial voussoirs of the archivolts, above the Christ in Majesty of the tympanum of Last Judgment. Suger inscribed verses on his tympanum; later Gothic artists abandoned the practice.

Italian Romanesque portals, on which verse inscriptions appeared as early as they did on the portals of France and Spain, were splendidly decorated, but the unifying typological allegory of Christ the door is less powerfully influential, or perhaps it would be better to say more discreetly implied. The decoration of Italian portals is subordinated to larger elements of design. A sign of Christ often appears somewhere on the vertical axis of the façade, though not necessarily immediately above the portal, where, if there is a carved tympanum, the axial figure is more likely to be the patron saint of the church.

The sculptural program of the west façade of the cathedral of San Geminiano of Modena dates from about 1106–10 (fig. 15). Its principal component is a marble Genesis frieze in four panels by the sculptor Wiligelmo. The panels are set in an up-down-up rhythm across the façade: the first, depicting the Creation of Adam and Eve and the Eating of the Forbidden Fruit, is above the left portal; the second, the Expulsion from the Garden of Eden, and third, the Story of Cain and Abel, are at eye level to the left and right of the central portal; and the last, the Death of Cain and the Story of Noah and the Ark, is above the right portal. Although the panels are related in a harmonious fashion to the portals, they do not serve to concentrate attention upon any of them. Instead, the visual narrative follows the up-down-up rhythm of the panels from left to right across the façade – initial promise, transgression, expulsion, murder, punishment, second promise. Each of the panels is framed on the top by an arcade of from nine to twelve arches. In the first panel a half-length figure of God, with a cruciform halo, appears at the far left in a mandorla supported by two angels (fig. 16). Wiligelmo did not even centre the figure under one of the arches of the arcade. A second representation of God, full-length this time, stands directly beside the first. He turns slightly to his left and places one hand on the head of the naked Adam. Again, he has a cruciform halo. The halo is inscribed on the arms of the cross with the word R/E/X. It is the same inscription that appears on the cruciform halos of Christ in the Last Judgment tympanum of Conques and the Ascension tympanum of Saint-Sernin of Toulouse (figs. 2, 10), and it parallels the word P/A/X inscribed on the cruciform halos of Christ in the Temptation and Flagellation tympana of Santiago of Compostela. These latter are the only four Romanesque tympana with halo 'anagrams,' and they are all from the very early twelfth century.[48] The idea is found earlier in manuscript illuminations.[49] One can hardly imagine a more striking confirmation of the internationalism of Romanesque art, of the movements of artists along the routes connecting northern Italy, southern France, and northern Spain, and at the same time of how differences in patronage and geographical location could radically affect the overall design of a portal or façade.

Tympana in the French manner can be found in northern Italy, but the informing conception of the axial figure of Christ is typically lacking. The sculptor Niccolò, who was a contemporary of Gislebertus, and worked at Ferrara, Piacenza, Sacra di San Michele, and Verona, favoured the use of the tympanum above the portal. His tympana usually display the Virgin Mary or the patron saint of the church in the axial position – the Virgin Mary at the cathedral of Verona, Saint Zeno at the abbey church of San Zeno in Verona, and Saint George at the cathedral of Ferrara (figs. 17–19). Only one of the tympana he created had Christ as the central figure – if the tympanum of Christ treading the basilisk and the asp of the Portal of the Months of Ferrara, which was destroyed in 1718, was by his hand.

Niccolò's west portal of the cathedral of Verona with its tympanum of the Virgin in Majesty (fig. 17) demonstrates that he was acquainted with the conception of the portal and its tympanum that we have been tracing. The single portal of the west façade is preceded by a two-storeyed porch. A Lamb of God occupies the axial position of the arch of the lower porch. Inside the porch, the tympanum rests on an oversized lintel on which there are three circular medallions in a horizontal row, which display the crowned figures of Faith, Charity, and Hope. Charity is on the central axis beneath the Virgin.

The tympanum is divided into three segments by the vertical rectangle of the Virgin in Majesty in the centre. This creates a pie-shaped quadrant on either side. In the left quadrant is the Annunciation to the Shepherds, and in the right, the Adoration of the Magi. A hexameter encircles the rim of the tympanum:

> Hic Dominus magnus leo Cristus cernitur agnus.[50]
> *(Here the Lord, the great lion Christ, is seen as a lamb.)*

The verse articulates and extends the complex symbolism of the tympanum and the façade. The Virgin is seated on a throne in the centre of the tympanum with the Christ Child in her lap. The Child is explicitly identified by the verse as the lamb. The Magi, who approach the Child on the right of the tympanum, are coming to worship the King of the Jews (Matt. 2:2), whom the verse associates with the royal beast, the Lion of Judah (Apoc. 5:5). The eye is carried down to the two couching lions which provide the base for the columns that support the porch. On the left of the tympanum are the shepherds. They are guarding their sheep against predatory beasts (such as the couching lions below). A watchdog turns his head to our left as if on the alert for a threat from outside the tympanum. An angel above the shepherds' heads gives them the news of the Christ Child (Luke 2:8–12) and points toward the Virgin and Child in the centre

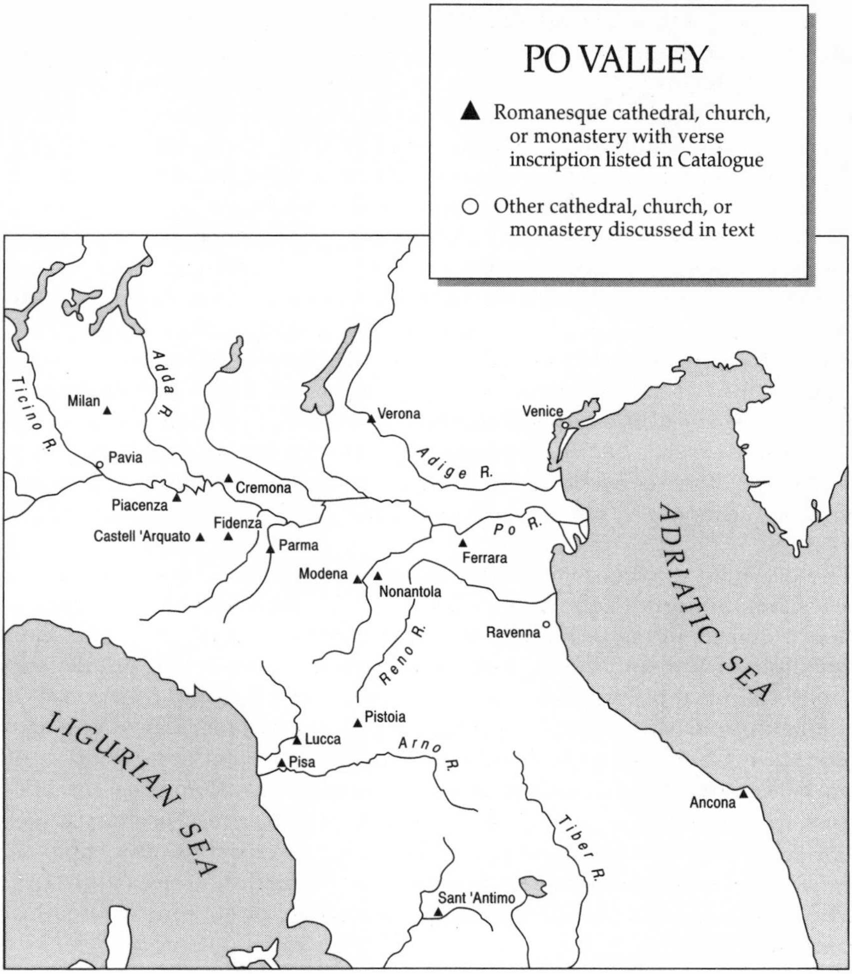
PO VALLEY
Romanesque cathedral, church, or monastery with verse inscription listed in Catalogue
Other cathedral, church, or monastery discussed in text
Ticino R.
Adda R.
Milan
Pavia
Cremona
Piacenza
Fidenza
Castell 'Arquato
Parma
Verona
Adige R.
Venice
Po R.
Ferrara
Modena
Nonantola
Reno R.
Ravenna
ADRIATIC SEA
LIGURIAN SEA
Pistoia
Lucca
Pisa
Arno R.
Tiber R.
Ancona
Sant 'Antimo

of the tympanum. The Lion of Judah is for them the Lamb of God. The *m* of *magnus* in the inscription is in the uncial form with a closed loop on the left.[51] According to Fred Gettings, this form of *m* is identical to the medieval sigil for the zodiacal sign Leo. He therefore sees a visual pun in *magnus* (Leo + Agnus).[52] The pun would be in keeping with the symbolism of the portal and with Niccolò's interest in the signs of the zodiac, as evidenced by his Zodiac Portal at Sacra di San Michele.

Although Niccolò borrowed elements of the French design for the Verona cathedral portal, the final effect is very different. Roland and Oliver, the heroes of the *Chanson de Roland*, are on the outer jambs of the portal, guarding the prophets of the Old Testament who are on the inner jambs. Roland's sword is inscribed DVRINDARDA, the Durendal of the epic poem. This monumental portal is symbolic of the Church Militant, a mighty fortress in the crusade against the infidels, as perhaps most medieval portals were; but it does not through the typological allegory of Christ the door concentrate the attention of the worshipper upon the urgent question of his or her personal salvation.

The typological allegory of Christ the door transcended regional boundaries. Beginning with the first tentative experiments with the reintroduction of monumental sculpture in the eleventh century, this informing principle of Romanesque iconography shaped the design of portals and their sculptural programs in most parts of western Europe. By the end of the century it had generated prototypical portal tympana in such major centres as Cluny and Jaca. Even where some of the resulting elements of portal design are relaxed or omitted, as in Italy, the influence of this allegory can be felt in nearly all Romanesque portals whose primary intention is to direct the worshipper rather than to celebrate any papal or episcopal patron. But its effect is most concentrated in French churches, where the door is Christ welcoming, forgiving, or judging those who come to him.

5

The Voice of Allegory: Language and Form in Romanesque Verse Inscriptions

The church addressed worshippers on the typological level of the allegory in the voice of Christ or the Church. This voice was given visible expression in the verses that were inscribed on the churches and their portals. Nearly all of these verses were composed in Latin in a single metre – the quantitative dactylic hexameter (including its dependent form, the pentameter of the elegiac couplet). There seems no obvious reason why this should be so. The choice of Latin is understandable. Latin was the sacred language of the Church. No vernacular language had yet acquired the prestige that would enable it to compete with Latin as the medium for public display of an inscription on a church building. So far as I know, the only vernacular poetic inscription on a Romanesque church in western Europe was a quatrain in Italian verse on the triumphal-arch mosaic of the cathedral of San Giorgio of Ferrara, which named the donor, a certain Guglielmo Ciptadin, and the builder, the sculptor Niccolò. The triumphal arch was torn down in 1712, and the authenticity of the quatrain, which was copied by Canon Baruffaldi just before the destruction of the arch, has been challenged. If it is genuine, it is said to be the oldest poetry (ca. 1135) in the Italian language.[1]

But the use of the quantitative dactylic hexameter to the exclusion of all other possible verse forms in Latin remains something of a mystery. The hexameter was, to be sure, a prestigious metre, and the staple of instruction in monastic schools. Yet the popularity of isosyllabic, rhymed, accentual meters, like the rhythmical trochaic septenarius, and their use in Christian hymns make one wonder why they were never employed for inscriptions. In many ways they would have been more suitable for the purpose. The great variety in the lengths of their lines meant that a metre could have been found that would have suited almost any available space.

A fixed number of syllables per line would have been easier to work with when fitting a stanza into place. And, finally, poets would not have had to concern themselves with syllabic quantities. Nevertheless, despite these advantages, poets never used them. Why? Perhaps the best answer is that by the Romanesque period the hexameter had been the preferred verse for church inscriptions for nearly a thousand years and no one thought to depart from tradition.

Monasteries and churches were islands of literacy in a sea of orality. Neither monks nor nuns were isolated from the dominant oral culture. In the Romanesque period they came from the same feudal society as their secular peers: Abbot Bernard of Clairvaux was the son of a noble who died fighting in the First Crusade.[2] They acquired literacy in the monastic schools, but they were profoundly influenced by the oral culture in which they were reared. Oral habits of thought have left their traces in these verse inscriptions. There are many indications that alphabetic literacy had not been deeply internalized.[3] In inscriptions as well as on parchment words appear to be semi-magical; they were treated as tokens which could be arranged into unexpected, inexplicable, patterns. Letters were interlaced in such a way that it took an effort of the mind to decipher their meaning (figs. 20, 21). Acrostics were formed from the initial or final letters of successive verses.

Writing was an instrument of social control. When the Church wielded not only supreme spiritual power but vast temporal power as well, its language, Latin, acquired special potency and prestige. In northern Europe, where Latin was always an alien tongue, strategies for dealing with it developed early. The Bible was translated into Old English (just as earlier it had been translated into Gothic by Bishop Ulfilas); it was paraphrased into Old Saxon. Latin had to be mastered, but it was equally important to cultivate literacy in one's own native language. This was perhaps a healthy counterbalance to the prestige of Latin. In southern Europe, by contrast, Latin stood in ambiguous relationship with the vernaculars. The separation of the vulgar tongues from the Latin of the educated classes of Rome can be traced back to the classical period, yet an awareness that the spoken language of the masses was in some sense a 'debased' form of the Latin taught in the schools lingered for centuries. The Romance languages were slower than their Germanic counterparts to be reduced to writing. Nevertheless, in Spain, in southern France, and above all in Italy, despite its inferior status, the spoken language of the vernacular influenced the way Latin was written in the verse inscriptions of the Romanesque period. Repeated echoes of the vernacular appear, for example, in verses that Wiligelmo inscribed on the Enoch and Elias plaque at the cathedral of Modena in about the year 1099 (fig. 22).[4] *Consendit* appears for *conscendit, sup tempore* for *sub tempore* (assimilation), *monos* for *uno, scultores* and *scultura* for *sculptores* and *sculptura,* and *onore* for *honore.*

Quantitative Latin hexameters were a product of the high culture of the Middle Ages. Poets and versifiers had to learn classical prosody in the schoolroom. This body of technical information was codified in the metrical handbooks that formed part of the instruction in grammar. But it was not enough to know the 'rules.' The metrical patterns of quantitative poetry were based on a linguistic distinction in the Latin language between 'long' and 'short' syllables. By the fourth or fifth century, that distinction had vanished; native speakers of Latin were no longer able to distinguish aurally the length of syllables.[5] From late antiquity through the Middle Ages (and after), men and women mastered the language to a high degree of proficiency, but the natural linguistic basis for composing quantitative verse was gone. Nor were there authoritative dictionaries of Latin in which they could look up the length of a syllable whose quantity was not apparent to the eye. In order to write quantitatively 'correct' verse, they had to know by heart thousands of lines of classical Latin poetry – a large enough number of lines to ensure that they had an authorized model for the length of every syllable of every word they wanted to use. No doubt the quantities of the syllables of common Latin words were drilled into every pupil's head, and this level of training would have sufficed for composing a simple hexameter or two. But fluent, confident verse composition implies a prodigiously stocked memory of Latin verses.

The poets of the versified portals of the twelfth century always used the standard or 'dactylic' form of the classical hexameter, in which each of the first four feet could be either a spondee (long, long) or a dactyl (long, short, short), the fifth foot was always a dactyl, and the sixth foot could be either a spondee or a trochee (long, short).[6] They translated the voice of God or the Church into an ornate, memorable form of the hexameter that could be made visible to the eyes of the faithful in a brief space. Rhyme is a vivid poetic device that can be seen as well as heard, which is one reason why there are so many rhymed verse inscriptions. Two kinds of rhyme were used with hexameters – leonine and disyllabic end rhyme.

Leonine or internal rhyme formed a special variety of quantitative hexameter known as leonine hexameter.[7] It was uniquely suited for brief inscriptions because it could visually display the poetic structure of even a single line of verse. Perhaps for this reason it was very widely used. In addition to the verse inscriptions that are the subject of this book, thousands of medieval epitaphs were composed in leonines, two of which are still familiar in the English-speaking world. One is the epitaph of the Venerable Bede, which is carved on his tomb in the Galilee Chapel of Durham Cathedral:[8]

Hac sunt in fossa | Baedae Venerabilis ossa.
(In this tomb are the bones of the Venerable Bede.)

The other is the epitaph of King Arthur as reported by Sir Thomas Malory:[9]

Hic iacet Arthurus, | rex quondam rexque futurus.
(Here lies Arthur, the once and future king.)

Both verses employ internal, disyllabic rhyme (*fossa/ossa*; *Arthurus/futurus*). This is what I call *full* leonine rhyme, to distinguish it from monosyllabic or *common* leonine rhyme.

Disyllabic end rhyme, the other kind of rhyme that is found in verse inscriptions in the Romanesque period, was not as widely used. It may have been considered less suitable for inscriptions simply because it was visually less prominent. It requires a minimum of two lines to display end rhyme, whereas a single line of verse suffices to display leonine. A couplet inscribed beneath the tympanum of Dinton in Buckinghamshire illustrates this type of rhyme:

Premia pro meritis si quis desperet hab*enda*,
Audiat hic precepta sibi que sit retin*enda*.[10]

Common leonine rhyme occurred sporadically in the hexameter and elegiac verse of the classical period, but conscious use of it dates from the Carolingian period. By the tenth century it had become the rule with some poets.[11] Full leonine rhyme developed in the eleventh century. William Beare cites as an early example a *Responsorium* attributed to Herimannus Contractus (1013–54).[12] Emperor Conrad II (1024–39) issued a bull proclaiming the dominion of Rome over the entire world in a full leonine rhyme:

Roma caput mundi | tenet orbis frena rotundi.[13]

Marbod of Rennes (ca. 1035–1123) composed many of his poems in full leonine hexameters; he also pioneered the use of disyllabic end rhyme in the hexameter.[14]

The classical hexameter consisted of six feet with an obligatory word break or caesura that usually occurred in the middle of the third foot. Medieval leonine hexameter nearly *always* put the caesura in the third foot. Thus, the structure of the leonine hexameter was rigidly prescribed as 2½ + 3½ feet, and rhyme linked the syllable(s) before the caesura with the final syllable(s) of the line. This is illustrated by the verse epitaphs quoted above, where a single bar (|) marks the caesura in the middle of the third foot.

The classical elegiac couplet could also be adapted for leonine rhyme. In the elegiac couplet, the first line is a hexameter and the second line is a pentameter. It is convenient to think of the pentameter as a doubling of the first 2½ feet of the hexameter, with an obligatory word break between them: 2½ + 2½ feet.[15] This full leonine elegiac couplet from the abbey church of Saint-Pé-de-Bigorre illustrates the form:

Est domus hic Domini, | via caeli, spes peregrini.
Haec data porta Petro: | vade maligne retro.[16]

The vogue for rhyme, and especially leonine rhyme, was in full swing in the twelfth century, and this is reflected in the statistics for the 607 verses in the Catalogue. Approximately 83 per cent of the verses (514/617) exhibit rhyme in some form, and 74 per cent (454/617) exhibit either full or common leonine rhyme.[17] Full leonines constitute 42 per cent (254/607) of all the verses. However, the distribution of full leonines by regions reveals that they were more popular in France and Spain than in Italy. Fifty per cent of the verse inscriptions in France (115/232) and a nearly equal percentage in Spain (27/56) are full leonines. In Italy the figure drops to 32 per cent (82/258). The discrepancy is more apparent than real, however, because Italian poets frequently substituted disyllabic slant rhyme for full leonine rhyme. Slant rhyme, that is, rhyme based on assonance or consonance, is virtually non-existent north and west of the Alps, except in Germany where there are several pockets of strong Italian influence. The statistics must be treated with caution, since there is an element of subjectivity in the identification of slant rhyme. Wiligelmo's verses on the Enoch and Elias plaque at Modena, for example, consist of four hexameters followed by an elegiac couplet (fig. 22).[18] Although one's first impression is that the poem is a mixture of unrhymed lines (1, 5) and common leonines (2–4, 6), all of the verses can be interpreted as displaying full leonine slant rhyme (*-ancer/-antes*; *-intis/-ensis*; *-arnis/annis*; *-ari/-ani*; *-ores/-ore*; *-tura/tua*). South of the Alps (Italy and Croatia) I find 49 full leonine slant rhymes out of 263 verses (19 per cent). In Germany, there are four full leonine slant rhymes out of 27 verses (15 per cent).[19] Elsewhere, the figures are six out of 327 (2 per cent).[20] The playfulness that Italian poets brought to their rhyming might have seemed frivolous in other parts of Europe.

Ten per cent of the verses (62/617) display disyllabic end rhyme (including four verses from Italy with disyllabic slant end rhyme[21]). Occasional variations and permutations of these principal forms occur, as, for example, identical trisyllabic end rhyme (*imago/imago*),[22] or tetrasyllabic end rhyme (*ingredientes/egredientes*),[23] or the combination in two consecutive lines of leonine and end rhyme (*forem/honorem // horrorem/priorem*).[24] Unrhymed hexameters and elegiac couplets comprise only about 17 per cent (103/617) of the total number of verse inscriptions.[25]

Several other characteristics of the verse forms employed in Romanesque inscriptions may be noted. Poets scrupulously observed classical quantities, with the following exceptions. Proper names, especially from Scripture or from other non-classical sources (including contemporary names), were arbitrarily scanned. *Ecclĕsia* was regularly scanned with a short antepenultimate syllable. Final *o* (except the dative or ablative ending) was routinely shortened. The lack of congruity between rhyme and metre reveals the artificial nature of vowel quantity and syllabic length. Rhyme ignores these distinctions; visual identity is all that counts. These full leonine hexameters from Corneilla-de-Conflent are typical:

> Heredes vite, | Dominam laudare venite,
> Per quam vita datur, | mundus per eam reparatur.[26]

The rhyme in both verses is quantitatively imperfect although the meter is correct: *vitē* (which is the standard medieval spelling for the classical *vitae*) with a long final vowel rhymes with *venitĕ* with a short one; *dătur* with a short penultimate vowel rhymes with *reparātur* with a long one. Both the spelling (*vitae*) and the non-visual common leonine rhyme (*vitae/me*) in this eleventh-century verse from Regensburg are truly exceptional:

Spes ego sum vitae | cunctis sperantibus in me.[27]

Poets avoided hiatus (the preservation of immediately adjacent vowels in successive words),[28] but they allowed the caesura to lengthen a short final vowel or syllable, as in *salutarē* in this full leonine hexameter from the cloister of the cathedral of Elne:

Ecce salutare | pariter fratres habitare.[29]

In classical Latin poetry a final vowel or nasalized vowel (vowel + *m*) was regularly suppressed or elided before a word beginning with a vowel or *h*. But in Romanesque verse inscriptions, the conditions for elision were studiously avoided. Therefore, non-elision must be regarded as a conscious poetic principle. Observance of the principle sometimes led versifiers into awkward straits. Four panels with bas-reliefs of the apostles from some unidentified church are displayed in the nave of the cathedral of Milan. One of the apostles is labelled with the following verse:

Cordis id est cultor es corculus atque Tadeus.[30]
(You are a dear little heart, that is, a worshipper of the heart, and also Thaddeus.)

Jude is included in the list of disciples in Luke (6:14–16) and Acts (1:13), but not in Matthew (10:3) and Mark (3:18), where his place is taken by Thaddeus. It was (and is) usually assumed that Jude and Thaddeus were the same person, which is what the poet was trying to say, perhaps a bit ineptly, in the verse. According to the etymological interpretation that was current in the Middle Ages, the name 'Jude' meant 'heart' (*cor*), and therefore the apostle Jude was familiarly called 'dear little heart' (*corculum*).[31] But *corculum* is neuter, and if it were placed before *atque*, the final -*um* would have to be elided. The poet invented a masculine form *corculus* to block the unwanted elision.

The principle of non-elision was more rigidly applied in verse inscriptions than in other poetry of the Romanesque period. Many poets from late antiquity onward tended to avoid elision, especially in rhythmical, but also in quantitative, verse. Some went further than others in this direction, but they seldom gave up its use altogether, and there were always poets throughout the Middle Ages who continued to employ elision in the classical manner.[32] Numerous elisions can be found in the mosaic verse inscriptions of Rome and in the verses composed by Carolingian poets for use as inscriptions. But in the Romanesque period, there are only four instances of elision among all the verse inscriptions that I have surveyed. One is at Mozac, in the verse that was copied from a poem inscribed on the Merovingian basilica of Saint-Martin of Tours.[33] Another is at Saint-Aventin in a line that does not in fact scan properly, and which may be an imperfectly remembered, garbled copy of a normal verse (without elision) from San Benito of Sahagún.[34] The two remaining elisions are, or were, both found at Cîteaux. This is sufficiently remarkable to justify a brief digression.

The abbey of Cîteaux, which was destroyed during the French Revolution, was visited by two Benedictines, Martène and Durand, early in the eighteenth century. They recorded numerous epitaphs in the church, as well as several inscriptions over various doors. The portal inscriptions may have been painted: the inscription over the main gate of the abbey is said to have been written in letters of gold. There is no way of judging from the comments of Martène and Durand when the inscriptions might have been added to the buildings. Given the Romanesque custom of inscribing portals with verses, it is possible that they went back to the time of construction. However, Cistercian abbeys were originally characterized by their unadorned simplicity, and the 'magnificence' that Martène and Durand observed represented the accumulation of centuries, so some caution in accepting these as verses of the late twelfth century is in order.

All of the portal inscriptions recorded by Martène and Durand invoked the Virgin Mary. Henry Kraus observes that the Cistercians 'dedicated all their churches to her and the mother-abbey at Cîteaux adopted as its device an image of Mary, under whose mantle the abbots of the order were shown kneeling while above the church portal verses in her honour were engraved.'[35] An unrhymed elegiac couplet was inscribed over the main gate of the abbey (the elided syllable is set off by parentheses):

Ad nos flect(e) oculos, dulcissima virgo Maria,
Et deffende tuam diva patrona domum.[36]
(Bend your eyes on us, sweetest Virgin Mary, and protect your house, blessed patroness.)

Two more unrhymed elegiac couplets were inscribed above the 'image' of the Patroness of the Order. Martène and Durand do not say where in the church this picture or carving was located, but presumably it was an organic part of the decor of the church, since the inscription refers to the building:

Haec caput et mater Cisterc(i) est ordinis aedes,
  Quae devota manet Virgo Maria tibi.
Auspice testantem, rogo, protege, porrige Christo
  Quae fiunt intus nocte dieque preces.[37]

(This building, which, O Virgin Mary, is dedicated to you, is the head and mother of the Cistercian Order. Look favourably on the donor [?], I beg, protect him, extend to Christ the prayers which are made within night and day.)

If these verses do go back as far as the end of the twelfth century, then the poet's decision to allow elision but to do without rhyme may reflect the Cistercians' wish to avoid a kind of poetic ornamental ostentation that they perhaps associated with the other monastic orders.

Medieval poets, as I have remarked above, regarded the caesura in the middle of the third foot as obligatory. It is lacking in only five verses in the Catalogue. Two of them are consecutive lines in a curious poem that is inscribed on the right-hand border of the labyrinth at Lucca:

Hic quem Creticus edit Dedalus est laberinthus,
De quo nullus vadere quivit qui fuit intus,
Ni Theseus gratis | Adriane [*sic*] stamine iutus.[38]

(This is the labyrinth that the Cretan, Daedalus, built, from which no one who was within was able to escape, except for Theseus freely helped by Ariadne's thread.)

There is no caesura in verses one and two. The author of these verses was not an ignorant man. Perhaps he intended the absence of the caesuras to be a kind of playful labyrinthine obscurantism from which the poem emerges in verse three. Even then, one must re-thread the spelling of Ariadne's name to obtain a proper scansion.

Two other verses without a caesura in the third foot come from widely separated churches in France.[39] Nevertheless, they are closely related. One is a verse on the book in Christ's hand in the Christ in Majesty tympanum from the abbey church of Saint-Bénigne of Dijon (fig. 20). The other is a lintel inscription on the tympanum of the First Vision of Saint John of the south portal of Saint-Pierre of La Lande-de-Fronsac, a small village about fifteen miles north-east of Bordeaux. Both are a cento of the words of Christ from the Apocalypse 1:8; 1:17–18; and John 1:1–18. The verse from the book in Christ's hand at Dijon reads:

Sum finis, | sum principium | mundique Creator.[40]

(I am the end, I am the beginning and the Creator of the world.)

This is an unrhymed hexameter without a word break in the third foot, but with caesuras in the second and fourth feet.

The lintel inscription from La Lande-de-Fronsac reads:

Principium | sine principio | finis sine fine.[41]
([I am] the beginningless beginning and the endless end.)

Again it is an unrhymed hexameter. Rhetorical balance together with word-initial internal rhyme (*prin-/sin-/fin-*) takes the place of leonine rhyme. The striking combination, in these two tympana, of the theme of the beginning and the end with the absence of the regular caesura cannot be accidental. The omission of the regular caesura perhaps symbolises unity (= the absence of the caesura) in Trinity (= the three-segment line).

In classical Latin poetry the word break in the hexameter could come after the first syllable of the foot (the 'masculine' caesura) or after the second syllable of a dactylic foot (the 'feminine' caesura). Poets composing verses for Romanesque churches avoided the feminine caesura; it is nearly as rare as the absence of a word break in the third foot. There are eight instances in the Catalogue.[42]

The spatial display of verses occasionally led to more elaborate formal devices and conceits. One such is a memorable acrostic, which is carved on the north nave wall in Saint-Trophime of Arles:

Terrarum Roma | **G**emina de luce magistr**A**
Ros missus semper | **A**derit velud incola Iose **P**
Olim contrito | **L**oeteo contulit Orch **O**[43]

The verses form three vertical acrostics by means of the initial and final letters of each line and the initial letters following the caesura, which are vertically aligned on the wall: TRO(phimus) GAL(liarum) APO(stolus), 'Trophime, the apostle of Gaul.'[44] Saint Trophime was believed to be a disciple of Saint Paul (Acts 20:4, 21:29; 2 Tim. 4:20), who had been sent to Arles to evangelize Gaul and who had been buried in the Christian cemetery in the Alyscamps. The cathedral of Arles was dedicated to Saint Stephen the protomartyr, but, following the transfer of Trophime's relics from the Alyscamps into the church in the tenth century, Trophime began to rival Stephen as patron, and in the reconstructed church, which was dedicated in 1152, he seems to have acquired pre-eminence. The acrostic verses were probably carved in connection with or soon after the dedication of the twelfth-century church.

The quantitative Latin hexameters that were inscribed on portals, mural surfaces, and capitals of churches, cloisters, and other monastic buildings in the eleventh and twelfth centuries went beyond the need for simple identification to offer matter for didactic instruction and contemplation. But above all, they functioned as visible speech. They were the primary medium through which the Romanesque church expressed itself as a multilevelled allegory. In them the portal found its voice.

6

The Portal as Christ: Personification or Real Presence?

A fine line separated the allegorical interpretation of the church as Christ from the idolatrous confusion of Christ's image above the portal with the reality that it represented. The novel appearance of large-scale sculpted images of God and the saints generated anxiety. The seated figure of Christ at Regensburg is about three feet high. His feet rest on a stool, on the front of which is a donor bust. An inscription around the circular rim of the donor bust allows the sculptures to be assigned to the time of Abbot Regenward (1048–64). There are verses on the frame that state: 'Since Christ is called a rock on account of his firm majesty, it is fitting enough that his image be in stone.'[1]

It is difficult for us, whose eyes have been saturated with images of every kind, to imagine the power and overwhelming effect images would have had in the mental landscape of people who had rarely seen a representation of a living thing. Large sculpted figures must have been awesome. Reinhold Lange is probably right in taking these verses at Regensburg as a justification for carving an image in stone.[2] The Mosaic prohibition against graven images ('Thou shalt not make to thyself a graven thing, nor the likeness of any thing that is in heaven above, or in the earth beneath, nor of those things that are in the waters under the earth,' Exod. 20:4, etc.), reaffirmed by Saint Paul (Rom. 1:23), remained a source of worry, even after bas-reliefs and statues became customary on church façades. Such images could be associated with the worship of pagan idols, and it was feared that the images might be mistaken for the persons they represented. When Bernard of Angers saw the seated statue of Saint Foy at Conques early in the eleventh century, he promptly thought of Venus and Diana.[3] A century later at the abbey church of Saint-Pierre at Vienne, the sculptor of a tympanum of Saint Peter holding the keys inscribed these verses on the background on either side of the figure of Peter: 'This stone is not Peter. Peter is at Rome and in heaven above. In his likeness the form of this statue is made.'[4]

But the deepest concern in the Romanesque mind was that the image of Christ might be thought to be the reality. The Portal of the Months (ca. 1138–40) of the cathedral of Ferrara, which was on the south façade of the nave, was demolished in 1718 during the course of repairs, but it was described by several persons who saw it before its destruction. The tympanum showed Christ treading the asp and the basilisk underfoot. This image was accompanied by a verse inscription, addressed to the viewer, which proclaimed: 'The image which you see is neither God nor man in the flesh, but it is God and man in the flesh which the image signifies.'[5] Nearly identical verses are found on the late-twelfth-century tympanum of the north portal of San Miguel of Estella in Navarre, where Christ in Majesty appears in a quadrilobed mandorla, surrounded by the Four Animals and two standing angels.[6] The unease that hovers about these verses is a measure of the powerful effect achieved by the association of the image of Christ with the portal. Since in the allegory of the church Christ was the door, he was invisibly present to the faithful when they entered through it. When his image appeared above the portal in sculptural form, might he not be conceived of as being present in the image? And from here, it would be but a short step to worshipping the image as God. The fact that artists and clergy felt obliged to assert repeatedly the distinction between representation and real presence in art suggests that the distinction was difficult to maintain as long as the church was perceived as an allegory in the here and now of Christ and the heavenly city.

A related issue concerns portal inscriptions that speak in the first person or directly address the worshipper. However seriously we as modern viewers may take the message of these inscriptions, our response is not likely to be coloured by any sense that we are actually hearing or seeing the voice of God or the Church. It is difficult to gauge the effect of these words in stone on a medieval audience, but the allegorization of the church invested the portal with a numinous quality that would have given its 'voice' a reality unlike that which any modern viewer is likely to experience. When God was believed to be an indwelling presence in the building of the church, then the metaphor that identified Christ with the door was more than a figure of speech. The words inscribed in stone were in some sense a material translation of Christ's ever-present, though inaudible, voice.

Consider, for example, the tympanum of Bourg-Argental, which displays in two registers Christ in Majesty and the Four Animals above scenes from the Nativity. The church of Bourg-Argental was completely rebuilt in 1854; the only vestige of the Romanesque church is its former west portal, which has been retained as the east portal of the new building.[7] In the tympanum Christ is seated in the axial position within a mandorla. He appears to hold the eucharistic wafer in his left hand, instead of the usual book. Using the principle of axial alignment, the sculptor has placed a second figure of Christ the Judge on the keystone of the inner archivolt, flanked on the archivolt with the Elders of the Apocalypse, and on the keystone of the outer archivolt he has placed the figure of David directing the choir of the angels, flanked by the Signs of the Zodiac.[8] An angel beneath Christ's feet on the lower register of the tympanum greets the shepherds watching their flocks by night. The lambs rather than the shepherds are in axial alignment with Christ.

Verse inscriptions on the arch of the tympanum above the upper register and on the horizontal band separating the registers declare, in the voice of Christ, 'You who are entering, why do you not come in haste? Provided that he come to me, he will escape the evils of hunger. And you who drink and by drinking thirst the more, if you drink of me, your thirst will be no more.'[9] The urgent injunctions of the inscriptions together with the visible sign of the wafer make manifest the eucharistic significance of Christ the door. His words seem designed to pierce the heart as only living words can. Perhaps they did.

There were epigraphic precedents for first-person portal inscriptions in three different types of objects in the ancient and medieval world. The first was the epitaph that spoke from the grave; the second was the tool, weapon, or other object that named its maker; and the third was the speaking cross of Anglo-Saxon England. They all involved a linguistic device related to the rhetorical figure of prosopopeia or personification. As it was commonly understood in the Middle Ages, prosopopeia was an abstract, lifeless literary convention. Isidore of Seville (560?–636) defined it as that figure which occurs whenever 'either humanity or speech is attributed to inanimate objects.' He added: 'Thus we introduce speaking mountains and rivers or trees, imposing humanity on a thing which does not have the power of speech.'[10] However, a material object inscribed with its own voice is quite different from personification in a literary text.

Greek and Latin epitaphs from the classical period sometimes employed the conceit of the voice from beyond the grave that speaks to the passer-by. The conceit was a conventional expression of appropriate sentiments. Of the class of epitaphs in which the dead person is represented as encouraging the survivors to stop lamenting, Richmond Lattimore concludes: 'This putting of words into the mouth of the dead is not, I think, to be understood as an implication of immortality; it is a device to make the whole relation between living and dead more gracious than if the composer of the epitaph avowed his own intention not to lament overlong.'[11] The same might be said of most epitaphs on other themes. What is important is that there were thousands of these first-person epitaphs, many of them in Latin hexameters or elegiacs, that were scattered throughout the lands of the former Roman Empire and available as models for Christian portal as well as sepulchral inscriptions. I have already drawn attention to their role in the development of Christian verse inscriptions in Rome.[12]

The material object that names its maker likewise has a long history. In Latin the formula *[X] me fecit*, which is common in Romanesque inscriptions naming the sculptor or artist, goes back to the earliest recorded period of the language in the sixth century BC, on the Praenestine fibula: MANIOS MED FHEFHAKED NVMASIOI, 'Manius made me for Numerius.'[13] Similar formulas in the older Germanic dialects of northern Europe were carved on personal objects, often in runes. One of the earliest, dating from the third century AD, is the maker's formula on a silver shield mount from Illerup on the Danish peninsula: *niþijo tawide*, 'Nithijo made [this?/me?].' A wooden box from a peat bog in Stenmagle, Sjælland, is similarly inscribed: *hagiradaR : tawide*, 'Hagiradar made [this/me].'[14] When the direct object of the verb was omitted, as they are here, it is impossible to know whether the inscription was in the first- or third-person voice. Sometimes the maker put himself in the first person, as in the fourth- or early-fifth-century runic verse inscription that was carved on the gold horn of Gallehus: *ek hlewagastiR : holtijaR : horna : tawido*, 'I, Hlewagastir, son of Holti, made the horn.'[15] The inscription in alphabetic letters on the ninth-century Anglo-Saxon Alfred Jewel, AELFRED MEC HEHT GEWYRCAN, '[King?] Alfred commanded me to be made,' can be equally well understood as a continuation of the Germanic tradition of runic inscriptions or as a translation of a variation of the Latin formula.[16]

These formulas, like the alphabetic signs by which they were expressed, have a hint of magic about them. In releasing the form of the object from the material in which it was embedded and then inscribing it with letters, the artist was giving it a kind of life and voice. In Germanic heroic epic, swords have personal names and semi-magical powers as if they were filled with a divine numen. The processional icons that Christianity took over from pagan religious customs in Europe were considered to be receptacles or possessors of the powers of the saints or deity that they represented.[17] These and other sacred objects, like reliquaries, candlesticks, and crosses, were often provided with inscriptions, which, quite apart from what they said, may have been regarded as visible signs of the objects' power. The treasury of Conques still preserves four reliquaries from the late eleventh and early twelfth centuries, all with leonine verse inscriptions.[18] Cluny possessed a great seven-branched altar candlestick of cast bronze, eighteen feet tall, whose symbolic form and healing powers were celebrated in the verses inscribed on it: 'God wished to give this form to the rule of faith. It teaches (us) like a rule to know Christ; from its sacred breath the full seven virtues flow and restore to health all things in everyone.'[19] No object had greater power than the cross. In the Saint Gall Plan, both the Altar of the Holy Cross in the centre of the church and the Cemetery Cross (presumably a free-standing cross of wood or stone) are given verse labels. The famous Bury Saint Edmunds Cross, now in the Cloisters in New York, which stands less than two feet in height, is carved with more than sixty inscriptions, including two hexameter couplets, with disyllabic end rhyme and internal rhyme.[20]

A fascinating anticipation of Romanesque portals and portal sculptures that speak in the first person is the Ruthwell Cross – one in a series of standing stone crosses of Northumbria. It now appears likely that the Ruthwell Cross was a work of the first half of the eighth century.[21] The Cross stands a little over seventeen feet in height. It is carved on the two narrower sides (east and west) of the shaft with birds and animals in an interlaced vine scroll and on the two broader faces (north and south) with scenes from the life of Christ and one scene showing the hermits Paul and Anthony breaking a loaf of bread. Appropriate Latin prose inscriptions, some of them taken from the Gospels, frame the scenes on the two broader faces. The vine scrolls are also framed by an inscription band, but the inscription is an Anglo-Saxon poem carved in runes. Whereas the Latin inscriptions merely identify and comment on the images of the north and south faces, the runic poem, astonishingly, speaks in the voice of the cross. It is as though the Germanic version of the *[X]-me-fecit* formula, which gave voice to the material object, had been suddenly, dramatically, expanded. On the east side the poem reads: 'God almighty stripped himself. When he wished to mount on the gallows, brave before all men, I did not dare turn away, but I had to stand fast. I raised up the powerful king, the Lord of heaven; I dared not bend. Men mocked us both together. I was drenched with blood, poured from the man's side, after he sent forth his spirit.'[22] On the west side, it goes on: 'Christ was on the cross. Eager ones came there from afar, noble ones to the solitary one. I beheld it all. I was painfully afflicted with sorrows; I bowed down to the hands of the men, wounded with nails. They laid him down, the limb-weary one; they stood by the head of his body. They beheld there the Lord of heaven; and he rested himself there for a time.'

This poem seems to have been much loved in England. A two-line echo of it is inscribed on a late-tenth- or early-eleventh-century silver reliquary from England, known as the Brussels Cross.[23] A longer version (156 lines), *The Dream of the Rood,* is preserved in a late-tenth-century English manuscript, which is now in the cathedral library of Vercelli in northern Italy.[24] It is a fascinating question, whether the inscription on the Ruthwell Cross is a quotation or brief adaptation from some early version of *The Dream of the Rood,* or if *The Dream of the Rood* is an expansion of the poem on the Ruthwell Cross. In *The Dream of the Rood,* although the cross speaks, it does so within a dream vision that is reported by the first-person narrator of the poem, the dreamer. Despite the fact that the voice of the cross is at one remove from direct address, *The Dream of the Rood* offers a memorable portrait of a believer listening to the words of a sacred material structure. As the cross spoke to receptive witnesses in Anglo-Saxon England, so, I suggest, the church was heard by worshippers in the eleventh and twelfth centuries.

Some portal inscriptions that addressed the viewer in the present moment may have been perceived, not as being recorded memoranda of speech, but rather as being 'voiced' in space rather than time, visually rather than audibly. If an inscribed voice ceased to be a mere quotation and 'spoke' in such a way that it gave the impression of articulating the words of Christ or the Church, the portal would have acquired a kind of 'presence.' The distinction between quotation and presence is difficult to make and impossible to prove. Each portal inscription has to be evaluated separately in the context in which it appears, and even then, one cannot be sure of the effect that it might have had on a medieval audience or how the effect might have differed from one member of that audience to another. First-person inscriptions may have raised the same concerns and anxieties that images did.

Would worshippers have taken Christ's words as being eternally present in the here and now when they were visibly marked as quotations from a text by being carved on a banderole, or on a book? Phrases like *Ego sum lux mundi,* 'I am the light of the world' (John 8:12), frequently appear on the book in Christ's hand when he appears seated in majesty, as, for example, on the tympanum of the south portal of Saint-Aventin in the French Pyrenees. Occasionally artists or their authors turned such phrases into verse. At the cathedral of Modena, on the segment of the marble Genesis frieze above the left portal that depicts the Creation of Adam and Eve and the Eating of the Forbidden Fruit, the inscription on the open book in God's hand is an unrhymed hexameter (fig. 16): 'I am the light of the world, the true way, life eternal.'[25] The verse is an amalgam of words and phrases spoken by Christ in the Gospel of John, including the phrase that was carved at Saint-Aventin (John 8:12, 9:5, and 14:6). Words like these might have been thought of as being immediately present rather than as reminders of what was spoken once in the past.

Sculpted figures of the prophets of the Old Testament and the disciples of Christ also carry banderoles or scrolls or open books on which their words are inscribed. These are typically quoted, sometimes in abbreviated form, either from the Bible or from some intermediate source, like a sermon. For example, the jambs on either side of the central portal of the cathedral of Ferrara are carved with statues of the prophets and Gabriel and Mary, holding scrolls (fig. 23). On the prophet Ezekiel's scroll is written VIDI PORTAM IN DOMO DOMINI CLAVSA, 'I saw the gate in the house of the Lord shut' (cf. Ezek. 44:1–4). Daniel's scroll contains words from a fifth-century sermon: 'Say, Saint Daniel, what you know about Christ. "When the holy of holies comes," he says, "your anointing will cease."'[26] The sculptural presentation of these inscriptions emphasizes their textual sources, and presence does not seem to be an issue.

Apart from these, it is rare to find sculpted figures who speak in the first person or use direct address. At San Zeno of Verona, we hear the voices of Adam and of Fortune. Both are on the west façade, but they belong to different phases of construction and therefore to different dates. Reliefs depicting scenes from the Old Testament on the right of the portal are the work of the sculptor Niccolò or an assistant working under his direction.[27] The panel at the top right shows Eve spinning, while nursing Cain and Abel, and Adam hewing wood (fig. 24). The inscription above them reads: 'You who are entering, I lament the sin of cruel Eve, who has inflicted perpetual woe on me [and] on you.'[28] This is the voice of Adam, addressing the people entering the church. The Wheel of Fortune window high above the portal is the work of the architect and sculptor Brioloto (ca. 1200). Fortune speaks in two full leonine hexameters that are inscribed in a circle on the inner hub of the wheel and can only be seen with the aid of binoculars: 'Lo, I, Fortune alone, govern mortals. I raise up, I dispose, I give good and evil to all.'[29]

The Lamb of God is sometimes set in a circular frame inscribed with the words of Christ. In a couple of instances, this variant raises some interesting questions about the inscription and its possible 'presence.' The image of the Lamb of God has a long history, and it appears in a number of places in the Romanesque period.[30] It was utilized ca. 1155 at the abbey church of Cluny for the keystone of the vault of the fifth bay of the narthex.[31] The keystone is now on display in the Musée Ochier. A full leonine hexameter is inscribed around the rim of the medallion, which says, in the voice of the Lamb:

> In celo magnus, hic parvus sculpor ut agnus.[32]
> *(In heaven I am the Great Lamb, here I am sculpted as a small lamb).*

The artist chose the thirteen-syllable hexameter line – the shortest standard hexameter – to fit his verse to the restricted space of the keystone medallion.[33] It could not have been seen from any normal viewing position in the church, which inevitably raises the question for modern viewers – for whom, or for what purpose, was it composed? Does it make sense to ask whether these words have presence? Is the question only appropriate for portal inscriptions?

The voice of the Lamb is juxtaposed with other voices on a tympanum of San Prudencio in the village of Armentia, which is now a suburb of Vitoria in Spain. The church has undergone considerable reconstruction since this sculptural program was created. The tympanum, which was originally above a portal, is now set into the wall of the south porch above a tomb sculpture. It is divided into two registers. A Lamb of God within a circular medallion is in the upper register, flanked by the kneeling figures of John the Baptist on the left and Isaiah on the right. John the Baptist holds a scroll on which are written his words, as reported by John the Evangelist, ECCE AGNVS DEI, 'behold, the lamb of God' (John 1:36). Isaiah holds a scroll with the phrase SI[CVT] OVIS, a reference to Isaiah's words: 'All we like sheep have gone astray, every one hath turned aside into his own way: and the Lord hath laid on him the iniquity of us all. He was offered because it was his own will, and he opened not his mouth: he shall be led *as a sheep* [*sicut ovis*] to the slaughter, and shall be dumb as a lamb before his shearer, and he shall not open his mouth' (Isa. 53:6–7) Both visually and verbally the composition of the tympanum ironically contradicts Isaiah. The Lamb lifts its head, and (arguably) opens its mouth, and speaks the full leonine hexameter that encircles the rim of the medallion:

Mors ego sum mortis, vocor Agnus, sum Leo fortis.[34]
(I am the death of death, I am called the Lamb, I am the strong Lion.)

Isaiah's words stress the humility of the sacrifice, but the verse asserts the triumph of Christ.

In the lower register of the tympanum two angels support a chrismon in a circular frame that sits directly beneath the medallion. The inscription band that separates the two registers displays a verse which establishes that the tympanum was once above a portal and the Lamb and the chrismon in the axial position: 'Through this gate the gate of heaven becomes accessible to each believer.'[35] This might be the voice of Christ or, more probably, the voice of the Church. Perhaps it is also the Church that speaks the verse on the rim of the tympanum: 'The great king of hosts is God and He is called the Lamb.'[36] Although the multiplicity of voices (there are also some simple labels and a donor inscription on the tympanum) may diminish the immediacy of the voice of the Lamb, it is nevertheless the case that the words of the inscriptions bring the somewhat abstract images of the sculpture remarkably to life.

Of all the inscriptions that appear on the Last Judgment tympanum of Conques, the only ones that are certainly in the voice of Christ the Judge are those on the partially unrolled scrolls in the hands of the two angels on either side of Christ's head (fig. 2). They are the words of Christ that are recorded in Matthew 25:34 and 25:41: *[Venite benedict]i patris mei p[oss]idete vo[bis paratum regnum]*, 'Come, blessed of my Father, take possession of the kingdom prepared for you,' and *Discedite a me [maledicti]*, 'Depart from me, accursed ones.'[37] These are the words that, as Christ informs his disciples, the King will speak on the day of judgment – that is, in the Gospel text, Christ prophesies the words that he speaks on the tympanum. They are not in the same time frame as the worshippers who view them, but the overwhelming presence of the massive figure of Christ may have made the day of judgment and his words more real than anything in time present.

The Last Judgment tympanum of the west portal of Autun (fig. 8) is a magnificent example of the projection of the voice of Christ through the use of verse inscriptions. The Autun poet responded totally to the mannered intensity of Gislebertus's sculpture. The words, the sounds, and even the rhythms of his verse seem to emerge from the scenes sculpted around them.

Christ in Majesty seated in a mandorla supported by four angels dominates the centre of the tympanum (fig. 25). His words are inscribed on the rim of the mandorla:

> Omnia dispono solus meritosque corono.
> Quos scelus exercet, me iudice, pena coercet.[38]
> *(I alone arrange all things and crown the deserving. Punishment, with me as judge, holds in check those whom vice stimulates.)*

The arrangement of these words and phrases mirrors the Last Judgment theme of the tympanum. The centre of each line, immediately following the caesura, is occupied by the epithet of the speaker, Christ, who is 'alone' (*solus*) or the 'judge' (*me iudice*), just as the figure of Christ is the overwhelming central image of the tympanum. The first verse, which is on Christ's right, the side of salvation, is simply but perfectly balanced: object + first-person verb + *solus* + object + first-person verb. The orderly syntax implies the order of God's creation and the justice of the rewards received by the deserving. Even the pattern of word accents harmonizes with Christ's unique simplicity. Every word is stressed on the vowel *o*:

> Ómnia dispóno sólus meritósque coróno.

Christ is the only figure in the tympanum who is full-front and completely symmetrical in posture (the arrangement of the folds of his robe introduces a slight touch of asymmetry). The Virgin Mary, seated on Christ's right hand, comes closest to recapitulating his timeless pose. All the other figures, even the angels and the apostles, turn aside or bend in some fashion. The damned and the demons positively writhe in contorted postures.

The second verse of the couplet, inscribed on Christ's left, the side of damnation, is still balanced, though not perfectly so, as if the disorder of the evil that Christ's words chastize troubles the lucid simplicity of his thought. The grammatical object, the damned (*quos*), standing at the left, shifts the paired subject + verb phrases slightly off centre. As if in compensation, the central *me* is qualified by its harsh pendant *iudice*. Underlying the actual verse is the orderly structure of the first verse: subject +

third-person verb + *me* + subject + third-person verb. Ultimately, order is not lost. The syntax of the second verse is appropriate to the visual scene in another way. Christ is the judge, yet he is detached. The work of separating the saved from the damned is carried out impersonally by the scales of justice watched over by Saint Michael and the Devil. In the verse Christ is insulated from direct involvement by the ablative absolute, *me iudice*, 'with me as judge,' just as in the composition he is isolated by his frontal posture within the mandorla.

A full leonine hexameter couplet that runs along the upper edge of the left side of the lintel (figs. 8, 25) offers hope to the faithful who have led a good life:

> Quisque resurget ita quem non trahit impia vita,
> Et lucebit ei sine fine lucerna diei.[39]
> *(Whoever is not seduced by an impious life will rise again in this way, and the light of day will shine on him or her forever.)*

These two verses are arranged on either side of the angel who stands in the middle of the line of the elect. Three naked children clutch his sheltering sleeves. Emile Mâle observed that visually the saved are already separated from the damned, even before the weighing of the souls.[40] But the first verse of the couplet mitigates this hint of predestination by the strong caesura after *ita*: '*Every one* will arise *in this way*' (that is, with the confident hope of the elect in the scene below) – pause – 'whom sin has not betrayed.' The second verse clarifies the postures of the figures on the lintel, who have just emerged from the grave and turn their faces toward the majestic Christ above their heads, as if bathing in the light that will shine on them forever.

In contrast, the men and women on the right side of the lintel bend beneath the weight of their sins and look anywhere but up. No light floods upon them. Along the upper edge of this side of the lintel, a couplet proclaims:

> Terreat hic terror quos terreus alligat error,
> Nam fore sic verum notat hic horror specierum.[41]
> *(May this terror terrify those whom earthly error binds, for the horror of these images here in this manner truly depicts what will be.)*

The nervous intensity of the couplet, especially the first verse, sharpens the edge of its verbal warning – a fitting counterpoint to the grotesque images of torment on the tympanum. Reiterated *er*'s and *or*'s weave a fatal knot around the damned (*quos*):

T*err*eat hic t*error* quos t*err*eus alligat *error*

The pressure of the alliteration on *t* ties *alligat* to *error*. *Error* returns to *terror*. There is no escape. Etymological wordplay provides the basis for these verbal effects. Medieval authors enjoyed contemplating real relationships where we find only chance resemblance. *Terreus/ terreat/ terror/ error/ horror* – this verbal morass must have seemed a significant revelation of the human meaning of the apocalyptic moment – the Last Judgment – which the tympanum depicts.

By whose authority is the promise of the couplet on the left side offered? Whose is the exhortation of the couplet on the right side? The future tense in the first and the hortatory subjunctive in the second give an urgent immediacy to these words. Is it the voice of the Church? Or is it possibly the voice of the Christ of the tympanum – the same voice that speaks the couplet of the mandorla?

One inscription stands apart from the rest for the simple reason that it is not in verse. This is the proud declaration, which is placed in the centre of the lintel, beneath the figure of Christ (fig. 25): *Gislebertus hoc fecit*, 'Gislebertus made this.' It is a variant of the formula, *[X] me fecit*, '[personal name] made me,' that artists used to sign their works.[42] 'Gislebertus made *this*,' however, is not quite the same as saying, 'Gislebertus made *me*.' This slight variation suggests that Gislebertus took all the verses of the Autun poet to be the voice of the Christ of the tympanum, not just in a fictive sense, but on some level as reality. By varying the formula he avoided the blasphemy of having God say, 'Gislebertus made me.' If to Gislebertus, then we may assume to the pilgrims contemplating it, the tympanum spoke in one voice and the voice was God's. All of which makes Gislebertus's signature no less audacious, for it is God who announces to the world that Gislebertus carved the tympanum!

7

Portal Inscriptions as 'Performatives'

When the Romanesque portal directly addressed the faithful, the voice of the portal was typically expressed as a command in the imperative or subjunctive mood, for example: 'enter,' 'do not enter,' 'change your ways.' Dante's imitation at the beginning of Canto 3 of the *Inferno* is exact, although demonically inverted. Over the gate of hell are inscribed the awful words:

> Per me si va ne la città dolente,
> Per me si va ne l'etterno dolore,
> Per me si va tra la perduta gente ...
> Dinanzi a me non fuor cose create
> Se non etterne, e io etterno duro.
> Lasciate ogne speranza, voi ch'intrate.
> *(Through me you enter the woeful city,*
> *Through me you enter eternal grief,*
> *Through me you enter among the lost ...*
> *Before me nothing was created*
> *If not eternal, and eternal I endure.*
> *Abandon every hope, you who enter.)*
> (*Inferno* 3, 1–3, 7–9)[1]

Every detail – the voice in the first person, the repeated phrase *per me*, the use of the imperative in the last line, the verb *intrate* – shows how thoroughly Dante had absorbed the convention. This is the voice of the gate of hell.

Pilgrims to Conques saw the two cities, heaven and hell, side by side in the Last Judgment tympanum above the double portal in which the two doors are separated by a massive central pier (fig. 1). A couplet on the lower edge of the lintel beneath the Heavenly City, which is depicted with its portal thrown open and an angel standing in it ready to welcome the saved, addressed the faithful in an imperative voice: 'Sinners, if you do not change your ways, know that a hard judgment will be upon you.'[2] This portion of the tympanum is above the left door. The inscription does not extend over the right door above which hell is depicted. From its location, I infer that lay worshippers entered through the left door, circulated clockwise around the interior and exited through the right door. The portal spoke as the gate of heaven; the idea of *entering* through the right door, directly beneath the Infernal City, might have been not so much repugnant as unimaginable to medieval Christians.

What can we make of the communication between the portal and its audience? Its message was conveyed in Latin – the sacred language of the western Church, but not a language any longer accessible to common people. Would the typical visitor have been able to read the words of the portal? The question is really twofold, because it involves not only the matter of comprehension, but also of visibility.

To take the latter point first, many portal inscriptions are today badly worn and degraded. Even with the aid of binoculars they can be hard to read. But, when they were newly carved and perhaps painted, would a viewer with normal eyesight have been able to distinguish all the letters without serious difficulty? (The question is really whether they were *intended* to be legible, but there is no way of answering this question directly.) We cannot always be sure that present viewing conditions correspond to the original ones. The inscriptions of Conques can easily be read with the naked eye from the parvis in front of the basilica. But if the tympanum was once enclosed within a narthex, or if, as one (unlikely) theory has it, it has been displaced from its original location within the church,[3] would the inscriptions have been as visible as they now are? The answer to this question would depend on our knowing both the amount of light that was available and the viewer's line of sight. However, it seems safe to assume that the penitential couplet on the lintel would have been readily visible to entering pilgrims, and probably most of the other inscriptions as well. The physical environment that determines the relationship between viewer and inscription varies tremendously. At one extreme, for example, is the monastic church of Santa María of Santa Cruz de la Serós. Santa Cruz is located in a narrow canyon in the mountain range just south of the valley of the river Aragón through which ran the pilgrimage road between

Jaca and Puente la Reina. The church, constructed for the Benedictine sisters of Saint John and dedicated to the Virgin Mary, was finished and decorated about 1100.[4] The community was not large; the secure residential chamber above the crossing could probably have held all the sisters in an emergency. Its west portal is deeply recessed in a low penthouse shelter, and the inscriptions on the tympanum, when they were in better condition than they now are, could probably have been read without difficulty (fig. 13). At the other extreme is the chapel of Loarre. The castle of Loarre is situated on a prominent hilltop about twenty miles south of Santa Cruz. After a successful battle against the Muslims near its site, Sancho Ramírez built the castle about 1070 as a frontier outpost, and with the assistance of the abbot of San Juan de la Peña installed a community of Augustinian canons in it.[5] Since the chapel is high up in the castle, its south portal is at the level of the crypt. The approach to the portal is narrowly hemmed in by the steepness of the terrain, and it is impossible to step back to get a good view of the frieze of Christ in Majesty above it. It is hard to imagine any circumstances in which the inscription on the frieze could have been read. Either the sculptor was unaware of the place for which the frieze was intended, or it simply did not matter to him that the words could not be seen. In general, however, the presence of portal inscriptions is obvious to the modern viewer, and for the most part it is probably safe to assume that they would have been legible when they had been freshly cut and painted.

It is difficult to estimate how many worshippers might have been functionally literate in Latin. No doubt most clergymen were literate, but not all of them. There was some lay literacy among both the aristocracy and the merchant and the artisan classes, particularly in southern Europe. The mercenary warrior chieftain El Cid, whose peregrinations may have taken him along the route between Jaca and Pamplona, and who died in Valencia (1099) just about the time the portal of Santa Cruz was being decorated, could read and write, and so, apparently, could his wife, Jimena. Pierre Riché calls attention to the development of a new phenomenon in the late eleventh and twelfth centuries, namely the existence of persons, both cleric and lay, male and female, who were literate in their own tongue, but not in Latin.[6] Certainly some pilgrims would have been able to read the inscriptions for themselves, but for many (the majority perhaps?), the words of the tympanum would have been unintelligible without the aid of an interpreter.

If commands of the kind that we have been considering on these portals were to be spoken by a living person in an appropriate social context, they would be, to use J.L. Austin's term, 'performatives.' Two of Austin's observations about performatives are relevant to portal inscriptions. He says: '[A] performative utterance will ... be *in a peculiar way* hollow or void if said by an actor on the stage, or if introduced in a poem, or spoken in soliloquy.'[7] And he also says: 'Unless a certain effect is achieved, the illocutionary act [= an action performed by saying or writing something (*New Shorter OED*)] will not have been happily, successfully performed ... I cannot be said to have warned an audience unless it hears what I say and takes what I say in a certain sense.'[8] Austin's remarks focus the problem precisely. I want to consider whether some inscriptions on Romanesque portals might be considered to be genuine performatives (as opposed to mimetic representations of performatives) and, if so, in what sense the directives of the portals might be called successful performative utterances.

It may appear that, in any logical sense of the term, the performative utterances of these portal inscriptions could only be described as being either 'hollow' or 'unhappy' or both. Insofar as we are dealing, not with spoken language, but with words memorialized in stone, the utterances might be said to have the same empty status as any speech composed by an author for a character to speak. And insofar as the performatives were not seen or comprehended by their audience, they might be said necessarily to fail in their effects.

Nevertheless, there is something unsatisfying about this preliminary judgment. Portal inscriptions themselves do not all share the same status as speech acts. Inscriptions that employ the first or second personal pronouns can be distinguished from those that do not. It is this class of utterances that seems in some cases to have had 'presence.'[9] It does not matter finally whether the speaker uses only the first person or only the second person or both, since I can only use the pronoun 'I' when I am addressing 'you,' and conversely the use of the pronoun 'you' implies an 'I' who uses it. As Émile Benveniste observes, 'it is a fact both original and fundamental that these 'pronominal' forms ["I" and "you"] do not refer to "reality" or to "objective" positions in space and time but to the utterance, unique each time, that contains them ... The importance of their function will be measured by the nature of the problem they serve to solve, which is none other than that of intersubjective communication.'[10] In Benveniste's sense, these voices all speak in performative utterances, apart from the question of whether they give specific commands, merely in utilizing the first- or second-person pronouns. They effect 'the conversion of language into discourse.' Benveniste goes on to say: 'Thus the indicators *I* and *you* cannot exist as potentialities; they exist only insofar as they are actualized in the instance of discourse, in which, by each of their own instances, they mark the process of appropriation by the speaker.'[11] Benveniste's formulation applies to spoken discourse. As phrased, it cannot literally be true of written texts, still less of words frozen in stone. Writing would seem to convert the pronouns *I* and *you* to 'potentialities' and the statements of which they are a part to mimetic representations of discourse. But there must be a class – indeed, a large class – of written utterances that have the potential to be reconverted to discourse at the moment they are read by a receptive reader or reported to a receptive listener.[12] In these cases it is the 'you' that actualizes the discourse. If the reader or listener accepts the role of 'you,' then it would appear that 'intersubjective communication' has taken place.

The voice of the portal was the voice of God or the Church. It was also, of course, the work of a human author (a monk in the local monastery, for example), writing in Latin in a conventional form of verse. No one would have doubted the human authorship of these inscriptions. However, it seems equally certain that they would not have been received by their audiences nor intended by their authors as scraps of a fictional monologue. The ontological status of the putative speaker (God or the Church) was radically different from any fictional character, or even from any historical person. Even though the form of the words (the use of Latin, the verse structure, the diction, the syntax) was the responsibility of their human author, their content was an expression of the divine message of God, ratified by the Church. In this sense, the human author functioned as a scribe or as a kind of simultaneous translator, very much in the way that medieval artists depicted the Evangelists writing the gospels from the dictation of an angel or the Holy Spirit whispering at their ear.[13]

Thus, it is possible to make a distinction between inscriptions that are (or were) performatives when they are actualized by their viewers and inscriptions that are mimetic performatives or merely descriptive utterances. The distinction can be illustrated by the north portal of the Cluniac abbey church of Notre-Dame of Déols. In the twelfth century, the abbey church, measuring some 370 feet in length, was one of the great structures of western Europe. This grandeur, however, offered it no protection from devastation during the Hundred Years' War and the Wars of Religion. It later served for two centuries as a stone quarry. Finally, in

1830, most of its remains, including the north porch, were auctioned off to a road contractor and demolished.[14] Fortunately, the ruins of the abbey, including the decoration of the north portal, were described by Father Dubouchat and by another traveller who visited the ruins about 1825.

From their descriptions we learn that the north portal of Déols was ornamented with a tympanum of Christ in Majesty with the Four Animals.[15] As at the Royal Portal of Chartres, to which this scheme was evidently related, the apocalyptic image of Christ in Majesty was accompanied by references to worship, the secular arts and sciences, and manual labour in three recessed orders of archivolts decorated with figures. The inner archivolt displayed angels in adoration; the keystone represented the Lamb of God. The middle archivolt displayed nine statues of the Arts and Sciences. At the summit of the archivolt was Philosophy with a banderole in her right hand which she offered to Grammar and another in her left hand which she offered to Dialectic. Standing beside Grammar were Rhetoric, Astronomy, and Arithmetic. Beside Dialectic were Geometry, Music, and Physics. The outer archivolt figured the Works of the Months.[16] A statue of the Virgin was mounted above the ensemble.

On the lower edge of the tympanum the voice of the portal addressed the pilgrim as an exile held captive in Babylon (earth) and promised passage to the road that led back to his or her native land (heaven): 'You wretch who are held captive in a wretched place, the way back from Babylon to your homeland lies open through me.'[17] Although faith and the Church were the necessary conditions for passage through the gate and onto the road home, the sculptural program of the portal offered work and study as palliatives to the misery of the human condition in exile. Philosophy addressed Grammar and Dialectic in verses that were inscribed on the banderoles in her hands. She said to Grammar: 'May the parts of speech sound as pleasing to the ear as sacred Scripture. Through you the other sciences and arts are known.'[18] And to Dialectic she added: 'May our faults of logic be made known to us through you.'[19] By stressing the value of grammar and dialectic for the pursuit of knowledge in the arts and sciences, the poet may have intended to emphasize the quality of the monastic school of Déols. They were the gates to higher education as the wordplay on the standard portal formula *per me* in both couplets makes clear.

Despite the fact that they were in the same verse form, there was a crucial difference between Philosophy's couplets and the couplet spoken by the portal. From the point of view of the worshipper, the voice of the portal addressed him or her directly, while the words of Philosophy, addressed to the statues on either side of her, could only have been representations of direct address. Thus, the performatives spoken by Philosophy were mimetic, but the portal inscription could be considered a genuine performative. If it no longer is, it is because the fragment of the tympanum with the fragment of the portal inscription on its lower edge is in a museum. The conditions for a performative are not 'happy,' not because the inscription is incomplete, but because it is not properly in place above the portal of a functioning church, which is (or was once thought to be) Christ and the gate of heaven.

Michael Hancher has described *fiat lux*, 'let there be light' (Gen. 1:3), as 'the supreme performative.'[20] This phrase comes to us as reported by the author of Genesis, in the Latin of Jerome's translation of the Hebrew text. It is necessarily a mimesis of a speech act that occurred once *in principio*, at the beginning of time. But if the words inscribed *on* the church were felt to be the words *of* the Church or *of* God, those words might have been thought immediately operative whether anyone 'heard' them or not. Moreover, the dual problem that some inscriptions were difficult or impossible to see and that some viewers could not read Latin could have been solved by the intervention of 'guides' or interpreters, whose function would be parallel to the human author of the sacred words. Although definitive evidence is lacking, I am persuaded of the likelihood that churches frequented by pilgrims would have provided commentators to explain the sculptures and translate the inscriptions of the portals.[21] A parallel to this practice is known in medieval Constantinople, where 'local guides instructed the pilgrims on addressing the icon or relic, which would answer their particular concern.'[22] Moving through the portal, worshippers passed from secular into sacred space. If personal transformation took place as a result, the 'message' of the portal, which was carried both by the verse inscription and by the art with which it was associated,[23] might be said, in the language I have been using here, to have been 'successfully' effected. Although the speech acts inscribed on the portals of Romanesque churches resemble *fiat lux* in being articulated in the Latin of a human translator, they were performatives that took effect not once in the past, but always and continually in the present, at the moment the receptive worshipper out of fear or hope accepted the role of 'you.'

8

Conditional Transcendence: Movement between the Literal and Spiritual Levels of the Allegory of the Church

When the church building was sacralized by the ceremony of dedication, it became the house of God, without ceasing to be a material structure in the temporal world. It existed on both levels at once. Its double nature might be differently experienced, depending on the individual worshipper's state of mind or soul. The aesthetic perfection of the building's structure was understood to have a transforming effect. The author of the *Pilgrim's Guide* praises the cathedral of Santiago of Compostela in these terms: 'In this church, in truth, one cannot find a single crack or defect: it is admirably built, large, spacious, luminous, of becoming dimensions, well proportioned in width, length and height, of incredibly marvelous workmanship and even built on two levels as a royal palace. He who walks through the aisles of the triforium above, if he ascended in a sad mood, having seen the superior beauty of this temple, will leave happy and contented ("si tristis ascendit, visa obtima pulcritudine ejusdem templi, letus et gavisus efficitur").'[1] One may wonder whether the author means to describe a spiritual transformation or merely an emotional response to the beauty of the interior as seen from the galleries, but the movement of transcendence is unmistakable.

Transcendence, defined as the temporary elevation of the worshipper into a state of grace, was the core experience of the allegory of the church. The portal was a particular locus of transcendence. Passing through it, the Christian could be spiritually exalted. Yet this liminal transformation was conditional, unstable, reversible. At any moment, the same worshipper might collapse back into the panic and terror of the unredeemed world.

The Benedictine abbey church of Notre-Dame des Moreaux near Poitiers was explicitly identified on the literal level with the temple of

Solomon. The west façade of the now-vanished church was described by three different archaeologists in the nineteenth century. It consisted of a single portal, surmounted by a round arch, with an inscription on the inner archivolt. A relief of a bishop standing on an animal was placed on each side of the arch. On the right, standing on a lion, was Bishop Adelelme of Poitiers, who died in 1140. In the corresponding position on the left, standing on a bull, was Bishop Grimoard, also of Poitiers, who died in 1142.[2] The portal was probably constructed shortly after Grimoard's death.

The inscription on the archivolt was recorded in the drawings of the nineteenth-century archaeologists. It consisted of two hexameters with disyllabic end rhyme:

> Ut fuit introitus templi sancti Salomonis,
> Sic est istius in medio bovis atque leonis.[3]
> *(As was the entrance to the temple of the holy Solomon, so the entrance of this is placed between an ox and a lion.)*

The couplet alludes to the fact that the entrance to Solomon's temple was decorated with brass basins adorned with figures of oxen and lions (cf. 3 Kings 7:29). The figure of a man standing on, or above, an animal signified transcendence from lower nature to higher nature, or from the secular to the spiritual realm. This is the meaning of the bishops standing upon the animals at the abbey. In the unredeemed world the church was the temple of Solomon, but for the faithful it was lifted up to become the Church of Christ.

In Italy and Provence transcendence was commonly signified by the columns on either side of a porch, which were mounted on the backs of couching lions, as, for example, at the cathedrals of Modena (fig. 15), Fidenza, and Embrun.[4] Griffins sometimes take the place of lions (e.g., the destroyed Portal of the Months at Ferrara; the cathedral of Verona). In the conventional symbolism of the parts of the church, the columns were said to be the bishops who supported the Church.[5] The design could be elaborated. There are three portals in the west façade of the cathedral of Piacenza.[6] Lions support the columns of the central porch, but the columns of the outer porches rest on the shoulders of seated men.[7] These elements are combined in the central porch of the cathedral of Ferrara (fig. 23). Two columns are on each side of the porch above a lion.[8] A platform is laid on the back of each lion. One column rests on the rear of the platform above the lion's hindquarters. In front of it there is a kind of backless chair on which sits a man who bears the weight of the other column on his neck and shoulders. According to Christine Verzár Bornstein, 'moralistic lions devouring beasts or humans are used for supports of a portal canopy for the first time in the Zodiac Portal of the Sagra di San Michele, then in the mature works of Nicholaus at Ferrara Cathedral, Verona Cathedral, and San Zeno.'[9] At Saint-Trophime of Arles and at Saint-Gilles, on the southern pilgrimage route from Arles to Compostela, transcendence is signified by the reliefs of two apostles on either side of the central portal that rest on lions mauling their prey of men or beasts.

A more profound expression of transcendence was achieved in churches in France where a tympanum with Christ in the axial position was structurally supported by a central pier or 'trumeau' on the same vertical axis. It belonged to the unredeemed world, but it carried the weight of the divine vision. The trumeau of the portal of the abbey church of Saint-Pierre of Beaulieu is decorated with elongated 'atlantes,' whose heads bend with the effort as they strain to uphold the tympanum of Last Judgment. One of them stands on a monstrous beast. The trumeau supporting the Christ-in-Majesty tympanum of the abbey church of Saint-Pierre of Moissac displays three crossed pairs of lactating lionesses and male lions[10] on the outer face with elongated figures of the prophet Jeremiah and Saint Paul on the lateral faces. Jeremiah and Paul represent the support of the Old and New Testaments, but the animals belong to the unredeemed world.

One of the last major halting-places on the pilgrimage route from Arles before it crossed the Pyrenees at the Somport Pass was Oloron,[11] where the Romanesque west portal with its sheltering porch still remains from the former cathedral of Sainte-Marie (the rest of the church has been rebuilt in the Gothic style). The trumeau supporting the tympanum of the west portal is a column resting on the heads and shoulders of two men who are chained at the waist (fig. 26). From their dress and features, they are thought to be modelled on Moorish slaves. What could this mean? Is it likely that the Church would be supported by Moors or even, as one suggestion has it, that the idea is the crushing of paganism?[12] The fortuitous discovery in 1934 of a fragment of the figure of a Moor and a capital with a verse inscription at the abbey of Santo Domingo de Silos in Spain helps in interpreting this conception. There, in the east walk of the cloister, a stairway leads through a double arch up to the Puerta de las Vírgenes, a portal that once opened into the Romanesque church. The figure and the capital are believed to have formed the central support of the double arch.[13] The abacus of the capital is carved with two lines of verse: 'The strong Moor laments as this is read: "The world marvels that I endure so great a weight."'[14] Given the axial position of the trumeau at Oloron and the (probably) similar configuration of the capital at Silos, the conception evidently parallels that of other trumeau designs in France. Moreover, the inscription aligns the meaning of the trumeau designs of France with the columns resting on the backs of men and lions in Italy. At the north portal of Piacenza one of the men bearing columns sits on a base with the (partly eroded) inscription, O QVAM GRANDE PONDVS SVPE[R]FERO, 'Oh, what a great weight I bear.'[15] The Church was founded on the strength and support of 'the citizens of the earthly Jerusalem,' who were nevertheless in bondage to the Old Law. In keeping with the medieval habit of transposing biblical events into contemporary settings (anachronism in the service of universal truth), the Moors would have been a familiar example, to Christians on either side of the Pyrenees, of a people who had not received the light. This configuration, which includes the column or arch above the Moors, combines the literal allegory of the unredeemed world with its transcendence to the spiritual level. The temple of Solomon carried on the back of the Moor is become the Church of Christ.

At Oloron, the trumeau column that is held up by the two chained Moors supports a tympanum of the Descent from the Cross (fig. 14). The cross rests on a chrismon, which in turn is above the head of an animal. There are two elaborately carved archivolts above the tympanum. In the outer archivolt are the Twenty-four Elders with the Lamb of God at the apex. The inner archivolt shows secular scenes that are perhaps related to the Labours of the Months. On the left, peasants slaughter and prepare a boar for feasting; on the right, they catch and prepare a giant salmon. In front of the lower portions of this archivolt, a demonic beast devours a man on one side, while a mounted cavalier rides above a prostrate man on the other. A monstrous animal head is in the axial position of the archivolt beneath the Lamb of God. The Lamb of God carries the inscription, *in cruce salus, in cruce vita,* 'in the cross, salvation, in the cross, life.'[16] Thus there is a constant alternation between the literal and the spiritual levels of allegory, between references to the fallen and to the redeemed world, along the axis that extends from the chained men at the bottom to the Lamb of God at the top – an alternation that is repeated between and along the archivolts and their bases.

Often, transcendence is expressed simply by the contrast between the tympanum and its archivolts. The Last Judgment tympanum of Saint-Lazare of Autun displays a multi-storeyed, arcaded heavenly city on the left side (fig. 8). Ruined towers on the right side indicate hell. In the outer archivolt circular medallions depicting the Signs of the Zodiac and the Labours of the Months encompass the tympanum in a great half-wheel. The sculptural program of the portal mediates between the temporal world (the archivolts) and eternity (the tympanum), between the literal level of unredeemed experience and the fearful hope that is anagogy. Human experience must have seemed double-edged, capable of moving in two directions, profoundly dualistic.

Lions support the columns of the porch of San Zeno of Verona, where another way of expressing conditional transcendence was employed somewhat later in the upper façade. A large circular window was inserted into the façade at the beginning of the thirteenth century. Though it looks like a typical rose window, it is in fact a wheel of fortune. John Leyerle points out that all rose windows have this aspect – that is, they may be seen as wheels of fortune rather than as roses (and, indeed, the term used to describe them was typically *rota*).[17] The wheel window at San Zeno has twelve spokes made of double columns that support round arches at the outer circumference. A small circular window with twelve scallops is inserted in the hub of the wheel. This repetition of the number 12 was undoubtedly meant to invoke the hours of the day and the months of the year – time's revolving cycles. Outside the wheel are six figures at the 2, 4, 6, 8, 10, and 12 o'clock positions. They are upright on the left side of the wheel and tumbling on the right side; the wheel therefore was imagined as rotating clockwise. Fortune turns the wheel from the still point of its centre, on the vertical axis of the façade. She is represented not by her image but by her voice, inscribed in verses on the inner hub of the wheel.[18] Passing into the church effects the transformation from the perspective of time to the perspective of eternity, or from the literal to the anagogical level. The vagaries of Fortune can be reinterpreted as the designs of Providence. For the worshipper who looks back out through the stained glass of the window, the wheel appears to have been transformed into a twelve-petalled flower.

There is a parallel to wheel windows in the labyrinths that were sometimes set into the pavements and sometimes displayed on the walls of medieval churches in Italy and France.[19] Like the wheel windows these were usually circular in shape. Although it is often asserted that the faithful got down on their hands and knees and made a 'pilgrimage' through the maze of the labyrinth to its centre in token of the pilgrimage to Jerusalem, no evidence survives from the Middle Ages to support this conclusion.[20] A mosaic labyrinth, dating from the beginning of the twelfth century, was once found in San Savino of Piacenza, perhaps in the pavement of the nave. It was accompanied by four leonine verses, which demonstrate that it was intended as an allegory of the unredeemed world: 'This labyrinth figuratively signifies this world, wide-open to anyone entering, but exceedingly narrow to the one going back out. Thus, in the grip of the world, burdened by a heap of sins, each person can only return with difficulty to the teaching of (eternal) life.'[21]

Elsewhere the labyrinth signified hell – not the hell that awaited unrepentant sinners, but rather hell as the end term of the unredeemed world before Christ offered the possibility of salvation. This seems to be the meaning of the images of Theseus and the Minotaur that were placed in the centre of the labyrinths at Pavia and Lucca. The labyrinth in San Michele Maggiore of Pavia shows Theseus slaying the Minotaur and a full leonine verse above them proclaims: 'Theseus entered and killed the hybrid monster.'[22] Adjacent scenes just outside the labyrinth depict David and Goliath and a man slaying a dragon, familiar types of Christ harrowing hell. Thus, Theseus too is a type of Christ, and the labyrinth can be read as a positive sign of resurrection.[23] The same may be true of the small labyrinth that is carved on a pillar of the west porch of the cathedral of Lucca. A representation of Theseus and the Minotaur was visible in its centre until about the middle of the eighteenth century, when it was finally effaced as a result of generations of visitors tracing the path of the labyrinth with their fingers.[24]

Still another manifestation of the literal level of the allegory and its transcendence occurs when the axial figure of Christ in Majesty or the chrismon on the tympanum is replaced or combined with a tree. The tree evokes the Tree of Life and the Tree of Knowledge from which, according to medieval legend, came the wood of the cross by way of the temple of Solomon.[25] It belongs to the natural world (and might be said to be the source of all of the images of nature that are found in the Romanesque church). On the tympanum of the south portal of the church at Dinton in Buckinghamshire, the axial tree is flanked by two animals who eat of its fruit. This is the negative vision of the fallen world, but the verses inscribed beneath it offer, in the voice of the Church, the possibility of transcendence: 'If anyone despairs of the rewards which are deserved for merited deeds, let him hear in this place the precepts which he ought to keep.'[26] Elsewhere, emphasis is placed on positive signs of the Saviour. On the south-portal tympanum of Kilpeck, in the district of

Hereford and Worcester in England, the axial plant is not a tree but a grapevine with ripe fruit hanging from its branches. Two lateral shoots droop gracefully to either side. The vine is a sign of Christ in the natural world.[27] On the west-portal tympanum of the hermitage of Puilampa, near Sádaba in the Spanish province of Zaragoza, five trees appear on the tympanum. Two are large, cone-bearing pine trees that flank an axial chrismon. The chrismon rests on a small tree on the central axis, and two other small trees, one on either side, lean in to support it. Christ appears to be the chief fruit of the natural world, and the verse on the implied lintel directs the viewer's attention to the anagogical meaning of the portal: 'Through this gate the gate of heaven becomes accessible to each believer'.[28] The sun and the moon – the lights that were added in the beginning (Gen. 1:16) and will be taken away at the end (Apoc. 21:23, etc.) – in the upper background of the tympanum are a reminder that the anagogical level of the allegory is a function of Last Judgment.

Representations of the virtues and vices relate to the spiritually ambivalent tropological allegory of the church. The struggle between virtue and vice is often one-sided, especially on the façades of Aquitainian churches, where the theme was frequently employed. Virtue is depicted as a female warrior, who stands upon the defeated figure of vice. Before the twelfth century, manuscript illustrations of Prudentius's *Psychomachia*, from which the image of the female warrior was derived, showed a more dynamic struggle, as if the issue were in doubt.[29] Linda Seidel claims that the 'transformation of the Prudentian imagery' into a static representation of the triumph of virtue can be traced to 'a Carolingian appropriation of a late antique motif' that the Carolingians associated with the triumph of Christ.[30] One reason for the sudden popularity of the static representation of the theme may have been that when the moral allegory of the church came to be depicted on the façade, particularly above the central portal that figured Christ, it seemed to demand a victorious resolution of the struggle against the sins of the unredeemed world (tropology thus verging on anagogy).

The dynamic conflict of the soul was mirrored in a different way. At Saint-Pierre of Aulnay the sculptural programs of the south transept portal and the window above it alternate between representations of the unredeemed world and images of transcendence.[31] Virtue triumphs over vice on the upper level around the window, where four female warriors with large pointed shields trample upon small human and animal figures.[32] The archivolts above the portal display an amazing variety of animal and human figures. Animals from the Bestiaries and the *Physiologus* make up the fourth, outer archivolt. The third archivolt shows the Elders of the Apocalypse. The Apostles and Prophets are displayed on the second. Flat animal figures amid floral vines decorate the inner archivolt. Thus, the dominant theme of the south-transept façade is the Janus-faced tropological allegory of the church as each of the faithful and as each saved soul. On the one hand, this allegory looks forward to the eternal stability of the soul in bliss in the static representation of the triumph of virtue. On the other hand, it looks back upon the experience of the individual in the sixth age and speaks to the need for spiritual transformation as well as the danger of relapse. The sculptural program embodies this dual focus of tropology.

The ambivalent multilayering of the allegory of the church and its deeply penitential implication are captured in the portal inscriptions of two churches in the French Pyrenees. The first is Saint-André of Luz-Saint-Sauveur, a fortified church built by the Knights Hospitallers at the end of the twelfth century.[33] Its north portal is decorated with a tympanum of Christ in Majesty with the Four Animals (fig. 27). A chrismon is carved on the innermost archivolt, in the axial position above Christ's head.[34] There is a single jamb column on either side of the door. The one on the right has a capital of a man between two animals – probably representing Daniel in the lions' den. David Simon has observed that this capital corresponds to the capital on the right side of the portal of the cathedral of Jaca, and he aligns the penitential message of the two portals.[35]

Verses inscribed around the arch of the tympanum and along the implied lintel frame the imposing figure of Christ. The ones around the arch are badly damaged. Originally, there were probably four hexameters; only portions of the last two remain, and even for these we have to rely on a doubtful transcription dating from the nineteenth century for some of the details. They may have said something like: 'The court of heaven is open to the righteous pilgrim, to whom Christ, born of the Virgin ...'[36] If we can accept the reading on which this translation is based, the anagogical and tropological elements of the allegory of the church are evident. The three hexameters on the lintel are in somewhat better condition. We can be reasonably confident of this much:

... spoliat serpens se pelle vetusta,
Est humilis multum. Lascivum neglige cultum.
Si cupis intrare, quoniam patet, hoc tibi quere.[37]

> *([When?] the serpent sheds his old skin, he is very humble. Despise lascivious dress (?) / a lascivious way of life (?) / lascivious worship (?) [probably a deliberate pun on* cultum*]. If you want to enter, since it lies open, seek this [= humility?] for yourself.)*

These verses, which are put in the voice of the Church (typology), confirm the penitential theme of the portal (tropology). Like the lion, the snake is an important example of the medieval habit of reading the signs in the book of nature *in bono* and *in malo*.[38] The serpent who sheds his old skin in humility is, according to the Bestiaries, the type of the Christian who puts off the old man and puts on the new man (Eph. 4:20–4).[39]

The left and right jamb columns, which support the third, half-round, archivolt, have inscriptions on their bases. In their own voice, the columns address those entering the church through the portal. The one on the left proclaims: 'If I am thus erect, I cannot be bent.'[40] And the column on the right adds: 'I sustain the worthy ... [I reject] the wicked.'[41] The columns speak for the Church; this is the typological level of the allegory. One must bear in mind the bent and enchained slaves supporting the trumeau column of the cathedral of Oloron (fig. 26) to register the full force of these verses. Nothing stands straight without the spiritual transformation effected by Christ and the Church. The possibility of transcendence and the threat of relapse into the unredeemed world are part of the deeper significance of this portal.

The other Pyrenean church with portal inscriptions illustrating the ambivalence and penitential implication of the allegory is Saint-Pé-de-Bigorre. Saint-Pé was a Benedictine abbey attached to Cluny. The church was dedicated and consecrated to Saints Peter and Paul on 14 October 1096. In the twelfth century it was enlarged to the west and given a western transept above which a magnificent dome was constructed. The enlargement constituted a second church, which was used by the monks, while the eleventh-century building was given over to the parish.[42] An interior portal in the south-west-corner tower, which is part of the enlarged, twelfth-century church, opens onto a staircase, which leads to a chamber above the transept where pilgrims were authorized to spend the night. Above this interior portal there is an effaced tympanum, which probably depicted two lions on either side of an axial figure. Élie Lambert suggests that the subject of the tympanum was Daniel between the lions. Pierre Pomès and Louis Michel believe that it depicted two lions facing a chrismon in the manner of the tympanum of Jaca (fig. 12).[43] The affronted lions, like the church in its literal sense as the temple of Solomon, belong to the fallen world that Christ came to redeem. They support the Church (or, it may be, they support Daniel who prefigures Christ). A leonine elegiac couplet is inscribed around the rim of the tympanum:

Est domus hic Domini, via caeli, spes peregrini.
Haec data porta Petro: vade maligne retro.[44]
(Here is the house of the Lord, the way of heaven, the hope of the pilgrim. This portal is dedicated to Peter: go back, wicked one.)

The first line of the couplet allegorizes the church in the three spiritual senses: it is the house of the Lord (typology), the path to heaven (anagogy), and the hope of the pilgrim (tropology). The last phrase of the pentameter is taken from Christ's rebuke to Peter, *Vade retro me, Satana*, 'Go behind me, Satan' (Mark 8:33). It was a vivid reminder of the conditional nature of the hope of redemption. Even Saint Peter, the rock on whom the Church was built and to whom this church was dedicated, fell from grace and reverted to the Old Man in a momentary fit of spiritual blindness. The unwary and impenitent pilgrim might wake to find himself a sinner in the temple of Solomon.

9

Anagogical Allegory and Imagery: Gate of Heaven, Gate of Life, Fountain of Life

The Romanesque church was, by anagogy, the heavenly city – the interpretation visually incorporated into the tympanum of Conques, where the heavenly city is represented by an image of the earthly church (fig. 2). Since the church was the heavenly city, its portal was the gate of heaven. Passage through the portal brought the worshipper into heaven itself. The interior of many of the larger basilicas, with their vaulted and/or painted ceilings, carved capitals, stained glass as that became fashionable, and other decoration, must have reinforced this interpretation – this moment of anagogical transcendence. But entrance into heaven was always conditional; the material church remained a man-made structure – the temple of Solomon on the literal level. Heaven was both immediately present and endlessly deferred. The interior spaces of the church were themselves hierarchical. Once through the portal, the worshipper's forward motion continued, blocked finally by the rood screen or other barrier separating the space of the laity from that of the clergy. Dimly glimpsed ahead, the clergy's space must have seemed more sacred, more heavenly. At Alpirsbach, the two columns on either side of the nave that marked the eastward limit of the laity's advance added the lower/higher vertical axis of hierarchy to the west/east horizontal axis. Monstrous animals inhabit the bases of these columns. An angel welcomes a saved soul on one of the capitals above, while a head gnawed by winged monsters suggests eternal damnation on the other. Below is the unredeemed world; above is the aftermath of Last Judgment – the final separation of the sheep from the goats. (The vertical hierarchy that puts hell below earth and heaven above it is foreign to the Romanesque visual imagination. Heaven and hell are both above.)

In this endless deferral of the anagogical interpretation of the church as the heavenly city, the instrumental function of the portal came to the fore, and by a kind of reverse synecdoche the church itself was allegorized as the gate of heaven. The church was the door through which the faithful had to pass – the means by which the heavenly city could be reached. The use of verbal images like 'the gate of heaven' and 'the gate of life' proliferated on twelfth-century portals, where it is not always easy to know whether their immediate reference (or the speaker) is the portal per se or the church.

Christ's words 'I am the door' fulfilled the verse of the Psalmist: *haec porta Domini, iusti intrabunt in eam*, 'this is the gate of the Lord, the just shall enter into it' (Ps. 117:20), as the artist who inscribed this verse on the banderole held by David at San Donnino of Fidenza (to the left of the central portal) understood.[1] The Carolingian scholar Alcuin composed a poem to be inscribed on the abbey church of Saint-Hilaire-le-Grand of Poitiers, which begins with an echo of Psalm 117:

> Porta domus Domini haec est et regia Caeli.
> Haec tibi pandit iter sancti et sacraria templi ...[2]
> *(This is the door of the house of the Lord and the royal gate of heaven. It opens for you the way to the sacred temple and the sanctuary ...)*

Similar phrasing appears in the leonine hexameters above the portal of Sant Pau del Camp in Barcelona and in the leonine elegiac couplet above the staircase portal of Saint-Pé-de-Bigorre.[3] Thus, the typological image of the door was easily transposed into the anagogical image of the gate of heaven.

The use of this image in connection with Romanesque portals can be traced to the last third of the eleventh century in Spain – to the Aragon of King Sancho Ramírez (1063–94) and his son Pedro I (1094–1104). It is implicit in the portal inscription of Nuestra Señora of Iguácel. Iguácel is a small eleventh-century church in the Pyrenees east of the pilgrimage road coming down from the Somport Pass to Jaca. Kingsley Porter first called attention to its importance in 1928. A Romanesque wooden statue of the Virgin in Majesty with the Child has made this shrine the object of a local pilgrimage.[4] Between the arch of the portal and the corbel table above it runs a horizontal inscription band, which reads: 'This is the gate of the Lord [*porta Domini*] through which the faithful enter into the house of the Lord [*domus Domini*] which is a church [*ecglesia*] founded in honour of Saint Mary. It was built on the order of Count Sancho together with his wife named Urraca. It was finished in the Era 1110 [= AD 1072] in the reign of King Sancho Ramírez in Aragon, who established for the sake of his soul in honour of Saint Mary the villa called Larrossa, so that the Lord may give him (?) eternal (?) rest. Amen.'[5] Some years after it was completed, probably in or just before 1094, the church was given to the monastery of San Juan de la Peña and monks were installed in it. This 'promotion' may have been the occasion for the addition of sculptural decorations, in crude imitation of the style of Jaca, to the unadorned structure, and for the placement of the inscription above the portal as a kind of 'document' recording the original endowment.[6]

On the literal level of the allegory of the church the *ecglesia* was the physical structure built by Count Sancho and Urraca in honour of the Virgin Mary. On the anagogical level it was the heavenly kingdom that was accessible to the faithful who passed through the *porta Domini* into the *domus Domini*. The images and language derive from Psalm 117 and from Jacob's outcry in Genesis 28:17: 'How terrible is this place! this is no other but the house of God [*domus Dei*] and the gate of heaven [*porta caeli*].' The verse from Genesis was recited in the liturgy for the dedication of a Christian church.[7]

Another image, which was to become associated with the gate of heaven, was the fountain of life (*fons vitae*). This image, with its reference to the sacrament of baptism, was connected with the portal on the basis of three passages in the Bible. In his second apocalyptic vision, John says: 'And he showed me a river of water of life, clear as crystal, proceeding from the throne of God and of the Lamb' (Apoc. 22:1). John's vision was interpreted by medieval exegetes with the help of two prophetic texts from the Old Testament. One was the vision of Ezekiel: 'And he brought me again to the gate of the house [*ad portam domus*], and behold waters issued out from under the threshold of the house toward the east: for the forefront of the house looked toward the east: but the waters came down to the right side of the temple to the south part of the altar' (Ezek. 47:1). The other was the words of the prophet Joel: 'And it shall come to pass in that day, that ... waters shall flow through all the rivers of Juda: and a fountain shall come forth of the house of the Lord, and shall water the torrent of thorns' (Joel 3:18).

One of the earliest Romanesque uses of the image of the fountain of life also goes back to Aragon, at the chapel of Loarre. A frieze of Christ in Majesty with angels, with an inscription around the mandorla, is set above the arch of the portal. The top half of the frieze was destroyed in the eighteenth century; the bottom half is mutilated. The inscription is so deteriorated that it can no longer be read, but early in this century Don Ricardo del Arco deciphered the words *fons ego sum vita(e)*, 'I am the fountain of life.'[8] This is the voice of Christ transposed to the anagogical level.

The portal of Loarre dates from about 1100, which means that it was contemporary with the tympanum of Santa Cruz de la Serós, where the metrical phrase *fons ego sum vitae* also appears (fig. 13). At Santa Cruz, the allegorical imagery of the portal as the gate of heaven was combined with the imagery of the fountain of life. Its rather crude tympanum, carved from a single slab of stone, bears some resemblance to the tympanum of Jaca (fig. 12).[9] A chrismon in the centre is flanked by two lions, each wearing a delicate chain collar and a ring about his tail just above the tuft. The lions face the chrismon. An eleven-petalled daisy is beneath the belly of the lion on the right. Both lions bare their teeth. The one on the left appears to be biting on a snake, or perhaps his own tongue, his right forepaw is raised, and his tail is curiously wrapped about his haunches like a girdle (a formula that was to become commonplace in the twelfth century).

Four leonine verses appear on the tympanum. Three of them run clockwise around the rim of the chrismon. The fourth is on the lower edge of the tympanum beneath the lions' feet. Christ the door speaks on the anagogical level as the gate of heaven and the fountain of life:

> Ianua sum perpes; per me transite, fideles.
> Fons ego sum vite; plus me quam vina sitite.
> Virginis hoc templum qui vis penetrare beatum,
> Corrige te primum, valeas quo poscere Christum.[10]
> *(I am the eternal door; pass through me, faithful ones. I am the fountain of life; thirst for me more than for wine. You who wish to enter this blessed church of the Virgin, reform yourself first, in order that you may be able to call upon Christ.)*

Isolated though their community was, it is unlikely that the sisters, who were in some sense already within the church, thought of themselves as the principal audience for these commands. The plural imperatives (*transite/sitite*) of the first two verses address the Christian community generally. The singular imperative (*corrige*) of the last two verses, which directs the individual worshipper to reform before entering the church, has a sharper tone. The intended audience may have been primarily penance-seeking pilgrims to Compostela travelling along the route between Jaca and Puente la Reina that passed within two or three miles of Santa Cruz.

Santa Cruz was the gateway to the powerful Cluniac monastery of San

Juan de la Peña in the hills behind it. The monastery is dug into the side of a massive overhanging cliff. A hermit named Juan took up residence here in the eighth century and built a little chapel. He was succeeded by two brothers, Voto and Felicio, who were knights from Zaragoza. Walter M. Whitehill recounts a romantic legend about one of the brothers who was a dedicated hunter:

> Voto, chasing a stag which disappeared over the cliff that now vaults the church, was saved from going over himself only by the miraculous intervention of St. John Baptist. Having dismounted, he was led by curiosity to clamber down and see what was below. He found a clear spring and a cave containing a chapel, on the floor of which was the dead body of a venerable old man, with a stone inscription telling his name, Juan de Atarés, and the story of his life as guardian of the chapel. Voto buried him, and soon after returned to the cave with his brother Felicio, where they carried on the life of hermits.[11]

About 1014 Sancho el Mayor brought the monastery under the rule of Cluny. The Archbishop of Bordeaux assisted by the bishops of Jaca and Maguelone consecrated the upper church on 4 December 1094.[12]

A portal on the south wall of the nave of San Juan de la Peña communicates with the cloister. The portal is capped with a Mozarabic horseshoe arch that may have been re-employed from the ninth-century lower church (fig. 28).[13] At some point an inscription was carved on it. The inscription faces the cloister so that the words are visible as one enters the church. It is a full leonine elegiac couplet, which reads:

> Porta per hanc caeli fit pervia cuique fideli,
> Si studead fidei iungere iussa Dei.[14]
> *(Through this gate the gate of heaven becomes accessible to each believer who strives to combine the commandments of God with faith.)*

Whitehill associates this couplet with the construction of the cloister in the twelfth century.[15] But the inscription is in Spanish Visigothic lettering characteristic of the late eleventh century,[16] which would coincide with the construction of the upper church and make it contemporary with the inscriptions of Santa Cruz and Loarre. The phrase 'this gate' implies a speaker who is on the scene. Thus, the statement, 'the gate of heaven is accessible through this gate,' which can only be validated by the active faith of the believer, is arguably the voice of the portal speaking on the typological level as the Church.

The allegorical imagery of the portal as the gate of heaven and the fountain of life did not originate in Aragon. Angel San Vicente remarks that the elegiac couplet of San Juan de la Peña 'resembles a couplet of the Carolingian poet Boniface, which was also composed for the portal of a basilica.'[17] I have not been able to find such a couplet in the poems of Boniface, but one of Alcuin's poems for the abbey church of Saint-Amand of Elnone begins,

Haec porta est caeli, aeternae haec est ianua vitae,
  Ista viatorem ducit ad astra suum.[18]

(This is the gate of heaven, this is the gate of eternal life, which leads the one passing through it to heaven.)

The image of the fountain of life (*fons hic est vitae*) occurs in the elegiac verses composed in the fifth century that are still to be seen carved on the octagonal architrave above the interior columns in the Baptistery of Saint John Lateran in Rome.[19] But the Aragonese portals are the oldest surviving Romanesque exemplars of the themes, which quickly spread throughout Spain. The hexameter from the elegiac couplet of the portal of San Juan de la Peña was copied on the tympanum of San Prudencio of Armentia, and at the beginning of the thirteenth century above the portal of the hermitage of Puilampa.[20]

Closer to the Byzantine Empire, the imagery of the gate of life, which Alcuin had offered as a synonym for the gate of heaven, gave rise to a somewhat different conception of the portal. In this new configuration of ideas, the Virgin Mary in her role as Queen of heaven sometimes took the place of Christ in the axial position. The typological equation of Mary with *ecclesia*, the Church, and her anagogical association with the heavenly kingdom as its Queen were fully developed notions in the exegetical tradition from which the allegory of the church sprang, but they were not exploited in portal programs until the extraordinary surge of Marian sentiment during the course of the twelfth century. Whether Christ or Mary was the axial figure, the idea of the gate of life was typically expressed in a leonine formula that rhymed *vite* with the imperative *venite*.

It is possible, though by no means certain, that the inspiration for substituting the Virgin Mary for Christ in the axial position and the choice of this particular leonine rhyme originated at the cathedral of San Marco in Venice. As currently constituted, both the exterior and interior mural surfaces above the central west portal leading from the main porch to the nave at San Marco are decorated with mosaics of the Virgin. The mosaics of the exterior wall are arranged in two series of niches. The upper series, above the portal, includes the standing figure of the Virgin holding the Child in the axial position. She is flanked on the left by the apostles Philip, Simon, James, and Peter, and on the right by Paul, Andrew, Thomas, and Bartholomew. The Evangelists Matthew and Mark are in the lower series on the left of the portal, and Luke and John on the right. Leonine inscriptions proclaim the typological link between Mary and the Church. The first, in a horizontal line above the lower niches, is in Mary's voice: 'I, the bride of God, a virgin, give birth virginally to sons, whom, being weak, I strengthen, [and] send fortified into heaven.'[21] As Otto Demus puts it, 'The *nati* ['sons'] refer to the apostles, and the Virgin is thus equated with the *Ecclesia* by the attribution of spiritual motherhood.'[22] The second inscription, in the four semicircular arches above the heads of the Evangelists, completes the typological equation: 'These are the four watchmen of the Church of Christ, whose sweet song resounds and moves heaven from all sides.'[23] The watchmen are the Evangelists, who look toward *ecclesia Christi* (= Mary) and whose sweet song moves heaven (= Mary and the Child on the anagogical level?). These mosaics date from the last quarter of the eleventh century[24] and demonstrate the formative power of the allegory of the church on portal design on the very border between the Byzantine and Western cultural-ecclesiastical zones.

On the interior wall above the west portal, there is a lunette mosaic of the Supplication of Christ or 'Deesis.' Christ is enthroned and is flanked by the standing figures of the Virgin Mary and Mark (taking the place of John – the traditional figure in the Deesis). An inscription in marble inlay runs around the rim of the lunette and there is a second inscription on the open book in Christ's hand. The lunette mosaic is from the second third of the thirteenth century, but the rim inscription is apparently considerably earlier.[25] In the voice of Christ, speaking as the gate of heaven, it says:

> Ianua sum vite, per me mea membra venite.[26]
> *(I am the gate of life, come through me my members.)*

Demus notes that this leonine verse is a paraphrase of John 10:9, 'I am the door,' etc., which is the inscription that appears in the book in Christ's hand in the lunette, and that both inscriptions 'stress the function of the mosaic as decor of the main porch ... One would actually expect to find a mosaic with these inscriptions on the outside above the main door, as, for instance, in Grottaferrata, where the inscription in the book is the same; or in Vatopedi, where the inscription reproduces John 8:12 ("I am the light of the world," etc., a text which is perhaps more appropriate to a placement in the apse). However, the outer face of the main door of San Marco was already filled with mosaics of the late eleventh century, so that there was no room for a monumental Deesis.'[27] Though multiple uncertainties are involved, it is possible that the thirteenth-century Deesis of the interior wall replaced an earlier one for which the frame inscription was equally appropriate, and also possible that this earlier Deesis went back to the middle of the twelfth century or before.

There is a mural painting of the Deesis at Payerne in Switzerland on the route from Italy over the Great Saint Bernard to northern Europe that is arguably based on the (earlier) Deesis of San Marco. The Payerne Deesis dates from ca. 1200. It is on the south wall of the narthex of the former abbey church. Christ is seated on a cushion throne flanked by the Virgin Mary and John (the traditional Byzantine configuration, as opposed to the Virgin Mary and Mark at Venice). Christ spreads his hands to display the wounds, but an open book is balanced on his left knee on the pages of which is inscribed the verse that at San Marco runs around the rim of the lunette. The only changes are the substitution of *regna* for *membra* and the imperative *subite* for *venite*:

> Ianua sum vite, per me mea regna subite.[28]
> *(I am the gate of life, enter my kingdom through me.)*

Other variants of this verse appeared even earlier in the twelfth century. One that is especially interesting is an inscription on the west portal of San Giorgio al Palazzo in Milan, which may be contemporary with the dedication of the church in 1129. The portal and its inscription still exist, but they are no longer visible, being completely enclosed by the present eighteenth-century baroque façade and portal of Francesco Bernardino Ferrario (1771).[29] They are known from the engraving of P. Giuseppe Allegranza (Milan, 1757).[30] This shows that in the eighteenth century a Renaissance coat-of-arms filled an otherwise blank tympanum above a blank lintel and that there was an inner archivolt with what appears to be a Latin inscription in Greek letters (the sense of which eludes me). If either the tympanum or the lintel were decorated in the twelfth century, we do not know what the subject or subjects were, but it is significant that the Chi-Rho monogram with the Alpha and Omega appeared in the axial position on the outer archivolt, on which were inscribed these leonine verses:

> Ianua sum vite, precor, omnes intro venite.
> Per me transibunt qui celi gaudia querunt.
> Virgine qui natus nullo de patre creatus
> Intrantes salvet redeuntes ipse gubernet.[31]
> *(I am the gate of life. Everyone come within, I beg. Those who seek the joys of heaven will pass through me. May he who was born of a virgin and not begot by a father save those who enter and guide those who go out.)*

If Dante ever wandered through the streets of Milan during his years of exile, he might well have got inspiration for the inscription on the lintel of the gate of hell from these verses.

Another variant is found at the late-twelfth-century church of the Benedictine priory of Saint-Marcel-lès-Sauzet in the hills along the east bank of the Rhone just outside of Montélimar. The priory was established in 985 by Lambert, the Count of Valence, and his wife Falectrude and later attached to Cluny. Above the portal is a Christ in Majesty tympanum with the Four Animals. Interestingly enough, given the dual orientation of the gate of life toward Christ and Mary, the Christ was replaced at some later date by a Virgin and Child.[32] The lower edge of the tympanum is inscribed with three full leonine hexameters:

> Vos qui transitis, qui crimina flere venitis,
> Per me transite quoniam sum ianua vite.
> Ianua sum vite. Volo parcere ... venite.[33]
> *(You who are passing through, you who are coming to weep for your sins, pass through me since I am the gate of life. I am the gate of life. I wish to spare ... come.)*

Here, as at San Marco and San Giorgio, the voice of the portal is Christ, speaking as the gate of life. The gate of eternal life is, of course, the gate of heaven, but the persistence of images of thirsting and weeping makes clear that the fountain of life is an underlying theme. These verses have close verbal affinities to Santa Cruz de la Serós, but the rapid diffusion of the leonine rhyme *vite/venite* and its variants throughout western Europe in the twelfth century, especially in the form *ianua sum vite/venite*, can perhaps best be understood as the result of the influence of prestigious centres like Venice and Milan.

The use of the Virgin Mary as the axial figure above the main portal of San Marco toward the end of the eleventh century and her possible appearance on the reverse side of the same portal in a twelfth-century Deesis next to a Christ who refers to himself as the gate of life may have inspired two portals north and east of Venice. These are, or were, the portals of the church of the Nonnberg convent in Salzburg and of the Romanesque cathedral of Esztergom in Hungary. In these, Mary, in her typological role as *ecclesia,* invites worshippers to enter the *porta vitae,* the 'gate of life,' which lies open before them. Both the phrasing and the typological associations are found in Bede, who comments on Genesis 3:20, 'And Adam called the name of his wife Eve, because she was the mother of all the living,' as follows: 'And it is an acknowledged fact that Adam bestowed this name [*Eva*] on his wife through divine inspiration, because it was so suitably appropriate for the holy Church [*Ave* = the Virgin Mary?], in whose unity alone, which is called 'catholic,' the gate of life lies open to all.'[34] The Nonnberg church is late-fifteenth-century, and the pointed-arch tympanum area of the south portal is filled by three re-employed reliefs: a Romanesque lintel of interlaced grape vines, a Gothic frieze, and a Romanesque round-arched tympanum of the Virgin in Majesty with the Child. I think it safe to assume that the lintel and tympanum originally belonged together because thematically and verbally they are so closely related. An inscription around the rim of the tympanum states in a non-defined voice:

> Splendor, imago Patris, fecundans viscera Matris.
> Ianua, lux, portus salvandis creditur ortus.[35]
> *(Radiance, the image of the Father, impregnating the womb of the Mother. His birth is believed to be the door, the light, the port for those who are to be saved.)*

On the lintel is the inscription in the voice of the Church:

> Porta patet vite. Cristus via vera. Venite.[36]
> *(The gate of [eternal] life lies open. Christ [is] the true way. Come.)*

The clipped, elliptical expression of these full leonine hexameters and the references to Christ the door (*ianua/porta*) suggest that they are the work of the same poet and intended for the same program.

The 'Porta Speciosa' of the cathedral of Esztergom no longer exists. It was the west portal of the building erected between 1188 and 1196 to replace an earlier structure that had burned. This portal was preserved when the rest of the church was torn down in 1763 to make way for the present cathedral building, but an accident destroyed it in the following year.[37] However, a detailed painting was made of the portal before the accident, and fragments of the tympanum and the rest of the sculptural program of the portal have survived. These enable the design of the Porta Speciosa to be reconstructed with confidence. The tympanum displayed the Virgin in Majesty with the Child. The Virgin was flanked by the standing figures of Saint Stephen, the first king of Hungary (1001–38) and founder of the archbishopric at Esztergom, and Bishop Adalbertus. In hexameters inscribed on scrolls in their hands, Stephen implored the Virgin to take the kingdom of Hungary under her protection, the Virgin promised to do so provided that Adalbertus took charge of the church; and Adalbertus accepted his responsibility.[38] The lintel was decorated with a wheel in the centre flanked by two angels and the kneeling figures of Job, archbishop of Esztergom (1184–1204), and Bela III, king of Hungary (1174–96), and by a church and castle. An inscription on the lower edge of the lintel, closely related to the one at Salzburg, proclaimed:

> Porta patet vite. Sponsus vocat. Intro venite.[39]
> *(The gate of life stands open. The Bridegroom calls. Come within.)*

The association of the Virgin Mary with the gate of life was largely confined to the eastern periphery of European Romanesque portal design. In Spain and France, Christ remained the axial figure. Typical are the portals of Sant Pau del Camp in Barcelona and Saint-Pierre of Maguelone. The Benedictine priory church of Sant Pau del Camp was a monastic dependency of Sant Cugat del Vallés. It was probably founded about 1117. The present church is thought to be the work of the beginning of the thirteenth century.[40] Although it is terribly weathered, the salient features of the west portal can still be made out. A tympanum of Christ in Majesty rests on a massive lintel. Saint Paul kneels at the right hand of Christ; Saint Peter at Christ's left. The Four Animals are arranged on the façade in counterclockwise order. The Hand of God appears on the façade between Matthew and John. A narrow inscription band frames the four sides of the lintel. This carries two full leonine hexameters and a prose statement possibly to the effect that Renard placed seven Arab workers (*Moabitinos*) in the construction project for his own sake and for the sake of the soul of his wife, Ramona.[41] The verses that run along the whole top edge and the left half of the bottom edge of the lintel read:

Hec Domini porta via ... est omnibus horta.
Ianua sum vite, per me gradiendo venite.[42]
(This is the gate of the Lord, the way ... is open to all. I am the gate of life, come and walk through me.)

The portal of Sant Pau may have been influenced by the west portal of Maguelone (fig. 29). More or less deserted now, Maguelone occupies a spot midway along the slender barrier island that shelters the mainland around Montpellier from the open Mediterranean. It stands on a tiny peninsula – an island at the time the cathedral was built in the twelfth century – jutting into the inland waterway. In its isolated solitude, it is difficult to imagine Maguelone as the bustling episcopal see it was from the sixth to the sixteenth centuries. The present fortified church is the product of two extended building campaigns (1104–58 for the apse and transepts and 1158–78 for the nave).[43] Its west portal is a curious heterogeneous mixture of sculptures from different periods, which in its present arrangement is not earlier than the thirteenth century. A tympanum of Christ in Majesty with the Four Animals sits above a large lintel. The lintel, which was fashioned from an ancient Roman milestone, is elegantly carved in a scroll pattern consisting of six acanthus leaf circles. Beautifully executed reliefs of Saint Paul and Saint Peter are set into the wall on either side of the square jambs that support the lintel. These reliefs are fragments from what appears to be an earlier tympanum, dating from the first half of the twelfth century. The Christ in Majesty tympanum, by contrast, which is unhappily diminished by the grand scale of the lintel, is later than both the reliefs and the lintel.

Although this hodgepodge might not lead one to suppose that any unified conception of the portal governed its final arrangement, comparison with Sant Pau del Camp offers reason for believing that the arrangement reproduces an earlier, more coherent one. The inscriptions that enclose the floral design of the lintel on all four sides are of two kinds. There is a prose inscription that gives us the name of the maker (in what sense is uncertain), Bernard de Tréviers, and the date, AD 1178. And there are four full leonine hexameters. This arrangement of the inscription bands around the four edges of the lintel, combining leonine verses with a prose inscription including a person's name, is identical to the arrangement of Sant Pau. The Sant Pau tympanum was arguably an imitation of the design of an early-twelfth-century tympanum of Maguelone, which was broken up and used to provide the kneeling figures of Paul and Peter that are now below the lintel on either side of the door.[44]

The verses of Maguelone read:

Ad portum vite sitientes quique venite;
Has intrando fores vestros componite mores.
Hinc intrans ora, tua semper crimina plora;
Quicquid peccatur lacrimarum fonte lavatur.[45]
(You who are thirsting, come to the port of eternal life; in entering these doors, correct your behaviour. Pray as you enter here, always weep for your sins; whatever is amiss is washed by the fountain of your tears.)

The shift from the plural imperatives of the first two verses to the singular of the second two parallels the shift at Santa Cruz de la Serós. Maguelone's location on an island in the inland waterway, with access to the Mediterranean through a narrow channel cut in the eleventh century by Bishop Arnaud, perhaps inspired the elegant pun in the first verse. The faithful are urged to come, not *ad portam*, to the gate, but *ad portum vitae*, to the port or harbour of life. Here we glimpse in embryo one of the seminal metaphors of the poetry of courtly love from the twelfth to the sixteenth centuries – the port that is the goal of so many tempest-tossed lovers adrift in the rudderless boats of their own unfulfilled desires.

10

Moral Allegory: Admonitory and *Pax* Portals and the Tympanum of Jaca

The literal level of the allegory, the church as the temple of Solomon, allowed for the possibility of unspiritualized entry into the church. Liminal inscriptions warned worshippers and pilgrims in severe tones to purify themselves before entering; otherwise the sacred space might be sullied by the presence of the impenitent. The instruction was tropological, though the voice of the instruction was Christ or the Church (typology).[1] At the abbey church of Sainte-Marie of Cassan in southern France, these verses are inscribed on a square marble plaque above the north portal: 'You, whoever you are – a man with a burden of deadly sin – who are reluctant to prostrate yourself in sorrow to the supreme Lord before this portal, the gate is entered in no other way, because it is held to be Christ.'[2] Portals with inscriptions of this kind constitute a thematically related group, which I call admonitory portals.[3]

Tropological injunctions bristled around the cathedral of Notre-Dame of Le Puy. The cathedral, which is built on the eroded core of an ancient volcano, is an extraordinary building by any standards. In consequence of its location and successive building campaigns, the nave and west façade, supported by a massive substructure, had been thrust out into space by the end of the twelfth century. The approach from the west up the steep slope of the hill did not bring worshippers to a portal leading into the nave, but to an arch beneath the nave through which they passed on a staircase that continued the ascent up under the centre of the church. A tunnel, now blocked, led directly to the main altar inside. A liminal inscription in leonine elegiac verse carved in the risers of the stairs underneath the west façade admonished the approaching worshipper: 'Unless you refrain from sin, do not contaminate this threshold, because the Queen of heaven wishes to be worshipped without sordidness.'[4] According to a seventeenth-century document, the portal of the south transept was provided with a similarly pointed liminal inscription: 'If your life has been lecherous, then avoid this threshold, and do not profane its sanctity as long as you smell of the evils of the flesh.'[5]

Other inscriptions at Le Puy offered the promise of healing. A well with spiritual curative powers stood in front of the east end of the church. Its position was marked by two leonine verses, which are still visible on the exterior wall of the apsidal chapel (the apse was completely rebuilt by the architect Mimey in the nineteenth century, but the lower portion was left in its original position[6]) (fig. 30):

> Fons ope divina languentibus est medicina,
> Subveniens gratis ubi deficit ars Ypocratis.[7]
> *(The fountain with its divine power is medicine for the sick, healing without charge when the art of Hippocrates fails.)*

There is a stone slab at the head of the stairway beneath the nave – the so-called Rock of Fevers – which was probably taken from a prehistoric dolmen. Vincent of Beauvais claimed that the original stone was polluted by an act of adultery and then broken into four pieces by an avenging stroke of lightning, one of which is the surviving rock.[8] Curative powers were attributed to it at an early date; its association with the cathedral appears to antedate the present Romanesque building. It was formerly placed at the foot of the main altar, which was approximately at the crossing of the east-west and north-south axes of the church. We know, again from a seventeenth-century source, that the rock was once accompanied by two leonine verses: 'People placed by this rock, having slept, become well. If you want to know why, the power is attributed to the altar.'[9] Like the liminal inscriptions, these verses combine typology with tropology; the church was Christ the healer and it was the people who needed healing.

In sum, the cruciform structure of the cathedral of Le Puy was delimited by leonine verses at the ends of the east-west axis (the apse inscription + the riser inscription), at the south end of the north-south axis (the south transept liminal inscription), and at the crossing of the two axes (the Rock of Fevers inscription). It is possible that the north transept portal was provided with a liminal inscription as well, though no record of it survives. The function of these verses seems to have been to prepare the sinner for the experience of spiritual transformation or healing, while at the same time to erect a verbal barrier at the principal portals against impenitent entry into the cathedral.

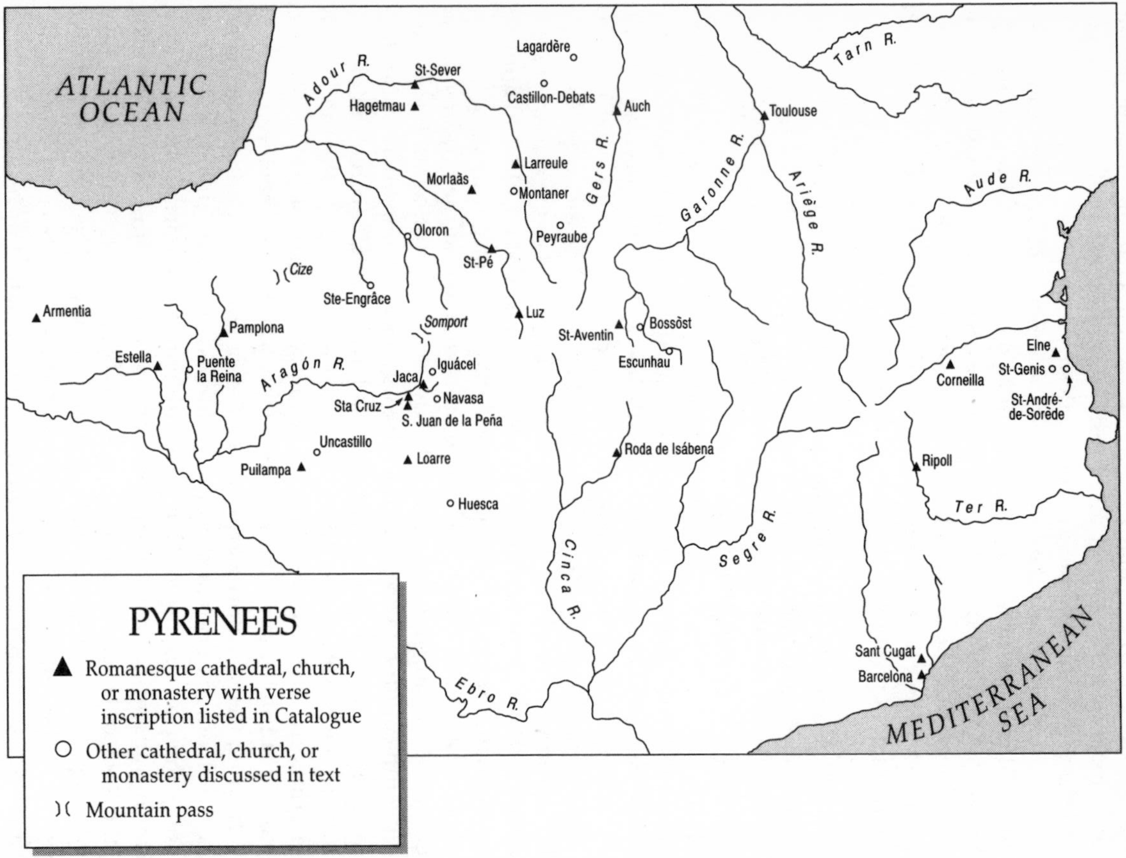
ATLANTIC OCEAN
MEDITERRANEAN SEA
PYRENEES
Romanesque cathedral, church, or monastery with verse inscription listed in Catalogue
Other cathedral, church, or monastery discussed in text
Mountain pass
Adour R.
Tarn R.
Gers R.
Garonne R.
Ariège R.
Aude R.
Aragón R.
Cinca R.
Segre R.
Ter R.
Ebro R.
St-Sever
Hagetmau
Lagardère
Castillon-Debats
Auch
Toulouse
Larreule
Morlaàs
Montaner
Peyraube
Oloron
St-Pé
Cize
Ste-Engrâce
Luz
Armentia
Pamplona
Somport
St-Aventin
Bossòst
Escunhau
Estella
Puente la Reina
Jaca
Iguácel
Sta Cruz
Navasa
S. Juan de la Peña
Uncastillo
Puilampa
Loarre
Huesca
Roda de Isábena
Elne
St-Genis
Corneilla
St-André-de-Sorède
Ripoll
Sant Cugat
Barcelona

There is another group of portals that are inscribed with the word *pax*, sometimes in anagrammatic form and sometimes as part of a cluster of associated words. *Pax* was a visible sign of the voice of Christ addressing the faithful – another manifestation of the allegory of the church on the typological level. If *pax* was encrypted in the chrismons of the tympana of Jaca and Santa Cruz de la Serós (figs. 12, 13), as I believe is the case, these churches belong to both groups – the admonitory portals and the *pax* portals – and the explicit tropological message of the liminal inscriptions helps shed light on the fuller meaning of the sign *pax*.

The iconographic theme of the tympanum of the west portal of Jaca is an 'exhortation to penitence' and this theme is supported by the sculpture of the capitals both of the portal and the nave.[10] The penitential symbolism of the portal is crucially dependent upon a heretofore unrecognized anagram of the sign *pax* in the tympanum.[11]

The tympanum (fig. 12) displays a chrismon – a wheel-shaped Chi-Rho monogram – in the centre. The monogram, which is augmented by an S entwined around the lower vertical bar of the Rho, stands for *XPistuS*. A horizontal bar extends through the chrismon from the ends of which hang the Greek letters Alpha and Omega. Two lions face the chrismon with their muzzles touching its rim. The lion on the left stands over a man who is on his hands and knees facing away from the chrismon. The man is clothed in a hooded garment. His feet are bare. He holds a snake at arm's length from his body. The lion pins down the man's legs with his left forepaw and treads on the snake with his left hindpaw. The lion on the right, baring his teeth, places his right forepaw firmly on the back of a smaller animal whose snout is to the ground. There is a winged creature with the tail of a snake under the lion's belly. The lion's right hindpaw rests on the tip of this creature's tail.

The symbolic meaning of these various creatures is crucial to understanding the iconography of the tympanum. The lions are types of Christ. The Christological symbolism of the king of the beasts was a medieval commonplace, and it is confirmed by the tympanum's verse inscriptions.[12] Two of the creatures under the lions are symmetrically positioned. The snake that the man holds under the hindquarters of the lion on the left is balanced by the fabulous bird-serpent under the hindquarters of the lion on the right. These are, or seem to be, the creatures referred to by the Psalmist when he says: 'Thou shalt walk upon the asp and the basilisk' (Ps. 90:13).[13] According to the twelfth-century commentator Honorius Augustodunensis the asp means sin and the basilisk death.[14] This interpretation applies to the creatures of Jaca, although it fails to capture the full richness of the symbolism. David Simon shows that the snake is also to be understood as the serpent of the Bestiaries that 'by virtue of the fact that it discards its skin after fasting for forty days, is a sign of the shedding of the old man.' It is, in short, a symbol of the humility that is the prerequisite for penitence.[15]

The creature under the right-hand lion's forepaw has been thought to be a bear.[16] In support of this assumption Werner Weisbach offers evidence that the bear was sometimes employed as a symbol for the Devil and sin. The symbolism is said to derive from 1 Kings (17:37): 'And David said: The Lord who delivered me out of the paw of the lion, and out of the paw of the bear, he will deliver me out of the hand of this Philistine.'[17] The branch of medieval allegory that dealt with the symbolism of animals, plants, and minerals of the natural world was notoriously freewheeling, but even so the claim that an allegorical interpretation of the bear and lion from whose paws David was delivered explains the image of a 'bear' being mauled by a lion is open to question. In the course of reexamining the verse inscriptions, I will propose a different identification for this creature.

Four sets of leonine hexameters accompany the sculpture. They were obviously intended to guide viewers to an authorized interpretation. In the background, above the lion on the left, is the verse 'The lion knows to spare the man who prostrates himself, and Christ knows to pardon the man who prays.'[18] The thought is based on traditional beast lore. Isidore of Seville, for example, states: 'Around man it is the nature of lions to be incapable of anger except when they are injured. Their pity is revealed by repeated examples, for they spare those who prostrate themselves.'[19] Medieval authorities interpreted this remarkable behaviour allegorically. As the verse makes clear, the lion that spares a penitent who prostrates himself in prayer is a type of Christ. The snake that the penitent holds in his hands is a dual symbol of the evil he has put away and the humility in which he has clothed himself.

Another verse appears in the background above the lion on the right: 'The strong lion tramples underfoot the sovereign power of death.'[20] Whatever the lion tramples underfoot must represent 'the sovereign power of death.' The basilisk, whose tail is under the lion's hindpaw, was a symbol of death, but the verse also directs our attention to the more visually prominent creature under the lion's forepaw, the one which is said to be a 'bear.' This is, I venture to suggest, the *leontophonos*, one of the rarest beasts in the menagerie of traditional beast lore. Pliny the

Elder included the *leontophonos* in his *Natural History* among a group of animals with remarkable urinary properties.[21] Solinus adapted Pliny's account for his description of Africa,[22] and Isidore of Seville put an abbreviated notice of this creature, taken from Solinus, in his *Etymologies.*[23] (Pliny and Isidore give the *leontophonos* an impeccable Spanish heritage.) None of the main branches of the *Physiologus* knows of the *leontophonos,* but it enters into at least one twelfth-century manuscript of the so-called second family of Bestiaries, as part of the general description of the lion.[24] According to this Bestiary (Cambridge, Cambridge University Library, MS II.4.26, fol. 3v): 'We read about certain creatures of moderate size, called Leontophontes, which people burn ... so that they may kill lions with meat which has been tainted by a sprinkling of their ash, and thrown down at crossroads between converging tracks, should the lions eat the least little bit of it. *Consequently lions instinctively pursue these creatures with hatred, and, when they get a chance, they do not actually bite them, but they lacerate and kill them with the weight of their paws* [emphasis mine].'[25]

The lion of Jaca keeps his head high to avoid biting the deadly *leontophonos,* while he kills him with the weight of his paw. That is (again, as the verse makes clear), Christ tramples under foot the sovereign power of death. The remarkably close fit between the text of Solinus and the sculpted images and verse makes it probable that the Jaca sculptor or his patron was familiar with a description of the *leontophonos* similar to the one I have quoted.[26]

In the vicinity of Jaca, the *leontophonos* seems to have made an impression, although it failed to capture the imagination of medieval artists and poets further afield. Marcel Durliat draws attention to two more images of a 'kind of bear' with its snout to the ground at Jaca, one on the cornice of the southern lateral apse and the other on a deposed capital.[27] The latter is snared around the paw by a twisted rope, which is tightly held by a seated man who looks away. This might be a scene of the trapping of a *leontophonos* before burning it for use as lion bait. The animal with its snout to the ground reappears on the tympanum of Navasa, where it resembles a boar more than a bear. In this simplified version of the scheme at Jaca, the chrismon in the axial position is flanked on the left by a lion and a man standing upright behind him and on the right by a bird standing on the back of the 'boar.' Possibly this is a confused attempt on the part of a provincial artist to assimilate the Jaca design to the theme of Christ in Majesty with the Four Animals.[28] But it is also possible that the artist has selectively employed key elements of that design in a new configuration in which salvation is promised by the positive signs of the lion and the risen man on the left (the privileged right-hand side from the perspective of the chrismon), and damnation is threatened by the negative signs of the *leontophonos* (or whatever the artist understood this creature to be) and the basilisk on the right.

A third inscription runs in a single line along the lower edge of the tympanum of Jaca beneath the feet of the lions and the wheel of the chrismon. Consisting of three leonine hexameters, it identifies this as an admonitory portal: 'If you who are bound by the law of death seek to live, come hither in prayer, renouncing the fomentations of poison. Cleanse your heart of vices, lest you perish in the second death.'[29] Christian theology attributed two deaths to the original sin of Adam and Eve. The first death was the death of the body; the second death was the damnation of the body and soul at Last Judgment. When Christ through his Passion made eternal life available to the Christian who sought his mercy, he conquered the 'law of death.' If the images were arranged according to the hierarchy of their symbolic importance, the basilisk under the lion's hindpaw may correspond to the provisional first death, and the *leontophonos* under his forepaw to the final second death.

These three hexameters confirm the penitential message of the tympanum. In a general sense it applied to every Christian visitor to the church. As they neared the portal, the faithful would see in the figure of the lion on the right that Christ had opened for them the door of eternal life by his conquest of death, and they would see in the figure of the lion on the left what they must do to pass through that door: namely, to repent humbly for their sins. Though they might have needed help with some of the visual details and perhaps with the Latin of the verses, they would surely have had little difficulty in comprehending this message. It seems designed to be accessible.

But one element in the penitential theme of the tympanum is not obvious, at least to the modern viewer. Encoded in the chrismon is a sign that may have been intended to convey a special meaning to the sinners who had come to undergo the rite of public penitence. In order to recover this sign and its meaning, it is necessary to consider the chrismon both alone and in the context of the tympanum as a whole. The inscription that runs around the rim of the wheel consists of three leonine hexameters, which read clockwise from the top:

Hac in sculptura, lector, sic noscere cura:
P Pater, A Genitus, duplex est Spiritus Almus.
Hii tres iure quidem Dominus sunt unus et idem.[30]

(In this sculpture, reader, take care to understand [the symbolism] in this way: P is the Father, A is the Son, duplex *is the Holy Spirit. These three are indeed rightly one and the same, the Lord.)*

The obscure phrasing of the second line suggests that it was intended as a puzzle. None of the solutions that have hitherto been proposed is without difficulties.[31] I believe that the path to a more satisfactory solution must begin with a consideration of *duplex*. The sculptor placed the word *duplex* at the bottom of the circular frame of the chrismon where it can be read most clearly. It demands to be contemplated. Whatever its specific meaning, it alludes to the double nature of things (the serpent, the lions, Christ).[32] *Duplex (littera)* was the regular technical term in medieval grammars for the Latin double consonant X [= *ks*].[33] I believe that this, rather than S or Omega, is the letter to which *duplex* refers.[34] Taking it in that sense, the verse directs the viewer to read the Greek letters *rho*, *alpha*, and *chi*, as the Latin letters P, A, and X, and to reinterpret them as a three-lettered anagram, *pax* ('peace'), signifying the Trinity. 'P is the Father, A is the Son, the double consonant [X] is the Holy Spirit. These three [PAX] are indeed rightly one and the same, the Lord.'[35]

With the *pax* anagram in mind, we can now examine the chrismon of Jaca in the context of the tympanum as a whole. The iconographic program of the tympanum identifies this as a 'penitential portal' in the sense defined by O.K. Werckmeister. Werckmeister hypothesized the existence of penitential portals when he demonstrated that the symbolism of penance found on the tympanum and lintel of the now-destroyed north portal of Autun was consistent with the liturgical rites of public penitence current in the twelfth century.[36]

The tympanum of Jaca confirms Werckmeister's hypothesis, although it suggests that the nature and function of the penitential portal exhibited local variations.[37] The special meaning of the tympanum depends on the association of *pax* with the chrismon and the way in which the symbolism of the chrismon and the anagram complements the penitential allegory of the scenes that flank it. The door of eternal salvation or 'peace,' which is Christ, lies open to the public penitent who follows the penitential instruction of the verses of the lintel.

Susan Havens Caldwell argues that the penitential theme of the tympanum reflects the Roman reform introduced at Jaca by the Augustinian order after 1076. This reform replaced the relatively relaxed penitential rites that had been the custom in the Spanish Church with the much stricter requirements of the Roman rite.[38] Whereas the Spanish Church had permitted penitents to mingle with the general congregation and to take part in a communal public ritual of contrition at different times during the year, the Roman reform required public penitents to be isolated from the rest of the congregation and allowed the ritual to be performed only at the Easter season in the presence of the bishop. Furthermore, the sacrament of penance could be performed only once, and penitents who had received it were not subsequently allowed to return to their regular life, but instead had to renounce the world and live like monks, without entering the monastic orders.

The ritual of public penitence that was imposed at Jaca after 1076 would have been the one recorded in *Ordo L*[39] embedded in the *Romano-Germanic Pontifical of the X Century*.[40] The ritual was described by Regino of Prüm (d. 915),[41] and in identical language by Burchard of Worms (d. 1025).[42] It unfolded in three stages. (1) Penitents were ceremonially expelled from the church on Ash Wednesday. (2) They were secluded in a special place during the period of Lent. (3) They were readmitted to the church in a ceremony of reconciliation on Maundy Thursday.[43]

In the version of the rite described by Regino and Burchard, on Ash Wednesday public penitents, barefoot and clothed in sackcloth, presented themselves before the bishop in front of the portal of the church. They fell prostrate, proclaiming by their dress and countenance that they were guilty. Then the bishop led them into the church and together with the clergy prostrated himself and tearfully sang the seven penitential psalms for their absolution. According to the version of the rite in *Ordo L*, which does not specify where this part of the ceremony should take place, after the penitential psalms and some additional prayers, the bishop ordered the penitent to get up from the ground. Thereupon he arose from his own chair, and both he and the penitent, supporting themselves on their knees and elbows, entered the church and chanted more psalms. Following mass, ashes were cast on the heads of the penitents, they were clothed in hair shirts, and expelled with rebuke from the church.[44]

The human figure in the tympanum of Jaca is barefoot and on his hands and knees[45] in what might be a hair shirt. His reversed position under the lion indicates that this is the climactic moment of the first phase of the ritual of penitence; he is being driven *out* of the church.[46]

At the end of Lent, on Maundy Thursday, penitents were readmitted to communion. There are two verbal elements in the ceremony of reconciliation and the mass that followed it to which the *pax* anagram may refer. One is found in Psalm 33, which the clergy chanted at the moment when the bishop took by the hand the first of the line of penitents in order to lead them back into the church.[47] The psalm is organized rhetorically around a series of imperative commands, which build to the climax: 'Turn away from evil and do good: seek after *peace* and pursue *it*' (33:15; emphasis mine).[48] The other is the salutation of the mass at the moment of the breaking of the bread, 'Pax Domini sit semper vobiscum.' The salutation was followed by the Kiss of Peace.

The liminal inscription of Jaca spoke typologically in the voice of the Church. The *pax* anagram unlocks its complex message, which is tropological. In its strict sense the message was directed to the public penitent. For such a person, who, like every sinner, was subject to physical death (the basilisk) and to spiritual death (the *leontophonos*), which Christ (the lion) has overcome, the way back to Christ (the chrismon), who is the door to eternal life, paradoxically took him out of the church (the reversed man) for a period of penitential exclusion during Lent. But he was not to despair. If he faithfully accomplished his act of public penitence, renouncing sin and adopting humility (the snake), he would be readmitted through the door to reconciliation (the *pax* anagram) on Maundy Thursday. The *pax* anagram, standing for the Trinity, symbolizes the ceremony that effected the reconciliation and offered the penitent peace.

The association of the word *pax* with the chrismon did not originate at Jaca, nor was its penitential admonition limited to public penitents there or elsewhere. There is an ancient tradition of wordplay involving the cluster *lex/rex/pax/lux*.[49] These four words appear in a variety of contexts from the earliest period of Christian art up through and beyond the Romanesque period. John Williams calls attention to the Cross Page prepared by the Castilian scribe Florentius in the 950s for a copy of the Homilies of Smaragdus now in Cordoba. The words are inscribed in the four quadrants formed by the arms of the cross, while the Alpha and Omega hang from the horizontal arm. PAX is in the upper-left quadrant and then in clockwise order LVX, REX, and LEX.[50]

The original significance of the cluster remains unclear. Whatever it may have been, letters or words which invoke or include one or more of the words of the cluster were frequently added to the chrismons sculpted in the tenth, eleventh, and twelfth centuries on both sides of the Pyrenees.[51] All four words of the cluster appear on the chrismons of Saint-Orens of Bostens, Saint-Avit, Lème, Saint-Pierre of Simacourbe, Saint-Orens of Larreule, and Saint-Michel of Séron.[52] CRVX / REX / LEX / LVX can, or could, be read on the chrismon of the church of Saint-Pé in the township of Castillon-Debats.[53] In the square chrismons of

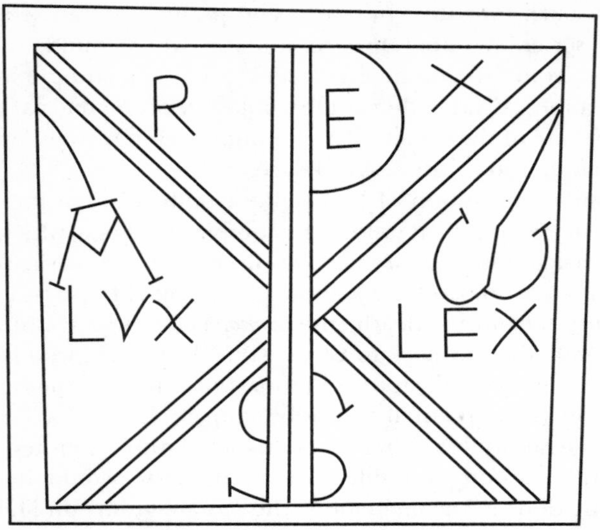

1 Square chrismon of Montaner

the churches of Montaner (text fig. 1) and Peyraube, LVX and LEX are inscribed beneath the Alpha and Omega and REX in the centre.[54] The last two examples raise the question of whether in these cases the missing *pax* was meant to be inferred anagrammatically from the Rho (P), Alpha (A), and Chi (X).

There is a chrismon from an altar dated by an inscription to the year 990 that is now preserved in the Château de Herrebouc near Saint-Jean-Poutge. In addition to the Alpha and Omega that hang from the upper arms of the Chi, a V-shaped crossbar between the lower arms of the Chi forms another A, which when taken with the Rho (P) and the Chi (X) makes up the anagram *pax*.[55] The word *rex* can be formed from the letters R and E, which are placed on either side of the Chi on the square chrismon of the church of Lagardère.[56] A similar configuration is on the chrismon in the tympanum of the church of Gellenave of Bouzon-Gellenave.[57]

The *lex/ rex/ pax/ lux* cluster seems to have functioned both as a decorative unit with symbolic overtones (each three-letter word ending in *x* being an attribute of Christ; the number four perhaps suggesting Incarnation) and as some kind of a mnemonic device related to various hexameter lines that were used for portal inscriptions. Variations or substitutions in the four words occur. CRVX takes the place of PAX on the chrismon at Castillon-Debats (see above); DVX replaces REX on the archivolts of the portal of Saint-Étienne d'Olérat of La Rochefoucauld.[58] The latter substitution is found in a hexameter of Marbod of Rennes (with the addition of a fifth term *vindex*):

Tu mihi rex, mihi lex, mihi lux, mihi dux, mihi vindex.[59]
(You are my king, my law, my light, my leader, my judge.)

Since each word in the cluster acts as a synonym for Christ, the words are in effect interchangeable and endlessly variable (three-letter monosyllables ending in *x*; four-letter monosyllables ending in *x*; disyllables ending in *x*; monosyllables ending in *s*; others).

A substitution formula based on the cluster generated numerous verses in the voice of Christ that were employed as portal inscriptions. The formula, which makes up the first two and a half feet of the hexameter (the portion up to the caesura), is *[X] ego sum [Y]*, where X = a long monosyllable from the cluster or a variable derived from it, and Y = a spondaic word, usually in the genitive. One of the panels of the Genesis frieze of the cathedral of Modena (the same frieze in which God's halo in the Creation of Adam and Eve panel is inscribed R/E/X) shows God seated in majesty holding an open book with the inscription (fig. 16)

Lux ego sum mundi, via verax, vita perennis.[60]
(I am the light of the world, the true way, life eternal.)

Similarly, we find *pax ego sum vobis*, 'I am your peace,' at San Bartolomeo in Pantano of Pistoia;[61] *fons ego sum vitae*, 'I am the fountain of life,' at Santa Cruz de la Serós;[62] *spes ego sum vitae*, 'I am the hope of life,' at Saint Emmeram of Regensburg;[63] *mors ego sum mortis*, 'I am the death of death,' at San Prudencio of Armentia;[64] and, with an initial trisyllabic dactyl, *ianua sum vitae*, 'I am the gate of life,' at San Giorgio of Milan and elsewhere;[65] and *ianua sum perpes*, 'I am the eternal door,' again at Santa Cruz.[66] The formula was used ca. 1200 on a processional icon of Christ the Redeemer at Trevignano. Christ holds a book inscribed with words in his own voice:

Rex ego sum celi populum qui de morte redemi.[67]
(I am the king of heaven who has redeemed the people from death.)

The word *pax* by itself does not seem to have been added to chrismons in portal sculpture before the anagram of the tympanum of Jaca at the end of the eleventh century.[68] In the twelfth century, however, there are a number of such additions, some of which may have been made in imitation of Jaca and with an understanding of the penitential implications of the *pax* anagram.

In the case of the tympanum of Santa Cruz de la Serós (fig. 13), the addition of the *pax* anagram in imitation of Jaca is nearly certain. A liminal inscription in the voice of Christ directs those who wish to enter to purify themselves first. There is a chrismon in the centre flanked by two lions. The chrismon has a horizontal crossbar; an Omega hangs from its left arm and an S is behind its right arm. A V-shaped crossbar connects the lower descender of the Rho with the lower-right arm of the Chi, forming an A.

The unusual order of the initials of the chrismon has baffled scholars, who are inclined to attribute it to ignorance.[69] However, Angel San Vicente argues that the chrismon's 'alphabetic signs are placed successively, turning in the direction of the hands of a watch, so that the eyes read them in a closed circuit from the first letter to the last.'[70] That is, we read Chi, and then clockwise from the top Rho, S (= XPistuS), and then Alpha and Omega. His suggestion is ingenious, but it leaves the essential question unasked: Why did the sculptor adopt this unorthodox order? The answer seems to be that the sculptor intended to replicate the symbolism of the chrismon of Jaca. By adopting this peculiar clockwise arrangement, he has aligned the initials P, A, and X on the vertical axis, visually emphasizing the presence of the symbolic *pax* anagram in the chrismon.

Other instances of the addition of *pax* to chrismons may owe more to the general diffusion of the *lex/rex/pax/lux* cluster than to the immediate influence of Jaca. Nevertheless I think there is a strong probability that penitential symbolism attached to the *pax* anagram wherever it appeared. In the western part of Catalonia, in the Valle de Arán, there is a curious modification of the chrismon on the lintel of the north portal of the small twelfth-century church of Bossòst (or Bosost).[71] The Alpha and Omega are reversed, the Omega being placed on the left and the Alpha on the right, and the lower-left arm of the Chi has a simple crossbar, making a new letter X.[72] In this case the *pax* anagram does not depend on the Chi, but reads clockwise from the P at the top around to the A and on to the X in the lower left.

The same modification was used in the chrismon of the church of Vilach also in the Valle de Arán.[73] A less radical version of the arrangement occurs nearby at Escunhau (or Escunyau), where the Alpha and

2 Wheel chrismon of Cazeaux in Laplume (reproduced from *Bulletin de la Société nationale des Antiquaires de France* [1892], 120)

Omega are in their normal positions, but the crossbar, which forms a new letter X, was placed on the lower-right arm of the Chi. Here the anagram reads counterclockwise.

It is unlikely that there were close connections between the Valle de Arán and the province of Huesca early in the twelfth century. If the *pax* anagram is found in both places, it must be because by this time the symbolism was widely understood and replicated in the pastoral effort to bring worshippers to penitence. And perhaps the reversal of the Alpha and Omega had begun to be associated with the anagram. The Alpha and Omega are reversed on the twelfth-century tympanum of the church of Sainte-Engrâce and there is an inscription around the chrismon that reads: PAX TECVM [*top*] BERNADVS [*sic*] ME FECIT [*bottom*] CHERVBIN [*left*] ET SERAPHIN [*right*]. Similarly, the Alpha and Omega are reversed in the chrismon of the north portal of San Pedro de la Rua in Estella.

A strange chrismon on the door of the chapel of Cazeaux in Laplume takes the shape of a wheel with eight spokes (the Chi and the cross combined) (text fig. 2). The Rho, the Alpha, and the Omega are missing.

3 Wheel chrismon of Cocumont, Gueyze, and Lagupie (reproduced from *Bulletin de la Société nationale des Antiquaires de France* [1892], 119)

Within the eight sections formed by the spokes of the wheel are inscribed, clockwise from above the left horizontal arm of the cross, the letters P, A, X, and V, and counterclockwise from below the left horizontal arm of the cross, O, B, I, and S; that is, PAX VOBIS. This chrismon inspired Vincent Durand, a nineteenth-century correspondent of the Société des Antiquaires de France, to interpret the chrismons of three other churches in Lot-et-Garonne (Cocumont, Gueyze, and Lagupie) as forming anagrams of *pax vobis.* In these, the chrismon took the shape of a six-spoke wheel (text fig. 3). Durand argued that the Rho = P, the Alpha = A, the Chi = X, the upper half of the Chi = V, the circle of the chrismon = O, the Omega closed by the horizontal arm of the crossbar = B, the staff of the Rho = I, and the S = S.[74]

There is a small, re-employed tympanum of Christ in Majesty with the Four Animals in the village of Lassouts in Rouergue (fig. 31). In this region of France, just as in the Pyrenees, the chrismon was still common. At Lassouts the sculptor seems to have regarded the Christ in Majesty as a visual expansion of the chrismon. The mandorla that encloses Christ is superimposed on a cross. Possibly because he did not wish to forgo any of the symbolism he associated with the chrismon, he included the Alpha and Omega and PAX in his design.[75]

Finally, the association of the *pax* anagram with the chrismon may explain several odd details on the south-transept façade of the cathedral of Santiago of Compostela. Although the sculptures have been rearranged, the *Pilgrim's Guide* explicitly locates the tympana with the Temptation and the Flagellation in their present positions and it speaks of the two lions on the trumeau, which are just below and in front of the chrismon on the vertical axis of the central pier.[76] The Alpha and Omega of the chrismon are reversed. The lower portion of the chrismon is partially screened by crossed lions, but so far as I can tell there is no evidence of a crossbar. Among the sculptures of the tympanum of the left portal is the Temptation of Christ. All the elements of the chrismon of Jaca are present. The figure of Christ replaces the Chi-Rho monogram, and PAX and the Alpha and Omega are inscribed on Christ's halo. (The head and halo are partially mutilated, but the letters A and X can still be made out on the vertical and right horizontal arms of the cross and the letters Alpha and Omega in the spaces between the arms.[77]) In the centre of the tympanum of the right portal is the Flagellation. Here again, Christ's halo is inscribed, this time with the Alpha and Omega on the left and right arms of the cross, the letters P and X in the spaces between the arms, and the letter A on the vertical arm.[78] These visual expansions of the chrismon, which are paralleled by the expansion at Lassouts, lend support to the conjecture that the sculptor might have had the *pax* anagram in mind when he reversed the Alpha and Omega on the chrismon of the central pier.

The *pax* anagram and its penitential implications may have been even more widely diffused and commonly understood in the Middle Ages than these numerous examples suggest. One can only guess at the missing links in the chain that connects the *pax* anagrams of twelfth century with the dream visions of Guillaume de Deguileville in the fourteenth century. In *Le pèlerinage de la vie humaine* (1330/55) Deguileville depicts two fine ladies, one with a broom in her mouth and the other with a document in her hand. The first lady is Penance; the second, Charity. After Penance explains her office, Charity reads the document that is a testament from Christ called the testament of peace. In it Christ, led by Charity, bequeaths a jewel, peace, to those unworthy to possess it. The jewel takes the form of a carpenter's square with the letter P at the end of one arm, the letter A in the corner, and the letter X at the end of the other arm.

> These three letters show that those who have been left the gift of this jewel must have peace in three ways. First, set high on a scaffold is the X, by which

> I am represented and signified. They should have perfect peace in such a way that they cease and correct all actions against my will. Next, lodged and fixed in the angle below, rests the A, which represents the soul [*âme/anima*] that is in the human body. It also should have true peace through the elimination of evil deeds. These must be wiped out and swept away by Penance ... Further still, they ought to be at peace with their neighbors [*prochain/proximus*], signified by the P at the other end.[79]

Pax portals constitute a group of thematically related portals, as do the admonitory ones. The *pax* anagram and the *lex/rex/pax/lux* cluster were primarily associated with the abstract sign of the chrismon, whereas the verse inscriptions of admonitory portals more often accompanied sculpted images of Christ. The portals of Jaca and Santa Cruz de la Serós belong to both groups. Given the traditional penitential associations of the word *pax*, it seems likely that the tropological message of the two groups was essentially the same. In both groups, the voice of the Church or Christ, visibly articulated in a verse inscription or the sign *pax*, directed all those about to enter to engage in penitential self-reflection and cleansing before undergoing liminal transformation at the moment of passing through the door, which was Christ.

11

Visions of Allegory: The Archivolts of Aquitaine

By virtue of its metaphysical assumptions and as an interpretative model, the allegory of the church profoundly influenced the architecture and decoration of Romanesque churches, but this almost never led to a systematic representation of all the different levels of the allegory in portal sculpture. Consequently, it is fascinating to find that artists visually projected a schematic idea of the multiple levels of the allegory of the church in the archivolts above the main portals of an important group of churches in the area of Aquitaine that includes Poitou, Vendée, and Saintonge.

Archivolts enlarged and proliferated early in the twelfth century in many parts of western Europe. Apparently, the semicircle of the archivolt was felt to be analogous to the diurnal path followed by the sun and the stars as they rose from the east, mounted to the zenith, and descended to the west, in a clockwise movement from left to right (facing the meridian). Hence, these semicircular mouldings were associated with the secular world and the cycles of time, and were often decorated with the Labours of the Months and the Signs of the Zodiac. When Christ appeared in the axial position on the tympanum beneath such an archivolt, the temporal and the eternal, the literal and spiritual levels of experience, were visibly juxtaposed, as notably at the west portals of Autun and Vézelay (figs. 8, 9). A similar conception may have governed the decoration of the outer moulding of the tympanum of Conques, where we see little figures peeling back a ribbon band and gazing out, as if, like us, they have been granted a vision of eternity (Christ in Judgment on the tympanum) from the perspective of everyday life in time (fig. 1).

Tympana were rarely employed over portals in Aquitaine, but portals in this region were often furnished with anywhere from two to five elaborately decorated archivolts. Some of these nested archivolts, like the ones above the west portals of Saint-Martial of Chalais, Parthenay-le-Vieux, and Saint-Symphorien, and the north portal of Notre-Dame of Fenioux, are made up of repetitive animal, floral, or geometrical patterns. These are no doubt purely decorative.[1] Other portals, however, are so constructed that images referring to different levels of the allegory of the church are lined up one above another on the vertical axis of the nested archivolts.

Possibly the first and certainly one of the most profound of all the attempts to create a vision of the allegory of the church is the west portal of the church of Sainte-Marie of Saintes, known as the Abbaye aux Dames (fig. 32). The church was built for a Benedictine convent by Geoffrey Martel and his wife Agnes of Burgundy, the count and countess of Anjou. It was dedicated on 2 November 1047.[2] The west portal is usually assigned to a period of reconstruction in the twelfth century, but there is considerable uncertainty involved and reason to think that decoration of the portal (and the whole of the lower façade) may in fact be earlier than is commonly thought.[3]

The portal is crowned with a nested series of four compound archivolts, which is to say that each archivolt has its own decorative moulding immediately above it. The four archivolts display (from bottom to top): (1) the Hand of God, supported by six adoring angels; (2) the Lamb of God, flanked by the Four Animals in a vine pattern; (3) forty-four executioners and victims, probably representing the theme of Holy Martyrdom;[4] and (4) the fifty-four Elders of the Apocalypse (fig. 33). The idea of fourfold allegory informs this arrangement, although it is not laid out in an absolutely systematic fashion. The Hand of God in the first archivolt points down from the clouds toward the portal, instead of out toward the Lamb as it does elsewhere in the soffits of Saint-Pierre of Pont-l'Abbé-d'Arnoult and Varaize. This would seem to be Christ pointing to himself as the door on the typological level of the allegory. It is also tropological, inasmuch as by the same gesture he is showing the path of salvation to the faithful who are about to enter. The Lamb in the second archivolt alludes to the anagogical level, but the harmonic relationship between typology and anagogy is nowhere more evident than here. The Four Animals are a verbal allegory for the four Evangelists, who record the earthly life of Christ. They are embedded in a vine scroll, which in this context is very likely another verbal allegory. 'I am the true vine; and my Father is the husbandman,' says Christ in John's Gospel (15:1). The Holy Martyrdom,

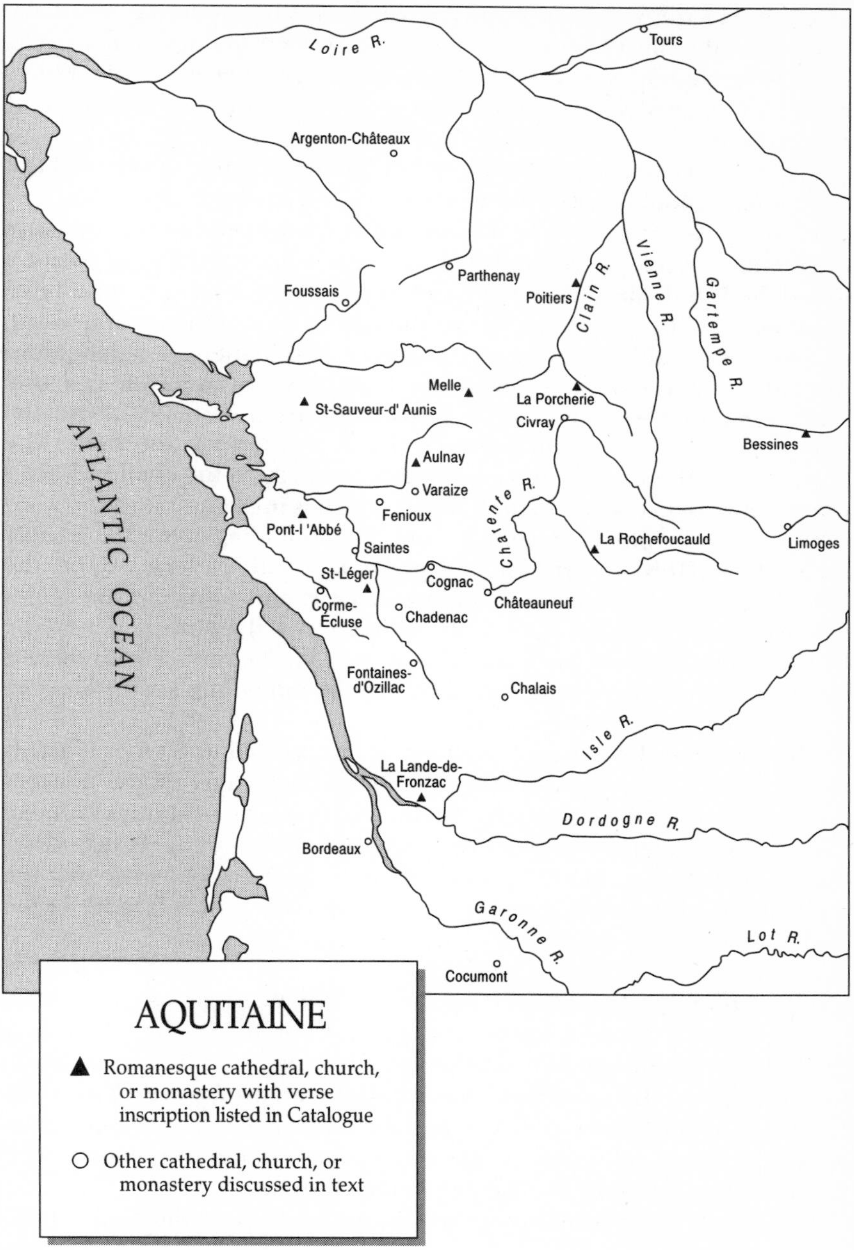

Loire R.
Tours
Argenton-Châteaux
Parthenay
Foussais
Poitiers
Clain R.
Vienne R.
Gartempe R.
Melle
St-Sauveur-d' Aunis
La Porcherie
Civray
Bessines
Aulnay
Varaize
Fenioux
Charente R.
Pont-l 'Abbé
Saintes
La Rochefoucauld
Limoges
St-Léger
Cognac
Châteauneuf
Corme-Écluse
Chadenac
ATLANTIC OCEAN
Fontaines-d'Ozillac
Chalais
Isle R.
La Lande-de-Fronzac
Dordogne R.
Bordeaux
Garonne R.
Lot R.
Cocumont
AQUITAINE
Romanesque cathedral, church, or monastery with verse inscription listed in Catalogue
Other cathedral, church, or monastery discussed in text

representing the persecution of the saints and the suffering of all the martyrs, in the third archivolt corresponds to the tropological interpretation of the church as each saved soul. I will suggest below that the Elders represent an allegory, on the literal level, of the world in expectation of redemption.

The secondary series of mouldings at Saintes belongs to the world of nature. The moulding above the Hand of God archivolt is another vine scroll. However, it cannot be interpreted as Christ because it culminates in an animal mask, off-centred slightly to the left from the axial position above the Hand. Masks can be images of hell;[5] in this context the animal mask seems to be a reminder of the ambiguous lure of the natural world, so green and fruitful, and yet to the unwary and inattentive a dangerous distraction. The moulding above the Lamb of God archivolt is a vine scroll interlaced with birds. Two birds drink from a chalice above the Lamb. Like the mask, they are off-centred; this time to the right. The cross behind the body of the Lamb points directly to the chalice. This is the positive aspect of the natural world, which is imprinted with the word of God for those who are willing to read. The moulding above the terrible archivolt of Holy Martyrdom is a graceful foliate pattern. Above the Elders is a more menacing moulding of lions and birds entwined in a vine. Each lion paws the flank of the lion in front; the birds perch on the backs of the lions and peck and claw at the lion behind. The archivolts allude to the allegory of the church, while the mouldings set the allegory in the restless, ambivalent world of nature.

The vision of the allegory of the church depicted at Saintes is richly obscure. One may surmise that the Benedictine nuns of the convent wanted a sculptural program that would give them opportunities for meditation. The relative chronology of the Aquitainian churches is still uncertain; if the façade of the Abbaye aux Dames is early, it is possible that the meditations of the nuns gave rise to the other allegorical façades of the region.

The west portal of Aulnay is a magnificent example of the use of axial figures to create a vision of the allegory of the church (fig. 34).[6] At Aulnay the vision is systematized in strict accord with the fourfold model. From top to bottom, the axial figures of the four archivolts are Cancer the Crab, Christ, the Crown of Virtue, and the Lamb of God. They permit the archivolts to be read as the literal, the typological, the tropological, and the anagogical levels of the allegory of the church.

The fourth or outermost archivolt of Aulnay depicts the Signs of the

Zodiac and the Labours of the Months. They are badly damaged, especially on the left side, but they are, or were, labelled with the names of the Signs and the Months, and enough remains to make the identification of most of the figures certain. The archivolt represents the year and the revolving cycles of time and life, which belong to the literal level of the allegory of the church. Cancer occupies the axial position at the top, in consequence of the symbolical alignment of the medieval divisions of the year and the sun with Christ.[7] The signs of the zodiac were governed by the solstices and equinoxes. The winter solstice ushered in the sign of Capricorn; the spring equinox, Aries; the summer solstice, Cancer; and the autumnal equinox, Libra. In the Roman calendar, which the Western world generally followed in the Middle Ages except for the purpose of calculating Easter, the summer solstice – the day from which Cancer took its beginning – occurred on the eighth calends of July, that is to say, 24 June.[8] Therefore the slim block to the left of Cancer on the archivolt marks the moment of time in the revolving cycle of the year when the sun reaches its highest point.[9]

This moment, when the sun is at the peak of its power in the natural world, explains the alignment of Cancer with Christ on the central axis. In the book of nature, the sun was a sign of Christ.[10] Cancer is at or beside the apex of the outer archivolt at several other churches in this region – Saint-Gilles of Argenton-Château,[11] Saint-Nicolas of Civray, Saint-Léger of Cognac, and Fenioux (fig. 35).[12]

One confusing complication must be addressed. The signs of the zodiac did not correspond precisely to the months of the year. Technically speaking, each sign stood, as it does in today's astrology, for the twelfth part of the year during which the sun rose in the zone of the sky containing the constellation named by the sign. According to this reckoning, therefore, Cancer designated a period of time that included the last week in June and roughly the first three and a half weeks of July. But in popular usage, each sign stood for the month in which it was entered by the sun. According to this way of looking at it, Cancer was synonymous with June, because the sun entered Cancer on 24 June.[13] Technically, the summer solstice fell between Gemini and Cancer, but, loosely speaking, it came after the sixth month, June, or between Cancer and Leo if they were thought of as naming the months in which they began.

Cancer is paired with Leo on the axis of the outer archivolt at Fenioux, and at Civray and Cognac carvings that might represent the solstice, a mask at Civray and a leaf at Cognac, stand between Cancer and Leo. Unfortunately, erosion has destroyed the signs at Argenton-Château, but it is thought that Cancer stood on the left and Leo on the right of a projection above the head of Christ.[14] This projection may have been something like the mask at Civray or the leaf at Cognac – that is, a mark that could have designated the solstice.

Two notable parallels to this symbolism are found in Burgundy. At Autun one of the two medallions directly above Christ's head is Cancer; the other is a youthful squatting human figure, which Denis Grivot and George Zarnecki identify as Annus, the Year (fig. 8).[15] Their identification is based on a manuscript illustration of the Labours of the Months and the Signs of the Zodiac, in which a hairy, bearded man holds the sun and the moon in his hands.[16] Except in the posture of its legs, it bears little resemblance to the youthful figure of Autun. Furthermore, the youthful figure separates the medallions of Gemini and Cancer, the juncture marked by the summer solstice. Although Grivot and Zarnecki reject as unsupported the conjecture that this figure represents the solstice, in light of Aulnay, the possibility must be reconsidered.

At Vézelay Cancer is displaced to the left from the axial position in the archivolt over Christ's head by three tumbling figures that interrupt the medallions of the Labours of the Months and the Signs of the Zodiac, and which may be another symbol of time's cycle (fig. 9).[17] Leo is in the medallion on the right of the tumbling figures. The artist was perhaps trying to pack more symbolism into his composition than he quite had space for. A stork with its neck bent around appears in a half medallion between Cancer and the tumbling figures; this has been said to symbolize the solstice.[18] If the stork represents the solstice it is, as we have seen, on the wrong side of the medallion of Cancer, technically speaking. But at Vézelay, as nearly everywhere else in Romanesque sculpture, the year begins with January and Aquarius on the left and ends with Capricornus and December on the right. Half the year (January/Aquarius–June/Cancer) falls in the left-hand quadrant of the archivolt and half (Leo/July–Capricornus/December) on the right. Here again, as at Fenioux, Civray, Cognac, and Argenton-Château, the solstice was thought of as coming between June and July. Certainly, the idea of the high point of the year is conveyed by the several related symbols at the top of the archivolt. The symbolism of the solstice extends to the trumeau. John the Baptist is the trumeau statue that extends the central axis of the tympanum. His feast day was celebrated on 24 June (Midsummer Day).

Cancer is the high point of the solar year, the moment of perfection when time brushes eternity, the temporal analogue of Christ. From this point the sun begins its decline. In the unredeemed world time is meaningless circularity, the revolving wheel of fortune that took Chaucer's Troilus 'fro wo to wele, and after out of joie.'[19]

The third archivolt at Aulnay depicts the Wise and Foolish Virgins (fig. 34). This subject was inspired by the parable in the Gospel of Matthew:

> Then shall the kingdom of heaven be like to ten virgins, who taking their lamps went out to meet the bridegroom and the bride. And five of them were foolish, and five wise. But the five foolish, having taken their lamps, did not take oil with them. But the wise took oil in their vessels with the lamps. And the bridegroom tarrying, they all slumbered and slept. And at midnight there was a cry made: Behold the bridegroom cometh, go ye forth to meet him. Then all those virgins arose and trimmed their lamps. And the foolish said to the wise: Give us of your oil, for our lamps are gone out. The wise answered, saying: Lest perhaps there be not enough for us and for you, go ye rather to them that sell, and buy for yourselves. Now whilst they went to buy, the bridegroom came: and they that were ready, went in with him to the marriage, and the door was shut. But at last came also the other virgins, saying: Lord, Lord, open to us. But he answering said: Amen I say to you, I know you not. (Matt. 25:1–12)

The five Virgins on the left hold their cups upright; the five on the right hold theirs upside down to show they are empty,[20] and the one closest to the top makes a gesture of despair. They move toward the figure of Christ on the vertical axis of the archivolt. No barrier blocks the approach of the Wise Virgins, but between Christ and the Foolish Virgins is a closed and bolted door. Christ beside a door is typology ('I am the door'). Christ is shown as a half-figure within a mandorla, rising, or perhaps enthroned, above the clouds. The bolted door is a miniature of the church of Aulnay; there are two pine-cone towers on the corners of the west façade, a line of arcades above the portal, a round-arched window on the second level, and a cross on the axial line above the roof (figs. 34, 36). The church is the body of Christ and the portal is the means of entry. The archivolt represents the typological level of the allegory of the church, but like every allegory, this is multi-referential. The Wise and Foolish Virgins remind the faithful to be prepared (tropology), and in combination with Christ they figure Last Judgment (anagogy).

Curiously, this side-by-side image of Christ and the door is used nowhere else in the region. Either the door is omitted and Christ appears within the mandorla above the clouds, as at Argenton-Château and Civray, or the clouds are omitted and Christ is shown within the door instead of beside it. At Saint-Martin of Chadenac (fig. 37), Saint-Nazaire of Corme-Royal, and Pont-l'Abbé, Christ stands beneath the central arch of an arcade and reaches behind the columns on either side of him. With his right hand in front of an open door he welcomes the Wise Virgins with a benediction; with his left hand he pulls a door shut before the Foolish Virgins. The Christ in the Door at Notre-Dame of Fenioux (fig. 35) is somewhat worn, but one can make out that the sculptor had conceived of a similar scheme.

In the second archivolt of Aulnay personified figures of virtue trample the vices beneath their feet (fig. 34). On the left side, Wrath is paired with Patience, Luxury with Chastity, Pride with Humility. On the right (from the top), Generosity is paired with Avarice, Faith with Idolatry, Concord with Discord.[21] These are loosely derived from the characters in Prudentius's *Psychomachia.*[22] The virtues are heroic female warriors; the vices are smaller, naked, grotesquely shaped, demonic figures. The two virtues nearest the top, Humility and Generosity, hold between them at the summit of the archivolt the Crown of Virtue, which is the reward of each saved soul. The archivolt therefore represents the tropological level of the allegory of the church. Small, fragile projections like the crowns of virtue rarely survived in the archivolts of this region, but they can be inferred from the nearly identical figures of the six virtues and vices at Argenton-Château,[23] Chadenac (fig. 37), Fenioux (fig. 35), Saint-Martin of Fontaines-d'Ozillac, and Notre-Dame de la Couldre of Parthenay.[24] There are six virtues and vices in the second archivolt of Pont-l'Abbé, but it would appear that the virtues at the top of the archivolt touched heads and there does not seem to be room for a crown. Likewise, heads probably touched at Varaize, where there are only four pairs of virtues and vices.

Finally, in the first, or innermost, archivolt of Aulnay, angels surround the mystical Lamb of God, which is placed on the vertical axis (fig. 34). The Lamb is a sign or, as Bede would say, a verbal allegory of Christ in Majesty and the heavenly Jerusalem. As a verbal allegory, it operates on at least two and possibly three levels, figuring typologically the incarnation of God in Christ on earth (Isa. 53:6–7; Jer. 11:19; John 10:11, etc.), anagogically the Christ in Majesty of the Second Coming and Last Judgment (Apoc. 5:6, etc.), and perhaps also tropologically each saved soul (as in the parable of the lost sheep, Luke 15:5). As an anagogy, the Lamb attracts and absorbs all of the apocalyptic imagery of the heavenly city. In the language of the Apocalypse, it is the temple, and the lamp for the temple that replaces the sun: 'For the Lord God Almighty is the temple thereof, and the Lamb. And the city hath no need of the sun, nor of the moon, to shine in it. For the glory of God hath enlightened it, and the Lamb is the lamp thereof' (Apoc. 21:22–3). The anagogical level of the allegory is always dominant in the image of the Lamb of God in Romanesque art, and it is emphasized in the archivolts of Aquitaine by the figures in the left and right quadrants of the archivolt. At Aulnay, and at Argenton-Château, Fenioux (fig. 35), Notre-Dame de la Couldre of Parthenay, Pont-l'Abbé, and Varaize, these are angels. At the Abbaye aux Dames of Saintes, as we have seen, the Lamb in the second archivolt is surrounded by a vine pattern in which are embedded the Four Animals (fig. 33). The Four Animals with a censing angel and another beast (?) appear at Saint-Pierre of Châteauneuf-sur-Charente. The Lamb is flanked by two censing angels and two Evangelists at Fontaines-d'Ozillac.

Several portals in Aquitaine closely parallel the allegorical vision of Aulnay. On the west portal of the Benedictine priory church of Pont-l'Abbé the Signs of the Zodiac and the Labours of the Months are absent.[25] There is, however, an enigmatic head of a king or queen in the axial position on the arch of the façade, whose relationship to the allegorical scheme is unclear, but which could conceivably belong to the literal level. The typological level is represented by the outer archivolt of Christ in the Door with the Wise and Foolish Virgins. The saints are on the third archivolt; on the second are the virtues and vices. Both archivolts belong to the tropological level. Finally, on the inner archivolt, angels flank the Lamb of God. The Lamb is in a circular medallion, on the rim of which is inscribed:

> Hic Deus est magnus quem signat misticus Agnus.[26]
> *(Here is [or perhaps, 'this is'] the great God whom the mystic Lamb signifies).*

The verse, which confirms the allegorical intention of the artist, identifies the Lamb on the mystical, or anagogical, level with the Lamb of the Apocalypse.

At Fenioux the innermost archivolt of the west portal was given an abstract floral design (fig. 35). Above it are four additional archivolts with the same axial figures that appear at Aulnay. Cancer is paired with Leo at the apex of the outermost, or fifth, archivolt. Then comes Christ in the Door in the fourth, the Lamb in the third, and the Crown of Virtue (broken off) in the second.

The temporal world seems to have been represented on the outer archivolts of the Abbaye aux Dames of Saintes and Notre-Dame de la

Couldre of Parthenay, not by means of the Signs of the Zodiac with the axial figure of Cancer, but rather with repeated images of the Elders of the Apocalypse. There are twenty-four Elders in John's vision (Apoc. 4:4). This number, which is typically maintained in Romanesque art when the Elders are shown with Christ in Majesty and the Four Animals or with the Lamb of God, is disregarded on these archivolts. Fifty-four Elders appear at Saintes (fig. 32) and only six at Parthenay, and there is no distinctive axial figure at the apex of either archivolt (although perhaps there could have been at Parthenay).[27] Biblical commentators explained that the Elders were figures for the twelve prophets and the twelve apostles, whose mission was to foretell and spread the news of Christ's coming.[28] Therefore, in the absence of an axial figure of Christ, the Elders could signify the world waiting to be redeemed, which is the domain of the literal level of allegory.

Artists and their patrons in Aquitaine did not always think in terms of the fourfold method of allegory. Archivolts sometimes come in sets of two; sets of three are common, and there are five at Argenton-Château and Fenioux. Nor do the number of archivolts necessarily correspond to the number of allegories represented. Sometimes two or perhaps even three archivolts depict the same allegorical level. It is the alignment of the axial figures of the archivolts that sets up an interplay – a movement back and forth – between different levels or allegories of redeemed and unredeemed experience.

At Notre-Dame of Corme-Écluse the two archivolts of the west portal may be purely decorative.[29] Six cat-like animals prowl through a vine pattern in the inner one; twelve birds, six to a side, flank a little human figure, without a halo, in the outer. However, the man, who seems to be emerging from waves or a cloud, is in the axial position. He holds two chalices from which two of the birds are drinking. This is very likely a Eucharistic theme.[30] It can be compared with the birds drinking from a common chalice above the Lamb of God at the Abbaye aux Dames of Saintes (fig. 33). Thus, the archivolts of Corme-Écluse, both of which belong to the literal level, may depict the signs of hope and despair, of union with Christ via the Eucharistic bread and wine or of descent into merely bestial prowling, that can be read in the book of nature. The spiritual level of the allegory of the church would then be signified by the portal beneath the archivolts.

Some portals with three archivolts confine themselves to this contrast between the spiritual and literal levels. At Châteauneuf-sur-Charente, the

Lamb of God is the axial figure in the inner archivolt and the other two archivolts belong to the unredeemed world. Men, monsters, and beasts inhabit a vine pattern on the middle archivolt. An archer is near but not in the axial position. Does this have something to do with the presence of evil or death in the natural world? The outer archivolt with its floral pattern seems more benign. At Foussais the inner archivolts are decorative (the blank innermost one is a modern restoration). Christ is at the apex of the outer archivolt. He is flanked by an angel and the Four Animals, apostles and abbots, and, finally, a musician, acrobats, and an animal and a siren at the far right. A moulding of cats and acanthus leaves encloses the archivolt. Since cats could be an erotic motif,[31] this might be interpreted as the fertile natural world surrounding the range of human experience from the sacred to the profane.

The four archivolts at Civray are closely related to the scheme at Aulnay, but whether they project a fourfold or a threefold allegory of the church depends on the interpretation of the axial figure of the third archivolt. To take the others first: Cancer is at the summit of the fourth, outermost archivolt with the Signs of the Zodiac and the Labours of the Months on either side, representing the literal level. The second archivolt, with Christ as the axial figure, is typological. Christ appears in a mandorla above the clouds with the five Wise and Foolish Virgins on either side. The keystone of the inner archivolt displays Christ in Majesty surrounded by the Four Animals and flanked by four censing angels. This is the anagogical level.

The axial figure of the third archivolt of Civray is a woman, crowned, within a mandorla. She is flanked by six adoring angels, the nearest of whom support the mandorla in their hands. Art historians interpret her as the Virgin in Majesty or the Virgin of the Assumption.[32] If she is, it would seem either that the crowned Virgin was understood to imply the salvation of the virtuous soul or that the artist substituted her for the crown of virtue, possibly as a figure for the Church on the typological level.[33]

Another interpretation might be considered. The Virgin Mary does not appear elsewhere in the archivolts of Aquitaine. In fact, the Virgin rarely appears by herself in Romanesque art. She is usually accompanied by some other person: in the Annunciation, by the angel; in the Visitation, by Elizabeth; in the Virgin in Majesty, by the Child; and so on. (One exception to this generalization is the Assumption of the Virgin in the tympanum of Saint-Pierre-le-Puellier of Bourges, where the Virgin, crowned, is in a mandorla supported by two angels. But that tympanum includes other scenes of the death and burial of the Virgin, which make the reference to her clear.) The closest analogue to the figure at Civray that I know of is the capital of 'the Assumption of the Virgin' at Saint-Caprais of Agen.[34] As at Civray, the woman is clothed and crowned and holds her hands, palms outward, in the *orans* position. The mandorla at Agen is inscribed with arcades that must represent the heavenly city. Why should we assume that either figure is the Virgin? The most prominent female figures in the archivolts of Aquitaine are the virtues, who offer the Crown of Virtue to the soul as her reward. Prudentius personified the soul as a woman when he described the marriage of the soul with the Holy Spirit in his *Psychomachia*. The stumbling block is that souls are usually depicted as naked figures in Romanesque art. However, an allegorical personification of the saved soul is not the same as the soul of a particular saint, and might well have been depicted with clothing.[35] For whatever reason, the artist at Civray decided not to include the triumph of the virtues over the vices on the archivolts of the portal (there is one above the upper window). In its place he may have substituted the triumphant ascent into heaven of the soul wearing the crown of virtue. If this is so, the theme is tropological, and all four levels of the allegory of the church are represented on the archivolts of the central portal at Civray.

It is just possible that the ascent of the virtuous soul also found a place on the west portal of Chadenac (fig. 37). A crowned figure in a mandorla occupies the axial position on the inner compound archivolt. It is surrounded by adoring angels and the virtues trampling the vices. According to François Eygun, the crowned figure represents the Ascension of Christ.[36] I am tempted to see it instead as a woman. The face is beardless, although there is no sign of long hair or a headdress. I cannot make out whether the garment is an ecclesiastical vestment or a simple gown. There appear to be arcades inscribed within the mandorla. If it were the ascent of the virtuous soul, it would provide a bridge to the ascent of the soul at Civray, because at Chadenac we find both the triumph of the virtues over the vices, which normally accompanies the Crown of Virtue, and the surrounding angels that lift the mandorla at Civray.

Aquitainian façades differ remarkably from most other Romanesque façades. Their multiple archivolts bend and concentrate all of the power of the allegory of the church onto the portals (fig. 32). Nevertheless, the systematic imaging of the allegory on the archivolts was an intellectualized construction that lent itself to the production of stereotypical formulas. If we may judge by the repetition of these formulas, some artists and their patrons came to understand the allegory as a source of decorative imagery rather than as a power capable of transforming the experience of the faithful at the moment of entrance. This stereotyping can be seen as one phase in a broader development that saw the transformation and eventual decline of the allegory of the church.

Part Four

Secular Transformations

12

The Search for the New: Politics, Pilgrimage, and Economics

The allegory of the church was not a doctrine, but a habit of mind, a mental framework, that manifested itself especially in the design of the Romanesque portal. To the extent that any particular church was perceived not merely to represent but to be Christ and his Church, it was natural for it to 'speak' in one voice or the other to the community of worshippers, and for that voice to be given visible expression in the Latin verses that were carved above (or below) the portal. But as time went on, the sense of 'real presence' diminished. Churches were more likely to be allegorized as symbols than as signs. Various influences combined in different degrees in different regions to effect this shift. These included the development of a new aesthetics of fashion, the utilization of art for political ends, an awareness of the economic advantages of promoting the cult of relics and pilgrimage traffic, the desire for fame and the beginnings of artistic autonomy, and patronage and the exaltation of the individual will – topics that will be explored in the final chapters.

The imperative to be up-to-date sets European culture after the year 1000 apart from most other cultures. People began to ask, and we have continued to ask ever since, not only, Is it the best? but also, Is it the latest? Changes in style and fashion occur over time in every culture, but the need to keep up with the latest fashion, to tear down and replace the outmoded style of yesterday, was new, and it has been an engine of rapid change and innovation.

Two related factors contributed to fostering an interest in keeping up with the latest in style. One was the developing sense that an unbridgeable chasm existed between the 'ancients' and the 'moderns.'[1] The ancients might be admired or despised, but their world could never be re-entered. There was a past with its own set of values that was distinctly 'past.' *Modernus,* the word for 'modern,' entered late Latin in the sixth century.[2] Although Christ inaugurated a new age, he belonged to the irrecoverable past of antiquity; he was not a modern. The other factor was the growing realization that the gulf between the ancients and the moderns, between 'them' and 'us,' was itself a long segment of historical time, a 'period.' Terms for that period like the 'Middle Ages' and the 'Dark Ages' had yet to be invented. But the perception of an intermediate past that was 'dark' in contrast to the light of the ancients and the light of the moderns lay behind the series of 'renaissances' that began with the Carolingians and extended to the Italian Renaissance.[3]

Novelty was in the air. Philosophers and theologians disputed over *quaestiones,* which led to new insights and to new uncertainties. Adventuresome minds delighted in the idea that they were exploring the frontiers of thought, while sober critics saw the dangers to faith posed by unrestrained questioning of the mysteries of religion. Toward the end of his life Gerhoh of Reichersberg (1093–1169) composed a *Liber de Novitatibus huius Temporis,* in which he deplored the fatuousness of those who, seduced by the wisdom of the world, called into question doctrines already settled by the doctors of the Church.[4] He was using the word *novitas* as a term of abuse, but, as Beryl Smalley has shown, during the course of the twelfth century words for the new and for change began to acquire a positive value. There were new orders of monks and friars, military orders, and orders of canons regular; new choices and opportunities for careers in the secular world; new kinds of learning; new forms in art and architecture; all of which were recognized and often approved of by contemporary witnesses.[5]

When western culture began to differentiate between the 'old-fashioned' and the 'up-to-date,' it necessarily gave more weight to the subjective aspect of beauty. Although beauty was not yet 'in the eye of the beholder,' it was treated as though it were located somewhere between the organic form and the perceiver rather than exclusively in divinely ordained proportions and harmonies. Umberto Eco documents movements toward a more subjectively determined concept of beauty in the theoreticians of the thirteenth century and after.[6] The seeds of this aesthetic shift were sown in the fertile soil of the early Romanesque.

The desire to be up-to-date, the determination to be *al of the newe jet,* as Chaucer says of the Pardoner in *The Canterbury Tales,*[7] can be discerned in the often-quoted words of the monk Raoul Glaber (ca. 985–ca. 1046):

> So on the threshold of the aforesaid thousandth year, some two or three years after it, it befell almost throughout the world, but especially in Italy and Gaul, that the fabrics of churches were rebuilt, although many of these were still seemly and needed no such care; but every nation of Christendom rivalled with the other, which should worship in the seemliest buildings. So it was as though the very world had shaken herself and cast off her old age, and were clothing herself everywhere in a white garment of churches.[8]

Raoul's primary concern is with splendour of form and renewal, not novelty. He makes clear that there was a competition to see what region could devise the most beautiful buildings.[9] But if a building were already beautiful and in good repair, and yet was replaced, what could this competition be except a search for new ways of achieving beauty?

Raoul Glaber was a monk at the abbey of Saint-Bénigne of Dijon during the abbacy of William of Volpiano. The abbey church of Saint-Bénigne was the site of a local pilgrimage to the tomb of Saint Benignus, the apostle of Burgundy. It was entirely rebuilt in the ninth century when the abbey accepted the Benedictine rule. William of Volpiano was sent there by Cluny and rebuilt the church again starting in the year 1001. William's church is famous because of the rotunda that he built, the crypt of which still survives as the crypt of the present church.[10] Then in 1137 the church was damaged by a disastrous fire. Abbot Peter of Geneva (1129–ca. 1141) and his successor Peter of Beaune (1142–5) undertook the rebuilding of the old church. Restoration work extended over the next decade. Peter of Geneva is believed to have engaged sculptors who had worked at Saint-Denis under Abbot Suger. A triple portal with symbolic ornamentation in the new fashion of Saint-Denis was added. Thus, the symbolic façade constituted a decisive break with the decoration of the old church.

This Romanesque church in its turn was torn down and replaced by a Gothic church in the thirteenth and fourteenth centuries, but a tympanum from one of the portals of the Romanesque church was re-employed, and so survived. Another tympanum that perhaps decorated the entrance to the cloister was buried beneath the foundations of a buttress on the north side of the church and was dug up in 1833. The theme of the portal tympanum is the Last Supper, and that of the cloister tympanum is Christ in Majesty.

In the portal tympanum of the Last Supper Christ is at the centre of the table, holding a circular loaf of bread. An inscription on the lintel declares in the voice of the Church:

Cum rudis ante forem, dedit hunc michi Petrus honorem.
Mutans horrorem forma meliore priorem.[11]
(Since I was formerly crude, Peter gave me this adornment, changing my previous uncouthness for a better form.)

In the cloister tympanum of Christ in Majesty, Christ is in a mandorla that is supported by four angels (fig. 20). The Four Animals are on the outer edges. Along the base of the tympanum a verse inscription, which is clearly related to the inscription in the same place on the tympanum of the Last Supper, states:

Reddidit amissum michi Petri cura decorem
Et dedit antiqua formam multo meliorem.[12]
(The care of Peter has restored my lost beauty and given me a form better by far than the old.)

'Peter' in both inscriptions probably refers to Abbot Peter of Geneva.

The two verse inscriptions drew the attention of worshippers to the contrast between the new symbolic façade and the old church, which appeared crude in comparison. In the verses, the words for beauty are *honor* ('adornment'), *decor* ('beauty'), and *forma* ('form'). The antithesis of beauty is expressed by the negative adjectives *rudis* ('crude') and *antiquus* ('old'), and by the noun *horror* ('uncouthness'). Of course, beauty that had been 'lost' as a result of a fire had to be 'restored.' But the old 'form,' that is, the church of William of Volpiano, one of those churches that to Raoul Glaber seemed to be clothing the world 'in a white garment,' was 'crude,' even a *horror*. A *horror* is something that literally makes your hair stand on end. Gislebertus used the word to describe the images of hell on his tympanum of Last Judgment at Autun (fig. 8). It expresses the extreme of deformity. The idea of beauty as an objectively determined, transcendental value, was subtly undermined when a building came to seem crude because it was old and out of date (even if Abbot Peter and his contemporaries believed that the builders of the earlier generation simply failed to imitate beauty adequately).

The allegory of the church was never insulated from the political turmoil of a dynamic era. Every portal asserts something about the beliefs and interests of its builders that goes beyond the strictly spiritual. The chrismon, the two lions, and the emphasis the inscriptions put upon the *duplex* nature of things in the tympanum of Jaca (fig. 12) are crucial to an understanding of its moral allegory, but they function as well to proclaim the importance of Jaca's dual role as the capital of a royal kingdom and the seat of a bishopric at a time during the Spanish Reconquest when its primacy was threatened by the recapture of the ancient episcopal see of Huesca by Christian forces in 1096.[13]

Strife within the bosom of the Church also worked its way into portal programs. A tympanum depicting Samson wrestling down the lion from the former Benedictine priory church of Saint-Pierre of Mauriac includes in the right-hand corner the figure of a man clothed in monastic garments and holding an abbot's staff. This personage witnesses the struggle and perhaps speaks the words inscribed on the lower frame: 'See Samson having overcome the lion with his hands.'[14] A turbulent episode in the priory's history probably explains this unique addition to the tympanum subject of Samson and the Lion. Mauriac was a dependency of the abbey of Saint-Pierre-le-Vif of Sens. However, at the beginning of the twelfth century, the bishop of Clermont attempted to wrest control of the priory away from the abbey. After being thwarted in an attempt to instal a nominee of his own as prior, the bishop secretly supported Pierre de la Balderie, the replacement named by the Council of Troyes in 1104. Prior Pierre was a man of a violent temper. He quarrelled with the parish priest of Mauriac, and when the priest complained of his treatment to the abbot of Saint-Pierre-le-Vif, Pierre had his eyes torn out. Abbot Arnauld summoned Pierre to Sens, but the prior refused to go. Arnauld then took his problem to a papal legate, who demanded that the bishop of Clermont excommunicate Pierre, which the bishop refused to do. Arnauld had to come in person to Mauriac in 1109 to expel the prior and replace him with a new one. No sooner had this been accomplished than Pierre led an armed revolt against Arnauld and the new prior. Arnauld appealed to the archbishop of Bourges and the king of France to intervene on his behalf with the papal legate, who finally came to Mauriac, excommunicated Pierre de la Balderie, and had him incarcerated in the castle of Ventadour in 1110. The bishop of Clermont repented of his actions and came for refuge to Mauriac, where he died the tenth of October, 1111. Thus, it seems likely that the monks of Mauriac saw in the theme of Samson triumphing over the lion, traditionally interpreted as a sign of the struggle of the Church against evil, a pertinent analogue to the triumph of the abbot of Sens over the revolted prior and the bishop of Clermont, and that, to make the analogy clearer, they added the figure of the observing abbot to the tympanum. They may even have seen a providential pun in the names 'Samson' [*Sanson*] and 'Sens' [*Senones*].[15]

The canons of Saint-Sernin of Toulouse used the extended programmatic space surrounding the tympanum of the Porte Miègeville to interpret some painful events of the last quarter of the eleventh century in a light favourable to themselves. The theme of the Ascension of Christ in the tympanum (fig. 10) is enriched by the sculptural program of the façade. The portal is enclosed by a shallow porch. At the level of the tympanum, the façade of the porch forms a large rectangular space enclosing the arch that frames the tympanum. On the left side of the rectangle, there is a bas-relief of Saint James the Greater; on the right side, there is a bas-relief of Saint Peter (fig. 38).

At Toulouse, both the cathedral of Saint-Étienne and the church of Saint-Sernin had been served in the eleventh century by canons closely tied to the local aristocracy. The canons of Saint-Sernin allowed the revenues of their church to be diverted to the interests of the city's leading families. It was abuse of this kind that led Pope Gregory VII (1073–85) to forbid clerical marriage and simony and to attack lay investiture. In that spirit Bishop Isarn of Toulouse (ca. 1072–1105) reformed the cathedral-chapter in 1073, imposing a rule of poverty, communal life, and obedience. Count William IV of Toulouse approved this reform and agreed to give up to the canons his inherited right to nominate the bishop. At about the same time the clergy of Saint-Sernin adopted the canonical life according to the Augustinian rule, but they chose to place themselves directly under the authority of the pope. Neither Bishop Isarn nor Count William was prepared to tolerate this challenge to their local authority. They expelled the canons in 1082 and installed Cluniac monks from Moissac under the ultimate authority of Abbot Hugh of Cluny. The canons appealed to the pope, who insisted firmly on the privileges he had granted. The canons were reinstated.[16]

Thus, the bas-relief of Saint Peter on the right side of the façade rectangle that encloses the Ascension tympanum of Saint-Sernin not only invokes the pilgrimage city of Rome but it also honours the papacy that had prevented the canons from being displaced by Cluniac monks, just as the bas-relief of Saint James the Greater on the left side of the rectangle stresses the importance of this church as one of the major stations on the pilgrimage route to Santiago of Compostela.

Rhetorically based principles of composition permitted complex and even discordant ideas to be economically expressed in Romanesque art.[17] Beneath Saint Peter there is a bas-relief of Simon Magus, which involves the use of comparison (juxtaposition), contrast (antithesis or dissimilitude), and paronomasia (verbal and visual punning).[18] The two reliefs are related by juxtaposition – they are aligned one above the other on the same vertical axis. Of course, the Simon Magus plaque is subordinated by its smaller size and its position beneath the feet of Peter (hierarchical antithesis). Since Saint Peter in the gospel account (Matt. 10:2) is referred to as 'Simon, called Peter,' the two reliefs pun on the name of *Simon.*

The story of Simon Magus, as told in the Bible, goes like this:

> Now a man named Simon had previously been practising sorcery in [the city of Samaria] and astounding the people of Samaria, claiming to be someone great ... And they gave heed to him because for a long time he had bewitched them with his sorceries. But when they believed Philip as he preached ... the name of Jesus Christ, they were baptized ... And Simon also himself believed ...; and at sight of the signs and exceedingly great miracles being wrought, he was amazed.
>
> Now when the apostles in Jerusalem heard that Samaria had received the word of God, they sent to them Peter and John ... Then they laid their hands on them and they received the Holy Spirit. But when Simon saw that the Holy Spirit was given through the laying on of the apostles' hands, he offered them money, saying, 'Give me also this power, so that anyone on whom I lay my hands may receive the Holy Spirit.' But Peter said to him, 'Thy money go to destruction with thee, because thou hast thought that the gift of God could be purchased with money ...' (Acts 8:9–24)

What the Middle Ages knew about Simon Magus was not limited to the Bible, however. There were apocryphal stories about him, which told how Peter and Simon Magus went to Rome in the time of the Emperor Nero, and how they challenged each other to feats of magic – contests that Peter inevitably won.[19] At last, as Simon's followers lost heart and began to fall away, he threatened to forsake them and fly up to God. The next day a crowd gathered at the Sacred Way to watch the flight, and Peter came too. Simon stood on a high place, and after a short speech rose into the air.

> And behold when he was lifted up on high, and all beheld him raised up above all Rome and the temples thereof and the mountains, the faithful looked toward Peter. And Peter seeing the strangeness of the sight cried unto the Lord Jesus Christ: If thou suffer this man to accomplish that which he hath set about, now will all they that have believed on thee be offended, and the signs and wonders which thou hast given them through me will not

> be believed: hasten thy grace, O Lord, and let him fall from the height and be disabled; and let him not die but be brought to nought, and break his leg in three places. And he fell from the height and brake his leg in three places.[20]

Evidently, the artist had some version of this apocryphal story in mind. Simon is holding his thigh – indicating that his leg was crushed in the fall. Two demons strain mightily to lift him up; their tongues hang out with the effort.

In the background above Simon's head is the word MAGVS. There is an inscription on the lower edge of the plaque beneath his feet, which can be transcribed as follows: 'ARTE FVREN MAGICA SIMON IN SVA COCI.' The word *Simon* is carved in larger letters than the rest of the inscription. Additional letters appear in the background between the legs of Simon and the demons: a backwards S, the word ARMA, and the letters DIT. The inscription makes no obvious sense, yet it cannot be dismissed as an ignorant blunder on the part of the sculptor. Too much care has been taken with the carving of the plaque and the inscription is too bizarre for this to be anything but a deliberate puzzle. It defeated the ingenuity of scholars until Robert Favreau and his colleagues proposed a common leonine hexameter as a solution:

> Arte furens magica Simon in sua occidit arma.[21]
> *(Led astray by his magical art, Simon succumbs to his own weapons.)*

They assume that the final letter of *furens* and the final syllable of *occidit* have been displaced to the background of the scene above, that the last word of the verse was placed just above the name *Simon*, and that the first two letters of *occidit* were transposed. Since the solution requires hiatus between the fourth and fifth feet (*sua:occidit*), it could be argued in support of it that the transposition of the first two letters of *occidit* was a device to block hiatus (*sua cocidit*). Similar wordplay occurs in the verses that were once inscribed on the west façade.[22] The disorder in the inscription might have been intended to mirror Simon's violation of the natural order in his magic arts.

Now we can see what the artist was trying to do in the scene under Peter's feet. He has interpreted the story of Simon Magus in relation to the story of Christ's Ascension (Acts 1:9–11) depicted on the tympanum and found a parallel. Simon is a type of the Antichrist. The aftermath of Simon's ill-fated flight is depicted as a failed, demonic ascension.[23] That is why the artist does not depict the flight itself. Simon has already fallen; the demons trying to lift him huff and puff, but get nowhere. But the two angels lifting Christ have no trouble at all.

Pope Gregory's attack on lay investiture and the buying and selling of church offices laid bare one of the most important and divisive issues of the eleventh century. Appointments to important positions in the Church had become inextricably mixed up with feudalism. Since so much real political power was in the hands of the Church, lay rulers felt they had the right to appoint the men they wanted to hold key offices and to demand payment for their appointment. This abuse (as Gregory and his successors saw it) was called 'simony' after Simon Magus.[24] So these reliefs cloak the quarrel of the canons of Saint-Sernin with Bishop Isarn and Count William in the mantle of contemporary political correctness. Isarn might have seen the issue differently. It was he, after all, who had instituted the reforms in Toulouse in the first place. Isarn's predecessor as bishop of Toulouse was Abbot Durand of Moissac (1047–72 / bishop 1060–72). Durand had been sent to Moissac from Cluny to reinvigorate the dilapidated monastery and make it a base for Cluny's policy of penetration into Spain. He and Isarn regarded the apostolic life as embodied in the Cluniac reform of the monastic order as the ideal model of communal living, and Isarn's move to instal Cluniac monks from Moissac in Saint-Sernin can be viewed as another reform effort, reflecting his preference for the monastic order over the canonical order.[25]

Under the statue of Saint James, there is a relief, corresponding to the Simon Magus plaque, of two women seated on lions and being embraced by a bearded man, which must have been intended to relate in some way to the Ascension theme of the portal and the political issues associated with it. It is in balanced 'asymmetrical opposition' to the Simon Magus plaque.[26] The women, it has been suggested, may represent Priscilla (Prisca) and Maximilla (Maximillia), prophets and followers of the second-century heresiarch Montanus. Canon Raymond Gayrard, who had charge of the second building campaign of Saint-Sernin, would thus have 'realised his goal "of making an apology and a praise of orthodox humility in contrast to the vanity of all heresies."'[27]

Another sculpture perhaps holds the key to the completion of the iconographical program of the Porte Miègeville. The sixteenth-century historian of Toulouse, Noguier, described a marble statue of a naked man that was in his time attached to one of the piers of the nave in Saint-Sernin. In 1651 it was removed on account of its nudity and was lost or destroyed.[28] The man was life-sized, his feet were together ('les piés ioints') and his arms extended downwards, palms out. He was set in a mandorla, on the rim of which was inscribed a rhymed hexameter couplet: 'After the meritorious death of the body, because of its pious service, the part [= the soul, represented by the Naked Man] which rises thus, that does not die, goes to heaven.'[29] The Naked Man was almost certainly a representation of the soul of the martyred Saint Sernin ascending to heaven.[30] This conjecture is strengthened by the fact that Noguier's description could be applied almost verbatim to the capital of the Soul of Saint Sernin in Glory in the east walk of the cloister of Moissac. To be sure, the size of the man is much reduced, but he is naked, his legs are tightly crossed ('les piés ioints'?), and his arms are extended downwards, palms out.[31]

Before its destruction in the French Revolution, the sculptural program of the west façade of Saint-Sernin featured Saint Sernin and Saint Martial. Marcel Durliat argues that the program was probably intended to include the Martyrdom of Saint Sernin, but that the death of Canon Raymond Gayrard in 1118 disrupted the work, and that the pieces already carved were set in place at random. He also thinks that other pieces that were once located elsewhere in the church, among them the Naked Man and a marble plaque of the Signs of the Lion and the Ram, may have been intended for this program.[32] Both the Porte des Comtes and the Porte Miègeville have also been proposed as locations for these two pieces.[33] Wherever the representation of Saint Sernin ascending to heaven was placed, it would have strengthened the grand theme of Ascension and tied in the Porte Miègeville with the martyr's cult. Not only was the basilica of Saint-Sernin a major station on the pilgrimage to Compostela, but Toulouse was the city that had given the First Crusade (1095–9) its first military leader, Count Raymond IV.[34] By contrasting the Christian faith of their martyr with the infidelity of Simon Magus, the canons of Saint-Sernin may have been claiming the merits of the saint for themselves and the Augustinian order of canons, as against Moissac (which appropriated the saint's glory even though it lost its claim to the saint's basilica) and the monastic orders, in the struggle against the pagan infidel both in Spain and Palestine that was so closely associated with Toulouse.

Surging numbers of people going on pilgrimage in the eleventh and twelfth centuries generated a creative ferment that upset the settled order of things and led to change. The most popular and influential pilgrimage in these years was not to Rome but to the shrine of Christ's disciple, Saint James the Greater, at Santiago of Compostela in north-west

Spain.[35] Early in the Christian era the doctrine of the *divisio apostolorum* developed, which assumed that a different portion of the world had been assigned to each of the apostles for their evangelic mission. Saint James was responsible for Spain and the west.[36] Sometime around the year 800, news spread through Europe that the saint's body had been found at Compostela.[37] After the Moors raided Compostela in 997, Saint James acquired a reputation as a champion against the Muslim infidels in the Spanish Reconquest, and in the course of time so many pilgrims flocked to his shrine that provision had to be made to accommodate them. Hospices and monasteries and other pilgrimage churches along the roads offered shelter and food a day's journey apart.

Artisans who worked on one pilgrimage church moved on or were sent on to another when they had finished, so that works by the same individual turn up hundreds of miles apart in different provinces and countries. Islamic designs and even Kufic inscriptions at places like Le Puy and Conques suggest that some of these workers came from Moorish backgrounds or had had contact with Moorish art.[38] Because they were itinerants, artists and builders had an economic incentive to promote the latest ideas in their trade as a way of gaining employment. By the same token, the monasteries that were their principal employers likewise had an economic incentive, even if they would not have seen it in quite those terms, to replace their outmoded churches and embellish them with the latest fashions in art. Pilgrimage traffic brought enormous wealth in treasure and lands to abbeys that were endowed with notable relics. The efficacy of the relics in restoring health to the body and the soul was paramount, but it is not difficult to understand that opinions on that point would have been influenced by the splendour of the art and the magnificence of the buildings that surrounded them, and that the abbeys recognized this fact. Competitive artistic ferment on the routes to Compostela put a premium on the new.

Like many of the churches along the routes, Conques was itself the object of pilgrimage. Crowds of pilgrims and the cult of relics created the need for pilgrimage churches to be constructed on a large scale and in an appropriate, functional design. The abbey of Conques is located in rugged mountainous country in south-central France, and there the present basilica was begun sometime after 1042. It is remote and difficult to reach even today, yet at the height of its power and prestige at the beginning of the twelfth century, the abbey ruled a monastic empire that rivalled Cluny in the number of its dependencies and its geographical reach.[39] It had possessions as far away as England. One of its monks became bishop of

Pamplona in about 1080. He consecrated an altar to Saint Foy in the cathedral of Compostela.[40] Monks from Conques constructed the monastic church of Sant'Antimo in Tuscany in 1118, at about the same time that the tympanum master of Conques or one of his disciples was employed at Compostela to work on the sculptures for the south transept portals. Taking the abbey church of Conques as representative of the great basilicas of the pilgrimage routes, two questions may be asked. What factors enabled the abbey to attract pilgrims and gain wealth and power? And how did the sculptural program of the church portal contribute to this prosperity?

The legend of Saint Foy (Latin – Sancta Fides; Spanish – Santa Fe; English – Saint Faith), the story of the theft and removal of her relics from their original resting place in Agen to Conques, and the miracles attributed to them provide a partial answer to the first question. The primary sources for these stories are the *Passion of Saints Faith and Caprasius*,[41] the *Metrical Passion* in leonine hexameters,[42] the *Chanson de Sainte Foy* in Provençal octosyllabics,[43] and the *Translation of Saint Faith.*[44] According to these tenth- and eleventh-century accounts, Saint Foy was born into an aristocratic Gallo-Roman family in the city of Agen, which is located on the Garonne River about a hundred miles west of Conques, late in the third century. In the course of the persecutions of Diocletian, the prefect Dacien arrived at Agen, and Saint Caprais and other Christians of the city fled into the hills. Dacien summoned Saint Foy, who was barely twelve years old,[45] into his presence. He demanded that she sacrifice to the goddess Diana, but she refused. She was stretched out on a grill of red-hot iron, and then beheaded. Saint Caprais beheld a vision of her crown of martyrdom and returned to Agen to suffer in his turn. Many years later Saint Foy's relics, which had been hidden from the persecutors, were recovered and placed in a mausoleum inside the church at Agen, where they performed miracles of healing.

Meanwhile, a Benedictine monastery was founded at Conques in the remote and isolated hills of Rouergue. Conques enjoyed the favour and support of Charlemagne and his son, Louis the Pious. For reasons that remain unstated in the *Translation*, but which may have been related to the monastery's isolation and lack of suitable relics,[46] the monks of Conques became obsessed with a desire to obtain for themselves the relics of Saint Foy. They sent one of their number, a monk by the name of Ariviscus or Arinisdus,[47] to Agen. Ariviscus dressed as a pilgrim priest and declared his intention of settling there. He gained such a reputation for sanctity that the brothers of the monastery that possessed the body of

Saint Foy asked him to join them, and after a time they appointed him guardian of the tomb. One night, when the brothers were dining in the refectory during the feast of the Epiphany, Ariviscus broke into the mausoleum, took the relics, and set out for Conques. The monks of Agen pursued him, but miraculously he escaped detection.[48] This theft, which the monks of Conques regarded as authorized by the saint, took place about 866.[49] From that time on, the prosperity and fame of Conques were assured.

Shortly after the arrival of her relics at Conques, late in the ninth century, a three-foot-high seated statue of Saint Foy, all in gold, was made to house them. It was placed on the main altar of the church. The statue is a heterogeneous Carolingian work of art, with bits and pieces of old jewellery stuck on all over – glowing testimony to the medieval fascination with radiance as an aesthetic principle. The shining of precious stones was a reflection of the divine light.[50]

When Bernard of Angers travelled through the Auvergne on his way to Conques in 1013, he was initially scandalized but nevertheless nearly overpowered by the sight of the seated statues, the 'majesties,' of the local saints that were displayed in the churches and carried in procession through the countryside: 'And I ... thought this practice seemed perverse and quite contrary to Christian law when for the first time I examined the statue of Saint Gerald placed above the altar [in Aurillac], gloriously fashioned out of the purest gold and the most precious stones. It was an image made with such precision to the face of the human form that it seemed to see with its attentive, observant gaze the great many peasants seeing it and to gently grant with its reflecting eyes the prayers of those praying before it.'[51] Three days later he saw the statue of Saint Foy. It is difficult to say what made the deeper impression: the human form of the statue, the beauty and value of its ornaments and of the other precious objects of the abbey, the relics it contained, or the riches that poured in on the abbey as a consequence of the miracles that Saint Foy performed. Not least in importance was the fact that the statue of Saint Foy had been remodelled according to contemporary taste:

> The image represents the pious memory of the holy virgin before which, quite properly and with abundant remorse, the faithful implore her intercession for their sins ... after the renown of the great miracle worked for Guibert (called 'the Illuminated') flew across the whole of Europe, many of the faithful made over their own manors and many other pious gifts to Sainte Foy by the authority of their wills. And though the abbey had long ago been

> poor, by these donations it began to grow rich and to be raised up in esteem. In the time before Guibert's era the place was not adorned with so many golden or silver reliquary boxes, nor so many crosses or great basins ... The most outstanding of the ornaments then was the splendid image, which was made long ago. Today it would be considered one of the poorer ornaments if it had not been reshaped anew and renovated into a better figure.[52]

Bernard's collection of miracle stories about Saint Foy was itself a vital factor in the development of her shrine into an international centre of pilgrimage.[53] The west portal of the eleventh-century basilica was designed to accommodate the ever larger number of pilgrims coming to venerate the relics. Early in the twelfth century the vast tympanum of Last Judgment was carved (fig. 1). To modern viewers, the tympanum is a work of art. The monks of Conques would surely have appreciated its aesthetic qualities; but as far as they were concerned, its primary function may have been a combination of the religious and the economic – specifically, the edification of the pilgrims who entered the basilica through the west portal and an appeal to their generosity. If Bernard of Angers was so moved by the majesty of Saint Foy in 1013, what an impact this tympanum must have had on pilgrims one hundred years later!

Perhaps the monks of Conques provided guides to explain the scenes and translate the inscriptions for the benefit of the pilgrims. One scene that the pilgrims might have viewed with greater comprehension if they had the benefit of a knowledgeable guide was the procession of persons approaching Christ from the left (from the viewer's perspective) (fig. 2). In the procession, only the Virgin Mary and Saint Peter on the right, and four small figures at the far left, have halos. The others, presumably, were important persons connected with the history of the abbey of Conques, who had not been officially sainted. The man next to Peter, facing full forward, is bearded and moustached. He leans on a hermit's staff, which is in the form of a T. This may be the hermit Dado, who founded the abbey.[54] Behind Dado is an abbot, probably one of the abbots of Conques, recognizable by his monk's tonsure and his abbot's staff. He is leading by the hand a figure wearing a crown and carrying a sceptre – a monarch, possibly Charlemagne, the legendary benefactor of the abbey.[55] A guide might have pointed out the discrepancy between the visual scene of the procession of the chosen toward Christ and the verse that accompanies it. The verse inscription above the heads of Charlemagne and the abbot announces: 'The assembly of saints stands joyfully before Christ the Judge.'[56] The abbot is erect and confident, but Charlemagne shuffles along with his head and shoulders hunched.[57] He seems far from certain of the reception he will get. Doubtless he has much to be pardoned for, but the two monks who follow him, one bearing a diptych, the other a reliquary delicately set on a cloth, bring the evidence for his defence – namely his generosity to the treasury of Conques.

This pointed pleasantry at the expense of their royal benefactor, evidently the result of collaboration between the tympanum master and the poet, acquires a sharper edge when the eye, guided by the principles of juxtaposition and contrast employed by the tympanum master, takes in the torments of hell. In the stone block on the right of the tympanum that corresponds to the one on the left with Charlemagne, there is another crowned king. A demon holds him by the hand. With his other hand the demon draws the king's head toward his mouth and prepares to swallow his crown. The king is naked and he points across the tympanum toward Charlemagne, perhaps as a despairing reminder of the opportunity for salvation that is forever lost to him. The abbot who holds Charlemagne's hand is in axial alignment with Abraham in the heavenly city in the lower register, just as the demon holding the hand of the naked king is in axial alignment with Satan in hell.

No sin is more prominently depicted or severely chastized on the tympanum than lack of generosity or avarice. A miser, suspended by a rope around his neck, with his bag of useless gold flopping against his chest, swings helplessly against Satan's left side.[58] His head droops to the right. One snake coils itself around his legs, while another attaches itself to his face. Satan's pointing finger rests on the front of his short skirt. The figure of the miser with his money bag about his neck was a popular image in Romanesque art. Meyer Schapiro attributes the increased emphasis on the sin of avarice in the twelfth century to the rise of an urban mercantile class and the growth of a money economy.[59] No doubt the monastic orders were sincere in deploring this sin, but perhaps the monks of Conques were not alone in using the image of the miser to imply a causal link between financial generosity to the abbey and salvation, and to show in the clearest manner the dire consequence of keeping one's wealth to oneself. They were surely aware of the economic benefits of promoting their abbey as a pilgrimage church. The message to pilgrims visiting Conques would have been obvious: a generous donation was their guarantee of salvation.

The need for change was an implicit message of the pilgrimage routes. This new preoccupation with keeping up-to-date with the latest in fashion was, at least in part, a product of the economic and spiritual rivalries of the monastic empires of the Romanesque period as they competed for the faithful admiration of the pilgrims. By directing the attention of builders and worshippers alike to the surface appearance of portal designs and how they compared with designs in other churches along the pilgrimage roads, monasteries emphasized the role of human agency and its purposes. What immediate effect, if any, this would have had on the way the church was allegorized is imponderable. But, over time, it might have done much to encourage the habit of looking at the church as though it were a text written by men referring to a reality to be found elsewhere – that is, as an allegory commemorating rather than embodying the things that it signified.

13

Artists and the Pursuit of Fame

The myth that artisans in the Middle Ages were content to labour humbly and anonymously for the glory of God on the construction of great churches and in the creation of magnificent art dies hard. In fact, many of them managed to inscribe their names, often prominently, somewhere on their work.[1] The desire for personal fame seems to have been just as deeply ingrained in men of the Romanesque period as at most other times in human history. It is true that artists were less likely to sign their names to large sculptural programs, particularly in monastic churches, than to smaller pieces of work, like an altar, a capital, or a door knocker. We do not know the names of the tympanum masters of Conques and Moissac, to take only two examples of early-twelfth-century artists with, we might guess, powerful personalities who worked on a large scale. The signatures of Girauldus (GIRAVLDVS / FECIT ISTAS PORTAS) on the tympanum of Saint-Ursin of Bourges and Gislebertus on the tympanum of Autun (fig. 25) are exceptional in France. Social custom and institutional constraints probably had more to do with this than any inability of the artists to conceive of themselves as autonomous individuals deserving of personal recognition. It may be that abbots regarded themselves as the only true 'makers' in their abbeys and were unwilling to tolerate competition from their subordinates and hirelings. In general, urban bishops seem to have been more relaxed in their attitude toward artists and more tolerant of their desire to record their names.

Who the person was whose name is carved in stone is not always easy to discover. It might be that of the sculptor or stonecutter, the masterbuilder, the author of the inscription, the abbot or bishop with immediate or ultimate responsibility for the project, or some wealthy donor or patron. Artisans were unlikely to have their names recorded in documentary sources. Often we have only the evidence of the inscriptions themselves, which can be bafflingly vague. Nevertheless, they do offer some clues. Most important is the help they give in distinguishing the work of the artisan from the role of the patron or administrator. Names were almost always inscribed in stereotyped phrases. There was one formula that applied to artists and another that was reserved for patronage, though the former could be used for patronage as well so that caution has to be exercized in drawing firm conclusions. Sculptors and other artists signed their works with the formula, *[X] me fecit*, '[name of artist] made me.'[2] In its simplest form, the formula used by patrons was *[X] me fieri fecit*, '[name of patron] caused me to be made.'[3] The artists' formula was almost always expressed in the 'voice' of the created object (the church, the sculpture, the mosaic, etc.); the patronage formula as often as not shifted to the third person: e.g., *[X] hoc opus fieri fecit*, '[name of patron] caused this work to be made.' And there were numerous variants.

By the end of the eleventh century, the *[X]-me-fecit* formula was already in use by sculptors. At Saint-Benoît-sur-Loire, perhaps in the 1080s, the sculptor Unbertus signed a capital in the porch VNBERTVS ME FECIT. In the interior of the south transept of Conques an angel carries a banderole with the inscription BERNARDVS ME FECIT.[4] Bernard Gelduin applied the formula to the marble altar table that he carved for Saint-Sernin of Toulouse in 1096. The woodcarver Gauzfredus employed it on the great wooden doors of the cathedral of Le Puy toward the middle of the twelfth century. Giralus or Giraldus inscribed it on one of the bronze door knockers he cast for Saint-Julien of Brioude. A *Rotbertus me fecit* signature identifies the sculptor Robert at Notre-Dame-du-Port of Clermont-Ferrand;[5] the sculptor Brunus signed his work in this fashion at Saint-Gilles.[6] The verb *facere* was ambiguous; it could also denote the activity of a patron, particularly one with executive responsibility for the work at hand. Sometimes more specific verbs were used, which leave no doubt that they referred to the labours of the artist. Italian artists favoured *sculpere*, a verb that also occurs in a verse on a keystone from the narthex of Cluny.[7] Gilabertus, who carved the sculptures for the chapter house of the cathedral of Toulouse, used the verb *celare*, 'to engrave, or carve.'[8]

Several sculptors in Italy in the first half of the twelfth century – Wiligelmo, Niccolò, and Niccolò's assistant Guglielmo – took advantage of the Romanesque taste for verse inscriptions to sign their names prominently and assertively to their works.

A dedication ceremony was held in June of the year 1099 to mark the beginning of the construction of the new cathedral of San Geminiano of Modena. The architect or master-builder of the cathedral was Lanfranc, who was also responsible for the cathedrals of Cremona and Piacenza and the abbey church of Nonantola.[9] Decoration was entrusted to the sculptor Wiligelmo. By 1106 construction had progressed to the point where the translation of the saint's relics into the new building could be undertaken. Lanfranc refused to continue work until this had been accomplished, probably because the old church, which occupied the site of the present nave, could then be demolished, permitting the next stage of construction to go forward.[10] Two dedication inscriptions in verse recorded the respective contributions of Lanfranc and Wiligelmo. They are, at present, at opposite ends of the church, though these are not their original locations, and one of them is a thirteenth-century copy. It appears that both were composed, at least in part, for the dedication ceremony in 1099. The one that mentions Lanfranc was the effort of a certain Canon Aimo; Wiligelmo may have composed the other himself. To the best of my knowledge this is the only Romanesque church for which we have the name of both the builder and the sculptor. Certainly no other church has two dedication plaques for the same date.

The plaque with Aimo's dedicatory verses is inserted into the exterior surface of the central apse above the lower apse window. It is a copy of the lost original, made at the order of Bozzalino, who was the foreman of the cathedral workshop from 1208 to 1225. Aimo's poem constitutes the first twelve lines, which are in Roman capitals; the last two lines of the inscription, in Gothic lettering, refer to Bozzalino. The inscription, with Bozzalino's addition, states:

> This cathedral gleams on every side with beautiful sculpted blocks of marble, where the body of Saint Geminianus lies at rest, whom, full of praise, the whole earth celebrates, and especially we the clergy whom he feeds, nourishes, and clothes. Whoever seeks here a true cure for limbs and soul, ... returns from here erect and with recovered health. Lanfranc, famed for his talent, learned and able, is the chief of this work, its guide and master. What he determined to be created, the present poem reveals [?]. Then, before the fifth day of the Ides of June [= 9 June] had gleamed, after 1099 years of the Lord [had passed], Aimo composed these verses suitable [?] for the occasion. – Bozzalino, the foreman of the workshop of San Geminiano, ordered this work to be done.[11]

Eric Fernie argues that Aimo could not have composed these verses until after the translation of Saint Geminianus into the cathedral in 1106 because the body is said to be inside.[12] But the inscription itself, if I have interpreted it correctly, states that Aimo composed it before the dedication ceremony in 1099. I do not see why he could not have anticipated the translation in his verses.

Nothing is certainly known of Wiligelmo beyond the fact that he carved the plaques on the west façade of Modena (fig. 15).[13] He may have been a German goldsmith,[14] although, if he wrote the verses for his sculptures, he seems to have been a fluent speaker of some dialect of Italian. He is sometimes tentatively identified with the sculptor who signed his name *Guillelmus* at San Zeno of Verona,[15] but M.F. Hearn gives convincing reasons for believing that the latter was an assistant of Niccolò, who was in turn trained by Wiligelmo at Modena.[16] As the years went by and the cathedral and its sculpted decoration came to completion, Aimo's poem may have rankled in Wiligelmo's mind. In it there was praise for the building and its sculpture, for its healing powers, for its architect Lanfranc, and for Aimo, but not a mention of the sculptor of those beautiful blocks of marble. Hearn has suggested that the marble plaque of the prophets Enoch and Elias, holding the dedication inscription with Wiligelmo's name (fig. 22), which is now high up on the west façade of the cathedral above one of the Genesis friezes, might have been placed originally on the wall in the crypt.[17] The inscription is in two parts – four hexameters which convey the dedication proper and an elegiac couplet which celebrates Wiligelmo:

Dum Gemini Cancer cursum consendit ovantes
Idibus in quintis Iunii sup tempore mensis
Mille Dei carnis monos centum minus annis,
Ista domus clari fundatur Geminiani.
Inter scultores quanto sis dignus onore,
  Claret scultura nunc, Wiligelme, tua.[18]

(While Cancer [June/July] mounts after triumphant Gemini [May/June] on the 5th Ides of the month of June [9 June] 1100 years minus one after the time of the Incarnation of God [1099], the foundation of this house of the illustrious Geminianus is laid. Now, Wiligelmo, this building shines with your sculpture; may you be worthy of as much honour among sculptors.)

Wiligelmo's inscription is oddly laid out. The first four verses are carved in large letters in ten lines. On this scale, there would have been room for eleven lines in all. It would have been nearly impossible to fit even one more verse in letters of the same size and spacing onto the plaque. Instead the elegiac couplet is carved in smaller letters[19] and squeezed into the remaining space in three lines. Perhaps Wiligelmo carved the first four verses at the time of the dedication of the cathedral in 1099 and added the elegiac couplet later, after he had completed the sculptural program of the west façade (ca. 1106–10). The added verses were apparently composed with a restricted space in mind, since they are made up of the minimum syllable count (13 + 12) for an elegiac couplet.

Immortality is the underlying theme of the inscription plaque with its sculpted figures of Enoch and Elias. Because they were believed to have ascended bodily to heaven (cf. Gen. 5:22–4 and 4 Kings 2:11), Enoch and Elias were considered to be prefigurations of the resurrection of the body and eternal life. Wiligelmo (assuming him to have been the poet as well as the sculptor) made a deliberate connection between Christian immortality (Enoch and Elias) and the immortality that comes from fame and that was his due as a sculptor.[20] By a play on words, visually emphasized by the placement of the name GEMINI/ANI on the inscription plaque, he linked the patron saint of the church, Geminianus, with *Gemini ovantes*, the 'triumphant Twins' (itself an allusion to that triumphant pair, Enoch and Elias), eternally wheeling in the sky, whose sign was ascendant at the moment when the church was dedicated. Just as the church was made beautiful or famous by the sculpture that he created, Wiligelmo in his turn hoped to achieve immortality through his work.

Self-confidence, pride, ambition, and an intense spirit of rivalry seem to have driven the men who worked on the cathedral of Modena. In this charged atmosphere it is easy to understand how Lanfranc and Wiligelmo came to regard the cathedral and the sculptural program as monuments to their own fame.

Niccolò belongs to the next generation of sculptors in Italy. Possibly taking a hint from his master Wiligelmo, he signed his name in verse on sculptural programs at four churches – Sacra di San Michele (ca. 1114–20), Ferrara (ca. 1132–5), San Zeno of Verona (ca. 1123–38), and the cathedral of Verona (ca. 1139–40). Niccolò's habit of repeating himself in verse enables us to identify him with virtual certainty as the sculptor at Piacenza (ca. 1107–20) as well.[21]

The Zodiac Portal (Porta dello Zodiaco) of Sacra di San Michele may have been one of Niccolò's first important commissions. The portal abuts the south side of the apse at the head of the Stairway of the Dead (Scalone dei Morti). The principal features of the decorative scheme that Niccolò carved for the portal are the signs of the zodiac and the stellar constellations on the inner (north) faces of the pilasters of the doorway. He signed his name on the pilaster on the west side of the doorway: 'Read the verses that Niccolò has written and carved [*descripsit Nicholaus*], you who are going up or perchance returning.'[22] The verses are in the voice of the portal that addresses the faithful who pass through it. But the voice refers back to the maker. Niccolò's choice of the verb *describere*, which means primarily 'to copy,' looks like a deliberate attempt on his part to find a word to express his dual role as poet and sculptor.[23] He probably meant that he both wrote and carved the verses.

Niccolò carved another verse on the pilaster on the opposite side of the doorway, which likewise refers to people coming and going through the portal. Although the end of the verse has been chipped away, it can be reconstructed because he put the same verse on the façade of the cathedral of Piacenza. At Piacenza it is on the lower edge of the lintel of the right portal, which depicts episodes in the life of Christ (the Presentation in the Temple, the Flight into Egypt, the Baptism in the Jordan, and three scenes from the Temptation on the Mountain): 'May this work guide whoever exits and enters as a good person.'[24]

From Piacenza Niccolò went on to the cathedral of Ferrara, where around 1135 he carved a tympanum of Saint George slaying the Dragon for the central portal (fig. 19). Here he took the bold step of inscribing verses with his name around the rim of the tympanum:

> Artificem gnarum qui sculpserit hec Nicolaum
> Huc concurrentes laudent per saecula gentes.[25]
> *(May the peoples coming to visit this place forever praise Niccolò, the skilled craftsman who sculpted this.)*

There is a significant difference between an artist's signature on a reliquary or a capital, or even the dedicatory plaque of Wiligelmo or Niccolò's own verses on the Zodiac Portal, and this extraordinary use of highly visible space on a tympanum. Even Gislebertus's signature on the Last Judgment tympanum of Autun (fig. 25), which is the only precedent for it (assuming Autun to be the prior work) is restrained in comparison. One must suppose that Niccolò had the permission of the cathedral chapter to do what he did. Apparently his reputation stood so high that the chapter was proud to boast of possessing his art. Church administrators were alive to the need to keep up with the latest fashions, and there is ample evidence that the artists of the twelfth century thirsted for fame.

In the conjunction of these twin ingredients, fashion and fame, there is the germ of the idea of the artist as an autonomous creator. If the ecclesiastical authorities were prepared to tolerate Niccolò's self-promotion because they recognized that he could give them what they wanted, namely, the latest in style, then it follows that he was thought of, and thought of himself, as an artistic innovator, as something like an 'artist' in the modern (beginning with the Renaissance) sense of the term. Per Nykrog argues that the 'figure of the author-writer came into existence in the years around 1170 after a gestation that lasted several decades.' He distinguishes the author from the oral storyteller on the grounds that the author

> produces his tale as an object existing outside himself and his mind, and in the shape of that object he will be present whenever and wherever it is 'performed' ... A creator who commits his work to oral tradition vanishes as an individual. The author who produces a written text remains as an individual person, as the one who left his mark on this text, from the level of more or less artfully calculated, more or less complex composition, down to the level of more or less subtle stylistic detail in the wording of the single sentence. He will remain in control, by means of the written text, even after he is dead and gone.[26]

The poet who, for Nykrog, exemplifies this new conception of the author is Chrétien de Troyes. In the prologue to *Erec et Enide* Chrétien announces:

> Des or comancerai l'estoire
> qui toz jorz mes iert an mimoire
> tant con durra chrestïantez;
> de ce s'est Chrestïens vantez.[27]
> *(I will begin the story from the beginning which will always remain in the memory as long as Christianity endures; that is Chrétien's boast.)*

The independent control of the artist over his material, the imposition of his individual style upon his work, and his confident conviction that his work would perpetuate his personal fame – these are the common features that link Nykrog's definition of the author to the conception of the artist that was beginning to emerge with Niccolò and other sculptors of the early twelfth century in northern Italy. Half a century before Chrétien wrote, the Arthurian legends that enabled him to break away from traditional narrative themes and assert his artistic independence had already stimulated the imagination of another artist, the sculptor at Modena who carved the north portal relief of the lady WINLOGEE's rescue by the knight ARTVS DE BRETANIA.[28]

Probably no artist in the twelfth century attained the degree of independent control that Chrétien enjoyed as an author; certainly as far as the sculptors who executed the major sculptural programs of the abbeys and cathedrals are concerned, their freedom of action must always have been narrowly circumscribed by the thematic requirements of the ecclesiastical authorities. The unifying conception of Christ the door and the themes that were elaborated upon it – notably, the Ascension, the Christ in Majesty, and the Last Judgment – offer a loose parallel to the stock of traditional narratives that were the common property of oral storytellers. They reduced, though they certainly did not eliminate, the scope for individual invention. In Italy, as we have seen, the typological allegory of Christ the door did not enjoy the pre-eminent dominance over the ecclesiastical imagination that it did elsewhere. This may have given Italian sculptors broader scope to exercise their powers of invention, even when the themes they worked with, like Niccolò's Saint George slaying the Dragon, were thoroughly conventional.[29] In any case, my purpose is not to imply that Niccolò enjoyed greater independent control over his material or better succeeded in imposing his personal style than his contemporaries in or out of Italy, but rather to argue that the inscriptions he composed and incised on his sculptures are proof that he, like Wiligelmo before him, conceived of himself as an artist in the same way that Chrétien would later conceive of himself as an author.

Shortly after his employment at Ferrara ended, Niccolò moved to Verona, where he may have spent the rest of his life working first on the abbey church of San Zeno and then on the cathedral. All of the wonderful stone sculptures on the lower portion of the west façade of San Zeno are the work of Niccolò and his assistant Guglielmo (fig. 24). For the tympanum of the portal Niccolò created the large, standing figure of Saint Zeno trampling a dragon beneath his feet (fig. 18).[30] Zeno is flanked by the military forces of Verona holding standards. A broad decorative semicircular border arches over the saint's head. On the outer rim of this border Niccolò inscribed a variant of the verses he used at Ferrara:

> Artificem gnarum qui sculpserit hec Nicolaum
> Omnes laudemus; Cristum Dominumque rogemus
> Celorum regnum sibi donet ut ipse supernum.[31]

(Let us all praise Niccolò, the skilled craftsman who sculpted this; and let us beg the Lord Christ to grant him the kingdom of heaven above.)

Niccolò may have seen a ciborium or ambo in the cathedral of Verona that the sculptor Pelegrinus signed with a similar movement of thought.[32] The signature verses are beneath the columns that frame the piece:

Sum Pelegrinus ego qui talia sic bene sculpo.
Quem Deus in altum faciat conscendere celum.
(I am Pelegrinus who sculpts these things so well. May God lift me up into high heaven.)

Niccolò's signature on the tympanum of San Zeno is prominent, but it does not engage the attention to quite the degree that his verses at Ferrara do. It is isolated from the subject of the tympanum by the width of the decorative border, and other verses on the tympanum distract the eye from it. On the other hand, Niccolò found new places to put his name on the façade of San Zeno. At one time, his signature could be seen on the lion that supports the north column of the porch sheltering the portal.[33] And it appears again with the reliefs depicting scenes from the Old and New Testaments that are placed on either side of the portal. The second panel from the bottom on the right of the portal shows in two scenes God creating the birds and the animals and God creating Adam. Niccolò included with the latter scene the verse 'Here examples of the merit of Niccolò can be derived.'[34] Christine Verzár Bornstein observes that this is a daring association of the artist with God the Creator.[35] Perhaps Niccolò's example emboldened his assistant to air his name on the string-course above the New Testament scenes on the left of the portal. But Guglielmo lacked Niccolò's assertive self-confidence: 'You who read this, try to placate the Son of holy Mary. May he save forever Guglielmo, who sculpted this. May all entering here come to the aid of this lost soul.'[36]

When the cathedral of Verona engaged his services ca. 1139, Niccolò had one more opportunity to carve a tympanum for a portal. The cathedral was dedicated to the Virgin, and for it he fashioned a tympanum of the Virgin in Majesty with the Annunciation to the Shepherds and the Adoration of the Magi (fig. 17). In the space around the rim, where, at Ferrara, he had put verses in honour of himself, he inscribed a single leonine hexameter celebrating the Lamb of God. Perhaps the chapter at Verona felt that this would be more suitable for the Virgin. But the chapter did permit Niccolò to carve a version of his Ferrara verses on the façade of the two-storeyed porch that shelters the tympanum. He arranged them so that the two verses are separated by the Lamb of God on the keystone of the porch's arch:

> Artificem gnarum qui sculpserit hec Nicolaum
> Hunc concurrentes laudant per secula gentes.[37]
> *(The peoples coming to visit forever praise him – Niccolò, the skilled craftsman who sculpted this.)*

Was it faulty memory or growing pride that caused him to put the verb 'praise' in the indicative, when earlier he had used the prayerful subjunctive?

No other Romanesque sculptor in or out of Italy quite matched Niccolò's talent for self-promotion. He was the only artist, so far as we now know, who ever managed to put his name in verse on a tympanum in the twelfth century. His contemporaries had to content themselves with more discreet spaces or more modest phrases. This may reflect a certain tension between the pride of the artists and the sense of decorum of the bishops and canons.

Nevertheless, Italian artists in the second half of the twelfth century and later continued the practice of signing their works. Several churches were constructed or renovated and decorated at Pistoia during the 1160s: Sant'Andrea, San Giovanni Fuorcivitas, the abbey church of San Bartolomeo in Pantano, and the cathedral of San Zenone. All except the cathedral are inscribed with the names of their builders or sculptors. For the decoration of the portals, fashion in Pistoia favoured a blank tympanum above an elegantly carved lintel. At Sant'Andrea the theme of the Magi was selected for the lintel of the central portal (fig. 39). From left to right, the Magi approach on horseback, they are warned to avoid Herod, and they present gifts to the Christ Child. The lintel rests on rectangular jamb capitals that depict the Visitation on the left and the Annunciation on the right. A prose inscription on the lower edge of the lintel declares: 'Good master Gruamons, together with his brother Adeodatus, made this work.'[38] 'This work' is ambiguous. It might refer to the construction of the church, but it is more likely to refer to the carving of the lintel: the brothers Gruamons and Adeodatus were probably sculptors. Another inscription on the underside of the lintel, which appears to have been executed by the same hand as the first, states: 'At that time the workmen [*operarii*, foremen?] were Villanus and Pathus the son of Ticnosus. A.D.

1166.'[39] If these two inscriptions were carved at the same time, the implication is that Gruamons had completed work at Sant'Andrea by 1166.

Construction of the abbey church of San Bartolomeo in Pantano of Pistoia began in 1159.[40] An inscription on the underside of the lintel, 'Rodolfinus the workman [foreman?], A.D. 1167,' dates the central portal of the west façade.[41] It is therefore almost exactly contemporary with the Magi lintel that Gruamons and Adeodatus carved for Sant'Andrea, and the two monuments are dated in the same manner.[42] Again, the design consists of a blank tympanum with a decorated lintel, this time of Christ and Doubting Thomas. Christ is in the centre, flanked by six apostles on each side and an angel at each end. There are inscription bands above and below the scene on the lintel. Five full leonine hexameters are inscribed on a single line in the upper band. They are in the voice of Christ: 'I am your peace, the one by whom peace is [made] most sure for us all (?). Discern separately that I am God, behold, see, and touch me, love (me) as you ought. Having been sent out through the four regions of the globe, convert the whole world, washed by the sacred fountain, from wickedness.'[43] The lower band, which is effaced in several places, labels the apostles. Although some details are unclear, both the letter forms, including numerous interlocked letters, and the use of full leonine rhymes distinguish this inscription from the practice of Gruamons. At least two different teams of builders and sculptors appear to have been employed in Pistoia; their rivalry was the kind that leads to variation within very narrow limits.

When the Romanesque façade was added in 1170 to the east front of the basilica of Saint John Lateran in Rome, the architect Niccolò di Angelo signed his name on the right-hand pier of the portico beneath the verse inscription of the architrave.[44] The thirteenth-century cloister of the basilica was the work of two of the Vassalletti, a father and son. The Vassalletti were builders and rivals of the Cosmati in ornamental work in stone and other materials. The elder Vassalletto was probably Pietro, whose work has been documented from ca. 1180 to 1230; his son (and perhaps other members of the family) flourished from ca. 1230 to 1260.[45] A mosaic inscription in a single line runs the length of the south walk, just above the arches of the columns. It is in bad shape, but there appear to have been at least ten full leonine hexameters, which addressed the canons on the theme of the relationship between the symbolism of the cloister design and the monastic vocation, rather in the manner of the cloister inscription of Vaison-la-Romaine.[46] Pietro Vassalletto's son completed the cloister and carved his name in a verse inscription on a pier in the south walk beneath the mosaic inscription: 'Nobly trained in this art, Vassalletto began this work with his father, which he finished himself alone.'[47] The absence of leonine rhyme in this inscription, in contrast to the leonines of the mosaic inscription above it, is worth noting. The younger Vassalletto may have felt that the Romanesque fashion of leonine rhyming had become out of date. One would like to know how he would have defined 'this art' in which he had been 'nobly trained.' The adverb certainly implies that in his own mind at least the artist's profession was a noble one.

In February 1178, the architect and sculptor Benedetto Antelami sculpted, dated, and signed the bishop's chair for the cathedral of Parma.[48] Eighteen years later, he began work on the octagonal baptistery across the piazza from the south-west corner of the cathedral.[49] It appears from the evidence of an inscription on the north portal that Antelami not only provided the sculptural program for the baptistery but also designed the building itself. The tympanum of the north portal, called the Portal of the Virgin, shows the Virgin in Majesty with the Child. Below it is a lintel in two registers. The lower register carries the inscription 'With twice two years subtracted from one thousand two hundred [= in the year 1196], the sculptor called Benedetto began this work.'[50]

Outside of Italy, the sculptor Gilabertus, who was the head of the workshop at the cathedral of Saint-Étienne of Toulouse in the 1120s or 1130s,[51] signed two apostle statues of the portal of the chapter house.[52] For the statue of Saint Thomas he used the standard *[X]-me-fecit* formula, but for the statue of Saint Andrew he came up with a clever adaptation of the formula in a full leonine hexameter that he inscribed on the base:[53]

> Vir non incertus me celavit Gilabertus.[54]
> *(Gilabertus, a man not unsure of himself, carved me.)*

Arnaldus Catellus constructed the cloister of the Benedictine abbey of Sant Cugat del Vallés near Barcelona around 1190. He took the unusual step of carving a portrait of himself on a capital adjoining the north-east pier (unfortunately the head has been destroyed),[55] and added two leonine hexameters on the blank face of the pier facing the east walk. By the very assertion that his cloister (with his portrait in it) would last forever, Arnaldus implied his own undying fame: 'This is the likeness of the sculptor Arnaldus Catellus, who constructed this cloister so that it will endure forever.'[56]

A forthright claim to fame in the Italian manner survives in the verses inscribed on the portal of the thirteenth-century cathedral of Trogir in Croatia. The portal was carved by the sculptor Radovan and his pupils in 1240. Radovan had trained in the workshop of Benedetto Antelami.[57] The tympanum depicts the Nativity and the Washing of the Infant Jesus. Radovan signed his name along the lower edge of the tympanum: 'The doors are fashioned in witness of (?) the childbirth of the holy Virgin by Radovan famed above all others (?) for this art, as is revealed by these very sculptures and low reliefs, in the year 1240 under Bishop Tuscan Treguan (?) of the city of Florence (?).'[58]

Perhaps the most intriguing of all the artists' names that the tradition of verse inscriptions has left us is 'Sabina.' In the seventeenth century Osée Schad reported that one of the statues of the twelve apostles that flanked the portal of the south transept of the cathedral of Strasbourg – the statue of John – carried a banderole on which was carved this leonine hexameter couplet:

> Gracia divinae pietatis adesto Savinae,
> De petra dura per quam sum facta figura.[59]
> *(May the grace of divine mercy be present to Sabina, by whom I am made a figure from hard stone.)*

These statues have since been destroyed. Legend has made Sabina into the daughter of Master Erwin 'of Steinbach,' the supposed designer of the west façade of the cathedral. The west façade was under construction from 1277 into the first two decades of the fourteenth century.[60] Since the apostle statues of the south transept portal have been dated to no later than ca. 1210–23,[61] Erwin cannot have been Sabina's father.

But who was Sabina? Was there really a woman sculptor working at Strasbourg at the beginning of the thirteenth century (or perhaps a little earlier)? Hans Reinhardt categorically rejects the idea. For him, the verse inscription refers to a donor by the name of Sabina, through whose generosity the statue was carved from stone.[62] The only basis for this claim seems to be the assumption that a woman could not have been a sculptor in the Middle Ages. The *[X]-me-fecit* formula, of which the second verse is a metrical variant is not decisive, although it usually refers to the artist. But nowhere else is the formula used to record the gift of a lay donor. If the person named at Strasbourg had been a man who was not known to have been a member of the ecclesiastical hierarchy of the cathedral, he would surely be assumed to be the sculptor. The apostle statues of the south transept portal, which are now represented by the heads that are conserved in the Musée de l'œuvre Notre-Dame, may be assigned, at least provisionally, to the hand of the sculptor Sabina. It would probably have been out of the question for a woman to have found employment in a monastery (which raises an interesting question about the artists who may have worked at convents for women; were there opportunities there for nuns or laywomen to become sculptors?). But if Sabina *was* the artist, it implies that in one town at least there was a workshop, perhaps a family enterprise, in which a woman was trained as a sculptor, and that no impediment barred her from exercising her talents on the façade of the cathedral and from publicly calling attention to the fact.

Sketchy though the evidence is, we may tentatively conclude that an artist was freer to sign his (or, in the case of Sabina, her) name to a large-scale façade program when the church was in an urban setting, especially if it was a cathedral rather than a monastic church. Verse inscriptions were a common adjunct to sculptural programs everywhere in the twelfth century, but the signed works that we have surveyed in this chapter are found almost exclusively in the towns and the cathedrals. Gislebertus at Autun (although Saint-Lazare was not elevated to the rank of cathedral until 1195), Wiligelmo at Modena, Niccolò at Ferrara and Verona, Gilabertus at Toulouse, Sabina at Strasbourg, and Radovan at Trogir all fit this pattern. Already in the twelfth century there were urban artisans who were conscious of themselves as autonomous artists and who took the means at their disposal to perpetuate their fame through their art.

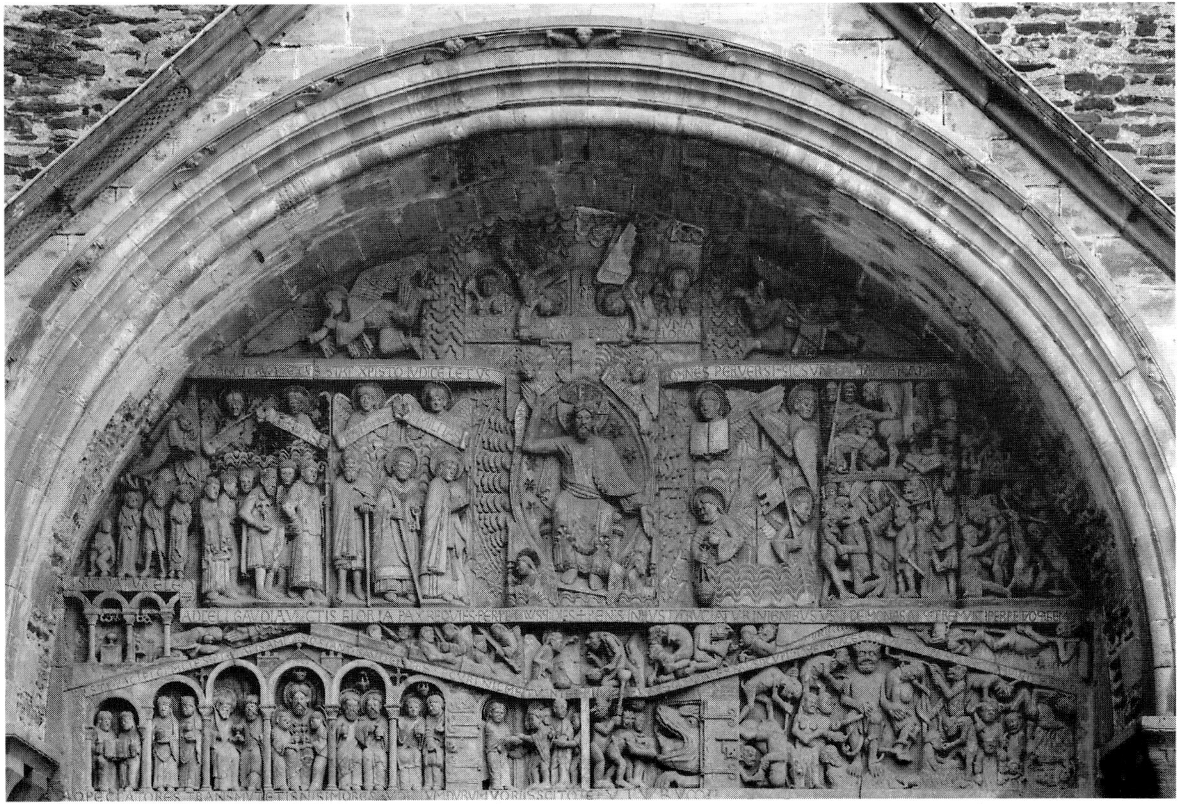

1. Conques. West portal, tympanum of Last Judgment

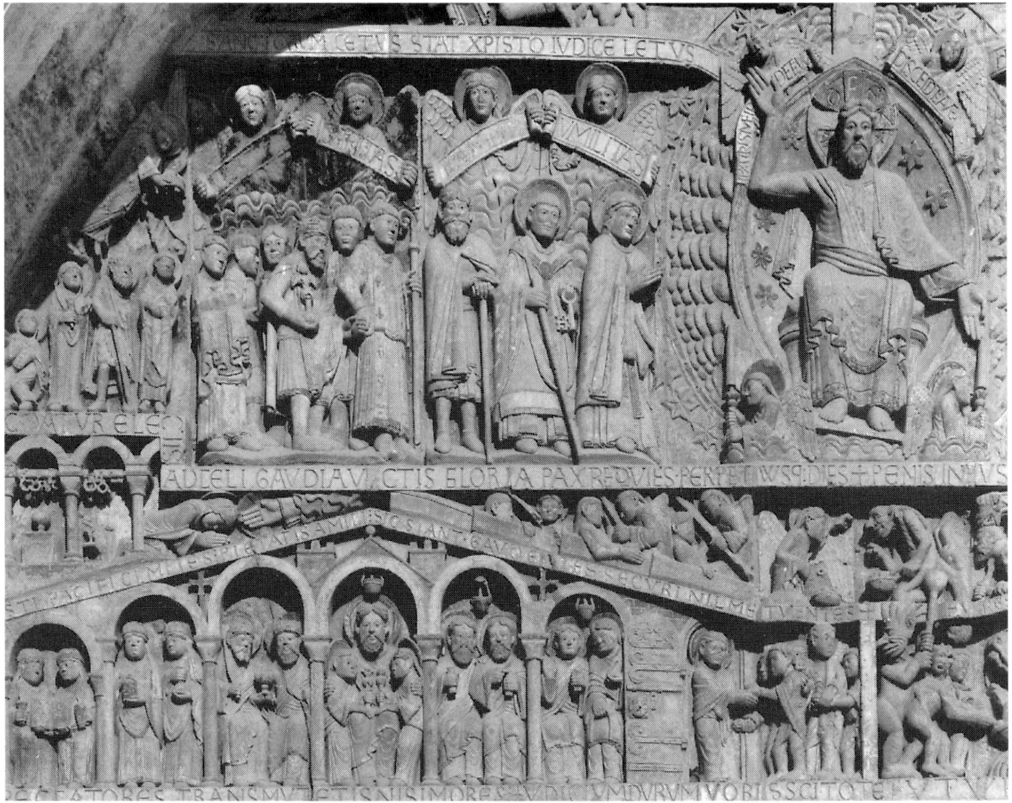

2. Conques. Tympanum, detail, left

3. Rome. Arch of Constantine: south face

4. Rome. Santi Cosma e Damiano: interior, apse mosaic of Christ with Saints Cosmas and Damian

5. Rome. Santa Maria in Domnica: interior, apse mosaic of the Virgin in Majesty with the Child

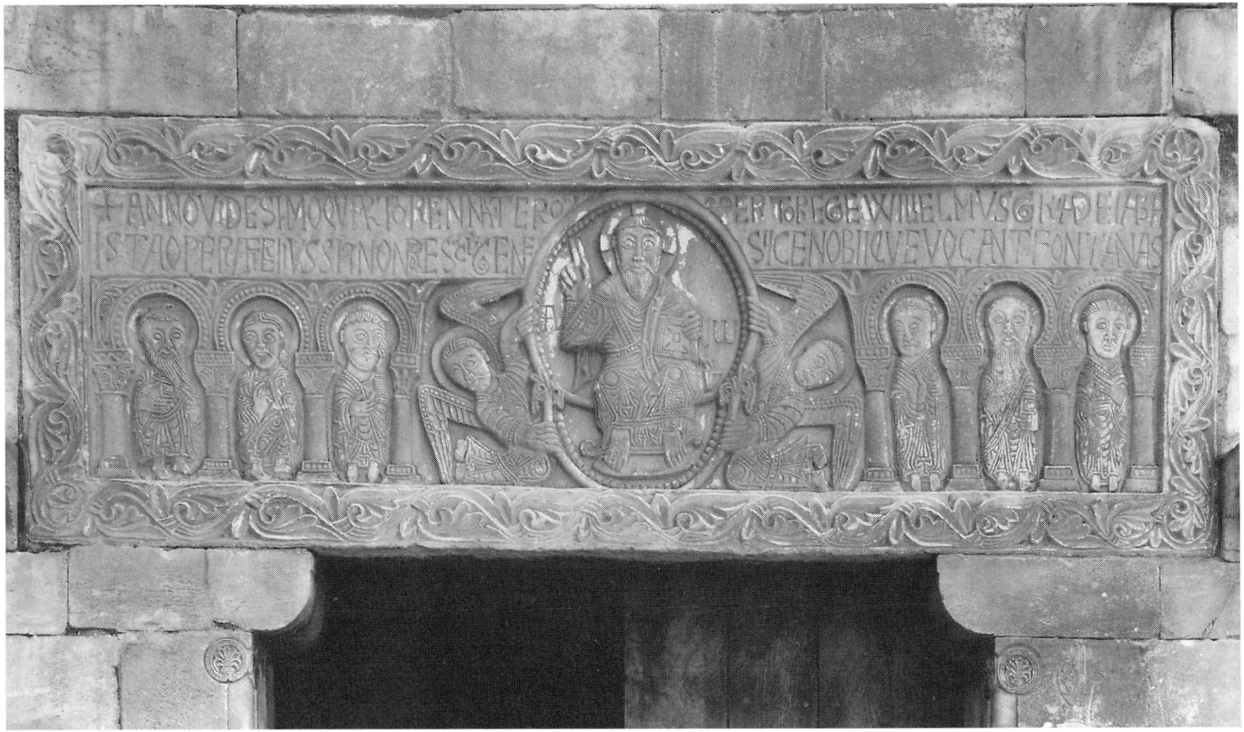

6. Saint-Genis-des-Fontaines. West portal, lintel of Christ with Apostles

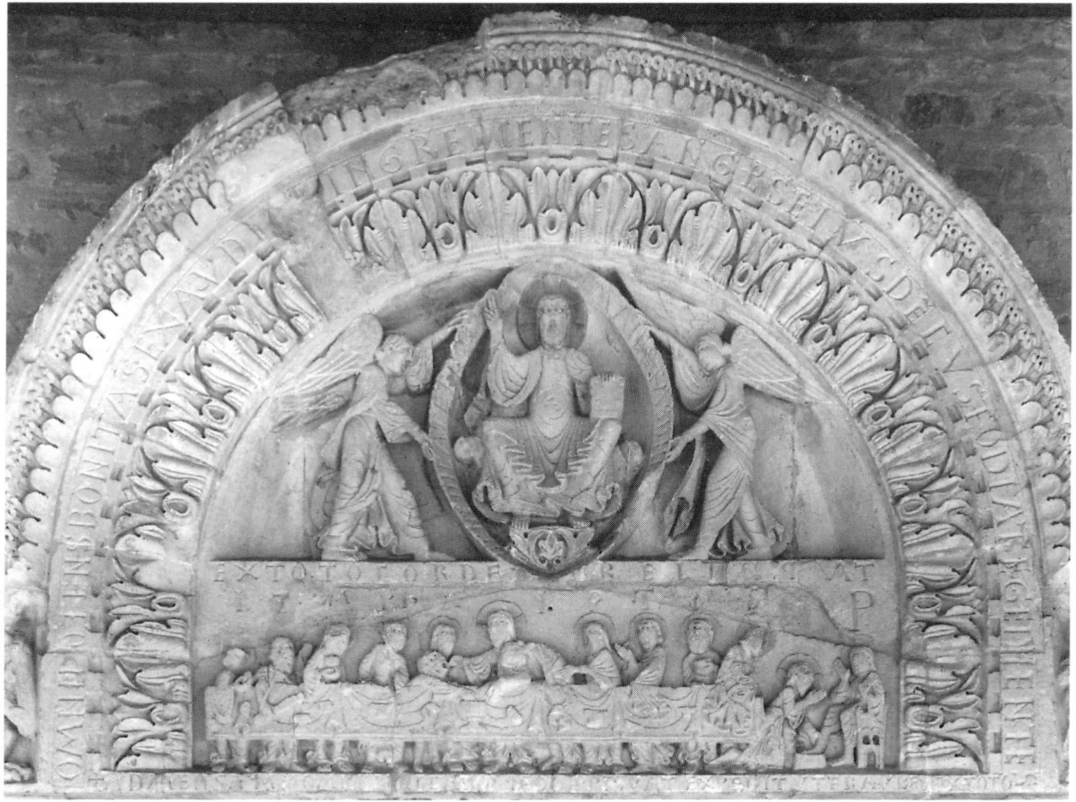

7. Vandeins. West portal, tympanum of Christ in Majesty

8. Autun. Cathedral: west portal, tympanum of Last Judgment

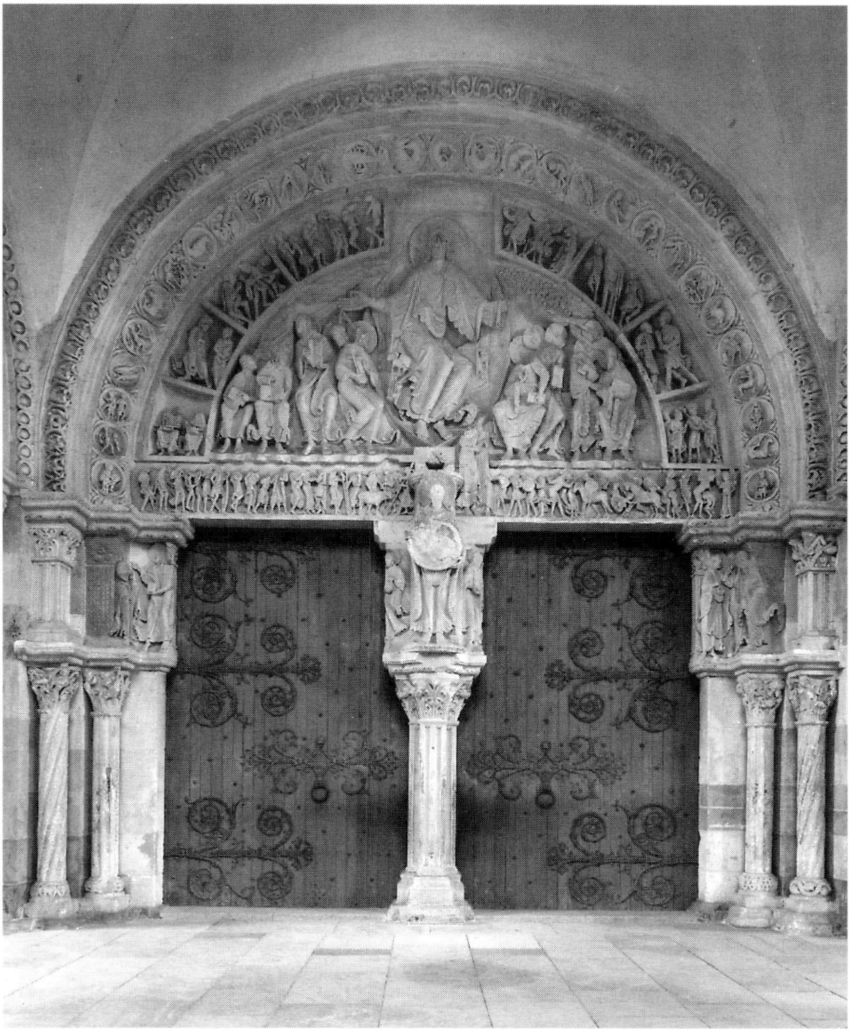

9. Vézelay. Narthex, inner central west portal

10. Toulouse. Saint-Sernin: south nave portal (Porte Miègeville), tympanum of the Ascension of Christ

11. Saint-Denis. Central west portal

12. Jaca. Cathedral: west portal, tympanum of Chrismon between two lions

13. Santa Cruz de la Serós. West portal, tympanum of Chrismon between two lions

14. Oloron-Sainte-Marie. West portal

15. Modena. Cathedral: west façade

16. Modena. West façade, Genesis frieze, panel of Creation of Adam and Eve

17. Verona. Cathedral: west portal, tympanum of the Virgin in Majesty

18. Verona. San Zeno: west portal, tympanum of Saint Zeno

19. Ferrara. Cathedral: central west portal, tympanum of Saint George

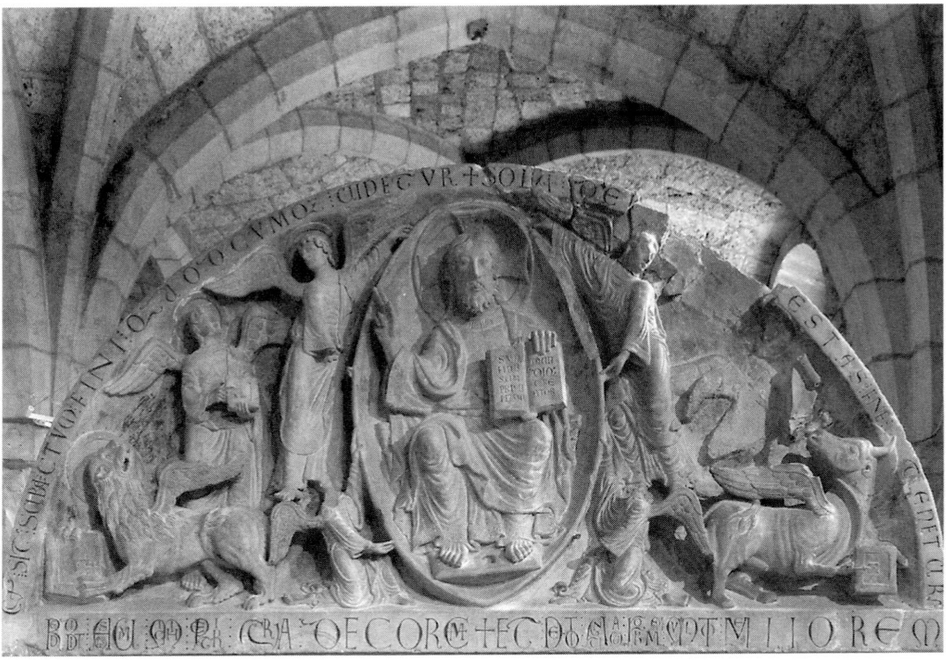

20. Dijon. Saint-Bénigne (in Musée archéologique): tympanum of Christ in Majesty

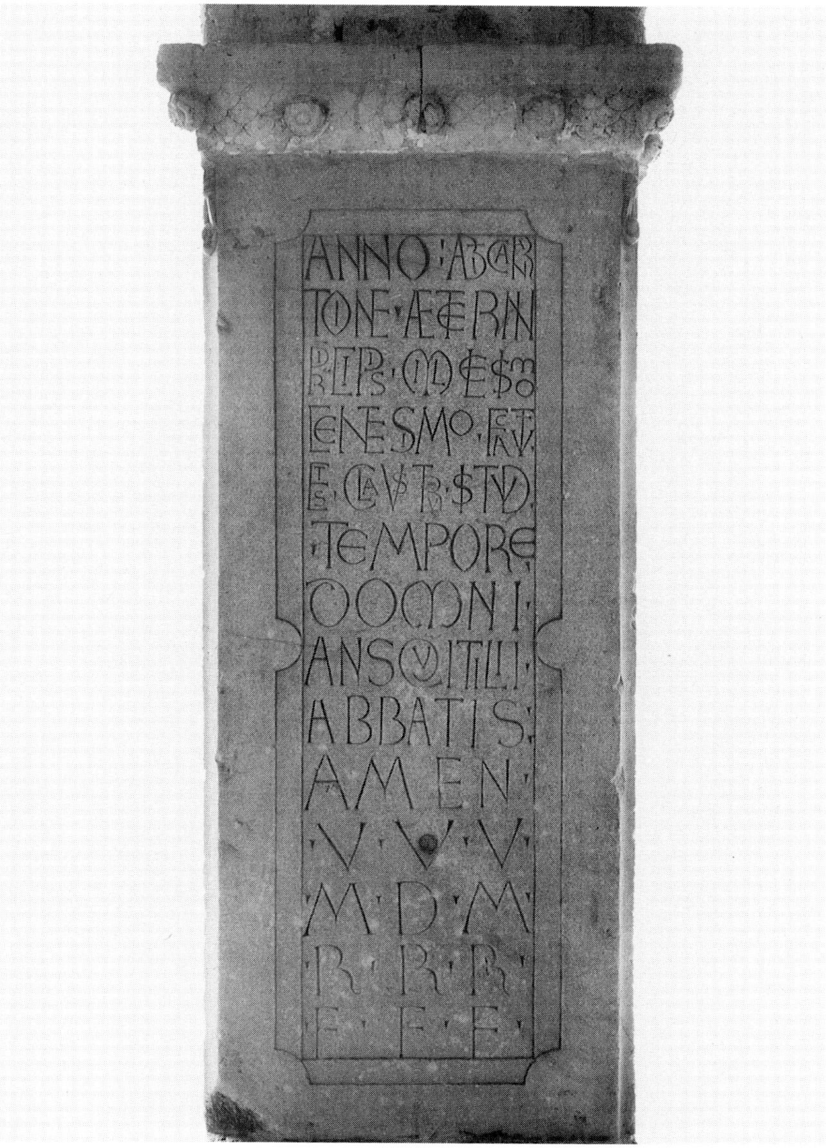

21. Moissac. Cloister, west walk, central pier, west face, dedication inscription

22. Modena. West façade, Enoch and Elias plaque

23. Ferrara. Central west portal

24. Verona. San Zeno: west façade, right of portal, relief of Adam and Eve

25. Autun. Tympanum, detail, centre

26. Oloron-Sainte-Marie. West portal, trumeau of Moorish slaves

27. Luz-Saint-Sauveur. North portal, tympanum of Christ in Majesty

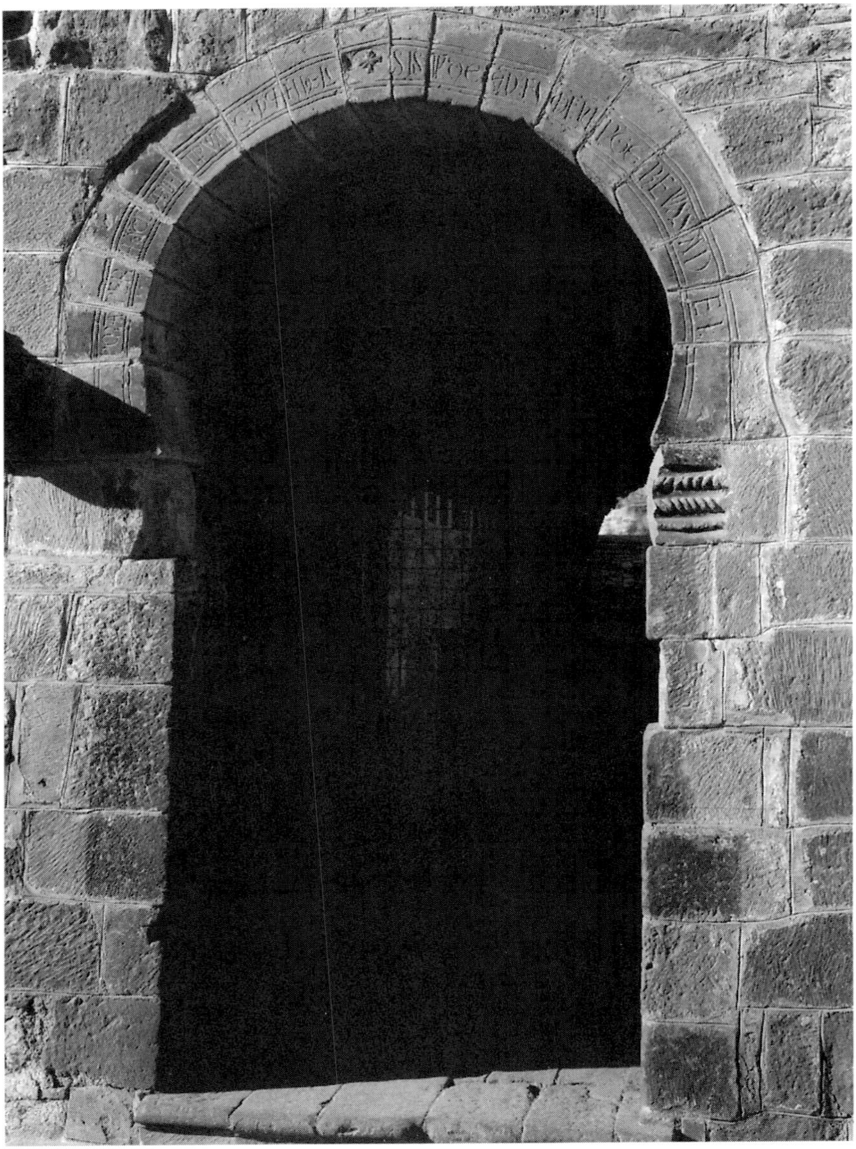

28. San Juan de la Peña. South nave portal (leading to cloister), portal inscription

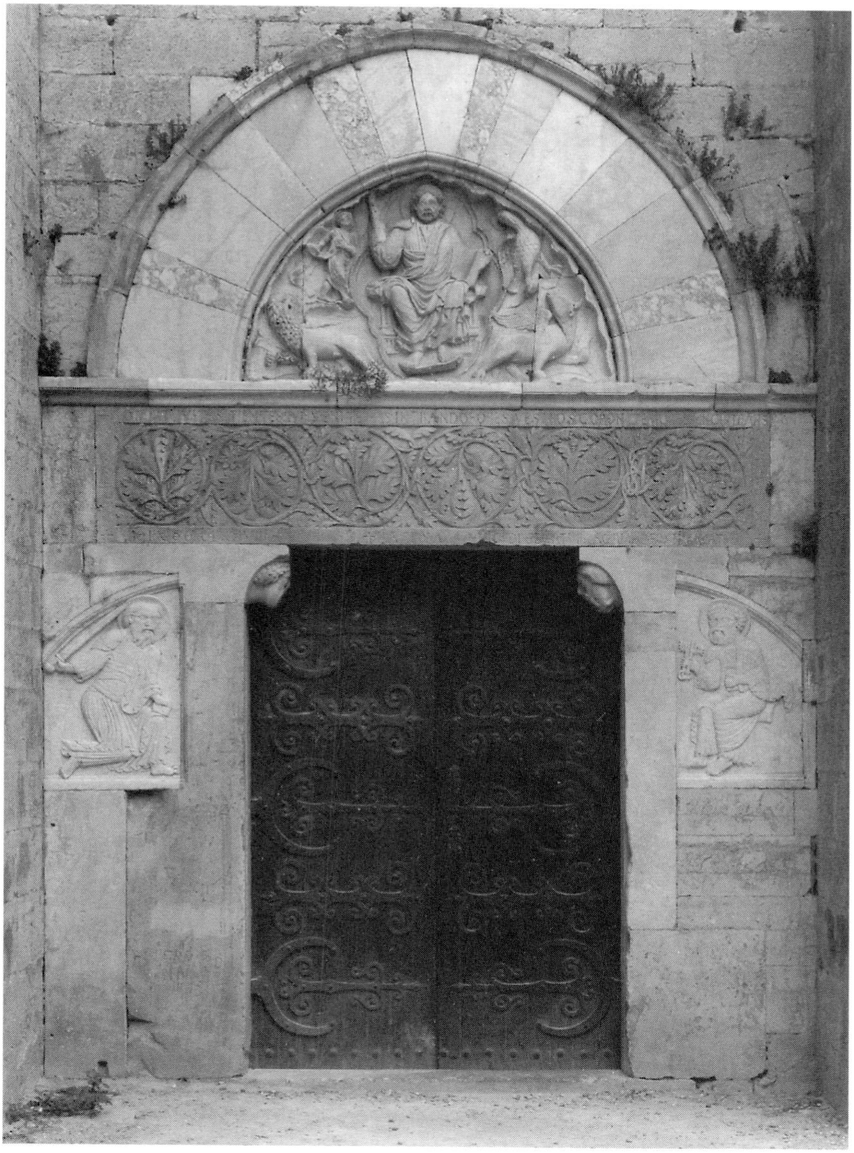

29. Maguelone. West portal

30. Le Puy. Cathedral: apse, exterior wall with inscription

31. Lassouts. West façade, tympanum of Christ in Majesty

32. Saintes. Abbaye aux Dames: west portal

39. Pistoia. Sant'Andrea: central west portal, lintel of Magi

40. Saint-Denis. Tympanum of Last Judgment, detail, lower centre

14

Allegory Undone: Patronage and the Shift to Representational Symbolism

The premises of the allegory of the church were fundamentally incompatible with the age-old tradition of patrons celebrating their patronage by means of prominently displayed inscriptions. The allegory of the church directed the self toward God and encouraged its absorption into Christ and the heavenly city; it would have worked to exclude almost all names outside those of the sacred persons. The display of a patron's name would have had the contrary effect of reminding worshippers that the church was a material object external to the self and dominated by the human will. And yet, despite this evident distraction from the church's spiritual purposes, men who were responsible for the building and decoration of churches in the eleventh and twelfth centuries often inscribed their names in prominent places. The more self-consciously and ostentatiously patrons, particularly abbots, stressed their responsibility for the projects they financed and directed, the less likely it is that they were responding to the allegory of the church on anything but a metaphorical level.

Lay patronage was an important financial mainstay of the ecclesiastical building programs of the Romanesque period. Abbots took on projects that were beyond their own resources. Kings and princes and eventually all the aristocracy considered it their duty to uphold the honour of the chivalric order by acts of generosity to the Church.[1] The wealth of the abbeys was owing in part to the magnificent treasures that secular authorities lavished upon them. It is surprising, therefore, how seldom lay donors had their names prominently inscribed on churches in the eleventh and twelfth centuries.[2] Among those who did were Count Sancho and his wife, Urraca, who provided funds for the church of Iguácel in what is now the Spanish province of Huesca.[3] Another was Countess

Petronella of Holland. Her patronage is recorded on a tympanum from the Benedictine abbey church of Saints Peter and Adelbert in Egmond Binnen – a church that was destroyed in 1572. The tympanum is now in the Rijksmuseum in Amsterdam. It was probably carved in the third decade of the twelfth century. Saint Peter with the key in his right hand and a crook in his left occupies the centre. Petronella and her son Count Dirk VI are on either side of him. Dirk faces Saint Peter in an attitude of prayer. His prayer is inscribed on the arch of the tympanum. Petronella looks out from the tympanum; she appears to be carrying an offering in her veiled hands. A verse on the lower edge of the tympanum announces: 'Here Dirk prays, Petronella adorns this work.'[4]

A handful of unidentified or uncertainly identified persons, some of whom may have been lay donors, have their names inscribed on scattered churches. Renard, together with his wife, Ramona, whose names appear after a verse inscription at Sant Pau del Camp of Barcelona but who are otherwise unknown, *misit in hac aula Moabitinos VII*, 'placed seven Arabic workers in [the construction of] the church.'[5] The Roderic who is named as *auctor huius operis* on the tympanum of San Prudencio of Armentia was probably neither the sculptor nor a lay donor but Rodrigo de Cascante, Bishop of Calahorra (1146–90).[6] Three names are carved on the lower edge of the Saint-Nicolas portal tympanum of Saint-Martin of Colmar: Cunradus, Utecha, and Nicolaus.[7] They may have been secular benefactors who donated money for the portal.

Secular donations ultimately made possible the monumental art of the twelfth century, but if the evidence of the inscriptions is representative, most church buildings and the sculptural decoration for their portals were commissioned and directed by the monastic hierarchy. Abbots appear disproportionately among the ranks of patrons and donors. They were in a position not merely to provide funds like the lay aristocracy, but also to plan and administer the work. It is probably for this reason that they tended to think of themselves as 'makers,' as is suggested by the occasional appearance of the verb *facere* in inscriptions that record their 'gifts.' When they had their names carved on their works, they paid tribute to their own administrative and executive genius, effectively turning the house of the Lord and the gate of heaven into monuments to the human will.

The number of churches and monasteries that were constructed or reconstructed and provided with decorated portals in the Romanesque period can be estimated in the tens of thousands. Many abbots had the opportunity to undertake a major building project. Some of them celebrated their accomplishments by having their own names carved in stone; others were fortunate enough to have a successor do it for them. Abbot William used the patronage formula to describe his role in commissioning the Christ in Majesty lintel for Saint-Genis-des-Fontaines in 1020 (fig. 6). The inscription along the upper portion of the lintel reads:

> Anno videsimo quarto rennate Rotberto rege Wilielmus gratia Dei aba ista opera fieri iussit in onore sancti Genesii cenobii que vocant Fontanas.
> *(In the 24th year of the reign of King Robert, William, by the grace of God abbot, ordered this work to be done in honour of the monastery of Saint Genis, which they call Fountains.)*

King Robert was Robert the Pious of France, who ruled from 996 to 1031. In his time Robert was praised 'for having contributed generously to the adornment of many churches.'[8] If the lintel at Saint-Genis was meant to commemorate a donation from the king, Abbot William chose a curiously oblique way of going about it, but there is no doubt about his own role.[9]

When Abbot Regenward had the north transept portal of Saint Emmeram of Regensburg decorated with the limestone relief plaques of Christ in Majesty, Saint Emmeram, and Saint Dionysius, one of his purposes was to substantiate his abbey's claim to have in its possession the (spurious) relics of Saint Denis (Dionysius) of France.[10] This is the point of the boastful verses around the frame of the Dionysius plaque: 'Tripartite Gaul laments its patron saint translated hither, which your image, holy Macharios Dionysius, reveals.'[11] (The claim provoked an excited reaction at Saint-Denis, where the monks decided to open the silver casket that contained the relics of Saint Denis and to expose them to a crowd of distinguished witnesses. When they did so, they found the saint's bones wrapped in very old textile.[12]) There is a donor bust with Abbot Regenward's portrait beneath Christ's feet on the central relief plaque. On the circular rim of the bust is this common leonine pentameter:

> Abba Regenwardus hoc fore iussit opus.[13]
> *(Abbot Regenward ordered this work to be made.)*

The poet (Regenward?) had to struggle to put the patronage formula, *[X] hoc fieri iussit,* into verse. I have discussed the anxieties generated by sculpted images of Christ like the Christ in Majesty above the donor bust.[14] Whether or not this was his intention, Regenward may have alleviated some of these anxieties by including his own portrait and signature in the sculptural ensemble. These would reassure viewers that the image of Christ was authorized by responsible authority and remind them that it was no different in nature from the portrait of the abbot.

Although we are told that the eleventh and twelfth centuries lacked the modern concept of 'personality,' the abbots of the more important monasteries made powerful impressions on their fellow monks.[15] Abbots Durand and Ansquitil of Moissac and Abbot Bego of Conques are cases in point. Momentous changes had taken place at Moissac during the course of the eleventh century. The old abbey was dilapidated when Odilo, the abbot of Cluny, secured its submission to his abbey in 1047.[16] He put in charge one of his own monks, Durand, an able and energetic man. In addition to being abbot of Moissac, Durand was made bishop of Toulouse. After his death in 1072, the monks of Moissac venerated him as a saint.[17] He and his immediate successors were great builders. Ansquitil was the one who built the cloister around 1100. On the centre pier of the east walk he placed a monumental portrait of Durand. The abbot, who is ceremoniously dressed, is in a pose that might have been imitated directly from a flat manuscript illustration. He is framed by two columns surmounted by an arch on which is carved his name and titles: SanCtuS DVRANNVS EPiscopuS TOLOSANVS ET ABBaS MOYSIACO, 'Saint Durand, bishop of Toulouse and abbot of Moissac.' Directly opposite Durand's portrait, on the centre pier of the west walk, is an inscription that fixes both the sculpture and the cloister precisely in time (fig. 21). The inscription is arranged in fourteen lines, divided into three groups of 5 + 5 + 4:

ANNO · AB InCARNA
TIONE · AETERNI
PRInCIPIS · MILLESIMO
CENTESIMO · FACTVm ·
EST · CLAVSTRVm · ISTVD ·
TEMPORE ·
DOMNI ·
ANSQVITILII ·
ABBATIS :
AMEN ·
·V·V·V·
·M·D·M·
·R·R·R·
·F·F·F·

(In the one thousand one hundredth year from the incarnation of the eternal Prince this cloister was made in the time of the lord Abbot Ansquitil. Amen. V.V.V. M.D.M. R.R.R. F.F.F.)

The first five lines are inscribed in elaborately interlocked, interlaced, raised and joined letters. It requires an effort to decipher the meaning of the attractive patterns they form. The last four lines at the bottom are a series of initials, arranged in four sets of three. Meyer Schapiro explains these as 'a variant of an inscription of mysterious alliterative initials often found in manuscripts since the ninth century and interpreted there as a prophecy of the fall of Rome ... V.V.V. is read as Venit Victor Validus or Victor Vitalis Veniet, M.M.M. as Monitus Monumentum Mortuus (*sic*), R.R.R. as Rex Romanorum Ruit, F.F.F. as Ferro Frigore Fame.'[18] Schapiro does not hazard a guess as to why the artist chose to put them on the cloister pier or what they might mean in this context, but their supposed import may have been well known to the monks. The substitution of D for M in the second set of initials may be a reference to Durand, whose image is on the cloister pier opposite. In contrast to the top five and the bottom four lines, the middle group of five lines, which refers to Abbot Ansquitil [*tempore Domni Ansquitilii Abbatis amen*], is perfectly clear (except for the interlocked QV and the reduced I's that allow the name 'Ansquitil' to occupy exactly one line). One's impression is that the inscription was intended to be visually attractive, but with enough obscurity to provide a satisfying exercise of the mind in interpreting it. But no one could fail to make out the name of Ansquitil. That, I imagine, was the point.

Ansquitil's contemporary at Conques was Abbot Bego. When Bego died, what his fellow monks remembered above all was that he had finished the cloister. One of the many tragedies involving Romanesque art is the loss of this cloister. It was pulled down early in the nineteenth century shortly before the visit of Prosper Mérimée in 1837 that saved the church. If we may judge from the fragments that remain, it was superb. A portion of the west walk that had been built into a later fifteenth-century structure and walled over was discovered in 1890. The abbey took a special interest in the work of its artisans. Among the extraordinarily fine capitals of this walk is a capital depicting the masons who were engaged in the construction of the cloister at the very time Abbot Ansquitil was directing the building of the cloister at Moissac.[19]

The monks of Conques built a decorated tomb for Abbot Bego with an epitaph commemorating his achievements. The tomb is now placed in a niche in the exterior south wall of the nave. A bricked-up door behind the tomb shows that this was not its original emplacement. Apparently, the architect who dismantled the cloister of Conques in 1830 moved Bego's tomb to its present location. Bego's successor, Abbot Boniface (ca. 1107–25), probably buried him in the cloister, just as Ansquitil commemorated Durand in the cloister at Moissac. Two green marble plaques set into the wall on either side of the tomb sculpture carry Bego's epitaph, which does for him what the cloister pier inscription did for Ansquitil.[20] The epitaph, consisting of six full leonine hexameters, says: 'Here is buried an abbot, skilled in divine law, a man pleasing to God, who was named Bego. He completed this cloister which extends to the south and accomplished many other useful works, all with expert care. This man should be venerated and praised through the ages. May he live forever, praising the King on high.'[21] Bego's role in the construction of the cloister is expressed with the verb *peragere*, 'to accomplish,' which probably has much the same force as the passive phrase *factum est* that was used to describe Ansquitil's role at Moissac.

Bego surely would not have objected to this posthumous celebration of himself, because three reliquaries that were fashioned during his lifetime at Conques are adorned with similar verses, also bearing his name.[22] The 'A of Charlemagne' is inscribed:

> Abbas formavit Bego reliquiasque locavit.
> *(Abbot Bego formed [this reliquary] and put relics [in it].)*

The verb *formare* is ambiguous. It could mean literally that Bego himself fashioned the reliquary.[23] Unless Bego liked to relax by puttering in the abbey workshop, however, it is more likely to mean that he conceived the idea for, or perhaps even designed (gave form to), the reliquary. There is no ambiguity in the inscription on the 'Reliquary of Pope Pascal,' which states, in the voice of the reliquary:

> Me fieri iussit Bego; clemens cui Dominus sit.
> *(Bego ordered me to be made; may the Lord be merciful to him.)*

This is the standard patronage formula.

Of course, Ansquitil and Bego were not the master masons who supervised the construction of the cloisters of their abbeys, but the inscriptions make clear that it was the energizing power of their will that drove these projects. Conques and Moissac were major halts about a six days' journey apart on the pilgrimage road from Le Puy to Compostela.[24] The poet who composed the *Chanson de Sainte Foy* in the Provençal tongue ca. 1065–70, possibly on the occasion of the translation of the relics of Saint Foy into the choir of the new basilica of Conques, was probably a monk there.[25] One of his sources appears to have been Lactantius's *De mortibus persecutorum*, the sole surviving manuscript of which was copied in the scriptorium of Moissac in the eleventh century, where the poet could have consulted it.[26] These are inferences, not facts, but they are consistent with the impression one has that the two abbeys enjoyed close relations. Ansquitil and Bego must have been intensely aware of one another. It is almost inconceivable that there would not have been a rivalry between them to see who could accomplish the more.[27]

The decisive importance of the administrative genius of the great twelfth-century abbots in the evolution and transformation of styles in architecture and monumental art is nowhere better illustrated than in the person of Abbot Suger of Saint-Denis. I am not here primarily concerned with the architectural innovations that effected the transition from Romanesque to Gothic style, although they are certainly part of the story. Instead, I want to focus on his involvement with the design and decoration of the portal and on his consciousness of his own role in the construction and ornamentation of the church. One runs the risk, in a discussion of this kind, of seeming to assign to Suger the artistic credit that properly belongs to his master masons and sculptors. Undoubtedly, his influence on the portal was more administrative and executive than artistic, though perhaps these strands cannot be entirely disentangled from one another.[28] But it is certain that he was widely travelled and had personally observed many of the great monuments of Europe,[29] and he could have supplemented his own observations with the reports of the many other intelligent men with whom he was in contact, including his own artists, who came 'from different regions.'[30] He imposed his authority and personality on nearly everything that was done at Saint-Denis during his time.

Abbot Suger decorated the west façade of his reconstructed abbey church between about 1137 and 1140. Although the Last Judgment tympanum of the central portal was recarved in the nineteenth century, it is known that the restorers preserved the essential composition of the original (fig. 11). For the Last Judgment Suger used a formula that had been tried at the Cluniac abbey church of Beaulieu on the river Dordogne.[31] Christ sits in majesty on a throne.[32] His arms are outstretched, palms open, in the form of the cross. As at Beaulieu, his right arm is bare and his left arm is draped with his garment, which is pulled away to display the wound in his side. A great cross is centred behind Christ. Its arms are flared at the ends and there is a circular disk at the crossing. Two angels hold up the arms of the cross at their outer ends. Two more angels bear the nails and the crown of thorns in the upper spaces defined by the arms of the cross. The twelve apostles, flanked by angels blowing the trumpets of Last Judgment, are seated below the arms of the cross, six on either side of Christ. The dead rise up from their coffins beneath the apostles. They are not separated into the saved and the damned, and there is no weighing of the souls, as is the case at Conques and Autun (figs. 2, 8).

With the exception of the centring of the cross, the features that I have emphasized at Saint-Denis seem to derive from Beaulieu. But I believe that Suger or his sculptor knew the Last Judgment tympanum of Conques (fig. 1) and took some hints from it. The organization of space into three horizontal registers is the same in both tympana. The upper register in both is occupied by angels. The middle register on the left is made up of a procession of figures. At Saint-Denis this is repeated on the right. The narrow bottom register of Saint-Denis expands one element of Conques – the raising of the dead – and again repeats it on the right. Christ at Saint-Denis holds two banderoles that extend the axis of his arms. The scroll in Christ's right hand reads: *Venite benedicti Patris mei*, 'Come, blessed of my Father' (Matt. 25:34), and the scroll in his left hand reads: *Discedite a me maledicti*, 'Depart from me, accursed ones' (Matt. 25:41). These are the same inscriptions that appear on the scrolls around the mandorla of Christ at Conques. Unfortunately, the inscriptions at Saint-Denis were recarved in the nineteenth century, and it is not known for certain whether they were the original ones. Although Emile Mâle was not prepared even to claim that the banderoles were part of the original configuration, Jacques Bousquet takes them as evidence of influence from Conques.[33]

The lintel of the central portal of Saint-Denis was destroyed in 1771 to enlarge the doorway. But we know that another inscription appeared on it – this one in hexameters with disyllabic end rhyme composed by Abbot Suger: 'Accept, strict Judge, the prayers of your Suger; grant that I be preserved among your own sheep.'[34] Suger, in his own voice, addresses the Christ of the tympanum – the Judge who has come to separate the sheep from the goats. A small figure of a monk kneeling in prayer, just in front of Christ's right foot, intersects the edge of the mandorla that encompasses the lower part of Christ's body (fig. 40). This must be Suger himself, uttering the verses that were carved on the lintel.[35] The inscription on the lintel was a mimesis of the prayer of the living Suger, not a performative utterance. It would have had the effect of transforming the figure of Christ on the tympanum above him into a representation as well.

Where did the audacious idea of putting himself into the sculpture come from? Suger could have seen how popes included themselves as donors in apse mosaics in Rome. At Santa Maria in Domnica, Pope Paschal kneels before the Virgin and Child in exactly the same relative position as Suger (fig. 5). He might have known how abbots like Durand and Ansquitil at Moissac, Bego at Conques, and Alberic at Baume[36] were commemorated; he might have seen, or heard of, Gislebertus's signature on the Last Judgment of Autun (fig. 25) and Regenward's donor bust at Regensburg (with the abbey's claim to possess relics of Saint Denis!). And there was a suggestive precedent at the abbey of Saint-Denis itself. Sometime before 1144 Suger transferred some old doors (probably the doors to the 'tower of William the Conqueror'[37]) to the north portal of the west façade. These wooden doors were covered with bronze panels that showed the monk Airard offering the doors to Saint Denis, with an inscription in elaborately interlaced letters: 'Behold, Airard, trusting in divine favour, offers this work to you, Saint Denis, gentle of heart.'[38] Almost certainly these doors were the work of the second half of the eleventh century. They would have provided Suger an example from the past of a donor who recorded his gift in this public manner right on the portal.

Abbot Suger's thirst for inscribing his name on the church of Saint-Denis and on its precious objects was unquenchable. In his naive egotism, moreover, he recorded many of these same verses in *De administratione*, the little book he wrote about his reconstruction of the abbey church. From this source we learn that his name appeared in copper-gilt letters on the main doors (chap. 27) as well as on the lintel above it, in the dedication inscription for the new choir (chap. 28), on the panel of the golden altar frontal in the choir (chap. 31), on a panel of the main altar (chap. 33), on a vase for the altar that Queen Eleanor of Aquitaine had presented as a wedding gift to her husband, King Louis VII (chap. 34a), and on another vase for the altar of similar material that Suger himself offered (ibid.). These verses give us a kind of glossary of the verbs and phrases Suger used to describe his role in the construction and adornment of the church or in the making and ornamentation of the precious objects in it. He says that he 'has worked for' (*studuit*) the adornment of the church, that he 'was in charge' (*me duce*) of the construction of the choir, that Saint Denis built a new home for himself 'with his (Suger's) aid' (*per nos*), that he 'set up' (*posuit*) the main altar panels, that he 'gave' (*dedit*) Eleanor's vase to the saints, and that he 'offers' (*offero*) his own vase to the Lord. Once at least he used the verb *facere* in this sense. This was on the back of a tabernacle in the shape of a miniature basilica that was placed above the tomb of the Patron Saints in the new choir. On it Suger inscribed a common leonine hexameter:

> Fecit utrumque latus, frontem, tectumque Sugerus.[39]
> *(Suger made [i.e., caused to be made] each side, the front, and the roof.)*

Suger had need of respectable contemporary thinking to defend his love of magnificence and ostentation in the ornamentation of his church against charges of materialism at a time when Bernard of Clairvaux was attacking the monastic art of the Benedictines as a distraction from their spiritual duties. From a variety of sources, including the writings of Dionysius the Pseudo-Areopagite, Suger borrowed and exploited an aesthetic of transcendental beauty to justify the use of beautiful objects.[40] The material things of this world were intended to lead the faithful toward the contemplation of the immaterial things of the next. On the gilded bronze doors beneath the tympanum, Suger inscribed these verses:

> Nobile claret opus, sed opus quod nobile claret
> Clarificet mentes, ut eant per lumina vera
> Ad verum lumen, ubi Christus ianua vera.[41]
> *(Bright is the noble work; but, being nobly bright, the work*
> *Should brighten the minds, so that they may travel, through the true lights,*
> *To the True Light where Christ is the true door.)*

Thus Suger reinterpreted the allegory of the church by means of his doctrine of transcendental beauty.[42] Quite apart from the politics involved, this reinterpretation suggests that Bedan allegorical hermeneutics as conventionally understood was no longer fully adequate to the task of mediating between man and God. The portal of the church, properly decorated, might be able to lift the minds of worshippers to the 'True Light,' but it was there in the Platonic realm of the ideal, not here in the material present, that Christ was the 'true door.' Sign gave way to symbol, which was defined by Hugh of Saint-Victor (1096–1141) as 'the bringing together of visible forms for the sake of revealing by analogy invisible realities.'[43] Wherever this aspect of the Sugerian aesthetic or the currents of thought that inspired it caught hold, prosopopeia in an inscription carved in stone could only be a mimesis of a speech act, not a 'real' voice.

In the years following Suger's rebuilding of the abbey church of Saint-Denis symbolism flourished, and all of human and divine knowledge was taken as a fit subject for display around the portals of the Gothic cathedrals. The programmatic juxtaposition of Old Testament types with New Testament antitypes, which had been rare before the second half of the twelfth century, became common from that time on. Emile Mâle argued that Suger himself was responsible for the reintroduction of this typological symbolism into medieval art after a lapse of some three and a half centuries.[44] But the representation of typology was a very different matter from the presence of Christ in the allegory of the church. In order adequately to depict the harmony of the two Testaments and all the other new topics of art, considerable display space was required. Portals were enlarged and multiplied, and the façades surrounding them were brought into use for sculptural programs. The main portal remained *a* focus, but was no longer *the* focus of the artists' attentions.

The allegory of the church was predicated on something like real presence. The portal was Christ; it spoke in his voice. When the portal ceased to address the faithful, the use of verse inscriptions on portal sculpture began to decline. Portal inscriptions in leonine verse are prima facie indicators of the Romanesque; their absence is Gothic. The further one moves from the epicentre of the Gothic revolution in Paris, the longer one finds the tradition of verse inscriptions to have lingered. This is especially true in Italy, where there are significant thirteenth-century examples. But in Italy the allegory of the church never completely took hold, and verse inscriptions were used on façades much as they had been for centuries in apse mosaics to claim credit for patronage. Verse inscriptions, which had served to articulate the voice of Christ and the Church, are not found with the sculptural programs on the façades of the major Gothic cathedrals. The voice of the portal fell silent.

Catalogue of Romanesque Verse Inscriptions

The Catalogue is an inventory of Latin verses carved in stone on mural surfaces, including columns, of churches and monasteries in western Europe from AD 1000 to the thirteenth century. Epitaphs and verses on movable objects, such as altars and baptismal fonts, are not included, unless special circumstances dictate otherwise. Dedication inscriptions are admitted only if they are associated with other verse inscriptions or have some claim to being part of the façade decoration. The beginning limit of the temporal range is arbitrary; the terminal limit is set by the exhaustion of the tradition of verse inscriptions in the thirteenth century. No inscriptions have been omitted because they are too 'late.' The inscriptions in this catalogue are arranged alphabetically, first by city and then by dedication of the church (with the cathedral first). The names of cities (except for Milan and Rome) and the dedications of French, Italian, and Spanish churches have not been Anglizised.

For further discussion of particular inscriptions in the text, the interested reader should consult the Index by place and person.

Key to transcriptions

Roman capitals are regularly used for all existing inscriptions. Conjectural restorations as well as letters and words that can no longer be seen, but which earlier photographs or other reliable reproductions reveal, are enclosed in square brackets. Suspensions and other standard abbreviations are expanded in lower-case roman. Brackets surrounding lower-case roman indicate that no marks of suspension are now visible. Letters, words, and phrases that were never carved and cannot be thought to be suspended or abbreviated, but which must be understood to complete the sense of the inscription, are in lower-case roman enclosed in angle brackets (< >). Standard upper and lower case is used when the inscription is quoted at second hand or when the primary source does not purport to be an exact transcription. Inscriptions and buildings or sculptures that no longer exist are preceded by an asterisk; such inscriptions are also given in upper and lower case.

The Greek letters *alpha, chi, rho, sigma,* and *omega* are transcribed as A, X, P, C, and W. Joined, interlocked, interlaced, and superimposed letters are indicated by underlining (e.g., OCCIDIT) or, for adjacent groups of such letters, by underlining and overstriking (e.g., MATTEus).

When an inscription begins a new line or recommences in a new position, the end of the preceding line is marked with a virgule (/). Occasionally, a double virgule (//) marks a more prominent break. Other separations, such as joints between blocks of stone or vertical alignments, are indicated by a vertical bar (|).

Sources of Transcriptions and Documentation

Unless otherwise indicated, transcriptions are given on my own authority from personal inspection. No attempt has been made to cite previous transcriptions, except where they help clarify obscurities or where controversies are involved. I do include references to a few standard collections of inscriptions, such as, for France, *CIFM*. Omission of the sign 'cf.' in front of a reference indicates that I have not seen the inscription in question and am relying solely on the referenced source.

Metrical description

Verses are described as hexameters or pentameters or elegiac couplets; as unrhymed or as end-rhymed or as leonines. 'Common' leonine means monosyllabic internal rhyme; 'full' leonine means disyllabic internal rhyme. (See chapter 5, pp. 71–4, for a description of the characteristics of these types of verse and their rhyming schemes.) All departures from 'normal' medieval practice, including false quantity, feminine caesura, absence of caesura, and so on, are marked.

1. **Agen** (Lot-et-Garonne). Cathedral (former collegiate church) of St.-Caprais.

Interior. NE pier of the crossing: capital of the Martyrdom of Saint Caprais. The capital shows the Roman governor Dacian on the left, ordering the execution of Caprais, the bishop of Agen at the time of Saint Foy; a soldier carrying it out on the front of the capital; and the soul of Caprais ascending to heaven on the right. The figures are labelled DACIANVS, MILES, and SanCtuS CAPRAS[i]VS. An inscription (a) runs around the base of the capital.

Early 12th century.

(a) PRAECIPIT OCCIDIT MORITVR CELESTIA SCAN[DIT]

A common leonine hexameter. Cf. *CIFM*, 6, 112.

'<Dacian> orders, <the soldier> kills, <and Saint Caprais> dies and ascends to heaven.'

The hexameter can only be understood by inserting the visual subjects that appear with their labels above the verse into the meaning of the line.

2. **Aix-en-Provence** (Bouches-du-Rhône). Cathedral of St-Sauveur.

Interior. S aisle: squinches decorated with the symbols of the four Evangelists. In the NE corner, the winged man (half-figure) of Matthew, holding a book, with an inscription (a) in the background and on the book; in the NW corner, the winged lion of Mark, holding a book, with an inscription (b) in the background and on the book; in the SE corner, the winged bull of Luke, holding a book, with an inscription (c) in the background; and in the SW corner, the eagle of John, holding a scroll (?), with an inscription (d) in the background.

End of 12th century?[1]

(a) HOC MA~~TTE~~us / A/GENS / HOMINEm / GENE/RA/LITER / IMPLET

(b) MAR/CVS VT / ALTA FRE/MEnS VOX / Per DE/SERTA / LEONIS

(c) IV/RA SA/CERDOCII / LVCAS / TENET / O/RE IV/VENCI

(d) MORE [VOLANS AQV]ILE V[ER]BO PETIT / AS/TRA / IO/HannES

Four unrhymed hexameters. *CIFM*, 14, 27–8. False quantity in *sacerdŏcii* (c).

'Matthew doing this fills generally the role of the man. Mark (is) as the deep voice of the lion, roaring through the desert. Luke guards the rights of the priesthood in the shape of the bull. Flying in the manner of the eagle, John seeks the stars by means of the word.'

Sedulius, *Carmen paschale* 1, 355–8. Sedulius: *fremit* for *fremens* (b); *sacerdotis* for *sacerdocii* (c) (eliminating the false quantity).

3. **Ancona** (Le Marche). Sta Maria della Piazza.

W portal. Tympanum of five figures above an oversized lintel, with an inscription (a) in six lines. The figures are cut off at or above the waist. They are bearded and have long flowing hair. The three in the middle cross their chests with their right hands, with the index finger extended. The two largest figures (centre and right of centre) hold what may be scrolls in their left hands. All five figures lean to the right, and the lean is progressively more pronounced from left to right. None of them has a crown or other distinguishing emblem.

AD 1210.[2]

(a) + AD MATREM XPIS[T]I · QVE TEMPLO PRESIDET ISTI ·/
· QVI LEGIS INGREDERE · [V]ENIAmQue PRECANDO MERERE ·/
· CVM BIS CENTENVS [C]LAVSISSET TEMPORA DENVS ·/
· ANNVS MILLENVS [F]LORERET ·I· PAPA SERENVS ·/
· IMPERIIQue DECVS · P[R]INCEPS ·O·TTO SVMERET EQVVS ·/
· HEC PHILIPPE · PIE · DE[C]ORASTI TEMPLA MARIE ·

Six full leonine hexameters. Final syllable of *ingredere* lengthened at caesura (2). The initial *i* (4), set off by points, stands for *Innocentius*; it must be read as a short syllable. False quantities in *Ŏtto* (5) and *Phīlippe* (6), although the poet may have directed that the first *o* of *Otto* be set off by points to mark it as a short syllable. *Equus* (5) appears to be a nominative used in place of an accusative for the sake of the leonine rhyme.

'To the mother of Christ, you who preside over this church. You who choose, enter and merit grace by prayer. When the year 1210 had rounded off the time [and] Pope Innocent the serene was flourishing, and Prince Otto, worthy of the empire, took horse (?), you, Philip, decorated this church of the holy Mary.'

In 1210, the pope was Innocent III (1198–1216), the Hohenstaufen emperor (Guelph) was Otto IV of Brunswick (1198–1215 [crowned emperor in 1209]; d. 1218). Otto was excommunicated by Innocent in 1210.

4. **Aosta** (Valle d'Aosta). S. Orso.

Cloister. S gallery, second column from SW corner: capital of stylized plants with horned animal heads at the four corners, with an inscription (a) on the abacus above.

Ca. 1133.[3]

(a) MARMORIBVS VARIIS · HEC · EST · DISTINCTA · DECENTER :
FABRICA · NEC · MINVS · EST · DISPOSITA · CONVENIENTER ·

Two hexameters with disyllabic end rhyme. False quantity in *dispōsita.*

'This (cloister) is becomingly adorned with various sculptures. The building also is suitably designed.'

5. **Arles** (Bouches-du-Rhône). Former cathedral of St-Trophime.

W porch. Statues on either side of the portal: eight apostles and Saints Stephen and Trophime, the patrons of the church. Starting from the inner flank, closest to the portal, they are, by pairs (left [L] and right [R]): (L1) Peter, holding the keys in his right hand, with an inscription (a) on a book held in his left hand, and (R1) Paul, with an inscription (b) on a scroll partially unrolled over his chest; (L2) John, with an inscription (c) on a book held in his left hand, and (R2) Andrew, with an effaced inscription of his name on a book held in his left hand; (L3) Trophime, with an inscription (d) on the *pallium* hanging down his front, and (R3) the Martyrdom of Stephen, with an effaced inscription, **Pro Christo protomartyr animam suam posuit Stephanus,*[4] on a ribbon band draped over the body of the martyr;[5] (L4) James, with his name inscribed on a book held in his left hand, and (R4) James,[6] with his name inscribed on an open book held in his two hands; (L5) Bartholomew, with his name inscribed on an open book held in his left hand, and (R5) Philip, with his name inscribed on a book held in his two hands. Some of the inscriptions are now illegible, or nearly so.

Between 1152 and 1180.[7]

(a) CRIMINIBVS / DEMPTIS RE/SERAT / PETRVS AS/TRA REDE/MPTIS

A full leonine hexameter. Cf. *CIFM*, 14, 41–3.

'Peter unlocks heaven for the redeemed after their sins have been taken away.'

(b) LEX MOISI / CELAT QVOD / PAVLI SERMO / REVELAT /
NVNC DATA / GRANA SI/NA PER EVM /SVNT FACTA / FARINA

Two full leonine hexameters.

'The law of Moses hides what the word of Paul reveals. The grain given by him at Sinai has been made into flour.'

Cf. the leonine verses that Abbot Suger composed for the 'Anagogical' window of St-Denis.

(c) XPistI / DILEC/TVS IOHanneS / EST IBI / SECTV/S

A full leonine hexameter.

'John the beloved of Christ is carved here.'

(d) CER/NITVR / EXI/MIVS / VIR / XP[ist]I / DISCI/PVLO/RVM /
DE NV[M]/ERO / TRO/PHI/MVS / HIC / SEP/TVA/GIN/TA /
DVO/RVM

Two hexameters with disyllabic end rhyme. Final syllable of *Trophimus* (2) lengthened at caesura.

'Here is seen the outstanding man, Trophimus, one of the company of the seventy-two disciples of Christ.'

6. **Arles**. St-Trophime.

Interior. Monumental wall inscription (a) in the first (eastern) bay of the N aisle of the nave. The letters in brackets were completely cut away when the tribune for the organ was inserted at the end of the 17th century, but they are known because the inscription was copied earlier in the century.[8]

Ca. 1152.[9]

(a) **TE**[RRAR]VM ROMA **G**EMINA DE LVCE MAGISTR**A** /
RO[S MISS]VS S[EMPER] **A**DERIT VELVD INCOLA IOSE**P** /
OL[IM CO]NT[RITO] **L**OETEO CONTVLIT ORCH**O**

Two common leonine hexameters (1, 3) and one unrhymed hexameter, with three vertical acrostics: TRO<phimus> GAL<liarum> APO<stolus>, 'Trophime, the apostle of Gaul.'

Cf. *CIFM*, 14, 39.

'The dew [= faith] sent from Rome, the mistress of the world, from its twin light [= Peter and Paul], will always be present, as once, in a strange land, Joseph distributed it, after he had conquered infernal death.'

My translation is based on the French translation of Dom Willibrord Witters.[10]

7. **Armentia** (Álava). S. Prudencio (formerly dedicated to Saint Andrew[11]).

S porch. Tympanum of the S portal, now located above a tomb sculpture set into the wall. The tympanum is in two registers. The upper register displays the Lamb in a circle, with an inscription (a) around the circle. In the lower register there is a chrismon held by two angels, with an inscription (b) on the horizontal band above the chrismon, and the words HVIus OPerIS AVCTORES RODERICVS EPiscopuS on the horizontal band beneath. The *p* and *s* of *episcopus* are uncertain. Finally, there are inscriptions around the rim of the tympanum. One is a verse (c) that is above the horizontal band dividing the tympanum into two registers.

Ca. 1190–1200.

(a) .+. MORS : EGO : SVM : MORTIS : VOCOR : AGNVS : SVM : LEO : FORTIS

A full leonine hexameter.

'I am the death of death, I am called the Lamb, I am the strong Lion.'

(b) .+. PORTA : Per : HANC : CELI : FIT : PERVIA : CVIQVE : FIDELI

A full leonine hexameter.

'Through this gate the gate of heaven becomes accessible to each believer.'

This is the first line of the elegiac couplet that is carved on the cloister portal at S. Juan de la Peña; it also appears at the hermitage of Puilampa.

(c) .+. REX : SABBAOTH : MAGNVS DEVS : EST : ET : DICITVR : AGNVS :

A full leonine hexameter. The Hebrew word *sabbaoth* is scanned arbitrarily either as an anapaest or as a spondee.

'The great king of hosts is God and He is called the Lamb.'

8. **Auch** (Gers). *St-Orens.

Stone from the *tympanum, now in the Château de Montesquiou in Marsan. Samson mastering the lion, with an inscription (a) in the background of the fragment.

End 11th century.[12]

(a) [VIRTV]S SAMSONIS SEVI DOMA[T] / ORA LEO/NIS

A full leonine hexameter. *CIFM*, 6, 56.

'The virtue of fierce Samson tames the mouth of the lion.'

Cf. Judg. 14:5–6.

9. **Augsburg** (Bayern). *Sts Ulrich and Afra.

*Cloister. *Portal to lavabo: tympanum of Christ washing the feet of Saint Peter. The tympanum is in the Maximilianmuseum in Augsburg. Peter sits on a chair at the left with the label S PETRVS by his head; Christ kneels in the centre marked by the letters Alpha and Omega; the allegorical figure of Humility holding a scroll inscribed BEATI MITES stands at the right with the label HVMILITAS by her head. There is an inscription (a) on the rim of the tympanum, and an inscription (b) on the implied lintel.

Ca. 1190–1200. These are the dates of Abbot Erchembold who built the cloister.[13] According the museum label, the tympanum is 'nach Mitte des 13. Jh.'

(a) · HERET · [SER]VORVM · P[EDI]BVS · DOMINVS · DOMINO[RVM]

A full leonine hexameter. Cf. *Suevia Sacra*, 96.

'The Lord of lords clings to the feet of his servants.'

Cf. John 13:5–16.

(b) SIC · DeuS · Est · HVMILIS · TVMET · VT · Q[ui]D · HOMVNTIO · VI[LIS] ·

A full leonine hexameter.

'God is so humble; why does vile little man swell in pride?'

10. **Aulnay** (Charente-Maritime). St-Pierre.

Interior. NW pillar of the transept: capital of Samson and Delilah, with an inscription (a) on the abacus, above the scene. Samson lies asleep on a bed. Delilah is shown twice: cutting his hair with a pair of scissors on the left, and tying his hands with a rope on the right.[14]

After 1122.[15]

(a) SAMSONEM VINCIT COMVNCS CRINEMO;

A common leonine hexameter? Cf. *CIFM*, 1:3, 82–3. The first two words are clear; the rest is somewhat doubtful. It appears that the carver was hurried and tried to squeeze in the letters after using too much space for the word *Samsonem*. The letters *munc* of *comuncs* are particularly ill formed, and the stone here appears to be slightly damaged. What I have taken as a mark of suspension in the shape of a semicolon after the last word may be simply more damage. Scholars have interpreted the inscription variously. Oursel, *Haut-Poitou roman*, 310, reads:

SAMSONEM VINCIT COMA, V(I)NC(TU)S CRINE MORATUR,

'La chevelure vainc (la force de) Samson; il git lié par les crins.'[16] The problems with this interpretation are three. First, there is no *a* after *com*; second, *vncs* is not a typical 12th-century abbreviation; and third, the word *moratur* was not completed. Tonnellier, *Aulnay de Saintonge*, 18, who rejects this reading, claims to be able to see SAMSONEMVINCITCORAMOVeNTeSCRINEMQvE, which he interprets as *Samsonen [*sic*] vincit; cor amoventes crinemqve*, '(Dalila) ligote Samson; (les Philistins) lui enlèvent sa force avec sa chevelure.' Favreau and Michaud, *CIFM*, 1:3, 83, propose SAMSONEM VINCIT COMA V[I]NC[TV]S CRINE MO[VETVR]. At the risk of multiplying unprofitable hypotheses, I will offer another suggestion: SAMSONEM VINCIT CONIVNCS CRINEMQue <totondit>. Evidently, the carver bungled the inscription. He may have mistaken *ni* for *m* in *comuncs* (= *coniunx*) in his copy text. The final *o* of *crinemo* lacks only the tail to make a *q*, and Q; is a regular 12th-century abbreviation for *-que*. Two actions in the sculpture and two direct objects in the inscription imply two verbs. *Totondit* fits the scene, and, not incidentally, completes a common leonine hexameter. There is room for it on the adjacent side of the abacus, but the space is blank.

'His wife binds Samson and cuts his hair.'

Cf. Judg. 16:4–21.

11. **Autry-Issards** (Allier). Ste-Trinité.

W portal. Gable-shaped lintel of Christ in Majesty (effaced) in a mandorla supported by the archangels Michael and Raphael with an inscription (a) on the lower edge, followed by the words NATALIS ME FE<cit>. The lintel is surmounted by a steeply pitched roof under non-decorated, rounded-arch archivolts, with an inscription (b) under the roof.

After ca. 1130. Dupont, *Nivernais-Bourbonnais roman*, 282. Lefèvre-Pontalis, 'Autry-Issard,' 228, dates the church to the first half of the 12th century; *CIFM*, 18, 4, assigns the inscriptions to the beginning of the 12th century.

(a) + CVNCTA DEVS FECI HOMO FACTVS CV[n]CTA REFECI :

A full leonine hexameter. Cf. CIFM, 18, 3. Elision is blocked by the consonant *h*.

'I, God, made all things; when I became man, I remade all things.'

(b) + / PENAS / REDDO MA/LIS PREMIA / DONO BONIS

A common leonine pentameter.

'I inflict punishment on the wicked; I bestow rewards upon the good.'

12. **Autun** (Saône-et-Loire). Cathedral of St-Lazare. St-Lazare was elevated to the rank of cathedral in 1195.[17]

W portal. Tympanum of the Last Judgment. There is an inscription (a) on the rim of the mandorla; and inscriptions on the upper edge of the lintel: on the left (b) above the raising of the elect and on the right (c) above the raising of the damned. The words GISLEBERTVS HOC FECIT appear in the centre, above the separation of the saved and the damned.

Ca. 1130–35.[18]

(a) OMNIA · DISPONO SOLVS MERITOSQue CORONO :
QVOS SCELVS EXERCET · ME IVDICE PENA COERCET ·

Two full leonine hexameters.

'I alone arrange all things and crown the deserving. Punishment, with me as judge, holds in check those whom vice stimulates.'

(b) QVISQue RESVRGET ITA : QVEM Non TRHAIT [*sic*] IMPIA VITA
ET LVCEBIT EI SINE FINE LVCERNA DIEI

Two full leonine hexameters. Final syllable of *ita* (1) lengthened at caesura. TRHAIT = *trahit.*

'Whoever is not seduced by an impious life will rise again in this way, and the light of day will shine on him forever.'

(c) : TERREAT HIC TERROR QVOS TERREVS ALLIGAT ERROR
NAM FORE SIC VERVM NOTAT HIC HORROR SPECIERVm

Two full leonine hexameters.

'May this terror terrify those whom earthly error binds, for the horror of these images here in this manner truly depicts what will be.'

13. **Barcelona** (Barcelona). Sant Pau del Camp.

W portal. Tympanum of Christ in Majesty with the apostles Paul (left) and Peter (right) above a lintel that displays a chrismon in the centre. There is an inscription (a) followed by the words RENARDVS Qui Per SE T ANIM VXOR [EIus RAI]MVNDA // + /M/IS/I/T // IN / HAC / AVLA / MOA/BITI/NOS / VII, forming a rectangle around the chrismon. The names of the two apostles are inscribed in the centre of the lintel.

Second half of the 12th century?[19]

(a) + HEC · D[omi]NI · PORTA VIA EST OMNIBVS HORTA :
IANVA SVM VITE // Per ME GRADIENDO VENITE:

Two full leonine hexameters. A syllable was apparently omitted from the first verse, between *via* and *est*, when it was carved. Final syllable of *porta* (1) lengthened at caesura. Double virgules mark the separation between top, bottom, right-side, and left-side inscriptions, respectively. Hübner, *Inscriptionum Hispaniae christianarum supplementum*, 130 (no. 521), reads HEC DomiNI PORTA VIA EST OM/NIBVS HORTA IANVA SVM VITE // P ME GRADIENDO VENITE R////NARDVS QP ET A[...] EXORE PRIVMVNDA // M/I/S/I/T // IN / HAC / NLA / MOX / B·T· / NOS VII. Cf. Ocón Alonso, 'Tímpanos románicos,' 1, 64, and n. 71 (p. 454).

'This is the gate of the Lord, the way is open to all. I am the gate of life, come through me by walking.'

For the phrase *ianua sum vite* and the leonine rhyme *vite / venite*, cf. S. Giorgio al Palazzo (Milan). The remainder of the inscription is not entirely clear. Possibly it should be interpreted to read *Renardus qui per se et animam uxoris eius Raimundae misit in hac aula moabitinos septem*, 'Renard, who for himself and for the soul of his wife Ramona placed seven Arabic workers in this church.'[20]

14. **Baume-les-Messieurs** (Jura). St-Pierre.

Centre pier of *porch.[21] This is now in the S aisle of the nave against the S wall. It was inscribed on opposite faces. The inscription on one side (a) is still legible; on the other side, the inscription (b) is now too obliterated to make out.

Before 1130.[22]

(a) ABB/AS AL/BRICus / QVOD / DAT / TIBI / SVS/CIPE / MV/NVS / PETRE / STRV/ENDO / DOMVm / FAM/VLI / NE D/ESPI/CE DO/NVM / QVI LE/GIS HaEC / DICAS AB/BAS IN / PACE QVI/ESCAS

Three common leonine hexameters.

'Take the gift which Abbot Alberic, in building your home, gives you, Peter – do not despise your servant's gift. May you who read this say: Abbot, may you rest in peace.'

(b) *Indicat istud opus quantum fuerit studiosus
Abbas Albricus Christo tibi reddere munus,
Quod forte acceptum tibi aut posse fore gratum
Crimine plecto, Patris Albrici memor esto.

Two common leonines followed by two unmetrical (?), internally rhymed lines. Martène and Durand, *Voyage litteraire* 1:1, 173. Probably these two lines were regular hexameters that had become garbled, or so worn as not to be entirely legible, when Martène and Durand saw them.

'This work indicates how eager Abbot Alberic was to return a gift to you, Christ ...' The sense of the last two lines is evidently something like: 'May the gift you have received be pleasing to you [Christ]. When his sins have been thoroughly read over, be mindful of Father Alberic.'

15. **Beaucaire** (Gard). Notre-Dame-des-Pommiers.

Central portion of the tympanum from the *Romanesque church, now in a private house in Beaucaire. From Millin's description (see note below), we know that the tympanum was still in place as late as ca. 1808. The fragment shows the Virgin in Majesty, holding the Child in her lap. The Virgin was flanked on the left by the Adoration of the Magi, and on the right by the Angel warning Joseph in a Dream.[23] There is an inscription (a) on the base of the throne beneath the Virgin's feet, and Millin reports that there were similar inscriptions (b) beneath the Adoration of the Magi and (c) beneath the Warning of Joseph.

Ca. 1160.[24]

(a) IN GREMIO MA T[r]IS · RESIDET · SAPIENTIA · PATRIS :

A full leonine hexameter. Stoddard, *Façade of Saint-Gilles*, fig. 237; Lasteyrie, 'Études sur la sculpture française,' fig. 32; *CIFM*, 13, 12; and Lombard, 'Beaucaire.'

'In the bosom of the Mother sits the Wisdom of the Father.'

The same verse is inscribed on a chalice of the church of Eichstädt and on a statue of Sta Maria della Pieve of Arezzo. Both objects have been dated in the second half of the twelfth century.[25]

(b) *Nostro divino dant tres tria munera trino

A full leonine hexameter. Millin, *Voyage*, 435. *CIFM*, 13, 12, reads *nutu divino.*

'The three [Magi] give three gifts to our triune God.'

Cf. Matt. 2:11.

(c) *Ducit in Aegyptum Joseph cum Virgine Christum

A common leonine hexameter. Millin, *Voyage*, 435.

'Joseph leads Christ with the Virgin into Egypt.'

Cf. Matt. 2:13–14.

16. **Bellegarde-du-Loiret** (Loiret). Notre-Dame.

W portal. Tympanum of decorative floral patterns, surmounted by elaborately ornamented archivolts, with an inscription (a) on the lower edge.

Ca. 1124.[26]

(a) + : HIC : FIVNT : IVSTI : VICIORVM SO[rdibus usti]

A full leonine hexameter? The conjectural restoration is from Läffler, 'Bellegarde-du-Loiret,' 105.

'Here those consumed by the sordidness of their sins are made upright.'

17. **Bessines-sur-Gartempe** (Haute-Vienne). Church.

N exterior wall. Plaque, set between 2nd and 3rd buttresses, of the Hand of God superimposed on the Cross, with the Alpha and Omega on either side, DEXTERA DEI VIVI on the bottom edge, and an inscription (a) along the other three sides.

12th century.[27]

(a) + QVOD FVIT EST ET / E|R||T | Per | M|E / C|O|NS|TA|RE | DO|CE|T|V|R :

An unrhymed hexameter. Cf. *CIFM*, 2, 92.

'It is taught that what was, is, and will be exists through me.'

18. **Bourg-Argental** (Loire). Church.

East (formerly west) portal. Tympanum in two registers of Christ in Majesty and the Four Animals above scenes from the Nativity, with an inscription (a) on the semicircular arch of the tympanum and a second inscription (b) on the horizontal band separating the two registers.

Ca. 1135–40.[28]

(a) VOS QVI TRANSITIS CVR NON PRO[PERANDO VENITIS
AD ME DVM VENIET DAMNA FAMIS FVGIET]

A full leonine elegiac couplet. Barthélemy, 'Rapport,' 595; *CIFM,* 18, 55–6. The inscriptions are now partly illegible; they are known from the 19th-century transcription of Barthélemy.

'You who are entering, why do you not come in haste? Provided that he come to me, he will escape the evils of hunger.'

(b) ET VOS QVI BIBITIS MAGIS ATQVE BIBENDO SITITIS
SI DE ME [BIBITIS NON ERIT VLTRA SITIS]

A full leonine elegiac couplet with disyllabic end rhyme.

'And you who drink and by drinking thirst the more, if you drink of me, your thirst will be no more.'

Cf. John 4:13.

19. **Bourges** (Cher). *St-Pierre-le-Puellier.

*W portal (?). Fragments of the tympanum of the Death, Burial, and Assumption of the Virgin Mary, with an inscription (a) on the lintel, and (b) on the rim.[29] The fragments are in storage at the Musée du Berry in Bourges. In addition to five major fragments (I–V) there are three small pieces (i–iii) from the lintel, which fit into fragment I (text fig. 4).

Ca. 1175–85.[30]

(a) [*Fragment I*:] PALMAM VICTRICI FERT ANGELVS [HIC]
[*Fragment i*:] [G]EN[I]
[*Fragment ii*:] TRICI
[*Fragment iii*:] · DESERATV[S] ...
[*Fragment II*:] ... I (?) MA[T]RIS DEFERT AD G (?) ...

Three full leonine hexameters? The leonine rhyme of the first verse is nearly certain:

Palmam victrici fert angelus hic genitrici.
Deseratus ...
... Matris defert ad ...

'An angel bears the palm to the victorious mother.'

(b) [*Fragment III*:] INPON[VNT] PVLCRVM CORP[V]
[*Fragment IV*:] S SINE FRAVDE SEPVLCRVM :
[*Fragment V*:] FILI[VS] AD PATREM FACIT ALMAM SCANDER[E]
[*Fragment II*:] MATREM :

Two full leonine hexameters, although several details remain doubtful:

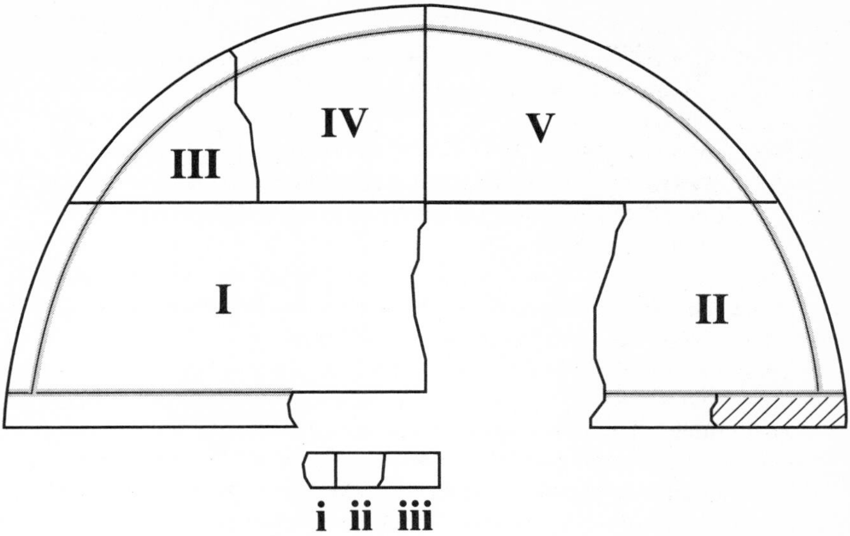

4 Tympanum of St-Pierre-le-Puellier of Bourges

Inponunt pulcrum corpus sine fraude sepulcrum.
Filius ad Patrem facit almam scandere Matrem.

On the rim of fragment I, which joins this from below, there is what appears to be a decorative Arabic (?) script. This is followed by the inscription on fragment III. After *Matrem*, there is a decorative Arabic (?) script.

'They (the apostles?) place the beautiful body, which is without stain, in the tomb. The Son has his blessed mother ascend to the Father.'

20. **Carpentras** (Vaucluse). Former cathedral of St-Siffrein.[31]

Interior. Pendentives of the cupola. The NW pendentive displays the eagle of John; the NE pendentive displays the lion of Mark; the SW pendentive displays the bull of Luke. The SE pendentive displays the winged man of Matthew, holding an open book with an inscription (a). The inscriptions can no longer be seen, but are known from earlier photographs.

Ca. 1180.

(a) FIT HO/MO MA/TRE DEVS // GENVS / INDICAT / ECCE MAT/TEVS

A full leonine hexameter. *CIFM*, 13, 141. The first syllable of *Matteus* is arbitrarily shortened.

'God becomes a man by a mother; behold, Matthew shows his descent.'

Cf. Matt. 1:1.

21. **Cassan** (Hérault). Ste-Marie.[32]

N portal (now walled up). A blank tympanum with a square marble plaque inserted in its centre, with an inscription (a).

First half of 12th century?

(a) QVISQVIS HOmO SCELERIS / FVNESTI MOLE GRAVARIS /
PRE FORIBVS DOMINO / MERENS ProSTerNERE SVMMO /
HAVD SECus InTRATur / Quia IANVA XPistuC HABETVR

Three common leonine hexameters.

'You, whoever you are – a man with a burden of deadly sin – who are reluctant to prostrate yourself in sorrow to the supreme Lord before this portal, the gate is entered in no other way, because it is held to be Christ.'

For the last line, cf. John 10:7, 9.

22. **Castell'Arquato** (Emilia-Romagna). Sta Maria Assunta.

N portal. Tympanum of the Virgin in Majesty seated with the Child in her lap. An inscription (a) extends the length of the lower border of the tympanum and continues on the right side of the curve of the semicircular border.

Ca. 1185.[33]

(a) + NATA GERIT NATVM · DE SE SINE SEMINE CRETVM ·
EST PATER IHC NATVS · NATE DE VEN/TRE CREATVS ·

Two leonine hexameters; the first common, the second full. The reversal of *i* and *h* in HIC appears to be a visual pun, since IHC is the regular suspension for *Iesus*.

'The daughter bears the Son, who came into existence from himself without seed. This son/Jesus is the Father born from the belly of his daughter.'

23. **Champeix** (Puy-de-Dôme). Church.

N transept portal. Gable-shaped lintel: the Trinity signified by the hand of God raised in blessing, the lamb, and the dove, with an inscription (a).

12th century.

(a) TRES TRINVM SIGNA~~NT~~ POLLEX PECCVS [*sic*] ATQue COLVmBA

An unrhymed hexameter. Cf. *CIFM*, 18, 156. *Peccus*, which spoils the meter, is an error for *pecus*.

'The three – hand, sheep, and dove – signify the Triune God.'

24. **Cîteaux** (Côte-d'Or). Abbey.

*Main gate of the abbey, with an inscription (a) in gold letters.

Ca. 1200?

(a) *Ad nos flecte oculos, dulcissima virgo Maria,
Et deffende tuam diva patrona domum.

An unrhymed elegiac couplet. Martène and Durand, *Voyage litteraire*, I, i, 217. Elision (1).

'Bend your eyes on us, sweetest Virgin Mary, and protect your house, blessed patroness.'

25. **Cîteaux**. *Abbey Church.

*Main portal, with an inscription (a).

Ca. 1200?

(a) *Salve, sancta parens, sub qua Cistercius ordo
Militat, & toto tamquam sol fulget in orbe.

Two unrhymed hexameters. Martène and Durand, *Voyage litteraire*, 1:1, 217.

'Hail, holy Mother, under whose banner the Cistercian Order marches, and shines like the sun over the whole world.'

26. **Cîteaux**. *Abbey Church.

*'Image' of the Patroness of the Order, surmounted by an inscription (a). Its location in the church is unknown.

Ca. 1200?

(a) *Haec caput & mater Cisterci est ordinis aedes
Quae devota manet Virgo Maria tibi.
Auspice testantem, rogo, protege, porrige Christo
Quae fiunt intus nocte dieque preces.

Two unrhymed elegiac couplets. Martène and Durand, *Voyage litteraire*, 1:1, 218. Elision (1). *Auspice* from unrecorded verb *auspicio* (?), or blunder for *aspice* (?).

'This building, which, O Virgin Mary, is dedicated to you, is the head and mother of the Cistercian Order. Look favourably on the donor (?), I beg, protect him, extend to Christ the prayers which are made within night and day.'

27. **Clermont-Ferrand** (Puy-de-Dôme). Notre-Dame-du-Port.

S nave portal. Tympanum of Christ in Majesty surrounded by the Four Animals and by the two Seraphim of the Vision of Isaiah (Isa. 6:1–3) above a gable-shaped lintel representing the Adoration of the Magi (left); the Presentation in the Temple (right centre); the Baptism of Christ (far right). There are inscriptions (a) on the left slope of the gable (above the Adoration of the Magi), (b) on the left lower edge of the lintel (below the Adoration of the Magi), (c) on the upper-right slope of the gable (above the Presentation in the Temple), (d) on the right-centre lower edge of the lintel (below the Presentation in the Temple), (e) on the lower-right slope and right vertical edge of the gable (above and to the right of the Baptism of Christ), and (f) on the far right edge of the lintel.

First half of 12th century? The tympanum and lintel are now generally thought to belong together, despite the superficial differences that led earlier scholars to separate them in time. The iconography of the tympanum shows no trace of the elaboration of the theme from the Vision of Isaiah such as we find at Moissac.[34] Jacques Bousquet points out that the epigraphy of the lintel is 'very archaic' and close to the epigraphy of Conques.[35]

(a) + ECCE MAGI NATO : DEPORTANT MVNERA · REGI

An unrhymed hexameter. Cf. *CIFM*, 18, 191–2.

'Behold, the Magi carry gifts to the new-born King.'

Cf. Matt. 2:1–12.

(b) HETHEREO REGI TRES DANT TRIA DONA SABEI

A common leonine hexameter.

'The three Sabaeans give three gifts to the heavenly King.'

(c) + IN TEMPLO DOMINO PVER OFFERTVR MATEP [*sic*] IHSu :

A garbled hexameter? or two separate phrases?

'In the temple the child is offered to the Lord. The Mother of Jesus.'

Cf. Luke 2:22–35.

(d) + HIC PVER EXCIPITVR IN VLNIS A SIMEONE

Another garbled hexameter?

'Here the Child is taken by Simeon in his arms.'

Cf. Luke 2:28.

(e) BAPTIIZAT PROLEM DomiNI / B|A|P|T|I|I|S|T|A / IO[hannis]

An unrhymed hexameter.

'John the Baptist baptizes the offspring of the Lord.'

Cf. Matt. 3:13–16; Mark 1:9; Luke 3:21; John 1:32–3.

(f) IHS[us] (?)

Possibly this is the last word of an otherwise effaced inscription on the far right edge of the lintel beneath the Baptism of Christ. There is sufficient space for a compact hexameter.

28. **Cluny** (Saône-et-Loire). Notre-Dame.

S portal. Tympanum of the Coronation of the Virgin (?), with an inscription (a) that was still visible in 1913. The sculpted figures of the tympanum have disappeared.

13th c.?

(a) *Sum quod eram, nec eram quod sum, nunc dicor utrumque

An unrhymed hexameter. Virey, 'Cluny,' 69.

'I am what I was, but I was not what I am; now I am called both.'

Probably this is to be interpreted: I am still a virgin, but I am also a mother, and now I am called the Virgin Mother.

29. **Cluny**. *St-Pierre-et-St-Paul [the 3rd abbey church, known as Cluny III].

*Interior. Capital of the first four tones of the Plain Chant (eight ambulatory capitals, three of them with inscriptions, were once set on eight columns arranged in a semicircle in the ambulatory; they are now displayed in the Musée du Farinier in Cluny): four figures within almond-shaped mandorlas, with inscriptions around the rim of the mandorlas. Figure #1, the First Tone, with an inscription (a), shows a man seated, playing a musical instrument. Figure #2, the Second Tone, with an inscription (b), shows a woman standing. Figure #3, the Third Tone, with an inscription (c), shows a man seated, playing an instrument that looks like a lyre. Figure #4, the Fourth Tone, with an inscription (d), shows a man with a bar over his shoulders on which two bells are hung.

Ca. 1088–1130.[36]

(a) HIC TONVS ORDITVR MODVL/A/MINA MVSICA PRIMVS

An unrhymed hexameter.

'This first tone begins the musical melodies.'

(b) SVBSEQV[ITV]R PTONGVS NV/MERO VeL LEGE SECVNDVS

A common leonine hexameter.

'The second tone follows by measure and rule.'

(c) TERTIVS IMPINGIT XPistuM/QVE RESVRGERE FINGIT ;

A full leonine hexameter.

'The third (tone) depicts and instructs that Christ rises again.'

(d) SVCCEDIT QVARTVS SIMVLA/N/S IN CARMINE PLANCTVS

A common leonine hexameter.

'The fourth (tone) follows, imitating in song the lamentations of mourning.'

30. **Cluny**. *St-Pierre-et-St-Paul.

*Interior. Capital of the second four tones of the Plain Chant: four figures separated by stylized acanthus-leaf scrolls, with a continuous inscription band around the middle. Each inscription is in two lines and is marked off from the one adjacent to it by a cross or a vertical line that extends the full height of the inscription band. Figure #1, with an inscription (a), is the Fifth Tone; figure #2, with an inscription (b), is the Sixth Tone; figure #3, with an inscription (c), is the Seventh Tone; and figure #4, with an inscription (d), is the Eighth Tone.

Ca. 1088–1130.

(a) OSTENDIT QVINTVS QVAM SIT / QVISQ[V]IS TVMET IMVS ; / +

A common leonine hexameter.

'The fifth (tone) shows how low he is who is puffed up.'

(b) SI CVPIS AFFECTVM PIETATIS / RESPICE SEXTVM : / +

A common leonine hexameter.

'If you wish a pious mood, give your attention to the sixth (tone).'

(c) INSINVAT FLATV[m] CV[m] DONIS / SEPTIMVS ALMVM :
A common leonine hexameter.

'The seventh (tone) insinuates the Holy Ghost with gifts (into the hearer).'

(d) OCTAVVS SANCTOS OM[ne]S / DOCET ESSE BEATOS :
A common leonine hexameter.

'The eighth (tone) teaches that all the saints are blessed.'

31. **Cluny**. *St-Pierre-et-St-Paul.

*Interior. Capital of the four Cardinal Virtues of Justice, Fortitude, Prudence, and Temperance (?): four figures within almond-shaped mandorlas, with inscriptions around the rim. Figure #1, Prudence, or 'Spring,' is a woman standing, holding a book in her hands, with an inscription (a). Figure #2, Justice (?), or 'Summer,' is a woman standing, with an inscription (b). The figure is damaged, but possibly she held the scales of justice in her hand.[37] Figure #3, Fortitude, or 'Avenging Prudence,' is a woman in armour, with an inscription (c). Figure #4, Temperance (?), or 'Warning Prudence,' is a woman facing a small figure (heavily damaged), with an inscription (d).

Ca. 1088–1130.

(a) + VER PRIMOS FLORES / PRIMOS ProDVCIT ODORES
A full leonine hexameter.

'Spring produces the first flower (and) the first odours.'

(b) [FALX RESECAT SPICAS FER]VENS / Q[V]AS DECOQ[VI]T AESTAS ;
A common leonine hexameter. The first portion of the inscription was painted; from ... VENS on it was carved. The painted portion can no longer be seen. For the restoration, see Evans, *Cluniac Art*, 113, and n. 9.

'The sickle cuts short the blades of wheat which the hot summer ripens.'

(c) DAT COGN[oscen]DV[m] PRVDENTIA Q[u]ID SIT /AGENDV[M]
A full leonine hexameter.

'Prudence gives knowledge of what ought to be done.'

(d) DAT NOS MONENDV[M] PRVDENTIA Q[u]ID SIT AGENDVM
A full leonine hexameter. Lloyd, 'Cluny Epigraphy,' 347, fig. 9D. False quantity in *mōnendum.* The inscription was painted, and cannot now be seen.

32. **Cluny**. *St-Pierre-et-St-Paul.

*Interior. Keystone of the vault of the fifth bay of the narthex: the Easter Lamb, with an encircling inscription (a). The keystone is displayed in the Musée Ochier.

Ca. 1155.[38]

(a) + IN CELO MAGNus : HIC PARVus SCVLPOR VT AGNus :
A full leonine hexameter. Final syllable of *magnus* lengthened at caesura.

'In heaven (I am) the Great Lamb; here I am sculpted as a small lamb.'

33. **Colmar** (Haut-Rhin). St-Martin.

S transept portal, the 'St.-Nicolas portal.' Composite tympanum of Christ resurrecting the dead (upper, Gothic) and of two scenes from the legend of Saint Nicholas (lower, Romanesque). There is an inscription (a) around the rim of the Romanesque tympanum; the names CVNRADVS, VTECHA, and NICOLAVS are inscribed along its lower edge.

Late 12th century?

(a) + DAT · CVLTOR · TRINI · TRIA · TRIS · VT · DET · [tr]IA · FINI
FAMA · FAMES · SCORT[us] · VT · CEDANT · CELITVS · ORTVS ·
AVREA · VIRGINIBus · DAT TrIA · DONA · TRIBVS ·
ERIPIS · HOS · MORTI · NICOLAE · NECISQue · COHORTI +

Four full leonines: a hexameter, an elegiac couplet, and a hexameter. Possibly the four lines were deliberately given an interlocking monosyllabic end rhyme: abba. Final syllable of *scortus* lengthened at caesura. The scansion of the tetrasyllabic *Nĭcolae* (vocative) is not classical (the first syllable should be long).

'... He [Saint Nicholas] gives three golden gifts to the three virgins. You, Nicholas, rescue these men from death and from the company of death.'

The first two lines are untranslatable as they stand. They may have been garbled before being carved, or perhaps they had a private meaning.

34. **Condeissiat** (Ain). St-Julien-et-St-Laurent.

W portal. Tympanum of Christ in Majesty, with an inscription (a) around the rim of the mandorla, and an inscription, IN NOMINE DomiNI NOSTRI IHsV XPistI ET BEATE SENPER VIRGI/NIS MARIE & SanCtI IVLIANI MARTIRIS, 'In the name of our Lord, Jesus Christ, and of the always blessed Virgin Mary and of Saint Julian the Martyr,' around the arch and on the lower edge of the tympanum.

Early 12th century.[39]

(a) SIC RESIDENS CELO N[o]B[is] XPistuS BENEDICIS

An unrhymed hexameter. Cf. *CIFM*, 17, 5. Guédel, *L'architecture romane en Dombes*, 61, reads: *Sic residens coelo B(eatus) Christus benedicis.*

'Sitting thus in heaven, you bless us, Christ.'

35. **Conques** (Aveyron). Ste-Foy.

W portal. Tympanum of the Last Judgment. There is an inscription, [R]/E/X IV/D/E/X, on the halo of Christ; the inscriptions <Venite benedict>I PATRIS MEI P<oss>IDETE VO<bis paratum regnum> / DISCEDITE A ME [MALEDicti], on scrolls held by the two angels who flank the upper edges of the mandorla; the inscriptions [I]E[SV]S REX IVDEORVM and SOL : LANCEA : CLAVI LVNA : / OC SIGNVm CRVCIS ERIT IN CELO CVM, on the upper vertical and the horizontal arms of the cross above Christ's head; inscriptions on the left (a) and right (b) of the upper inscription band, referring to the scenes below in the middle register; the inscriptions [FIDES SPES] / CARITAS / [CONSTANCIA] / VMILITAS, on the scrolls held by the angels on the left side of the middle register; an inscription, SIGNATVR LIBER [VI]TE, on the book held by an angel on the right side of the middle register; an inscription, EXIBVNT ANGELI ET SEPARA<bunt malos de medio iustorum> (Matt. 13:49), on the shield of an angel on the right side of the middle register; inscriptions on the left (c) and right (d) of the middle inscription band, referring to scenes below in the lower register; an inscription (e) on the angled slopes above the Heavenly City, referring to the scene beneath; an inscription (f) on the angled slopes above Hell, referring to the scene beneath; and an inscription (g) on the bottom edge of the tympanum beneath the Heavenly City and the Weighing of the Souls. The author of these verses (a–g) also composed verses for the reliquaries in the Treasury and the verse epitaph for Abbot Bego's tomb in 1107.[40]

In addition there are several inscriptions that are not visible to the viewer. These include the word CVNEVS or CVNEI on a coin of the counterfeiter on the right side of the middle register; the word IERONIMVS on a banderole held by a monk on the left side of the middle register; and an inscription in Arabic characters on the lower edge of the robe of the angel blowing the trumpet in the upper right of the tympanum.

Ca. 1105–15.[41]

(a) SANCTORVM CETVS STAT XPISTO IVDICE LETVS

A full leonine hexameter. Cf. *CIFM*, 9, 17–25.

'The assembly of saints stands joyfully before Christ the Judge.'

(b) HOMNES PERVERSI – SIC SVNT IN TARTARA MERS[I]

A full leonine hexameter. The poet substituted *homnes* for the anapaestic *homines* (with a pun on *omnes*) to secure an initial long syllable.

'Wicked men – thus they are plunged into hell.'

(c) SIC DATVR ELE/CTIS / AD CELI GAVDIA V[E]CTIS
GLORIA PAX REQVIES · PERPETVVSQue DIES

A full leonine elegiac couplet.

'Thus is given to the elect, who have been borne to the joys of heaven, glory, peace, rest, and eternal light.'

(d) + PENIS INIVSTI CRVCIANTVR IN IGNIBVS VSTI
DEMONAS ATQue TREMVNT : PERPETVOQue GEMVNT :

A full leonine elegiac couplet. The Greek accusative plural in *-ăs* is used to secure a short syllable in place of the regular cretic form *dēmŏnēs* (2).

'The unjust, burned in fires, are tormented by punishments, and they shudder at the demons and groan endlessly.'

(e) CASTI PACIFICI MITES : PIETATIS AMICI : I
SIC STANT · GAVDENTES · SECVRI NIL ME/TVENTES

Two full leonine hexameters.

'The chaste, the peace-loving, the gentle ones, the lovers of piety – thus they remain rejoicing, secure, fearing nothing.'

(f) + FVRES MENDACES FALSD [*sic*] CVPIDIQVE RAPACES I
SIC SVNT DAMPNATI CVNCTI SIMVL ET SCELERATI

Two full leonine hexameters. FALSD is an error for *falsi* (1).

'Thieves, liars, hypocrites, and the rapaciously avaricious – thus they are condemned and defiled at the same moment.'

(g) O PECCATORES TRANSMVTETIS NISI MORES :
IVDICIVM DVRVM VOBIS SCITOTE FVTVRVM :

Two full leonine hexameters.

'Sinners, if you do not change your ways, know that a hard judgment will be upon you.'

36. **Conques**. Ste-Foy.

*Cloister. Lintel from an *entrance door, with an inscription (a). The lintel is now housed with the treasure of Conques in the building labelled 'Trésor II.'

Ca. 1095–1105.

(a) HAS BENEDIC VALVAS QVI / MVNDVM REX BONE SALVAS /
ET NOS DE PORTIS SIMVL / OMNES ERIPE MORTIS :

Two full leonine hexameters. Cf. *CIFM*, 9, 38.

'Bless these doors, good King, you who save the world, and at the same time snatch us all from the gates of death.'

37. **Conques**. Ste-Foy.

Gable-shaped lintel from an entrance door to a storage room in the *monastic school (?), with an inscription (a). It is now placed in the W walk of the cloister.

Ca. 1095–1105.

(a) ISTE MAGISTRORVM LOCVS EST SIMVL ET PVERORVM /
MITTVNT QVANDO VOLVNT HIC RES QVAS PERDERE NOLVNT

Two full leonine hexameters. Cf. *CIFM*, 9, 37–8.

'This is the place both of the masters and the boys. When they wish, they send to this place the things which they do not want to lose.'

38. **Corneilla-de-Conflent** (Pyrénées-Orientales). Notre-Dame.

W portal. Tympanum of the Virgin in Majesty with the Child, with an inscription (a) around the arch of the tympanum.

Second half of the 12th century.[42]

(a) HEREDES · V·I··T··E· : DOMINAM : LAVDARE : VENITE :
PER QVAM VITA DATVR : MVNDVS PER EAM REPARATVR

Two full leonine hexameters.

'Heirs of (eternal) life, come praise the Lady, by whom life is given, and by whom the world is renewed.'

The phrase *haeredes vitae aeternae* is found in Titus 3:7 and 1 Peter 3:22.[43] The couplet is nearly identical to one in the subterranean church of the Death of the Virgin in Jerusalem, which reads: 'Haeredes vitae Dominam laudare venite / Per quam vita datur mundique salus reparatur.'[44]

39. **Cremona** (Lombardia). *Santi Vito e Modesto.

*Portal. Tympanum of the miracles of Saint Vitus, now in the Museo Civico. On the left, the saint frees the son of the Emperor Diocletian from a demon. On the right, he tames a lion that the emperor had thrown him to. The hand of God appears at the top centre. A double row of inscriptions (a) runs on the semicircular blocks that form an arch around the tympanum.

Second half of 12th century.[45]

(a) VT MOX ConCESSIT LEO CEPIT CVI FAMVLARI /
+ DEMOn DISCESSIT DE REGIS CORPORE NATI

Two unrhymed hexameters. Cf. Francovich, *Benedetto Antelami*, 1, 35. The verse in the first line is preceded by four (?) words, QVI VITI Non SVPerATI, and the verse in the second line is followed by two words, IMPIO CESSIT, that are not metrical and do not make sense as they stand.

'As soon as the lion yielded, he began to serve him. The demon has departed from the body of the king's son.'

40. **Déols** (Indre). *Notre-Dame of Bourg-Dieu.

*N portal. Tympanum of Christ in Majesty with the Four Animals, surmounted by three recessed orders of arches decorated with figures. Only a fragment of the tympanum and the Lamb of God remain. These are displayed in the Musée Bertrand in Châteauroux. An inscription (a) appeared on the lintel of the tympanum. The inner arch displayed angels in adoration; the keystone represented the Lamb of God. The middle arch displayed nine statues of the Arts and Sciences. At the summit of the arch was Philosophy with a banderole in her right hand with an inscription (b) and a banderole in her left hand with an inscription (c). These she offered respectively to Grammar and Dialectic.

Ca. 1145–60.[46]

(a) QVI CAPTIVARIS MISER IN MISERA REGIONE
AD | PATRIAM R[EDITVS PER ME PATET EX BABYLONE]

Two hexameters with disyllabic end rhyme. The right side of the tympanum with the Eagle and the Bull and the rest of the inscription is missing. The missing words are supplied from the transcription of Father Dubouchat.[47]

'You wretch who are held captive in a wretched place, the way back from Babylon to your homeland lies open through me.'

(b) *Auri grata sonent sicut sacra dictio partes
Per te doctrine relique noscuntur et artes

Two hexameters with disyllabic end rhyme. Father Dubouchat transcribed this as *Auri grata sonent sunt sacra dictio partes – Per te doctrina reliqua noscuntur et artes.*[48] Jean Hubert proposes several corrections, which, with the exception of *noscantur* for *noscuntur*, I have adopted.[49]

'May the parts of speech sound as pleasing to the ear as sacred Scripture. Through you the other sciences and arts are known.'

(c) *Altera que docent sic sit ne filia monstra
Notaque sint nostris per te sophismata nostra

Two hexameters with disyllabic end rhyme. Father Dubouchat's transcription is *Altera que docent sic sit ne filia monstra – note que sint nostris per te sophismata nostra.*[50] Hubert emends the first verse to *Altera que docuit succincte filia monstra.*[51] This is too radical a change to carry complete conviction, nor is the meaning that it gives persuasive. I have accepted Hubert's emendation in the second verse. False quantity in *dōcent* (1). In *sophismata* (2), *-ph* is allowed to lengthen the first syllable.[52]

'May our faults of logic be made known to us through you.'

The first verse is too faulty to be translated.

41. **Dijon** (Côte-d'Or). Cathedral (former abbey church) of St-Bénigne.

*Left W portal. *Tympanum of the Martyrdom of Saint Benignus.[53] It was reproduced in a drawing by Dom Plancher[54] and in a similar drawing in the Bibliothèque nationale, Bourgogne, ms. 14, fol. 122.[55] There were inscriptions (a) on the lintel, and (b) on the arch of the tympanum. In addition to the verses given below, the inscriptions included several labels and in (b) several letters from what may have been a second hexameter.

Ca. 1140–60.[56]

(a) + MACTANT Non DIGNVm TAm SEVA MORTE BENIGNVm +

A full leonine hexameter.

'They [Count Terentius and King Aurelianus] are killing Benignus who is not deserving of so cruel a death.'

(b) + NunC TIBI VIVERE · DONAT IN ETHERE VISIO XPistI

An unrhymed hexameter. Feminine caesura. This verse was probably balanced by another hexameter on the left curve of the rim of the tympanum (only fragments of which remained when the tympanum was drawn).

'Now the sight of Christ gives you life in heaven.'

42. **Dijon**. St-Bénigne.

*Right W portal. Tympanum of the Last Supper.[57] There is an inscription (a) on the lintel, and several letters from what may have been another inscription around the arch of the tympanum. The tympanum is now in the Musée archéologique of Dijon.

Ca. 1140–60.

(a) + CVm : RVDIS : AN~~TE~~ : FO~~RE~~M : DE~~DI~~T : HunC : MICHI : PETR~~VS~~ : HONOREM

+ MVTANS : HORROREM : FORMA : MELIORE : PRIO[REM]

Two full leonine hexameters with disyllabic end rhyme.

'Since I was formerly crude, Peter gave me this adornment, changing my previous uncouthness for a better form.'

43. **Dijon**. St-Bénigne.

*Portal leading from church to cloister (?).[58] Tympanum of Christ in Majesty with the Four Animals, with inscriptions (a) on the lintel, (b) on the arch of the tympanum, and (c) on the book held by Christ in his left hand. The tympanum is now in the Musée archéologique of Dijon.

Ca. 1140–60.

(a) RED~~DIDIT~~ : AMISS~~VM~~ : MICHI : PET~~RI~~ : CVRA : DECOREM

+ ET : DE~~DIT~~ : ANTI~~QVA~~ : FOR~~MAM~~ : MVL~~TO~~ : MELIOREM

Two hexameters with disyllabic end rhyme.

'The care of Peter has restored my lost beauty and given me a form better by far than the old.'

(b) CVm : SIT : SVBIECTVM : FINI : QVODCVMQue : VIDETVR

+ SOLA : DEI [MVNDI (?) MAI]ESTAS : FINE : TENETVR :

Two hexameters with disyllabic end rhyme.

'Since all things visible must have an end, only the majesty (?) of God is maintained at the end (of the world?).'

(c) SVM / FINIS / SVM / PRINCI/PIVM // MVN/DIQue / CRE/ATOR

An unrhymed hexameter. Caesuras in the second and fourth feet, but not in the third.

'I am the end, I am the beginning and the Creator of the world.'

44. **Dinton** (Buckinghamshire). Sts Peter and Paul.

S portal. Tympanum of two monsters eating fruit from a tree and a lintel of leviathan facing an angel. A two-line inscription (a) is in raised lettering within a rectangular frame. The first line is on the lower edge of the tympanum. The second is on the upper bevelled edge of the lintel, which cannot be seen from a normal standing position.

Mid-13th century.[59]

(a) + PREMIA PRO MERITIS SI Q[u]IS DESPE[re]T HABENDA /

AVDIAT HIC PREC[e]PTA SIBI QVE SIT RETINENDA

Two hexameters with disyllabic end rhyme. Feminine caesura (2).

'If anyone despairs of the rewards which are deserved for merited deeds, let him hear in this place the precepts which he ought to keep.'

45. **Egmond Binnen** (Noord Holland). *Sts Peter and Adelbert.

Tympanum of Saint Peter with the praying figures of Dirk VI, Count of Holland (1122–57), and his mother the Countess Petronella. There is an inscription (a) on the rim of the tympanum; and (b) on its lower edge. The tympanum is in the Rijksmuseum, Amsterdam (inventory number 1914, catalogue number 1).

Ca. 1122–32 (museum catalogue).

(a) [I]ANITOR · O · CELI · TIBI · ProNVm · MENTE · FIDELI

:+: INTROMITTE · GREGEM · SV[PER]Vm PLACANS · SIBI REGEM

Two full leonine hexameters. Cf. Deijk, *Pays-Bas romans*, 329.

'O gatekeeper of heaven, by appeasing the heavenly King, let in your flock who prostrate themselves before you with faithful hearts.'

(b) +HIC THIDERIC ORAT OPVS H[o]C · PET[r]ONILLA DEC[o]RAT

A full leonine hexameter. Cf. Deijk, *Pays-Bas romans*, 329. False quantity in *decōrat*.

'Here Dirk prays, Petronella adorns this work [= the church?].'

46. **Elne** (Pyrénées-Orientales). Former cathedral of Ste-Eulalie.

S walk of cloister. Third pillar (from W) with frieze of interlaced medallions enclosing a dragon, a lion, and facing peacocks, with an inscription (a) on the W face (above a lion and dragon opposed) and a prose inscription, ECCE QVAm BONVm ET QVAm IOCVNDVM HABITARE FRATRES IN VNVM (Ps. 132:1), on the S face (above the facing peacocks).

Ca. 1180.[60]

(a) ECCE · SALVTARE · PARITER · FRATRES HABITARE :

A full leonine hexameter. Final vowel of *salutare* lengthened at caesura.

'Behold, [how] salutary it is for the brothers to live together.'

47. **Estella** (Navarra). S. Miguel.

N portal. Tympanum of Christ in Majesty in a quadrilobed mandorla, surrounded by the Four Animals and two standing angels. A very worn, nearly illegible inscription (a) runs clockwise around the rim of the mandorla.

Ca. 1187–beginning of the 13th century.[61]

(a) NEC DEVS EST NEC HOMO PRESENS QVAM CERNIS IMAGO

SET DEVS EST ET HOMO QVEM SACRA FIGVRAT IMAGO

Two common leonine hexameters with identical trisyllabic end rhyme. Cf. Favreau, 'L'inscription du tympan nord,' 237.

'The present image which you see is not God nor man, but it is God and man whom the sacred image figures.'
This couplet was carved on the tympanum of the Portal of the Months at Ferrara.

48. **Esztergom** (Komárom). Cathedral (1822–69).

The W portal of the late Romanesque church survived until 1764.[62]

*W portal (the 'Porta Speciosa'). *Tympanum of the Virgin in Majesty with the Child, flanked by Saint Adalbertus on her right and Saint Stephen on her left. Two angels were at the Virgin's head; a smaller standing figure accompanied each saint; there was a very small tree in each corner. Stephen held a scroll with an inscription (a); the Virgin held a scroll with an inscription (b); Adalbertus held a scroll with an inscription (c). The lintel was decorated with a wheel in the centre, inscribed **rota in medio rotae* (Ezek. 1:16), flanked by two angels and the kneeling figures of Job (left), archbishop of Esztergom (1184–1204), and Bela III (right), king of Hungary (1174–96), and by a church and castle, all with labelling inscriptions. Archbishop Job carried a scroll inscribed **Deus propitius esto mihi peccatori* (Luke 18:13) and King Bela a scroll inscribed **qui plasmasti me miserere mei.* There was an inscription (d) on the lower edge of the lintel.

AD 1188–96.

(a) *Suscipe Virgo pia mea regna regenda Maria

A full leonine hexameter. Máthes, *Veteris Arcis Strigoniensis,* 36 (based on an 18th-century painting of the portal). Final vowel of *pia* lengthened at caesura.

'Receive into your protection, Holy Virgin Mary, my kingdoms.'
These are the words of King Stephen, the first king of Hungary (1001–38) and founder of the archbishopric at Esztergom, addressed to the Virgin.

(b) SVSSCI[pio serv]/ANDA · TVI[s si iura sacrorum
Su]/MET · ADA[lbertus sicut petis]

An unrhymed hexameter followed by the first four feet of a second hexameter. A surviving fragment of the scroll in Mary's hand shows portions of the inscription (photograph in Dercsényi, 'La "Porta Speciosa,"' fig. 17). The remainder of the inscription (in square brackets) is from Máthes, *Veteris Arcis Strigoniensis,* 36. There is no indication that the second verse was ever completed.

'I undertake to protect your kingdoms, if Adalbertus will assume the authority over the church as you ask ...'
The Virgin replies to King Stephen.

(c) *Annuo Virgo tuis iussis ac exequar ut vis

A common leonine hexameter. Máthes, *Veteris Arcis Strigoniensis,* 36. False quantity in *ā c.*

'I agree, Virgin, to your commands and I will do as you wish.'
This is Bishop Adalbertus responding to the Virgin Mary.

(d) *Porta patet vite sponsus vocat intro venite
A full leonine hexameter. Bogyay, 'L'iconographie de la «Porta Speciosa» d'Esztergom,' 89, n. 2 (Máthes, *Veteris Arcis Strigoniensis,* 35, reads *Porta patet, vitae Sponsus vocat, introvenite*).

'The gate of life stands open. The Bridegroom calls. Come within.'
Cf. Salzburg, church of the Nonnberg convent.

49. **Ferrara** (Emilia-Romagna). Cathedral of S. Giorgio.

W porch. Ornamented archivolt with keystone of the Lamb of God and a horizontal inscription band (a) above. John the Evangelist is in the left spandrel; John the Baptist is in the right spandrel.

Ca. 1132–5.[63]

(a) + ANNO MILLENO CENTENO TER QVOQVE DENO /
+ QVINQVE SVPERLATIS STRVITVR DOMVS HEC PIETATIS
Two full leonine hexameters.

'In the one-thousand one-hundred and thirtieth year, with five years added on, this house of religion is constructed.'[64]

50. **Ferrara**. S. Giorgio.

Central W portal. Tympanum of Saint George slaying the Dragon, with an inscription (a) around the rim.

Ca. 1132–5.

(a) + ARTIFICEm GNARVm Qui SCVLPSERIT HEC NICOLAVm
+ HVC [CON]CVRRENTES LAVDENT Per SaeCuLA GENTES ·
Two full leonine hexameters with slant rhyme in the first verse. The missing letters have been supplied on the basis of the nearly identical inscription at the Cathedral of Verona. The scansion of *Nĭcolaum* is not classical.

'May the peoples coming to visit this place forever praise Niccolò, the skilled craftsman who sculpted this.'
Cf. the similar inscriptions at S. Zeno and the Cathedral of Verona.

51. **Ferrara**. S. Giorgio.

S façade. *Portal of the Months (Porta dei Mesi). The portal was described by several persons in the eighteenth century, including Borsetti in a work published in 1735.[65] The tympanum showed Christ treading the basilisk and the asp underfoot, with an inscription (a).[66] Reliefs on either side of the portal showed the history of mankind as narrated in the Old Testament from Creation to the Sacrifice of Isaac, with an inscription (b), which includes some non-metrical material not reproduced here.

Ca. 1135–40. This date is based on the assumption that the Porta dei Mesi was the work of Niccolò.[67]

(a) *Nec Deus est, nec Homo praesens quam cernis imago
Sed Deus est, & Homo praesens quam signat imago.

Two common leonine hexameters with trisyllabic end rhyme. Borsetti, cited by Porter, *Lombard Architecture* 2, 416, n. 47, and by Krautheimer-Hess, 'The Original Porta Dei Mesi at Ferrara,' 156 (Krautheimer-Hess omits *praesens* in line 2). Probably line 2 should read *quem signat imago.*

'The image which you see is neither God nor man in the flesh, but it is God and man in the flesh which the image signifies.'

Nearly identical verses appear on the tympanum of the N portal of S. Miguel of Estella.

(b) *Omne genus rerum processit sorte dierum
Adam de limo formatur tempore primo
Viva primeva de costa fingitur Eva
Livor serpentis mutavit jura parentis
Ostia fert damnum placet his qui detulit agnum
Justus Abel moritur et fratris fuste feritur.

Six full leonine hexameters. Giglioli, cited by Krautheimer-Hess, 'The Original Porta Dei Mesi,' 154, n. 20. The verse *Justus Abel* etc. appears in nearly identical wording on the Zodiac Portal of Sacra di S. Michele. *His* (5) = *is.*

'Every race of beings came forth according to the order of the days. Adam is formed from the mud in the first age. Eve is fashioned from the living primeval rib. The envy of the serpent changed the rights of the parent. The offering [of grain] carries damnation; he who offered the lamb is acceptable [to God]. Righteous Abel dies and he is struck by his brother's club.'

52. **Fidenza** (known as *Borgo San Donnino* until 1927) (Emilia-Romagna). Cathedral of S. Donnino.

W façade, left of central portal. (The W façade and central porch are elaborately ornamented with sculptures accompanied by non-metrical inscriptions. The sculptures are the work of Benedetto Antelami and his school.) Statue of King David in a niche, with the Presentation in the Temple above his head. David holds a scroll, the lower section of which is inscribed with the words HEC PORTA DOMINI IVSTI INTRANT PER EAM, 'This is the gate of the Lord, the just enter through it' (cf. Ps. 117:20).[68] On the surface above the niche and above the Presentation in the Temple, there is an inscription (a) in two rows.

Ca. 1202–16.[69]

(a) D<u>AN</u>S B<u>LA</u>NDVm M<u>VR</u>MVR [FERTVR P]RO MVN[ERE TVRTVR] /
SVSCIPIT OB<u>LA</u>TVm SYMEON DE VIRGINE NATVM

Two full leonine hexameters with slant rhyme in the first verse. Cf. Saporetti, *Iscrizioni romaniche*, 23–4, 26–40. Francovich, *Benedetto Antelami*, 1, 321–2, n. 23, reconstructs the verse as *Dans blandum murmur puer raro munere fertur*, which is almost certainly incorrect, both because the sense is inferior and because the leonine rhyme is not full.

'Making an alluring murmur, the dove is carried as a valuable gift. Simeon receives the Child offered by the Virgin.'

53. **Fidenza** (Emilia-Romagna). S. Donnino.

W façade, right of central portal. Statue of the prophet Ezekiel in a niche, with the Virgin and Child above his head. Ezekiel holds a scroll, the lower section of which is inscribed with the words VIDI PORTAM IN DOMO DOMINI CLAVSAM, 'I saw the gate in the house of the Lord which was shut' (cf. Ezek. 44:1–2);[70] on the surface above the niche and above the Virgin and Child, there is an inscription (a) in two rows. Above the statue is a frieze of a miracle of Saint Donnino and above that, plaques of Enoch between two men in trees and of Elias (Elijah) in a cart drawn by two horses followed by Eliseus (Elisha).[71]

Ca. 1202–16

(a) + VIRGA · VIRTVTIS · PROTVLIT · FRVCTVmQVE · SALVTIS /

+ VIRGA : FLOX · NATVS · EST · CARNE · DEVS · TRABEATVS

Two full leonine hexameters. Cf. Saporetti, *Iscrizioni romaniche*, 23–4, 26–40. Final syllable of *natus* lengthened at caesura.

'From the rod of virtue [God] has brought forth the fruit of salvation. The flower born from the rod is God clothed in flesh.'

54. **Gellerup** (near Herning) (Jutland: Ringkøbing Amt). Church.

Medieval Danish village churches were constructed with a door in the S wall of the nave for men and a door in the N wall for women. These were located in the western third of the nave.[72] At Gellerup these doors were each surmounted by a simple tympanum displaying a Greek Cross. The portals with the tympana have now been walled up. The tympana are known from engravings published in 1903 by H. Storck.[73]

*S portal. Tympanum of a Greek Cross, with an inscription (a) running around the rim and continuing across the lintel. The inscription begins with a date: ANNO M° C° XL° INCARNATIONIS DominI.

AD 1140.

(a) EST HIC FVNDA/TA SVB HONORE DEI DOMVS ISTA ;

A common leonine hexameter. Mackeprang, *Jydske Granitportaler*, fig. 110a. Final syllable of *fundata* lengthened at caesura.

'This church was founded here in honour of God.'

55. **Gellerup**. Church.

*N portal. Tympanum of a Greek Cross, with an inscription (a) running around the rim and continuing across the lintel.

AD 1140.

(a) INGREDIENS AVLAM CVLPAS ABICIT REVS ISTAM /
ET QVOD IVSTE PETIT DONANDO DEVS PIVS AVDIT

Two common leonine hexameters. Mackeprang, *Jydske Granitportaler*, fig. 110b. False quantity in *iustĕ*.

'Entering this church, the guilty one casts aside sins, and merciful God approves by giving what is justly asked.'

56. **Goslar** (Niedersachsen). Sts Simon and Jude (known as the Cathedral). Only the N porch is still standing.

N porch portal. Central column: capital of human masks surrounded by winged monsters, with an inscription (a) on three faces. The inscription begins on the N face; the E face is blank.

Ca. 1150.[74]

(a) ·+· HARTMANNVS · STA/TVAM · FECIT · BASIS / · QVE · FIGVRAM ·

A full slant leonine hexameter. Cf. Wulf, *Saxe romane*, 149. False quantity in *bāsisque.*

'Hartmann made the image and the figure of the base.'

Perhaps *statuam* refers to the large statues in niches above the portal and *basis* to the central column.

57. **Goslar**. Sancta Maria in Horto (known as the Neuwerk Church).

Interior. Relief plaque of an angel above first intermediate pier of S wall of nave, with an inscription (a) on the banderole in the angel's hands, and the name of the sculptor, WILHELMI, inscribed on the console.

Ca. 1200.[75]

(a) MIRI · FACTA · VIDE · LAV/DANDO VIRI · LAPICIDE ·

A full leonine hexameter. Cf. Wulf, *Saxe romane*, 155. Wulf reads *laudanda*, which was probably the poet's intention.

'See the praiseworthy deeds of a man [who is] a marvellous sculptor.'

58. **Hagetmau** (Landes). St-Girons. The church was destroyed in 1904; only the crypt remains.

Crypt interior. S wall, capital, with three faces, of Saint Peter delivered from prison by an angel, with an inscription (a) on four arches that enclose four separate figures. Guards, labelled CVSTODES, are under the first two arches on the left; Peter is under the third arch; and the angel who frees him, using the point of a spear to cut through Peter's ropes, is under the fourth arch. This action is labelled SOLVERE ANGELVS PETRVM.

12th century.[76]

(a) FEREA QVID / MIRVM SIC CEDVNT / HOSTIA PETRO

An unrhymed hexameter. Cf. *CIFM*, 6, 95. *Ferea* = *ferrea*; *hostia* = *ostia*.

'Iron doors (what wonder!) yield thus to Peter.'

Cf. Acts 12:3–10.

59. **Huy** (Liège). St-Mort (or St-Maur). The present church is Gothic.

*Portal of the Romanesque church. Tympanum of Christ in Majesty, flanked by the Virgin Mary and John and two angels. Christ holds a book in his left hand, which is inscribed EGO SVm OSTIVm. The Alpha and Omega are inscribed above Christ's head. The Virgin Mary, robed and crowned, stands on his right, holding a book in her left hand and a scroll in her right hand. The book is inscribed PORTA CELI. An inscription (a) runs around the rim of the tympanum and along its lower border.

1st half of 12th century, towards 1150.[77]

(a) + ORA · VIRGO · PIA · NOSTRA · PRO · PACE · MARIA ·
IOHannES · CARE · XPISTO · BONA · NOSTRA PRECARE /
VOTA TVE GENTIS DeuS AVDI · PARCE REDEmpTIS
P[ost?]QVAm VICISTI MORTEM VITAmQue DEDISTI

Four full leonine hexameters with slant rhyme (3). Barral i Altet, *Belgique romane*, 281. Final vowels of *pia* and *care* lengthened at caesura (1, 2).

'Pray for our salvation, holy Virgin Mary. John, beloved of Christ, pray for our good. God, hear the prayers of your people; spare those you have redeemed, after you have conquered death and given life.'

60. **Isen** (Bayern). St Zeno.

W portal. Tympanum of Christ seated on a lion and a dragon, with an inscription (a) in two lines on the semicircular rim of the tympanum.

Ca. 1180–1212. These are the dates of Prior Ulrich, who was apparently the principal donor for the new church.[78]

(a) VODALRICE DeI · FLAGRANS · IN AMORE · FIDEI · /
HOC · OPVS · AVCXISTI · PATEAT · TIBI · GRATIA · XPistI ·

Two full leonine hexameters. Cf. Strobel and Weis, *Bavière romane*, 354. Strobel and Weis transcribe the first word as VOLDARICE.

'Ulrich, inflamed with the love of God, you have enlarged this work of faith; may the grace of Christ be extended to you.'

61. **Jaca** (Huesca). Cathedral of S. Pedro.

W portal. Tympanum. The tympanum displays a chrismon in the centre. The chrismon contains the Chi-Rho monogram with an S entwined around the lower vertical bar of the P (rho) = XPistuS. A horizontal bar extends through the monogram from the ends of which hang the Alpha and Omega. There is an inscription (a) around the rim of the chrismon. On the left of the chrismon there is a lion sparing a man, who holds a snake in his hands away from his body, with an inscription (b) above; on the right there is a lion mastering a bear-like animal, together with a basilisk under the belly of the lion, with an inscription (c) above; and finally there is an inscription (d) on the lintel. Cf. Durán Gudiol, 'Las inscripciones medievales,' 100–2 (no. 69).

Ca. 1095–1100.[79]

(a) + HAC IN SCVLPTVRA LECTOR SIC NOSCERE CVRA ·,·
P PATER · A GENITVS · DVPLEX EST SPirituS ALMVS ·,·
HII TRES IVRE QVIDEM DOMINVS SVNT VNVS ET IDEM

Two full (1,3) and one common leonine hexameter.

'In this sculpture, reader, take care to understand [the symbolism] in this way: P is for the Father, A is for the Son, the double consonant [X] is for the Holy Spirit. These three [PAX] are indeed rightly one and the same, the Lord.'

(b) PARCERE STERNENTI / LEO SCIT XPistuSQue PETENTI ·,·

A full leonine hexameter.

'The lion knows to spare the man who prostrates himself, and Christ knows to pardon the man who prays.'

(c) IMPerIVM MORTIS CON/CVLCANS Est LEO FORTIS

A full leonine hexameter.

'The strong lion is trampling underfoot the sovereign power of death.'

(d) VIVERE SI QVERIS QVI MORTIS LEGE TENERIS :
HVC SVPLICANDO VENI · RENVENS FOMENTA VENENI ·
COR VICIIS MVNDA · PEREAS NE MORTE SECVNDA

Three full leonine hexameters. The initial syllable of *sŭplicando* (= *supplicando*) has been shortened by the suppression of the first *p* of the consonant cluster *ppl*.[80]

'If you who are bound by the law of death seek to live, come hither in prayer, renouncing the fomentations of poison. Cleanse your heart of vices, lest you perish in the second death.'

62. **Jaillans** (Drôme). Ste-Marie.[81]

Interior. Gallery, N wall: westernmost capital, of Daniel, with an inscription (a) in two lines on the S face of the abacus and in one line on the E face. The line on the E face (the word *Danielis*) continues from the top line on the S face.

12th century?

(a) QVAnTA : DeI : PIETAS : QVAnTVm : MERITVm / DANIELis
// BESTIA : PLENA : DOLi : NOn EST

Two unrhymed (?) hexameters, the second incomplete. *CIFM*, 16, 144.

'As much as is the compassion of God, so much is the merit of Daniel. The beast is not full of deceit ...'

Cf. Dan. 6:23.

63. **Königslutter am Elm** (Niedersachsen). Sts Peter and Paul.

Central E apse. 'Frieze of the Hunt,' with an inscription (a). The 'frieze' consists of a series of separate scenes of men and animals hunting or fighting alternating with acanthus-leaf rosettes under the arches of a Lombard band that helps divide the half-round exterior surface of the apse into an upper and lower register. Three windows are set into the upper register; the lower register is divided into three panels (NE, E, & SE) by pilasters. The inscription extends the length of the NE panel, above the Lombard band. It seems to proceed from the horn of a huntsman (?) at the extreme right of the band. A similar man with a horn appears at the extreme left of the SE panel, but there are no inscriptions in either the E or the SE panels.

Ca. 1137–50.

(a) + HOC OPVS EXIMIVM VARIO CELAMINE MIRVM
+ SC<ulpsit>

A full slant leonine hexameter and possibly the beginning of a second verse. Cf. Wulf, *Saxe romane*, 314. The inscription is carved in mirror lettering reading from right to left.

'[...] sculpted (?) this outstanding work, wondrous with varied carving.'

This appears to be the beginning of a sculptor's signature. Stylistically, the sculptures of the apse have been compared with the Italian artist Niccolò's work. It has even been suggested that the sculpture of a hunter bringing home a hare under the space where the artist's name might have been, had the inscription been completed, is a rebus for Niccolò (in Greek, Niko-lagos, 'hunter of hare,' = Nikolaos).[82] Niccolò (like several others) used the phrase *hoc opus* at the beginning of his verses (Piacenza, Sacra di S. Michele).

64. **La Lande-de-Fronsac** (Gironde). St-Pierre.

S portal. Tympanum of Christ, standing, with John inclining under Christ's right arm and a sword coming out from Christ's mouth, with an inscription (a) on the lintel and the words, IOH[ann]ES VII ECCL[es]IIS QVE SVNT IN [ASIA VIDI]T FILIV[m] HO[MINIS IN]TER VII CANDELABRA AV<rea> 'John to the seven churches which are in Asia. He saw the Son of man in the midst of seven golden candlesticks' (Apoc. 1:4, 12–13), inscribed around the arch of the tympanum.

Middle of the 12th century?[83]

(a) PRINCIPIVm [SINE PRINCIPIO FINIS SINE FINE]

An unrhymed hexameter. Cf. *CIFM*, 5, 110–11. The lintel is badly eroded; no trace of the words in brackets, which are supplied by Dubourg-Noves, *Guyenne romane*, 293, can now be seen. No caesura in third foot.

'(I am) the beginningless beginning and the endless end.'

Cf. Apoc. 1:8, 17–18; John 1:1–18.

65. **Larreule** (Hautes-Pyrénées). St-Orens.

S portal.[84] Stone plaque of Christ in Majesty with the Four Animals re-employed as tympanum. Christ is seated within a mandorla, which carries an inscription (a).

12th century.[85]

(a) SIC SEDET AE~~TE~~RNE DEITATIS IMAGO PATERNE ·
CVNCTA REPLENDO REGIT SVSTI~~NE~~T ATQVE TEGIT ·

A full leonine elegiac couplet. Cf. *CIFM*, 8, 92.

'Thus the image of the eternal paternal Deity sits. He rules, sustains, and protects by permeating everything.'

66. **Lent** (Ain). Chapel of Longchamp.

W façade. A stone plaque of the Cross with five four-petalled flowers decorating its arms and crossing, re-employed, probably from above a portal, and set into the wall to the left of the portal. There is an inscription (a) in the background in the upper-left quadrant and an inscription (b) in the upper-right quadrant.

11/12th century.[86]

(a) + Est VIA Ce/LESTIS DO/MVS HEC / ET PORTA / SALVTIS

A common leonine hexameter. *CIFM*, 17, 7.

'This church is the road to heaven and the gate of salvation.'

(b) OSPICIVM / PA[cis]

Probably the beginning of a leonine hexameter. *CIFM*, 17, 7. There is space for the remainder of the verse, but the carving is unfinished.

'The hospice of peace ...'

67. **Lérins, Iles de** (Alpes-Maritimes). St-Honorat.

Cloister.[87] S walk: an antique sarcophagus re-employed as a lavabo is set into the arcades of the S walk parallel to the rectory. One long side of the lavabo faces the cloister garden and the other faces the walk. An inscription (a) in rather small letters in a single line is scratched (it is hardly more than this and quite difficult to see) on the side facing the walk.

Ca. 1100? Similarities of phrasing and rhyme link it closely with the epitaph of Aldebertus (d. 1101).[88]

(a) XPistE TVA DEXTRA : QVE MuNDAT : ET INTus ET EXTRA

:|: INTERIVs MVNDA : MVNDARE QuoD HEC NEQVIT VNDA :

Two full leonine hexameters. Cf. *CIFM*, 14, 7–8.

'Christ, with your right hand which purifies both within and without, purify inwardly that which this water cannot purify.'

For the phrase *intus et extra*, cf. St-Sauveur of Nevers.

68. **Loarre** (Huesca). Castle Chapel.

S portal. Frieze of Christ in Majesty with angels, with an inscription (a) around the mandorla. The inscription is no longer legible.

Ca. 1100.[89]

(a) [...]NIAS INVICTAS VBI TI[...]

FONS EGO SVM VITA[e ...]

Two hexameters? Whitehill, *Spanish Romanesque Architecture*, 245 (citing the transcription of Don Ricardo del Arco; my lineation and reading of *vitae* for *vita*). The first phrase, if correctly transcribed, is unmetrical; the second phrase appears as the first segment of a leonine hexameter at Santa Cruz de la Serós.

'... I am the fountain of life ...'

69. **Lucca** (Toscana). Cathedral of S. Martino.

W façade, left of left portal. Inscription (a) in white marble.

AD 1070/1233? These verses give every indication of having been composed for the consecration of the cathedral in 1070. However, the letter forms appear to be contemporary with, though somewhat more elegant than, the letter forms of the Saint Martin panels, which are dated to 1233. One possibility is that this inscription plaque is a copy of an earlier one and was set in place ca. 1233 when the surface decoration of the interior façade was completed.

(a) HVIVS · QVE · CELSI · RADIANT · FASTIGIA · TEMPLI ·; /

SVNT · SVB ALEXANDRO · PAPA · CONSTRVCTA · SECVNDO ·; /

AD CVRAM · CVIVS · PROPRIOS · ET PRESVLIS · VSVS ·; /

IPSE · DOMOS · SEDES · PRESENTES · STRVXIT · ET EDES ·; /

IN QVIBVS · HOSPITIVM · FACIENS · TERRENA · POTESTAS ·; /

VT SIT · IN ETERNO · STATVENS · ANATHEMATE · SANXIT ·; /

MILLE · QVE · SEX DENIS · TEMPLVM · FVMDAMINE [*sic*] · IACTO ·; /

LVSTRO · SVB BINO · SACRVM STAT · FINE · PER · ACTO ·;

Eight hexameters; verses 1–4 and 8 are common or (4) full leonines, the others, unrhymed. *Fumdamine* (7) = *fundamine.*

'The roofs of this lofty church which gleam were constructed under Pope Alexander the Second [1061–73], for the administration and particular needs of this bishop. He himself constructed the present dwellings, seats, and buildings, creating in them a place of comfort. Earthly power decreeing that it be as a sacred gift forever, he sanctified the church in the year 1060, after the foundation was laid. In the second lustrum (= 1070) with the (W?) end completed, the church stands consecrated.'

70. **Lucca**. S. Martino.

W façade, left and right of central portal. Four marble panels of scenes from the life of Saint Martin. In the panel at the far left, Saint Martin revives a dead man, with an inscription (a). In the next panel, Martin is made bishop, with an inscription (b). In the panel on the near right-hand side of the portal, miraculous fire appears around Martin's head as he celebrates mass, with an inscription (c). In the panel on the far right, Martin expels a demon, with an inscription (d). All the inscriptions are in a single line on the lower edge of the panels.

AD 1233.

(a) MARTINVS MONACHus DEFVNTVM VIVERE FECIT

An unrhymed hexameter.

'Martin has brought a dead man back to life.'

(b) DE MONACHO PRESVL ES TV MARTINE VOCATVS

An unrhymed hexameter. Final syllable of *presul* lengthened at caesura.

'You, Martin, are called from being a monk to being a bishop.'

(c) IGNIS ADEST CAPITI MARTINO SACRA LITANTI

A common leonine hexameter.

'Fire hovers about Martin's head as he celebrates mass.'

(d) DEMONE VEXATVM SALVAS MARTINE BEATE

An unrhymed hexameter.

'You heal a man tormented by a demon, blessed Martin.'

71. **Lucca**. S. Martino.

W porch. Right pillar, N face: labyrinth carved in stone, with an inscription (a) on its right border.

Ca. 1200.[90]

(a) HIC · QVEM · / CRETICVS / EDIT · DEDA/LVS · EST / LABERINT/HVS :
DE Q[u]/O · NVLLV/S · VADER/E · QVIVIT · / QVI · FVIT · / INTVS ·
NI THESE/VS GRAT/IS ADRIAN/E · STAMI/NE IVTVS ·

Three hexameters with di- and monosyllabic (3) end rhyme. No caesura in third foot (1, 2). *Ădrĭānē* (3) is scanned as though it were correctly spelled *Ariadne.*

'This is the labyrinth that the Cretan, Daedalus, built, from which no one who was within was able to escape, except for Theseus freely helped by Ariadne's thread.'

72. **Lucca**. S. Giovanni.

W portal. Blank tympanum (with a small, inset rose window) above a lintel decorated with the Assumption of the Virgin Mary. Mary stands in the centre, flanked by two angels and the twelve apostles; all the figures in the scene are identified by initial letters above their heads. An inscription (a) in a single line runs along the edge of the lintel beneath their feet.

AD 1187.[91]

(a) HOC DORM[...]M ILLI :
PresByteR(?) VGVICIO : BENEDICTVS E TERCIVS ECCE :
DISPENSATOR ERAT OPIZO SETIR AGMIRE QVARTVS :
SACRA DABANT POPVLOS ORIENTES MVNIA LAVDIS :
[...]AQue CANA VILLANV NEmPE(?) MAGISTRVm

These appear to be five unrhymed hexameters, although I am unable to make sense of them.

73. **Lugo** (Lugo). Cathedral.

N transept portal. Hanging capital of the Last Supper, beneath a tympanum of Christ in Majesty, with an inscription (a) on the E, N, and W faces.

Late 12th century?

(a) DISC[i]PVLVS DomiNI · PLACI~~DE~~ DANS / MEMBRA QVIECI ;
DVM CVBAC IN CENA / CELES~~TIA~~ VI~~DIC~~ AMENA

Two leonine hexameters, one common and one full.

'The disciple of the Lord quietly giving his limbs to rest – while he reclines in the pleasant Supper, he sees a heavenly vision.'

Cf. John 13:23–6.

74. **Luz-St-Sauveur** (Hautes-Pyrénées). St-André.

N portal. Tympanum of Christ in Majesty with the Four Animals, with inscriptions (a) on the arch and (b) on the lintel.

End of the 12th century. The porch was completed in 1200.[92]

(a) [MIGRANTI IVSTO COELEST]IS PA[n]DIT[ur] AVLA
CVI XPistuS P[...]H[...]L[...]MO[...] VI[r]GI NIS OR[TVS]

Two (?) unrhymed hexameters. Cf. *CIFM*, 8, 94–5. Only the portion of the inscription on the right quarter of the rim of the tympanum is still partially legible. Laplace, *Notice sur l'église*, 10, at the end of the 19th century was able to see more than is now visible, although it is clear from his remarks that he relied on guesswork for some of his reconstruction. Porter appears to have based his transcription on Laplace (though he does not say so), corrected from his own observation.[93] Laplace reads MIGRANTI JUSTO COELESTIS PANDITUR AULA / CUI CHRISTOS THALAMOS VIRGINES [*sic*] ORTUS. Porter reads (MIGRANTI JUSTI [*sic*] COELEST)IS PADIT' AULA CVI XPS (THA)LAMOS VIRGINIS OR(TUS).

'The court of heaven is open to the righteous pilgrim, to whom Christ, born of the Virgin ... '

(b) [... SPOLIAT S]ERPEnS SE PELLE VETVSTA
EST HVMILIS MVLTVm LASCIVVm NEGLIGE CVLTVm
SI CVPIS INTRARE QVONIAM PATET HOC T[IBI] QVERE

One unrhymed, one full, and one common leonine hexameter. Cf. Laplace, *Notice sur l'église*, 10. Final vowel of *intrare* (3) lengthened at caesura. Porter reads (SPOLIAT S)ERPĒS SE PELLE VETUSTA EST HVMILIS MVLTŪ LASCIV̄ NEGLIGE CULTV̄ SI CVPIS INTRARE QVONIAM PATET HOC T(IBI) QVERE. *CIFM* follows the reading of Father Abadie, cited in F. Galan (*Église fortifiée de Luz-Saint-Sauveur* [Bagnères-de-Bigorre, n.d.], 3–4): [QVOTANNIS SPOLIATA (*sic*) S]ERPENS SE PELLE VETVSTA EST HVMILIS MVLTVM LASCIVVM NEGLIGE CVLTVM SI CVPIS INTRARE QVOD IAM [*sic*] PATET HOC T[IBI] QVA[ERE].

'[When?] the serpent sheds his old skin, he is very humble. Despise lascivious dress/way of life/worship (?). If you want to enter, since it lies open, seek this [= humility?] for yourself.'

75. **Luz-St-Sauveur**. St-André.

N portal. Left- and right-jamb columns on either side of the door, with inscriptions (a) and (b) on the top surfaces of their bases. The right column has a capital of a man between two animals – probably representing Daniel in the lions' den.[94]

End of the 12th century.

(a) FLECTI NOn POSS[VM] SI RECT[VS?] SIC EGO SVm

A full leonine pentameter? Cf. *CIFM*, 8, 94–5. Laplace, *Notice sur l'église*, 9, transcribed the line as he saw it in the 19th century as FLECTI NON POSSUM – SI RECTUS EGO SUM. Laplace may have inferred the reading *rectus* from the *s* of *sic* (which he does not record). Porter reads FLECTI NŌ POSSV̄ SI RECT' SIC EGO SV̄. *CIFM* reads FLECTI NON POSSVM SI RECTVS SICVT [*sic*] EGO SV̄. The verse is corrupt: if *rĕctŭs* is the correct reading there are two false quantities. Nevertheless, the rhyme between *possum* and *ego sum* and the metrical cadences at both ends of the line make it likely that a leonine pentameter was intended. If *CIFM*'s reading *sicut* could be justified (I am unable to make out any mark of suspension, but the stone is very rough), it is possible that the poet intended the *o* of *ego* to be taken as long. This would permit the line to be read as a full leonine hexameter.

'If I am thus erect, I cannot be bent.'

(b) SVSTINEO DIGNOS [... MALI]GNOS

A full leonine hexameter? Cf. Laplace, *Notice sur l'église*, 8, who could still see the letters that I have put in brackets. He translates 'Je soutiens ceux qui sont dignes ..., je repousse les méchants.' This is apparently the source of Porter's reading SVSTINET [*sic*] DIGNOS (REPELLO MALI)GNOS. *CIFM* reads SVSTINEO DIGNOS QV[ONIAM CONFVNDO] MALIGNOS; this conjecture is plausible.

'I sustain the worthy ... [I reject] the wicked.'

76. **Maastricht** (Limburg). Former cathedral of Our Lady.

Interior. Choir: quadruple capital of the story of Jacob and Esau, with an inscription (a) on the abacus. The inscription, which is partly effaced, appears to have been displaced by a quarter-turn with respect to the corresponding scenes on the multiple faces of the capital.[95]

Ca. 1150–1200.[96]

(a) [...]DENTIS · HEC · / SVMIT DONA PARENTIS /
+ ETHEREOS CET[us] CER/NIT Per SOMNIA LET[us]

Two full leonine hexameters. Cf. Deijk, *Pays-Bas romans*, 134. Deijk's reconstruction of the missing portion as [MISIS BI]DENTIS etc. is unacceptable. Final syllable of *-dentis* lengthened at the caesura (1).

'[...] he [Jacob] takes this blessing of his father [Isaac]. He [Jacob] joyfully sees the heavenly hosts in his vision.'

Cf. Gen. 27:22–9; 28:10–12.

77. **Maastricht**. Our Lady.

Interior. Choir: twin capital of the story of Abraham, with an inscription (a) on the abacus.

Ca. 1150–1200.

(a) + QVE TR[...] / VENERATVR ET ORAT /
ESSAT SPECTAT[ur] VIVV[s] / MANEAT TIBI NATVS

Two unrhymed hexameters (?). Cf. Deijk, *Pays-Bas romans*, 134–5.

'[...] he [Abraham] worships and prays. Isaac [?] is seen alive; may your son remain with you.'

Cf. Gen. 22:10–13.

78. **Maastricht**. St Servaas.

N nave portal (formerly the pilgrims' entrance to the tomb of Saint Servais; now the portal communicating between the nave and the E walk of the cloister). Tympanum of Christ in Majesty with the Four Animals, with an inscription (a) in two lines around the rim of the tympanum, and an inscription (b) along the implied lintel. Christ's cruciform halo is inscribed D/C/O, which is said to be an abbreviation for *Deus creator omnipotens*,[97] and the book in his left hand is inscribed EGO SVm VIA VERITAS VITA (John 14:6).

Ca. 1175–1200.[98]

(a) + HEC DOMVS · ORANDI · DOMVS · EST · PECCATA LAVANDI + /
+ HOC SVBEAS LIMEN PVRGARE VOLENS HOMO CRIMEN

Two full leonine hexameters. Cf. Deijk, *Pays-Bas romans*, 97.

'This house of prayer is the house for washing away sins. May you cross this threshold as a man wishing to purge his sin.'

(b) + INTVS PECCATIS · LAVA[CR]VM · DAT · FONS PIETATIS

A full leonine hexameter. Cf. Deijk, *Pays-Bas romans*, 97.

'Within [the church] the fountain of mercy gives cleansing to sins.'

79. **Maastricht**. St Servaas.

Interior. Bas-relief in two parts marking the entrance to the two-storey western choir. The semicircular upper part depicts Christ enthroned between the kneeling figures of Saint Peter (left) with the keys and Saint Servais (right). The Alpha and Omega are inscribed on either side of Christ's cruciform halo. The rim of the false tympanum carries an inscription (a) on the outer edge. Saints Peter and Servais are labelled on the inner edge of the rim. The implied lintel has an inscription (b). The rectangular lower part of the sculpted block represents the Virgin in Majesty with the Child in a mandorla supported by two angels. There is an inscription (c) around the mandorla.

Ca. 1150–75.[99]

(a) VERA SALVS · HOMINIS PRO SE · CERTAMINA · PASSIS
POST · CARNIS · FINEM VITE LARGITVR HONOREM

Two common leonine hexameters. Cf. Deijk, *Pays-Bas romans*, 102.

'The true salvation of man bestows the honour of [eternal] life after the death of the flesh upon those who have endured battle for him.'

(b) TV SIS SALVATRIX ET · VIRGINITATIS FICTRIX
ARAQue REGALIS ATTRITTIO VERA · DRACONIS

Two common leonine hexameters. Cf. Deijk, *Pays-Bas romans*, 102. The first verse is a spondaic hexameter. Final syllable of *regalis* lengthened at caesura (2). Final *o* treated as short (2).

'May you be the saviour and the moulder of virginity, the royal altar and the true chastisement of the dragon.'

(c) VIRGO DEV[m] PEPERIT DO[...]
[...]VI SERVIT CVRIA CELI

Probably two leonine hexameters. Cf. Deijk, *Pays-Bas romans*, 102.

'The Virgin gives birth to God ... the court of heaven serves ...'

80. **Maguelone** (Hérault). Former cathedral of St-Pierre.

W portal. Tympanum of Christ in Majesty with the Four Animals, above a lintel in a scroll pattern consisting of six circles with acanthus leaves and an inscription (a) on the top edge, right edge, and right two-thirds of the bottom edge, and a prose inscription, B<ernardus> D<e>' III VIIS FECIT HOC + AnNO INCarnationis Domini M.C.LXX.VIII.,[100] 'Bernard de Tréviers [Tres-viis] made this in 1178,' on the left edge, and left third of the bottom edge.

AD 1178. The lintel is dated by the inscription. The present tympanum is later than the lintel and dates from the end of the 12th or beginning of the 13th century.

(a) + AD PORTVm VITE : SITIENTES QVIQue VENITE :
HAS INTRANDO FORES : VESTROS COmPONITE MORES
HINC INTRANS / OR/A : / TV/A / SEmPer / CRI/MI/+NA PLORA :
QVICQuID PECCATVR : LACRIMARum FONTE LAVATVR +

Four full leonine hexameters.

'You who are thirsting, come to the port of eternal life; in entering these doors, correct your behaviour. Pray as you enter here, always weep for your sins; whatever is amiss is washed by the fountain of your tears.'

81. **Mauriac** (Cantal). Notre-Dame-des-Miracles.

W portal. Tympanum of the Ascension. The tympanum is divided into two registers by a horizontal band. The twelve apostles and the Virgin Mary stand in the lower register. There are inscriptions (a) on the implied lintel, and (b) on the lower, bevelled edge of the middle band.

Ca. 1151–74?[101]

(a) + TRES · SVNT · ATQue DECEM · QVI CERNVNT · SCANDERE REGEM :
CELVm · CVNCTORVm · CRISTVm · DOMINVM · DOMINORVM

Two full leonine hexameters with slant rhyme (1). Cf. *CIFM*, 18, 43.

'There are thirteen who see the King ascend to heaven – Christ, Lord of all lords.'

Cf. Acts. 1:6–11.

(b) S[CA]NDIT · SVBLIMIS · CELESTIA · IESVS · AB IMIS /
QVOD BENE TESTANT[ur] QVI · IVGI · LVCE · BEANTVR

Two full leonine hexameters.

'Jesus, borne aloft, ascends heaven from the depths, which they well testify who are blessed with perpetual light.'

82. **Mauriac**. *St-Pierre.

*Portal. Tympanum of Samson wrestling the lion of Thamnatha with his bare hands, with an inscription (a) on the lower border. There is a mutilated figure of an abbot in the right corner of the tympanum. The tympanum has been re-employed above the portal of the sub-prefecture of Mauriac.

First quarter of 12th century?[102]

(a) ASPICE · S[A]NSONEM · [MANIBV]S · [SV]PERASSE (?) · LEONEM ·

A full leonine hexameter. Mayeux, 'Tympan sculpté de Mauriac,' 234 (reading *exidisse*); *CIFM*, 18, 44–5 (reading *superesse*). With the exception of a few letters, the inscription is no longer legible. According to Mayeux, 'La lecture du mot *exidisse* n'est pas certaine, les cinq premières lettres étant en partie effacées.' I venture to propose *superasse*.

'See Samson having overcome the lion with his hands.'

Cf. Judg. 14:5–6.

83. **Melle** (Deux-Sèvres). St-Savinien.

Interior. Transept: NE capital, S face, of three persons (all their heads have been chiselled off), presumably including Saint Savinianus and Aurelianus, with an inscription (a).

End 11th / beginning 12th century.[103]

(a) EST SAVINIA/NVS · QVEM SIC · / NECAT AVRELIAN/VS

A full leonine hexameter. *CIFM*, 1:3, 138. Arbitrary scansion of proper names: *Saviniănus, Aurĕlianus.*

'This is Savinianus whom Aurelianus kills in this manner.'

See Jacobus de Voragine, *The Golden Legend*, 510–12.

84. **Milan** (Lombardia). Cathedral.

Interior. N wall of nave (second bay from the W): four panels, each with two apostles, with inscriptions (a) below the first panel of James the Greater and another apostle, (b) in two rows above the head of Jude, who is also identified as Thaddeus, on the third panel, (c) above James the Less on the third panel, and (d) below the third panel. The sculptures are based on the apostle statues of St-Trophime of Arles; their provenance is unknown. Cf. Francovich, *Benedetto Antelami*, 1, 87, n. 119.

Ca. 1180–90.[104]

(a) HOS DEVS ELEGIT : PER QVOS MVNDANA SVREGIT

A full leonine hexameter. The form *sŭregit* is attested from Livius Andronicus, *Oxford Latin Dictionary*, s.v. *surgo*, but it seems likely that the poet coined it (in place of *surrexit*) for the sake of the meter and leonine rhyme.

'God chose these men through whom he resurrected the world.'

(b) CORDIS ID EST CVLTOR : ES / CORCVLVS ATQue TADEVS

An unrhymed hexameter.

'You [Jude] are a dear little heart, that is, a worshipper of the heart, and also Thaddeus.'

(c) ALPHEI IACOBVS EST SVPLAN/TATOR ALVMNVS

A common leonine hexameter. Final syllable of *Iacobus* lengthened at caesura.

'The apostle James the son of Alpheus is the "supplanter."'

The name of the patriarch Jacob is said in the Bible to mean 'supplanter,' because he supplanted his brother Esau (Gen. 27:36). The etymology has here been applied to James the Less, as it is elsewhere applied to James the Greater.[105]

(d) [...]STO FRATRES FIDEI COMPAGE SODALES

A full slant leonine hexameter.

'The brothers [are] companions in the bond of faith.'

85. **Milan**. S. Giorgio al Palazzo.

W Portal. Blank tympanum, with an inscription (a) in two lines on the outer archivolt. The tympanum and its inscription still exist, but are completely covered and hidden by the present baroque façade.

Ca. 1129. The Romanesque church was finished and consecrated in 1129.[106]

(a) + IANVA SVM VITE PRECOR OMneS INTRO VENITE |
PER ME TRANSIBVNT Qui CELI GAVDIA QVERVNT /
VIRGINE Qui NATVS NVLLO DE PATRE CREATVS |
INTRANTES SALVET REDEVNTES IPSE GVBERNET

Two full (1,3) and two common leonine hexameters. Colombo, *San Giorgio al Palazzo*, pl. 1. A Chi-Rho monogram with the Alpha and Omega at the apex of the outer archivolt separates the two lines of verse on the left (1,3) from those on the right (2, 4).

'I am the gate of life. Everyone come within, I beg. Those who seek the joys of heaven will pass through me. May he who was born of a virgin and not begot by a father save those who enter and guide those who go out.'

For similar verses, cf. Sant Pau del Camp (Barcelona), Esztergom, Saint-Marcel-lès-Sauzet, Nonnberg Convent (Salzburg), S. Marco of Venice ('Ianua sum vite per me mea membra venite'), and Wrocław.

86. **Modena** (Emilia-Romagna). Cathedral of S. Geminiano.

W façade. Marble Genesis frieze in four panels. The first panel is above the left portal; panels two and three are on the left and right, respectively, of the central portal, and the fourth panel is above the right portal.

The first panel depicts the Creation of Adam and Eve and the Eating of the Forbidden Fruit. God appears twice. At the left he holds an open book, on which is an inscription (a). Then he is shown creating Adam. The letters REX are inscribed on his cruciform halo.

The second panel depicts the Expulsion from the Garden of Eden. At the left,

God, holding an unrolled scroll, with the inscription DVm DEAmBVLARET DOMINVS In PARADISVm, 'While the Lord was walking in the garden' (cf. Gen. 3:8), confronts Adam and Eve.

The third panel depicts the Story of Cain and Abel. Abel is on the left, bringing a sheep as an offering, with an inscription (b) beneath the sheep. Next to him is a double panel: God appears in the upper part, holding an open book, on which is the inscription QVI SEQVITVR ME NON AmBV<lat>, 'He who follows me does not walk [in the darkness, but will have the light of life]' (John 8:12); below is the altar on which the sacrifice is to be made: a kneeling figure supports it on his shoulder, with an inscription (c) to the side. On the far right, God, holding a partially unrolled scroll, with the inscription VBI EST ABEL FRATer TVVS, 'Where is your brother Abel?' (Gen. 4:9), questions Cain.

The fourth panel depicts the Death of Cain and the Story of Noah and the Ark.

Ca. 1106–10.[107]

(a) LVX / EGO / SVm MV/NDI // VIA VE/RAX / VI~~TA~~ PER/ENNIS

An unrhymed hexameter.

'I am the light of the world, the true way, life eternal.'

Cf. John 8:12; 9:5; 14:6.

(b) PRIMVS / ABEL IVS/TVS / DEFERT / PLACA/BILE MV/NVS

A common leonine hexameter.

'First righteous Abel contributes the placatory offering.'

Cf. Gen. 4:3.

(c) HIC PreMIT / HIC PLORAT / GEMIT HIC / NIMIS ISTE / LABORAT

A full leonine hexameter. Schapiro, 'From Mozarabic to Romanesque,' n. 171 (p. 93), gives PORT(at) for PLORAT; the correct reading brings this verse closer to the other examples of the formula that Schapiro discusses, 58–9, and n. 171. Cf. Santo Domingo de Silos.

'This one presses, this one weeps, this one groans, that one labours exceedingly.'

This formula normally distinguishes the actions of different persons, but it is not clear which of the figures in panel three are meant. Possibly, '<God> presses down, <Cain> weeps, <Abel> groans, <the Atlas> labours exceedingly.'[108] Another possibility is that all the pronouns and verbs refer to one person, namely, the Atlas.[109] He might be said to 'press' up against the world, and to 'weep' and 'groan' as he labours exceedingly. At Cremona, there is a caryatid with the inscription HIC PREMITVR.[110]

87. **Modena**. S. Geminiano.

W façade. Marble plaque set above panel two of the Genesis frieze (see above).

It shows the prophets Enoch and Elias, holding between them a plaque with an inscription (a).

Ca. 1099.

(a) DVm GEMINI CANCER / CVRSVm CONSENDIT / OVANTES ;
IDIBVS / IN QVINTIS IVNII SVP TemPoRe / MENSIS ·
MILLE DEI / CARNIS MONOS CEN/TVm MINVS ANNIS ; /
ISTA DOMVS CLARI / FVNDATVR GEMINI/ANI ;
INTER SCVLTORES QVAN/TO SIS DIGNVS ONORE ;
CLA/RET SCVLTVRA NV[n]C WILIGELME TVA

Four full slant leonine hexameters, followed by a full slant leonine elegiac couplet. False quantity in *mōnos* (3).

'While Cancer [June/July] mounts after triumphant Gemini [May/June] on the 5th Ides of the month of June [= 9 June] 1100 years minus one after the time of the incarnation of God [= 1099], the foundation of this house of the illustrious Geminiano is laid. Now, Wiligelmo, this building shines with your sculpture; may you be worthy of as much honour among sculptors.'

88. **Modena**. S. Geminiano.

S (western nave) portal (Porta dei Principi). Lintel of six scenes from the life of Saint Geminiano, each accompanied by an inscription (a–f) in a continuous line on the upper edge. According to legend, the daughter of the Emperor Jovian was possessed by a devil. She learned in a vision that she could only be cured by a holy man named Geminiano. The Emperor sent out men to search his empire until Geminiano, the bishop of Modena, was found and brought to Constantinople.[111] The first scene shows Geminiano setting out on horseback with an assistant for Constantinople. In the second, Geminiano crosses the sea in a boat with his assistant and a sailor. In the third, the Emperor presents his daughter to Geminiano. A devil appears over her head. The fourth scene shows the Emperor rewarding Geminiano with gifts. In the fifth, Geminiano returns to Modena and is welcomed at the gates of the city by the people. The last scene depicts the death of Geminiano mourned by the people.

Ca. 1110?

(a) SCANDIT EQVVm LETus DVm TENDIT / AD / EQVORA PRESVL ·
(b) PASTOR PreCLARV[s] MARE TRANSIT GEMINIANVS ·
(c) PRINCIPIS / HIC / NATAm DAT PVLSO DEMONE SANAM ·
(d) DONA CAPIT REGIS CALICEm CVm CODICE LEGIS ·
(e) DVm REDIT EConTRA SIBI CVRRIT ConTIO CVNCTA ;
(f) POST REDITVm FORTIS PerSOLVIT DEBITA MORTIS ·

Two full (4,6) and four full slant leonine hexameters. Quintavalle, *La Cattedrale di Modena*, 1, 208, reads *en contra* for *econtra* (5).

'(a) The bishop joyfully mounts his horse as he heads for the sea. (b) The illustrious bishop Geminiano crosses the sea. (c) He gives back the daughter of the Emperor restored to health with the demon expelled. (d) He accepts the gifts of the king – a chalice with a book of the law. (e) When he returns, all the people run to meet him. (f) After his return the brave man pays the debt of death.'

89. **Modena**. S. Geminiano.

S façade. Nave wall between the Porta dei Principi and the Porta Regia: relief plaque, which was partially destroyed during the Second World War. Its original position is unknown.[112] Photographs taken before the war show better what it was like.[113] On the left, Jacob wrestles with the Angel. Above them is the inscription [DIMIT]TE ME AVRORA EST RESPONDIT Non DIMITTAm TE NISI BENEDIX[eris] ME, '[The angel said,] "Let me go; it is dawn." [But Jacob] answered, "I will not let you go till you bless me"' (Gen. 32:26). On the right, Truth pierces the tongue of Fraud with a spear. Beside them is an inscription (a).

Second quarter of 12th century?[114]

(a) VERIDIC<u>VS</u> / LINGVAM / FRAVDIS / DE GVT/TVRA STIR/PAT

An unrhymed hexameter. The *a* of *guttura* is probably a blunder for *e*. Since *gutture* restores both grammatical sense and metre, it appears that the carver rather than the poet was at fault here. Porter, *Lombard Architecture*, 3, 43, n. 155, divides DE GVTTVR ASTIRPAT.

'Truth tears out the tongue from the throat of Fraud.'

Cf. Prudentius, *Psychomachia*, lines 715–19. In Prudentius, it is Faith who transfixes the tongue of Discord.

90. **Modena**. S. Geminiano.

S (eastern nave) portal (Porta Regia). Lintel with an inscription (a) on the upper edge.

Ca. 1220? The portal was constructed about this time, replacing the earlier portal (the Porta dei Principi), which was relocated three bays to the W. The jamb capitals were carved in the time of Wiligelmo and re-employed.[115] Possibly the lintel inscription was copied from an earlier version.

(a) HINC VOS PERGENTES CVM CORPORE FLECTITE MENTES

A full leonine hexameter.

'As you proceed from here, bow down your mind with your body.'

91. **Modena**. S. Geminiano.

Apse. Plaque with a dedication inscription (a) inserted into the wall of the central apse above the lower apse window. The inscription concludes with the words BOCALINVS MASSARIVS SANCTI IEMINIANI HOC OPVS FIERI FECIT, 'Bozzalino, the foreman of the workshop of S. Geminiano, ordered this work to be done.'

Composed in 1099 by Canon Aimo; the plaque was carved between 1208 and 1225, during the administration of Bozzalino.[116]

(a) MARMORIBus SCVLPTIS DOMus HEC MICAT VNDIQue PVLCHRIS · /
QVA CORPVS SanCtI REQVIESCIT GEMINIANI · /
QVEm PLENVm LAVDIS TERRARVm CELEBRAT ORBIS · /
NOSQue MAGIS QVOS PASCIT ALIT VESTITQue MINISTRI · /
QVI PETIT IC VERAM MENBRIS ANIMEQue MEDELAm · /
[*blank space*] RECTA REDIT HINCQue SALVTE RECEPTA · /
INGENIO CLARVS LANFRANCVS DOCTVS ET APTVS · /
EST OPERIS PRINCEPS HVIVS · RECTORQue MAGISTER · /
QVO FIERI CEPIT DEMONSTRAT LITTERA PRESENS · /
ANTE DIES QVINTVS IVNII TVNC FVLSERAT IDVS · /
ANNI POST MILLE DOMINI NONAGINTA NOVEMQue /
HOS VTILES FACTO VERSVS COMPOSVIT AIMO

Three unrhymed (4, 8, 9), two common leonine (3, 11), and seven full slant leonine hexameters. Cf. the Enoch/Elias inscription plaque on the W façade. The final two verses display several false quantities: final vowel of *mille* (11) lengthened at caesura; *nŏnăgintă* (11), *ŭtiles* (12), *compōsuit* (12).

'This cathedral gleams on every side with beautiful sculpted blocks of marble, where the body of Saint Geminiano lies at rest, whom, full of praise, the whole earth celebrates, and we clergy even more whom he feeds, nourishes, and clothes. Whoever seeks here a true cure for limbs and soul, ... returns from here erect and with recovered health. Lanfranc, famed for his talent, learned and able, is the chief of this work, its guide and master. What he determined to be created, the present poem reveals (?). Then, before the 5th day of the Ides of June [= 9 June] had gleamed, after 1099 years of the Lord [had passed], Aimo composed these verses suitable (?) for the occasion.'

92. **Moosburg** (Bayern). St Kastulus.

W portal. Tympanum of Christ in Majesty flanked by the standing figures of the Virgin Mary and Saint Castulus and the kneeling figures of the Holy Roman emperor Henry II (1002–24), holding the document of donation, and Bishop Adalbert of Freising (1158–84), presenting a model of the church. The various figures are labelled on the semicircular rim of the tympanum, HAINRICVS IMPerATOR, SanCtA ΘEWTOcRWC = 'Theotokos,' 'God-bearer,' CASTVLVS MAPTYP = 'Martyr,' and ADELBERTVS EPiscopuC, and there is an inscription (a) in two lines on the lintel.

Ca. 1170–1212. The church was under construction after 1170, and was consecrated in 1212.[117]

(a) HOS TA MAGNIFICVm ·T· DEERT : CASTVLE TENPLVm ·
FELIX · ANTISTES · CVIV(?)S · PA · TemPoRA : PreSTES /

PO · CP · Sit REQuiEM · QuI · RESTITVIT · TIBI · LVMEN ;

AVCRNS (?) · PerPETVO · SVBTRACTVm · TemPoRE · LONGO ·

Evidently, these constitute four hexameters, three of which (if not all four) are common leonines. Strobel and Weis, *Bavière romane*, 346–7, transcribe them as HOC TAMEN MAGNIFICUM TIBI DEFERT CASTULE TEMPLUM. FELIX ANTISTES, CUI SIS PATRONA POTESTAS. PROPITIUS SIT REX QUI RESTITUIT TIBI LUMEN LUCEM PERPETUO SUBSTRACTUM TEMPORE LONGO, and translate: 'Ce temple magnifique, Castule, l'heureux évêque te le donne. Sois pour lui un puissant protecteur. Que lui soit favorable aussi le Roi qui t'a rendu à jamais la splendeur dont tu avais été privé si longtemps.'

93. **Morlaàs** (Pyrénées-Atlantiques). Ste-Foy.

W portal. Tympanum of Christ in Majesty, with an inscription (a) on the rim of the mandorla. The entire W façade is a 19th-century restoration by Viollet-le-Duc. He based his design of the tympanum on the fragmentary remains of the old one.[118] Two smaller tympana are inscribed within the large tympanum. On the left is the Massacre of the Innocents, with an inscription (b) around the rim. On the right is the Flight into Egypt, inscribed + FVGIEBAT MORTEM VT NOS REDIMERET. ANGELVS SALVTIFERO MONSTRABAT VIAM SALVTIS +, 'He fled death in order to redeem us. An angel showed the path of safety to the Redeemer.'[119]

Ca. 1140.[120]

(a) + REX SVM · CAELORV[M ME]RCES · CONDIGNA · MEORVM

+ ME · QVICVMQVE · COLIT · PRO VITA · PerDERE · NOLIT ·

Two full leonine hexameters. Cf. *CIFM*, 6, 158.

'I am the King, the merited reward of my heaven. Whoever cherishes me more than life will not lose it.'

(b) ERODES DomInuM DVm QVERIT PerDERE XPistuM :

EXTiNXIT PVEROS FIDEI IAm FONTE RENATOS

Two common leonine hexameters. This is the 19th-century restoration, but the authenticity of the verses is confirmed by a transcription by Abbé Laplace and photographs made before the restoration.[121] *CIFM* reads EXSTINXIT. Abbé Laplace transcribed the second verse *Exstinxit pueros fide iafoni ... natos.*[122]

'Herod, while he sought to destroy Christ the Lord, killed the children since reborn by the fountain of faith.'

94. **Mozac** (Puy-de-Dôme). St-Pierre.

N portal. The portal has an unadorned archivolt. Above it has been set in an older archivolt, with an inscription (a). This archivolt encloses a blank tympanum[123] on which has been painted a dedication dated 1802.

First quarter of the 12th century? The Romanesque church was probably erected shortly after the affiliation of the abbey with Cluny.[124] The archivolt belongs to this period. As a result of a series of earthquakes in the 15th century, a large part of the church was pulled down and rebuilt. It seems likely that the archivolt was taken down and reinstalled in its present place at that time.

(a) IN|G|RE|DI|EN|S | TE|M|PL|VM | RE|FE|RAT | AD | SV|BLI|M|A | VV|LTVm|

IN|TR|A|TV|R|I A|VL|A|M |VE|NE|RA|NSQ|[ue] | LI|M|I|NA | XP[ist]|I

Two imperfect hexameter lines, the first with incidental common leonine rhyme. Cf. *CIFM*, 18, 222–3. The vertical bars (|) mark the forty arch-stones – twenty for each verse. These lines have been variously misquoted.[125] The final syllable of *referat* (1) is metrically superfluous; the final syllable of *veneransquĕ* (2) ought to be long. Elision (2).

'May he who is entering the church lift up his face to the highest things; worshipping, he [plural] is about to enter the court and the gates of Christ' (?). This is as close to a literal translation of the inscription in its present state as I can get.[126] The source of this inscription is the first lines of two poems that were inscribed after AD 470 on the basilica of St-Martin of Tours.[127]

95. **Nantua** (Ain). St-Michel (former Cluniac priory of St-Pierre).

W portal. Tympanum of Christ in Majesty (effaced) with a lintel of the Last Supper, with an inscription (a) along the lower edge of the lintel.

Ca. 1145.[128]

(a) + NE RES PRETERITAS · VALEAT · DAMPNARE · VETVSTAS

+ ISTE · REI · GESTE · DAT · SIGNA · LAPIS MANIFESTE +

Two leonine hexameters, the first common, the second full. Cf. *CIFM*, 17, 13. Oursel deciphers SIGNA LAPIS as SIGNA EPSI, which he takes to be a mistake for *signa ipse*.[129]

'In order that antiquity not have the power to condemn to oblivion past actions, this stone clearly gives a sign of the deed.'

96. **Nevers** (Nièvre). *St-Sauveur.

*S transept portal. Tympanum of Christ giving the keys to Saint Peter. The tympanum is in the Musée archéologique. There are inscriptions (a) on the background of the tympanum above the heads of four apostles, and (b) on the lower edge of the lintel. The word MAVO, which follows (b) and has been thought to record the sculptor or donor of the tympanum,[130] is probably only a graffito.[131]

1100/1150?[132]

(a) + VISIBus HVMANIS M[ONS]/TRATVR MISTICA [CL]AVIS

A common leonine hexameter. The facsimile transcription in Bourassé, *Dictionnaire d'épigraphie chrétienne*, 1, 983, shows all the missing letters.

'The mystical key is shown to human eyes.'

(b) + PORTA POLI PATEAT HVC EVNTIBus INTVS ET EXTRA +

An unrhymed hexameter? The final syllable of *pateat* is lengthened at caesura and there is a false quantity in *hŭc.*

'The gate of heaven lies open to those going to this place inside and out.'

97. **Nonantola** (Emilia-Romagna). S. Silvestro.

W portal. Tympanum of Christ in Majesty, with an inscription (a) on the lintel.

Ca. 1121. The church was severely damaged or destroyed by a violent earthquake in 1117. Reconstruction began four years later.[133]

(a) + SILVESTRI CELSI CECIDERVNT CVLMINA TEmPLI ·
MILLE REDEmPTORIS LAPSIS VERTIGI~~NE~~ SOLIS /
ANNIS CENTENIS SEPTEm NECNON QVO·Que DENIS ·
QVOD REFICI MAGNOS CEPIT POST QVATVOR ANNOS

One full (3) and three full slant leonine hexameters.

'The roofs of the lofty church of Silvester fell, with the passing, by the revolution of the sun, of one thousand one hundred seven and ten years of the Redeemer. It began to be restored after four great (?) years.'

98. **Pamplona** (Navarra). Cathedral.

*W portal. Console, with an inscription (a), now in the Museo de Navarra. Portions of the portal survived the destruction of the Romanesque façade at the end of the 18th century, and are preserved in the museum. Two consoles, which supported the tympanum, are trimmed with lions, the first with its victim in its jaws, the second holding its victim between its paws.[134]

Ca. 1120–30.[134]

(a) [Virginis ecclesiam praesul sanctissimus olim
Hanc rexit sede(m) Petrus ista(m) fecit et aedem
Ex quo sancta piae domus est incepta Mariae
Tempus protentum fert annos milique centum]
EX INCARNATI DE VIRGINE TEMPORE CHRISTI

Three common and two full (3,4) leonine hexameters. Emended from the text printed by Lojendio, *Navarre romane*, 18. The first four lines are known only from a copy of the inscription made by Sandoval before the destruction of the W façade. The last line is carved on one of the two surviving consoles. The second line, as copied by Sandoval, reads HANC REXIT. SEDE PETRVS IN ISTA FECIT ET AEDEM. I read *sedem* for *sede* and *istam* for *in ista.* The first emendation is virtually certain. It restores normal meter and the leonine rhyme that characterizes the other four lines. The second emendation involves a greater change and can only be regarded as a (plausible?) guess.

'A very holy bishop once ruled this cathedral, a church dedicated to the Virgin. Peter also constructed this building. From the time when the holy house of pious Mary was begun, time stretching back adds up to a thousand and a hundred years from the time of Christ born in the flesh from the Virgin.'

Peter of Roda was the bishop of Pamplona who undertook the construction of the Romanesque cathedral. Construction began in 1100 and was finished perhaps in the 1120s (when the W façade was built and decorated).[136]

99. **Parma** (Emilia-Romagna). Cathedral.

Interior. Tribune level (not open to the public). Pilaster capital, N side, second pier, E face:[137] two wolves dressed as monks being taught by an ass dressed as a monk, with an inscription (a).

Post 1106–ca. 1130.

(a) EST MO/NACHVS / FACTVS LVPVS / HIC SVB DOG/MATE TRACTVS

A full leonine hexameter. Quintavalle, *La Cattedrale di Parma*, pl. 507; Tassi, *Il Duomo di Parma*, pl. 97.

'Here a wolf lured by the power of Christian doctrine has become a monk.'

100. **Parma**. Baptistery.

N portal (the Portal of the Virgin). Tympanum of the Virgin in Majesty with the Child above a lintel in two registers. The upper register depicts from left to right the Baptism of Christ, the Banquet of Herod, and the Beheading of John the Baptist. The lower register carries an inscription (a).

1196–ca. 1216.

(a) BIS : BINIS : DEMPTIS : / ANNIS : DE MILLE : / DVCENTIS : //
IN[C]EPIT : DICTVS : / O[P]VS : HOC : SCVLTOR / B[E]NEDICTVS :

Two full leonine hexameters, the first with slant rhyme.

'With twice two years subtracted from one thousand two hundred [= in the year 1196], the sculptor called Benedetto began this work.'

The baptistery and its sculptures are (almost certainly) the work of Benedetto Antelami, who had earlier (1178) sculpted, dated, and signed the bishop's chair.[138]

101. **Parma**. Baptistery.

Left of the N portal. Relief of Chastity, seated, with Patience on the right and Humility on the left, with an inscription (a) above.

1196–ca. 1216.

(a) + PONITVR IN MEDIO VIRTVS QVE CASTA TVETVr /

CVIVS ADORNATVm RESIDET PACIENCIA DEX/TRA
ET FACIENS HVMILEm COGNOSCITVR / ALTERA LEVA

Three unrhymed hexameters. Cf. Francovich, *Benedetto Antelami*, 1, 174.

'The virtue which chastely beholds her (?) adornment is placed in the middle. Patience sits on the right, and the other [virtue] on the left is recognized making herself humble.'

Cuius perhaps refers to the Virgin of the tympanum.

102. **Parma**. Baptistery.

Right of the N portal. Relief of Charity (?), seated, with two minor virtues, with a tablet with an inscription (a).

1196–ca. 1216.

(a) + HIC RESI[DET] ... TE ...
TATE SINISTR[A]
NOVIT RED[I]

Probably this consisted of one or more hexameters. Cf. Francovich, *Benedetto Antelami*, 1, 174. Now only fragments of four letters remain.

103. **Parma**. Baptistery.

W portal (the Portal of the Redeemer). Tympanum of the Last Judgment. There are inscriptions on the horizontal band separating the tympanum from the lintel. The first (a) is on the left, and the second (b) on the right.

1196–ca. 1216.

(a) SVRGITE DEFVnCTI · RECTOREm CERNITE MVnDI

A full slant leonine hexameter. Cf. Francovich, *Benedetto Antelami*, 1, 171.

'Arise dead ones; see the Ruler of the world.'

(b) VOS Qui DORMITIS IAm SVRGITE NunCIVS INQVID

An unrhymed hexameter.

'You who are asleep, arise now, the angel says.'

104. **Parma**. Baptistery.

W portal. Left jamb: the Works of Mercy, in six panels. From bottom to top, the panels depict: lodging the pilgrim, with an inscription (a); caring for the sick, with an inscription (b); feeding the hungry, with an inscription (c); giving drink to the thirsty, with an inscription (d); visiting the prisoner, with an inscription (e); and clothing the naked, with an inscription (f). The inscriptions are on the lower borders of the panels.

1196–ca. 1216.

(a) ... PLVM PEREGRINIS HOSTIA PANDAS :

An unrhymed hexameter. Cf. Francovich, *Benedetto Antelami*, 1, 169–70; the conjectural restoration of the first words as *iuxta hoc exemplum* is rendered doubtful by the necessity for elision, which is almost unheard of in Romanesque inscriptions.

'... open your doors to pilgrims.'

(b) CVM MVLTA CVRA LAVAT HIC EGRO SVA CRVRA :

A full leonine hexameter.

'With much care, this one washes the legs of a sick man.'

(c) ESCAM LARGA MANVS HEC PORRIGIT ESVRIENTI ·;

An unrhymed hexameter. Final syllable of *manus* lengthened at caesura.

'This generous hand offers food to the hungry.'

(d) HIC QVOD QVESIERAT SICIENTI POCVLA PRESTAT :·

A common leonine hexameter.

'This one offers a cup to a thirsting man, because he had asked (for a drink).'

(e) NON SPERNENS LAPSVM VENIT HIC AD CARCERE CLAVSVM :

A common leonine hexameter.

'Not despising the sinner, this one comes to a man shut up in prison.'

(f) EST HIC NVDATVS QVEM VVLT VESTIRE BEATVS :

A full leonine hexameter.

'This is the naked one whom the blessed man wishes to clothe.'

105. **Parma**. Baptistery.

Left of the W portal. Relief of Faith, seated, with Justice on the left and Peace on the right, with an inscription (a).

1196–ca. 1216.

(a) + [H]AC HABRAAM XPistO PLACVIT / [VI]RTVTE ProBATVS :

LEVE IVSTICI/A PAX DEXTRE CONSOCIATVR :

Two unrhymed hexameters. Cf. Francovich, *Benedetto Antelami*, 1, 174; Francovich, 1, 178, n. 73, reads ‿PRATVS (1).

'Abraham, tested and approved for this virtue [i.e., faith], was pleasing to Christ. Peace to the right is accompanied by Justice to the left.'

106. **Parma**. Baptistery.

Right of the W portal. Relief of Hope, seated, with Modesty on the left and Prudence on the right, with an inscription (a).

1196–ca. 1216.

(a) + SPES Est QVAM CERNIS PRVDENCI[A] / DEXTRA SODALIS :

SIGNATVR LAPID/ES ET PARTE MODESTIA LEVA :

Two unrhymed hexameters. Cf. Francovich, *Benedetto Antelami*, 1, 174.

'It is Hope that you see; Prudence [is] the right-hand companion. And Modesty is represented in stone (?) on the left side.'

107. **Parma**. Baptistery.

Interior. Above W portal: sculpture of David playing the harp, with an inscription (a) in a single line beneath.

1196–ca. 1216?

(a) REX DAVID INVITAT PSALLENS CAnTARE SODALES :

VT BENE DESIGNAnT SCVLTIQue MOLARES :

Two hexameters with trisyllabic slant end rhyme. *Dăvĭd* was normally scanned with two long syllables, but arbitrary scansion of biblical names was common.

'King David, playing the harp, invites his companions to sing, as the sculpted stones well show.'

108. **Petershausen** (Baden-Württemberg). *Church.

*E portal. Tympanum of the Ascension, now in the Badisches Landesmuseum, Karlsruhe. Christ stands within an almond-shaped mandorla. Mary and the twelve apostles are on the lintel. The name of the sculptor, WEZIL (Wezilo of Konstanz), is inscribed to the right of Mary. There is an inscription (a) on the rim of the mandorla; (b) in a double band above the line of apostles; and (c) beneath the feet of the apostles.

A.D. 1173–80.

(a) [+ PRESIDET HIS · PORTIS · QVI · SOLVIT ·] VINCVLA · MORTIS

+ SVM · Q[VI · PerDVRO · NON · SEDEO · CVM · PERIT...]

Two full leonine hexameters? Cf. Kraus, *Die christlichen Inschriften,* 2, 32. The bracketed words are no longer visible. An 18th-century engraving photographically enlarged on the museum wall helps recover some of the lost material. Kraus completes the last word of the second verse as *perituro.* False quantity in *sēdeo* (2) (this reading is open to question).

'He presides over these doors who loosens the bonds of death. I, who am eternal, do not sit with one who will perish' (?).

(b) + FILIVS · ECCE · DE[i QVEM] · CER[nit]IS · O · GALILEI ·

+ IPSE · REVerT[etuR · Non · MITIS · Vt · ISTE VIDETVr] /

+ [vos oli]M · MECVM · FRATRES · TRACTABITIs EQV[um]

[+ OM]NIBVS · VT · VOB[IS · ME]RCEDEm [· REDDO · LABoris]

Four full leonine hexameters: two with slant rhyme (3–4).

'Behold the Son of God, whom you see, o Galileans. He will not return as lenient as he seems here. You will hereafter treat the brothers [= the disciples (?)] equally with me, just as I pay the wages of your work to you all.'

(c) + RECTORES · ISTI · MALA · TOLL[E]NT · SVB · VICE · XPistI ·

+ QVOS · NE · DAMN[EMVR · VENER]ANTE[s] · Q[ui]Que · PreCEMVR ·

Two full leonine hexameters.

'These masters [= the disciples and Mary], like Christ, will take away our sins. Let each of us, venerating them, pray that we not be damned.'

109. **Piacenza** (Emilia-Romagna). Cathedral.

Right W portal. Blank tympanum with lintel of episodes in the life of Christ (the Presentation in the Temple, the Flight into Egypt, the Baptism in the Jordan, and three scenes from the Temptation on the Mountain), with inscriptions (a) on upper edge and (b) on lower edge.

Ca. 1110–15 or a little later? The sculptures of the lintel are ascribed to Niccolò, who was working at Sacra di S. Michele before 1120, and who is known to have been at Ferrara ca. 1135.[139]

(a) OFFERTVR DEVS · ATQue FVGIT · SIC FONTE LAVATVR ·
TEMPTATVR TRIPLICI DEVS · ARTE DOLI SE[? *or* I?]NA[? *or* I?]

Two unrhymed hexameters? Feminine caesura (1).

'God is presented [in the Temple], and He flees [into Egypt], thus He is baptized in the river [Jordan: literally, 'thus He is washed in the fountain']. God is tempted by the triple art of deception [?] ...'

The three clauses of the first verse correspond to the first three scenes on the lintel. The second verse relates to the three scenes of the Temptation of Christ on the Mountain.

(b) + HOC OPVS INTENDAT QVISQVIS BONVS EXIT ET INTRA[T]

A common leonine hexameter.

'May this work guide whoever exits and enters as a good person.'

The same verse is found on the Zodiac Portal of Sacra di S. Michele, where it is accompanied by another verse signed by Niccolò.

110. **Piacenza**. Cathedral.

Right W porch. Lower stage of porch, with an inscription (a) carved on the upper edge between two prophets in the spandrels (one at left labelled HELIAS; the other at right with a label that I have not been able to decipher, but which is said to be Enoch[140]).

AD 1122? Quintavalle thinks that the inscription, in which he has little confidence, possibly refers to a reconsecration of the cathedral that may have taken place in 1122 or thereabouts.[141] If Robb is correct about the provenance of the inscription (see below), it might have been carved on the base of a column of one of the lateral portals at about the time of the supposed reconsecration.

(a) + CENTVM VICENI DVO XP[ist]I POST MILLE FVERE /
ANNO CVM INCEPTVM FVIT HOC LAVDABILE TEMPLVM ›

Two garbled hexameters, the second with common leonine rhyme. This 'is a modern carved inscription ... duplicating an earlier one painted in the same place which in turn was derived from an inscription cut in the base of one of the columns of the portal.'[142] The original verses can be reconstructed from the *Chronicon Placentinum* of Giovanni da Musso (quoted from Muratori, *Rerum Italicarum Scriptores*, 16, 452, by Robb, 'Niccolò,' 385–6): *Centum viceni duo Christi mille fuere / Anni cum coeptum fuit hoc venerabile templum.*

'It was one thousand one hundred twenty-two years after Christ, when this venerable church was begun.'

111. **Pisa** (Toscana). Cathedral of Sta Maria Assunta.

In 1063, the Pisan fleet, under Giovanni Orlando, seized Palermo from the Saracens and occupied the city. With the booty from this campaign, the cathedral was begun by the architect Buschetto Pisano and consecrated by Pope Gelasius II in 1118. Its W façade was completed by Rainaldo in the period 1261–72.[143]

W façade. Marble slab, inset to the left of the central portal, with a carved inscription (a).

Ca. 1118/1261–72? It seems likely that the verses were composed for the dedication of the cathedral, within living memory of the event that it describes. The commemorative plaque might have been carved at that time and later inserted into the 13th-century W façade or perhaps the verses were re-inscribed in the 13th century at the time of the completion of the W façade.

(a) + ANNO QVO XPistuS DE VIRGINE NATVS AB ILLO ;
TRANSIERANT MILLE DECIES SEX TRESQue SVBINDE : /
PISANI CIVES CELEBRI VIRTVTE POTENTES ;
ISTIVS ECCLesiE PRIMORDIA DANTur INISSE : /
ANNO QVO SICVLAS EST STOLVS FACTVS AD ORAS ;
QuoD SIMVL ARMATI MVLTA CVM CLASSE PROEECTI [*sic*] ; /
OMneS MAIORES MEDII PARITERQVE MINORES ;
INTENDERE VIAM PRIMAm SVB SORTE PANORMAm ; /
INTRANTES RVPTA PORTVm PVGNANDO CATENA ;
SEX CAPIVNT MAGNAS NAVES OPIBVSQue REPLETAS ; /
VNAm VENDENTES RELIQVAS PRIVS IGNE CREMANTES ;
QVO PRETIO MVROS CONSTAT HOS ESSE LEVATOS ; /
POST HINC DIGRESSI PARVm TERRAQue POTITI ;
QVA FLVVII CVRSVm MARE SENTIT SOLIS ADORTVM ; /
MOX EQVITVm TurBA PEDITVm COMITANTE CATERVA ;
ARMIS ACCINGVNT SESE CLASSEmQue RELINQVVNT ; /
INVADVNT HOSTES CONTRA SINE MORE FVRENTES ;
SED PRIOR INCVRSVS MVTANS DISCRIMINA CASVS ; /
ISTOS VICTORES ILLOS DEDIT ESSE FVGACES ;

QVOS CIVES ISTI FERIENTES VVLNERE TRISTI ; /
PLVRIMA Pro PORTIS STRAVERVNT MILIA MORTI ;
CONVERSIQue CITO TENTORIA LITORE FIGVNT ; /
IGNIBus ET FERRO VASTANTES OMnIA CIRCVm ;
VICTORES VICTIS SIC FACTA CE~~DE~~ RELICTIS ;
INCO~~LV~~MES MVLTO PISAm REDIERE TRIVMPHO ;

Three unrhymed (1, 21, 22), three full (7, 20, 24), three full slant (11, 16, 21), and sixteen common leonine hexameters. Final syllable of *mille* (2) lengthened at caesura. False quantities in post-classical *stōlus* (5), in *constāt* (12) (or *h* makes position), and in *pārum* (13). *Panormam* (8) = *Panormum* (f.); possibly the shift to the first declension is for the sake of the leonine rhyme.

'From that year when Christ [was] born of the Virgin, one thousand sixty-three [years] had afterwards passed. The citizens of Pisa, potent with celebrated virtue, are enabled to have undertaken the beginnings of this church, in that year when the fleet was formed for the Sicilian shores, because as soon as they were armed and were proceeding with a numerous fleet, as fate would have it, all the upper, middle, and lower classes together directed their primary course to Palermo. After breaking the chain and fighting their way into the port, they seize six ships, large and filled with wealth, selling one before burning the rest by fire. With that prize it is well known that these walls have been raised. Then, shifting a bit from this place and seizing land where the sea feels the current of the river to the east, presently with a squadron of cavalry (and) with an accompanying troop of foot-soldiers they gird themselves with arms and leave the fleet. The enemy, who are raging without control, counterattack, but, the odds being altered by the previous assault, the fortunes of war brought it about that the Pisans were the victors (and) that the enemy were put to flight. The Pisans, striking those citizens with heavy injuries, laid out many thousands for death before the gates, and turning about they quickly fix their tents on the shore. Wasting with fire and sword all things round about, the victors, finishing up the slaughter in this fashion (and) leaving behind the vanquished, returned safe and sound in great triumph to Pisa.'

112. **Pistoia** (Toscana). Cathedral of S. Zenone.

Right W portal. Blank tympanum, with lintel decorated with a floral design. There is an inscription (a) on the upper and lower border of the design.

Late 12th century?

(a) ADVENIENS DISCAS QVID XPICTI CVRIA DICAT : /
QVISQue MALVM VITES BONA FAC PER SECVLA VIVES :

Two full slant leonine hexameters.

'Approaching, learn what the court of Christ says. May each of you avoid evil; do good; may you live forever.'

113. **Pistoia**. S. Bartolomeo in Pantano.

Central W portal. Blank tympanum, with lintel of Doubting Thomas. Christ, flanked by six apostles on each side and an angel at each end. There is an inscription (a) on a band above the scene on the lintel, the apostles are labelled on a band below the scene on the lintel, and the words RODOLFINus OPerarius ANNI DomiNI MCLXVII, 'Rodolfinus the workman (foreman?), AD 1167,' are inscribed on the underside of the lintel.

AD 1167.

(a) + PAX EGO SVm VOBis QuO SIT FIRMIS[s]IMA D/N(?)OBis
CERNITE Dis(?)CRETE Q[ui?]A Sum D[eu]S ECCE V[i]DE~~TE~~
ME QuOQue PALPATE SICVT DE~~BE~~TIS AMATE
EXPLOSI MORBis Per CLI~~MA~~TA QVATTVOR ORBis
FONTE SACRO LOTVm MVN~~DV~~m ConVERTI~~TE~~ TOTVm

Five full leonine hexameters. Final syllable of *discrete* (2) and *palpate* (3) lengthened at caesura. For the long initial syllable in *clīmata*, see Blaise, *Dictionnaire latin-français*, s.v. *clima*.

'I am your peace, the one by whom peace is [made] most sure for us all (?). Discern separately that I am God, behold, see, and touch me, love (me) as you ought. Having been sent out through the four regions of the globe, convert the whole world, washed by the sacred fountain, from wickedness (*morbis*).'

Cf. John 20:19–31. Some of the uncertainties and difficulties of this translation may stem from faults in my transcription.

114. **Pistoia**. S. Giovanni Fuorcivitas.

N portal. Blank tympanum above lintel of the Last Supper, with an inscription (a) in a single line above the scene of the Last Supper. The arch of the tympanum springs on each side from the back of a lion crouching over its prey, with the inscription GRVAMONS MAGISTER BONVS FECit HOC OPVS, 'Good master Gruamons made this work,' on the white marble blocks of the arch.

Ca. 1160–70. Gruamons's signature appears also on Sant'Andrea.

(a) + CENANS DISCIPVLIS CRISTVS DAT VERBA SAL[VTIS]
[...]VA TRIBVIT LEGE[m] VETEREM QVOQVE FINIT

Two common leonine hexameters? The conjecture *salutis* seems fairly certain, given the evidence of common leonine rhyme in the second verse.

'Dining with his disciples, Christ gives words of salvation. He assigns ... and also finishes the old law.'

The last clause is a reference to the new law of charity (Matt. 22:39; John 13:34).

115. **Poitiers** (Vienne). St-Porchaire. Only the combination bell-tower and narthex of the W front remains.

Narthex. Historiated capital of right-jamb column of W arcade, W face: Daniel in the Lions' Den, with an inscription (a) around the mandorla.

Second half of the 11th century? The bell-tower/narthex is assumed to have been built after the submission of the priory to the Benedictine abbey of Bourgueil in 1068.[144] Favreau and Michaud date the capital to the second half of the 11th century.[145] However, Oursel argues that the style of the capital indicates the first half of the 11th century.[146]

(a) HIC DANIEL DOMINO VI[n]C[IT] COETVM LEONINVM

An unrhymed hexameter? Cf. *CIFM*, 1:1, 93, where the reading is VI[NCIT]. The inscription is now badly eroded and cannot be accurately read; even in 1874 (photo in *CIFM*, 1:1, pl. 33, fig. 65) it was not entirely clear. False quantity in *lĕōninum.*

'Here Daniel with (the help of) the Lord conquers a pride of lions.'
Cf. Dan. 14:30–1.

116. **Poitiers** (Vienne). Ste-Radegonde.

Interior. *Entrance to the night-stairs.[147] Fragment of an undecorated gable-shaped lintel, with an inscription (a). The lintel is now housed in the Musée Ste-Croix of Poitiers (item #481). The left edge of the lintel is broken off. A vertical gouge on the right side of the lintel goes through the last letters of the verses.

End 11th/12th century?[148]

(a) [TV] QuI ES : PraeCLARA : DIES : NOS · XPistE GVB[ERN]A /
[NOCTI]BVS · OMnIBVS : INTRO IACENTIBVS ESTO · LVCERN[A]

Two hexameters with full disyllabic and partial trisyllabic end rhyme. Cf. *CIFM*, 1:1, 117. *CIFM* reads *introiacentibus* as one word (eliminating the medial caesura). Hiatus in line 1 (*qui* : *es*). Feminine caesura (1, 2).

'Guide us, O Christ, you who are the shining day. Be the lamp for all those who are lying within.'

117. **Pont-l'Abbé-d'Arnoult** (Charente-Maritime). St-Pierre.

Central W portal. Inner archivolt: Lamb of God in a circular medallion, on the rim of which is an inscription (a), at the apex of the archivolt.

Mid-12 century? *CIFM*, 1:3, 100, puts the date as early as the end of the 11th century.

(a) [HIC] / D[eu]S / E[st] / MAGNVS / QVEm / SIGN[AT] / MISTICus / AGNus

A full leonine hexameter. Cf. *CIFM*, 1:3, 100–1. The inscription is damaged; I supply the missing letters from Eygun, *Saintonge romane*, 147, who bases his transcription on the authority of Canon Tonnellier. However, neither of them recognize this as a leonine verse, and hence both expand and interpret it incorrectly.

In the words of Eygun: 'Autour, le chanoine Tonnelier [*sic*] a lu: HIC / DS / E / MAGNVS / QVE / SIGNAT / MISTIC' / AGN' (Hic Deus est Magnus; quare signatur misticus Agnus) ...'

'Here is the great God whom the mystic Lamb signifies.'

Cf. Ps. 94:3. See the closely related verses on the tympanum of the Cathedral of Verona.

118. **La Porcherie** (Vienne). *Notre-Dame des Moreaux.

All that remains of the abbey, which suffered in the Hundred Years' War and during the Wars of Religion, are fragments of the ancient construction that are incorporated into some of the buildings of a farm outside the hamlet of la Porcherie, some two kilometres west of Sommières-du-Clain.

*W portal. *Inner archivolt, with an inscription (a). Two life-sized reliefs of bishops Grimoard and Adelelme standing on animals flanked the arch of the portal. Bishop Grimoard (d. 1142) was identified by an inscription, DeuS MISEREATVR GRIMOARDI / PICTAVENSIS EPiscopI ET ARNAVDI / ARCHIDIACONI PATer NosteR, 'May God have mercy on Grimoardus, Bishop of Poitiers, and on Arnaudus the archdeacon. Our Father.' Bishop Adelelme (d. 1140) was identified by an inscription, DeuS MISEREATVR GVILELMI ADALELMI / PICTAVENSIS EPiscopI ET ARNAVDI ARCHID[I]/ACONI PATer NosteR, 'May God have mercy on Guilelmus Adalelmus, Bishop of Poitiers, and on Arnaudus the archdeacon. Our Father.' The two inscription blocks are currently displayed beneath the animals, but the drawings of the 19th-century archaeologists reveal that they were placed in the spandrels between the figures of the bishops and the outer curve of the arch.[149] When Porter photographed the portal in 1921, the sculptures were still in place. Since then the archivolt with its inscription has disappeared,[150] and the sculptures are in the Allen Memorial Art Museum of Oberlin College, Oberlin, Ohio.[151]

Ca. 1142–55. Stechow shows that these sculptures must have been placed by Archdeacon Arnaud, who was active between 1142 and 1155.[152]

(a) *VT : FVIT : INTROITVS TEMPLI : SanCtI : SALOMONIS :

\+ SIC : EST : ISTIVS : IN : MEDIO : BOVIS : ATQue : LEONIS :

Two hexameters with disyllabic end rhyme. *CIFM*, 1:2, 8. From a drawing of Brouillet reproduced by Favreau and Michaud. Genitive singular *istĭus* is common in the 12th century (see Langosch, *Lateinisches Mittelalter*, 54).

'As was the entrance to the holy temple of Solomon, so the entrance of this is placed between an ox and a lion.'

119. **Puilampa** (near Sádaba) (Zaragoza). Hermitage.

W portal. Tympanum of a chrismon flanked by two pine trees and the sun and moon, with an inscription on the lintel (a). The roll moulding above the tympanum is inscribed BERNARDVS ME FECIT.[153]

First quarter of 13th century.[154]

(a) + PORTA : PER : HANC CELI : FIT : PERVIA CVIQVE : FIDELI

A full leonine hexameter.

'Through this gate the gate of heaven becomes accessible to each believer.' This is the first of two verses inscribed on the portal of S. Juan de la Peña.

120. **Le Puy-en-Velay** (Haute-Loire). Cathedral of Notre-Dame.

W façade. Grand stairway leading to the 'porte dorée.' The stairway rises up in four stages under the last four bays of the nave. There is an inscription (a) on the seventh and eighth risers of the third set of stairs (under the third bay from the W of the nave). At one point in the 12th century, what is now the third bay from the W was the last bay of the nave, and the steps beneath it on which the inscription appears marked the limit of the W façade and the entrance to the church.[155]

Ca. 1150–75? It seems likely that the inscription would have been added at the time (not precisely known) in the 12th century when the late-11th-century church was extended by two bays, but before the final two bays were added at the end of the century.[156]

(a) [*Upper riser*:] + NI CAVEAS CRIMEN CAVEAS CONTINGERE LIMEN

[*Lower riser*:] NAM REGINA POLI VVLT SIN[E SORDE C]OLI

A full leonine elegiac couplet. Cf. Paul and Paul, *Notre-Dame du Puy*, 103; *CIFM*, 18, 110–11. The risers were restored between 1878 and 1881. Two fragments of stone from the original stairs with a few of the same letters are in the Musée Crozatier. The first, item BC 5, contains the letters NI (the first word of line 1); the second, item BC 6, contains the letters M RE (from the first two words of line 2).

'Unless you refrain from sin, do not contaminate this threshold, because the Queen of heaven wishes to be worshipped without sordidness.'

121. **Le Puy-en-Velay**. Notre-Dame.

W façade. The Rock of Fevers, with an *inscription (a). The Rock is now placed at the head of the grand stairway under the fourth bay from the W, but once was placed at the foot of the main altar.[157]

Ca. 1150–75?

(a) *Plebs hac rupe sita, fit sana sopore potita,

Si quaeras, quare: virtus adscribitur Arae.

Two full leonine hexameters. Gissey, *Discours historiques*, 91. One assumes from Gissey's description that these were painted on the picture, but Paul and Paul, *Notre-Dame du Puy*, 6, speak as though they were (and still are?) painted (?) or carved (?) on the frame of the rock. Nothing is now visible on the frame or the rock. They quote the same verses, but instead of *potita*, they read *sopita*. Final syllable of *sita* (1) lengthened at caesura.

'People placed by this rock, having slept, become well. If you want to know why, the power is attributed to the altar.'

122. **Le Puy-en-Velay**. Notre-Dame.

Apse. Exterior wall of the flat-headed apsidal chapel, with an inscription (a).

Ca. 1150–75.[158]

(a) FONS · OPE · DIVINA · LANGVENTIBVS · Est · MEDICINA · /
SVBVENIENS · GRATIS · VBI · DEFICIT · ARS · YPOCRATIS

Two full leonine hexameters. Cf. *CIFM*, 18, 116. *Ȳpŏcrātēs* is probably not a matter of false quantities but rather a characteristic medieval deformation of the name *Hippocrates* (cf. OF/ME *ypocras*).

'The fountain with its divine power is medicine for the sick, healing without charge when the art of Hippocrates fails.'

123. **Le Puy-en-Velay**. Notre-Dame.

Porche du For (SE porch). Grand portal opening into the S transept, with an *inscription (a) on the left side.[159]

Ca. 1150–75?

(a) *Lubrica si vita fuerit tunc limina vita
Sanctaque ne violes dum mala carnis oles

A full leonine elegiac couplet. Paul and Paul, *Notre-Dame du Puy*, 111; *CIFM*, 18, 115 (reading *fuerit vita*). According to *CIFM*, the couplet was published by Mathurin des Roys, *Fondation de la saincte et dévote Église de Notre-Dame du Puy* (Lyon, 1523). Final syllable of *vita* (1) lengthened at caesura.

'If your life has been lecherous, then avoid this threshold, and do not profane its sanctity as long as you smell of the evils of the flesh.'

124. **Regensburg** (Bayern). St Emmeram.

N transept portal. Limestone relief plaques installed above the twin doors, representing Saint Emmeram (left), Christ in Majesty (centre), and Saint Dionysius (right). The relief of Saint Emmeram is inscribed (a) along three sides of its rectangular frame. The centre relief shows Christ in Majesty with a book in his left hand. His feet rest on a stool, on the front of which is a donor bust. The plaque has an inscription (b) around three sides of the rectangular frame. There is an inscription (c) on the open book. There is also an inscription (d) around the circular rim of the donor bust. The relief of Saint Dionysius has an inscription (e) along three sides of its rectangular frame.

Ca. 1050. The donor bust assigns the sculptures to the time of Abbot Regenwardus (1048–64).

(a) [...] INTRANTES BENEDIC AVDIQ[ue] PRE/CAN<u>TE</u>S
EMMER/AMME TVI CVSTOS FIDISSI<u>ME</u> TEMPLI

Two leonine hexameters: the first full, and the second common. Cf. Porter, *Romanesque Sculpture*, 9, pl. 1281; Strobel and Weis, *Bavière romane*, 60–1.

'Bless those entering, and hear those praying, O Emmeram, most faithful guardian of your church.'

(b) + CVM PETRA SIT DICTVS STABILI P[ro] NVMINE / XP[istu]C
ILLIVS / IN SAXO SATIS APTE CONSTAT IMAGO

Two common leonine hexameters. Lange, *Die Byzantinische Reliefikone*, 31, reads PNOMINE; Hearn, following Lange, interprets this as P[rae]NOMINE, and translates 'Since he was called Petra in spite of his confirmed praenomen XPC his likeness in stone is completely appropriate.'[160] The inscription clearly reads P NVMINE.

'Since Christ is called a rock on account of his firm majesty, it is fitting enough that his image be in stone.'

(c) SPES EGO SVm / VITAE CVNC/TIS SPERAN/TIBVS IN ME

A common leonine hexameter.

'I am the hope of life for all who hope in me.'

(d) + ABBA REGENWARDVS HOC FORE IVSSIT OPVS

A common leonine pentameter.

'Abbot Regenwardus ordered this work to be made.'

(e) GALLIA TRANSLATVm GEMIT HVC QVEM TRINA / PATRONV[m]
EXSTAT / IMAGO TVI PIE MACHARIOS DIONISI

Two common leonine hexameters.

'Tripartite Gaul laments its patron saint translated hither, which your image, holy Macharios Dionysius, reveals.'

125. **Ribe** (Jutland: Ribe Amt). Cathedral of Our Lady.

S Portal (called the 'Cat's Head' doorway from its medieval knocker). Tympanum of the Descent from the Cross, with labels around the rim, and an inscription (a) along the base of the tympanum and continuing back up the right end of the rim.

Ca. 1130.[161]

(a) REX · OBIT [HA]EC PLOR[AT C]ARVS [D]OLET · IM<u>PI</u>/V[s] · OR<u>AT</u> ·

A full leonine hexameter. Cf. Mackeprang, *Jydske Granitportaler*, 160. The bracketed letters are no longer legible (and some of the others are partially effaced), but can be filled in on the basis of an etching made by Terpager in 1736, which reads: REX OBIT · IDCORI · OBT · CARVS · DOLET · IMP/V · OR<u>AT</u> ·,[162] and from the inscription at Santo Domingo de Silos.

'The King dies, she [Mary] weeps, the dear one [John] grieves, the sinner prays.'

The 'sinner' at Silos is Adam, who is depicted lifting the lid of his coffin beneath the cross. Adam is not represented on the tympanum of Ribe.

126. **Ripoll** (Gerona). Sta Maria.

W façade and portal. The whole is badly eroded and damaged, and inscriptions that are reported by earlier authorities are now too worn to be read with confidence, if at all. The façade presents a large rectangular surface into which is inserted a monumental recessed central portal. The façade projects slightly from the church so that the surface extends around onto a short N and S wall. It is divided horizontally into three major areas, with various subdivisions. No inscriptions are associated with the upper and lower areas.

The middle area, in two registers, depicts scenes from the life of David and Moses. The scenes associated with David are on the left of the portal. The four panels in the upper register have been variously identified, and no certainty is possible. There is an inscription (a) above the upper register. In the lower register, which is divided into three panels, the first panel from the left depicts the transporting of the Ark of the Covenant. A standing figure on the left blows a horn, while two small bulls draw the Ark. There is an inscription (b) above this panel. The other two panels depict the plague and Gad addressing David. There is an inscription (c) above these panels. On the right of the portal, with Moses, there is an inscription (d) on the upper register, and an inscription (e) on the lower register.

The recessed jambs and statue columns of the portal correspond to the lower area of the façade. The outer-jamb column on the left is a statue of Saint Peter who holds a key in one hand and a book in the other, with an inscription (f). The outer-jamb column on the right is a statue of Saint Paul who holds a banderole. The banderole may once have been inscribed. Numerous non-metrical inscriptions appear on the archivolts of the portal.

Ca. 1150–75.[163]

(a) Iudicat hinc populum ... ieste do ...

The beginning (+ a fragment) of one or perhaps two leonine verses? Cf. Sanoner, 'Le portail de Ripoll,' 371–2, 379, 386, 388–94.

'He judges the people from here ...'

(b) Archam cantantes deducunt et iubi[lantes]

A full leonine hexameter.

'Singing and shouting, they conduct the ark.'

Cf. 2 Kings 6:2–5, 12; 1 Para. 13:5–8; 15:24–8.

(c) Angelus est vindex sceleris sed gad ne[ci iu]dex

A common leonine hexameter. If *necĭ* is the correct reading (dative singular of *nex*), then there is a false quantity in the second syllable.

'The angel is the avenger of crime but Gad [is] the judge for the slaughter.'
Cf. 2 Kings 24:11–16; 1 Para. 21:9–15.

(d) Virga la ... moyses reserat ferit unda et aquatur ... a ... data coturnix

Two (garbled) hexameters? The reference seems to be to the times when Moses parted the Red Sea with his rod (Exod. 14:16–22) and when God provided the children of Israel with quails and manna (Exod. 16:2–13).

(e) Ur et aaron relevant manuum moyse gravitatem
dum [iosue] popul[usque leva]nt amalehc ferita[te]m

Two hexameters with trisyllabic end rhyme? The regular genitive singular of *Moyses* is *Moysi*, but Souter, *Glossary*, indicates that there are a number of variations of which *Moysē* (1) might be one. My tentative reconstruction of the second verse is based on speculation in Sanoner, 'Le portail de Ripoll,' 372.

'Hur and Aaron relieve the weight of the hands of Moses, while Josue and the people relieve the ferocity of Amalech.'
Cf. Exod. 17:10–13.

(f) [Pe]trus it[er p]andit e[t] plebs a[d] sidera scandit

A full leonine hexameter. Sanoner reads *flebs* for *plebs.*

'Peter opens the way and the people ascend to heaven.'

127. **La Rochefoucauld** (Charente). St-Étienne d'Olérat.

W portal. Sculptures of the Lamb of God and the Four Animals, with an inscription (a) around the edges of the diamond-shaped plaque that surrounds the Lamb. The letters SVN I [*two blank stones*] I C I [*blank*] I V I [*two blank*] I PTIS I LAVA are inscribed on the inner archivolt of the portal, and the letters PAX I LEX I DVX I [*blank*] I CVSS I ET I MAR I X VI I RAN I RTVS I SCR I VCAS I OMNI I ETLV on the outer archivolt. Cf. *CIFM,* 1:3, 66. The blocks of the archivolts have been reset without regard for their original order. *CIFM* partially reconstructs the outer inscription as PAX LEX DVX ET LV[X] VIRTVS MARCVS S[ANCTVS L]VCAS ET. The sequence *pax, lex, dux, lux* is a variant of *pax, lex, rex, lux,* which is found in a number of places elsewhere.[164]

End 11th/beginning 12th century.[165]

(a) DA PACEM NO/BIS QVI MVN[...]

Cf. *CIFM,* which completes the inscription as DA PACEM NOBIS QVI MVN[di peccata tollis], with the suggestion that it was intended as a (common leonine) hexameter, despite the false quantity in *peccăta.* The blocks forming the edges of the diamond-shaped frame are out of order; possibly the missing portions of the inscription were on one or two blocks that have disappeared and been replaced. The first part of the inscription (*da pacem no*) is on the block the forms the left half of the upper-right edge; the second part is on the block that forms the left half of the upper-left edge.

'Give peace to us, you who take away the sins of the world.'
Cf. John 1:29.

128. **Roda de Isábena** (Huesca). Cathedral.

Interior. Pilaster on the right side of the nave before the choir, with a plaque bearing an inscription (a), preceded by the date [Anno M. CC. XXV]. I have not been able to find the plaque and it is not clear to me whether the inscription is carved or painted.

AD 1225.

(a) [Pax hic intranti sint prospera cuncta precanti
Pontifices sancti septem sunt hic tumulati
Rotenses episcopi venite prandete]
PONTIFICum : DICTA Q[uo]R[u]M SVNT NOmInA SCriPTA
CORPorA SVnT / SACRO COnDITA QuIP[p]E LOCO
HOC VIVIT TVMuLO SAnCTVS / RAIM[un]Dus IN ISTO
PR[i]Mus ODISSE[n]Dus ATO FVIT SECVnDus
TeRCIO / BORELLus AIMERICus QVOQue Q[u]ARTus
Q[ui]NTus FVIT ARNVLFus SEXTus et / IPsE LVPus
SEPTIMus EST IACOBus IVSTus CASTus REVEreNDus /
CVNCTIS PROPICIus SIT DEVS IPsE PIVS

Eleven (?) verses. Verses 1–2 are leonine hexameters, verse 1 with full, verse 2 with common leonine rhyme. Verse 3 is unmetrical. Verses 4–11 make up four common leonine elegiac couplets. Durán Gudiol, 'Las inscripciones medievales,' 107–9 (no. 79). The first portion of the inscription (in square brackets) is now lost, but is known from earlier transcriptions. Final syllable of *dicta* (4) lengthened at caesura. False quantities in *secŭndus* (7), *prōpicius* (11). Extra-metrical syllable in *Quin(tus)* (9). Arbitrary scansion of proper names.

'Peace to the one entering here! May all good fortune be to the one praying. Seven holy bishops are buried here. Bishops of Roda, come, eat (?). The aforesaid bodies of the bishops whose names are written are buried indeed in this sacred place. In this tomb lives Saint Raymond [Raymond Guillelmus, prior of St-Sernin of Toulouse, and bishop of Roda (1104–25), d. 1126]; in this, first, bishop Odisendus [956–76]; Ato [son of the count of Ribagorza; brother of Odisendus] was second; in the third Borrellus [taken prisoner by Muslims in 1006]; Aimericus [metropolitan bishop of Narbonne in the time of Odisendus][166] likewise the fourth; fifth was Arnulfus; sixth Lupus himself; the seventh is James, just, chaste, and revered. May holy God himself be propitious to all.'
The first verse (for which, cf. St.-Léger-en-Pons) seems more appropriate to a portal inscription.

129. **Rome** (Lazio). Cathedral of Saint John Lateran (S. Giovanni in Laterano).

E façade. Architrave of portico: an inscription (a) preserved from the *portico of the old façade. The portico was constructed by Niccolò di Angelo ca. 1170.[167] An inscription recording his name was located on the right-hand pier of the old portico, beneath the inscription of the architrave: *NICOLAVS ANGELI FECIT HOC OPVS (Armellini, *Le chiese di Roma*, 1, 124).

Ca. 1170/1733–5.

(a) DOGMATE PAPALI DATVR AC SIMVL IMPERIALI /
QVOD SIM CVNCTARVM MATER CAPVT ECCLESIARum /
HINC SALV/ATORIS/ COELE/STIA REG/NA DATORIS :
NOMINE SANCXERV/NT CVM CV/NCTA / PERACTA / FVERVNT /
SIC NOS EX TOTO CONVERSI SVPPLICE VOTO /
NOSTRA QVOD HEC AEDES TIBI XPiCte SIT INCLITA SEDES

Six full leonine hexameters.

'By papal decree and also by imperial decree it is granted that I be the mother (and) head of all churches. From henceforward, after everything has been finished, they have consecrated this heavenly kingdom with the name of the Saviour and Creator. Thus we (have been) persuaded wholly (*ex toto*) by humble prayer that this our celebrated temple be your home, Christ.'

130. **Rome**. Saint John Lateran.

Cloister. S walk, second intermediate pier from left: impost (N face), with an inscription (a). (There is a mosaic inscription in a single line running the length of the S walk of the cloister, just above the arches of the columns.)

Ca. 1215–1232/6.[168]

(a) + NOBILITer DOCTus HAC / VASSALLECTVS In ARTE : /
CVm PATRE CEPIT OPVS / QvoD SOLus PERFICIT IPsE

Two unrhymed hexameters.

'Nobly trained in this art, Vassalletto began this work with his father, which he finished himself alone.'

131. **Rome**. S. Giorgio in Velabro.

S portico (the portico was almost entirely destroyed by a terrorist bomb on 27 July 1993). Entablature, supported by corner piers and four Ionic columns, with an inscription (a) in a single line above the piers and columns, and an inscription (b) in a single line on the entablature of the E side of the porch. This inscription is preceded by the letters [...]VI.

Beginning of the 13th century.[169]

(a) + STEFANVS · EX STELLA CVPIEnS CAPTARE SVPerNA ·

ELOQuiO RARVS VIRTVTVm LVMINE CLARVS ·
EXPENDENS AVRVm STVDVIT RENOVARE ProAVLVm ·
SVmPTIBVS EX ProPRIIS TibI FECIT SanCtE GEORGI ·
CLerICus HIC CVIus PrIOR ECCLesIE FVIT HVIus ·

One unrhymed (4), two full (2,5), one full slant (3), and one common (1) leonine hexameter. Arbitrary quantity in proper name (*Stēfanus*, 1). *Proaulum* (3) for *proaulam* (for the sake of the rhyme?).

'Stephan of Stella, wishing to lay siege to heaven, outstanding in eloquence, bright with the light of his virtues, paying out gold, was eager to renovate the portico. At his own expense, he made [it?] for you, Saint George, whose cleric he was (and) prior of this church.'

(b) HIC LOCus AD VELVm PreNOmInE DICITVR AVRI ·

An unrhymed hexameter.

'This place is nicknamed "ad velum auri" [at the shelter of gold].'

132. **Rome**. Sta Pudenziana.

E façade. Portico supported by two columns with spiral fluting, with an ornamental lintel and a triangular pediment above. The lintel frieze consists of five medallions on a background of interlaced vines. The Lamb of God, with a cruciform nimbus, is in the centre medallion. There are portrait busts in the other four medallions. The Good Shepherd is on the far left; Saint Pudentiana is on the near left; Saint Praxedes is on the near right; Saint Pudens, the supposed father of the virgins Pudentiana and Praxedes, is on the far right (this is the Pudens mentioned by Paul in his letter to Timothy [2 Tim. 4:21]).

A horizontal band with an inscription (a) in a single line runs above the three inner medallions. There are circular inscriptions (b–f) around the five medallions.

Early 12th century (?). Estimates range from the late 8th to the 12th century.[172] The use of full leonine slant rhyme in the inscriptions points to the 12th century for the sculpture of the lintel.

(a) [A]D REQVIEm VITE CVPIS · O TV QuiQue VENIRE :
EN PATET INGRESSVs FVERIS · SI RI~~TE~~ REVERSVs : /
ADVOCAT IPSE QuiDEm VIA · DVX ET IANITOR IDEm :
GAV~~DI~~A ProMIT~~TE~~NS ET CRIMI~~NA~~ QVEQue REMI<tt>ENS :

Two full (3,4) and two full slant leonine hexameters. Cf. Buchowiecki, *Handbuch*, 3, 665, who gives *ad* (1) and *remittens* (4) without comment and reads *quoque* for *quique* (1).

'O you who wish to come to life's eternal rest, lo, the entrance lies open if you turn back correctly. And indeed, the way itself, the guide and also the keeper of the gate, calls, promising joys and remitting all sins.'

(b) + HIC CVNCTIS VITE PASTOR DAT DOGMATE SanCtE

+ SanCtE PRECOR PASTOR Pro NOBIS ESTO ROGATOR ·

One common and one full slant leonine hexameter.

'Here the Shepherd gives the doctrine of holy life to all. Holy Shepherd, be an intercessor for us, I pray.'

(c) + VIRGO PVDENQueTIANA · CORAm STAT LAmPADE PLENA

+ ProTEGE PRECLARA NOS VIRGO PVDENQueTIANA :

Two common leonine hexameters. Feminine caesura (1). False quantity in *cŏram* (1). Final syllable of *preclara* (2) lengthened at caesura. The spelling *Pudenquetiana* for *Pudentiana* seems to be an artificial device for eliminating an internal trochee, which would preclude the use of the name in hexameter.

'The virgin Pudentiana stands in the presence (of God) with her lamp full. Protect us, o noble virgin Pudentiana.'

Saint Pudentiana is associated with the wise virgins of the parable (Matt. 25:1–13), who kept their lamps filled with oil.

(d) + HIC AGNVS MVNDVm · RESTAVRAT SANGVINE LAPSVM

+ MORTVVS ET VIVVS · IDEM SVm PASTOR ET AGNVS

Two common leonine hexameters.

'Here the Lamb restores the fallen world with his blood. "Dead and alive, I am equally the Shepherd and the Lamb."'

(e) + OCCVRRIT SPONSO · PRAXEDIS LVMINE CLARO ·

+ NOS PIA PRAXEDIS · PRECE SanCtAS ConFER AD EDIS :

One common and one full leonine hexameter. Cf. Buchowiecki, *Handbuch*, 3, 665, who reads: S(an)C(t)A S(an)C(tas) FER for *sanctas confer* (2).

'Saint Praxedes runs to meet the Bridegroom with her bright light. Holy Praxedes, convey us to the holy church with your prayer.'

Saint Praxedes, like Saint Pudentiana, is associated with the wise virgins of the parable.

(f) + ALMVS ET ISTE DOCET · PVDENS AD SIDERA CALLES ·

+ TE ROGO PVDENS [S]anCtE · NOs PVRGA CRIMINA TRVDENS

One unrhymed and one full leonine hexameter. Cf. Buchowiecki, *Handbuch*, 3, 665, who reads *CA(e)LES* for *calles* (1). False quantity in *Pŭdens* (1). The stone carver has inadvertently reversed the words *sancte Pudens* (2), upsetting both the metre and the leonine rhyme.

'And this holy Pudens teaches the path to the stars. I beg you, Saint Pudens, purify us, expelling our sins.'

133. **Rome**. Santi Giovanni e Paulo.

S portico. Entablature, supported by eight columns, with an inscription (a) in a single line.

Ca. 1154–9.[170]

(a) + PRESBITER ECCLESIE ROMANE RITE IOHANNES ;
HEC ANIMI VOTO DONA VOVENDO DEDIT ;
MARTIRIBVS CRISTI PAVLO PARITERQVE IOHANNI :
PASSIO QVOS EADEM CONTVLIT ESSE PARES

Two unrhymed elegiac couplets (line 3 with common leonine rhyme).

'John, duly ordained priest of the Roman church, has given these gifts, in fulfilment of his soul's vow (*animi voto vovendo* [?]), to the martyrs of Christ, Paul and John alike, whom the same suffering made companions.'

The priest John was Cardinal Giovanni di Sutri, who was responsible for the construction of the portico.[171]

134. **Rothenkirchenhof** (near Kirchheim-Bolanden) (Rheinland-Pfalz). *Monastery of Rothenkirchenhof. The refectory, now part of a farm building, still stands.

Refectory portal. Tympanum, with an inscription (a) around its frame.

Ca. 1200?[173]

(a) Sedibus his panem carni Verbum dabis auri
Deliciis verbi sacius quam pane cibaris

Two unrhymed hexameters. Winterfeld, *Palatinat roman*, p. 324.

'In this place you will give bread to the flesh [and] the word to the ear. You are fed better by the delights of the word than by the bread.'

135. **Sacra di San Michele** (Piemonte). S. Michele.

S side of the apse. 'Zodiac Portal' (Porta dello Zodiaco) at the head of the 'Stairway of the Dead' (Scalone dei Morti), executed by the sculptor Niccolò. A row of columns and pilasters with ornamented capitals and a continuous frieze moulding above decorates the inner face of each side of the Zodiac Portal. It is generally agreed that these decorative members of the portal were brought here from somewhere else.[174] However, they must have been intended as part of a church entrance (see inscription [a] below).

On the left (W) side of the portal, the capital of the second column shows naked figures wrestling, with an inscription (a) on the S and E faces of the abacus above their heads. The centre pilaster of the pier is decorated with the signs of the zodiac on the inner (N) face, inscribed on the left edge: CHAP<u>RI</u>CORN[VS] SAGITARIVS SCORPIVS <u>LI</u>BRA VIRGO LEO CANCER GEMINI TAVRVS ARIES PISCES AQVARIVS; the inside (E) face is decorated with a floral scroll pattern embracing bird, animal, and human figures, with an inscription (b) on the left and right edges of the lower block. The capital of the third column depicts the story of Cain and Abel, with inscriptions (c) and (d) on the N and E faces of the abacus.

On the right (E) side of the portal, the centre pilaster of the pier is decorated only on the inner (N) and inside (W) faces. The inner face depicts a number of stellar constellations in floral-patterned squares, with labelling inscriptions on the right edge of the two blocks that make up the pilaster: HYDRA ARA NOTHIVS CETVS CENTAVRVS ERIDANVS PISTRIX ANTICANIS CANIS LEPVS ORION DELTOTON PEGASVS DELFINVS.[175] The left edge of the upper block shows an inscription (e). The upper block of the inside face of the pilaster, which is decorated with another floral scroll pattern enclosing various animal and bird figures, has an inscription (f) on the left edge and another (g) on the right edge.

Ca. 1114–20.[176] The church itself in which the portal now is incorporated had not been begun in 1120.[177]

(a) [...]VS EST PACIS / CAVSAS DEPONITE L ...

A hexameter, probably common leonine. Cf. Porter, *Lombard Architecture*, 3, 346, who reads [DOMV]S EST etc. This conjecture seems probable.[178] The reading DEPONITIS is incorrect.[179] Perhaps [HAEC DOM]VS EST PACIS CAVSAS DEPONITE L[EGIS].

'(This is a house) of peace; lay aside your suits (of law?).'

(b) VOS LEGITE VERSVS :· QVOS DESCRIPSIT NICHOLAVS /
VOS QVI TRANSITIS SVRSVM VEL FORTE REDITIS

One common and one full leonine hexameter. Final syllable of *legitē* (1) lengthened. For the scansion of *Nicholaus*, see S. Giorgio of Ferrara.

'Read the verses which Niccolò has written and carved,[180] you who are going up or perchance returning.'

(c) MVNVS ABEL GRATVm CONSTATQ[ue] CAIN RE/PROBATVM

A full leonine hexameter.

'It is known that the gift of Abel was pleasing (to God) and that the gift of Cain was rejected.'

Cf. Gen. 4:4–5.

(d) IVSTVS ABEL MORITur · CVm FRatrIS FVSTE FERITur

A full leonine hexameter.

'Righteous Abel dies when he is struck by his brother's club.'

Cf. Gen. 4:8. This verse once appeared on the S façade of the cathedral of Ferrara.

(e) HOC OPVS ORTATVR · SEPIVS VT ASPICIA[T]VR

A full leonine hexameter. False quantity in *sepīus.*

'This work demands to be viewed again and again.'

(f) HOC OPVS INTENDAT · QVISQVIS BONVS EXI[T ET INTRAT]

A common leonine hexameter. The missing letters are supplied on the basis of the same verse that appears at Piacenza; Robb, 'Niccolò,' 377, reports seeing ... AT at the end of the verse.

'May this work guide whoever exits and enters as a good person.'

(g) FLORES CVM BELVIS · COMIXTOS CE[RNERE QVITIS (?)]

A common leonine hexameter? Cf. Robb, 'Niccolò,' 377, who reports COMIXTOS CV ...' Porter, *Lombard Architecture*, 3, 346, reads CE[RNIS]; Chierici, in Chierici and Citi, *Piémont-Ligurie roman*, 83, reads CERNITIS (without any indication that the last part of the word is conjectural). Neither conjecture completes the verse. Since all the other verses at S. Michele are either common or full leonines, this probably was too. My conjecture preserves the sense of Porter's and Chierici's versions and provides a common leonine rhyme. False quantity in *bĕluis*.

'You can see flowers mingled with wild beasts.'

136. **Sahaqún** (León). *S. Benito.

*Portal. Marble plaque of the Virgin and Child, now in the Museo Arqueológico Nacional in Madrid. According to Porter, this relief 'no doubt originally formed the central part of a tympanum representing the Adoration of the Magi.'[181] The Virgin is seated in majesty with the Child in her lap. There is an inscription (a) on the background beside the head and left shoulder of the Virgin.

Early 12th century? The tympanum must be earlier than the plaque at St-Aventin. Porter dates it to the time of the consecration of the church (AD 1099).[182]

(a) RES MIRA/NDA SAT/IS ; BENE / CONPLA/CITVRA / BEA/T/I/S

A full leonine hexameter.

'An object which is worthy of being fully admired will please the blessed very well.'

137. **Saint-Aventin** (Haute-Garonne). St-Aventin.

S portal. Marble plaque set into the right pillar: relief of the Virgin in Majesty with the Child. There is an inscription (a) on the arch.

Mid-12th century?[183]

(a) RES MI|RANDA NI|MIS MA~~TE~~R | DEI ERAT | VI NIMI|S

A garbled full leonine hexameter? The vertical bars (|) indicate the placement of floral buttons. Elision. Spondee in fifth foot; iamb in sixth foot.

'An exceedingly remarkable thing – the mother of God was exceedingly powerful.'

The line appears to have been modelled directly or indirectly on the full leonine hexameter that is inscribed on the plaque of the Virgin and Child of Sahagún.

138. **Saint-Aventin**. St-Aventin.

S façade. Bas-relief of Saint Aventin set in the first buttress to the right of the S portal. The relief depicts a bull, inspired by an angel, digging up the grave of Saint Aventin. There is an inscription (a) on the side of Aventin's tomb.

Mid-12th century?[184]

(a) SIC INNOTESCIT SanCtuS QV[A] / PARTE / QVIESCIT
A full leonine hexameter.

'Thus he makes known in what place the saint rests.'

139. **Saint-Denis** (Seine-Saint-Denis). Cathedral (former abbey church) of St-Denis.

Central W portal. Tympanum of the Last Judgment, with an *inscription (a) on the *lintel, which was destroyed in 1771 to enlarge the doorway.[185] VENITE BENEDICTI PATRIS MEI, 'Come, blessed of my Father' (Matt. 25:34) is inscribed on the banderole extending from Christ's right hand, and DISCEDITE A ME MALEDICTI, 'Depart from me, accursed ones' (Matt. 25:41), on the banderole extending from his left hand. These inscriptions were recarved in the 19th century.

Ca. 1135–40.

(a) *Suscipe vota tui iudex districte Sugeri
Inter oves proprias fac me clementer haberi
Two hexameters with disyllabic end rhyme. Suger, *De Administratione* 27: Panofsky, *Abbot Suger*, 48. The first syllable of *Sŭgēri* is here treated as short and the second, long. In the consecration inscriptions at St-Denis (for which see Suger, *De Administratione* 27–8: Panofsky, *Abbot Suger*, 46, 50) the first syllable is lengthened by doubling the *g* and the second syllable is common (*Sūggĕrius / Sūggērus*).

'Accept, strict Judge, the prayers of your Suger; grant that I be preserved among your own sheep.'

140. **Saint-Georges-de-Camboulas** (Aveyron). St-Georges-de-Camboulas. The church was rebuilt in the 14th century and in recent times has been used as a farmhouse.

Fragment of a tympanum, presumably from the Romanesque church, of the Last Judgment. It is now set in the wall above the S portal. The block displays Christ seated in judgment in a mandorla, with his right hand raised and his left lowered. It is closely modelled on the tympanum of Conques. Angels hold banderoles on either side of the mandorla. There is an inscription (a) on the left banderole, which is broken off at either end, an inscription (b) on the right banderole, which is broken off at the left (top) end, and an inscription (c) on the lower edge of the block that may have extended to adjacent blocks in the original tympanum.

After ca. 1115.

(a) [A]D : REGNV[m] : VITE : AGMINA : SanCtA : [VENITE?]
A full leonine hexameter? Cf. *CIFM*, 9, 66. Bousquet, *La sculpture à Conques*, 934, proposes to complete the verse with *venite.*

'(Come), you holy hosts, to the kingdom of life.'
Cf. Matt. 25:34.

(b) [...]NAS : DIGNI : Qu<u>I</u>BVS : ESTIS : A<u>B</u>ITE : MALIGNI :+:

A full leonine hexameter? Cf. Bousquet, *La sculpture à Conques*, 934, who proposes [AD PE]NAS. However, the remaining stroke of the letter before -*nas* does not look as though it could be an *e* (it resembles a short *i*). The inscription is badly eroded. *CIFM* reads [AD:] IMAS : DIGNI : QVIBVS : ESTIS : ARTE : [M]ALIGNI.

'Depart, evil ones, [to the punishments?] of which you are deserving.'

Cf. Matt. 25:41.

(c) [...]S : PRO : PLEBE : FIDEL[I]

+ SIC : PENSABVNTVR : R[...] SEV : MA[...]

Probably the end of one hexameter, and the beginning of another. Cf. Bousquet, *La sculpture à Conques*, 934, who proposes S(IGNVM) PRO PLEBE FIDELI. / SIC PENSABVNTVR B(ONI) SEV MALI. Though (c) is not fully intelligible, *pensabuntur* seems a clear reference to a Weighing of Souls that must have appeared beneath Christ. Thus (c) may have extended to the left and right of the present block. If so, the first *s* would be the final letter of a word (and not, as Bousquet would have it, an abbreviation for *signum*, which is in any case unlikely).

'... for the faithful. Thus they will be weighed ...'

141. **Saint-Léger-en-Pons** (Charente-Maritime). St- Léger.

W portal. Inner archivolt, composed of sixteen blocks, with an inscription (a). The phrase NOMINE SPIRITVS is carved in two lines on the last block at right angles to the lettering of the rest of the inscription. The lettering is crude, and the blocks look quite modern. There are no sculptures. Has an old inscription been reproduced?

12th century.[186]

(a) SIT I PAX I INTIRANITI I FEILIIX I SIT I CESISVIS EIVNITIS

An unrhymed hexameter. Cf. *CIFM*, 1:3, 108–9.

'May peace be to the one entering; may the departure of one going out be happy. In the name of the Spirit.'

Cf. Deut. 28:6; John 10:9. For a similar verse, cf. Roda de Isábena.

142. **Saint-Marcel-lès-Sauzet** (Drôme). St-Marcel.

W portal. Tympanum of Christ in Majesty with the Four Animals (the Christ has been replaced by a Virgin and Child). There is an inscription (a) on the bottom edge of the lintel.

Second half of the 12th century?[187]

(a) VOS : QVI : TRAN:SITIS : QVI : CRI:MI:NA : FLE:RE : VE:NITIS :

PER : ME : TRAN:SITE : QVO:NI:AM : SVM : IA:NV:A : VI:TE :

IANVA : SVM : VITE : VOLO : PARCERE : CL[AMO] VENITE :

Three full leonine hexameters. Cf. *CIFM*, 16, 183–4. Final syllable of *transite* (1) lengthened at caesura.

'You who are passing through, you who are coming to lament your sins, pass through me since I am the gate of life. I am the gate of life. I wish to spare. I cry out, come.'
Cf. Lam. 1:12, 'O vos omnes qui transitis per viam,' and, for similar verses, S. Giorgio al Palazzo (Milan).

143. **Saint-Paul-de-Mausole** (Saint-Rémy-de-Provence) (Bouches-du-Rhône). St-Paul.

*Portal, with an inscription (a).

12th century.

(a) *Hanc quicumque domum modo vis intrare sacratam
Corrige te primum quod possis poscere Christum

One unrhymed and one common leonine hexameter. *CIFM*, 14, 126, citing H. Rolland, *Saint-Rémy-de-Provence* (Bergerac, 1934), 132; Gérard Giordanengo, 'Un monastère de chanoines réguliers. Saint-Paul-de-Mausole,' *Congrès archéologique de France, 1976, Pays d'Arles*, 157, 163.

'You, whoever you are, who wish to enter this sacred house, first correct yourself, so that you may be able to call upon Christ.'
These are similar to two verses at Sta Cruz de la Serós.

144. **Saint-Paul-de-Varax** (Ain). St-Paul.

Central W portal. Tympanum of the Ascension above a lintel of Mary and the Twelve Apostles. There is an inscription (a) on the lower edge of the lintel. The arch of the tympanum is inscribed: IN NOMINE DomiNI NOSTRI IHsV XP[ist]I ET IN ONORE BEATE S[em]Per VIRGINIS MARIE ET S[an]C[t]I PAVLI APostolI ET OM[n]IVm SanCtOrum DEI, 'In the name of our Lord, Jesus Christ, and in honour of the always blessed Virgin Mary and of Saint Paul the Apostle and of all the saints of God.'

First quarter of the 12th century?

(a) + CVm PIRECIBus LACRIMAS SI FVnDA I AVE I REDIE[n]TES
GRAC[...]ENIA COMI(?) ABITV I EGREDI/EnITES

Two hexameters with tetrasyllabic end rhyme? Cf. *CIFM*, 17, 18. The inscription has been garbled. Possibly, *cum precibus lacrimas si fundant ingredientes, / [...] egredientes.* For the rhyme, cf. Vandeins. Guédel accepts for the second verse the suggestion *gracia cum venia compleat abitu egredientes.*[188] However, this is metrically impossible.

'If they would pour forth tears with their prayers on entering, ... on exiting.'

145. **Saint-Paul-de-Varax**. St-Paul.

S portal. Tympanum of Saint Anthony and the Faun. There is an inscription (a) around the arch of the tympanum.

First quarter of the 12th century: contemporary with the W portal?[189]

(a) ABBAS QVEREBAT PAVLVm FAVNusQue DOCEB/A<t>

A full leonine hexameter. Cf. *CIFM*, 17, 20. The *a* of *docebat* appears over the first *a* of *abbas*; the *t* was apparently never carved.

'The abbot sought Paul and a faun gave him instructions.'

Cf. Jerome's Life of Saint Paul the First Hermit.

146. **Saint-Pé-de-Bigorre** (Hautes-Pyrénées). St-Pierre.

Interior. Portal in SW corner tower of the church, leading to circular staircase: tympanum (effaced) with an inscription (a) around the rim. The inscription has been freshened up with gold paint. Another inscription, now almost entirely effaced, appears on the lower horizontal border. Only the word LEONES can still be made out.[190]

12th century.

(a) EST DOMus HIC DomiNI · VIA CAELI · SPES PEREGRINI :
HAEC DATA PORTA PETRO VADE MALIGNE RETRO ·

A full leonine elegiac couplet. Cf. *CIFM*, 8, 104.

'Here is the house of the Lord, the way of heaven, the hope of the pilgrim. This portal is dedicated to Peter: go back, wicked one.'

See Mark 8:33.

147. **Saint-Rémy-de-Provence** (Bouches-du-Rhône). *St-Pierre-le-Mévolier.

*Portal, with an inscription (a). Revoil and Rolland assign this inscription to St-Paul-de-Mausole, but the verses imply a church dedicated to Saint Peter.[191]

12th century.

(a) *Si Christus Deus est et Petrus claviger eius
Iam nisi per Petrum nemo videbit eum

Elegiac couplet with common leonine rhyme in the pentameter. *CIFM*, 14, 137, citing Henri Revoil, *Architecture roman du Midi de la France*, 2 (Paris, 1874), 3; H. Rolland, *Saint-Rémy-de-Provence* (Bergerac, 1934), 132, 157; Gérard Giordanengo, 'Un monastère de chanoines réguliers. Saint-Paul-de-Mausole,' *Congrès archéologique de France, 1976, Pays d'Arles*, 163, n. 4.

'If Christ is God and Peter is his gate-keeper, now no one will see him except through Peter.'

148. **Saint-Sauveur-d'Aunis** (Charente-Maritime). St-Sauveur.

Interior. Transept: SW capital, N face, of monstrous beast, with an inscription (a) above.

2nd half of 11th century?[192]

(a) PREBVIT EXEMPLVM CVM : FIT DIABOLICE / TEMP[VS?]

An unrhymed hexameter? *CIFM,* 1:3, 111. False quantity in *diabōlice.*

'It (the beast) served as an example when the time of the devil arrived.'[193]

149. **Saint-Sever** (Landes). St-Sever.

Interior. Historiated capital in the nave (western bay, S aisle) showing scenes from the story of the Beheading of John the Baptist, with an inscription (a) on the astragal.

Ca. 1096–1107?[194]

(a) HIC PATITV[R] ...
[...] MVNERE MORTEM
IPSAQ[ue] DAT MATRI BABTISTE COLLA IHOanniS

Three (?) unrhymed hexameters. Cf. *CIFM,* 6, 107. Cabanot, *Gascogne roman,* 120, reads HIC PATITU(r) ... MUNERE MORTEM / IPSA DAT MATRI BABTISTE COLLA IH ... S. The capital has three faces. The scene on the left face is the beheading; the scene on the centre face is the dance of Salomé before Herod and his guests; the scene on the right face is Salomé presenting to her mother the head of John the Baptist.

'Here suffers [John the Baptist ...]. [Salomé asks] as a gift the death [of John the Baptist]. And she gives the head of John the Baptist to her mother.'

Cf. Matt. 14:1–11; Mark 6:14–28.

150. **Salzburg** (Salzburg). Nonnberg convent. The church is late-15th-century.

S portal (1497/9), with pointed-arched tympanum area filled by three re-employed reliefs: a Romanesque lintel, a Gothic frieze, and a Romanesque round-arched tympanum. Lintel of interlaced grape vines, with an inscription (a) on the lower edge. Tympanum of the Virgin in Majesty with the Child. The Virgin is flanked by the standing figure of an angel and the kneeling figure of a nun on the left and by the standing figures of a saint holding a book and a praying nun on the right, with an inscription (b) around the rim of the tympanum. It does not appear to be certain whether or not the lintel and tympanum originally belonged together.

12th century.

(a) + PORTA PATET VITE XP[istu]C VIA VERA VENITE +

A full leonine hexameter. Cf. Ragusa, '*Porta patet vitae,*' 350.

'The gate of (eternal) life lies open. Christ (is) the true way. Come.'

Cf. the similar inscription at Esztergom.

(b) + SPLENDOR · IMAGO · PATRIS · FECVNDANS · VISCERA · MATRIS
+ IANVA · LVX · PORTVS · SALVANDIS · CREDITVR · ORTVS +

Two full leonine hexameters.

'Radiance, the image of the Father, impregnating the womb of the Mother.

His birth is believed to be the door, the light, the port for those who are to be saved.'

151. **San Juan de la Peña** (Huesca). S. Juan de la Peña.

S nave portal leading to cloister. The portal is capped with a horseshoe arch that is thought to be contemporary with the crypt (9th-century). It was relocated when the cloister was constructed in the 12th century, and an inscription (a) was then carved on the exterior (cloister) side in Visigothic (?) script.[195]

Second half of 12th century. Angel San Vicente records the belief of Father Pinedo that the author of the elegiac couplet inscribed on the arch was Don Rodrigo de Cascante, bishop of Calahorra from 1146 to 1190.[196]

(a) PORTA | PER | HAnC : C|AELI : FI|T : PerVIA | : CVIQue | FIDELI |
+ | SI S|TVDE|AD : FI|DEI : IV|NGE|RE : IVSS|A : D|EI :

A full leonine elegiac couplet. Cf. Durán Gudiol, 'Las inscripciones medievales,' 84 (no. 17). Joints between the blocks of the arch are indicated by vertical bars.

'Through this gate the gate of heaven becomes accessible to each believer who strives to combine the commands of God with faith.'

The first line was copied at Armentia and on the lintel of the tympanum of the portal of the hermitage of Puilampa.

152. **Santa Cruz de la Serós** (Huesca). Sta María.

W portal. Tympanum: chrismon flanked by two lions. The chrismon has a horizontal crossbar; an omega hangs from its left arm and an S is behind its right arm. A V-shaped crossbar connects the lower descender of the P (rho) with the lower-right arm of the X (chi) forming an A. These initials, P (= rho), A (= alpha), and X (= chi), form an acrostic (= the Trinity), which reads 'peace' (*pax*) (cf. Jaca). An inscription (a) encircles the rim of the chrismon and continues on the lintel beneath the lions' feet.

Ca. 1100? There is documentary evidence that the church was in construction in 1095.[197] The tympanum almost certainly derives from the tympanum of Jaca. It cannot therefore be earlier than ca. 1095–1100, if the date proposed for the tympanum of Jaca is correct.[198]

(a) + IANVA SVM PerPES [:] Per ME TRANSITE FIDELES :
FONS EGO SVM VITE [:] PLVS ME QVAM VINA SITITE
VIRGINIS H[oc] TEMPLVM Qui VIS PENETRARE BEATVM /
+ CORRIGE TE PRIMVM VALEAS QVO POSCERE XPISTVM

One full (2) and three common leonine hexameters. Cf. Durán Gudiol, 'Las inscripciones medievales,' 105–6 (no. 78). Lampérez, in a transcription published in 1899, reported colons after the caesuras in lines 1 and 2, as well as *hoc* and *quisquis* [instead of *qui vis*]. He erroneously transcribed *perpes* as *praepes*.[199]

'I am the eternal door; pass through me, faithful ones. I am the fountain of life; thirst for me more than for wine. You who wish to enter this blessed church of the Virgin, reform yourself first in order that you may be able to call upon Christ.'

153. **Sant'Antimo** (Toscana). Sant'Antimo.

W portal. Blank tympanum with a broad lintel of foliage above an inscription band (a) in two lines.

After 1118.[200]

(a) VIR BONVS IN XPistO MAGNVS VIRTVTIBVS AZZO :
CENOBII MONACHVS PVER HVIVS POSTQVE DECANVS
ISTIVS EGREGIE FVIT AVCTOR PREVIVS AVLE :
ATQVE LIBENS OPERIS PORTAVIT PONDERA TANTI :
PROGE/[NIE] TVSCVS PORCORVM SANGVINE CRETVS :
PRO QVO XPistICOLE CVNCTI D[omi]N[u]M ROGITATE :
DET SIBI PerPETVE CVM SanCtIS GAVDIA VITE :
MARTYR ET EXIMIVS SIT CVSTOS ANTIMVS EIVS

Seven common leonine and one (4) unrhymed hexameter.[201]

'Azzo, a man good in Christ and great in virtues, monk of this monastery as a boy and later dean, was the guiding author of this outstanding church, and willingly carried the burdens of so great a work. (He was) Tuscan by race, grown from the blood of pigs [= of the Porcari?]. Keep praying to the Lord for him, all you Christians. May He give the joys of eternal life with the saints to him, and may the worthy martyr Antimo be his guardian.'

Dean Azzo may have been deceased when these verses were composed. Enlart interprets the inscription as meaning that he was 'of the line of the Porcari, a family from Lucca.'[202] For Moretti and Stopani, he is 'the monk Azzo dei Porcari.' They describe him as 'the promoter of the construction, if not the architect himself.'[203]

154. **Sant Cugat del Vallés** (Barcelona). Sant Cugat.

Cloister. NE pier with adjoining capital depicting the sculptor Arnaldus Catellus. An inscription (a) is on the blank face of the pier facing the E walk.

Ca. 1190.[204]

(a) HEC EST ARNALLI : / SCVLPTORIS FORMA CATELLI : /
QVI CLAVSTRVM TALE : / CONSTRVXIT PerPETVALE :

Two full leonine hexameters with slant rhyme in line 1.

'This is the likeness of the sculptor Arnaldus Catellus, who constructed this cloister so that it will endure forever.'

155. **Santiago de Compostela** (La Coruña). Cathedral of Santiago.

S transept façade (Puerta de las Platerías). Reliefs above the double portal: figure of Saint James between two cypress trunks, probably re-employed from W portal, with the inscriptions PAX VOBI[s] on the book in his hands, IACOBus ZEBEDEI on his halo, ANFus REX on the background next to the cypress on the right, and an inscription (a) on either side of the cypress on the left. *Anfus rex* apparently refers to Alfonso VII, who was crowned in the cathedral as king of Galicia in 1111, entered the city again in triumph in 1116, and was temporarily deposed by his sister Urraca in 1122.[205]

Ca. 1116/ca. 1122 (dates of W portal).[206]

(a) H/I/C/ IN / MO/N*/TE / IHE/S*/Vm* / MI/R/A*/<u>TV</u>/R* / G/L*/O/RI/FI*/CA/<u>TVm</u>*

A common leonine hexameter? The inscription reads down on the right side of the cypress, with several letters marked (*) on the left side. If this is a verse, there is a false quantity in the first syllable of *Ihesum*, which is normally a spondee (with initial consonantal *i*). However, a poet might have shortened the first syllable in conformity with the medieval habit of scanning proper names arbitrarily.

'Here on the mountain he [Saint James] looks with wonder on Jesus glorified.' Cf. Matt. 17:1–8; Luke 9:28–36.

156. **Santo Domingo de Silos** (Burgos). Sto Domingo.

Double arch on stairway leading to the Puerta de las Vírgenes, a portal that once opened into the Romanesque church. A capital, discovered in 1934, is believed to have formed part of the central support of the double arch.[207] The abacus of the capital is carved with an inscription (a).

AD 1088 to 1100?

(a) MAVRVS CONQVERITVR FORTIS VT HIC LEGITVR
MIRATVR MVNDVS QVOD TANTVM SVF[FER]O PONDVS

A full leonine pentameter followed by a full slant leonine hexameter. Whitehill, *Spanish Romanesque Architecture*, 164, n. 4.

'The strong Moor laments as this is read: "The world marvels that I endure so great a weight."'

157. **Santo Domingo de Silos**. Sto Domingo.

Cloister reliefs and capitals. Saint Domingo was buried (1073?) in the N walk of the cloister before the door of the church, but his body was translated three years later (1076?) to a tomb within the church.[208] This must have been the cloister that preceded the present one, construction of which was begun sometime between 1088 and 1158, probably at or near the earlier date.[209] A portion of Domingo's epitaph (a) was carved on the abacus of a cluster of four capitals supported by five columns depicting Harpies in the N walk nearest the spot of his original burial.

There is now a 13th-century tomb of Domingo in the N walk, nearly adjacent to the cluster of capitals, with the same version of his epitaph carved upon it.

The corner piers are carved with flat reliefs on their inner faces (i.e., the faces visible from the cloister walks). The NE pier depicts the Three Women at the Tomb, who are labelled MARIA MAGDALENE MARIA IACOBI SALOME, with an inscription (b), and the Descent from the Cross with an inscription (c). The inscriptions follow the semicircular frame of the relief in the manner of the ambulatory reliefs of St-Sernin of Toulouse and the cloister piers of Moissac.

AD 1088 to 1100.[210] Porter, *Spanish Romanesque Sculpture*, 1, 76, argues that the abacus (= a) was carved 'between 1073 and 1076.'

(a) HAC : TVMBA : TEGITVR : DIV/A QVI LVCEBEATVR :
DICTVS D[omi]NICVS NOMINE CONSPI[CVVS] /
[ORBI QVEM SPECVLVM] / XPistuS CONCES[s]IT HONESTVM :
PROTEGAT : HIC PLEBES : SIBI FIDA MENTE : FIDELES :

An elegiac couplet plus two hexameters, all with common leonine rhyme. These are lines 1–3 and 7 of an eight-line epitaph in elegiac couplets, which Domingo's biographer, Grimaldo, inserted into his Life.[211] Schapiro assumes that Grimaldo was its author.[212]

'In this tomb is buried one who is blessed with divine light, called Domingo, made illustrious by his name. Christ yielded him as a virtuous mirror to the world. May he protect the people who are faithful to him with a faithful mind.'

(b) NIL : FORMIDETIS : VIVIT DEVS : ECCE VIDETIS

A full leonine hexameter.

'Fear nothing, God lives, behold you see [the place where the Lord was laid].' Mark 16:1, 6; cf. Matt. 28:5–6. The verse is spoken by the angel on the left of the Three Women. What they see is that the tomb is empty (what the spectator sees is Joseph of Arimathea and Nicodemus laying the body in the tomb). Schapiro calls attention to a similar verse from the *tituli* of Ekkehard IV for the paintings of Mainz. It is the words of the angel to Elizabeth: 'Ne timeas, vates: Ego sum Gabrihel, age grates!'[213]

(c) H[i]C OBIT : HEC PLORAT CARVS DOLET : IMPIVS ORAT :

A full leonine hexameter.[214]

'He [Christ] dies; she [the Virgin Mary] weeps; the beloved [John] grieves; the sinner [Adam] prays.'

The four clauses cannot be understood without reference to the visual scene. The subjects of the four clauses in the verse are each separately labelled within the scene. The other two, unlabelled, figures are Joseph of Arimathea and Nicodemus. The four clauses are ordered hierarchically (Christ, Mary, John, Adam). Schapiro documents similar inscriptions from Lombardy, Germany, Denmark, and western France, which 'indicate a common tradition of descriptive tituli in the arts of these regions.'[215]

158. **Schleswig** (Schleswig-Holstein). Cathedral of St Peter.

S portal ('Saint Peter's Doorway'). Tympanum of Christ in Majesty with the Four Animals. Saint Paul stands on the right; Saint Peter stands on the left. Christ holds a banderole in his left hand that crosses in front of Saint Paul. There is an inscription (a), partially effaced, on the banderole. The inscription continues on the rim of the tympanum beside the figure of Paul, and finishes beneath Paul's feet.

Ca. 1180.[216]

(a) TV MICHI V[...] FVNDI DEPELLE TY/RANNVM

ET REVOCA GEN/[TES ...] COLENTES

Two full leonine hexameters (the conjectural restoration *gentes* is probable). Cf. Mackeprang, *Jydske Granitportaler*, 176. Among the proposals for completing the verses are: *Tu michi vesanum fundi depelle tyrannum / Et revoca gentes Petrum pietate colentes* and *Tum michi vesanum fundi depelle tyrannum / Et revoca gentes ad me mundana colentes.*[217]

'Expel from me the tyrant of the depths (?), and call back the worshipping people.'

159. **Strasbourg** (Bas-Rhin). Cathedral of Notre-Dame.

S transept portal. *Statue columns (now destroyed): column of Saint John, holding a banderole with an inscription (a).

Ca. 1210–23 (?). This is the estimate of Reinhardt.[218] It is based on comparative criteria that are far from conclusive. The verse inscription would be consistent with an earlier date, sometime before the end of the twelfth century.

(a) *Gratia divinae pietatis adesto Savinae,

De petra dura per quam sum facta figura.

Two full leonine hexameters. Geyer, 'Le mythe d'Erwin de Steinbach,' 327–8; Reinhardt, *La cathédrale de Strasbourg*, 222. The source appears to be Osée Schad, *Summum Argentoratensium Templum* (Strasbourg, 1617), who printed an engraving of Isaac Brunn in which the inscription can be seen. The engraving is reproduced in Reinhardt, *La cathédrale de Strasbourg*, fig. 88.

'May the grace of divine mercy be present to Sabina, by whom I was made a figure from hard stone.'

160. **Strasbourg**. Notre-Dame.

N transept portal (an enclosed porch now stands in front of the portal). Tympanum of the Adoration of the Magi; the Return of the Magi; and King David

Playing the Harp, with an inscription (a) above. The figures of the tympanum were destroyed during the French Revolution, but traces of them could still be seen in 1850, together with the inscription.

End of 12th century?

(a) + SVSCIPE · TRINE · DEVS · QVE · FERT · T[ri]A · DONA · SABEVS · +
HEC · TIBI · QVI · DEDERIT · DONA · BEATVS · ERIT · +
AVRO · DONANTIS · VIRTVSQ[ue] · PROBATVR · AMANTIS · +
IN · MIRRA · BONA · SPES · THVRE · BEATA · FIDES.

Two full leonine elegiac couplets (common leonine rhyme in the final pentameter verse). Kraus, *Die christlichen Inschriften*, 2, 55, citing Schneegans, *Revue d'Alsace* 1850, 274.

'Take, triune God, the three gifts which the Sabaean bears. He who gives these gifts to you will be blessed. With gold the virtue of the loving donor is proved; in myrrh the good hope; with frankincense the blessed faith.'

These are closely related to the verses at Notre-Dame-du-Port of Clermont-Ferrand.

161. **Tarascon** (Bouches-du-Rhône). Ste-Marthe. The previously existing church was reconstructed beginning in AD 1187 in order to receive the relics of Saint Martha; the new church was dedicated by the archbishop of Arles on 1 June 1197.[219]

Right wall of S portal. Dedication plaque with three scenes from the life of Saint Martha at the top and an inscription (a) beneath. The three scenes represent from left to right the discovery of Saint Martha's body, the ascent of her soul borne by angels to heaven, and the consecration of the church by Archbishop Imbertus of Arles (1191–1202) and Archbishop Rostagnus of Avignon (1185–ca. 1198).[220]

AD 1197.

(a) VIGInTI : NOVIES : SEPTEm : Cvm : MILLE : RE/LAPSIS :
ANnO : POSTREMO : NOBIS : PA/TET : OSPITA : XPistI : /
MILLE : DVCEnTIS / TRAnSACTIS : MINVS AT TRIBVS : AN/NIS
IMBERTVS : PRESVL : ROSTAG/NO : PRESVLE : SECVM : /
IN PRIMA : IVNII : CONSECRAT : ECCLESIAM :

Four unrhymed hexameters and a final unrhymed pentameter. No caesura in third foot (3). Cf. *CIFM*, 14, 140–2.

'Nine times twenty, and seven, with a thousand, years having passed away [i.e., 1187, the year the portal was begun], in the last year of the church [= 1187], the hostess of Christ is revealed to us [i.e., the body of Saint Martha was discovered at Tarascon, which prompted the rebuilding of the church]. One thousand two hundred years less but three having been completed [i.e., 1197, the year of the dedication], Imbertus the bishop, with Rostagnus the bishop in attendance with him, consecrates the church on the first of June.'

The phrase *ospita Cristi* refers to Martha's role in receiving Christ into her house in Bethany (Luke 10:38–42; John 12:1–2). Martha was the sister of Lazarus and Mary.

162. **Thines** (Ardèche). Notre-Dame.

S portal. Lintel of three scenes of the life of Christ (the tympanum is blank): the Entry into Jerusalem, the Last Supper, and the Betrayal of Christ, with an inscription (a) in a single line along the lower edge. The inscription begins with the non-metrical phrase INGREDIENTE DO[MINO ...]AM CIVITATEM, 'the Lord entering the city.'

Ca. 1175–1209?[221]

(a) DVM CENAT XPHistuS [*sic*] IVDAS SIBI PREPA[RAT IN]TVS :
ORE DATIS SIGNIS · REX TRADITVR E[...]NIS :

Two hexameters with common leonine rhyme? Cf. *CIFM*, 16, 80; Bacconnier, *Notre-Dame de Thines*, 51, and n. 50 (pp. 93–4). I accept *CIFM*'s conjecture for PREPA[RAT IN]TVS. Bacconnier proposes PREPA[RAT TRADI]TVS. The conjecture PREPA[RA]TVR, which goes back to the 19th century, does not adequately fill the space.[222]

'While Christ dines, Judas prepares himself inwardly. After the sign is given by a kiss, the King is betrayed ...'

163. **Torre de Passeri** (Abruzzo). S. Clemente a Casauria.

Central W portal. Tympanum and lintel of Saint Clement. The tympanum shows Saint Clement seated in the centre, with Saint Cornelius and Saint Phoebus standing on the left, and Abbot Leonatus kneeling, presenting a model of the church, on the right. There is an inscription (a) in the background on either side of the head of Abbot Leonatus. The lintel displays scenes of the Translation of Saint Clement. In one of the scenes Pope Adrian II, seated on a throne, offers a reliquary chest to Emperor Louis II. An inscription (b) is beneath the chest. There is an inscription (c) around the frame of the lintel. Numerous non-metrical inscriptions are found both on the tympanum and the lintel.

AD 1176–80.[223]

(a) + SVSCIPE SanCtE CLE|MENS / + TIBI REGIA TEmPLA | PARATA ·; /
RETRIBVENS CELO LEO|NATI REGNA / BEATA ·;

Two hexameters with disyllabic end rhyme. The vertical bars (|) mark where the head of Leonatus intersects the inscription. The first syllable of *retribuens* is lengthened (as occasionally in classical verse).

'Receive, Saint Clement, the regal church prepared for you, paying back to heaven the blessed reign of Leonatus.'

A dangling participial construction of this kind is unusual in medieval verse inscriptions.

(b) CESA/RIS AD / VOTVM / CLEMenTEm Con/FERO TOTVm

A full leonine hexameter.

'In accordance with the emperor's vow, I [= Pope Adrian II] confer (on you) *all* of Clement.'

(c) + / ECCE / PATER / PATRIE / MAGNVm / TIBI / ConFERO / MVNVS /
CLEM[en]TIS CORPVS TV SACRVM SVSCIP[e] FVNVS ·ʾ
MA[RT]IRIS EXIMII CLEMENTIS SVSCIPE CORPVS ·ʾ
INSVLA PISCARIE PARADISI FLORIDVS ORTVS ·;
SCEPTRO FIRMAMVS REGIMen TIBI SVME ROGAMVS ·;
INSVLA PISCARIE QVE NOSTRI IVRIS HABETVR
LIBERA Per PRETIA TVA CESAR / IVRE / VOCE/TVR ;

Seven hexameters. Lines 1/2, 3/4, and 6/7 display disyllabic end rhyme (slant rhyme in 3/4). Line 5 is a full leonine hexameter. Final vowel of *pretia* (7) lengthened at caesura. The left portion of the bottom line of the inscription is blocked from ground-level view by the jamb capital that supports the lintel. The hidden portion has been recarved on the abacus of the capital: CONFERO MVNVS CLEN[*sic*]ET[...]RPVS TV SACRVM SVSCIPE / FVNVS.

'[Pope Adrian II to Emperor Louis II:] "Behold, father of the country [= Louis], I confer a great gift on you – the body of Clement. Take the sacred corpse." [Louis to Brothers Celsus and Reatus:] "Take the body of the outstanding martyr Clement." [Louis and the first abbot of S. Clemente:] "Island of the Pescara, flowery source of Paradise, we affirm with the sceptre dominion over you; take [the body of Clement], we beg." [Louis to Sisenandus and Bishop Grillus?:] "Island of the Pescara, which is considered to be under our jurisdiction, deliver [us?/me?] by your worth." [Count Heribaidus?:] "May he rightly be called Caesar."'

164. **Toulouse** (Haute-Garonne). Cathedral of St-Étienne.

*Cloister. SE angle pillar:[224] statues of Saint Peter and Saint Sernin, with an inscription (a) accompanying the figure of Saint Peter, and another (b) accompanying the figure of Saint Sernin. NW angle pillar: statues of Saint Exupère and a deacon, with an inscription (c) accompanying the figure of Saint Exupère, and an inscription (d) accompanying the deacon. The statues are now in the Musée des Augustins in Toulouse.

Early 12th century.[225]

(a) *Petrus pontificem benedicens mittit ad urbem
Pro populi cura concessit ei sua iura

One common and one full leonine hexameter. Noguier, *Histoire tolosaine,* 60–1; *CIFM,* 7, 11–14.

'Peter, blessing the bishop [= Saint Sernin], sends him to the city [= Toulouse]; he yielded his rights to him out of care for the people.'

(b) *Curva trahit quos recta regit pars ultima pungit

A hexameter, with internal, triple monosyllabic rhyme (the first two at the trihemimeral and hephthemimeral caesuras: *curva trahit* | *quos recta regit* | *pars ultima pungit*). The penthemimeral caesura is feminine.

'The curved part draws in those whom the upright part guides, and the end point goads.'

The figure of Saint Sernin was shown holding a bishop's staff.[226]

(c) *Ecce Deo dignus vir pauperibus[que] benignus

A full leonine hexameter.

'Behold a man worthy of God and kind to the poor.'

(d) *Sacramenta parat pia pontificique ministrat
Offert vas vitreum [...] vimineumque canistrum

Two common leonine hexameters. There appears to be one or two syllables missing from the second verse.

'He prepares the holy sacraments and serves the bishop. He offers the glass vase and the wicker basket.'

165. **Toulouse**. St-Étienne.

*Chapter house portal. Statue of Saint Andrew, with an *inscription (a) beneath its feet. The statue is in the Musée des Augustins.

Ca. 1135–40.[227]

(a) *VIR N[on] INCERTVS ME CELAVIT GILABERTVS

A full leonine hexameter. Transcription by Castellane (reproduced by Seidel, *Romanesque Sculpture of Saint-Etienne*, fig. 29); cf. Mesplé, *Les sculptures romanes*, no. 22; *CIFM*, 7, 64. This inscription was on a part of the base that has disappeared since the publication of the 1864 catalogue.[228] For some time it was mistakenly thought to have appeared on the base of the statue of Saint Thomas.

'Gilabertus, a man not unsure of himself, carved me.'

Gilabertus was the head of the workshop. He signed the statue of Saint Thomas GILABERTVS ME FECIT.

166. **Toulouse**. *St-Jean.

Chrismon plaque from a portal of the church. The plaque is now in the Musée des Augustins in Toulouse. An inscription (a) is above and outside the circle of the chrismon.

12th century?

(a) HI[c] : DeuS : ORATur : DOMVS / EIVS : ET : IS/TA : VOCAT[ur] //
HVC : ERGO : VENIAT / QVEm : COnSCIA : / CVLPA : FA/TIGAT

One full and one full slant leonine hexameter. Cf. *CIFM*, 7, 97.

'Here God is worshipped, and this is called his house. Let him, therefore, who is wearied by the knowledge of guilt, come hither.'

167. **Toulouse**. St-Sernin.

W façade. *Grand entrance of le Peyrou: reliefs in marble. The façade is now bare. Surviving fragments of the sculptural program are in the Musée des Augustins. The façade and its program was described in the 16th century by Nicolas Bertrand (1515 and 1517) and Antoine Noguier (1556), in the 17th century by Guillaume de Catel (1663), and in the 19th century by Alexandre Du Mège (1814, 1818–35, 1847, and 1854).[229]

King Antonius (fragment in the Musée des Augustins) seated on a throne in a long robe, crowned, with an inscription (a), was paired, probably on the left of the portal, with Saint Sernin [Saturninus] (destroyed[230]), with inscriptions (b) and (c), and a bull beneath his feet (possibly on a separate plaque[231]). Saint Martial (destroyed) holding a pastoral cross, with an inscription (d), was paired, probably on the right, with Saint Sernin (destroyed) baptizing the virgin Austris, with inscriptions (e) and (f). A Harpy (fragment in the Musée des Augustins) holding a Crocodile, labelled [CO]CODRILLVS, in her claws, with an inscription (g), was directly beneath Saint Martial. Sagittarius (destroyed), with an inscription (h), was by the side of the Harpy, directly beneath the Baptism of Austris. There were also a Bishop (destroyed) holding a book on which was inscribed *pax vobis* and another Figure (destroyed), with an inscription (i). Scott believes that the Bishop was placed in the centre of the program, between the two doors.[232]

Ca. 1115–18.[233]

(a) [IVDICAT ANTONIVS REX SERVVM REGIS] ALIVS

A full leonine hexameter. In the photograph in Mesplé, *Les sculptures romanes*, no. 207, the lower part of the *s* of *regis* appears to be visible, but now only the bottom portions of the last word remain. The full inscription was quoted by Noguier, *Histoire tolosaine*, 58, and by Catel (cited by Scott, 'The West Portal Relief Decoration of Saint-Sernin,' 277). The *o* of *Antŏnius* was long in classical Latin.

'King Antonius judges the servant [i.e., Saint Sernin] of another King.'

(b) *Cum docet Antonium non timet exitium

A full leonine pentameter. Noguier, *Histoire tolosaine*, 58–9, makes it clear that the two verses associated with the figure of Saint Sernin ran down either side of the relief. This one (Noguier, p. 58) was undoubtedly on the left side, completing the elegiac couplet begun in (a).

'When [Saint Sernin] teaches Antonius; he does not fear destruction.'

(c) *Ecce Saturninus quem miserat ordo latinus

A full leonine hexameter. Noguier, *Histoire tolosaine*, 59.

'Behold Sernin whom the church of Rome had sent.'

There is a local tradition that Saint Sernin had in fact been sent on his mission by Saint Peter.[234]

(d) *Hic socius socio subvenit auxilio

A full leonine pentameter. Reported by Noguier, *Histoire tolosaine*, 63 (also by Bertrand [1515 and 1517], cited by Durliat, 'Le portail occidental de Saint-Sernin,' 219). Probably this was meant to be associated with the hexameter in (e), forming an elegiac couplet.

'Here one companion assists the other.'

A comment of Bertrand (1517) makes clear that Austris was jointly baptized by the two saints, Sernin and Martial.[235]

(e) *Iure nove legis sanatur filia regis

A full leonine hexameter. Noguier, *Histoire tolosaine*, 63 (also Bertrand [1515 and 1517], cited by Durliat, 'Le portail occidental de Saint-Sernin,' 219; Catel, cited by Scott, 'The West Portal Relief Decoration of Saint-Sernin,' 277, and Du Mège [1847], cited by Scott, 280, n. 34, read *novae*). Noguier put the inscription 'à côté de ladite statue de Saint Sernin.' Bertrand (1515 and 1517) located it beside Saint Martial. Clearly, it was inscribed between the two reliefs, and may have been intended to be read with (d).

'By the privilege of the New Law, the king's daughter is healed.'

(f) *Cum baptizatur mox mordax lepra fugatur

A full leonine hexameter. Noguier, *Histoire tolosaine*, 63 (Bertrand [1515] reads *Quum baptisatur*, etc.; and [1517] *Quin baptisatur nuper morborum lepra fugatur*, cited by Durliat, 'Le portail occidental de Saint-Sernin,' 219; Du Mège [1847], cited by Scott, 'The West Portal Relief Decoration of Saint-Sernin,' 280, n. 34, reads *baptisatur*).

'When [Austris] is baptized her corrosive leprosy is soon put to flight.'

(g) [COR]PVs AVIS F[ACIES / [HO]MINIS VO[LVCRI] / MANET / ISTI

An unrhymed hexameter. Cf. Mesplé, *Les sculptures romanes*, no. 208; *CIFM*, 7, 48–9.

'The body of a bird and the face of a human are found in this winged creature.'

(h) *Iuncta simul faciunt unum duo corpora corpus
Pars prior est hominis altera constat equo

An unrhymed elegiac couplet. Noguier, *Histoire tolosaine*, 65; *CIFM*, 7, 48–9. The first verse was inscribed in the following order:

IVNCTA SIMVL FACIVNT / O.VN / COVM / RDV / PORA / CORPus

Noguier, *Histoire tolosaine*, 64 (the second, third, fourth, and fifth lines are lined up under the last five letters of *faciunt*; the last word is written CORP', where the apostrophe represents *-us*). The inscription was placed 'Haut derriere la tête dudit Sagitaire.' Bizarre as this looks, Noguier was able, with the help of a friend, to puzzle out a solution.[236] With the letters rearranged, the second half of the line reads: VNVM DVO CORPORA CORPus. The method of deciphering the reading is indicated by the capital letters:

oVN | coVM | rDV / Oun | COum | Rdu / PORA | CORP[VS].

The second verse appeared this way:

CON	PARS
STAT	PRIO
EQVO	REST
	HOminIS
	ALTE
	RA

Final syllable of *hominis* (2) lengthened at caesura.

'Two bodies joined together make one body. The forward part belongs to a man, the other part to a horse.'

(i) *[...] fit corpus victima XP[ist]i

The last three and one-half feet of an hexameter. Du Mège (1854, cited by Scott, 'The West Portal Relief Decoration of Saint-Sernin,' 281, n. 43).

'The body [of Saint Sernin?] becomes a martyr of Christ.'

Possibly this relief depicted the martyrdom of Saint Sernin.

168. **Toulouse**. St-Sernin.

S portal (Porte Miègeville). Plaque of Simon Magus on spandrel to right of tympanum of the Ascension of Christ. In the background above the head of Simon is the word MAGVS. Two winged demons attempt to lift him up. There is an inscription (a) on the lower edge of the plaque beneath Simon's feet, with additional letters (b) on the sloping surface above the edge and between Simon's feet, on the background (c) between the feet of the demon on the left, and (d) between Simon's left leg and the legs of the demon on the right. These four inscriptions can be recombined to form a hexameter.

Beginning of the 12th century.

(a) AR<u>TE</u> | <u>FV</u>|RE|N | MAGICA SIMON IN S<u>VA</u> COC|I

Cf. *CIFM*, 7, 44. The claws of the demons intersect the inscription at the points indicated by the vertical bars (|). *Simon* is carved in larger letters than the rest of the inscription.

(b) ARMA

(c) S

The *s* is reversed.

(d) DIT

(a–d) *Arte furens magica Simon in sua occidit arma*

A common leonine hexameter? This is the solution proposed by *CIFM*. Hiatus between fourth and fifth foot (*sua* | *occidit*).

'Led astray by his magical art, Simon succumbs to his own weapons.'

Based on the French translation in *CIFM*: 'Egaré par son art magique, Simon succombe à ses propres armes' (p. 44).

169. **Toulouse**. St-Sernin.

Interior. *A marble figure of a Nude Man (destroyed) with his legs together and his arms extended downwards, palms out, in a mandorla with an inscription around the rim (a). It was in the 16th century attached to one of the piers of the nave.[237] In 1651 it was removed on account of its nudity.[238]

Ca. 1115–18?

(a) *Post obitum car*n*is meritum propter pia castra
Pars que sic oritur quod non moritur petit astra

Hexameter couplet, with disyllabic end rhyme. Noguier, *Histoire tolosaine*, 52 (Noguier reads *cardis* for *carnis* [1]). This is an interesting variant of what has been called 'versus trinini salientes.'[239] The first verse displays the normal form with internal disyllabic rhyme at the trihemimeral and hephthemimeral caesuras, but the second verse shifts the caesuras one position to the right:

Post obitum | carnis meritum | propter pia castra
Pars que sic oritur | quod non moritur | petit astra.

'After the meritorious death of the body, because of its pious service, the part [= the soul] which rises thus, that does not die, goes to heaven.'

The reference is undoubtedly to the martyrdom of Saint Sernin.[240]

170. **Toulouse**. St-Sernin.

Interior. Ambulatory crypt: seven marble plaques set into the wall of the raised crypt in the ambulatory. Christ in Majesty, holding a book in his left hand inscribed PAX VOBIS, and with a cruciform halo behind his head with the letters Alpha and Omega inscribed on the horizontal arms and the letter R[ex] on the vertical arm, is in the centre. On his right is a Cherub, with an inscription (a) on an arch above its head, and the words ET CLAMANT S<anctu>S S<anctu>S S<anctu>S, 'And they cry out: Holy, holy, holy' (cf. Isa. 6:3), on a partially unrolled phylactery in its hand. Further to his right are two angels (neither of these plaques has inscriptions). On his left is a Seraph, with an inscription (b) on an arch above its head, and the words ET CLAMANT S<anctu>S S<anctu>S S<anctu>S, on a partially unrolled phylactery in its hand. Further to his left are two apostles (again, neither has inscriptions). The plaques might once have been set in a semicircle in the brick wall of the apse of the earlier church that was preserved as the shrine of Saint Sernin surrounding the marble table-altar.[241]

Ca. 1096.[242]

(a) AD DEXTRAm PATRIS : CHERVBIN STAT CVNCTIPOTENTIS

A common leonine hexameter.

'A cherub stands on the right hand of the almighty Father.'

(b) POSSIDET INDE SACRAM : SERAFIN : SINE : FINE : SINISTRAM
A common leonine hexameter.

'The seraph thenceforward occupies the sacred left-hand side eternally.'

171. **Toulouse**. Musée des Augustins. Capital from an unknown church of the musicians of King David, with an inscription (a). No. 473.

End 11th century.[243]

(a) [QVATVOR / HIC / SOCI/I / CONCI/TANTVR / IN / ORDINE / DAVID]
An unrhymed hexameter? *CIFM*, 7, 70, citing Rachou, *Pierre romanes*, 144. The text is not now visible. There is a superfluous short syllable in *concĭtantur*.

'Here four companions of David are arranged (?) in order.'

172. **Trogir** (**Traù**) (Croatia). Cathedral.

Portal (I have not been able to verify that this is the W portal, but from the placement of Eve on the left and Adam on the right, which would suggest the north and the south, I suspect that it is). The fully ornamented portal, which was carved by the sculptor Radovan and his pupils in 1240, is surmounted by a tympanum with two archivolts. The tympanum depicts the Nativity (above) and the Washing of the Infant Jesus (below), with an inscription (a).

AD 1240.

(a) + FVNDANTVR VALVE / POST PARTVM VIRGINIS ALME
PER RADVANVM CVNCTIS HAC ARTE PRECLARVM
VT PATET EX IP[S]IS SCVLPTVRIS ET EX ANAGLIPHIS
ANNO MILLENO DVCENO BISQ[VE] VICENO
PRESVLE TVSCANO FLORIS / EX VRBE TREGVANO

Five full leonine hexameters, the first three with slant rhyme. Fiskovič and Szabo, *Radovan*, vii. Like some of the Italians of the 12th century, Radovan, or the poet who composed the verses for him, was careless of quantity and clumsy in diction. There are false quantities in *prĕclarum* (2), *sculpturĭs* (3), and *vĭceno* (4). These suggest that he followed the rules for quantity only to the extent that he always made a closed syllable long. Arbitrary scansion of proper names.

'The doors are fashioned in witness of (?) the childbirth of the holy Virgin by Radovan famed above all others (?) for this art, as is revealed by these very sculptures and low reliefs, in the year 1240 under Tuscan Bishop Treguan (?) of the city of Florence (?).'

173. **Vaison-la-Romaine** (Vaucluse). Former cathedral of Notre-Dame-de-Nazareth.

Exterior N wall of nave. Monumental mural inscription (a), followed by the phrase PAX VHIC DOMVI, 'peace to this house' (Matt. 10:12).

Ca. 1150–60.[244]

(a) OBSECRO VOS FRATRES AQuiLONIS VINCITE PARTES ·
SECTANTES CLAVS~~TR~~VM QuiA SIC VENIETIS AD AVSTRVm ·
TRIFIDA QVADRIFIDVm MEMORET SVCCENDERE NIDVM ·
IGNEA BISSENIS LAPIDVM SIT VT ADDITA VENIS

Four full leonine hexameters with slant rhyme in (1). False quantity in *trīfida* (3).

'I beseech you, brothers, conquer the region of the north (wind), frequenting the cloister, because thus you will come to the south. May the triple fire remember to kindle the fourfold residence in order that it (the fire) may be added to the twice-six veins of the stones.'

174. **Vandeins** (Ain). St-Pierre.

W portal. Tympanum of Christ in Majesty seated within a mandorla supported by two angels above a gable-shaped lintel of the Last Supper and (on the far right) the Washing of the Feet. The rim of the mandorla is inscribed with the words BENEDICAT ET EDEM MAIESTAS D[omi]NI, 'May you also bless this house, Majesty of the Lord.' There are inscriptions (a) around the arch of the tympanum and (b) on the lower edge of the lintel, continued above the Last Supper on the lower edge of the tympanum proper.

Late in the first quarter of the 12th century? Cf. Condeissiat and St-Paul-de-Varax for similar monuments and epigraphy; St-Paul-de-Varax was probably the model for the other two.[245]

(a) OMNIPOTENS BONITAS EXAVDI[AT] INGREDIENTES
ANGeLuS EIVSDE[m] CVSTODIAT EG[r]EDIENTES

Two hexameters with tetrasyllabic end rhyme. Cf. Guédel, *L'architecture romane en Dombes*, 56, who reads: *Omnipotens Bonitas exaudiat ingredientes / Ange(lu)s ejus Dei custodiat egredientes*; *CIFM*, 17, 21.

'May the omnipotent Goodness hear the prayers of those who enter, and His angel watch over those who go out.'

(b) + AD MENSAM DOMINI [PE]CCATOR [QVANDO PROPINQV]AT
EXPEDIT VT FRAVDES EX TOTO / EX TOTO CORDE RELINQVAT

Two hexameters (deleting the second *ex toto*) with disyllabic end rhyme. Guédel, *L'architecture romane en Dombes*, 56, provides the missing letters on the authority of the earlier transcription of Leymarie (in *Album de l'Ain*, Bourg, 1836).[246] *Ex toto* has been repeated, like the catchword on a manuscript.

'When the sinner approaches the table of the Lord, it is proper for him to repudiate his sins with all his heart.'

175. **Vercelli** (Piemonte). Sant'Andrea. Cardinal Guala Bicherio laid the cornerstone of the church on 19 February 1219.[247]

Central W portal. Tympanum of the martyrdom of Saint Andrew, with an inscribed lintel (a). The tympanum may be the work of Benedetto Antelami, who is best known as the architect and sculptor of the Baptistery of Parma (ca. 1196–1216).[248] Saint Andrew is tied to the cross (the scene is closely modelled on the Descent from the Cross; the fact that Andrew is tied rather than nailed and the absence of an inscribed cross in his halo are the chief visual clues distinguishing this from a Descent). Two executioners are securing him to the cross at the direction of the proconsul Aegeus, who sits at the right. Two men and a woman stand on the left (they represent the twenty thousand people who listened to Andrew preach for two days from the cross; the woman specifically represents Maximilla, the wife of Aegeus, whom Andrew had baptized, and who buried him with honour after his death).[249] The lintel is modern, but the verses may be presumed to copy faithfully verses that appeared on the original lintel.

Ca. 1219.[250]

(a) PREDICAT ANDREAS PACIENS PLEBS CREDIT EGEAS
CREDERE QVI RENVIT DEMONIS ARTE RVIT
CONDIT SARCHOFAGO QVEDAM DEVOTA VIRAGO
ET PIA NON MODICVM CORPVS APOSTOLICVM

Two full leonine elegiac couplets. The spelling and scansion of *Ĕgēās* (for *Aegeus*) are dictated by the requirements of metre and rhyme.

'Saint Andrew preaches while suffering on the cross; the people believe; Aegeus, who refuses to believe, is destroyed by the art of a demon. A devout and holy woman buries the remarkable body of the apostle in a coffin.'

According to the *Golden Legend*, Aegeus, returning to his house after the execution, was seized in the street by a demon and died. After Maximilla buried Andrew's body, manna and scented oil issued from the tomb.[251] Only the first line of the first couplet refers to the scene depicted on the tympanum. It resembles other leonines with multiple subjects, such as the verse that accompanies the Deposition from the Cross at Santo Domingo de Silos. However, it is oddly asymmetrical in comparison with those, and although Aegeus, the third subject, is represented on the tympanum, he is not shown being destroyed as stated by the predicate in line 2.

176. **Vercelli**. Sant'Andrea.

Left W portal. Tympanum of Cardinal Guala offering a model of the church to Saint Andrew,[252] with an inscribed lintel (a). The lintel is modern (see above, central portal).

Ca. 1219.

(a) LVX CLERI · PAT[ri]EQue DECVS · CAR GVALA DINALIS /
QVEm CANOR AC ARTES · QVEm SANCTIO CANONICALIS /
QVEm LEX DOTAVIT · QVEm PAGINA SPiritVALIS /
CVIus IN ORE FVIT GEMINIS DOCT[ri]NA SVB ALIS /

CVIus ERAT STVDIVm LVX VITAQue PERPETVALIS /
VERAX ET NVmQVAm SERMONE SVPerFICIALIS /
SED TALIS VERBO COnCEPTus PECTORE QVALIS /
HIC VT HONORETVR ANDREAS MORTE PATRALIS /
HIC VT SIT CVLTus QVEm TERRA COLIT SCOCIALIS /
PER TE FACTA FVIT DOTATAQue FABRICA TALIS //
+ PARS TOTV[m] FORMA[m] DESIGNAT FORMVLA CAVSA /
EXPRIMIT EFFECTVS ET GENITVRA PATREM · /
CARDO GVALA PATer · PreSENS OP[us] EST GENITVRA · /
DAT PATer ANDREE QVOD GENERAVIT OPVS ·

Ten hexameters with disyllabic end rhyme (*-alis*), followed by two unrhymed elegiac couplets. Feminine caesura (1); tmesis: *car Guala dinalis* = *cardinalis Guala* (1); false quantity in *cā̆nonicalis* (2); final syllable of *honoretur* (8) lengthened at caesura.

'Light of the clergy and glory of the city, Cardinal Guala, whom poetry and the arts, whom canon and civil law, whom holy scripture enriched, in whose mouth doctrine was under the two wings (of the two Testaments?), whose study was the light and eternal life, truthful and never superficial in speech, but so expressed in word as in heart, in order that Andrew, an inhabitant of Patras (in Achaea, Greece) at the time of his death, should be honoured here, in order that he, whom the Scottish earth worships, be worshipped here, such a building was built and endowed by you. The part signifies the whole, the pattern signifies the form, the cause expresses the effects and that which is engendered expresses the father. "Cardinal" Guala is the father, the present work is the offspring. The father gives to Andrew that which [i.e., the model] begot the work.'

177. **Verona** (Veneto). Cathedral of Sta Maria.

W portal. Tympanum of the Virgin in Majesty, the Annunciation to the Shepherds, and the Adoration of the Magi, with an inscription (a) around the rim.

Ca. 1139–40.[253] The cathedral was reconstructed beginning in 1139 and consecrated by Pope Urban III in 1187. There is evidence that the high altar was in place in 1153, which indicates that the rebuilding proceeded rapidly.[254] The W portal must belong to an early phase of the reconstruction, because it is the work of Niccolò, who was at Piacenza and Sacra di S. Michele ca. 1107–20.

(a) + HIC DOMINVS · MAGNVS · LEO CRISTVS CERNITVR AGNVS ~

A full leonine hexameter.

'Here the Lord, the great lion Christ, is seen as a lamb.'

178. **Verona**. Sta Maria.

W. façade. Two-storeyed porch sheltering a tympanum, with an inscription (a) along the upper edge of the lower storey. The figures of John the Evangelist and

John the Baptist are placed in the lower spandrels on the left and right, respectively. The inscription ECCE AGNVS DEI appears beside John the Baptist.

Ca. 1139–40.

(a) + ARTIFICEM GNARVM QVI SCVLPSERIT HEC NICOLAVM ~

~ HVNC CONCVRRENTES · LAVDANT PER SECVLA GENTES ~

Two full leonine hexameters with slant rhyme in (1). First syllable of *Nĭcolaum* (1) long in classical Latin.

'The peoples coming to visit forever praise him – Niccolò, the skilled craftsman who sculpted this.'

Niccolò employed variants of this formula at S. Zeno and at the Cathedral of Ferrara, and used a similar formula at Sacra di S. Michele.

179. **Verona** Sta Maria.

S porch. Two sets of superimposed columns. The upper capitals depict the Annunciation. According to Porter, there is an inscription (a) on the abacus of one of these.[255]

Ca. 1139–40.

(a) + ANGeLuS INGRESSVS DOMINAm FAM/VLANDO SALVTAT.

INQ[ui]D [AV]E TECVm DomiNuS NAm[?] MVNERE PLENA

Two unrhymed hexameters. Porter, *Lombard Architecture* 3, 478. Porter places a horizontal suspension bar over the *n* of *nam*. Possibly another word is meant.

'The angel, having entered in, adoring the Lady greets her. He says: Hail, the Lord is with you, for you are full of grace.'

Cf. Luke 1:28.

180. **Verona**. S. Zeno Maggiore.

W portal. Tympanum of S. Zeno. The large, standing figure of the saint, trampling a dragon beneath his feet, occupies the centre. Zeno is flanked by the military forces of Verona holding standards.[256] The infantry is on his right; the cavalry on his left. A broad decorative semicircular border arches over the saint's head. A similar border, exhibiting four episodes, in a series of eight arcades, from the life of the saint,[257] forms the lintel of the tympanum (a more massive double lintel supports the tympanum). In the first (from the left), the Emperor Gallienus seeks Saint Zeno. In the second, the saint casts out the devil from the Emperor's daughter. The third depicts the miracle of the fish that the legates of the Emperor had stolen from the saint and which could not be cooked. In the last (the four arcades on the right side), Zeno saves a peasant who had been thrown into the river Adige with his cart and oxen by the devil. There are inscriptions (a) around the outer rim of the decorative border; (b) around the inner rim; and (c) on the upper edge of the lintel.

Ca. 1120–38.[258] The W portal is the work of Niccolò[259] with the help of an assistant named Guglielmo.[260]

(a) + ARTIFICEM GNARVM QVI SCVLPSERIT HEC NICOLAVM
+ OMNES LAVDEMVS CRISTVM · DomiNuMQue ROGEMVS
+ CELORVm REGNVM SIBI DONET VT IPSE SVPerNVm

Three full leonines, two with slant rhyme (1, 3).

'Let us all praise Niccolò, the skilled craftsman who sculpted this; and let us beg the Lord Christ to grant him the kingdom of heaven above.'

Cf. the similar inscriptions at Ferrara and the cathedral of Verona.

(b) + DAT PRESVL SIGGNVM [*sic*] · POPVLO · MVNIMINE
DIGNVM + VEXILLVM ZENO · LARGITVR CORDE SERENO

Two full leonine hexameters.

'The bishop gives to the people a standard worth having for defence. Zeno gives a banner with a serene heart.'

The first verse refers to the scene on the left side of the tympanum, which depicts the infantry. The second verse refers to the scene on the right, which depicts the cavalry.

(c) [*On the left side of the central figure of Zeno:*]
+ REX GALIENVS ZENO<nem> QVERIT · ANELVS ·
PISCES LEGATIS · TRES DAT BONITAS SVA GRA/TIS ~
[*On the right side of Zeno:*]
ZENO PISCATVR · VIR STAT · DEMONQVE FVGATVR ~

Three full leonine hexameters. Both sense and metre require the accusative form *Zenonem* (1). The *i* of *Galienus* (1) is lengthened *metri causa.*

'King Gallienus breathlessly seeks Zeno. His [Zeno's] goodness gives three fishes to the legates for free. Zeno fishes, the man stands [i.e., the peasant survives], and the devil is put to flight.'

The three verses apply to the first, third, and fourth episodes from the miracles of Saint Zeno that are carved on the lintel.

181. **Verona**. S. Zeno Maggiore.

W façade (lower). Reliefs depicting scenes from the Old Testament on the right side of the portal. They are the work of Niccolò or an assistant working under his direction.[261] The panels are arranged in pairs vertically and read from bottom to top.

The lowest pair depicts the legend of King Theodoric who asked the devil, his father, for a gift of a horse and dogs. When they arrived, he leapt naked from his bath and rode off on a hunt from which he never returned.[262] On the left, Theodoric rides off. There is an inscription (a) on the upper background. On the right, a deer is pursed by two dogs watched by the devil. There is an inscription

(b) on the background above one of the dogs that is leaping on the deer.

The second pair shows God creating the birds and the animals on the left, with an inscription (c) above, and God creating Adam on the right, with an inscription (d) above and another inscription (e) identifying the sculptor as Niccolò.

The third pair depicts on the left God creating Eve from Adam's rib, with an inscription (f) above, and on the right the Sin of Adam and Eve, with an inscription (g) above.

The fourth (top) pair shows on the left God expelling Adam and Eve from Paradise, with an inscription (h) above, and on the right Eve spinning while nursing Cain and Abel and Adam hewing wood, with an inscription (i) above.

Ca. 1120–38.

(a) + O REGEM · STVLTVm PETIT INFERNALE TRIBVTVm /
MOXQue PARATVR EQVVS · QVEm MISIT DEMON INIQVVS /
EXIT AQVAm NVDVS PE/TIT INFERA NON REDITV/RVS

One common (2) and two full slant leonine hexameters. False quantity in *demŏn* (2).

'O foolish king! He seeks a gift from hell, and soon a horse appears which the wicked devil sent. He gets out of the water naked. He seeks hell and will not return.'

(b) NISVS EQVVS · CERVVS CANIS HVIC / DATVR · HOS DAT AVERNus

A full slant leonine hexameter.

'A labouring horse, a stag, a dog is given to him [i.e., Theodoric]; hell gives them.'

(c) FACTOR TERRARVm GENVS HIC CREAT OMnE FERARVM

A full leonine hexameter.

'Here the Maker of the world creates every kind of animal.'

Cf. Gen. 1:20–5.

(d) + VT SIT REX RERVm DEDIT ADE SEXTA DIERVM

A full leonine hexameter.

'(God) gave (life) to Adam on the sixth of the days (of creation) in order that he might be king of all things' (?).

The verse scarcely makes grammatical sense. If *sexta dierum* is intended as an ablative of time, there is a false quantity in *sextă*. Porter, *Lombard Architecture*, 3, 530, translates 'Adam was created on the sixth day in order that he might be king of all things.' Cf. Gen. 1:26–31.

(e) HIC EXEmPLA TRAI POSSVnT LAVD[i]S NICO/LAI

A full leonine hexameter. For scansion of *Nicolai*, see cathedral of Verona, W porch.

'Here examples of the merit of Niccolò can be derived.'

(f) + COSTA[m] FVR[a]TVR DeuS VTI VIRAGO CREATVR

A full leonine hexameter. Porter, *Lombard Architecture*, 3, 531, n. 69, reads VN for

VTI. If *uti* is correct, it is an infinitive used to express purpose (common in medieval Latin), and its final vowel is shortened.

'God takes a rib to use; the woman is created.'

Cf. Gen. 2:21–4.

(g) + IDRA DAT EVA VIRO VIR MORDET FEDERE DIRO

A full leonine hexameter.

'The serpent gives [the fruit to Eve], Eve gives it to her husband, her husband bites it despite the awful prohibition.'

The construction of this verse is unusually elliptical. Eve is virtually equated with the serpent ('the serpent, Eve, gives to the man'). The ablative phrase *federe diro* stands in uncertain relationship with the rest of the sentence. I take it, as did Porter,[263] to be a reference to God's prohibition against eating the fruit of the tree of the knowledge of good and evil (Gen. 2:17). But it might imply that a horrible bond was established between Satan and mankind at the moment the fruit was tasted. Cf. Gen. 3:1–6.

(h) LEX DATVR OFFENDIT · PENAS Pro CRIMINE PEND[IT]

A full leonine hexameter. Porter, *Lombard Architecture*, 3, 531, n. 71, incorrectly reads OFFENDITVR.

'The law is given, Adam breaks it, he pays the penalty for the crime.'

(i) CONQVEROR INTR[a]NTES DE SEVE FRAVDIBVS EVE · /
QVE M<ih>I QV[E VO]BIS INFLIXIT PERPETVM VE

Two hexameters with monosyllabic end rhyme. The final letter of the second *que* and the first two letters of *vobis* are chipped away; I supply them on the authority of Porter, *Lombard Architecture*, 3, 531, n. 72, whose reading of the second line is QVE MI QVE VOBIS INFLIXIT PERPETVO VIVIS.

'You who are entering, I lament the sin of cruel Eve, who has inflicted perpetual woe on me [and] on you.'

182. **Verona**. S. Zeno Maggiore.

W façade (lower). String-course with an inscription (a) above reliefs depicting scenes from the New Testament on the left side of the portal. These panels are the work of Guglielmo, who seems to have been a pupil of Niccolò.[264] None of the panels is accompanied by a verse inscription. The final line of the inscription (a) is on a separate lunette underneath the string-course. The Hand of God appears on this lunette. It is flanked by two kneeling figures that hold up the string-course above. The inscription is on the background on either side of the Hand of God.

Ca. 1120–38.

(a) Qui LEGIS ISTA PIE NATVM PLACATO MARIE
SALVET In ETERNV[m] Q[VI] SCVLP[SE]RIT ISTA GVILLELMVM /
+ INTRANTES CVNCTI / [SV]CVRRANT HVIC PEREVNTI

Three full leonine hexameters with slant rhyme in lines 2 and 3. Arbitrary scansion in *Guĭllelmum* (2). The last two letters of *ista* and all of *pie* are chipped away on the upper portions. I supply them and portions of the second and third lines that were not visible to me on the two occasions when I examined them from Porter, *Lombard Architecture*, 3, 532.

'You who read this, try to placate the Son of holy Mary. May He save forever Guglielmo, who sculpted this. May all entering here come to the aid of this lost soul.'

183. **Verona**. S. Zeno Maggiore.

W porch façade. The porch shelters the tympanum. The Hand of God is at the top. The Evangelist John is on the left, holding a book, which is inscribed IN PRINCIPIO ERAT VERBVM, 'In the beginning was the Word' (John 1:1). John the Baptist is on the right, holding a scroll, which is inscribed HECCE AGNVS DEI, 'Behold the Lamb of God' (John 1:29), in one hand and pointing with the other. The Lamb of God is at the top of the supporting arch, beneath the Hand of God. There are inscriptions (a) in a circle around the Hand of God; (b) above the Lamb of God; (c) above and to the right of the head of John the Evangelist; and (d) above and to the left of the head of John the Baptist.

Ca. 1120–38.

(a) + DEXTRA DEI GENTES BE<u>NE</u>DICAT SACRA PETENTES

A full leonine hexameter.

'May the sacred right hand of God bless those peoples who seek Him.'

(b) + AGNVS HIC EST CVNCTI QVI | TOLLIT CRIMINA MVNDI ;

A full slant leonine hexameter. The vertical bar (|) marks where the head of the Lamb intersects the inscription.

'This is the Lamb who takes away the sins of the whole world.'

Cf. John 1:29.

(c) + ASTRA PETENS ALES BIBIT ALTA / FLVENTA IOHanneS ·
PECTORE DE / XPistI GVSTANS ARCHANA / MAGISTRI

Two full slant leonine hexameters.

'The eagle, John, seeking the stars, drinks the flowing deeps, tasting the secrets of the Master from the breast of Christ.'

(d) + SENSIT PR[EDI]XIT MONSTRAVIT / GVRGITE [T]INXIT ;

A full slant leonine hexameter.

'He perceived the truth, he preached, he showed the way, he baptized in the river.'

184. **Verona**. S. Zeno Maggiore.

W façade (upper). The Wheel of Fortune window above the W portal, executed by Brioloto (fl. 1189–1226). A clockwise inscription (a) runs around the inner hub of the Wheel. Another inscription (b) is said to appear on the inside of the Wheel, although I have never been able to see it.

Ca. 1200. The upper part of the W façade was the work of Brioloto and Adamino di S. Giorgio.[265]

(a) + EN EGO FORTVNA MODEROR MORTALIBVS VNA
ELEVO DEPONO BONA CVNCTIS VEL MALA DONO

Two full leonine hexameters. Final vowel of *Fortuna* (1) lengthened at caesura.

'Lo, I, Fortune alone, govern mortals. I raise up, I depose, I give good and evil to all.'

(b) Induo nudatos, denudo veste paratos.
In me confidit si quis, derisus abibit.

Two full leonine hexameters. Ederle, *The Basilica of St. Zeno,* 16.

'I clothe the naked, I strip those who are provided with clothing. If anyone trusts in me completely, he will depart as an object of scorn.'

185. **Vézelay** (Yonne). Ste-Marie-Madeleine.

Interior. Central W portal (the portal is sheltered by a narthex) tympanum of Christ in Majesty giving to the apostles the mission of converting the peoples of the world, with an inner archivolt depicting the Labours of the Months and the Signs of the Zodiac in twenty-nine medallions; December (the 29th medallion), a man holding a cup of wine, with an inscription (a) around the left rim of the medallion. The right half of the rim is blank, as are the rims of all the other medallions.

Ca. 1125.[266]

(a) + OMnIBVS IN MEMBRIS DESIGNAT IMAGO DECE[m]BRIS

A full leonine hexameter.

'In all its parts the image of December represents ...'

The thought appears to be incomplete. There is room on the medallion for another verse.

186. **Vézelay**. Ste-Marie-Madeleine.

Interior. Central W portal: trumeau statue column of John the Baptist, with an inscription (a) around the base of the column. John holds the Lamb in a circular dish or mandorla. There was formerly an inscription on the mandorla surrounding the Lamb. Traces of letters are visible on the lower rim.

Ca. 1125.

(a) AGNOSCANT OMneS QVIA DICITVR ISTE IOHanneS +
Cum RETINET POPuLuM DEMONSTRANS INDICE XP[istu]M

Two common leonine hexameters. The words *cum retinet* are uncertain. Salet, *La*

Madeleine de Vézelay, 174, reads AGNOSCANT OMNES QVIA DICITVR ISTE IOHANNES / CVM (?) RETINET POPVLVM DEMONSTRANS INDICE CHRISTVM. Evans, *Cluniac Art,* 19, n. 4, reads AGNOSCANT OMNES QVIA DICITVR ISTE IOHANNES / QVI RETINET POPVLVM INDICE MONSTRANS CHRISTVM.[267]

'Let all realize that this is meant to be John when he holds the attention of the people, pointing out Christ with his finger' (?).

187. **Vézelay**. Ste-Marie-Madeleine.

Interior. Keystone medallion, 3rd arcade, S side of nave. The medallion shows a seated woman, crowned, holding a standard in her right hand and a church in her left. There is an inscription (a) around the rim.

Ca. 1120–32.[268]

(a) SVm MODO FVMOSA SED ERO I POST HEC SPECIOSA

A full leonine hexameter. The vertical bar (I) marks where the footstool of the seated woman intersects the rim. Final vowel of *fumosa* lengthened at caesura. If this is the original position of the keystone, the inscription could never have been read from any position in the church. There is no gallery from which it might be viewed more or less straight on. The lower rim of the medallion faces upward and therefore the lower portions of the inscription cannot be seen from the floor of the nave. An excellent photograph in Oursel, *Routes romanes,* 1, 48, shows all details of the inscription clearly.

'Now I am smoke-stained, but later I will be beautiful.'

188. **Vezzolano** (Piemonte). Church.

Interior. Double frieze in nave, with an inscription (a) beneath. The verses are followed by the words ANN[O AB INCARNATIONE ...].

12th century?

(a) HEC [SERIES SANCTAM PRODVXIT IN ORBE MARIAM
QVE PEPERIT VERAM SINE SEMINE MVNDA SOPHIAM]

Two common leonine hexameters. Cf. Chierici and Citi, *Piémont-Ligurie roman* 99. The inscription is now almost entirely obliterated. I can see the first word *hec* and below it the first three letters of *anno. Sophīam* (2) retains its Greek accent with arbitrary lengthening of the vowel.

'This line [of patriarchs] produced Saint Mary in the world, who, chaste, gave birth to the true Wisdom without seed.'

189. **Vienne** (Isère). St-Pierre.

S portal (communicating with the cloister). Tympanum of Saint Peter holding the keys, with an inscription (a) in the background on either side of the figure.

Second quarter of the 12th century.[269]

(a) + NON PETRVS HEC PETRA / ROMaE PETRVS ET SVPer aETHRA //
+ AD FORMAM CVIVS / SPECIES FIT IMAGINIS HVIVS

Two full leonine hexameters. Cf. *CIFM*, 15, 142. Final vowel of *petra* (1) lengthened at caesura.

'This stone is not Peter. Peter is at Rome and in heaven above. In his likeness the form of this statue is made.'

190. **Vieu** (Ain). Notre-Dame de l'Assomption.

W porch. Lintel with an inscription (a).

Beginning of 12th century.[270]

(a) HVC · SINE · MENTE · BONA · NEQVE · VOTA · VALENT · NEQVE · DONA /
ERGO MALAS MENTES DEPONANT INGREDIENTES

Two full leonine hexameters. *CIFM*, 17, 23.

'In this place without a pure mind neither prayers nor gifts avail. Therefore, let those entering put aside their evil thoughts.'

191. **Wrocław** (Wrocław). Museum of Architecture.

Tympanum of Jaxa. With an inscription (a).

Ca. 1160–3.

(a) Ianua sum vite, per me quicumque venite

A full leonine hexameter. *CIFM*, 16, 184, citing *Ornamenta ecclesiae. Kunst und Künstler der Romanik* 1, *Katalog* ... (Cologne, 1985), 161.

'I am the gate of life. Come through me, whoever you are.'

192. **Zwolle** (Overijssel). St Michaël. The church dates from the 14th century.

Apse. SE exterior wall: re-employed tympanum of Three Souls in the Bosom of Abraham, with an inscription (a) around the rim, and the words PATER ABRAHAM in the background on either side of the patriarch's head. Abraham and the three souls in his bosom are all half-figures; both of Abraham's hands are raised, palms out, and his right hand has two fingers extended in blessing.

Beginning of 13th century.[271]

(a) PR[e]M[i]A · F[e]RT · VITE LOC[VS V]T DOMVS · ISTA VENITE

A full leonine hexameter. Cf. Deijk, *Pays-Bas romans*, 330.

'A place like this church offers the reward of (eternal) life. Come.'

Notes

Chapter 1: The Allegory of the Church

1 Lehmann, 'The Dome of Heaven,' pp. 1–27. Dome mosaics, like the east dome of S. Marco in Venice or the Scarsella vault of the Baptistery of Florence (Lehmann, figs. 1, 41), were sometimes inscribed with hexameters.

2 'Haec est illa domus, quam mater numinis alti / incolitans seruat uasti sub culmine caeli. // omnes ast sancti medii pauimenta sacelli / seruantes colitant per tempora cuncta maniplis / innumeris.' Æthelwulf, *De Abbatibus* 434–5; 441–3 (Campbell, 34–7). See Taylor, 'The Architectural Interest of Æthelwulf's *De Abbatibus*,' 165, 167.

3 I use 'liminal' here and throughout in its primary etymological sense as an adjective referring to the threshold, but with a glance at the anthropological use of the term to refer to a space or condition in which settled categories are in flux and the possibility of spiritual transformation exists. For a summary of the latter usage, see 'Pilgrimage as a Liminoid Phenomenon,' in Turner and Turner, *Image and Pilgrimage*, 1–39.

4 A corpus of these verse inscriptions is gathered in the Catalogue of Romanesque Verse Inscriptions, commencing on p. 199.

5 Simson, *The Gothic Cathedral*, xiv, endeavours 'to understand Gothic architecture as an *image*, more precisely, as the *representation* of supernatural reality' (emphases mine). He does not say this in order to set up a contrast with Romanesque architecture, but I think it is appropriate to do so. If the Gothic church was a 'representation of supernatural reality,' then the Romanesque church was in some sense the supernatural reality itself.

6 So called because its principles as applied to the Bible can be traced to Philo of Alexandria, and to distinguish it from 'Antiochene' exegesis, which had little influence in the West. See Smalley, *The Study of the Bible*, 2–20. The best

short introduction to the subject is still Mâle, *Religious Art, 13th Century*, 137–45.

7 Bede divided human history from Creation to the end of the world into six ages. The sixth age extended from the Incarnation to the Second Coming; it therefore included the 'present.' See Bede, *De Temporum Ratione* 10 (Jones, *Bedae Opera de Temporibus*, 201–2), and Jones's note, p. 345; Brown, *Bede the Venerable*, 37–40.

8 Spicq, *Esquisse*, 98–9.

9 'Sciendum uero est, quod quaedam historica expositione transcurrimus et per allegoriam quaedam typica inuestigatione perscrutamur, quaedam per sola allegoricae moralitatis instrumenta discutimus, nonnulla autem per cuncta simul sollicitius exquirentes tripliciter indagamus. Nam primum quidem fundamenta historiae ponimus; deinde per significationem typicam in arcem fidei fabricam mentis erigimus; ad extremum quoque per moralitatis gratiam, quasi superducto aedificium colore uestimus.' Gregory the Great, *Moralia in Iob*, Epistola Fratri Leandro Coepiscopo 3, in *CC*, 143, 4.

10 Auerbach, 'Figura,' 11–76.

11 'Typology' and 'typological' are modern forms based on such medieval terms as *typus*, *typicus*, and *typice*. The usual term for 'typology' in medieval formulations of the fourfold method was *allegoria*. I use 'typology' to avoid confusion with 'allegory' in the broader sense of that word.

12 'Theoretice vero in duas dividitur partes, id est, in historicam interpretationem, et intelligentiam spiritalem ... Spiritalis autem scientiae genera sunt, tropologia, allegoria, anagoge.' Cassian, *Collationes XXIV* 14.8 (*PL*, 49, col. 962).

13 'Tropologia est moralis explanatio, ad emendationem vitae et instructionem pertinens actualem ... ea quae in veritate gestae sunt, alterius sacramenti formam praefigurasse dicuntur ... ad sublimiora quaedam et sacratiora coelorum secreta.' Cassian, *Collationes XXIV* 14.8 (*PL*, 49, col. 963).

14 Jones, 'Bede's Commentary on Genesis,' 135–6.

15 Lubac, *Exégèse médiévale*, 139–57.

16 Kendall, 'Imitation and the Venerable Bede's *Historia Ecclesiastica*,' 161–90.

17 Krautheimer, 'Introduction to an "Iconography of Mediaeval Architecture,"' esp. 3, 13–17. See also Ousterhout, 'Loca Sancta,' 109–24.

18 Krautheimer, 'Introduction to an "Iconography of Mediaeval Architecture,"' 5, 10.

19 Lubac, *Exégèse médiévale*, 664.

20 Bede, *De Schematibus et Tropis* (*CC*, 123A, 142–71). Bede offers a briefer treatment of the fourfold method in *De Tabernaculo* 1 (*CC*, 119A, 24–5). Like other commentators, Bede shifted easily between the threefold and fourfold meth-

ods. See Plummer, *Venerabilis Baedae Opera Historica*, 1, lxii, and n. 1. On the fourfold method of scriptural interpretation, see also Caplan, 'The Four Senses of Scriptural Interpretation,' 282–90.

21 Kendall, *De Arte Metrica et De Schematibus et Tropis*, 60–76.

22 *De Schematibus et Tropis* 2.12 (*CC*, 123A, 161–9; for historical and verbal allegory, pp. 164–6). See Strubel, '*Allegoria in factis et Allegoria in verbis*,' esp. 347–53.

23 'According to St. Augustine, the "wood" is a sign of the cross. The "stone" and the "beast" represent the human nature of Christ.' Robertson, *Augustine's On Christian Doctrine*, 8, n. 6.

24 Augustine, *De Doctrina Christiana* 1.2.2 (Robertson, *Augustine's On Christian Doctrine*, 8–9).

25 Eco, *The Aesthetics of Thomas Aquinas*, 151–2.

26 Jones, 'Bede's Commentary on Genesis,' 118.

27 *De Schematibus et Tropis* 2.12 (Kendall, *Bede's Art of Poetry and Rhetoric*, 203). I cite the Bible in Latin from the Vulgate Edition and in English from the Challoner revision of the Douay-Rheims translation of the Vulgate; punctuation and capitalization are mine. I occasionally alter the English translation slightly to bring it closer to the Latin of the Vulgate or to eliminate an archaism.

28 Despite appearances, Bede has not really added another level of meaning to the 'fourfold' method. He simply isolates 'sign' from the things that it signifies on the literal, typological, tropological, and anagogical levels.

29 Bede, *De Schematibus and Tropis* 2.12 (Kendall, *Bede's Art of Poetry and Rhetoric*, 207).

30 Bede probably had in mind St Paul's saying, *Vos enim estis templum Dei* (2 Rom. 6:16), which he quoted, for example, in his commentaries *In Genesim* 4.18 (*CC*, 118A, 213), and *De Tabernaculo* 2 (*CC*, 119A, 43).

31 It is perhaps relevant to note that laymen rather than clerics tended to be praised as 'Solomons' in their role as patrons of new buildings. See Cahn, 'Solomonic Elements in Romanesque Art,' 57, and n. 33.

32 Lubac, *Exégèse médiévale*, 155.

33 Bede, *De Schematibus and Tropis* 2.12 (Kendall, *Bede's Art of Poetry and Rhetoric*, 207). Bede's allegorical interpretation of Jerusalem, which he expands in his commentary *In Cantica Canticorum* 4.11 (*CC*, 119b, 260), derives from Cassian's *Collationes XXIV* 14.8 (*PL*, 49, cols. 963–4).

34 Psalm 47:2–3 makes this identification explicit: 'Great is the Lord, and exceedingly to be praised in the city of our God, in his holy mountain. With the joy of the whole earth is mount Sion founded ..., the city of the great king.'

35 See chapter 3.

36 Bouillet, *Liber miraculorum* 1.31; Sheingorn, *The Book of Sainte Foy*, 102.

37 'Ipsa vero ecclesia eam utique Ecclesiam designat, quae in ea continetur, id est multitudinem: unde et am [*sic*: etiam?] ecclesia vocatur, eo quod Ecclesiam contineat. Haec enim figura a grammaticis metonymia dicitur, quando id quod continet, ponitur pro eo quod continetur. Quale est illud, quod in Evangelio Dominus ait: "Jerusalem, Jerusalem, quae occidis prophetas": cum utique non ipsa Jerusalem, sed ejus habitatores prophetas occiderint. Sic etiam dicere solemus: Illa domus bona est, eo quod bonos habeat habitatores; et illa mala est, eo quod mali habitatores habitent in ea. Secundum hanc igitur significationem, haec ecclesia ex lignis, lapidibusque constructa, eam Ecclesiam designat, quae ex vivis lapidibus aedificatur; cujus lapides non calce, sed charitate junguntur et uniuntur; cujus fundamentum Christus est; cujus portae apostoli sunt; cujus columnae episcopi sunt et doctores, in quo unusquisque lapis tanto amplius rutilat, quanto fidelior et melior est.' Bruno of Asti, *De Sacramentis Ecclesiae*, *PL*, 165, col. 1092.

38 Carlsson, *The Iconology of Tectonics in Romanesque Art*, esp. chaps. 2–6, provides a series of excerpts from the Bible and the Church Fathers, including Bede, that supports this conclusion.

39 'Cujus principia bona fuerunt, novissima vero mala.' Isidore, *De Ortu et Obitu Patrum*, 34, *PL*, 83, col. 140.

40 Simson, *The Gothic Cathedral*, 11.

41 Cahn, 'Solomonic Elements in Romanesque Art,' 52–3, 56–7.

42 Verzár Bornstein, *Portals and Politics*, 66.

43 *Religious Art, 12th Century*, 341.

44 Durliat, *La sculpture romane*, 391; Lyman, 'Raymond Gairard,' 88, notes that *membrum* can denote 'aisle' and raises the possibility that *capitis membrum* refers to 'the continuous aisle enclosing the entire choir, and part of the nave.'

45 Heer, *The Medieval World*, 380–1.

46 Durliat, *La sculpture romane*, 324, and fig. 344.

47 See chapter 4.

48 Catalogue no. 187a (Vézelay).

49 See, for example, Isidore, *Allegoriae quaedam Scripturae Sacrae*, *PL*, 83, col. 117: 'Maria autem Ecclesiam significat, quae cum sit desponsata Christo, virgo nos de Spiritu sancto concepit, virgo etiam parit.'

50 Prudentius, *Psychomachia*, preface, lines 59–68.

51 Ibid., lines 902–15.

52 Ibid., lines 803–87.

53 Colgrave and Mynors, *Bede's Ecclesiastical History*, 338–9.

54 Holder, 'Allegory and History,' 115–31.

55 The western towers of the basilica were pulled down in the 16th century; the

upper portion of the west façade and the towers with their spires are 19th-century restorations.

56 Buchowiecki, *Handbuch*, 1, 62. The design of the older façade is known from a 17th-century drawing by Francesco Borromini, in which a portion of the inscription can be read. Buchowiecki, *Handbuch*, 1, 65; the drawing is reproduced in ibid., 66, and in Armellini, *Le chiese di Roma*, 1, 122. Fragments of the original 12th-century inscription are preserved in the cloister. The 18th-century stonecutters carefully imitated the letter forms of the 12th century.

57 The dedication to Christ the Saviour is Constantinian. Its better known dedication to St John the Baptist dates from the time of Pope Gregory the Great and was definitively established by Pope Sergius III (904–11). See Buchowiecki, *Handbuch*, 1, 62.

58 Catalogue no. 129a (Rome).

Chapter 2: Constantine and the Mosaics of Rome

1 Favreau, *Les inscriptions médiévales*, 10, n. 2.

2 Luke 23:36–8; see also Matt. 27:37; Mark 15:26; John 19:19.

3 'St. Ambrose in 382 was among the first to emphasize that the cross plan of the church of the Holy Apostles at Milan, which he laid out, was meant to symbolize the victory of Christ and of His cross.' Krautheimer, 'Introduction to an "Iconography of Mediaeval Architecture,"' 8.

4 For numerous examples, see Lattimore, *Themes in Greek and Latin Epitaphs*.

5 Fox, *Pagans and Christians*, 169–82, 202–4, 231–5.

6 *Imp(eratori) Caes(ari) Fl(avio) Constantino Maximo / P(io) F(elici) Augusto, S(enatus) P(opulus)q(ue) R(omanus), / quod instinctu divinitatis, mentis / magnitudine, cum exercitu suo / tam de tyranno quam de omni eius / factione, uno tempore, iustis / rem publicam ultus est armis, / arcum triumphis insignem dicavit.* Latin text and English translation (rearranged) from Gordon, *Latin Epigraphy*, 168–9 (no. 82). The inscription is identical on both faces.

7 Buchowiecki, *Handbuch*, 1, 105.

8 'Constantinus imperator in musivo depictus, literis aureis ostendens Salvatori et beato Petro ecclesiam Sancti Petri.' Jacobacci, *De concilio*, Rome, 1538, cited by Duchesne, *Liber Pontificalis*, 1, 193. The date of the mosaic is in dispute. It may not be Constantinian; it could even be a work of the Carolingian period. See Arbeiter, *Alt-St. Peter*, 215–16, and n. 501, for details of the controversy. The inscription, however, is certainly Constantinian.

9 Duchesne, *Liber Pontificalis*, 1, 193 (from de Rossi).

10 The term 'triumphal arch' as applied to ecclesiastical architecture goes back

to the Carolingian period, and possibly derives from the inscription on the Arch of Constantine. See Krautheimer, 'Carolingian Revival,' 34 and nn. 191–3. Mathews, *The Clash of Gods*, 15, calls into question the association of the 'triumphal arches' of early Christian churches with the triumphal arches of imperial Rome.

11 Duchesne, *Liber Pontificalis*, 1, 193.

12 For the origin of representations of Christ in Majesty in Roman imperial iconography, with particular reference to the scene of the emperor bestowing largess on the frieze of the Arch of Constantine, see Grabar, *Christian Iconography*, 43–4, and pl. 116; for a counter-argument, deriving it from anti-imperial motives and Roman images of the gods, see Mathews, *The Clash of Gods*, 92–114.

13 *Martyrium flammis olim levvita subisti. / Iure tuis templis lux beneranda <r>edit.* The first and last parts of the inscription have been restored. The last word now reads *dedit.* See the copy of a drawing in the Vatican Library in Armellini, *Le chiese di Roma*, 2, pl. 43 (facing p. 1080), and Duchesne, *Liber Pontificalis*, 1, 310.

14 For illustrations of the first type, see Lattimore, *Themes in Greek and Latin Epitaphs*, e.g., 217–20; for the second, see Lattimore, e.g., 275–7.

15 *O veneranda mihi, sanctum decus, alma, pudoris, / Ut Damasi precibus faveas precor, inclyta martyr.*

16 Arbeiter, *Alt-St. Peter*, pp. 55–6, and nn. 104–7.

17 The mosaic was destroyed in 1631. It is known from a fresco in the Vatican Grottoes and sketches in two Vatican manuscripts. The fresco is reproduced in Oakeshott, *The Mosaics of Rome*, pl. 29.

18 For the verses, see Oakeshott, *The Mosaics of Rome*, 67; Buchowiecki, *Handbuch*, 1, 113.

19 *Aula Dei claris radiat speciosa metallis, / In qua plus fidei lux pretiosa micat. / Martyribus medicis, populo spes certa salutis / Venit, et ex sacro crevit honore locus. / Optulit hoc Domino Felix antistite dignum / Munus, ut aetheria vivat in arce poli.*

20 In origin this was a chapel added to the 4th-century basilica of Constantia, which has almost entirely disappeared. The chapel was rebuilt by Pope Honorius.

21 *Aurea concisis surgit pictura metallis, / Et conplexa simul, clauditur ipsa dies. / Fontibus e nibeis credas aurora surire, / Correptas nubes, ruribus arva ricans, / Vel qualem inter sidera lucem proferet irim, / Purpureusque pavo ipse colore nitens. / Qui potuit noctis vel lucis reddere finem / Marturum e bustis hinc reppulit ille chaos. / Sursum versa nutu quod cunctis cernitur uno / Praesul Honorius haec vota dicata dedit. / Vestibus et factis signantur illius ora, / Lucet et aspectu, lucida corda cerens.* It is not easy to distinguish spellings that may be characteristic of the orthography of the 7th century from modern errors of restoration. My translation is tentative. See Duchesne, *Liber Pontificalis*, 1, 325–6, for commentary.

22 Buchowiecki, *Handbuch*, 1, 93; Oakeshott, *The Mosaics of Rome*, 150.

23 *Martyribus Cristi Domini pia vota Iohannes / Reddidit antistes, sanctificante Deo./ At sacri fontis simili fulgente metallo / Providus instanter hoc copulavit opus. / Quo quisquis gradiens et Cristum pronus adorans / Effusasque preces <mittit ad aethra> suas.* The bracketed letters in the last line are the original reading (Armellini, *Le chiese di Roma,* 1, 137). They have been replaced by *impetrat ille.*

24 *Ista domus pridem fuerat confracta ruinis. / Nunc rutilat iugiter variis decorata metallis, / Et decus ecce suus splendet ceu Phoebus in orbe, / Qui post furva fugans tetrae velamina noctis / Virgo Maria tibi Paschalis praesul honestus / Condidit hanc aulam laetus per saecla manendam.* Cf. Duemmler, *Poetae Latini Aevi Carolini,* 2, 686. Duemmler reads *nunc iugiter rutilat* (2). The syntax of these verses is not entirely clear.

25 Bede, *Ecclesiastical History* 5.11 (Colgrave and Mynors, 484–5).

26 Krautheimer, 'Carolingian Revival,' 13, and n. 93; Geary, *Furta Sacra,* esp. 18, 28–32.

27 Mâle, *Early Churches,* 89, derives this design from the apse mosaic of Santi Cosma e Damiano.

28 *Emicat aula piae variis decorata metallis / Praxedis Domino super aethra placentis honore, / Pontificis summi studio Paschalis alumni / Sedis apostolicae passim qui corpora condens, / Plurima Sanctorum subter haec moenia ponit, / Fretus ut his limen mereatur adire polorum.* Cf. Duemmler, *Poetae Latini Aevi Carolini,* 2, 662. Duemmler reads *pia e variis* (1).

29 *Haec domus ampla micat variis fabricata metallis, / Olim quae fuerat confracta sub tempore prisco./ Condidit in melius Paschalis praesul opimus. / Hanc aulam Domini formans fundamine claro. / Aurea gemmatis resonant haec dindima templi. / Laetus amore Dei hic coniunxit corpora sancta / Caeciliae et sociis rutilat hic flore iuventus / Quae pridem in cruptis pausabant membra beata. / Roma resultat ovans semper ornata per aevum.* Cf. Duemmler, *Poetae Latini Aevi Carolini,* 2, 662.

30 Oursel, *Invention,* 227–8.

31 Horn and Born, *The Plan of St. Gall,* 3, 28–9, captions 46, 49–51.

32 Mâle, *Early Churches,* 87–91; Krautheimer, 'Carolingian Revival,' 14–15, and n. 109. On Byzantine iconoclasm, see Belting, *Likeness and Presence,* 146–9.

33 See Ouspensky, *Theology of the Icon,* 1, 112, on the emigration of large numbers of monastic iconographers to Italy in this period.

34 Boyle, *St. Clement's Rome,* 28, repeats a suggestion that 'the mosaic is simply a reproduction or, possibly, a remodelling on a smaller scale, of the mosaic that decorated the apse of the abandoned [4th-century] basilica below.' He adds (p. 30), 'The only element that is not typical, perhaps, is the Crucifixion scene in the centre. For here there seems to be a conflict between explicitness and symbolism that may be attributed to the twelfth-century resetting of the earlier motifs.'

35 Ibid., 12, 28.

36 For an account of this fire, see Mâle, *Early Churches*, 123–7.
37 Oakeshott, *The Mosaics of Rome*, 248.
38 Cf. Matthiae, *Mosaici medioevali*, 2, fig. 228.
39 Oakeshott, *The Mosaics of Rome*, 250.
40 *Ye Solace of Pilgrims*, A Description of Rome *circa* A.D. 1450 by John Capgrave. Text quoted by Boyle, in *St. Clement's Rome*, 79.
41 *De cruce Laurenti Paulo famulare docenti*, 'Lawrence, serve Paul teaching about the Cross.' *Respice promissum Clemens a me tibi Cristum*, 'Clement, regard Christ, whom I promised to you.' Boyle, *St. Clement's Rome*, 32, takes the speaker of the second verse to be Peter rather than Jeremiah.
42 Mâle, *Early Churches*, 132–3.
43 *Hec in honore tuo prefulgida, Mater honoris, / Regia divini rutilat fulgore decoris. / In qua, Criste, sedes manet ultra secula sedes. / Digna tuis dextris est, quam tegit aurea vestis. / Cum moles ruitura vetus foret, hinc oriundus / Innocentius hanc renovavit Papa Secundus*. Cf. Matthiae, *Mosaici medioevali*, 2, fig. 229; Oakeshott, *The Mosaics of Rome*, fig. 173.
44 Oakeshott, *The Mosaics of Rome*, 373.

Chapter 3: Portal Inscriptions, Liminal Transformation, and the Creation of Sacred Space

1 Mâle, *La fin du paganisme en Gaule*, 124, and n. 1. The inscription was recorded by the 10th-century chronicler Flodoard.
2 'Intus lux micat atque bratteatum / Sol sic sollicitatur ad lacunar, / Fulvo ut concolor erret in metallo.' Sidonius, *Epistulae* 2. 10 (lines 8–10) (Luetjohann, *Apollinaris Sidonii Epistulae et Carmina*, 33–5). Sidonius mentions the poems of Constantius and Secundinus in this letter to his friend Hesperius. The letters in book 2 were written before ca. 472 (Mommsen, in Luetjohann, li).
3 Unrhymed hexameters are found in the panels of Constantine and Melchisedech beneath the apsidal semidome mosaic of Sant'Apollinare.
4 E.g., *Cuius in humano consistunt pectore tenpla / Fundamen Petrus, Petrus fundator et aula* ..., 'The temple stands in the human heart of which Peter is the foundation, Peter is the founder, and the building ...' *Cunctaque sidereo percussa in murice saxa. / Autoris pretio splendescunt munera Petri* ..., 'And all the stones [are] stamped in gleaming purple. The gifts of the patron Peter become splendid with value ...'
5 *Huc veniens fundat parituros gaudia fletus / Contritam solidans percusso in pectore mentem / Ne iaceat, se sternat humo morbosque latentes / Ante pedes medici cura properante recludat. / Saepe metus mortis vitae fit causa beatae.*
6 As a technical term, *loca sancta* may be restricted to places visited by God. For

the most part these were in Palestine. I refer to the venerated sites of western Europe as 'holy places' to preserve the distinction.

7 The church for the monastery was constructed within the walls of the Roman villa sometime in the decade 361–71. It consisted of a rectangular nave with a semicircular apse. Oursel, *Invention*, 226–7.

8 It was built between 466 and 470. See Conant, *Carolingian and Romanesque Architecture*, 40–1, and n. 12 (p. 467).

9 Sidonius, *Epistulae* 4.18 (Luetjohann, *Apollinaris Sidonii Epistulae et Carmina*, 69–70).

10 Gregory, *Historiae Francorum*, 2.14 (Thorpe, *The History of the Franks*, 130).

11 Ibid., 5.37.

12 Quicherat, *Mélanges d'archéologie et d'histoire*, 32, and n. 1; Le Blant, *Inscriptions chrétiennes*, 1, 231–9 (nos. 170–3, 176). For the manuscripts, which are in the Bibliothèque nationale, see Le Blant, 1, 227–8, and 227, n. 2. The attribution of these poems to Sulpicius Severus is spurious: see Dekkers and Gaar, *Clavis Patrum Latinorum*, 110 (no. 478).

13 Quicherat's assumption (*Mélanges d'archéologie et d'histoire*, 32) that all the inscriptions, whether engraved, painted, or mosaic, accompanied *interior* decorations is unwarranted.

14 *Quisque solo adclinis mersisti in pulvere vultum, / Humidaque inlisae pressisti lumina terrae. / Attolens oculos, trepido miracula visu / Concipe et eximio causam committe patrono. / Nulla potest tantas complecti pagina vires, / Quanquam ipsa his titulis caementa et saxa notentur. / ... / Qui flens adfuerit, laetus redit; omnia cedunt / Nubila; quod meritum turbat, medicina serenat / Expete praesidium; non frustra haec limina pulsas. / In cunctum pergit pietas tam prodiga mundum.* Quicherat, *Mélanges d'archéologie et d'histoire*, 37–8 (lines 1–6, 22–5).

15 Ibid., 38.

16 *Quisquis templa Dei petiturus mente serena, / Ingrederis veniam culpis deposcere seris. / Non animo debes non titubare fide. / Quae petis impetras si puro pectore poscas. / Fides ut ipse ait, sic tua salus erit.* Le Blant, *Inscriptions chrétiennes*, 1, 233 (no. 172); Quicherat, *Mélanges d'archéologie et d'histoire*, 42.

17 Lasteyrie, *L'architecture religieuse*, 382, and n. 4, is certain that this tower could not have been located in front of the apse.

18 *Ingrediens templum refer ad sublimia vultum, / Excelsos aditus suspicit alta fides. / Esto humilis sensu sed spe sectare vocantem. / Martinus reserat quas venerare fores. / Haec tuta est turris trepidis obiecta superbis, / Elata excludens mitia corda tegens. / Celsior illa tamen quae coeli vexit ad arcem / Martinum astrigeris ambitiosa viis, / Unde vocat populos qui praevius ad bona Christi / Sidereum ingressus sanctificavit iter.* Le Blant, *Inscriptions chrétiennes*, 1, 231–2 (no. 170); Quicherat, *Mélanges d'archéologie et d'histoire*, 42.

19 *La fin du paganisme en Gaule*, 143. His argument for a crossing tower does not rest on this evidence alone.

20 *Intraturi aulam venerantes limina Christi / Pellite mundanas toto de pectore curas, / Et desideriis animum vacuate profanis. / Votorum compos remeat qui iusta precatur.* Le Blant, *Inscriptions chrétiennes*, 1, 233 (no. 171); Quicherat, *Mélanges d'archéologie et d'histoire*, 42.

21 Le Blant, *Inscriptions chrétiennes*, 1, 234–5 (no. 173); Quicherat, *Mélanges d'archéologie et d'histoire*, 36.

22 Le Blant, *Inscriptions chrétiennes*, 1, 235–6 (no. 174); Quicherat, *Mélanges d'archéologie et d'histoire*, 36–7.

23 *Sanctissima Christi ecclesia quae est mater omnium ecclesiarum. Quam fundaverant apostoli in qua descendit Spiritus Sanctus super apostolos. In specie ignis linguarum in ea positus est thronus Iacobi apostoli et columna in qua verberatus est Christus.* Le Blant, *Inscriptions chrétiennes*, 1, 236–7 (no. 175); Quicherat, *Mélanges d'archéologie et d'histoire*, 37. My punctuation indicates the arrangement of the lines in the manuscripts. It somewhat distorts the meaning.

24 Bede, *De Locis Sanctis* (Tobler, *Itinera*, 1, 218). Cf. Theodoric, *De Locis Sanctis* (Sandoli, *Itinera Hierosolymitana*, 2, 348, 354). Jerome mentions the column in Epistula 108, 9 (*Lettres*, 5, 167–8), and Prudentius describes it in *Dittochaeon* 41 (*Collected Works*, 2, 364–6).

25 Loerke, '"Real Presence" in Early Christian Art,' esp. 30–6 (quotation, p. 34). On the organization of the sites in Palestine, see further MacCormack, 'Loca Sancta,' 8–40; Wilkinson, 'Jewish Holy Places,' 42–53; and Sivan, 'Pilgrimage, Monasticism, and the Emergence of Christian Palestine,' 55–65.

26 Lienhard, *Paulinus of Nola*, 58–81, reviews the evidence and concludes that the label is appropriate.

27 Ibid., 24–8.

28 Sulpicius Severus, *Vita Sancti Martini*, chap. 19 (Fontaine, *Vie de Saint Martin*, 1, 292–5).

29 Lienhard, *Paulinus of Nola*, 29–32. See also Farmer, *The Oxford Dictionary of Saints*, s.v. 'Paulinus of Nola'; Goldschmidt, *Paulinus' Churches at Nola*, 3–6; Labriolle, *Histoire de la littérature latine chrétienne*, 481–7; Raby, *Christian-Latin Poetry*, 101–7.

30 In these early churches, the priest stood behind the altar and faced the congregation as he celebrated mass. See Mâle, *La fin du paganisme en Gaule*, 118–21; Nussbaum, *Der Standort des Liturgen am christlichen Altar*, 395–408. Waddell, 'The Reform of the Liturgy,' 96, describes the practice of priests' turning their backs on the congregation as being 'characteristic' by the year 1000, implying a rather long period of transition.

31 'Prospectus vero basilicae non, ut usitatior mos est, orientem spectat, sed ad

domini mei beati Felicis basilicam pertinet, memoriam eius adspiciens.' Paulinus, Epistula 32 (Goldschmidt, *Paulinus' Churches at Nola,* 40).

32 'Laetissimo vero conspectu tota simul haec basilica in basilicam memorati confessoris aperitur trinis arcubus paribus perlucente transenna, per quam vicissim sibi tecta ac spatia basilicae utriusque iunguntur. Nam quia novam a veteri paries abside cuiusdam monumenti interposita obstructus excluderet, totidem ianuis patefactus a latere confessoris quot a fronte ingressus sui foribus nova reserabatur, quasi diatritam speciem ab utraque in utramque spectantibus praebet, sicut datis inter utrasque ianuas titulis indicatur' (Goldschmidt, *Paulinus' Churches at Nola,* 40–2).

33 Conant, *Carolingian and Romanesque Architecture,* 39, fig. 3.

34 *Pleno coruscat trinitas mysterio: / Stat Christus agno, vox Patris caelo tonat, / Et per columbam Spiritus Sanctus fluit. / Crucem corona lucido cingit globo, / Cui coronae sunt corona apostoli, / Quorum figura est in columbarum choro. / Pia Trinitatis unitas Christo coit / Habente et ipsa trinitate insignia: / Deum revelat vox paterna et Spiritus, / Sanctam fatentur Crux et Agnus victimam, / Regnum et triumphum purpura et palma indicant. / Petram superstat ipse, petra ecclesiae, / De qua sonori quattuor fontes meant, / Evangelistae, viva Christi flumina.* Paulinus, Epistula 32 (Goldschmidt, *Paulinus' Churches at Nola,* 38, with minor adjustments of spelling and punctuation, here and below).

35 *Quam bene iunguntur ligno Crucis ossa piorum, / Pro Cruce ut occisis in Cruce sit requies!* Paulinus, Epistula 32 (Goldschmidt, *Paulinus' Churches at Nola,* 38–40, lines 9–10).

36 Epistula 32; see Lienhard, *Paulinus of Nola,* 97.

37 *Ut medium valli, pax nostra, resolvit Iesus / Et Cruce discidium perimens duo fecit in unum, / Sic nova destructo veteris discrimine tecti / Culmina conspicimus portarum foedere iungi.* Paulinus, Epistula 32 (Goldschmidt, *Paulinus' Churches at Nola,* 42, lines 1–4).

38 *Tergeminis geminae patuerunt arcubus aulae, / Miranturque suos per mutua limina cultus.* Paulinus, Epistula 32 (Goldschmidt, *Paulinus' Churches at Nola,* 44).

39 *Una fides trino sub nomine quae colit unum / Unanimes trino suscipit introitu.* Paulinus, Epistula 32 (Goldschmidt, *Paulinus' Churches at Nola,* 44).

40 *Pax tibi sit, quicumque Dei penetralia Christi / Pectore pacifico candidus ingrederis.* Paulinus, Epistula 32 (Goldschmidt, *Paulinus' Churches at Nola,* 40).

41 *Cerne coronatam Domini super atria Christi / Stare Crucem duro spondentem celsa labori / Praemia; tolle Crucem, qui vis auferre coronam.* Paulinus, Epistula 32 (Goldschmidt, *Paulinus' Churches at Nola,* 40).

42 *Caelestes intrate vias per amoena virecta, / Christicolae; et laetis decet huc ingressus ab hortis, / Unde sacrum meritis datur exitus in paradisum.* Paulinus, Epistula 32 (Goldschmidt, *Paulinus' Churches at Nola,* 40).

43 Paulinus, Carmen 27, lines 542–95; Carmen 28, lines 167–74 (Goldschmidt, *Paulinus' Churches at Nola*, 62–4, 80).

44 Paulinus, Carmen 28, lines 167–79 (Goldschmidt, *Paulinus' Churches at Nola*, 80).

45 Prudentius mentions Paulinus in his *Contra Orationem Symmachi* 1, lines 558-60 (Prudentius, *Collected Works*, 1, 392–3). Nothing further is known of their possible relationship.

46 The word is usually interpreted as 'twofold nourishment,' but it has been suggested that it might be a corruption of a word meaning 'bi-mural.' See Raby, *Christian-Latin Poetry*, 67, n. 1.

47 The *Dittochaeon* is edited and translated by Thompson, in Prudentius, *Collected Works*, 2, 346–71.

48 Raby, *Christian-Latin Poetry*, 67.

49 Davis-Weyer, *Early Medieval Art*, 25.

50 Ghellinck, *L'essor de la littérature latine*, 309, 401–2.

51 Mâle, *Religious Art, 12th Century*, 161; Schanz, *Geschichte der römischen Literatur*, 4:2, 389–91.

52 Bede, *Historia Abbatum* 9 (Webb and Farmer, *The Age of Bede*, 194).

53 See chapter 11.

54 Duemmler, *Poetae Latini Aevi Carolini*, 1, 326, line 11.

55 Lasteyrie, *L'architecture religieuse*, 38.

56 For these dates, see Conant, *Carolingian and Romanesque Architecture*, 475.

57 Catalogue no. 94a (Mozac).

58 The inscriptions at Tours were collected for the use of pilgrims, so that the designer might have seen them in a manuscript. See Vaucelle, *La collégiale de Saint-Martin de Tours*, 392.

59 Duemmler, *Poetae Latini Aevi Carolini*, 1, 305–47.

60 It is difficult to judge whether any of Fortunatus's poems were actually intended to be inscribed on the churches that they celebrate. See esp. Carm. 1.2–13; 2.7; 2.10–13; 10.5–6; 10.10–11 (Leo, ed., *Opera Poetica*, 8–15; 35–6; 39–42; 234–8; 244–6).

61 *Cum lapides vivi pacis compage ligantur, / Inque pares numeros omnia conveniunt, / Claret opus Domini totam qui construit aulam, / Effectusque piis dat studiis hominum, / Quorum perpetui decoris structura manebit, / Si perfecta Auctor protegat atque regat. / Sic Deus hoc tutum stabili fundamine templum, / Quod Carolus princeps condidit, esse velit.* This mosaic inscription dates from the 19th century, but replaces the original in red paint on white marble that went back to Charlemagne's time.

62 Horn and Born, *The Plan of St. Gall*, 3, 9. Haito retired as abbot of Reichenau in 823 but lived on until 836.

63 Kendall, 'The Plan of St. Gall,' 279, and n. 3.

64 As noted by Horn and Born, *The Plan of St. Gall*, 1, 13.

65 Ibid., 2, 268–70.

66 *Quaeque vides ospes pendencia celsa vel ima / Vir Domini Iosue struxit cum fratribus una*, 'Whatever lofty structures you see here, traveller, extending from low on high, were built by the servant of the Lord, Iosue, and his brother monks.' Mitchell, 'Literacy Displayed,' 205–9; text and translation, p. 207, and n. 38. See also Favole (with Del Vitto), *Abruzzes Molise romans*, 248–9.

67 CIVITATEM ISTAM / TV CIRCVMDA DomiNE ET / ANGELI TVI CVSTO/ DIANT MVROS EIVS. The plaque on the outside wall is a copy; the original has been removed to an interior wall in the second storey of the Emperor's gallery.

68 *Parvula Tecta Tenent*; Duemmler, *Poetae Latini Aevi Carolini*, 1, 332.

69 *Fercula Nostra Pius*; Duemmler, *Poetae Latini Aevi Carolini*, 1, 332.

70 *Qui Vim Ventorum*; Duemmler, *Poetae Latini Aevi Carolini*, 1, 321.

71 *Luxuriam ventris, lector, cognosce vorantis, / Putrida qui sentis stercora nare tuo. / Ingluviem fugito ventris quapropter in ore: / Tempore sit certo sobria vita tibi.* Duemmler, *Poetae Latini Aevi Carolini*, 1, 321.

72 *En Patet Ista Domus*; Duemmler, *Poetae Latini Aevi Carolini*, 1, 554–5. See also *Pauperibus Pateat, Praesul*; Duemmler, 1, 556.

73 *Qui Sim Nosse Volens* and *Qui Cupis Esse Bonus*; Duemmler, *Poetae Latini Aevi Carolini*, 1, 540.

74 *Percepi Numquam Quod* and *Pervigil Aeterna Mundum*; Duemmler, *Poetae Latini Aevi Carolini*, 2, 409.

75 *Haec Domus Officii*; Traube, *Poetae Latini Aevi Carolini*, 3, 296.

76 *Parva Domus Iugiter*; Traube, *Poetae Latini Aevi Carolini*, 3, 320.

77 *Corporis hic faciem lavo, sed peccamina mentis / Deluat, oro humilis, gratia summa Dei.* Traube, *Poetae Latini Aevi Carolini*, 3, 318.

78 *Hic redolere solent autumni pendula mala / Tempore, sed rigida diffugiunt hiemis.* Traube, *Poetae Latini Aevi Carolini*, 3, 323.

79 Judging from their paucity in Strecker, *Die lateinischen Dichter*, 5:1–2, and Silagi, *Die lateinischen Dichter*, 5:3.

80 Catalogue no. 67a (Lérins).

81 Catalogue no. 116a (Poitiers).

82 Catalogue no. 134a (Rothenkirchenhof).

83 Mérimée's report to the Minister of the Interior was instrumental in saving the basilica of Conques from being torn down. See Mérimée, 'Extrait d'un rapport,' 225–42.

84 Catalogue no. 36a (Conques).

85 Mérimée, 'Extrait d'un rapport,' 240.

86 Catalogue no. 37a (Conques).

87 In the building labelled 'Trésor II.'

Chapter 4: 'I am the door'

1 + EGO · SVM · OSTIVM · DICIT · DOMINVS · PER ME · SI QUIS · INTROIERIT · SALVABITVR · +

2 Demus, *The Mosaics of San Marco, 13th Century*, 68; pl. 102 (+ EGO SVM HOSTIVm Per ME SI Quis INTrOIERIT SALVABITVR ET PASCVA InVENiet). Demus notes that the inscription is also found above the main door at Grottaferrata.

3 On the lack of emphasis on the façade of early Roman basilicas, see Krautheimer, 'Carolingian Revival,' 29.

4 Hearn, *Romanesque Sculpture*, 26–31; Klein, 'Les portails. I: Saint Genis,' 121–42; 'Les portails. II: Saint-André-de-Sorède,' 159–72.

5 This evidence must be treated with caution – the façades of St-Genis and St-André have been rebuilt, and it has been argued that their lintels were originally intended as altar frontals, although this now seems unlikely. Klein, 'Les portails. I: Saint Genis,' 121–30, 142; 'Les portails. II: Saint–André-de-Sorède,' 170.

6 Mathews, *The Clash of Gods*, 142–76; esp. 150.

7 Durliat, *La sculpture romane*, 102–3. Durliat stresses the relationship, both in organization and in iconography, between the portals of St Emmeram and St-Sernin.

8 The *Pilgrim's Guide* is the fifth book of the *Liber Sancti Jacobi* or *Codex Calixtinus*, a collection of materials relating to the cult of St James the Greater and the pilgrimage to Compostela that was probably compiled between 1139 and 1173. The description of the basilica of Santiago in the *Guide* is based on reports that may date from 1122 to 1135 (Conant, *The Cathedral of Santiago de Compostela*, 23). The *Guide* describes the pilgrimage routes through France leading to the Pyrenees and thence across northern Spain to Compostela, and some of the important relics and churches to be found along the way. A convenient edition of the Latin text of the *Guide* is Vielliard, *Le guide du pèlerin* (with a French translation); an English version is Melczer, *The Pilgrim's Guide*. Conant, 49–58, translates the portion of the *Guide* that describes the basilica of Santiago.

9 'Super vero columpnam que est inter duos portales deforis in pariete, residet Dominus in sede majestatis et manu dextera benedictionem innuit et in sinistra librum tenet. Et in circuitu troni ejus sunt quatuor evangeliste quasi tronum sustinentes ...' (Vielliard, *Le guide du pèlerin*, 96–8), 'On a column erected between the two portals, on the outside wall, the Lord is seated in maj-

esty giving the blessing with his right hand while holding a book in the left. The four Evangelists are all around his throne, as if sustaining it' (Melczer, *The Pilgrim's Guide*, 123).

10 For a discussion of the complex history of the Romanesque portals of Santiago, see Durliat, *La sculpture romane*, 326–52.

11 Oursel, *Floraison*, 2, 346, puts the first appearances of the sculpted tympanum 'scarcely before the years 1080–1100.'

12 Christe, *Les grands portails romans*, 11; Durliat, *La sculpture romane*, 454.

13 It occurred to Mâle that the Christ in Majesty tympanum of Charlieu might be an Ascension (*Religious Art, 12th Century*, 405). Klein, 'Les portails. I: Saint Genis,' 141–2, finds the combination of these two themes (Second Coming and Ascension) in the lintels of St-Genis and St-André and situates them at the beginning of a series of portals that includes Charlieu, Cluny III, Anzy-le-Duc, and the north narthex portal of Charlieu.

14 The scheme of Christ in Majesty surrounded by the Four Animals can be traced back to Byzantine apse mosaics of the 5th century. See Mathews, *The Clash of Gods*, 115–17, and figs. 88–9.

15 For the possible priority of the tympanum of Cluny III and its relationship to the tympanum of Charlieu, see Hearn, *Romanesque Sculpture*, 132–9.

16 Catalogue no. 34a (Condeissiat).

17 Catalogue no. 144 (St-Paul-de-Varax).

18 Catalogue no. 144a (St-Paul-de-Varax).

19 Catalogue no. 174 (Vandeins).

20 Catalogue no. 174a (Vandeins).

21 Catalogue no. 174b (Vandeins). Mâle, *Religious Art, 12th Century*, 421, on the basis of this inscription, inferred that the intention of the artist was to symbolize the sacraments of Penance and the Eucharist in the Washing of the Feet and the Last Supper.

22 Salet, *La Madeleine de Vézelay*, 66–7, 162–7; Grivot and Zarnecki, *Gislebertus*, 174–5.

23 For a discussion of these verses and their relation to the tympanum, see chapter 6.

24 Actually, the orientation of the cathedral is almost NNW and the hill slopes down NW to the Arroux.

25 The statue of John the Baptist was not originally designed to project onto the lintel. See Salet, *La Madeleine de Vézelay*, 42.

26 Catalogue no. 186a (Vézelay).

27 Catalogue no. 185a (Vézelay).

28 Catalogue no. 166a–i (Toulouse).

29 These inscriptions echo the relief plaque of Christ in Majesty with the Four

Animals (ca. 1096), attributed to Bernard Gelduin, which is now in the ambulatory. It displays the letter R (= *rex*?) on the vertical arm of Christ's cruciform halo and the Alpha and Omega on the horizontal arms. See Catalogue no. 170 (Toulouse).

30 Schapiro, 'The Romanesque Sculpture of Moissac,' 203.

31 Durliat, *La sculpture romane*, 443, assigns the arrival of the tympanum master at Conques to ca. 1140.

32 Kendall, 'The Voice in the Stone,' 163–82.

33 Durliat, *La sculpture romane*, 165–7; *Haut-Languedoc roman*, 175–7.

34 For all of the inscriptions on the tympanum, see Catalogue no. 35 (Conques).

35 The word could be LEX, but REX seems more likely. See Bousquet, 'Les nimbes à anagramme,' 101, and n. 2.

36 Or could this be St Foy, as Mérimée ('Extrait d'un rapport,' 235) guessed? There are no particularizing details that permit a definitive identification.

37 See chapter 12.

38 Vielliard, *Le guide du pèlerin*, 4.

39 For a review of this claim and the reasons for its abandonment, see Simon, 'El tímpano de la catedral de Jaca,' 407–8.

40 Moralejo Alvarez, 'La sculpture romane de Jaca,' 79–85; 'Une sculpture à Jaca,' 7–10.

41 Simon, 'L'art roman,' 257–66.

42 Moralejo Alvarez, 'La sculpture romane de Jaca,' 99–105.

43 Durliat, *La sculpture romane*, 238–9. There is a prose inscription, in the voice of Christ, on the left third of the rim of the tympanum of the south transept portal of S. Isidoro. The tympanum is a composite of the Ascension (left), the Deposition (centre), and the Three Marys at the Tomb (right). The inscription in interlocked letters reads: + ASCENDO AD PATREM MEVm ET PATREM VestRuM, 'I ascend to my Father and your Father.'

44 Focillon, *The Art of the West*, 1, 118–33.

45 See chapter 11.

46 On the possible influence of the archivolts of south-western France on St-Denis and Chartres, see Stoddard, *Sculptors of the West Portals of Chartres Cathedral*, 178.

47 Gerson, 'The Iconography of the Trinity,' 73, argues that this is God the Father holding the Lamb and that with the Dove it is the first known representation of the Trinity in monumental sculpture.

48 Bousquet, 'Les nimbes à anagramme,' 103. At Fidenza, there is a sculpture of Christ and the expulsion of the rebel angels on a pilaster in the nave in which the halo of Christ is inscribed LVX. See Saporetti, *Iscrizioni romaniche*, 42.

49 Bousquet, 'Les nimbes à anagramme,' 111–12, cites two examples of PAX

arranged as an anagram on halos of Christ in the Evangelistary of Poussay (ca. 970–80) and a third example in the Bible of Saint-Vaast of Arras (ca. 1025–50).

50 Catalogue no. 177a (Verona).

51 Deschamps, 'Étude sur la paléographie,' 74; e.g., 1165, Vienne.

52 Gettings, *The Secret Zodiac*, 123.

Chapter 5: The Voice of Allegory

1 Krautheimer-Hess, 'The Original Porta Dei Mesi,' 158, and n. 65; Stocchi, *Émilie romane*, 368; Verzár Bornstein, *Portals and Politics*, 92, and n. 5 (p. 111).

2 Crosby, *The Royal Abbey of Saint-Denis*, 109.

3 Ong, *Orality and Literacy*, 96.

4 Catalogue no. 86a (Modena).

5 St Augustine says, 'African ears cannot distinguish between short and long vowels' (*Afrae aures de correptione vocalium aut productione non iudicant*; *De Doctrina Christiana*, 4.24); Nicolau, 'Versification latine accentuelle,' 57, says this was true in all parts of the Empire, even in Italy. See also Grandgent, *Vulgar Latin*, 75–6.

6 There is only one unquestionable 'spondaic' hexameter (that is, a hexameter with a spondee in the fifth foot) in the Catalogue: see no. 79b (Maastricht); one other is doubtful: see no. 137a (St-Aventin).

7 The origin of the term 'leonine' is uncertain. The earliest citation in *Le Petit Robert: Dictionnaire alphabétique et analogique de la langue française*, s.v. *léonin*, is 1175.

8 The tomb was constructed in 1542, and the epitaph was added in 1831. Although the verse as applied to Bede goes back only to the 17th century (see Plummer, *Venerabilis Baedae Opera Historica*, xlviii–xlix, and n. 1 [p. xlix]), the epitaphic formula with leonine rhyme *Hac sunt in fossa* [name + title] *ossa* can be traced to the epitaph of Bishop Egino of Verona, who died in 802 and was buried in the church he founded at Niederzell (Reichenau). See Strecker, 'Studien zu karolingischen Dichtern,' 211.

9 Malory, *Works* (bk. 21, chap. 4), 873.

10 Catalogue no. 44a (Dinton).

11 Strecker, 'Studien zu karolingischen Dichtern,' 218; *Introduction*, 74.

12 Beare, *Latin Verse and European Song*, 277.

13 Cited by Benson, 'Political *Renovatio*,' 371 (see also 374). The bull was issued in 1033.

14 Beare, *Latin Verse and European Song*, 277; Raby, *Secular Latin Poetry*, 1, 329–37.

15 In the first half of the pentameter, each of the first two feet may be either a

spondee or a dactyl and the half foot is a long syllable; in the second half, the first two feet must be dactyls and the half foot is a long syllable.

16 Catalogue no. 146a (St-Pé-de-Bigorre).

17 Given the number of imperfectly preserved and garbled verse inscriptions in the Catalogue, these figures are arbitrary and include some guesswork. For the record, I have not counted Catalogue nos. 19a (Bourges) (2 of 3), 27c and 27f (Clermont-Ferrand), 63a (Königslutter) (1 of 2), 66b (Lent), 68a (Loarre), 72a (Lucca), 79c (Maastricht), 92a (Moosburg), 102a (Parma), 126a and 126d (Ripoll), 127a (La Rochefoucauld), 128a (Roda de Isábena) (1 of 11), 140c (St-Georges-de-Camboulas), and 149a (St-Sever) (2 of 3).

18 Catalogue no. 87a (Modena).

19 Catalogue nos. 56a (Goslar), 63a (Königslutter), and 108b (Petershausen) (2×).

20 Catalogue nos. 59a (Huy), 81a (Mauriac), 154a (Sant Cugat), 156a (Sto Domingo de Silos), 166a (Toulouse), and 173a (Vaison-la-Romaine).

21 Catalogue nos. 107a (Parma) (actually, trisyllabic slant end rhyme: *sodales/ molares*) and 163c (Torre de Passeri).

22 Catalogue no. 47a (Estella).

23 Catalogue no. 174a (Vandeins).

24 Catalogue no. 42a (Dijon).

25 This group includes sporadic cases of monosyllabic end rhyme and non-leonine internal rhyme.

26 Catalogue no. 38a (Corneilla-de-Conflent).

27 Catalogue no. 124c (Regensburg).

28 There are only two instances of hiatus in the Catalogue. See nos. 116a (Poitiers) and 167a–d (Toulouse). Since elision was blocked by the consonant *h*, as it was not in classical Latin, unelided final vowel + initial *h* did not constitute hiatus. For an example, see Catalogue no. 11a (Autry-Issards).

29 Catalogue no. 46a (Elne).

30 Catalogue no. 84b (Milan).

31 See, for example, Isidore, *Etymologiae*, 7.9.19: 'Iudas Iacobi, qui alibi appellatur Lebbaeus, figuratum nomen habet a corde, quod nos diminutive corculum possumus appellare; ipse in alio evangelista Thaddaeus scribitur ...'

32 Norberg, *Introduction*, 32–3.

33 *Intratur(i) aulam veneransque limina Cristi.* Catalogue no. 94a (Mozac).

34 *Res miranda nimis mater De(i) erat vi nimis.* See Catalogue nos. 137a (St-Aventin) and 136a (Sahagún).

35 Kraus, *Living Theatre*, 45.

36 Catalogue no. 24a (Cîteaux).

37 Catalogue no. 26a (Cîteaux).

38 Catalogue no. 71a (Lucca).

39 For the fifth verse without a caesura, see Catalogue no. 161 (Tarascon).

40 Catalogue no. 43c (Dijon).

41 Catalogue no. 64a (La Land-de-Fronsac).

42 Catalogue nos. 41b (Dijon), 44a (Dinton), 109a (Piacenza), 116a (Poitiers) (2×), 133c (Rome), 164b (Toulouse), and 176a (Vercelli). Not counted is a feminine caesura in a conjectural restoration, Catalogue no. 126e (Ripoll).

43 Catalogue no. 6a (Arles).

44 This expansion follows Rouquette, *Provence romane*, 321. For the acrostic system, compare the epitaph of Abbot Benedict (d. ca. 1040) of the abbey of Montmajour, which spells out (in ten hexameter lines) *Benedictus abbas verus istic situs*, 'Benedict the true abbot is buried here.' *CIFM*, 14, 79–80.

Chapter 6: The Portal as Christ

1 Catalogue no. 124b (Regensburg).

2 Lange, *Die Byzantinische Reliefikone*, 31.

3 Bouillet, *Liber miraculorum* 1.13 (Sheingorn, *The Book of Sainte Foy*, 78).

4 Catalogue no. 189a (Vienne).

5 Catalogue no. 51a (Ferrara).

6 Catalogue no. 47a (Estella). According to Bugge, '*Effigiem Christi*,' 133–5, the couplet is found in the works of the Benedictines Hildebertus Cenomanensis (1054–1136) and Baudry of Bourgueil (1046–1130), who were acquaintances of each other, but it was perhaps already a commonplace. A 12th-century mosaic of Christ in the Cappella di S. Clemente of S. Marco in Venice is inscribed *Nam Deus est quod imago docet set non Deus ipsa / Hanc videas set mente colas quod noscis in ipsa* (Demus, *The Mosaics of San Marco, 11th and 12th Centuries*, 56; pl. 83). Similar verses were carved around the quadrilobed mandorla of Christ on a stone retable of the altar of St Firmin at St-Denis. Formigé, *L'abbaye royale de Saint-Denis*, 130, believes that the retable dates from the end of the twelfth or the beginning of the 13th century. He gives the inscription as *Hic Deus est et homo quem presens signat ymago / Ergo rogabit homo quem sculta figurat ymago.* A gilded monstrance of the beginning of the 13th century at St-Denis showed the figure of Christ with the inscription *Hic Deus est nec homo quem presens signat imago / Sed Deus est et homo quem sculpta figurat imago* (Guilhermy and Lasteyrie, *Inscriptions de la France*, 2, 123–4, cited by Favreau, 'L'inscription du tympan nord,' 240). By the time it reached St-Denis, the original sense of the couplet seems to have been lost.

7 Beigbeder and Oursel, *Forez-Velay roman*, 40; *CIFM*, 18, 55.

8 Beigbeder, *Lexique des symboles*, 354.

9 Catalogue no. 18a–b (Bourg-Argental).
10 'Prosopoeia [*sic*] est, cum inanimalium et persona et sermo fingitur ... Sic et montes et flumina vel arbores loquentes inducimus, personam inponentes rei quae non habet naturam loquendi.' Isidore, *Etymologiae*, 2.13.
11 Lattimore, *Themes in Greek and Latin Epitaphs*, 217.
12 See chapter 2.
13 *CIL*, 14 (no. 4123); Lindsay, *The Latin Language*, 188, 305.
14 Page, *Runes*, 23, 29.
15 Ibid., 28–9; Lehmann, *Germanic Verse Form*, 28–9.
16 Webster and Backhouse, *The Making of England*, 282–3.
17 Belting, *Likeness and Presence*, esp. 47.
18 Kendall, 'The Voice in the Stone,' 171–2.
19 *Ad fidei normam voluit Deus hanc dare formam, / Quae quasi praescriptum doceat cognoscere Christum: / De quo septenae sacro spiramine plenae / Virtutes manant, et in omnibus omnia sanant.* Marrier and Quercetanus, *Bibliotheca cluniacensis*, col. 1640.
20 For the inscriptions, see Hoving, 'The Bury St. Edmunds Cross,' 317–40; Beckwith, *Ivory Carving in Early Medieval England*, 141–3; Parker and Little, *The Cloisters Cross*, 52, 241–52.
21 Mac Lean, 'The Date of the Ruthwell Cross,' 49–70, esp. 69–70.
22 I base my translation on the text in Howlett, 'Inscriptions and Design of the Ruthwell Cross,' 88.
23 Dobbie, *The Anglo-Saxon Minor Poems*, 115.
24 Krapp, *The Vercelli Book*, 61–5.
25 Catalogue no. 86a (Modena).
26 From the *Sermo contra Judaeos, Paganos et Arianos*, attributed to Quodvultdeus, the bishop of Carthage (437–53), *PL*, 42, col. 1124; cf. Dan. 9:24. See Mâle, *Religious Art, 13th Century*, 167–8. Some of the same figures and inscriptions are found at Cremona, Fidenza, and Verona.
27 Crichton, *Romanesque Sculpture*, 33.
28 Catalogue no. 181i (Verona).
29 Catalogue no. 184a (Verona).
30 A mosaic of the Lamb of God in a circular frame appears, for example, in the vault of S. Vitale (6th century) in Ravenna. The Lamb of God in the keystone of the arch of the west-porch façade of S. Zeno of Verona, which is accompanied by a leonine hexameter spread out along the surface above the arch, is another example. The Lamb is not in a medallion and the verse does not encircle it. The leonine rhyme *magnus / Agnus* appeared in the first line of a poem that accompanied the great wall painting of the Last Judgment in the refectory of Cluny. The painting dated from the end of the 11th century. Another curi-

ous anticipation is the altar of 1050 of the cathedral of Besançon (for which see Tournier et al., *Franche-Comté romane*, 26, and pl. 82). This is a round table with a raised border that marks out eight interior lobes – spaces reserved for unconsecrated wafers. The Lamb of God is represented in a shallow relief in the flat central surface. A single hexameter is inscribed around the upper surface of the raised border, which reads (in the eight spaces formed by the lobes): HOC SIGNVM I PRAESITAT I POPVLIS I CAELESITIA I REGINA, 'this sign offers to the people the heavenly kingdom.' For the Lamb of God medallion with a verse inscription at Pont-l'Abbé-d'Arnoult, see chapter 11.

31 Conant, *Cluny*, 26, n. 23.

32 Catalogue no. 32a (Cluny).

33 The verse is not always recognized as such. Oursel, *Bourgogne romane*, 138, reads, 'Hic parvus sculpor [*sic*, omitting *ut*] Agnus / In celo magnus.'

34 Catalogue no. 7a (Armentia).

35 Catalogue no. 7b (Armentia). The verse is copied from the cloister portal of the monastery of S. Juan de la Peña (see Catalogue no. 151a).

36 Catalogue no. 7c (Armentia).

37 Catalogue no. 35 (Conques). The bracketed words and letters are not part of the carving. I give them to complete the sense.

38 Catalogue no. 12a (Autun).

39 Catalogue no. 12b (Autun).

40 Mâle, *Religious Art, 12th Century*, 418.

41 Catalogue no. 12c (Autun).

42 On this formula, see chapter 13. 'Gislebertus' is not certainly the name of the sculptor: see Oursel, *Evocation*, 144–7. In a forthcoming book, Linda Seidel will suggest that 'Gislebertus' designates a putative patron of Autun (personal communication).

Chapter 7: Portal Inscriptions as 'Performatives'

1 Text and translation, *The Divine Comedy*, ed. Singleton.

2 Catalogue no. 35g (Conques).

3 Balsan and Surchamp in Gaillard et al., *Rouergue roman*, 29–34.

4 Canellas López and San Vicente, *Aragon roman*, 235.

5 Whitehill, *Spanish Romanesque Architecture*, 243–4.

6 Riché, 'Recherches sur l'instruction des laïcs,' 175–82: for El Cid and his wife, see Riché, 176, and n. 10, and Fletcher, *The Quest for El Cid*, 109.

7 Austin, *How to Do Things with Words*, 22.

8 Ibid., 115.

9 See chapter 6.

10 Benveniste, 'The Nature of Pronouns,' in his *Problems in General Linguistics,* 217–22; 219.
11 Ibid., 220.
12 Austin accepts many varieties of written discourse as genuine performatives, or, ultimately, following his collapse of the categories of performatives and constatives, as illocutionary acts. Some of his illustrations of performative utterances, for example, are taken from legal texts.
13 See, for example, the portrait of St John in the Evangelistary of Liessies reproduced in H. Oursel et al., *Nord roman,* pl. 136.
14 Details summarized from Favière, *Berry roman,* 200–1.
15 Reported by Hubert, 'L'abbatiale Notre-Dame de Déols,' 46–57. Only a fragment of the tympanum and the Lamb-of-God keystone of the inner archivolt remain. These are displayed in the Musée Bertrand in Châteauroux.
16 The adoring angels of the inner archivolt at Déols corresponded to the twenty-four Elders of the archivolts of the central (Christ in Majesty) tympanum of Chartres; the arts and sciences of the middle archivolt corresponded to the Seven Liberal Arts of the right (Incarnation) tympanum of Chartres; the Works of the Months of the outer archivolt corresponded to the archivolt of the left (Ascension) tympanum of Chartres.
17 Catalogue no. 40a (Déols). Weisbach, *Religiöse Reform,* 204, n. 106, calls attention to the inscription, *adest porta per quam iusti redeunt ad patriam,* 'this is the door through which the just return to their native land,' which appears around an ornamented door pull on the west portal of the church of Ébreuil in the Auvergne.
18 Catalogue no. 40b (Déols).
19 Catalogue no. 40c (Déols). The first verse of this couplet does not make sense in Father Dubouchat's transcription.
20 Hancher, 'Performative Utterance,' 36.
21 On the presence of illiterates and semiliterates in 'medieval textual communities' and the routine expectation that they would 'participate in textual culture, having the necessary texts, and their interpretation, read to them,' see Irvine, 'Medieval Textuality,' 185, and n. 11 (p. 277).
22 Belting, *Likeness and Presence,* 192.
23 On the fallacy of the assumption that religious art by itself could be directly 'read' by illiterates, see Duggan, 'Was Art Really the "Book of the Illiterate?,"' 227–51.

Chapter 8: Conditional Transcendence

1 Melczer, *The Pilgrim's Guide,* 121. Latin text, Vielliard, *Le guide du pèlerin,* 90–2.

2 Inscriptions enable us to identify the bishops. See Catalogue no. 118 (La Porcherie).
3 Catalogue no. 118a (La Porcherie).
4 The earliest examples are at Modena (Verzár Bornstein, *Portals and Politics*, 34). Other meanings or functions are not excluded. It is frequently asserted (e.g., Melzcer, *The Pilgrim's Guide*, n. 460 [p. 207]) that the lions have the apotropaic function of guarding the door. Likewise, 'It has been suggested that the location of lions as symbols of authority and justice flanking a portal, *inter leonese*, marks the place where jurisdictional matters were judged.' (Stoddard, *Façade of Saint-Gilles*, 54). Verzár Bornstein, 36, suggests that the lion 'became a potent symbol of papal Rome and of the *Ecclesia Romana* itself, representing the Holy City and the *imperium romanum* now governed by the popes.'
5 See, for example, Bruno of Asti, *De Sacramentis Ecclesiae*, *PL*, 165, col. 1092 (quoted in chapter 1); Honorius Augustodunensis, *Gemma Animae* 1, chap. 131, *PL*, 172, col. 586.
6 The two lateral portals were probably transferred from the nave flanks to the west façade at the beginning of the 13th century. See Quintavalle, 'Piacenza Cathedral,' 52–4.
7 The lions of the central porch are restored (Verzár Bornstein, *Portals and Politics*, 66), but the lions of the lateral porches are original.
8 The sculptures are 19th-century replicas; the originals are in the Museo del Duomo. See Verzár Bornstein, *Portals and Politics*, 93.
9 Ibid., n. 14 (p. 46).
10 Schapiro, 'The Romanesque Sculpture of Moissac,' 250–1.
11 Now Oloron-Ste-Marie.
12 Durliat and Allègre, *Pyrénées romanes*, 293.
13 Whitehill, *Spanish Romanesque Architecture*, 164, n. 4.
14 Catalogue no. 156a (Sto Domingo de Silos).
15 Verzár Bornstein, *Portals and Politics*, 60; 'Text and Image,' 132–3.
16 Compare the hexameter inscription for the cross above the Altar of the Holy Cross on the Plan of St Gall: *crux pia vita salus miserique redemptio mundi*, 'Holy cross, the life, salvation, and redemption of the wretched world.'
17 Leyerle, 'The Rose-Wheel Design,' 283, 287–9, 302–3. In addition to S. Zeno, there are extant four other wheel windows with figures on the rim: in the north transept of St-Étienne of Beauvais (ca. 1120–40); in the north transept of the cathedral of Basel (late 12th century); in the north transept of the cathedral of Trento (ca. 1200–20); and in the south transept of the cathedral of Amiens (2nd half of 13th century) (Leyerle, 283, and n. 5 [p. 306]).
18 Catalogue no. 184a–b (Verona). Fortune is visually depicted on the hub at

Trento and in Villard de Honnecourt's drawing of a wheel window. See Leyerle, 'The Rose-Wheel Design,' 283, and figs. 2–3.

19 On labyrinths in medieval churches, see Doob, *The Idea of the Labyrinth*, 117–33.

20 Ibid., 118–21.

21 *Hunc mundum tipice laberinthus denotat iste, / Intranti largus, redeunti set nimis artus. / Sic mundo captus, viciorum mole gravatus, / Vix valet ad vite doctrinam quisque redire.* Kern, *Labirinthi*, 211.

22 *Theseus intravit monstrumque biforme necavit.* Kern, *Labirinthi*, 210. The Minotaur is depicted as a centaur; hence, it is *biforme.*

23 Doob, *The Idea of the Labyrinth*, 127.

24 Matthews, *Mazes and Labyrinths*, 56; Kern, *Labirinthi*, 206.

25 See the Invention of the Holy Cross, in Jacobus de Voragine, *The Golden Legend*, 269–76.

26 Catalogue no. 44a (Dinton).

27 Cf. John 15:1–17.

28 Catalogue no. 119a (Puilampa).

29 Katzenellenbogen, *Allegories of the Virtues and Vices*, 1–13.

30 Seidel, *Songs of Glory*, 49–50.

31 For Aulnay, south portal, see Oursel, *Haut-Poitou roman*, 311–29.

32 Katzenellenbogen, *Allegories of the Virtues and Vices*, 17, calls this the earliest example of the portrayal of the triumph of virtue over vice in the archivolts of Saintonge and Poitou. He dates the south transept to ca. 1130.

33 Durliat and Allègre, *Pyrénées romanes*, 311–16.

34 Laplace, *Notice sur l'église*, 9, notes that the chrismon consists of a Greek cross with the four majuscule letters P/F/A/O, which he explains as standing for 'the beginning and the end' (*principium/finis/alpha/omega*). Unless there are four small letters that I am unable to see inscribed somewhere in the chrismon, Laplace must be referring to the *alpha* and *omega* hanging from the upper arms of the *chi*, and to the *rho* that has a crossbar beneath the upper loop (there is also an S entwined about the lower arm of the descender of the *rho*). I do not think the latter could be interpreted as a P + F.

35 Simon, 'El tímpano de la catedral de Jaca,' 407–19.

36 Catalogue no. 74a (Luz-St-Sauveur).

37 Catalogue no. 74b (Luz-St-Sauveur).

38 Simon, 'El tímpano de la catedral de Jaca,' 414–15.

39 White, *The Bestiary*, 187; Simon, 'El tímpano de la catedral de Jaca,' esp. 413–14.

40 Catalogue no. 75a (Luz-St-Sauveur).

41 Catalogue no. 75b (Luz-St-Sauveur).

42 Lambert, 'L'ancienne abbaye de Saint-Pé de Bigorre,' 109–27.

43 Ibid., 119; Pomès and Michel, *L'église de Saint-Pé-de-Bigorre*, 27. The word LEONES on the lower edge of the tympanum, all that can be read of another inscription, supports the assumption of Lambert and of Pomès and Michel that the tympanum depicted affronted lions. The lions themselves can be interpreted as figures of Christ, although I do not believe that that meaning is the dominant one. Affronted lions supporting a central figure or image representing Christ have more in common with lions supporting columns on either side of a portal.

44 Catalogue no. 146a (St-Pé-de-Bigorre).

Chapter 9: Anagogical Allegory and Imagery

1 Catalogue no. 52 (Fidenza).

2 Duemmler, *Poetae Latini Aevi Carolini*, 1, 326.

3 Catalogue nos. 13a (Barcelona) and 145a (St-Pé-de-Bigorre).

4 Porter, 'Iguácel and More Romanesque Art of Aragón,' 115–16; see also Porter, *Spanish Romanesque Sculpture*, 1, 63; Canellas López and San Vicente, *Aragon roman*, 165–89.

5 HEC EST PORTA DomiNI VNDE INGREDIVNTVR FIDELES IN DOMVM DomiNI QVE EST ECGLESIA IN HO~~NO~~RE SanCtE MARIE FVN|DATA : IVSSV SAN~~CI~~ONI COMITIS EST FABRI~~CA~~TA / VNA CVm SVA CONIVGE NomiNE VRRA~~CC~~A : IN ERA T : CENTE~~SI~~MA XA EST EXPLI~~CI~~TA : REGNANTE REGE SAN~~CI~~O R[A]DI~~MI~~RIZ IN ARAGONE QVI POSVIT PRO SVA ANI~~MA~~ IN HO~~NO~~RE SanCtE MA~~RI~~E : VI~~LLA~~[m?] \ NomiNE LA\RR~~OS~~SA VT DE~~T EI~~ DomiNuS RE~~QVI~~EM AM \ AMEN \

Superscript words and syllables in blocks nine and ten are marked by left-sloping virgules (\). The final letters of the line, which other scholars have transcribed as *eternam*, are very worn and very uncertain. I see, faintly, the superimposed letters *am*, which might correspond to the *amen* carved above the line. There is not sufficient room for *eternam* unless it was radically abbreviated. Cf. Durán Gudiol, 'Las inscripciones medievales,' 76 (no. 4). The transcriptions of Porter and of Canellas López and San Vicente, *Aragon roman*, 187, differ in some details.

6 Durliat, *La sculpture romane*, 253–4.

7 Simson, *The Gothic Cathedral*, xv; 44, n. 57.

8 Catalogue no. 68a (Loarre).

9 However, Porter's remark (*Spanish Romanesque Sculpture*, 1, 70) that it is 'a debased copy of the one at Jaca' is misleading.

10 Catalogue no. 152a (Sta Cruz de la Serós).

11 Whitehill, *Spanish Romanesque Architecture*, 251, n. 2.
12 Ibid., 252.
13 Canellas López and San Vicente, *Aragon roman*, 77.
14 Catalogue no. 151a (S. Juan de la Peña).
15 Whitehill, *Spanish Romanesque Architecture*, 253–5.
16 Canellas López and San Vicente, *Aragon roman*, 78.
17 Ibid., 77–8.
18 Duemmler, *Poetae Latini Aevi Carolini*, 1, 306.
19 Buchowiecki, *Handbuch*, 1, 91.
20 Catalogue nos. 7b (Armentia) and 119a (Puilampa).
21 *Sponsa Deo* [sic] *gigno natos ex virgine Virgo, / Quos fragiles firmo, fortes super aethera mitto.* Cf. Demus, *The Mosaics of San Marco, 11th and 12th Centuries*, 22; pls. 14–15. Kloos (Demus, *The Mosaics of San Marco, 11th and 12th Centuries*, n. 21 [p. 383]) regards DEO as the work of a 'later, restoring hand,' and notes that the original reading must have been DEI.
22 Demus, *The Mosaics of San Marco, 11th and 12th Centuries*, 22.
23 *Ecclesiae Cristi vigiles sunt quattuor isti, / Quorum dulce melos sonat et movet undique celos.* Cf. Demus, *The Mosaics of San Marco, 11th and 12th Centuries*, 22; pls. 14–15.
24 Demus, *The Mosaics of San Marco, 11th and 12th Centuries*, 29. Although Demus declares, n. 12 (p. 316), that the inscriptions *might* have been added later, his collaborator, the palaeographer Rudolf M. Kloos (*The Mosaics of San Marco, 11th and 12th Centuries*, 296–7), dates the inscriptions to the same period (1060/90) as the mosaics (in Kloos's chapter on the palaeography of the inscriptions).
25 'An unresolved problem is presented by the fact that the inscription of the frame, "Janua sum vite," etc., cannot be later than 1230 – and is probably a good deal earlier – for palaeographic reasons (according to Dr. R. M. Kloos: letter of 1 January 1979); the ornamental motif is also early in character; the frame would thus have preceded the mosaic by a considerable time. This could be explained in several ways: (1) the frame may have remained empty in the intermediate period; (2) it may have been filled with a fresco, to be replaced by the present mosaic; (3) an early mosaic may have been replaced by the present one because of damage or for other reasons, iconographic or artistic' (Demus, *The Mosaics of San Marco, 13th Century*, n. 343 [p. 245]).
26 Demus, ibid., 68.
27 Ibid.
28 Meier, *Suisse romane*, 171.
29 Colombo, *San Giorgio al Palazzo*, 16.
30 Reproduced by Colombo, *San Giorgio al Palazzo*, pl. 1.

31 Catalogue no. 85a (Milan).
32 Evans, *Romanesque Architecture*, 29, n. 8; Rouquette, *Provence romane*, 50.
33 Catalogue no. 142a (St-Marcel-lès–Sauzet).
34 'Et hoc nomen Adam diuino instinctu constat uxori suae posuisse, quod aptissime congruit ecclesiae sanctae, in cuius solum unitate quae "catholica" uocatur uitae cunctis ianua patet.' Bede, *In Genesim* 1 (*CC*, 118A, 69).
35 Catalogue no. 150b (Salzburg).
36 Catalogue no. 150a (Salzburg).
37 Ragusa, '*Porta patet vitae*,' 346, n. 6.
38 Catalogue no. 48a–c (Esztergom).
39 Catalogue no. 48d (Esztergom).
40 Junyent, *Catalogne romane*, 2, 50–75; for the date of the foundation, see p. 50; for the date of the construction, see p. 73. Porter, *Spanish Romanesque Sculpture*, 1, 71, associates the west portal with the foundation of the monastery in 1117. In light of the probable (to me) dependence of the portal decoration on Maguelone (see below), Porter's inference seems untenable.
41 Catalogue no. 13 (Barcelona). The inscription is so badly worn that it cannot be read with certainty. Another possibility is that Renard gave seven gold coins (*Mo[r]abitinos*) for the project. See Junyent, *Catalogne romane*, 2, 73.
42 Catalogue no. 13a (Barcelona).
43 Lugand, Nougaret, and Saint-Jean, *Languedoc roman*, 231–3.
44 For the probable existence of this hypothetical earlier tympanum at Maguelone, see Lugand, Nougaret, and Saint-Jean, *Languedoc roman*, 235–6.
45 Catalogue no. 80a (Maguelone).

Chapter 10: Moral Allegory

1 William Durandus, in the 14th century, defined tropology as 'an injunction unto morality; or a moral speech, either with a symbolical or an obvious bearing, devised to evince and instruct our behaviour.' Durandus, *The Symbolism of Churches*, 6–7.
2 Catalogue no. 21a (Cassan).
3 In France they would include the cathedrals of Le Puy and Maguelone and the monastic churches of Cassan, Conques, Luz-St-Sauveur, St-Marcel-lès-Sauzet, St-Paul-de-Mausole, and St-Paul-de-Varax; in Italy, the cathedrals of Modena and Pistoia; in the Netherlands, the monastic church of Egmond Binnen; and in Spain, the cathedral of Jaca and the monastic church of Sta Cruz de la Serós.
4 Catalogue no. 120a (Le Puy).
5 Catalogue no. 123a (Le Puy).

6 Paul and Paul, *Notre-Dame du Puy*, 79; see the drawing of Mallay, reproduced by Paul and Paul, facing p. 70.
7 Catalogue no. 122a (Le Puy).
8 Paul and Paul, *Notre-Dame du Puy*, 6.
9 Catalogue no. 121a (Le Puy).
10 Moralejo Alvarez, 'Aportaciones,' 173–98; 'La sculpture romane de Jaca,' 94–5; Caldwell, 'Penance, Baptism, Apocalypse,' 25–40.
11 See Kendall, 'The Verse Inscriptions of Jaca,' from which this chapter is, in part, adapted.
12 Gaillard, 'Notes,' 233–5, calls attention to Hugh of St-Victor's discussion of the Christological symbolism of the lion, which is, in turn, grounded in the Bestiaries. The biblical source for this symbolism is Apocalypse 5:5: 'behold the lion of the tribe of Juda, the root of David, hath prevailed to open the book, and to loose the seven seals thereof.'
13 Ibid., 234–5, and n. 18.
14 *Speculum Ecclesiae*, *PL*, 172, cols. 913–15. Mâle, *Religious Art, 13th Century*, 46–8, calls attention to the interpretation of Honorius.
15 Simon, 'El tímpano de la catedral de Jaca,' 411–13: 'Teniendo en cuenta que la serpiente pierde su piel tras cuarenta días de ayuno, puede entenderse como un símbolo del "hombre viejo" que se despoja de sus vestiduras' (412).
16 Whitehill, *Spanish Romanesque Architecture*, 240; Weisbach, *Religiöse Reform*, 125–6; Moralejo Alvarez, 'La sculpture romane de Jaca,' 93, etc. By contrast, Gaillard ('Notes,' 234–5; *Les débuts de la sculpture romane espagnole*, 108) identifies it as the asp because it approaches its head to the ground (the asp was said to press one ear to the ground and to put its tail in the other to shut out the alluring songs of an approaching snake-charmer).
17 Weisbach, *Religiöse Reform*, 125–6; for additional references, see Caamaño Martínez, 'En torno al tímpano de Jaca,' 206–7, and n. 34.
18 Catalogue no. 61b (Jaca).
19 'Circa hominem leonum natura est ut nisi laesi nequeant irasci. Patet enim eorum misericordia exemplis assiduis. Prostratis enim parcunt ...' *Etymologiae*, 12.2.6.
20 Catalogue no. 61c (Jaca).
21 Pliny, *Naturalis Historia*, 8.57.136.
22 Solinus, *Collectanea Rerum Memorabilium*, 27.21–2.
23 Isidore, *Etymologiae*, 12.2.34.
24 McCulloch, *Mediaeval Latin and French Bestiaries*, 34–8.
25 White, *The Bestiary*, 11. The Latin text in the Cambridge manuscript is taken word for word from Solinus (not Isidore, as stated by McCulloch, *Mediaeval Latin and French Bestiaries*, 138), the only variants being *leontophontes* for *leon-*

tophonos and *modicas bestias* for *bestias modicas*: 'Leontophontes vocari accipimus modicas bestias, quae captae exuruntur, ut earum cineris aspergine carnes pollutae iactaeque per conpita concurrentium semitarum leones necent, si quantulumcumque ex illis sumpserint. Propterea leones naturali eas premunt odio atque ubi facultas data est, morsu quidem abstinent, sed dilancinatas exanimant pedum nisibus.' I am grateful to my colleague David Wallace for examining this manuscript for me.

26 On the widespread utilization of Solinus in the earlier Middle Ages and especially in the 12th century, see Ghellinck, *L'essor de la littérature latine*, 306.

27 Durliat, *La sculpture romane*, 227, 230, and 245.

28 Simon, 'L'art roman,' 266.

29 Catalogue no. 61d (Jaca).

30 Catalogue no. 61a (Jaca).

31 For details, see Kendall, 'The Verse Inscriptions of Jaca,' 412.

32 Simon, 'El tímpano de la catedral de Jaca,' 415–18.

33 Cf. Isidore, *Etymologiae*, 1.4.14; Bede, *De Arte Metrica* 1 (*CC*, 123A, 85).

34 My argument for *duplex* = X has been independently corroborated by Esteban, 'Las inscripciones del tímpano de la Catedral de Jaca,' 143–61.

35 Hrabanus Maurus, *Allegoriae in Sacram Scripturam*, *PL*, 112, col. 1016, glosses *pax* as 'penitence' and 'Christ.' See also Honorius Augustodunensis, *Gemma Animae*, *PL*, 172, col. 563.

36 Werckmeister, 'The Lintel Fragment from Autun,' esp. 21–3.

37 Moralejo Alvarez, 'La sculpture romane de Jaca,' 96, and Caldwell, 'Penance, Baptism, Apocalypse,' n. 55 (p. 39), point out the relevance to Jaca of Werckmeister's discussion of Autun.

38 Caldwell, 'Penance, Baptism, Apocalypse,' 28–35.

39 Andrieu, *Ordines romani*. The rite of public penitence is found on pp. 108–24 (Ash Wednesday) and pp. 192–207 (Maundy Thursday). See Werckmeister, 'The Lintel Fragment from Autun,' 17–21.

40 Vogel and Elze, *Le pontifical romano-germanique*, 14–21; 59–67.

41 *De synodalibus causis* 1.295 (Wasserschleben, *Reginonis abbatis Prumiensis*, 136).

42 *Decretum* 19.26, *PL*, 140, col. 984; also in Andrieu, *Ordines romani*, appendix I, pp. 367–8.

43 Vogel, 'Les rites de la pénitence publique,' 138–44.

44 Werckmeister, 'The Lintel Fragment from Autun,' 18–19.

45 To be sure, he is not literally on his elbows, but the discrepancy is not, I think, significant.

46 The identification of this figure as an image of the penitent described in the rite of public penitence is made by Moralejo Alvarez, 'La sculpture romane de Jaca,' 94–5.

47 Vogel, 'Les rites de la pénitence publique,' 144.
48 'Diverte a malo et fac bonum, / inquire pacem et persequere eam.'
49 Bousquet, 'Les nimbes à anagramme,' 101–21.
50 Williams, 'The *Moralia in Iob* of 945,' 225–6, and fig. 4. The Cross Page is Córdoba Cath., cod. 1, f. 2v.
51 *CIFM,* 10 (*Chrismes du sud-ouest*), esp. 5–12; Mesplé, 'Les chrismes du département du Gers'; Sené, 'Quelques remarques'; Torres Balbás, 'La escultura románica aragonesa.' Caamaño Martínez, 'En torno al tímpano de Jaca,' n. 24 (p. 207), provides a bibliography.
52 *CIFM,* 10, 115–16, 121, 148–9, 158, 190–1, 202–3.
53 Mesplé, 'Les chrismes du département du Gers,' 80 (note the substitution of CRVX for PAX). I have been unable to locate the chrismon.
54 Beigbeder, *Lexique des symboles,* 327 (s.v. 'nombres: six').
55 *CIFM,* 10, 100. The same design appears on a chrismon of a tympanum (12th/13th century) in the church of St-Vincent of Les Peintures: see *CIFM,* 10, 109.
56 Cf. Mesplé, 'Les chrismes du département du Gers,' 80.
57 Ibid., 73. I have been unable to find this chrismon.
58 Catalogue no. 127 (La Rochefoucauld).
59 Cited by Raby, *Secular Latin Poetry,* 1, 330.
60 Catalogue no. 86a (Modena). The Genesis frieze is on the west façade; the admonitory portal at Modena is the Royal Portal of the south façade.
61 Catalogue no. 113a (Pistoia). This is the voice of Christ speaking to Doubting Thomas and the other apostles carved on the lintel.
62 Catalogue no. 152a (Sta Cruz de la Serós).
63 Catalogue no. 124c (Regensburg).
64 Catalogue no. 7a (Armentia).
65 Catalogue nos. 13a (Barcelona), 85a (Milan), 142a (St-Marcel-lès-Sauzet), and 191a (Wrocław).
66 Catalogue no. 152a (Sta Cruz de la Serós).
67 Belting, *Likeness and Presence,* 313, n. 12 (p. 587), and fig. 193.
68 But note the 10th-century chrismon with *pax* in the Château de Herrebouc, cited above.
69 Gaillard, 'Notes,' 233; Sené, 'Quelques remarques,' 374.
70 In Canellas López and San Vicente, *Aragon roman,* 233: 'ses [the chrismon's] signes alphabétiques sont placés successivement en tournant dans le sens des aiguilles d'une montre, de sorte que les yeux en font la lecture selon un circuit continu et fermé, depuis la première lettre jusqu'à la dernière, contrairement à la lecture en croix qu'impose la distribution habituelle des signes composant l'anagramme du Christ ...'
71 Ocón Alonso, '*Tímpanos románicos,*' 1, 106–10. See also Durliat, in Durliat and

Allègre, *Pyrénées romanes,* 203. The identical configuration occurs in the chrismon on the tympanum of the south portal of Bossòst. I take this to be a slightly later copy (Durliat tentatively assigns it to the beginning of the 13th century).

72 This may be a displacement of the crossbar that frequently, and here as well, appears in chrismons on the staff of the Rho (elsewhere, e.g., on the Tomb of Doña Sancha at Jaca), and which functions as a sign of abbreviation.

73 Mesplé, 'Les chrismes du département du Gers,' 85, and fig. 4.

74 Durand, 'Roues symboliques,' 119–20. Durand's interpretation failed to convince Mesplé ('Les chrismes du département du Gers,' 80), but deserves to be reconsidered.

75 Bousquet, 'Les nimbes à anagramme,' 103, accepts these letters as original, and Fau, *Rouergue roman,* 331–2, records the inscription without questioning it. But see Gaillard, in Gaillard et al., *Rouergue roman,* 230.

76 Vielliard, *Le Guide du pèlerin,* 98–102. Hearn, *Romanesque Sculpture,* 145, points out that the description in the *Guide* 'can represent only a remodeling which took place before 1139, the earliest date when Picaud [the supposed author of the Guide] could have written.'

77 Chamoso Lamas et al., *Galice romane,* 102.

78 Ibid., pl. 25.

79 Deguileville, *Le pèlerinage de la vie humaine,* 1, 2531–59 (Clasby, ed., *The Pilgrimage of Human Life,* 35). See Keen, 'Documenting Salvation,' 6–7.

Chapter 11: Visions of Allegory

1 For Parthenay-le-Vieux, west portal, see Dillange, *Vendée romane,* 115; for St-Symphorien, west portal, see Eygun, *Saintonge romane,* 184–6.

2 Eygun, *Saintonge romane,* 89–91.

3 Mendell, *Romanesque Sculpture in Saintonge,* 62, calls the façade 'probably the oldest in Saintonge on which iconographic sculpture appears.'

4 In recent years, the theme of this archivolt has been accepted as being the Massacre of the Innocents, an identification originally made by Mendell, *Romanesque Sculpture in Saintonge,* 63. See Eygun, *Saintonge romane,* 95–6; Seidel, *Songs of Glory,* 45. In an as yet unpublished paper, Marguerite Ragnow shows that the older interpretation of the archivolt as representing Holy Martyrdom is undoubtedly to be preferred, and she finds a plausible source for the theme in Prudentius's collection of hymns on various early martyrs, the *Peristephanon Liber.* I am indebted to Ragnow for allowing me to benefit from the results of her investigations into the Abbaye aux Dames.

5 Beigbeder, *Lexique des symboles,* 306: 'les masques, images de l'enfer, menacent ceux qui restent inactifs ...'

6 For Aulnay, west portal, see Tonnellier, *Aulnay de Saintonge*, 28–32; and Oursel, *Haut-Poitou roman*, 329–31. Katzenellenbogen, *Allegories of the Virtues and Vices*, 18, dates the west portal to ca. 1140. Seidel, *Songs of Glory*, 51–4, discusses the allegorical symbolism of Aquitainian façades, and especially the west façade of Aulnay.

7 According to Tonnellier, *Aulnay de Saintonge*, 28, the beast on the left of Cancer is Leo the Lion (and he notes the same inversion on the west façade of Notre-Dame of Paris). I am unsure of this identification. It is an odd pose for a lion.

8 In the Roman calendar dates were reckoned backwards from three fixed points in the month, the calends, the nones, and the ides. The calends of July = 1 July, the second calends = 30 June, etc. The winter solstice occurred on the eighth calends of January (= 25 December); the vernal and autumnal equinoxes on the eighth calends of April (= 25 March) and October (= 24 September). In reckoning Easter the vernal equinox was taken to occur on the twelfth calends of April (= 21 March) rather than the eighth calends (= 25 March). See Bede, *De Temporum Ratione* 30.

9 Tonnellier, *Aulnay de Saintonge*, 29–30.

10 See, for example, Isidore, *De Natura Rerum*, 15.3, *PL*, 83, col. 988: 'At vero juxta spiritualem intelligentiam, sol Christus est, sicut in Malachia scriptum est: Vobis autem credentibus justitiae sol orietur, et sanitas in pinnis ejus.'

11 The sign is no longer visible at Argenton-Château, but it can be inferred with virtual certainty.

12 According to Katzenellenbogen, *Allegories of the Virtues and Vices*, 18, and 19, n. 1 (following Porter, *Romanesque Sculpture*, 1, 333), the west portals of Argenton-Château and Aulnay are the work of the same artist. He dates Argenton-Château ca. 1135, Aulnay ca. 1140, Fenioux ca. 1150, and Civray ca. 1165.

13 Occasionally, the sign designated the month in which it spent the greater amount of time. Capricorn = January at Chartres. See Mâle, *Religious Art, 13th Century*, 69–71.

14 Sanoner, 'Analyse du portail,' 401.

15 Grivot and Zarnecki, *Gislebertus*, 29.

16 Ibid., 24, fig. j.

17 Beigbeder, *Lexique des symboles*, s.v. 'acrobate.'

18 Ibid., s.v. 'zodiaque.'

19 Chaucer, *Troilus and Criseyde* 1.4.

20 It was this detail, which is not mentioned in the gospel text, that led Mâle, *Religious Art, 12th Century*, 152–3, to link the theme of the Wise and Foolish Virgins in art to the liturgical drama of the Virgins that was performed at St-Martial of Limoges from the beginning of the 12th century.

21 The inscriptions read from left to right: IRA PACIENCIA : LVXVRIA : CASTITAS : SVPERBIA : HVMILITAS : + : LARGITAS : AVARICIA : FIDES : IDOLATRIA : : CONCORDIA : DISCORDIA. See Deschamps, 'Le combat des vertus et des vices,' 314.

22 The more-or-less equivalent conflicts in the *Psychomachia* are: *Patientia* vs. *Ira* (lines 109–177); *Pudicitia* vs. *Sodomita Libido* (lines 40–108); *Sobrietas* vs. *Luxuria* (lines 310–453); *Mens Humilis* vs. *Superbia* (lines 178–309); *Ratio* and *Operatio* (who gives all she has to the poor, lines 577–81) vs. *Avaritia* (lines 454–628); *Fides* vs. *Cultura Veterum Deorum* (lines 21–39); *Pax* and *Concordia* vs. *Discordia*, also known as *Heresis* (lines 629–725). The correspondences are far from exact. See Mâle, *Religious Art, 13th Century*, 101–7; Katzenellenbogen, *Allegories of the Virtues and Vices*, 1–13.

23 The pairs at Argenton-Château are labelled LIBIDO : CASTITAS + IRA : PACIENCIA + SVPerBIA : HVMILITAS : + : FIDES : IDOLATRIA + LARGITAS : AVARICIA + CONCORDIA : DISCORD[i]A. See Deschamps, 'Le combat des vertus et des vices,' 314; Katzenellenbogen, *Allegories of the Virtues and Vices*, 17–18, and n. 5 (pp. 17–18).

24 In 1912, the crown was apparently still in place at Fontaines and Parthenay, as well as at Aulnay. See Deschamps, 'Le combat des vertus et des vices,' 314–15. Deschamps lists Argenton-Château, Fenioux, and Civray as places where the crown had disappeared. The virtues and vices are above the upper window at Civray. Chadenac differs in that it is a crowned figure (either Christ or possibly, as I argue below, the virtuous soul) rather than a crown alone that is at the summit between the virtues and vices.

25 The abbey was founded in the 11th century by Geoffrey Martel, Count of Anjou. Only the west façade remains of the Romanesque church. The tympanum of the central portal is an unfortunate early modern addition. See Eygun, *Saintonge romane*, 147.

26 Catalogue no. 117a (Pont-l'Abbé-d'Arnoult). It is nearly identical to the verse inscription on the mosaic of the Scarsella vault of the baptistery of Florence, which is the work of Iacopo da Torrita (ca. 1225): *Hic Deus est magnus mitis quem denotat Agnus.* The configuration – the Lamb in a medallion with a verse inscription – relates the scheme to Cluny and Armentia.

27 At least one of the badly mutilated figures in the outer archivolt of Chadenac may have been an Elder. See Eygun, *Saintonge romane*, 182.

28 E.g., Walahfrid Strabo, *Glossa Ordinaria, Apocalypsis Ioannis*, 4:4, *PL*, 114, col. 718; Anselm of Laon, *Enarrationes in Apocalypsin*, 4, *PL*, 162, col. 1517.

29 This is the conclusion of Eygun, *Saintonge romane*, 271.

30 Seidel, *Songs of Glory*, 47.

31 Ibid., 66.

32 Oursel, *Haut-Poitou roman*, 333 (Virgin in Majesty); Mâle, *Religious Art, 12th Century*, 443 (Assumption of the Virgin).

33 In this case Civray would have two typological archivolts. Since the archivolt seems to suggest an *ascent*, this solution seems less likely.

34 Durliat, *La sculpture romane*, 463, and fig. 473.

35 There is, however, a naked figure of 'the saved soul' in a mandorla supported by angels on a capital at León: see Durliat, *La sculpture romane*, 373, and fig. 395.

36 Eygun, *Saintonge romane*, 181. Mendell, *Romanesque Sculpture in Saintonge*, 68, sees it as Christ and the surrounding figures as 'perhaps the Four Evangelists.'

Chapter 12: The Search for the New

1 On an awareness of the historical distance of the past in the 11th and 12th centuries, see Constable, 'Renewal and Reform in Religious Life,' 38, and n. 7, and pp. 54 and 63. For a different view, see Ladner, 'Terms and Ideals of Renewal,' 9, and n. 50.

2 Curtius, *European Literature*, 254. See his remarks on 'The "Ancients" and the "Moderns,"' 251–5.

3 On the other hand, in the 12th century Frederick Barbarossa chose to regard the period from Charlemagne to his own time as the 'modern' age in contrast to the Roman empire, both pagan and Christian. Benson, 'Political *Renovatio*,' 382. Benson (p. 383) finds 'an intensified consciousness of historical period' in the 12th century. 'For the twelfth century was cultivating a new and sharpened sense of "modernity" (one encounters the term *modernitas* late in the century), of the distance between past and present, as well as between a more remote and a more recent past, or, as we would say, of the break between Antiquity and Middle Ages.'

4 Lubac, *Exégèse médiévale*, 94–110.

5 Smalley, 'Ecclesiastical Attitudes to Novelty,' 113–31.

6 Eco, *Art and Beauty in the Middle Ages*, 65–115.

7 General Prologue 682.

8 Glaber, *Historiarum* 3.4.13 (Davis-Weyer, *Early Medieval Art*, 124).

9 Constable, 'Renewal and Reform in Religious Life,' 44, emphasizes that an 'important aspect of the reform movement [in the religious life of the 11th and 12th centuries] was the rebuilding and repair of the ecclesiastical buildings that had been neglected or destroyed in the ninth and tenth centuries.'

10 Conant, *Carolingian and Romanesque Architecture*, 149–51. See also Quarré, 'Saint-Bénigne de Dijon,' 177–94.

11 Catalogue no. 42a (Dijon).

12 Catalogue no. 43a (Dijon).

13 Simon, 'El tímpano de la catedral de Jaca,' 416–19.
14 Catalogue no. 82a (Mauriac).
15 Summarizing the argument of Mayeux, 'Tympan sculpté de Mauriac,' 235–6.
16 Durliat, *Haut-Languedoc roman*, 67–8; *La sculpture romane*, 81.
17 See Lyman, 'Le style comme symbole,' 165–79, for an important discussion of Romanesque principles of composition in relation to the Porte Miègeville.
18 On the sculptor's use of antithesis in this iconographic program, see Durliat, *La sculpture romane*, 406–7.
19 For a useful account of Simon Magus and medieval ideas of magic, see Flint, *The Rise of Magic*, 338–44.
20 *The Acts of Peter* (The Vercelli Acts), chaps. 31–2 (James, trans., *The Apocryphal New Testament*, 331–2). Simon has himself carried from Rome, but eventually dies at the hands of two incompetent physicians. Jacobus de Voragine, *The Golden Legend*, 335–6, sums up other versions in which he is killed outright in the fall.
21 Catalogue no. 168a–d (Toulouse).
22 Catalogue no. 167h (Toulouse).
23 On the relationship of Simon Magus to the legend of the Antichrist, see McGinn, *Antichrist*, esp. 70–1, and n. 64 (p. 300). McGinn argues that the story of Simon's flight influenced later accounts of the ascension of the Antichrist. Durliat, *La sculpture romane*, 237, sees a kind of 'Annonciation démoniaque' in the antithesis between a woman with a snake around her neck and the Virgin Mary on a capital at Jaca.
24 Blumenthal, *The Investiture Controversy*, 113–27.
25 Durliat, *La sculpture romane*, 118–19.
26 Lyman, 'Le style comme symbole,' 170.
27 Ibid., 171–2: the quotation, citing Anna Maria Cetto ('Raymond Gayrard ... aurait réalisé son but «de faire une apologie et une louange d'une orthodoxe humilité en regard de la vanité de toutes les hérésies»'), is on p. 172.
28 Durliat, 'Le portail occidental de Saint-Sernin,' 222.
29 Catalogue no. 169a (Toulouse).
30 Durliat, 'Le portail occidental de Saint-Sernin,' 222.
31 Schapiro, 'The Romanesque Sculpture of Moissac,' fig. 63 (facing p. 178).
32 Durliat, 'Le portail occidental de Saint-Sernin,' 220–3.
33 *CIFM*, 7, 41–3.
34 Runciman, *A History of the Crusades*, 1, 110–12.
35 In 1300, Pope Boniface VIII instituted the practice of holding 'Jubilee Years' at Rome, which restored the Roman pilgrimage to favour. See Oursel, *Pèlerins du Moyen Age*, 34–5.
36 Durliat, *La sculpture romane*, 17.

37 Bottineau, *Les chemins de Saint-Jacques*, 14–15.
38 Fikry, *L'art roman du Puy*, 263; Bousquet, *La sculpture à Conques*, 141.
39 On the power and prestige of Conques, its numerous priories in France and Spain, and its rivalry with Cluny, see Deschamps, 'Étude sur les sculptures,' 243–5.
40 Durliat, *La sculpture romane*, 46.
41 *Passio Sanctorum Fidis et Caprasii*, *Acta Sanctorum*, 3, cols. 288–9; another edition in Alfaric, *La Chanson de Sainte Foy*, 2, 179–88; trans. Sheingorn, *The Book of Sainte Foy*, 33–8.
42 *Passio Metrica Sanctorum Fidis et Caprasii*, *Acta Sanctorum*, 8, cols. 826–8; repr. in Alfaric, *La Chanson de Sainte Foy*, 2, 189–97.
43 Hoepffner, *La Chanson de Sainte Foy*, 1, 253–337; trans. Clark, in Sheingorn, *The Book of Sainte Foy*, 275–84.
44 *Translatio Sanctae Fidis ad Monasterium Conchacense*, *Acta Sanctorum*, 3, cols. 294–9; trans. Sheingorn, *The Book of Sainte Foy*, 263–74.
45 *Chanson*, line 80. Bouillet and Servières, *Sainte Foy*, put her birth ca. 290–2 (pp. 21, 404–5) and her martyrdom ca. 302–4 (pp. 25, 406–7).
46 Although, according to Bouillet and Servières (*Sainte Foy*, 61–2), Conques had relics of Christ, St Peter, and the Virgin Mary; the church that preceded the present basilica was dedicated to these three.
47 The name is variously spelled.
48 The real impetus for the theft may have been Conque's need to counter the increasing success of a neighbouring monastery in Figeac. See Geary, *Furta Sacra*, 58–63, 138–41.
49 Gaillard, in Gaillard et al., *Rouergue roman*, 39: between 877 and 883 according to Bouillet and Servières, *Sainte Foy*, 57.
50 The statue continued to be altered over the centuries. Originally St Foy held the grill on which she was roasted; now there are little holders for flowers in her hands.
51 Bouillet, *Liber miraculorum* 1.13 (Sheingorn, *The Book of Sainte Foy*, 77).
52 Bouillet, *Liber miraculorum* 1.13, 17 (Sheingorn, *The Book of Sainte Foy*, 79, 82). See Belting, *Likeness and Presence*, 299–301.
53 Ashley and Sheingorn, 'The Translations of Foy,' 33.
54 For the legend of Dado, see Sheingorn, *The Book of Sainte Foy*, 6–8.
55 Or possibly Charlemagne's son, Louis the Pious. The *Translation* credits them jointly with restoring the abbey and endowing it with privileges: see Sheingorn, *The Book of Sainte Foy*, 266.
56 Catalogue no. 35a (Conques).
57 As Mérimée, 'Extrait d'un rapport,' 235, observed.
58 Fau, *Rouergue roman*, 172, calls him a 'usurer.'

59 Schapiro, 'From Mozarabic to Romanesque in Silos,' 37, and n. 32 (p. 72).

Chapter 13: Artists and the Pursuit of Fame

1 Schapiro, 'On the Aesthetic Attitude,' 22–3; Oursel, *Floraison*, 2, 11–35; Verzár Bornstein, 'Text and Image,' 122.
2 For the earlier history of this formula, see chapter 6.
3 On these formulas, see Oursel, *Floraison*, 2, 11–17.
4 Gaillard et al., *Rouergue roman*, 48.
5 Bréhier, 'Les traits originaux,' 398.
6 Porter, *Romanesque Sculpture*, 1, 274.
7 Catalogue nos. 32a (Cluny), 50a (Ferrara), 91a (Modena), 178a (Verona), 180a (Verona), 182a (Verona). See also Catalogue no. 63a (Königslutter).
8 Catalogue no. 165a (Toulouse). The same verb is used in the epitaph of Berengar, an architect and sculptor who worked at the Abbaye aux Dames of Saintes: see Eygun, *Saintonge romane*, 91.
9 Quintavalle, 'Piacenza Cathedral,' 52–4.
10 Porter, *Lombard Architecture*, 3, 15–16; Crichton, *Romanesque Sculpture*, 4.
11 Catalogue no. 91/91a (Modena). For a slightly different translation, see Porter, *Medieval Architecture*, 1, 229.
12 Fernie, 'Notes on the Sculpture of Modena Cathedral,' 90.
13 The 'style' or 'school' of Wiligelmo is recognized in other Emilian sculpture, as at Cremona and Piacenza. See Quintavalle, 'Piacenza Cathedral,' 46, 50.
14 Hearn, *Romanesque Sculpture*, 95, and n. 70.
15 E.g., Oursel, *Floraison*, 2, 17.
16 Hearn, *Romanesque Sculpture*, 163.
17 Ibid., 92.
18 Catalogue no. 87a (Modena).
19 Hearn, *Romanesque Sculpture*, 87, calls this 'a different type of lettering.' The letters in the couplet are slightly less elegantly carved and arranged, certainly more squeezed looking, but to my eye essentially the same. Compare, for example, the *g* of *Geminiani* (line 9) with the *g* of *Wiligelme* (line 12).
20 Niccolò at Piacenza and, later, Benedetto Antelami at Fidenza incorporated sculptural representations of Enoch and Elias in their programs. It is tempting to imagine that they knew of Wiligelmo's association of these figures with the fame of the artist and alluded to it in their work.
21 The order of Niccolò's works is not entirely settled. I follow Verzár Bornstein, *Portals and Politics*, 14–15, 57. She observes (p. 58), 'It is possible that an artist's signature, possibly that of Nicholaus, would originally have been placed on the central portal [of Piacenza] and has since been lost.'

22 Catalogue no. 135b (Sacra di S. Michele).
23 Oursel, *Floraison*, 2, 18.
24 Catalogue nos. 109b (Piacenza) and 135f (Sacra di S. Michele).
25 Catalogue no. 50a (Ferrara). The first three letters of *concurrentes* are chipped away, but can be confidently restored on the basis of the nearly identical verses at the cathedral of Verona (Catalogue no. 178a).
26 Nykrog, 'The Rise of Literary Fiction,' 594.
27 *Erec et Enide*, 1.23–6; cited by Nykrog, 603, n. 10.
28 Nykrog, 'The Rise of Literary Fiction,' 605. The names of the lady and the knight are inscribed on the relief.
29 On the development of this theme, see Mâle, *Religious Art, 13th Century*, 288.
30 Kain, 'The Marble Reliefs,' 368–9, 372, argues that the standing figure of Zeno in the tympanum is a later insertion, replacing an earlier, probably seated, figure. Furthermore, she proposes that Guglielmo was neither Niccolò's assistant nor the artist responsible for the New Testament panels of the west portal, but rather a co-worker of Brioloto's and 'quite possibly the individual responsible for the incorporation and adaptation of the Niccolò workshop sculpture to the façade of 1200' (p. 372). Her arguments are rejected by Verzár Bornstein, *Portals and Politics*, 140–1, and n. 4 (p. 154).
31 Catalogue no. 180a (Verona).
32 A large fragment of this work is preserved in the Museo di Castelvecchio. Pelegrinus or Peregrinus was active in Verona ca. 1120–6. Verzár Bornstein, *Portals and Politics*, 15.
33 The inscription is now too badly worn to be legible. See Porter, *Lombard Architecture*, 3, 529.
34 Catalogue no. 181e (Verona).
35 Verzár Bornstein, *Portals and Politics*, 16; see also 138.
36 Catalogue no. 182a (Verona).
37 Catalogue no. 178a (Verona).
38 *Fecit hoc opus Gruamons magister bonus et Adeodatus frater eius.*
39 *Tunc erant opera(r)ii Villanus et Pathus filius Ticnosi / A.D. MCLXVI.*
40 Moretti and Stopani, *Toscane romane*, 285.
41 Catalogue no. 113 (Pistoia).
42 According to Porter, *Romanesque Sculpture*, 1, 160, n. 2, the artist who created the lintel at S. Bartolomeo was Guglielmo da Innspruch.
43 Catalogue no. 113a (Pistoia).
44 Catalogue no. 129 (Rome).
45 Golzio and Zander, *Le chiese di Roma*, 55, 61–2; Claussen, *Magistri Doctissimi Romani*, 101–44.

46 Claussen, *Magistri Doctissimi Romani,* 132, and n. 732; Catalogue no. 173a (Vaison-la-Romaine).
47 Catalogue no. 130a (Rome).
48 For the verse inscription, see Quintavalle, *La Cattedrale di Parma,* 339.
49 Francovich, *Benedetto Antelami,* 1, 167; Stocchi, *Émilie romane,* 222.
50 Catalogue no. 100a (Parma).
51 Durliat, *Haut-Languedoc roman,* 204, dates these sculptures ca. 1135–40. Seidel, *Romanesque Sculpture of Saint-Etienne,* 157, prefers an earlier date, ca. 1125.
52 The statues are preserved in the Musée des Augustins.
53 The verse was transcribed by Castellane for the 1864 catalogue of the museum. Since then the part of the base that held the inscription has disappeared.
54 Catalogue no. 165a (Toulouse). Schapiro, 'From Mozarabic to Romanesque in Silos,' 46, comments: 'Like certain Romanesque sculptors of the South, the jongleurs conceived of their art as ingenious, intricate, and woven. The terms in which they describe their poetry apply also to sculptures of the region. They show similar conceits of manipulation; and it is hardly by accident that Gilabertus of Toulouse signs his sculpture as the work of *vir non incertus,* like his contemporary, the jongleuresque troubador William of Aquitaine, who refers to himself in one of his poems as *maiestre certa.*'
55 I do not know of any certain example of an artist's self-portrait in monumental Romanesque sculpture previous to this. Verzár Bornstein, *Portals and Politics,* 102, has proposed that the south-west corner capital of the lower façade gallery of the cathedral of Ferrara, which shows a figure wearing a tunic with a knotted rope, might be a portrait of Niccolò.
56 Catalogue no. 154a (Sant Cugat).
57 Verzár Bornstein, *Portals and Politics,* n. 24 (pp. 134–5).
58 Catalogue no. 172a (Trogir).
59 Catalogue no. 159a (Strasbourg).
60 Bony, *French Gothic Architecture,* 425–6. For problems with accepting the attribution of the façade to Erwin, see Geyer, 'Le mythe d'Erwin de Steinbach,' 322–9.
61 Reinhardt, *La cathédrale de Strasbourg,* 105. Reinhardt assigns the Angel Pillar, the two tympana of the double portal, and the statues of the Church and the Synagogue to a later sculptor.
62 Reinhardt, *La cathédrale de Strasbourg,* 101.

Chapter 14: Allegory Undone

1 Summarizing the argument of Duby, 'The Culture of the Knightly Class,' 252–5.

2 More common are donor inscriptions on capitals. For two examples in the Auvergne, see Bréhier, 'Les traits originaux,' 396.
3 See chapter 9.
4 Catalogue no. 45b (Egmond Binnen).
5 Catalogue no. 13 (Barcelona).
6 Catalogue no. 7 (Armentia).
7 Catalogue no. 33 (Colmar).
8 Duby, 'The Culture of the Knightly Class,' 253 and n. 7.
9 The same patronage formula appears in the Auvergne on a capital in the choir of Notre-Dame-du-Port of Clermont-Ferrand: IN ONORE S[anctae] MARIA[e] STEFANVS ME FIERI IVSSIT. See Bréhier, 'Les traits originaux,' 396.
10 Porter, *Spanish Romanesque Sculpture*, 1, 40; Strobel and Weis, *Bavière romane*, 57–8, 61–2.
11 Catalogue no. 124e (Regensburg).
12 Crosby, *The Royal Abbey of Saint-Denis*, 97, 114. News of the claim apparently reached St-Denis in 1049; the opening of the casket took place on 9 June 1053.
13 Catalogue no. 124d (Regensburg).
14 See chapter 6.
15 For the difference between the 12th-century concept of self and the modern view of personality, see Benton, 'Consciousness of Self,' 284–7. Benton, p. 283, remarks on the monks' submergence of their own wills in the authority of the abbot in the Benedictine community. This has a bearing on the way medieval abbots tend to be thrown into strong relief.
16 Odilo is commemorated as founder in two common leonine hexameters that are carved in the oak door of the Cluniac priory church of Lavoûte-Chilhac (Haute-Loire). The door is thought to date from the middle of the 11th century (after the death of Odilo in 1049). See Evans, *Cluniac Art*, 17.
17 Summarized from Schapiro, 'The Romanesque Sculpture of Moissac,' 136–7.
18 Schapiro, 'The Romanesque Sculpture of Moissac,' n. 66 (p. 258), with references. The MMM phrase could be translated (taking *monitus* as a masculine 4th-declension noun): 'the monument [is] a dead omen.' The FFF phrase is especially puzzling. If *fame* is from *famis*, then perhaps it goes with RRR: 'The king of the Romans has fallen by war, age, or famine.'
19 Durliat, *La sculpture romane*, 428–30.
20 Kendall, 'The Voice in the Stone,' 170–1.
21 *Hic est abba situs, divina lege peritus, / Vir Domino gratus, de nomine Bego vocatus. / Hoc peragens claustrum quod versus tendit ad Austrum, / Sollerti cura, bona gessit et altera plura. / Hic est laudandus per secula vir venerandus. / Vivat in eternum Regem laudando supernum.*

22 For details, see Kendall, 'The Voice in the Stone,' 171–2; in addition to the 'A of Charlemagne' (a reliquary in the shape of the letter A, supposed to have been the gift of Charlemagne) and the 'Reliquary of Pope Pascal' discussed here, Bego was named on the 'Lantern of Bego' (see 172, and n. 39).

23 Mély, 'Signatures de primitifs,' 15, describes Bego, on the evidence of the A of Charlemagne, as 'un des plus habiles orfèvres de son temps.'

24 The *Pilgrim's Guide* describes the route from Le Puy thus: 'alia [via] per Sanctam Mariam Podii et Sanctam Fidem de Conquis et Sanctum Petrum de Moyssaco incedit' (Vielliard, *Le guide du pèlerin*, 2), 'another route leads through Sainte-Marie of Le Puy and Sainte-Foy of Conques and Saint-Pierre of Moissac.' For the stages of the journey between Conques and Moissac, see Oursel, *Routes romanes*, 2, 100, and fig. 10.

25 Sheingorn, *The Book of Sainte Foy*, 26–7.

26 Alfaric, *La Chanson de Sainte Foy*, 2, 28–30. I am grateful to my colleague Oliver Nicholson for calling my attention to this connection.

27 On the rivalry among abbots, priors, and bishops to outdo each other in building and rebuilding their monasteries and churches, see Duby, 'The Culture of the Knightly Class,' 252.

28 Panofsky, *Abbot Suger*, 35–7.

29 Suger visited Mainz in 1125 (Panofsky, *Abbot Suger*, 200); he saw the bronze doors of Monte Sant'Angelo and the triumphal arch of Montecassino on a pilgrimage in 1123 (pp. 164, 169); he visited Rome on several occasions (p. 169).

30 Suger, *De administratione* 24 (Panofsky, *Abbot Suger*, 42–3). See also Porter, 'Two Romanesque Sculptures in France,' 132–5.

31 Mâle, *Religious Art, 12th Century*, 179–81, points out the influence of Beaulieu on St-Denis; see also Crosby, *L'abbaye royale de Saint-Denis*, 36–7. However, the assumption of the priority of Beaulieu over St-Denis has been questioned: see Crosby, *The Royal Abbey of Saint-Denis*, 186–7.

32 Only the lower half of Christ's body, including the throne, is enclosed in a mandorla. This is a unique feature. For an elaborate interpretation of its meaning, see Rudolph, *Artistic Change at St-Denis*, 37–40.

33 Mâle, *Religious Art, 12th Century*, 476, n. 77; Bousquet, *La sculpture à Conques*, 613.

34 Catalogue no. 139a (St-Denis).

35 Crosby, *L'abbaye royale de Saint-Denis*, 37, accepts the conclusion that this is Suger. St Foy kneels in prayer on the tympanum of Conques.

36 Catalogue no. 14a–b (Baume-les-Messieurs).

37 This was a 'westwork' for the Carolingian basilica that was donated by William the Conqueror. See Hubert, 'La tour occidentale de Saint-Denis,' 137–40.

38 *Hoc opus Airardus caelesti munere fretus / Offert ecce tibi, Dionysi, pectore miti.* Mon-

tesquiou-Fezensac, 'Les portes de bronze de Saint-Denis,' 134–5; Montesquiou-Fezensac reproduces the drawing of Peiresc, made early in the 17th century, from a manuscript in Carpentras. See also Panofsky, *Abbot Suger*, 159. Panofsky's reading of *mitis* for *miti* is in error.

39 For this verse, which Suger does not mention in *De administratione*, see Panofsky, *Abbot Suger*, 173.

40 On the pervasiveness of a 12th-century transcendental aesthetics based on measure and light, its Neoplatonic and Augustinian roots, and its contemporary proponents, see Simson, *The Gothic Cathedral*, 21–58.

41 Suger, *De administratione*, chap. 27; trans. Panofsky, *Abbot Suger*, 47–9.

42 Rudolph, *Artistic Change at St-Denis*, 52–4, argues that these verses are only superficially Dionysian, and that their philosophical core is Augustinian.

43 *Commentarii in Hierarchiam Coelestem*, *PL*, 175, col. 941: 'Symbolum est collatio formarum visibilium ad invisibilium demonstrationem.' Cited by de Bruyne, *Études d'esthétique médiévale*, 2, 213.

44 Mâle, *Religious Art, 12th Century*, 160–2.

Catalogue of Romanesque Verse Inscriptions

1 *CIFM*, 14, 29.

2 Favole, *Marches romanes*, 93–4.

3 Chierici and Citi, *Piémont-Ligurie roman*, 234.

4 *CIFM*, 14, 43; cf. pl. 12, fig. 26.

5 Millin, *Voyage*, 594, mistook the ribbon band for a kind of sword, and saw, but was unable to read, the inscription.

6 James the Greater and James the Less are paired on the west face of the monumental arch that acts as a porch – one on each side. Both are bearded. I have not found any way to distinguish them. Stoddard, *The Façade of Saint-Gilles*, 278–83, and figs. 387 and 389, and *CIFM*, 14, 42–3, say that (R4) is James the Greater and (L4) is James the Less. Rouquette, *Provence romane*, 278–9, 281, says that (R4) is James the Less and (L4) is James the Greater.

7 Cf. Rouquette, *Provence romane*, 275. Porter, *Romanesque Sculpture*, 1, 298, argues that the façade of Arles must have been constructed between ca. 1142 and 1152.

8 Millin, *Voyage*, 597; Rouquette, *Provence romane*, 273–4, 321.

9 Rouquette, *Provence romane*, 321.

10 See Witters's discussion of this text in Rouquette, *Provence romane*, 343–4.

11 Ocón Alonso, 'Tímpanos románicos,' 1, 43.

12 *CIFM*, 6, 56–7.

13 *Suevia Sacra*, 95–6.

14 Tonnellier, *Aulnay de Saintonge*, 16–18, argues that the figure on the left with the scissors is not a woman, but the barber whom Delilah summoned (Judg. 16:19). He claims to see a beard and moustache. But the figure wears a wimple and woman's clothing and, to my eye, the 'moustache' is a prominent upper lip (cf. the figure of Delilah tying Samson's hands), and the 'beard' is a couple of gouges in the chin.

15 Cf. Oursel, *Haut-Poitou roman*, 307. According to Labande-Mailfert, *Poitou roman*, 214, 'M. Aubert a proposé les dates de 1150–70.' *CIFM*, 1:3, 82, puts the date in the second half of the 12th century.

16 Oursel's reading corrects the reading of Lefèvre-Pontalis, 'Aulnay-de-Saintonge,' 102.

17 Oursel, *Bourgogne romane*, 225–6.

18 Cf. Grivot and Zarnecki, *Gislebertus*, 162.

19 Ocón Alonso, 'Tímpanos románicos,' 1, 67. Junyent, *Catalogne romane*, 2, 73, argues for the beginning of the 13th century.

20 Junyent, *Catalogne romane*, 2, 73.

21 Martène and Durand, *Voyage litteraire*, 1:1, 172, remarked, when they visited Baume in the early 18th century: 'Il ne faut pas oublier, qu'on nous fit voir à l'entrée du monastere devant l'église une grande colonne taillée en quarré, d'un ouvrage Corinthien, tirée d'un bâtiment qui étoit à l'entrée de l'église, & qui apparemment étoit le portique ...'

22 Aubert, *Romanesque Cathedrals*, 524. Alberic died ca. 1139 (Deschamps, 'Paléographie,' 37, n. 2).

23 Millin, *Voyage*, 434–5.

24 This is the estimate of Stoddard, *The Façade of Saint-Gilles*, 196. Mâle, *Religious Art, 12th Century*, 429, who believed that this preceded the tympanum of St-Gilles, dated it 'about 1150.' Lugand, Nougaret, and Saint-Jean, *Languedoc roman*, 26, and *CIFM*, 13, 12, locate it in the second half of the 12th century.

25 *CIFM*, 1:1, 18–20; *CIFM*, 13, 12–13.

26 A note inside the church states: 'La façade et le porche, construits à partir du mois d'aout 1124 ...' Evans, *Cluniac Art*, fig. 56, says 'early 12th century.'

27 *CIFM*, 2, 92–3.

28 Porter, 'Two Romanesque Sculptures in France,' 125.

29 Deshoulières, 'Saint-Pierre,' 44, transcribes the inscriptions thus: PALMAM VITRICI FERT ANGELVS. HIC GENITRIS (?) DES ... RATUS ... (*Corpus*) MATRIS DEI FERTVR AD C(*oelum*) ... IMPONI(*tur*) PVLCRVM CORPUS SINE FRAVDE SEPULCRUM. I(*esus*) AD PATREM FACIT ALMAM SCANDERE MATREM.

30 Cf. Deshoulières, 'Saint-Pierre,' 46; Mâle, *Religious Art, 12th Century*, 438.

31 Rouquette, *Provence romane*, 33–4; *CIFM*, 13, 139.

32 Lugand, Nougaret, and Saint-Jean, *Languedoc roman*, 40–1.
33 Stocchi, *Émilie romane*, 71 (citing Kingsley Porter).
34 Christe, *Les grands portails romans*, 25–6.
35 Bousquet, *La sculpture à Conques*, 682, n. 215.
36 Hearn, *Romanesque Sculpture*, 106–9. Lloyd, 'Cluny Epigraphy,' 344, concludes that 'the date 1088–1095 is acceptable for the Cluny inscriptions.'
37 Hearn, *Romanesque Sculpture*, 112.
38 Conant, *Cluny*, 26, n. 23.
39 *CIFM*, 17, 5.
40 Kendall, 'The Voice in the Stone,' 163–82.
41 Ibid. *CIFM*, 9, 17–25, puts the date of the tympanum at the beginning of the 12th century. The remarks of Porter (*Spanish Romanesque Sculpture*, 2, 4) are still apposite to the problem of the date: 'In the sculptures of the western tympanum [of Conques] critics with antennae will recognize the personality of one of the sculptors of the Puerta de las Platerías, at a later and more accomplished stage of his development. How much this artist owed to Spain may be realized by comparing the western tympanum of Conques with the tomb of Bégon III of 1107.'
42 Durliat, *Roussillon roman*, 238.
43 *CIFM*, 11, 48.
44 *CIFM*, 11, 48, citing Sandoli, *Corpus inscriptionum crucesignatorum terrae sanctae (1099–1291)* (Jerusalem, 1974), no. 239, p. 177.
45 Francovich, *Benedetto Antelami*, 1, 35, n. 58.
46 Hubert, 'L'abbatiale Notre-Dame de Déols,' 55.
47 Reprinted by Hubert, 'L'abbatiale Notre-Dame de Déols,' p. 48.
48 Ibid., 50, n. 2.
49 Ibid., 50.
50 Ibid., 50, n. 3.
51 Ibid., 50.
52 Cf. Strecker, *Introduction*, 59, s.v. *sophia*.
53 Kerber, *Burgund*, 43, says the tympanum came from the north (i.e., left) portal. I have not found the evidence on which he bases this statement.
54 Reprinted in Mâle, *Religious Art, 12th Century*, fig. 175.
55 Reprinted in Quarré, 'Saint-Bénigne de Dijon,' fig. 6.
56 Ibid., 186; Sauerländer, *Gotische Skulptur*, 74–5.
57 Kerber, *Burgund*, 41. See above, note on the tympanum of St Benignus.
58 Quarré, 'Saint-Bénigne de Dijon,' 179.
59 Musset, *Angleterre romane*, 323.
60 Durliat, *La sculpture romane en Roussillon*, 48, 68.
61 Sené, 'Quelques remarques,' 369; Ocón Alonso, 'Tímpanos románicos,' 1, 196–7.

62 Ragusa, '*Porta patet vitae*,' 346, n. 6.
63 Verzár Bornstein, *Portals and Politics*, 14–15; see also Krautheimer-Hess, 'The Original Porta Dei Mesi,' 159–60; Porter, *Lombard Architecture*, 2, 407–8.
64 I follow Robb, 'Niccolò,' 394, in taking *superlatis* as one word. Krautheimer-Hess, 'The Original Porta Dei Mesi,' 159, n. 69, takes *struitur* to mean 'begins to be constructed.'
65 Porter, *Lombard Architecture*, 2, 413; 416, n. 47; Krautheimer-Hess, 'The Original Porta Dei Mesi,' 152, n. 2.
66 A fragment of a relief with a basilisk that was found in the pavement of the atrium at Ferrara has been claimed as being from the tympanum by Krautheimer-Hess, 'The Original Porta Dei Mesi,' 156–7.
67 Krautheimer-Hess, 'The Original Porta Dei Mesi,' 152–74; Verzár Bornstein, *Portals and Politics*, 108–10.
68 Cf. Francovich, *Benedetto Antelami*, 2, fig. 410; Saporetti, *Iscrizioni romaniche*, 28, and fig. 5/a.
69 Stocchi, *Émilie romane*, 85–6.
70 Cf. Francovich, *Benedetto Antelami*, 2, fig. 388; Saporetti, *Iscrizioni romaniche*, 38–9, and fig. 10/a. The same inscription is found on the tympanum of St George of the cathedral of S. Giorgio of Ferrara.
71 A marble plaque of Enoch and Elias appears above the Genesis frieze on the west façade of the cathedral of Modena.
72 Mackeprang, *Jydske Granitportaler*, 349.
73 Reproduced in ibid., figs. 110a–b, and Bæksted, *Danske Indskrifter*, figs. 11–12.
74 Wulf, *Saxe romane*, 149–50.
75 Ibid., 155.
76 *CIFM*, 6, 95–6.
77 Barral i Altet, *Belgique romane*, 282.
78 Strobel and Weis, *Bavière romane*, 353.
79 Moralejo Alvarez, 'La sculpture romane de Jaca,' 85; 'Une sculpture à Jaca,' 7, 12; Ocón Alonso, 'Tímpanos románicos,' 1, 244.
80 For this scansion, see Kendall, 'The Verse Inscriptions of Jaca,' n. 27 (pp. 427–8).
81 Barruol, *Dauphiné roman*, 323, states explicitly that the church is dedicated to the Virgin; *CIFM*, 16, 144, describes it as 'Église Sainte-Lucie.'
82 Wulf, *Saxe romane*, 310. Wulf thinks Niccolò's engagements in Italy make his personal presence in north Germany unlikely, but Verzár Bornstein, 'Text and Image,' 126–8, is certain that he was the sculptor at Königslutter.
83 Dubourg-Noves, *Guyenne romane*, 293; he notes that Francis Salet proposed a date ca. 1120.
84 Not 'north' as stated in *CIFM*, 8, 92.
85 *CIFM*, 8, 92.

86 *CIFM*, 17, 7.

87 The cloister dates (probably) from the end of the 11th century. However, Thirion, *Alpes romanes*, 139, dates the cloister 'à l'extrême fin du XIIe siècle ou dans la première moitié du XIIIe.' By contrast, the brother who took me into the cloister in April 1985 asserted that one portion of it went back to the 7th century.

88 Text of epitaph in *CIFM*, 14, 9.

89 Durliat, *La sculpture romane*, 266–8.

90 Kern, *Labirinti*, 206–7.

91 All the guide books give the date of the lintel as 1187, although I have not yet been able to discover the grounds for this. The missing portion of the first-verse of the inscription may have given a date.

92 Durliat and Allègre, *Pyrénées romanes*, 315–16.

93 Porter, *Spanish Romanesque Sculpture*, 1, n. 567.

94 Laplace, *Notice sur l'église*, 9.

95 Deijk, *Pays-Bas romans*, 134.

96 Ibid., 107.

97 Ibid., 97.

98 Ibid., 63–4.

99 Ibid., 102.

100 The period after B appears to be intentional. Porter, *Romanesque Sculpture*, 1, 268, n. 1, does not recognize it, and interprets BD' as *Bernardus*. I have followed Vallery-Radot, 'L'ancienne cathédrale de Maguelone,' 87, and Lugand, Nougaret, and Saint-Jean, *Languedoc roman*, 236.

101 For various conjectures about the date, see Craplet, *Auvergne romane* (1978), 305; Deschamps, *French Sculpture*, fig. 55; Quarré, 'Le portail de Mauriac,' 136–9; and Vidal et al., *Quercy roman*, 199.

102 *CIFM*, 18, 45, assigns the tympanum to the first half of the 12th century.

103 *CIFM*, 1:3, 138–9.

104 Crichton, *Romanesque Sculpture*, 81.

105 In the *Breviarium apostolorum* (6/7th century): 'Jacobus qui interpretatur subplantator filius Zebedei frater Johannis' (cited by Melczer, *The Pilgrim's Guide*, 10).

106 Porter, *Medieval Architecture*, 1, 223.

107 Cf. Hearn, *Romanesque Sculpture*, 91.

108 Porter, *Lombard Architecture*, 3, 36, translates, 'Cain chafes, Cain weeps, Cain groans; Abel is in great danger.' See, further, Salvini, *Wiligelmo*, 110, n. 17.

109 Verzár Bornstein, 'Text and Image,' 132.

110 Porter, *Lombard Architecture*, 2, 389.

111 For details of the life and legend of Geminiano (312–98), see Porter, *Lombard Architecture*, 3, 39–42, and Stocchi, *Émilie romane*, 249, 283.

112 Porter, *Lombard Architecture*, 3, 43.

113 Ibid., 4, pl. 145, no. 1; Quintavalle, *La Cattedrale di Modena*, 2, pls. 157–8; Salvini, *Wiligelmo*, pl. 160. Its present appearance can be seen in Salvini, *Wiligelmo*, pls. 161–2.

114 Salvini, *Wiligelmo*, 163–6.

115 Stocchi, *Émilie romane*, 283–4.

116 Ibid., 284; cf. Salvini, *Wiligelmo*, 96–7, n. 1.

117 Strobel and Weis, *Bavière romane*, 345–6.

118 These remains, which were rediscovered in 1974, are at present displayed inthe north apsidal chapel.

119 'Le texte gravé sur celui [the tympanum] de gauche est connu par les relevés avant restauration et les photographies des Monuments historiques, ainsi que par une inscription lue par l'abbé Laplace. L'authenticité du second texte, gravé sur le tympanon de droite, est beaucoup moins certaine, l'inscription n'étant mentionnée ni par l'abbé Laplace, ni lors des travaux de restauration.' *CIFM*, 6, 158.

120 Evans, *Cluniac Art*, fig. 103.

121 *CIFM*, 6, 158.

122 *CIFM*, 6, 158, n. 2.

123 Apparently there is no justification for associating this archivolt, as both Mâle (*Religious Art, 12th Century*, 377) and Evans (*Cluniac Art*, 20–1) do, with the tympanum of the Virgin Mary in the south transept, which belonged to the portal leading to the cloister (now gone). See Craplet, *Auvergne romane* (1978), 128.

124 Craplet, *Auvergne romane* (1978), 122.

125 E.g., by Mâle, *Religious Art, 12th Century*, 377, n. 2; and Evans, *Cluniac Art*, 21. According to Craplet, *Auvergne romane* (1978), 123, the source of some of these errors was Abbé Cohadon, *Tablettes historiques d'Auvergne* (1842), 30. Le Blant, *Inscriptions chrétiennes*, 1, 232, printed INGREDIENS TEMPLVM REFER AD SVBLIMIA VVLTVM / INTRATVRI AVLAM VENERANSQ LIMINA XPI on the basis of a copy made for him on the spot by François Lenormant; another copy, sent him by M. Faure, the curate of Mozac, was similar except in reading VENERANDO for VENERANSQ in the second line. In 1913, the Abbé Luzuy, 'Mozac,' 135, read INGREDIENS TEMPLVM REFER AD SVBLIMIA VVLTVM / INTRATVRI AVLAM VENITE IN SOLEMNIA CHRISTI. Craplet, *Auvergne romane* (1978), 124, having corrected these errors, introduces a new misreading in the first line: *vultus* (for *vultum*).

126 Craplet, *Auvergne romane* (1955), 227; *Auvergne romane* (1978), 125.

127 Printed by Le Blant, *Inscriptions chrétiennes*, 1, 231–3 (nos. 170, 171). See chapter 3.

128 Evans, *Cluniac Art*, 62, n. 9.

129 Oursel, *Lyonnais et Savoie romans*, 342.
130 Serbat, 'Nevers,' 366; Evans, *Cluniac Art*, n. 6.
131 Dupont, *Nivernais-Bourbonnais roman*, 37.
132 Evans, *Cluniac Art*, fig. 17a (ca. 1100); Serbat, 'Nevers,' 353 (ca. 1150).
133 Stocchi, *Émilie romane*, 293, 297.
134 Lojendio, *Navarre romane*, 17–19.
135 Ibid., 18.
136 Ibid., 17–18
137 Quintavalle, *La Cattedrale di Parma*, plan XLIX, no. 9.
138 In three hexameters, the first and third of which are full leonines: ANNO MILLENO CENTENO SEPTVAGENO / OCTAVO SCVLTOR PATRAVIT MENSE SECVNDO / ANTELAMI DICTVS SCVLPTOR FVIT HIC BENEDICTVS ('In the year one thousand one hundred seventy-eight, in the second month, the sculptor finished. This sculptor was called Benedetto Antelami'). See Quintavalle, *La Cattedrale di Parma*, 339.
139 Quintavalle, 'Piacenza Cathedral,' 46, 54; Stocchi, *Émilie romane*, 52–3; Verzár Bornstein, *Portals and Politics*, 14–15.
140 Robb, 'Niccolò,' 385.
141 Quintavalle, 'Piacenza Cathedral,' 43–4.
142 Robb, 'Niccolò,' 385: Robb cites Porter, *Lombard Architecture*, 3, 241f. See also Porter, *Medieval Architecture*, 1, 230, n.
143 Conant, *Carolingian and Romanesque Architecture*, 377–9; Moretti and Stopani, *Toscane romane*, 74–5.
144 Labande-Mailfert, *Poitou roman*, 42.
145 *CIFM*, 1:1, 93.
146 Oursel, *Haut-Poitou roman*, 203.
147 Martène and Durand, *Voyage litteraire*, 1:1, 11. From the transcription that Martène and Durand give, it is clear that the left portion of the lintel was missing when they saw it.
148 *CIFM*, 1:1, 117, dates the inscription a full century or more earlier. The complicated triple rhymes of the verse point to the 12th century, although there can be no certainty about this.
149 Horste, 'Romanesque Sculpture,' figs. 15 and 16.
150 It can be seen in part in Porter, *Romanesque Sculpture*, 7, pl. 1065.
151 For details, see Stechow, 'Two Romanesque Statues,' and Horste, 'Romanesque Sculpture,' 122–25.
152 Stechow, 'Two Romanesque Statues,' 33–4, 38. See also Gaillard, 'Deux sculptures de l'Abbaye des Moreaux,' 392.
153 Cf. Abbad Ríos, *El Románico en Cinco Villas*, 67; Ocón Alonso, 'Tímpanos románicos,' 1, 326–7.

154 Ocón Alonso, 'Tímpanos románicos,' 1, 327.
155 Paul and Paul, *Notre-Dame du Puy*, 103, n. 1.
156 'On peut attribuer ce texte à la fin du XIe ou au début du XIIe s.' *CIFM*, 18, 110. This seems too early.
157 Paul and Paul, *Notre-Dame du Puy*, 6.
158 Cf. *CIFM*, 18, 116.
159 Paul and Paul, *Notre-Dame du Puy*, 111.
160 Hearn, *Romanesque Sculpture*, 60.
161 Mackeprang, *Jydske Granitportaler*, 353.
162 Terpager, *Ripae Cimbricae seu Urbis Ripensis in Cimbria* [n.p.].
163 Sanoner, 'Le portail de Ripoll,' 355.
164 See chapter 10.
165 *CIFM*, 1:3, 66–7.
166 Parenthetical details from Canellas López and San Vicente, *Aragon roman*, 56.
167 Buchowiecki, *Handbuch*, 1, 62.
168 Golzio and Zander, *Le chiese di Roma*, 55; Buchowiecki, *Handbuch*, 1, 85; Claussen, *Magistri Doctissimi Romani*, 127.
169 Krautheimer, *Corpus Basilicarum*, 1, 245; Buchowiecki, *Handbuch*, 2, 53–4.
170 Krautheimer, *Corpus Basilicarum*, 1, 270; Buchowiecki, *Handbuch*, 2, 131.
171 Krautheimer, *Corpus Basilicarum*, 1, 270, 273; Buchowiecki, *Handbuch*, 2, 131.
172 Buchowiecki, *Handbuch*, 3, 665–6.
173 According to Winterfeld, *Palatinat roman*, 324, this is the date of the refectory. The tympanum probably is contemporary.
174 Porter, *Lombard Architecture*, 3, 346; Chierici and Citi, *Piémont-Ligurie roman*, 63; Gettings, *The Secret Zodiac*, 166.
175 See Gettings, *The Secret Zodiac*, 167, for a technical discussion of these names for the constellations. Robb, 'Niccolò,' 377, n. 5, points out that Eridanus is also the ancient Greek name for the river Po.
176 Verzár Bornstein, *Portals and Politics*, 57. Ca. 1120: Porter, *Lombard Architecture*, 3, 347; Robb, 'Niccolò,' 381; Verzár, *Die romanischen Skulpturen*, 97. Ferrari would date the portal ca. 1125–35, after the period of Niccolò's work at Piacenza: cf. Chierici and Citi, *Piémont-Ligurie roman*, 83.
177 Debove, 'La Sacra di S. Michele,' 28.
178 Debove ('La Sacra di S. Michele,' 28, fig. 27) says that the inscription reads *locus est pacis causas deponite.* He does not give a source for this, but *locus* would work as well as *domus.* Verzár, *Die romanischen Skulpturen*, 80, reads *hic locus est pacis causas deponite litium. Litium* cannot be right because it spoils the verse. In 'Matilda of Canossa,' 149, she asserts that the inscription reads *Deponite litium, locum pacis est.*
179 Robb, 'Niccolò,' 377.

180 The Latin word *describere* means primarily 'to copy.' See the discussion of Oursel, *Floraison*, 2, 18. Niccolò probably means that he both wrote and carved the verses.

181 Porter, *Spanish Romanesque Sculpture*, 1, 60.

182 Ibid.

183 Durliat and Allègre, *Pyrénées romanes*, 64, date all the sculptures at St-Aventin to the second half of the 12th century; *CIFM*, 8, 49, dates the relief of the Virgin to the first half of the 12th century.

184 *CIFM*, 8, 47, dates the relief of St Aventin on the basis of the epigraphy to the end of the 11th century or at the latest to the first years of the 12th century. This seems too early.

185 Crosby, *L'abbaye royale*, 36.

186 *CIFM*, 1:3, 109.

187 Evans, *Romanesque Architecture*, 65.

188 Guédel, *L'architecture romane en Dombes*, 29.

189 Guédel, *L'architecture romane en Dombes*, 38, on the basis of the epigraphy, suggests the end of the 12th or the beginning of the 13th century. I cannot agree that the epigraphy is significantly different from, or later than, that of the west façade.

190 Pomès and Michel, *L'église de Saint-Pé-de-Bigorre*, 27.

191 *CIFM*, 14, 137.

192 *CIFM*, 1:3, 111.

193 Based on the French translation in *CIFM*, 'Elle (la Bête) servit d'exemple lorsqu'arriva le temps du diable.'

194 Cabanot, *Gascogne roman*, 95, 120.

195 Whitehill, *Spanish Romanesque Architecture*, 253–5.

196 Canellas López and San Vicente, *Aragon roman*, 78.

197 Ibid., 235; Whitehill, *Spanish Romanesque Architecture*, 255–6.

198 See also Ocón Alonso, 'Tímpanos románicos,' 1, 364.

199 Whitehill, *Spanish Romanesque Architecture*, 257, and Canellas López and San Vicente, *Aragon roman*, 233, give the transcription of Lampérez.

200 Cf. Moretti and Stopani, *Toscane romane*, 142–3.

201 My reconstruction (in brackets) is supported by the text of the inscription as given in Enlart, 'L'église abbatiale de Sant'Antimo,' 12. However, Enlart's text is faulty at a number of points and is not entirely to be trusted.

202 Enlart, 'L'église abbatiale de Sant'Antimo en Toscane,' 12.

203 Moretti and Stopani, *Toscane romane*, 143.

204 Junyent, *Catalogne romane*, 2, 145.

205 Durliat, *La sculpture romane*, 356.

206 Ibid.

207 Whitehill, *Spanish Romanesque Architecture*, 164, n. 4.
208 For these details, see ibid., 155–60.
209 Ibid., 191–2.
210 The dating of Silos is open to question. Spanish scholars have tended to push back the dates well into the 11th century; French scholars to prefer the 12th century. See the review of the quarrel by Oursel, *Floraison*, 1, 335–9. See also Whitehill, *Spanish Romanesque Architecture*, 192; Schapiro, 'From Mozarabic to Romanesque,' 58, 62. Hearn, *Romanesque Sculpture*, 68, n. 1, opts for 'a date well into the twelfth century, perhaps c. 1135/1140.'
211 Whitehill, *Spanish Romanesque Architecture*, 160, n. 1, quotes the epitaph in full:

Hac tumba tegitur . diva qui luce beatur
Dictus Dominicus . nomine conspicuus.
Orbi quem speculum Christus concessit honestum.
Exhortando bonos . corripiendo malos.
Solsticium mundo dum dat brumalis origo
Subtrahitur mundo . iungitur et domino.
Protegat hic plebes. sibi fida mente fideles.
Nuncque tuendo suos . post trahat ad superos.

This may be translated: 'In this tomb is buried one who is blessed with divine light, called Domingo, made illustrious by his name. Christ yielded him as a virtuous mirror to the world for the sake of encouraging the good and correcting the wicked. While a wintry beginning gives the solstice to the world, he is taken from the world and is joined with the Lord. May he protect the people who are faithful to him with a faithful mind, and by watching over his own now, may he afterwards lead them to the angels.' The rather tortured lines about the winter solstice (lines 5–6) allude to the fact that Sto Domingo died on 20 December 1073 (Whitehill, *Spanish Romanesque Architecture*, 159).
212 Schapiro, 'From Mozarabic to Romanesque,' 59.
213 Ibid., n. 179 (p. 94).
214 Ibid., 58.
215 Ibid., 58–9, and nn. 171–7 (pp. 93–4).
216 Mackeprang, *Jydske Granitportaler*, 353.
217 Ibid., 176–7.
218 Reinhardt, *La cathédrale de Strasbourg*, 105.
219 Rouquette, *Provence romane*, 53.
220 *CIFM*, 14, 141–2.
221 Bacconnier, *Notre-Dame de Thines*, 22–3. Saint-Jean, in Saint-Jean and Nou-

garet, *Vivarais Gévaudan romans*, 241, places the construction of the church in the second half of the 12th century.

222 Proposed by O. de Valgorge (see Bacconnier, *Notre-Dame de Thines*, n. 50 [pp. 93–4]).

223 Favole (with Del Vitto), *Abruzzes Molise romans*, 54.

224 The location and orientation of these statues is discussed by Seidel, *Romanesque Sculpture of Saint-Etienne*, 15–16.

225 Ibid., 7.

226 Ibid., 16. *CIFM*, 7, 12, explains: 'Le vers gravé sous les pieds de saint Sernin se rapporte au bâton pastoral, signe du pouvoir donné à l'évêque. La signification de l'hexamètre découle de la forme du bâton: la volute est faite pour rassembler le troupeau confié au pasteur, la partie médiane, rectiligne, sert à guider, et l'extremité, en forme d'aiguillon, stimule les négligents. Cette explication symbolique est donnée par Hugues de Saint-Victor, et sera reprise par Sicard de Crémone qui donne le même texte que celui de l'inscription toulousaine en remplaçant le terme *recta* par le substantif *virga*.'

227 Durliat, *Haut-Languedoc roman*, 204; Seidel, *Romanesque Sculpture of Saint-Etienne*, 157, prefers an earlier date, ca. 1125.

228 See Seidel, *Romanesque Sculpture of Saint-Etienne*, 46–52, for a discussion of the circumstances of this disappearance.

229 See Scott, 'The West Portal Relief Decoration of Saint-Sernin,' and Durliat, 'Le portail occidental de Saint-Sernin,' for analysis of these descriptions and proposals for restoration of the decorative program.

230 Mâle, *Religious Art, 12th Century*, 189, citing Jules de Lahondès, *Toulouse Chrétienne, l'église Saint-Etienne, cathédrale de Toulouse*, 32, associates this statue with the canons' cloister of St-Étienne, and comments, 'St. Sernin stood beside St. Peter, because according to a tradition then current the apostle of Toulouse had received his mission from the first of the popes.' However, Noguier, *Histoire tolosaine*, 59, clearly locates the statue with its inscription on the west façade of St-Sernin.

231 Scott, 'The West Portal Relief Decoration of Saint-Sernin,' 277.

232 Ibid., 278.

233 Ibid., 275, supported by Durliat, 'Le portail occidental de Saint-Sernin,' 223.

234 Mâle, *Religious Art, 12th Century*, 189.

235 Cited by Durliat, 'Le portail occidental de Saint-Sernin,' 219.

236 Noguier, *Histoire tolosaine*, 64–5.

237 According to Noguier, *Histoire tolosaine*, 52: 'Ce Marc Fonteic [Préteur de la Gaule] fit ériger plusieurs effigies de marbre à l'honneur de César, dont entre autres en i a deux affichees en l'eglise de saint Sernin en Tolose: l'une êt au pillier vis à vis de la porte d'icelle qui regarde la grande rue: cette pierre

de marbre êt assez grande, en laquelle êt une statue d'homme nu de taille relevee à la grandeur du naturel, tenant les piés ioints, les bras étendus en bas, et les mains ouvertes, montrant leurs concavités, le tout dans un ovale aussi de taille relevee, à l'entour duquel ces vers sont gravés en lettre antique.'

238 Durliat, 'Le portail occidental de Saint-Sernin,' 222.

239 Norberg, *Introduction*, 66.

240 Durliat, 'Le portail occidental de Saint-Sernin,' 222.

241 Dated from the table-altar of Bernard Gilduin: see Hearn, *Romanesque Sculpture*, 69, 77–8.

242 Hearn, *Romanesque Sculpture*, 69.

243 *CIFM*, 7, 69.

244 Rouquette, *Provence romane*, 142, 152. Rambaud, 'Le quatrain mystique,' 160, would date it perhaps between 1150–60 (the date of the wall) and ca. 1200 (the date of the upper frieze).

245 Guédel, *L'architecture romane en Dombes*, 55–6.

246 His reading is *Ap* [sic] *mensam Domini peccator q(u)ando proppiquat* [sic] / *Expedit ut fraudes ex toto-ex toto corde relinquat.*

247 Francovich, *Benedetto Antelami*, 1, 387.

248 Crichton, *Romanesque Sculpture*, 57–75, 80–1; Francovich, *Benedetto Antelami*, 1, 387–92.

249 For details of the martyrdom of St Andrew, see Jacobus de Voragine, *The Golden Legend*, 10–13.

250 Crichton, *Romanesque Sculpture*, 80.

251 Jacobus de Voragine, *The Golden Legend*, 13.

252 Francovich, *Benedetto Antelami*, 1, 390, identifies this figure as Christ the Redeemer. The figure is seated. Its left hand is lowered on a book that rests on its left knee. Its right hand is held out at about the same level with the palm turned *down*. The figure has a halo, which is not, so far as I can see, cruciform. The verses on the lintel (which are not without ambiguities) say that Cardinal Guala gives the model to Andrew.

253 Porter, *Lombard Architecture*, 3, 478–9; Verzár Bornstein, *Portals and Politics*, 14–15.

254 Porter, *Lombard Architecture*, 3, 469.

255 Ibid., 3, 478.

256 'Military standards, originally of profane origin, began in the West to receive the blessing and approval of the Church about the tenth century.' Crichton, *Romanesque Sculpture*, 31.

257 Porter, *Lombard Architecture*, 1, 425–8, gives a résumé of the life of St Zeno.

258 Verzár Bornstein, *Portals and Politics*, 14–15. Ca. 1138: Porter, *Lombard Architecture*, 3, 525.

259 In addition to the verses around the outer rim of the tympanum, Niccolò's signature appeared on the northern lion, but this inscription is now too badly worn to be legible (Porter, *Lombard Architecture*, 529). Robb, 'Niccolò,' 405, reports SCVLPSIT ... S DOGMATE CLARVS, and notes, 'although it cannot be proven, it seems at least possible that at one time, the hiatus was filled with the name NICOLAVS.'

260 Porter, *Lombard Architecture*, 3, 532; Hearn, *Romanesque Sculpture*, 163.

261 Niccolò's signature appears on the plaque of God creating Adam, but the style of most of these relief sculptures is thought to be unlike his. Crichton, *Romanesque Sculpture*, 33, believes that only the panels of Theodoric and possibly the images of God are the work of Niccolò.

262 For the legend and these panels, see Porter, *Lombard Architecture*, 3, 530–2.

263 Porter, *Lombard Architecture*, 3, 531, translates, 'thereby breaking the dire command of God.'

264 Crichton, *Romanesque Sculpture*, 32.

265 Ibid., 83.

266 Salet, *La Madeleine de Vézelay*, 148.

267 Castellane, 'Inscriptions du XIe au XIIe siècle,' 56, following Mérimée, gives the inscription as 'Agnoscant omnes quia dicitur iste Johannes, / ... Populum, demonstrans indice Christum,' with the remark, 'un mot reste encore à déchiffrer.'

268 Lasteyrie, *L'architecture religieuse*, 425.

269 Barruol, *Dauphiné roman*, 160.

270 *CIFM*, 17, 23.

271 Deijk, *Pays-Bas romans*, 331.

Bibliography of Works Cited

AB *Art Bulletin*
BM *Bulletin monumental*
CC *Corpus Christianorum, series latina*
CIFM *Corpus des inscriptions de la France médiévale*
CIL *Corpus Inscriptionum Latinarum*
CSMC *Les cahiers de Saint-Michel de Cuxa*
CTSEEH Collection de textes pour servir à l'étude et à l'enseignement de l'histoire.
GBA *Gazette des beaux-arts*
MGH *Monumenta Germaniae Historica*
Monuments Piot Académie des inscriptions et belles-lettres, Paris. Commission de la Fondation Piot, *Monuments et mémoires.* Paris: E. Leroux.
PL *Patrologiae cursus completus, series latina*

Abbad Ríos, Francisco. *El Románico en Cinco Villas.* Zaragoza: Institucion 'Fernando el Católico,' 1979.

Acta Sanctorum. 3rd ed., 62 vols. Paris, 1863–1925.

Æthelwulf. *De Abbatibus.* Ed. and trans. A. Campbell, Oxford: Clarendon Press, 1967.

Alfaric, *La Chanson de Sainte Foy. See* Hoepffner and Alfaric.

Andrieu, Michel, ed. *Les* Ordines romani *du haut moyen age. V: Les textes (suite) (Ordo L).* Spicilegium Sacrum Lovaniense, 29. Louvain, 1961.

Anselm of Laon. *Enarrationes in Apocalypsin.* In Migne, *PL*, 162, cols. 1499–1586.

Arbeiter, Achim. *Alt-St. Peter in Geschichte und Wissenschaft: Abfolge der Bauten, Rekonstruktion, Architeckturprogramm.* Berlin: Gebr. Mann Verlag, 1988.

Armellini, Mariano. *Le chiese di Roma dal secolo IV al XIX.* Rev. and ed. Carlo Cecchelli, 2 vols. (continuously paged). Rome: Edizione R.O.R.E. di Nicola Ruffolo, 1942.

Ashley, Kathleen, and Pamela Sheingorn. 'The Translations of Foy: Bodies, Texts and Places.' In Ellis and Tixier, *The Medieval Translator*, 29–49.

Aubert, Marcel. *Romanesque Cathedrals and Abbeys of France*. Trans. Cuthbert Girdlestone. London, 1966.

Auerbach, Erich. 'Figura.' Trans. Ralph Manheim, from *Neue Dantestudien* (Istanbul, 1944), 11–71, in *Scenes from the Drama of European Literature*, 11–76.

– *Scenes from the Drama of European Literature*. 1959; repr. Gloucester, Mass.: Peter Smith, 1973.

Augustine, Saint. *De Doctrina Christiana*. Ed. J. Martin. In *CC*, 32.

– *On Christian Doctrine*. Ed. and trans. D.W. Robertson, Jr. Indianapolis and New York, 1958.

Austin, J.L. *How to Do Things with Words*. 2nd ed., ed. J.O. Urmson and Marina Sbisa. Cambridge: Harvard University Press, 1975.

Bacconnier, Raoul. *L'église romane Notre-Dame de Thines-en-Vivarais*. Lavilledieu: Les Editions de Candide, 1991.

Badisches Landesmuseum Karlsruhe: Meisterwerke aus den Sammlungen des wiedereröffneten Museums. Karlsruhe: C.F. Müller, 1959.

Bæksted, Anders. *Danske Indskrifter: En Indledning til Studiet af Dansk Epigrafik*. Copenhagen: Dansk Historisk Fællesforening, 1968.

Baker, Derek, ed. *Church, Society, and Politics: Papers Read at the Thirteenth Summer Meeting and the Fourteenth Winter Meeting of the Ecclesiastical History Society*. Oxford: Basil Blackwell, 1975.

Barral i Altet, Xavier. *Belgique romane et Grand-Duché de Luxembourg*. Saint-Léger-Vauban: Zodiaque, 1989.

Barruol, Guy. *Dauphiné roman*. Saint-Léger-Vauban: Zodiaque, 1992.

Barthélemy, Anatole de. 'Rapport: Église de Bourg-Argental.' *BM* 7 (1841), 595–6.

Beare, William. *Latin Verse and European Song: A Study in Accent and Rhythm*. London: Methuen, 1957.

Beckwith, John. *Ivory Carving in Early Medieval England*. London: Harvey Miller & Medcalf, 1972.

Bede, the Venerable. *De Arte Metrica et De Schematibus et Tropis*. Ed. Calvin B. Kendall. In *CC*, 123A, 59–171.

– *Bedae Opera de Temporibus*. Ed. Charles W. Jones, Cambridge, Mass.: The Mediaeval Academy of America, 1943.

– *In Cantica Canticorum*. Ed. David Hurst. In *CC*, 119B, 175–375.

– *The Ecclesiastical History of the English People*. Ed. Bertram Colgrave and R.A.B. Mynors. Oxford: Clarendon Press, 1969.

– *In Genesim*. Ed. Charles W. Jones. In *CC*, 118A.

– *Historia Abbatum*. Ed. Charles Plummer. In Plummer, *Venerabilis Baedae Opera Historica*, 364–87.

– *Libri II De Arte Metrica et De Schematibus et Tropis – The Art of Poetry and Rhetoric.* Latin text with English translation by Calvin B. Kendall. Bibliotheca Germanica, series nova, 2. Saarbrücken: AQ-Verlag, 1991.

– *Lives of the Abbots of Wearmouth and Jarrow.* Trans. D.H. Farmer. In Webb and Farmer, *The Age of Bede.*

– *De Locis Sanctis.* In Tobler, *Itinera.*

– *De Tabernaculo.* Ed. David Hurst. In *CC,* 119A, 1–139.

– *De Temporum Ratione.* In Jones, *Bedae Opera de Temporibus,* 173–291.

– *Venerabilis Baedae Opera Historica.* Ed. Charles Plummer. 2 vols. Oxford: Clarendon Press, 1896.

Beigbeder, Olivier. *Lexique des symboles.* 2nd ed. Saint-Léger-Vauban: Zodiaque, 1989.

Beigbeder, Olivier, and Raymond Oursel. *Forez-Velay roman.* 2nd ed. Saint-Léger-Vauban: Zodiaque, 1981.

Belting, Hans. *Likeness and Presence: A History of the Image before the Era of Art.* Trans. Edmund Jephcott. Chicago: University of Chicago Press, 1994.

Benson, Robert L. 'Political *Renovatio*: Two Models from Roman Antiquity.' In Benson and Constable, *Renaissance and Renewal,* 339–86.

Benson, Robert L., and Giles Constable, with Carol D. Lanham, eds. *Renaissance and Renewal in the Twelfth Century.* Cambridge: Harvard University Press, 1982.

Benton, John F. 'Consciousness of Self and Perceptions of Individuality.' In Benson and Constable, *Renaissance and Renewal,* 263–95.

Benveniste, Émile. *Problems in General Linguistics.* Trans. Mary Elizabeth Meek. Coral Gables, Fla.: University of Miami Press, 1971.

Bernard, Vital. *Le miroir des chanoines.* Paris: Jacques Quesnel, 1630.

Bible. Biblia Sacra Vulgatae Editionis. Turin: Marietti, 1959.

– *The Holy Bible Translated from the Latin Vulgate.* The Douay-Rheims translation, rev. Bishop Richard Challoner. Rockford, Ill.: Tan Books and Publishers, Inc., 1989.

Blaise, Albert. *Dictionnaire latin-français des auteurs chrétiens.* Turnhout: Brepols, 1954.

Blumenthal, Uta-Renate. *The Investiture Controversy: Church and Monarchy from the Ninth to the Twelfth Century.* Philadelphia: University of Pennsylvania Press, 1988.

Bogyay, Thomas. 'L'iconographie de la «Porta Speciosa» d'Esztergom et ses sources d'inspiration.' *Revue des Etudes Byzantines* 8 (1950), 85–129.

Bonne, Jean-Claude. *L'art roman de face et de profil: Le tympan de Conques.* Paris: Le Sycomore, 1984.

Bony, Jean. *French Gothic Architecture of the 12th and 13th Centuries.* California Studies in the History of Art, 20. Berkeley and Los Angeles, 1983.

Bornstein, Christine Verzár. *See* Verzár Bornstein, Christine.

Bottineau, Yves. *Les chemins de Saint-Jacques.* 2nd ed. Paris: Arthaud, 1983.

Bouillet, Auguste, ed. *Liber miraculorum sancte Fidis.* CTSEEH, 21. Paris: Alphonse Picard et fils, 1897. For English translation, *see* Sheingorn, *The Book of Sainte Foy,* 39–261.

Bouillet, Auguste, and L. Servières. *Sainte Foy: Vierge & martyre.* Rodez: E. Carrère, 1900.

Bourassé, J.J. *Dictionnaire d'épigraphie chrétienne.* 2 vols. Paris, 1852.

Bousquet, Jacques. *La sculpture à Conques aux XIe et XIIe siècles: Essai de chronologie comparée.* Diss., Toulouse, 1971. Photographically reproduced in 3 vols. Lille, 1973.

– 'Les nimbes à anagramme: Origines et brève fortune d'un motif roman.' *CSMC* 11 (1980), 101–21.

Bovini, Giuseppe. *La Cattedra eburnea del Vescovo Massimiano di Ravenna.* With appendix by Vanda Frattini Gaddoni, 'Breve guida alla visita del complesso storico monumentale della Cattedrale di Ravenna (Cattedrale, Battistero, Museo e Cappella Arcivescovili).' Ravenna: Edizioni 'Giorgio La Pira Soc. Coop. a.r.l.,' 1990.

Boyle, Leonard, OP. *A Short Guide to St. Clement's Rome.* Corrected reprint, Rome: Collegio San Clemente, 1989.

Bréhier, Louis. 'Les traits originaux de l'iconographie dans la sculpture romane de l'Auvergne.' In Koehler, *Medieval Studies in Memory of A. Kingsley Porter,* 2, 389–403.

Brown, George Hardin. *Bede the Venerable.* Boston: Twayne Publishers, 1987.

Bruno of Asti. *De Sacramentis Ecclesiae, Mysteriis atque Ecclesiasticis ritibus.* In Migne, *PL,* 165, cols. 1089–1110.

Bruyne, Edgar de. *Études d'esthétique médiévale.* 4 vols. Brugge: «De Tempel», 1946.

Buchowiecki, Walther. *Handbuch der Kirchen Roms: Der römische Sakralbau in Geschichte und Kunst von der altchristlichen Zeit bis zur Gegenwart.* 3 vols. Vienna: Verlag Brüder Hollinek, 1967–74.

Bugge, Ragne. '*Effigiem Christi, qui transis, semper honora*: Verses Condemning the Cult of Sacred Images in Art and Literature.' *Acta ad Archaeologiam et Artium Historiam pertinentia, Institutum Romanum Norvegiae* 6 (1976), 127–39.

Burchard of Worms. *Decretum.* In Migne, *PL,* 140, cols. 537–1058.

Caamaño Martinez, Jesus M.ª 'En torno al tímpano de Jaca.' *Goya: Revista de arte* 142 (1978), 200–7.

Cabanot, Jean. *Gascogne roman.* Saint-Léger-Vauban: Zodiaque, 1978.

Cahn, Walter. *The Romanesque Wooden Doors of Auvergne.* New York: New York University Press, 1974.

– 'Solomonic Elements in Romanesque Art.' In Gutmann, *The Temple of Solomon,* 45–72.

Caldwell, Susan Havens. 'Penance, Baptism, Apocalypse: The Easter Context of Jaca Cathedral's West Tympanum.' *Art History* 3 (1980), 25–40.

Canellas López, Angel, and Angel San Vicente. *Aragon roman.* Saint-Léger-Vauban: Zodiaque, 1971.

Caplan, Harry. 'The Four Senses of Scriptural Interpretation and the Mediaeval Theory of Preaching.' *Speculum* 4 (1929), 282–90.

Carlsson, Frans. *The Iconology of Tectonics in Romanesque Art.* Hässleholm: Am-Tryck, 1976.

Cassian, John. *Collationes XXIV.* In Migne, *PL*, 49, cols. 477–1328.

Cassidy, Brendan, ed. *The Ruthwell Cross: Papers from the Colloquium Sponsored by the Index of Christian Art, Princeton University, 8 December 1989.* Princeton: Princeton University Press, 1992.

Castellane, Marquis de H. 'Inscriptions du XIe au XIIe siècle, recueillies principalement dans le Midi de la France.' *Memoires de la Société archéologique du Midi de la France* 3 (1836–7), 53–107.

Chamoso Lamas, Manuel, Victoriano González, and Bernardo Regal. *Galice romane.* Trans. from Spanish into French by Norbert Vaillant. Saint-Léger-Vauban: Zodiaque, 1973.

Chierici, Sandro, and Duilio Citi. *Piémont-Ligurie roman.* Trans. from Italian into French by Norbert Vaillant. Saint-Léger-Vauban: Zodiaque, 1979.

Christe, Yves. *Les grands portails romans: Études sur l'iconologie des théophanies romanes.* Geneva: Librairie Droz, 1969.

Claussen, Peter Cornelius. *Magistri Doctissimi Romani: Die römischen Marmorkünstler des Mittelalters (corpus Cosmatorum I).* Forschungen zur Kunstgeschichte und christlichen Archäologie, 14. Stuttgart: Franz Steiner Verlag Wiesbaden GMBH, 1987.

Colgrave, Bertram, and R.A.B. Mynors, eds. *Bede's Ecclesiastical History. See* Bede, *The Ecclesiastical History of the English People.*

Colombo, Giulio. *San Giorgio al Palazzo: Guida descrittiva con note storiche.* Milan: Parrocchia di S. Giorgio, 1974.

Conant, Kenneth John. *Carolingian and Romanesque Architecture 800 to 1200.* 2nd integrated paperback ed. Harmondsworth: Penguin Books, 1978.

– *Cluny: Les églises et la maison du chef d'ordre.* Mediaeval Academy of America Publication no. 77. Mâcon: Protat Frères, 1968.

– *The Early Architectural History of the Cathedral of Santiago de Compostela.* Cambridge: Harvard University Press, 1926.

Constable, Giles. 'Renewal and Reform in Religious Life: Concepts and Realities.' In Benson and Constable, *Renaissance and Renewal*, 37–67.

Corpus Christianorum, series latina. Turnhout: Brepols, 1954–.

Corpus Inscriptionum Latinarum. Berlin, 1863–.

Craplet, Bernard. *Auvergne romane.* 1st ed. Saint-Léger-Vauban: Zodiaque, 1955.
– *Auvergne romane.* 5th ed. Saint-Léger-Vauban: Zodiaque, 1978.
Crichton, G.H. *Romanesque Sculpture in Italy.* London: Routledge & Kegan Paul, 1954.
Crosby, Sumner McKnight. *L'abbaye royale de Saint-Denis.* Paris: Paul Hartmann, 1953.
– *The Royal Abbey of Saint-Denis from Its Beginnings to the Death of Suger, 475–1151.* Ed. and completed by Pamela Z. Blum. New Haven: Yale University Press, 1987.
Curtius, Ernst Robert. *European Literature and the Latin Middle Ages.* Bollingen Series, 36. Trans. Willard R. Trask. New York: Pantheon Books, 1953.
Dante Alighieri. *The Divine Comedy.* Bollingen Series, 80. Ed. and trans. Charles S. Singleton. Princeton: Princeton University Press, 1970.
Davis-Weyer, Caecilia. *Early Medieval Art 300–1150: Sources and Documents.* Medieval Academy Reprints for Teaching, 17. Toronto: University of Toronto Press, 1986.
Debove, Guido. 'La Sacra di S. Michele in Val di Susa.' *Arte lombarda: Rivista di storia dell'arte* 10:2 (1965), 11–32.
Deguileville, Guillaume de. *The Pilgrimage of Human Life (Le Pèlerinage de la vie humaine).* Trans. Eugene Clasby. New York: Garland Publishing, 1992.
Deijk, Ada van. *Pays-Bas romans.* Trans. from Dutch into French by Annick van der Does de Willebois. Saint-Léger-Vauban: Zodiaque, 1994.
Dekkers, Eligius, and Aemilius Gaar, ed. *Clavis Patrum Latinorum.* 2nd ed. (*Sacris Erudiri* 3). Brugge: Karel Beyaert, 1961.
Demus, Otto. *The Mosaics of San Marco in Venice. 1: The Eleventh and Twelfth Centuries.* 2 vols. (vol. 1: Text; vol. 2: Plates). Chicago: University of Chicago Press, 1984.
– *The Mosaics of San Marco in Venice. 2: The Thirteenth Century.* 2 vols. (vol. 1: Text; vol. 2: Plates). Chicago: University of Chicago Press, 1984.
Dercsényi, Dezsö. 'La "Porta Speciosa" dell'antica Cattedrale di Esztergom.' *Annuario dell'Istituto Ungherese di Storia dell'Arte di Firenze* (1947), 22–46.
Deschamps, Paul. 'Le combat des vertus et des vices sur les portails romans de la Saintonge et du Poitou.' *Congrès archéologique de France* 79 (1912), vol. 2, 309–24.
– 'Étude sur la paléographie des inscriptions lapidaires de la fin de l'époque mérovingienne aux dernières années du XIIe siècle.' *BM* 88 (1929), 5–86.
– 'Étude sur les sculptures de Sainte-Foy de Conques et de Saint-Sernin de Toulouse et leurs relations avec celles de Saint-Isidore de León et de Saint-Jacques de Compostelle.' *BM* 100 (1941), 239–64.
– *French Sculpture of the Romanesque Period: Eleventh and Twelfth Centuries.* 1930; repr. New York: Hacker Art Books, 1972.
Deshoulières, François-Thabaud. 'Le tympan de l'église Saint-Pierre-le-Puellier.' *Mémoires de la Société des Antiquaires du Centre* 38 (1917–18), 38–46.

Dillange, Michel. *Vendée romane. Bas-Poitou roman.* Saint-Léger-Vauban: Zodiaque, 1976.

Dobbie, Elliott Van Kirk, ed. *The Anglo-Saxon Minor Poems.* The Anglo-Saxon Poetic Records, 6. New York: Columbia University Press, 1942.

Doob, Penelope Reed. *The Idea of the Labyrinth from Classical Antiquity through the Middle Ages.* Ithaca: Cornell University Press, 1990.

Dubourg-Noves, Pierre. *Guyenne romane.* Saint-Léger-Vauban: Zodiaque, 1979.

Duby, Georges. 'The Culture of the Knightly Class: Audience and Patronage.' In Benson and Constable, *Renaissance and Renewal*, 248–62.

Duchesne, (Abbé) L. *Le Liber Pontificalis: Texte, introduction et commentaire.* 2nd ed., 3 vols. Paris: E. De Boccard, 1955–7.

Duemmler, Ernest, ed. *Poetae Latini Aevi Carolini.* In *MGH*: *Poetarum Latinorum Medii Aevi.* Vol. 1 (2 parts in 1, continuously paged), Berlin, 1880–1; vol. 2, Berlin, 1884. *See also* Traube.

Duggan, Lawrence G. 'Was Art Really the "Book of the Illiterate?"' *Word & Image* 5 (1989), 227–51.

Dupont, Jean. *Nivernais-Bourbonnais roman.* Saint-Léger-Vauban: Zodiaque, 1976.

Durán Gudiol, Antonio. 'Las inscripciones medievales de la provincia de Huesca.' *Estudios de edad media de la corona de Aragón* (Consejo superior de investigaciones científicas. Escuela de estudios medievales. Estudios, 39) 8 (1967), 45–153.

Durand, Vincent. 'Roues symboliques avec le monogramme du Christ.' *Bulletin de la Société nationale des Antiquaires de France* (1892), 119–20.

Durandus, William. *The Symbolism of Churches and Church Ornaments: A Translation of the First Book of the Rationale Divinorum Officiorum.* Trans., with intro. and notes, John Mason Neale and Benjamin Webb, 1843; repr. London: Gibbings & Co., 1893.

Durliat, Marcel. *Haut-Languedoc roman.* Saint-Léger-Vauban: Zodiaque, 1978.

– 'Le portail occidental de Saint-Sernin de Toulouse.' *Annales du Midi* 77 (1965), 215–23.

– *Roussillon roman.* Saint-Léger-Vauban: Zodiaque, 1958.

– *La sculpture romane de la route de Saint-Jacques: De Conques à Compostelle.* Mont-de-Marsan: Comité d'Études sur l'Histoire et l'Art de la Gascogne, 1990.

– *La sculpture romane en Roussillon.* Vol. 2: Corneilla-de-Conflent, Elne. Perpignan, 1949.

Durliat, Marcel, and Victor Allègre. *Pyrénées romanes.* 2nd ed. Saint-Léger-Vauban: Zodiaque, 1978.

Eco, Umberto. *The Aesthetics of Thomas Aquinas.* Trans. Hugh Bredin. Cambridge: Harvard University Press, 1988.

– *Art and Beauty in the Middle Ages.* Trans. Hugh Bredin. New Haven and London: Yale University Press, 1986.

Ederle, Guglielmo. *The Basilica of St. Zeno.* Trans. Laura Severi. Verona: Edizioni di 'Vita Veronese,' 1962.

Ellis, Roger, and René Tixier, eds. *The Medieval Translator / Traduire au Moyen Age,* vol. 5 (Proceedings of the International Conference of Conques [26–29 July 1993]). Turnhout: Brepols, 1996.

Enlart, Camille. 'L'église abbatiale de Sant'Antimo de Toscane.' *Revue de l'art chrétien* 63 (1913), 1–14.

Esteban Lorente, Juan F. 'Las inscripciones del tímpano de la Catedral de Jaca.' *Artigrama: Revista del Departamento de Historia del Arte* [Universidad de Zaragoza] 10 (1993), 143–61.

Evans, Joan. *Cluniac Art of the Romanesque Period.* Cambridge: Cambridge University Press, 1950.

– *The Romanesque Architecture of the Order of Cluny.* Cambridge: Cambridge University Press, 1938.

Eygun, François, with the assistance of Jean Dupont. *Saintonge romane.* 2nd ed. Saint-Léger-Vauban: Zodiaque, 1979.

Farmer, David Hugh. *The Oxford Dictionary of Saints.* 1978; repr. with corrections. Oxford: Oxford University Press, 1983.

Fau, Jean-Claude. *Rouergue roman.* 3rd ed. Saint-Léger-Vauban: Zodiaque, 1990. *See also* 2nd edition by Georges Gaillard et al.

Favière, Jean. *Berry roman.* 2nd ed. Saint-Léger-Vauban: Zodiaque, 1976.

Favole, Paolo. *Marches romanes.* Saint-Léger-Vauban: Zodiaque, 1993.

Favole, Paolo, with collaboration of Francesca Del Vitto. *Abruzzes Molise romans.* Saint-Léger-Vauban: Zodiaque, 1990.

Favreau, Robert. 'L'inscription du tympan nord de San Miguel d'Estella.' *Bibliothèque de l'École des Chartes* 133 (1975), 237–46.

– *Les inscriptions médiévales.* Typologie des sources du Moyen Age occidental, fasc. 35. Turnhout: Brepols, 1979.

Favreau, Robert, and Jean Michaud. *Corpus des inscriptions de la France médiévale [CIFM].* Vol. 1, pt 1: Ville de Poitiers. Poitiers: Éditions du Centre National de la Recherche Scientifique [C.N.R.S.], 1974.

– *CIFM.* Vol. 1, pt 2: Département de la Vienne (excepté la ville de Poitiers). Poitiers: Éditions du C.N.R.S., 1975.

– *CIFM.* Vol. 1, pt 3: Charente, Charente-Maritime, Deux-Sèvres. Poitiers: Éditions du C.N.R.S., 1977.

– *CIFM.* Vol. 2: Limousin: Correze, Creuse, Haute-Vienne. Poitiers: Éditions du C.N.R.S., 1978.

Favreau, Robert, Bernadette Leplant, and Jean Michaud. *CIFM.* Vol. 5: Dordogne, Gironde. Poitiers: Éditions du C.N.R.S., 1979. [As a result of a renumbering, vols. 1:1–3 and 2 are now considered vols. 1–4; hence vol. 5 is the next in the series.]

– *CIFM*. Vol. 6: Gers, Landes, Lot-et-Garonne, Pyrénées-Atlantiques. Paris: Éditions du C.N.R.S., 1981.
– *CIFM*. Vol. 7: Ville de Toulouse. Paris: Éditions du C.N.R.S., 1982.
– *CIFM*. Vol. 8: Ariège, Haute-Garonne, Hautes-Pyrénées, Tarn-et-Garonne. Paris: Éditions du C.N.R.S., 1982.
– *CIFM*. Vol. 9: Aveyron, Lot, Tarn. Paris: Éditions du C.N.R.S., 1984.
Favreau, Robert, Jean Michaud, and Bernadette Mora. *CIFM*. Vol. 10: Chrismes du sud-ouest. Paris: Éditions du C.N.R.S., 1985.
– *CIFM*. Vol. 11: Pyrénées-Orientales. Paris: Éditions du C.N.R.S., 1986.
– *CIFM*. Vol. 12: Aude, Hérault. Paris: Éditions du C.N.R.S., 1988.
– *CIFM*. Vol. 13: Gard, Lozère, Vaucluse. Paris: Éditions du C.N.R.S., 1988.
– *CIFM*. Vol. 14: Alpes-Maritimes, Bouches-du-Rhône, Var. Paris: Éditions du C.N.R.S., 1989.
– *CIFM*. Vol. 15: La ville de Vienne en Dauphiné. Paris: Éditions du C.N.R.S., 1990.
– *CIFM*. Vol. 16: Alpes-de-Haute-Provence, Hautes-Alpes, Ardèche, Drôme. Paris: Éditions du C.N.R.S., 1992.
– *CIFM*. Vol. 17: Ain, Isère (sauf Vienne), Rhône, Savoie, Haute-Savoie. Paris: Éditions du C.N.R.S., 1994.
– *CIFM*. Vol. 18: Allier, Cantal, Loire, Haute-Loire, Puy-de-Dôme. Paris: Éditions du C.N.R.S., 1995.
Fernie, Eric. 'Notes on the Sculpture of Modena Cathedral.' *Arte lombarda: Rivista di storia dell'arte* 14:2 (1969), 88–93.
Fikry, Ahmad. *L'art roman du Puy et les influences islamiques*. 1934; repr. Soest: Davaco Publishers, 1974.
Fiskovič, Cvito, and Marijan Szabo. *Radovan: Portal Katedrale u Trogiru*. Zagreb: Državno Izdavače Poduzeče Hrvatske, 1951. (English summary, pp. xxxvi–xl.)
Fletcher, Richard. *The Quest for El Cid*. New York: Alfred A. Knopf, 1990.
Flint, Valerie I.J. *The Rise of Magic in Early Medieval Europe*. Princeton: Princeton University Press, 1991.
Focillon, Henri. *The Art of the West*. Vol. 1: Romanesque Art. Trans. Donald King, 1963; repr. Ithaca: Cornell University Press, 1980.
Fontaine, Jacques. *Vie de Saint Martin*. 3 vols. Paris: Les Éditions du Cerf, 1967–9.
Formigé, Jules. *L'abbaye royale de Saint-Denis: Recherches nouvelles*. Paris: Presses universitaires de France, 1960.
Fortunatus, Venantius. *Opera Poetica*, Ed. Fridericus Leo. In *MGH*: *Auctores Antiquissimi*, 4:1. Berlin, 1881.
Fox, Robin Lane. *Pagans and Christians*. 1986; repr. New York: HarperCollins, 1988.
Francovich, Geza de. *Benedetto Antelami: Architetto e scultore e l'arte del suo tempo*. 2 vols. Milan: Electa Editrice, 1952.

Frantzen, Allen J., ed. *Speaking Two Languages: Traditional Disciplines and Comtemporary Theory in Medieval Studies.* Albany: State University of New York Press, 1991.

Gaddoni, Vanda Frattini. 'Breve guida alla visita del complesso storico monumentale della Cattedrale di Ravenna (Cattedrale, Battistero, Museo e Cappella Arcivescovili).' In Bovini, *La Cattedra eburnea del Vescovo Massimiano di Ravenna,* 47–83.

Gaillard, Georges. *Les débuts de la sculpture romane espagnole: Leon, Jaca, Compostelle.* Paris: P. Hartmann, 1938.

– 'Deux sculptures de l'Abbaye des Moreaux à Oberlin (Ohio).' *GBA,* 6th ser., 44 (1954), 81–90; repr. in Gaillard, *Études d'art roman,* 389–97.

– *Études d'art roman.* Paris: Presses universitaires de France, 1972.

– 'Notes sur les tympans aragonais.' *Bulletin hispanique* 30 (1928), 193–203; repr. in Gaillard, *Études d'art roman,* 231–9.

Gaillard, Georges, Marie-Madeleine S. Gauthier, Louis Balsan, and Dom Angelico Surchamp. *Rouergue roman.* 2nd ed. Saint-Léger-Vauban: Zodiaque, 1974. *See also* 3rd edition by Jean-Claude Fau.

Gallacher, Patrick J., and Helen Damico, eds. *Hermeneutics and Medieval Culture.* Albany: State University of New York Press, 1989.

Gallais, Pierre, and Yves-Jean Riou, eds. *Mélanges offerts à René Crozet à l'occasion de son soixante-dixième anniversaire.* Vol. 1. Poitiers: Société d'Études Médiévales, 1966.

Geary, Patrick J. *Furta Sacra: Thefts of Relics in the Central Middle Ages.* Rev. ed. Princeton: Princeton University Press, 1990.

Gerson, Paula Lieber. 'The Iconography of the Trinity at Saint-Denis.' *Gesta* 17 (1978), 73.

Gettings, Fred. *The Secret Zodiac: The Hidden Art in Mediaeval Astrology.* London: Routledge & Kegan Paul, 1987.

Geyer, Marie-Jeanne. 'Le mythe d'Erwin de Steinbach.' In Recht, *Les bâtisseurs des cathédrales gothiques,* 322–29.

Ghellinck, J. de, SJ. *L'essor de la littérature latine au XIIe siècle.* 2nd ed. Brussels: Desclée de Brouwer, 1955.

Gissey, Odo de. *Discours historiques de la très ancienne dévotion de Nostre Dame du Puy.* 3rd ed. Le Puy, 1644.

Glaber, Raoul. *Historiarum Sui Temporis libri quinque.* In Mortet, *Recueil de textes.*

Goldschmidt, Rudolf Carel. *Paulinus' Churches at Nola: Texts, Translations and Commentary.* Amsterdam: N.V. Noord-Hollandsche Uitgevers Maatschappij, 1940.

Golzio, Vincenzo, and Giuseppe Zander. *Le chiese di Roma: dall' XI al XVI secolo.* Roma cristiana, 4. Bologna: Casa Editrice Licinio Cappelli, 1963.

Gordon, Arthur E. *Illustrated Introduction to Latin Epigraphy.* Berkeley and Los Angeles: University of California Press, 1983.

Grabar, André. *Christian Iconography: A Study of Its Origins.* Bollingen Series, 35.10. Princeton: Princeton University Press, 1968.

Grandgent, C.H. *An Introduction to Vulgar Latin.* 1934; repr. New York: Hafner Publishing Co., 1962.

Gregory the Great. *Moralia in Iob (Libri I–X).* Ed. Marcus Adriaen. In *CC*, 143.

Gregory of Tours. *Historiae Francorum.* Ed. W. Arndt and Bruno Krusch. In *MGH: Scriptores rerum Merovingicarum.* Vol. 1, Hanover, 1885; repr. 1961. For English translation, *see* Thorpe.

Grivot, Denis, and George Zarnecki. *Gislebertus: Sculptor of Autun.* New York: Orion Press, 1961.

Guédel, Jean. *L'architecture romane en Dombes.* Bourg: Courrier de l'Ain, 1911.

Guilhermy, F. de, and R. de Lasteyrie. *Inscriptions de la France du Ve siècle au XVIIIe.* Collection de documents inédits sur l'histoire de France, 3rd ser., archéologie. Vol. 5, Paris: Imprimerie nationale, 1883.

Gutmann, Joseph, ed. *The Temple of Solomon: Archaeological Fact and Medieval Tradition in Christian, Islamic and Jewish Art.* Missoula: Scholars Press, 1976.

Hancher, Michael. 'Performative Utterance, the Word of God, and the Death of the Author.' *Semeia* 41 (1988), 27–40.

Hearn, M.F. *Romanesque Sculpture: The Revival of Monumental Stone Sculpture in the Eleventh and Twelfth Centuries.* Oxford: Phaidon Press, 1981.

Heer, Friedrich. *The Medieval World: Europe 1100–1350.* Trans. Janet Sondheimer. New York: New American Library, 1962.

Hoepffner, Ernest, and Prosper Alfaric. *La Chanson de Sainte Foy.* Vol. 1: Fac-similé du manuscrit et texte critique, introduction et commentaire philologiques par Ernest Hoepffner. Vol. 2: Traduction française et sources latines, introduction et commentaire historiques par Prosper Alfaric. Publications de la Faculté des Lettres de l'Université de Strasbourg, 32–3. 2 vols. Paris: Société d'Édition: Les Belles Lettres, 1926.

Holder, Arthur G. 'Allegory and History in Bede's Interpretation of Sacred Architecture.' *American Benedictine Review* 40 (1989), 115–31.

Honorius Augustodunensis. *Gemma Animae.* In Migne, *PL*, 172, cols. 541–738.

Horn, Walter, and Ernest Born. *The Plan of St. Gall.* 3 vols. Berkeley and Los Angeles: University of California Press, 1979.

Horste, Kathryn. 'Romanesque Sculpture in American Collections, XX: Ohio & Michigan.' *Gesta* 21 (1982), 107–34.

Hoving, Thomas P.F. 'The Bury St. Edmunds Cross.' *Metropolitan Museum of Art Bulletin* 22 (June 1964), 317–40.

Howlett, David. 'Inscriptions and Design of the Ruthwell Cross.' In Cassidy, *The Ruthwell Cross*, 71–93.

Hrabanus Maurus. *Allegoriae in Universam Sacram Scripturam.* In Migne, *PL*, 112, cols. 849–1088.

Hubert, Jean. 'L'abbatiale Notre-Dame de Déols.' *BM* 86 (1927), 5–66.

– 'La tour occidentale de Saint-Denis.' *Bulletin de la Société nationale des Antiquaires de France 1945–1946–1947* (1950), 137–40.

Hübner, Aemilius [Emile]. *Inscriptionum Hispaniae Christianarum Supplementum.* Berlin: Georgius Reimer, 1900.

Hugh of Saint-Victor. *Commentarii in Hierarchiam Coelestem Sancti Dionysii Areopagitae.* In Migne, *PL*, 175, cols. 923–1154.

Irvine, Martin J. 'Medieval Textuality and the Archaeology of the Text.' In Frantzen, *Speaking Two Languages*, 181–210.

Isidore of Seville. *Allegoriae quaedam Scripturae Sacrae.* In Migne, *PL*, 83, cols. 97–130.

– *Etymologiarum sive Originum libri XX.* Ed. W.M. Lindsay. 2 vols. Oxford: Clarendon Press, 1911.

– *De Natura Rerum Liber.* In Migne, *PL*, 83, cols. 963–1018.

– *De Ortu et Obitu Patrum, Ex Veteri Testamento.* In Migne, *PL*, 83, cols. 129–56.

Jacobus de Voragine. *The Golden Legend.* Trans. Granger Ryan and Helmut Ripperger. 1941; repr. New York: Arno Press, 1969.

James, Montague Rhodes, trans. *The Apocryphal New Testament: Being the Apocryphal Gospels, Acts, Epistles, and Apocalypses.* 1924; corrected repr. Oxford: Clarendon Press, 1953.

Jerome, Saint. *Lettres.* Ed. Jérome Labourt. Vol. 5. Paris: Société d'Édition «Les Belles Lettres», 1955.

Jones, Charles W. 'Some Introductory Remarks on Bede's Commentary on Genesis.' *Sacris Erudiri* 19 (1969/70), 115–98.

Jones, Charles W., ed. *Bedae Opera de Temporibus. See* Bede, *Bedae Opera de Temporibus.*

Junyent, Edouard. *Catalogne romane.* Vol. 2, trans. from Catalan into French by Emmanuel Companys. Saint-Léger-Vauban: Zodiaque, 1961.

Kahn, Deborah, ed. *The Romanesque Frieze and Its Spectator: The Lincoln Symposium Papers.* London: Harvey Miller Publishers, 1992.

Kain, Evelyn. 'The Marble Reliefs on the Façade of S. Zeno, Verona.' *AB* 63 (1981), 358–74.

Katzenellenbogen, Adolf. *Allegories of the Virtues and Vices in Medieval Art: From Early Christian Times to the Thirteenth Century.* 1939; repr. Toronto: University of Toronto Press, 1989.

Keen, Jill A. 'Documenting Salvation: Charters and Pardons in "þou Wommon Boute Uére," the Charters of Christ and *Piers Plowman.*' PhD diss., University of Minnesota, 1995.

Kendall, Calvin B. 'Imitation and the Venerable Bede's *Historia Ecclesiastica.*' In King and Stevens, *Saints, Scholars, and Heroes*, 1, 161–90.

– 'The Plan of St. Gall: An Argument for a 320-Foot Church Prototype.' *Mediaeval Studies* 56 (1994), 279–97.

– 'The Verse Inscriptions of the Tympanum of Jaca and the PAX Anagram.' *Mediaevalia* 19 (1996), 405–34.

– 'The Voice in the Stone: The Verse Inscriptions of Ste.-Foy of Conques and the Date of the Tympanum.' In Gallacher and Damico, *Hermeneutics and Medieval Culture*, 163–82.

Kendall, Calvin B., ed. *Bede's Art of Poetry and Rhetoric. See* Bede, *Libri II De Arte Metrica.*

– *De Arte Metrica et De Schematibus et Tropis. See* Bede, *De Arte Metrica.*

Kerber, Bernhard. *Burgund und die Entwicklung der französischen Kathedralskulptur im zwölften Jahrhundert.* Recklinghausen: Verlag Aurel Bongers, 1966.

Kern, Hermann. *Labirinti: Forme e interpretazioni: 5000 anni di presenza di un archetipo.* Trans. Libero Sosio, 3rd ed. Milan: Giangiacomo Feltrinelli Editore, 1981.

King, Margot H., and Wesley M. Stevens, eds. *Saints, Scholars, and Heroes: Studies in Medieval Culture in Honour of Charles W. Jones.* 2 vols. Collegeville, Minn.: Hill Monastic Manuscript Library, 1979.

Klein, Peter. 'Les portails de Saint-Genis-des-Fontaines et de Saint-André-de-Sorède. I: Le linteau de Saint Genis.' *CSMC* 20 (1989), 121–42.

– 'Les portails. II: Le linteau et la fenêtre de Saint-André-de-Sorède.' *CSMC* 21 (1990), 159–72.

Koehler, Wilhelm R.W., ed. *Medieval Studies in Memory of A. Kingsley Porter.* 2 vols. Cambridge: Harvard University Press, 1939.

Krapp, George Philip, ed. *The Vercelli Book.* The Anglo-Saxon Poetic Records, 2. New York: Columbia University Press, 1932.

Kraus, Franz Xaver. *Die christlichen Inschriften der Rheinlande.* Vol. 2: Die christlichen Inschriften der Rheinlande von der Mitte des achten bis zur Mitte des dreizehnten Jahrhunderts. Freiburg i. B.: Paul Siebeck, 1894.

Kraus, Henry. *The Living Theatre of Medieval Art.* Philadelphia: University of Pennsylvania Press, 1967.

Krautheimer, Richard. 'The Carolingian Revival of Early Christian Architecture.' *AB* 24 (1942), 1–38. New York, 1969.

– *Corpus Basilicarum Christianarum Romae: The Early Christian Basilicas of Rome (IV–IX Cent.).* Vol. 1., Vatican City: Pontificio Istituto di Archeologia Cristiana, 1937.

– 'Introduction to an "Iconography of Mediaeval Architecture."' *Journal of the Warburg and Courtauld Institutes* 5 (1942), 1–33.

Krautheimer-Hess, Trude. 'The Original Porta Dei Mesi at Ferrara and the Art of Niccolo.' *AB* 26 (1944), 152–74.

Labande-Mailfert, Yvonne. *Poitou roman.* 2nd ed. Saint-Léger-Vauban: Zodiaque, 1962.

Labriolle, Pierre de. *Historie de la littérature latine chrétienne.* 3rd ed., rev. and enlarged by Gustave Bardy, 2 vols. (continuously paged). Paris: Société d'Édition «Les Belles-Lettres», 1947.

Ladner, Gerhart B. 'Terms and Ideas of Renewal.' In Benson and Constable, *Renaissance and Renewal*, 1–33.

Läffler, L.-Fr. 'Restitution d'une inscription latine incomplète du Moyen-age sur le linteau du portail de l'église de Bellegarde-du-Loiret.' *Bulletin de la Société archéologique et historique de l'Orléanais* 19 (no. 218) (1920–1), 104–6.

Lambert, Élie. 'L'ancienne abbaye de Saint-Pé de Bigorre' (1943). Repr. in *Études médiévales*, 2, 109–31.

– *Études médiévales.* 4 vols. Toulouse: Privat-Didier, 1956–7.

Lampérez, Vicente. 'Notas de une excursión.' *Boletín de la Sociedad Española de excursiones* (1899), 192–3.

Lange, Reinhold. *Die Byzantinische Reliefikone.* Recklinghausen: Verlag Aurel Bongers, 1964.

Langosch, Karl. *Lateinisches Mittelalter: Einleitung in Sprache und Literatur.* Darmstadt: Wissenschaftliche Buchgesellschaft, 1969.

Laplace, P.-L. *Notice sur l'église de St-André de Luz-en-Barèges.* Pau: H. Maurin, 1899.

Lasteyrie, R. de. *L'architecture religieuse en France à l'époque romane.* 2nd ed., rev. Marcel Aubert. Paris, 1929.

– 'Études sur la sculpture française au moyen âge.' *Monuments Piot* 8 (1902), 118–27.

Lattimore, Richmond. *Themes in Greek and Latin Epitaphs.* Illinois Studies in Language and Literature 28, nos. 1–2. Urbana: University of Illinois Press, 1942.

Le Blant, Edmond. *Inscriptions chrétiennes de la Gaule antérieures au VIIIe siècle.* 2 vols. Paris, 1856–65.

Lefèvre-Pontalis, E. 'Église d'Aulnay-de-Saintonge.' *Congrès archéologique de France* 79 (1912), vol. 1, 95–111.

– 'Église d'Autry-Issard.' *Congrès archéologique de France* 80 (1913), 228–32.

Lehmann, Karl. 'The Dome of Heaven.' *AB* 27 (1945), 1–27.

Lehmann, Winfred P. *The Development of Germanic Verse Form.* 1956; repr. New York: Gordian Press, 1971.

Leo, Fridericus, ed. Venantius Fortunatus, *Opera Poetica. See* Fortunatus, *Opera Poetica.*

Leo of Ostia. *Chronicon Monasterii Casinensis.* In Migne, *PL*, 173, cols. 479–812.

Leyerle, John. 'The Rose-Wheel Design and Dante's *Paradiso*.' *University of Toronto Quarterly* 46 (1977), 280–308.

Lienhard, Joseph T. *Paulinus of Nola and Early Western Monasticism: With a Study of the Chronology of His Works and an Annotated Bibliography, 1879–1976.* Cologne/Bonn: Peter Hanstein Verlag, 1977.

Lindsay, W.M. *The Latin Language: An Historical Account of Latin Sounds, Stems, and Flexions.* 1894; repr. New York: Hafner Publishing, 1963.
Lloyd, Richard Wingate. 'Cluny Epigraphy.' *Speculum* 7 (1932), 336–49.
Loerke, William. '"Real Presence" in Early Christian Art.' In Verdon, *Monasticism and the Arts*, 29–51.
Lojendio, Luis-Maria de. *Navarre romane.* Trans. from Spanish into French by Norbert Vaillant. Saint-Léger-Vauban: Zodiaque, 1967.
Lombard, O. 'Les sculptures romanes de Beaucaire.' *Bulletin de la Société d'histoire et d'archéologie de Beaucaire*, no. 20 (1969), n. p.
Lubac, Henri de, SJ. *Exégèse médiévale: Les quatre sens de l'Écriture.* 2 vols. (continuously paged). Paris: Aubier, 1959.
Luetjohann, Christian, ed. *Apollinaris Sidonii Epistulae et Carmina. See* Sidonius Apollinaris, *Apollinaris Sidonii Epistulae et Carmina.*
Lugand, Jacques, Jean Nougaret, and Robert Saint-Jean. *Languedoc roman: Le Languedoc méditerranéen.* Saint-Léger-Vauban: Zodiaque, 1975.
Luzuy, l'Abbé. 'Mozac.' *Congrès archéologique de France* 80 (1913), 124–43.
Lyman, Thomas. 'Raymond Gairard and Romanesque Building Campaigns at Saint-Sernin in Toulouse.' *Journal of the Society of Architectural Historians* 37 (1978), 71–91.
– 'Le style comme symbole chez les sculpteurs romans: Essai d'interprétation de quelques inventions thématiques à la Porte Miègeville de Saint-Sernin.' *CSMC* 12 (1981), 161–79.
MacCormack, Sabine. 'Loca Sancta: The Organization of Sacred Topography in Late Antiquity.' In Ousterhout, *The Blessings of Pilgrimage*, 8–40.
McCulloch, Florence. *Mediaeval Latin and French Bestiaries*, University of North Carolina Studies in the Romance Languages and Literatures, 33. Rev. ed. Chapel Hill: University of North Carolina Press, 1962.
McGinn, Bernard. *Antichrist: Two Thousand Years of the Human Fascination with Evil.* New York: HarperCollins, 1994.
Mackeprang, M. *Jydske Granitportaler.* Copenhagen: Andr. Fred. Høst & Søns Forlag, 1948.
McKitterick, Rosamond, ed. *The Uses of Literacy in Early Mediaeval Europe.* Cambridge: Cambridge University Press, 1990.
Mac Lean, Douglas. 'The Date of the Ruthwell Cross.' In Cassidy, *The Ruthwell Cross*, 49–70.
Mâle, Emile. *The Early Churches of Rome.* Trans. David Buxton. Chicago: Quadrangle Books, 1960.
– *La fin du paganisme en Gaule et les plus anciennes basiliques chrétiennes.* Paris: Flammarion, 1950.
– *Religious Art in France, The Twelfth Century: A Study of the Origins of Medieval Iconog-*

raphy. Bollingen Series, 90.1. Ed. Harry Bober, trans. Marthiel Mathews (from 1953 Paris ed.). Princeton: Princeton University Press, 1978.

– *Religious Art in France, The Thirteenth Century: A Study of Medieval Iconography and Its Sources.* Bollingen Series, 90.2. Ed. Harry Bober, trans. Marthiel Mathews (from 1958 Paris ed.). Princeton: Princeton University Press, 1984.

Malory, Sir Thomas. *The Works of Sir Thomas Malory.* Ed. Eugène Vinaver. London: Oxford University Press, 1954.

Marrier, Dom Martinus, and Andreas Quercetanus. *Bibliotheca cluniacensis.* Paris, 1614.

Martène, Edmond, and Ursin Durand. *Voyage litteraire de deux religieux Benedictins de la Congregation de Saint Maur.* 2 vols., Paris, 1717–24; photographically repr., Westmead, Farnborough, Hants.: Gregg International Publishers, 1969. Vol. 1 is in two parts, separately paginated.

Máthes, Joanne N. *Veteris Arcis Strigoniensis, Monumentorum Ibidem Erutorum, Aliarumque Antiquitatum Lythographicis Tabulis Ornata Descriptio.* Esztergom, 1827.

Mathews, Thomas F. *The Clash of Gods: A Reinterpretation of Early Christian Art.* Princeton: Princeton University Press, 1993.

Matthews, W.H. *Mazes and Labyrinths: A General Account of Their History and Developments.* London: Longmans, Green and Co., 1922.

Matthiae, Guglielmo. *Mosaici medioevali delle chiese di Roma.* 2 vols. (vol. 1, text; vol. 2, plates). Rome: Istituto poligrafico dello stato, 1967.

Mayeux, A. 'Tympan sculpté de la porte du doyenné de Mauriac.' *Bulletin de la Société nationale des Antiquaires de France,* 1927, 232–6.

Meier, Hans Rudolf. *Suisse romane.* 3rd ed., trans. from German into French by Angelico Surchamp, Rouin Leblanc, and Norbert Vaillant. Saint-Léger-Vauban: Zodiaque, 1996.

Melczer, William, ed. *The Pilgrim's Guide to Santiago de Compostela.* New York: Italica Press, 1993.

Mély, F. de. 'Signatures de primitifs (XIe–XIIe siècles): De Cluny à Compostelle.' *GBA,* 5th ser., 10 (1924), 1–24.

Mendell, Elizabeth L. *Romanesque Sculpture in Saintonge.* New Haven: Yale University Press, 1940.

Mérimée, Prosper. 'Extrait d'un rapport adressé au Ministre de l'Intérieur, sur l'abbaye de Conques.' *BM* 4 (1838), 225–42.

Mesplé, Paul. 'Les chrismes du département du Gers: Observation sur l'évolution et le groupement des chrismes au nord et au sud des Pyrénées.' *Mémoires de la Société archéologique du Midi de la France* (Toulouse, 1970), 71–90.

– *Les sculptures romanes: Toulouse. Musée des Augustins.* Paris, 1961.

Migne, J.-P., ed. *PL.* 217 vols. Paris, 1844–1905.

Millin, Aubin-Louis. *Voyage dans les départemens du Midi de la France.* Vol. 3. Paris, 1808.

Mitchell, John. 'Literacy Displayed: The Use of Inscriptions at the Monastery of San Vincenzo al Volturno in the Early Ninth Century.' In McKitterick, *The Uses of Literacy in Early Mediaeval Europe*, 186–225.

Montesquiou-Fezensac, Comte Blaise de. 'Les portes de bronze de Saint-Denis.' *Bulletin de la Société nationale des Antiquaires de France 1945–1946–1947* (1950), 128–37.

Moralejo Alvarez, Serafín. 'Aportaciones a la interpretación del programa iconográfico de la catedral de Jaca.' In *Homenaje a don José María Lacarra de Miguel*, 1 (Saragossa, 1977), 173–98.

– 'Une sculpture du style de Bernard Gilduin à Jaca.' *BM* 131 (1973), 7–16.

– 'La sculpture romane de la cathédrale de Jaca: État des questions.' *CSMC* 10 (1979), 79–106.

Moretti, Italo, and Renato Stopani. *Toscane romane.* Saint-Léger-Vauban: Zodiaque, 1982.

Mortet, Victor, ed. *Recueil de textes relatifs à l'histoire de l'architecture et à la condition des architectes en France au moyen âge (XI–XII siècles)*, CTSEEH, 44 (Paris: Alphonse Picard et fils, 1911).

Musset, Lucien. *Angleterre romane: Le sud d'Angleterre.* Saint-Léger-Vauban: Zodiaque, 1983.

Nicolau, Mathieu. 'Les deux sources de la versification latine accentuelle.' *Archivum Latinitatis Medii Aevi* (*Bulletin du Cange*) 9 (1934), 55–87.

Noguier, Antoine. *Histoire tolosaine.* Toulouse, 1556 (another edition, identical, is dated 1559).

Norberg, Dag. *Introduction à l'étude de la versification latine médiévale.* Stockholm: Almqvist & Wiksell, 1958.

Nussbaum, Otto. *Der Standort des Liturgen am christlichen Altar vor dem Jahre 1000: Eine archäologische und liturgiegeschichtliche Untersuchung.* 2 vols. (vol. 1, text; vol. 2, plates). Bonn: Peter Hanstein Verlag, 1965.

Nykrog, Per. 'The Rise of Literary Fiction.' In Benson and Constable, *Renaissance and Renewal*, 593–612.

Oakeshott, Walter. *The Mosaics of Rome from the Third to the Fourteenth Centuries.* London: Thames and Hudson, 1967.

Ocón Alonso, Dulce. 'Tímpanos románicos españoles: Reinos de Navarra y Aragón.' PhD diss., University of Madrid, 1987. 2 vols., separately paginated.

Ong, Walter J., SJ. *Orality and Literacy: The Technologizing of the Word.* London: Methuen, 1982.

Oursel, Hervé, Colette Deremble-Manhès, and Jacques Thiébaut. *Nord roman: Flandre, Artois, Picardie, Laonnois.* Saint-Léger-Vauban: Zodiaque, 1994.

Oursel, Raymond. *Bourgogne romane.* 7th ed. Saint-Léger-Vauban: Zodiaque, 1979.
– *Évocation de la chrétienté romane.* Saint-Léger-Vauban: Zodiaque, 1968.
– *Floraison de la sculpture romane.* 2 vols. Saint-Léger-Vauban: Zodiaque, 1973–6.
– *Haut-Poitou roman.* 2nd ed. Saint-Léger-Vauban: Zodiaque, 1984.
– *Invention de l'architecture romane.* 2nd ed. Saint-Léger-Vauban: Zodiaque, 1986.
– *Lyonnais, Dombes, Bugey et Savoie romans.* Saint-Léger-Vauban: Zodiaque, 1990.
– *Pèlerins du Moyen Age: Les hommes, les chemins, les sanctuaires.* 2nd ed. Paris: Fayard, 1978.
– *Routes romanes.* 3 vols. Saint-Léger-Vauban: Zodiaque, 1982–6.
Ouspensky, Leonid. *Theology of the Icon.* Vol. 1, trans. Anthony Gythiel and Elizabeth Meyendorff. Crestwood, NY: St Vladimir's Seminary Press, 1992.
Ousterhout, Robert. 'Loca Sancta and the Architectural Response to Pilgrimage.' In Ousterhout, *The Blessings of Pilgrimage,* 109–24.
Ousterhout, Robert, ed. *The Blessings of Pilgrimage.* Urbana: University of Illinois Press, 1990.
Page, Raymond I. *Runes.* Berkeley and Los Angeles: University of California Press / British Museum, 1987.
Panofsky, Erwin. *Abbot Suger on the Abbey Church of St.-Denis and Its Art Treasures.* 2nd ed., ed. Gerda Panofsky-Soergel. Princeton: Princeton University Press, 1979.
Parker, Elizabeth C., and Charles T. Little. *The Cloisters Cross: Its Art and Meaning.* New York: Metropolitan Museum of Art, 1994.
Paul, Georges, and Pierre Paul. *Notre-Dame du Puy: Essai historique et archéologique.* Le Puy: Cazes-Bonneton, 1950.
Paulinus of Nola. Epistula 32, Carmina 27–8. *See* Goldschmidt, *Paulinus' Churches at Nola*; also in Migne, *PL,* 61, cols. 330–43.
Physiologus. See White.
Pliny the Elder. *Naturalis Historia.* Ed. and trans. H. Rackham and W.H.S. Jones. Loeb Classical Library.
Plummer, Charles, ed. *Venerabilis Baedae Opera Historica. See* Bede, *Venerabilis Baedae Opera Historica.*
Pomès, Pierre, and Louis Michel. *L'église de Saint-Pé-de-Bigorre.* Pau: Marrimpouey Jeune, [1980].
Porter, Arthur Kingsley. 'Iguácel and More Romanesque Art of Aragón.' *The Burlington Magazine* 52 (1928), 115–27.
– *Lombard Architecture.* 4 vols. New Haven: Yale University Press, 1915–17.
– *Medieval Architecture: Its Origins and Development.* Vol. 1: The Origins. New York and London, 1909.
– *Romanesque Sculpture of the Pilgrimage Roads.* 10 vols. Boston: Marshall Jones, 1923.
– *Spanish Romanesque Sculpture.* 2 vols. Florence: Pantheon, Casa Editrice, 1928.

– 'Two Romanesque Sculptures in France by Italian Masters.' *American Journal of Archaeology*, 2nd ser., 24 (1920), 121–35.

Prudentius. *Collected Works.* 2 vols., ed. H.J. Thompson (Loeb Classical Library). Cambridge: Harvard University Press, and London: William Heinemann, 1949–53.

– *Contra Orationem Symmachi.* In *Collected Works,* 1, 344–401; 2, 2–97.

– *Dittochaeon.* In *Collected Works,* 2, 346–71.

– *Psychomachia.* In *Collected Works,* 1, 274–343.

Quarré, Pierre. 'Le portail de Mauriac et le porche d'Ydes: Leurs rapports avec l'art du Languedoc et du Limousin.' *BM* 98 (1939), 129–51.

– 'La sculpture des anciens portails de Saint-Bénigne de Dijon.' *GBA*, 6th ser., 50 (1957), 177–94.

Quicherat, Jules. *Mélanges d'archéologie et d'histoire: Archéologie du moyen âge.* Ed. Robert de Lasteyrie. Paris: Alphonse Picard, 1886.

Quintavalle, Arturo Carlo. *La Cattedrale di Modena: Problemi di romanico emiliano.* 2 vols. Modena: Bassi & Nipoti, 1964–5.

– *La Cattedrale di Parma et il Romanico Europeo.* Parma: Università di Parma, Istituto di Storia dell'Arte, 1974.

– 'Piacenza Cathedral, Lanfranco, and the School of Wiligelmo.' *AB* 55 (1973), 40–57.

Raby, F.J.E. *A History of Christian-Latin Poetry from the Beginnings to the Close of the Middle Ages.* 2nd ed. Oxford: Clarendon Press, 1953.

– *A History of Secular Latin Poetry in the Middle Ages.* 2nd ed., 2 vols. Oxford: Clarendon Press, 1957.

Ragusa, Isa. '*Porta patet vitae sponsus vocat intro venite* and the Inscriptions of the Lost Portal of the Cathedral of Esztergom.' *Zeitschrift für Kunstgeschichte* 43 (1980), 345–51.

Rambaud, Michel. 'Le quatrain mystique de Vaison-la-Romaine.' *BM* 109 (1951), 157–74.

Recht, Roland, ed. *Les bâtisseurs des cathédrales gothiques.* Strasbourg: Éditions Les Musées de la ville de Strasbourg, 1989.

Regino of Prüm. *De synodalibus causis. See* Wasserschleben, *Reginonis abbatis Prumiensis.*

Reinhardt, Hans. *La cathédrale de Strasbourg.* Paris: Arthaud, 1972.

Riché, Pierre. 'Recherches sur l'instruction des laïcs du IXe au XIIe siècle.' *Cahiers de civilisation médiévale X^e^–XIIe siècles* 5 (1962), 175–82.

Robb, David M. 'Niccolò: A North Italian Sculptor of the Twelfth Century.' *AB* 12 (1930), 374–420.

Robertson, D.W., Jr. *Augustine's On Christian Doctrine. See* Augustine, *On Christian Doctrine.*

Rouquette, Jean-Maurice. *Provence romane: La Provence rhodanienne.* 2nd ed. Saint-Léger-Vauban: Zodiaque, 1980.

Rudolph, Conrad. *Artistic Change at St-Denis: Abbot Suger's Program and the Early Twelfth-Century Controversy over Art.* Princeton: Princeton University Press, 1990.

Runciman, Steven. *A History of the Crusades.* Vol. 1: The First Crusade and the Foundation of the Kingdom of Jerusalem. 1951; repr. New York: Harper & Row, 1964.

Saint-Jean, Robert, and Jean Nougaret. *Vivarais Gévaudan romans.* Saint-Léger-Vauban: Zodiaque, 1991.

Salet, Francis. *La Madeleine de Vézelay: Étude iconographique par Jean Adhémar.* Melun: Librairie d'Argences, 1948.

Salvini, Roberto. *Wiligelmo e le origini della scultura romanica.* Milan: Aldo Martello, 1956.

Sandoli, Sabino de, ed. *Itinera Hierosolymitana Crucesignatorum (saec. XII–XIII).* Vol. 2: Tempore Regum Francorum (1100–1187). Jerusalem: Franciscan Printing Press, 1980.

Sanoner, G. 'Analyse du portail de l'église St-Gilles à Argenton-Château (Deux-Sèvres).' *Revue de l'art chrétien* 46 (1903), 397–405.

– 'Le portail de Santa Maria de Ripoll.' *BM* 82 (1923), 350–99.

Saporetti, Claudio. *Iscrizioni romaniche del Duomo di Fidenza.* 2nd ed. Parma: Presso la Deputazione di Storia Patria per le Province Parmensi, 1981.

Sauerländer, Willibald. *Gotische Skulptur in Frankreich 1140–1270.* Munich: Hirmer Verlag, 1970.

Schanz, Martin. *Geschichte der römischen Literatur bis zum Gesetzgebungswerk des Kaisers Justinian.* Vol. 4, pt 2: Die Literatur des fünften und sechsten Jahrhunderts, by Martin Schanz, Carl Hosius, and Gustav Krüger. 1920; repr. Munich: C.H. Beck'sche Verlagsbuchhandlung, 1959.

Schapiro, Meyer. 'On the Aesthetic Attitude in Romanesque Art' (1947). Repr. in Schapiro, *Romanesque Art,* 1–27.

– 'From Mozarabic to Romanesque in Silos' (1939). Repr. in Schapiro, *Romanesque Art,* 28–101.

– 'The Romanesque Sculpture of Moissac I & II' (1931). Repr. in Schapiro, *Romanesque Art,* 131–263.

– *Romanesque Art.* New York: George Braziller, 1977.

Scott, David W. 'A Restoration of the West Portal Relief Decoration of Saint-Sernin of Toulouse.' *AB* 46 (1964), 271–82.

Sedulius. *Sedulii opera omnia.* Ed. J. Huemer. Vienna, 1885.

Seidel, Linda. *Romanesque Sculpture from the Cathedral of Saint-Etienne, Toulouse.* Harvard thesis, 1964; repr. New York and London: Garland Publishing, 1977.

– *Songs of Glory: The Romanesque Façades of Aquitaine.* Chicago: University of Chicago Press, 1981.

Sené, Alain. 'Quelques remarques sur les tympans romans à chrisme en Aragon et en Navarre.' In Gallais and Riou, *Mélanges offerts à René Crozet*, 365–81.
Serbat, Louis. 'Nevers.' *Congrès archéologique de France* 80 (1913), 300–73.
Sermo contra Judaeos, Paganos et Arianos. In Migne, *PL*, 42, cols. 1117–30. (Now attributed to Quodvultdeus, bishop of Carthage [437–53]: *see* Dekkers and Gaar, *Clavis Patrum Latinorum*, no. 404.)
Sheingorn, Pamela, ed. *The Book of Sainte Foy.* Trans. with intro. and notes; with Song of Sainte Foy, trans. Robert L.A. Clark. Philadelphia: University of Pennsylvania Press, 1995.
Sidonius Apollinaris. *Apollinaris Sidonii Epistulae et Carmina*, ed. Christian Luetjohann. In *MGH: Auctores Antiquissimi*, 8. Berlin: Weidmann, 1887.
Silagi, Gabriel, ed., with collaboration of Bernard Bischoff. *Die lateinischen Dichter des deutschen Mittelalters: Die Ottonenzeit.* In *MGH: Poetarum Latinorum Medii Aevi*, vol. 5:3. Munich: Monumenta Germaniae Historica, 1979. *See also* Strecker, ed.
Simon, David L. 'L'art roman, source de l'art roman.' *CSMC* 11 (1980), 249–67.
– 'El tímpano de la catedral de Jaca.' *XV Congreso de Historia de la Corona de Aragón, Actas III: Jaca en la Corona de Aragón (Siglos XII–XVIII)*, 1994, 406–19.
Simson, Otto von. *The Gothic Cathedral: Origins of Gothic Architecture and the Medieval Concept of Order.* 1956; 1962; 2nd rev. ed., repr. New York: Harper Torchbooks, 1964.
Sivan, Hagith S. 'Pilgrimage, Monasticism, and the Emergence of Christian Palestine in the 4th Century.' In Ousterhout, *The Blessings of Pilgrimage*, 55–65.
Smalley, Beryl. 'Ecclesiastical Attitudes to Novelty c. 1100–c. 1250.' In Baker, *Church, Society, and Politics*, 113–31.
– *The Study of the Bible in the Middle Ages.* 1952; repr. Notre Dame, Ind.: University of Notre Dame Press, 1964.
Solinus. *Collectanea Rerum Memorabilium*, ed. Th. Mommsen. Berlin, 1895.
Souter, Alexander. *A Glossary of Later Latin to 600 A.D.* Oxford: Clarendon Press, 1949; corrected repr. 1957.
Spicq, Ceslas. *Esquisse d'une histoire de l'exégèse latine au moyen âge.* Paris: J. Vrin, 1944.
Stechow, Wolfgang. 'Two Romanesque Statues from Poitou.' *Bulletin of the Dudley Peter Allen Memorial Art Museum* (Oberlin College) 7 (Winter 1949/50), 29–38.
Stern, Henri. 'Mosaïques de pavement préromanes et romanes en France.' *Cahiers de civilisation médiévale X^e–XIIe siècles* 5 (1962), 13–33.
Stocchi, Sergio. *Émilie romane: Plaine du Po.* Trans. from Italian into French by Norbert Vaillant. Saint-Léger-Vauban: Zodiaque, 1984.
Stoddard, Whitney S. *The Façade of Saint-Gilles-du-Gard: Its Influence on French Sculpture.* Middletown, Conn.: Wesleyan University Press, 1973.
– *Sculptors of the West Portals of Chartres Cathedral: Their Origins in Romanesque and*

Their Role in Chartrain Sculpture; Including the West Portals of Saint-Denis and Chartres. New York: W.W. Norton, 1987.

Strecker, Karl. *Introduction to Mediaeval Latin.* Trans. and rev. Robert B. Palmer. Berlin: Weidmann, 1957.

– 'Studien zu karolingischen Dichtern.' *Neues Archiv der Gesellschaft für ältere deutsche Geschichtskunde* 44 (1922), 209–51.

Strecker, Karl, ed. *Die lateinischen Dichter des deutschen Mittelalters: Die Ottonenzeit.* In *MGH: Poetarum Latinorum Medii Aevi.* Vol. 5:1, Leipzig: Verlag Karl W. Hiersemann, 1937; vol. 5:2, Berlin: Weidmann, 1939. *See also* Silagi.

Strobel, Richard, and Markus Weis. *Bavière romane.* Trans. from German into French by Wolfgang Haas, Saint-Léger-Vauban: Zodiaque, 1995.

Strubel, Armand. '*Allegoria in factis et Allegoria in verbis.*' *Poetique* 6 (1975), 342–57.

Suevia Sacra: Frühe Kunst in Schwaben. 3rd ed. Augsburg: H. Mühlberger, 1973.

Suger, Abbot. *Liber de rebus in administratione sua gestis.* Ed. and trans. Erwin Panofsky (q.v.).

Sulpicius Severus. *Vita Sancti Martini.* Ed. and trans. into French by Jacques Fontaine (q.v.).

Tassi, Roberto. *Il Duomo di Parma: I. Il Tempo Romanico.* Parma: Amilcare Pizzi, 1966.

Taylor, H.M. 'The Architectural Interest of Æthelwulf's *De Abbatibus.*' *Anglo-Saxon England* 3 (1974), 163–73.

Terpager, Peter. *Ripae Cimbricae seu Urbis Ripensis in Cimbria sitae Descriptio.* Flensburg, 1736.

Theodoric. *De Locis Sanctis.* In Sandoli, *Itinera Hierosolymitana,* 2, 309–92.

Thirion, Jacques. *Alpes romanes.* Saint-Léger-Vauban: Zodiaque, 1980.

Tobler, Titus, ed. *Itinera et Descriptiones Terrae Sanctae.* Vol. 1 (two parts in one, continuously paged): Itinera Hierosolymitana et Descriptiones Terrae Sanctae, ed. Titus Tobler and Augustus Molinier. Geneva: J.-G. Fick, 1879–80.

Tonnellier, le Chanoine. *Aulnay de Saintonge.* Saintes: Delavaud, n.d.

Torres Balbás, Leopoldo. 'La escultura románica aragonesa y el crismón de los tímpanos de las iglesias de la región pirenaica.' *Archivo Español de Arte y Arqueologia* 2 (1926), 287–91.

Tournier, René, Willibald Sauerländer, and Raymond Oursel. *Franche-Comté romane: Bresse romane.* Saint-Léger-Vauban: Zodiaque, 1979.

Traube, Ludwig, ed. *Poetae Latini Aevi Carolini.* In *MGH: Poetarum Latinorum Medii Aevi,* vol. 3 (2 parts in 1, continuously paged). Berlin, 1886–96. *See also* Duemmler.

Les trésors des églises de France. Paris: Musée des arts décoratifs, 1965.

Turner, Victor, and Edith Turner. *Image and Pilgrimage in Christian Culture: Anthropological Perspectives.* New York: Columbia University Press, 1978.

Vallery-Radot, Jean. 'L'ancienne cathédrale de Maguelone.' *Congrès archéologique de France* 108 (1950), 60–89.

Vaucelle, l'Abbé E.-R. *La collégiale de Saint-Martin de Tours: Des origines à l'avènement des Valois (397–1328)*. Paris: Alphonse Picard et fils, 1908.

Venantius Fortunatus. *See* Fortunatus.

Verdon, Timothy Gregory, with assistance of John Dally, ed. *Monasticism and the Arts*. Syracuse: Syracuse University Press, 1984.

Verzár, Christine. *Die romanischen Skulpturen der Abtei Sagra di San Michele: Studien zu Meister Nicolaus und zur 'Scuola di Piacenza.'* Basler Studien zur Kunstgeschichte, 10. Bern: Francke Verlag, 1968.

Verzár Bornstein, Christine. 'Matilda of Canossa, Papal Rome and the Earliest Italian Porch Portals.' In *Romanico padano, Romanico europeo*, 143–58. Parma: Istituto di Storia dell'Arte, Università di di Parma, 1982.

– *Portals and Politics in the Early Italian City-State: The Sculpture of Nicholaus in Context*. Parma: Istituto di Storia dell'Arte, Università di Parma, 1988.

– 'Text and Image in North Italian Romanesque Sculpture.' In Kahn, *The Romanesque Frieze*, 121–40.

Vidal, Marguerite, Jean Maury, and Jean Porcher. *Quercy roman*. 3rd ed. Saint-Léger-Vauban: Zodiaque, 1979.

Vielliard, Jeanne, ed. *Le guide du pèlerin de Saint-Jacques de Compostelle*. 5th ed. Macon: Protat Frères, 1978.

Virey, Jean. 'Cluny.' *Congrès archéologique de France* 80 (1913), 65–91.

Vogel, Cyrille. 'Les rites de la pénitence publique aux Xe et XIe siècles.' In Gallais and Riou, *Mélanges offerts à René Crozet*, 1, 137–44.

Vogel, Cyrille, and Reinhard Elze, eds. *Le pontifical romano-germanique du dixième siècle: Le texte*, 2, Studi e testi, 207. Vatican City, 1963.

Waddell, Chrysogonus. 'The Reform of the Liturgy from a Renaissance Perspective.' In Benson and Constable, *Renaissance and Renewal*, 88–109.

Walahfrid Strabo. *Glossa Ordinaria*. In Migne, *PL*, 113–14.

Wasserschleben, F.W.H., ed. *Reginonis abbatis Prumiensis, libri duo de synodalibus causis et disciplinis ecclesiasticis*. Leipzig, 1840.

Webb, J.F., and D.H. Farmer. *The Age of Bede. Bede: Life of Cuthbert. Eddius Stephanus: Life of Wilfrid. Bede: Lives of the Abbots of Wearmouth and Jarrow. With the Voyage of St Brendan*. Rev. ed. Harmondsworth: Penguin, 1983.

Webster, Leslie, and Janet Backhouse. *The Making of England: Anglo-Saxon Art and Culture AD 600–900*. Toronto: University of Toronto Press, 1991.

Weisbach, Werner. *Religiöse Reform und mittelalterliche Kunst*. Einsiedeln/Zürich: Verlagsanstalt Benziger, 1945.

Werckmeister, O.K. 'The Lintel Fragment Representing Eve from Saint-Lazare, Autun.' *Journal of the Warburg and Courtauld Institutes* 35 (1972), 1–30.

White, T.H. *The Bestiary: A Book of Beasts.* New York: G.P. Putnam's Sons (Capricorn Books), 1960.

Whitehill, Walter Muir. *Spanish Romanesque Architecture of the Eleventh Century.* London: Oxford University Press, 1941.

Wilkinson, John. 'Jewish Holy Places and the Origins of Christian Pilgrimage.' In Ousterhout, *The Blessings of Pilgrimage,* 42–53.

Williams, John. 'The *Moralia in Iob* of 945: Some Iconographic Sources.' *Archivo Español de Arqueologia* 45–7 (1972–4), 223–50.

Winterfeld, Dethard von. *Palatinat roman.* Trans. from German into French by Gosbert Schecher. Saint-Léger-Vauban: Zodiaque, 1993.

Wulf, Walter. *Saxe romane.* Saint-Léger-Vauban: Zodiaque, 1996.

Index

Numbers in parentheses after names of churches refer to numbered entries in the Catalogue of Romanesque Verse Inscriptions, pp. 201–300; numbers in italics refer to the illustrations, following p. 184.

[redacted]